DO GREAT CASES MAKE BAD LAW?

Do Great Cases Make Bad Law?

Lackland H. Bloom, Jr.

OXFORD
UNIVERSITY PRESS

UNIVERSITY PRESS

Oxford University Press is a department of the University of Oxford. It furthers the University's objective of excellence in research, scholarship, and education by publishing worldwide.

Oxford   New York
Auckland   Cape Town   Dar es Salaam   Hong Kong   Karachi   Kuala Lumpur   Madrid
Melbourne   Mexico City   Nairobi   New Delhi   Shanghai   Taipei   Toronto

With offices in
Argentina   Austria   Brazil   Chile   Czech Republic   France   Greece   Guatemala   Hungary
Italy   Japan   Poland   Portugal   Singapore   South Korea   Switzerland   Thailand
Turkey   Ukraine   Vietnam

Oxford is a registered trademark of Oxford University Press in the UK and certain other countries.

Published in the United States of America by
Oxford University Press
198 Madison Avenue, New York, NY 10016

© Oxford University Press 2014

Library of Congress Cataloging-in-Publication Data
Bloom, Lackland H., Jr., author.
  Do great cases make bad law? / Lackland H. Bloom, Jr.
     pages cm
  Includes bibliographical references and index.
  ISBN 978-0-19-976588-1 ((hardback) : alk. paper)
1. United States. Supreme Court. 2. Constitutional law—United States—Cases.
3. Political questions and judicial power—United States—Cases. I. Title.
  KF8748.B56 2014
  342.73'00264—dc23
                                                                    2013034368

9 8 7 6 5 4 3 2

Printed in the United States of America on acid-free paper

Note to Readers
This publication is designed to provide accurate and authoritative information in regard to the subject matter covered. It is based upon sources believed to be accurate and reliable and is intended to be current as of the time it was written. It is sold with the understanding that the publisher is not engaged in rendering legal, accounting, or other professional services. If legal advice or other expert assistance is required, the services of a competent professional person should be sought. Also, to confirm that the information has not been affected or changed by recent developments, traditional legal research techniques should be used, including checking primary sources where appropriate.

(Based on the Declaration of Principles jointly adopted by a Committee of the American Bar Association and a Committee of Publishers and Associations.)

> **You may order this or any other Oxford University Press publication by visiting the Oxford University Press website at www.oup.com.**

This book is dedicated to my wife Janice who contributed so much time, effort and love toward the completion of this book, and to my daughter, Sylvia, for the patience and love she has provided throughout this project.

Table of Contents

Acknowledgments

I AM THANKFUL for the hard work and dedication of my assistant, Michele Oswald, and Debbie Seiter in the preparation of this manuscript, and research librarians Donna Wolff and Laura Justiss for the gathering of information and resources to aid my research, and for the generous financial support provided by the Law School Excellence Fund of the Dedman School of Law. Finally, I am grateful to my wife Janice for her editorial contributions, and for always staying one step ahead of me.

Introduction

"GREAT CASES, LIKE hard cases, make bad law. For great cases are called great, not by reason of their real importance in shaping the law of the future, but because of some accident of immediate overwhelming interest which appeals to the feelings and distorts the judgment. These immediate interests exercise a kind of hydraulic pressure which makes what previously was clear seem doubtful and before which even well-settled principles of law will bend."

So spoke Justice Holmes in his famous dissent in *Northern Securities Co. v. United States.*[1] *Northern Securities* was indeed a great case. It involved an attempt by the United States to use the Sherman Antitrust Act to prohibit a merger between two major competing railroads. The transactions at issue involved well-known financiers and railroad barons J.P. Morgan, Edward Harriman, and J.J. Hill. The case did indeed attract an extreme amount of attention, especially for a business decision. In a majority opinion by Justice Harlan, the Court held that the Sherman Act by its terms prohibited all restraints of trade that affected interstate commerce. Holmes disagreed vigorously, maintaining that as a matter of common sense and consistent with the Act's common law heritage, it was intended to prohibit only "unreasonable" restraints of trade. Over time, Holmes's approach largely prevailed. Thus at least in terms of durability, the majority opinion did make bad law, at least in the sense that it did not endure. The case also raised a question as to whether the Act could constitutionally be applied to the stock purchases in question; however Holmes was most concerned with the statutory question.

Holmes's sentence "[g]reat cases, like hard cases, make bad law" is one of the most familiar statements in American jurisprudence. But was Holmes correct? Do great cases

---

[1] 193 U.S. 197, 400-01 (1904).

make bad law? That is the subject that this book will attempt to explore. At the outset this project raises crucial definitional questions. First, what is a great case? Second, what is bad law? And third, assuming that we can answer the first two, can we determine whether a great case did, in fact, make bad law? None of these questions can be answered in an objective manner. Each is fraught with value judgement and speculation. Recognizing the subjectivity of the enterprise, this book will attempt to examine Holmes's thesis as applied to 24 great cases decided over a period of 210 years. The project is limited to constitutional cases although it should encompass most of the truly great cases.

Holmes explained what he meant by the great case. It was a case "by some accident of immediate overwhelming interest which appeals to the feelings and distorts the judgment." In other words, it was the type of case in which the media and the public take a consuming interest in the proceeding, seemingly causing the Court to be subjected to unusual pressure in reaching and explaining its decision. Holmes seems to distinguish great cases as so defined from landmark cases—that is, cases that are in fact important in shaping the law of the future. The distinction is not generally recognized in modern parlance. Indeed many would define the great case as the one that is great or famous because of the positive impact it had on the path of the law. But that is clearly not what Holmes had in mind. On the other hand, it is unlikely that Holmes meant that the great case and the landmark case were mutually exclusive. If Holmes meant that a great case was simply a highly publicized case that inevitably made bad law, then he stated nothing more than a tautology—great cases make bad law because that is essentially the definition of a great case. Presumably, Holmes recognized that a great case could make good law but usually did not. Otherwise his statement is unworthy of its celebrity.

In fact, many cases that should be considered great cases under the Holmes definition, cases where the hydraulic pressures of public interest were in play, are also legitimate landmark cases in that they have in fact had a significant, positive, and lasting influence on the shape of the law. In many instances there is almost certainly a consensus that they made good law. However, there are certainly instances in which the great case did indeed illustrate Holmes's point. Although he did not cite any specific examples, it is likely that Holmes had three specific cases in mind that had been decided within his lifetime: *Scott v. Sanford* (the *Dred Scott* Case), *Hepburn v. Griswold* and the *Legal Tender Cases*, and *Pollack v. Farmers Loan and Trust* (the Income Tax Case decided less than a decade earlier). Indeed it was these three decisions that Chief Justice Hughes later referred to as the Court's self-inflicted wounds.[2] However there were and are other great cases that are more reputable.

This study will define the great case somewhat more broadly than did Holmes. Holmes seemed to contemplate cases in which external factors led to an unusual public interest in the case, resulting in a unique degree of pressure being brought to bear on the Court. The great majority of cases discussed in this book fit that description. However, a few seemingly do not. The *Slaughter-House Cases* was not a highly publicized dispute and yet the justices themselves clearly recognized that they were deciding one of the most crucial cases ever presented to the Court. It is fair to say that the hydraulic pressure of which Holmes spoke was as present in that case as in almost any other great case although it

---

[2] CHARLES EVANS HUGHES, THE SUPREME COURT OF THE UNITED STATES 50–54 (1928).

was generated internally rather than externally. Likewise, *New York Times v. Sullivan* may not have caught the public's attention in the way that many great cases did, yet it was truly a clash of the titans forcing the Court to negotiate a seeming conflict between the law of libel, freedom of the press, and the civil rights movement. Both the cast of characters and the enormous legal and societal stakes certainly qualify it as a great case broadly understood. Perhaps the same can be said of the Reapportionment Cases. The public at large may not have been paying close attention but the legal and political elites including the justices understood that these cases were among the most important ever presented to the Court. These cases are worthy of consideration although not clearly the type of cases that Holmes had in mind.

Perhaps the most difficult aspect of this project was the selection of cases to discuss. The problem was one of exclusion rather than inclusion. Given that the Court has been at the center of many of the most significant social and political disputes in the history of the nation, there have been a plethora of great cases. There would probably be a consensus that most of the cases discussed in this book would qualify as great cases. Indeed, all have been described as such though not always in the sense that Holmes employed the phrase. Many cases have been omitted however that readily could have been included. The number of cases discussed was limited to 24 in order to permit fairly thorough consideration of each case. Hopefully, nearly all of the cases that students of the Court would classify as great in the Holmesian sense have been included.

There is an attempt to consider cases decided throughout the entire history of the Court. That in itself poses difficulties in that great cases have not necessarily been randomly disbursed but rather have often been bunched together in relatively short time frames. Three Marshall court cases are included in the book. The Marshall court was relatively aggressive, and considering that it was in a position to have the first opportunity to interpret many crucial constitutional provisions, it is not surprising that it was confronted with many great cases. Beyond the three discussed in the book, *Marbury v. Madison*, *McCulloch v. Maryland*, and *Gibbons v. Ogden*, others could have been included as well such as *Martin v. Hunter's Lessee*, *Cohens v. Virginia*, *Fletcher v. Peck*, *Trustees of Dartmouth College v. Woodward*, and *Worcester v. Georgia*.

Prigg v. Pennsylvania is probably the best example from the Taney period prior to *Dred Scott*. The period surrounding the Civil War was almost by definition a dysfunctional time in American constitutional history and as such gave rise to quite a number of great cases. In addition to the *Dred Scott* Case, the *Legal Tender Cases*, and the *Slaughter-House Cases* several others might have been included such as the Prize Cases, *Ex Parte McCardle*, *Mississippi v. Johnson*, *Georgia v. Stanton*, and *Texas v. White*. The Civil Rights Cases and the Income Tax Case are sterling examples of great cases that were decided during the last two decades of the nineteenth century.

The book does not include any cases decided during the 40-year period from 1896 to 1937. Ironically, this excludes any case in which Justice Holmes himself participated. The Court rendered many important decisions during this period including its foundational freedom of speech opinions in *Schenk v. United States*, and *Abrams v. United States* as well as the infamous decision in *Lochner v. New York* and the massive decision in *Myers v United States*; yet none of the decisions during this period seemed to quite fit the great case template as considered in this volume.

During the New Deal period of the 1930s, the Court assumed center stage and decided a large number of cases that could qualify as great cases both with respect to federal and state authority. *NLRB v. Jones & Laughlin Steel* was arguably the most crucial and as such is representative of the era. However for the period from 1934 through 1937 it seemed as though the Court was deciding one great case after another.

The decade following the end of the World War II era also gave rise to several great cases in a very short period of time. *Dennis v. United States, Youngstown Sheet & Tube v. Sawyer*, and finally *Brown v. Board of Education* were decided within a three-year period. During the 1960s the aggressiveness of the Warren court led to several great cases in a relatively short time period including the Reapportionment decisions, *New York Times v. Sullivan*, and *Miranda v. Arizona*. The school prayer decisions could be included as well. The pace with which great cases reached the Court continued under the Burger court in the 1970s with the Pentagon Papers Case, *Roe v. Wade, United States v. Nixon*, and *Regents of the University of California v. Bakke*. The death penalty and campaign finance decisions during this era might also have been included. Sequels to the abortion and affirmative action decisions also qualify as great cases in their own right. Finally, *Bush v. Gore* and the *National Federation v. Sebelius* healthcare decision are certainly recent examples of great cases. *Lawrence v. Texas, Citizens United v. FEC*, and the recent gay marriage cases could also have been considered.

As we have now settled on a collection of great cases for examination, the next issue is how we determine whether these cases did or did not make bad law. Obviously the very question of what qualifies as bad law is in itself highly subjective and controversial. This examination will focus on four criteria in an attempt to draw conclusions.

First, is there reason to believe that the hydraulic pressure that Holmes mentioned had an adverse effect on the Court's decision-making process? That is not easy to evaluate under any circumstances and particularly difficult because of lack of evidence with respect to cases decided during the nineteenth and early part of the twentieth century. Until relatively recently with a few exceptions, perhaps most notably the *Dred Scott* Case, there is little if any memoranda as to what did in fact occur inside of the Court as it reached its decision and drafted its opinion. There were sometimes unsubstantiated rumors and statements made often long after the fact in correspondence and memoirs but there is often reason to doubt the credibility of these sources. At most they tend to provide some basis for speculation. That changed during the second half of the twentieth century when the conference notes of certain justices along with opinion drafts and inter-office memoranda became widely available following the deaths of the justices. Moreover, contemporaneous leaks to the media with respect to the internal operations of the Court, especially in great cases, as well as the production of more detailed judicial biographies has greatly increased the amount of material purporting to describe the Court's internal decision-making processes. As with any historical data, this must be viewed with some skepticism. However, at least some of this data appears to be substantiated and reliable. Thus from the 1940s on, it is at least possible to attempt to determine whether the internal deliberations of the justices were affected by the greatness of the case.

The second criteria and unquestionably the single most significant piece of evidence with respect to the impact of the greatness of the case is the opinions of the justices themselves. The opinions present the Court's decision of the case as well as its public reasoning process. They provide the foundation from which any subsequent precedent and legal doctrine is derived. The opinions are truly the key to determining whether the greatness of the case made bad law. As such, the opinions will be discussed in great detail in this book in an attempt to understand the justices' reasoning process. There will be an attempt to critique the legal reasoning and to determine, if at all possible, to what extent the hydraulic pressure of the case may have had an impact.

The third criteria for evaluating the impact of the greatness of the case is to attempt to assess whether in some absolute sense, the law that developed from the case can be considered good or bad. That of course will entail highly subjective judgments on which reasonable people can, and will, disagree. Still there is room for a fair degree of consensus on some point; for instance the law of *Dred Scott* was quite bad whereas that of *Brown v. Board of Education* was good. Between those extremes there is much room for argument. Account will be taken of the scholarly opinion as to the quality of the law produced by the cases although there is frequently disagreement.

Finally, there will be consideration of the lasting impact of the case on jurisprudence. In certain instances, it is difficult to say that the case made good or bad law in that it made very little law at all in the sense that its principles and doctrine are unique, so they are virtually never applied. In some instances the holding and doctrine of a great case have been decisively rejected either by subsequent courts or by constitutional amendment. Such a case can hardly be claimed to have created good law. In other instances, great cases have in fact become landmark cases in that they have been fountain heads of subsequent jurisprudence. Whether or not the law is good or bad in terms of some external standard of evaluation, there is much to be said for a case that is the source of heavily relied upon precedent and doctrine over an extended period of time.

It is fair to say that every great case is different and as such it is hazardous to draw general conclusions. Most conclusions that can be drawn are best stated after the individual cases have been reviewed. A few highlights can be noted at the outset however. First, the great case is by definition a product of its own historical context. The circumstances of how and why these cases come before the Supreme Court vary greatly. Some great cases were forced upon the Court, others arose in the normal course of business, and in certain instances the Court reached out to consider great cases when it scarcely needed to do so.

Often, the Court has taken full advantage of the greatness of the case to render a much broader decision than necessary. The Court has sometimes used the great case to create a landmark case although not always successfully. Chief Justice Marshall was especially inclined to do just that. However the courts have not always exploited the greatness of the case in a positive way. On some occasions, the Court has used the great case to take the law in the wrong direction, either because it has been caught up in the excitement of the event as Holmes seemed to suggest or perhaps because the justices in the majority deliberately used the occasion to launch an ill-fated vision or agenda. Generally, great cases have offered the Court modest alternatives for deciding the matter on narrow and unremarkable grounds. Most great cases could have been disposed of with little lasting impact. As it happens, the justices have almost always chosen to ignore the potential narrow or non-controversial grounds for a decision. Perhaps this is attributable to the fact that there has almost always been one or more extremely confident justices driving the decision in the great case. Whether prophetic or misguided, a relatively self-assured

Court has almost always been present in the great case. As such, more often than not the great case has been welcomed by the Court rather than feared.

Great cases create momentum on the Court to decide more great cases in the future. If the Court resolves controversial societal disputes without too much damage to its institutional position, both society and the justices themselves may conclude that the resolution of such disputes is precisely what the Court is supposed to do. At many points during the Court's history, it has seemed to relish the spotlight provided by the great case. Litigants have been only too happy to accommodate. One might think that with the expansion of the media, the greater legalization of society, and the explosion of the amicus brief, there is now greater interest and public awareness of the Court and consequently more potential for great cases to arise today. That would not seem to be true however. The Court has in fact been near the center of public attention throughout its existence. The excitement surrounding the great cases of the Marshall court era certainly rivals that of the great cases of today. The very existence of the great case throughout the Court's history is probably most attributable to its constitutional position as a coequal branch of the federal government.

"[Marbury] exerts an enormous magnetic pull. It is…a great historic event, a famous victory…one of the foundation stones of the Republic. It is hallowed. It is revered. If it had a physical presence like the Alamo or Gettysburg, it would be a tourist attraction."[1]

ALEXANDER BICKEL

1

Marbury v. Madison

THE SPECIFIC QUESTION presented in *Marbury v. Madison*[2] was whether a local businessman in the District of Columbia was entitled to a commission as a justice of the peace, a relatively minor political office. As so described it would scarcely seem to be the stuff of which great cases are made. But of course there was more to it. *Marbury* arose in the direct aftermath of the bitterly contested presidential election of 1800 in which Thomas Jefferson defeated the incumbent John Adams.[3] Only slightly beneath the surface, the case pitted Jefferson and his secretary of state, James Madison, against arch rival the new chief justice, John Marshall, in a face-off between the executive and judicial branches. The outgoing Adams administration had passed the Circuit Courts Act creating a new level of federal judgeships staffed with loyal Federalists. The new Jeffersonian congress promptly repealed the Act, thus dismissing the Federalist judges. The *Marbury* litigation was the outgrowth of a partisan political battle over the extent to which the executive and legislative branches could exercise control over the judicial branch. In the background was a movement to impeach recalcitrant federal judges. At the center was a dispute between two very different philosophies of American government and the Constitution. The lawsuit was essentially an attempt to embarrass President Jefferson politically. Contemptuous of the whole proceeding, he simply declined to participate. Chief Justice Marshall was scarcely a disinterested umpire having been deeply involved in the controversy that gave rise to the litigation while serving as secretary of state. As the case was brought within the original jurisdiction of the Court, it gave rise to the

---

[1] ALEXANDER M. BICKEL, THE LEAST DANGEROUS BRANCH: THE SUPREME COURT AT THE BAR OF POLITICS 74 (1962).

[2] 5 U.S. 137 (1803).

[3] Two excellent relatively recent books have provided a detailed review of that election. EDWARD J. LARSON, A MAGNIFICENT CATASTROPHE: THE TUMULTUOUS ELECTION OF 1800, AMERICA'S FIRST PRESIDENTIAL CAMPAIGN (2007); JOHN E. FERLING, ADAMS VS. JEFFERSON: THE TUMULTUOUS ELECTION OF 1800 (2004).

unusual spectacle of a mini-trial before the Supreme Court itself. *Marbury* is considered one of the greatest of great cases ever decided by the Court, not on account of all of the above-described circumstances but rather because Marshall used the opportunity that it presented to establish the foundational constitutional principle that the Court could invalidate an unconstitutional act of Congress, an issue that no one in the litigation had anticipated or discussed.

THE POLITICAL CONTEXT

The election of 1800 marked the first instance in American history in which one presidential administration was replaced by another of a different political persuasion. The Republican Jefferson defeated the Federalist Adams to become the third president of the United States. However it was not quite that simple. Under the Constitution as it then existed, the candidate with the highest electoral vote total became president and the runner-up vice president. This had allowed Adams's opponent Jefferson to become vice president in the Adams administration in the election of 1796. Jefferson easily defeated Adams in the next election; however he received the exact same number of electoral votes as his vice presidential running mate Aaron Burr. Under the Constitution, the winner would be selected by the House of Representative with each state delegation casting one ballot. Rather than gracefully withdrawing, Burr held his ground, hoping with anti-Jeffersonian Federalist support in the House to edge out Jefferson for the presidency. Jefferson finally prevailed however in mid-February of 1801 after 36 ballots.

As this was taking place, the outgoing Adams administration was doing what it could to entrench some of its adherents in the judicial branch. Adams close confidant John Marshall had been serving as secretary of state. Chief Justice Oliver Ellsworth tendered his resignation due to old age and poor health. After John Jay declined reappointment to the Court, Adams nominated Marshall, who was confirmed by the Senate on February 4, 1801. He continued to serve as secretary of state as well until the end of the Adams administration a month later. In fact Jefferson actually prevailed upon him to stay on for a few days during the transition.

The Republicans had ousted the Federalists from control of the Congress in the election of 1800 as well. Before relinquishing power however, the Federalist-dominated Congress turned its attention to the judiciary. First, it enacted the Circuit Court Act, which created 16 new circuit judgeships to be quickly filled by Federalist appointees. In addition, it relieved Supreme Court justices of the arduous task of riding circuit and decreased the size of the Court from six to five justices as of the next vacancy. Then, Congress enacted the Organic Act of the District of Columbia creating 42 new judgeships including several justice of the peace positions.

During the final two weeks of his administration, Adams was busy nominating judges and signing their commissions after confirmation by the Senate. Secretary of State (and Chief Justice) Marshall was responsible for sealing the commissions and seeing that they were delivered. On his final night in office, Adams signed several commissions for justice of the peace, sending them to Marshall for sealing and delivery. All of the commissions were signed and sealed but several went undelivered, including one confirming the appointment of a local businessman and ardent Federalist William Marbury to a position of justice of the peace in the District of Columbia. There is some dispute as to the signifi-cance of this post. It has been described as an important local office with a combination of executive, legislative, and judicial powers.[4] However it has also been described as "a sorry little thing...[that] had been stripped of many of its functions."[5] The failure to deliver that commission would ultimately result in one of the great constitutional deci-sions in U.S. history.

The following day, Chief Justice Marshall swore in his second cousin and personal and political foe, Thomas Jefferson, as president. James Madison would be the new secretary of state but would remain in Virginia until May wrapping up the estate of his recently deceased father. A day or two later on a visit to the Department of State, Jefferson appar-ently discovered the stack of undelivered commissions and directed his new attorney general and acting secretary of state, Levi Lincoln, not to deliver them.[6] Jefferson and the Republican Congress were incensed by the attempt by Adams and the Federalist Congress to pack the courts with Federalist appointees shortly before leaving office. Consequently, Jefferson decided to withhold some though not all of the undelivered commissions. The Republicans disliked the federal courts, considering them aristocratic and insufficiently protective of the rights of individuals and the prerogatives of the states.[7]

After a lengthy debate, Congress voted to repeal the Circuit Court Act eliminating the 16 judgeships that had been created. Fearing that the Court might invalidate the repeal, Congress also canceled the next term of the Supreme Court, effectively forcing the jus-tices to decide whether to return to riding circuit. Although Marshall believed that the Repeal Act was unconstitutional, the justices determined to acquiesce and resume circuit riding duties. Jefferson and the Republicans in Congress made it clear that they greatly resented the lame duck effort by the Adams administration to entrench itself in the judi-ciary. There were rumblings about the need to impeach certain judges and justices, and impeachment proceedings were commenced against District Judge William Pickering who appeared to be both a drunkard and insane.

MARBURY'S LAWSUIT

Perhaps in an attempt to embarrass the new administration, Marbury and three other appointees to the office of justice of the peace in the District of Columbia whose com-missions had not been delivered filed suit in the Supreme Court in its December 1801 term invoking its original jurisdiction.[8] They requested Secretary of State Madison to show cause why a writ of mandamus should not issue directing him to deliver the missing

---

[4] David F. Forte, *Marbury's Travail: Federalist Politics and William Marbury's Appointment as Justice of the Peace*, 45 CATH. U. L. REV. 349, 354 (1996).

[5] James M. O'Fallon, *Marbury*, 44 STAN. L. REV. 219, 241 (1992).

[6] CLIFF SLOAN & DAVID MCKEAN, THE GREAT DECISION: JEFFERSON, ADAMS, MARSHALL, AND THE BAT-TLE FOR THE SUPREME COURT 76 (2009). In a letter to Justice William Johnson, June 12, 1823, Jefferson declared, "I found them on the table...and I forbade their delivery." XV THE WRITINGS OF THOMAS JEF-FERSON 439, 447 (Library ed. 1904).

[7] GEORGE LEE HASKINS & HERBERT A.JOHNSON, FOUNDATIONS OF POWER: JOHN MARSHALL, 1801–1815, at 156–58 (1981).

[8] The three others were Dennis Ramsay, William Harper, and Robert Townshend Hooe.

commissions. The plaintiffs were represented by Charles Lee who had served as attorney general under both Presidents Washington and Adams. Marshall and the Court ruled that the action could proceed at the next term. The Republican press attacked the decision to hear the case, period.[9] Presumably, Marbury and his co-plaintiffs could have commenced their lawsuit in the recently created Circuit Court of the District of Columbia but chose to bring it in the Supreme Court instead.[10] Apparently the filing of the lawsuit in *Marbury* played a major role in persuading the Republican Congress to repeal the Circuit Court Act.[11]

In view of the cancellation of the 1802 term, the Court did not reconvene until February 1803 and promptly returned to the suit filed by Marbury and the three other appointees. Quite ominously, Secretary of State Madison declined to make an appearance through counsel, signaling that the executive branch held the entire proceeding in contempt. Lawsuits are rarely commenced as an original matter in the Supreme Court. The Court's original jurisdiction is quite discrete and limited. Beyond that however, virtually all lawsuits involve contested factual issues that the Court is ill-equipped to resolve.

THE "TRIAL" AND ARGUMENT

Marbury's counsel was faced with the problem of establishing that the commission in question had in fact been signed and sealed, but had not been delivered. That in turn resulted in the very unusual spectacle of a mini-trial before the Court itself. Charles Lee, Marbury's attorney, began by presenting affidavits by the plaintiffs asserting that they were aware that they had been nominated to the judgeships and that their nominations had been confirmed by the Senate.[12] They also noted that they had petitioned Madison to explain what had become of the commissions but he had declined to respond. In addition they had requested the Senate to produce a record of the confirmations and it had failed to reply. Lee called two former clerks who had aided Secretary of State Marshall in processing the commissions. They testified that they had seen the commissions but could not verify that Marbury's was among them

Lee then called Attorney General Lincoln who was present in Court observing the proceedings. He had served as acting secretary of state at the outset of the Jefferson administration. Lincoln requested that questions be posed to him in writing, to which the Court agreed. He indicated that he did not want to incriminate himself, which suggested that perhaps he had destroyed the commissions. He also noted that it was inappropriate for a high government official to be questioned in court about the performance of his official duties; however he agreed to respond to written questions. Like the clerks, he indicated that he had seen several signed and sealed commissions but could not say whether any of them were for the plaintiffs.[13] He declined to answer the questions as to what became

---

[9] SLOAN & MCKEAN, *supra* note 6, at 100.

[10] Susan Low Bloch, *The Marbury Mystery: Why Did William Marbury Sue in the Supreme Court?*, 18 CONST. COMM. 607 (2001).

[11] Dean Alfange, Jr., Marbury v. Madison *and Original Understandings of Judicial Review: In Defense of Traditional Wisdom*, 1993 SUP. CT. REV. 329, 354-55.

[12] Marbury v. Madison, 5 U.S. 137 (1803).

[13] *Id.* at 145.

of the commissions. James Marshall, the chief justice's brother, submitted an affidavit to the effect that he had attempted but had been unable to deliver all of the commissions on the evening of March 3. Lee then presented an argument on behalf of the plaintiffs. He emphasized that the duty to deliver the commission was ministerial in nature and that the order was not directed at the president. A few days later, he presented the Court with an affidavit from yet another clerk who had been unavailable previously, stating that he had in fact seen Marbury's commission signed and sealed in the Secretary's office.

THE DECISION

One-and-a-half weeks after the end of Lee's presentation, Marshall delivered the opinion for the unanimous Court dismissing Marbury's suit for lack of jurisdiction. Given that one of the justices was too ill to cross the street to the Court's chambers in the basement of the Capitol, Marshall read the opinion in the sitting room of the Stelle boarding house, where the justices stayed while in Washington.[14] Marshall has been subject to criticism for failing to recuse himself considering that he was so deeply involved in the underlying events.[15] A modern justice certainly would not have participated in the case under these circumstances. Indeed when witnesses were testifying before the Court as to whether Marbury's commission had been signed and sealed, Marshall himself almost certainly could have provided the answer given that he was the one who had sealed it. And it was not as though the concept of recusal was unknown to Marshall. He declined to participate in the decision of *Stuart v. Laird* issued six days after Marbury given that he had decided the case below while riding circuit.[16] Likewise in *Martin v. Hunter's Lessee*,[17] Marshall recused himself because he was attempting to purchase the property at issue in the case. The temptation of shaping the decision in *Marbury* must have been too great for Marshall to resist highlighting the political significance of the case. In any event, considering that Madison did not appear through counsel, there was no one before the Court to suggest that Marshall should not participate.

Marshall began the opinion by stating the issues and the order in which they would be addressed.[18] First, he explained that the Court must determine whether Marbury had a right to the commission. If he did, then the Court must consider whether the right had been violated and whether he was entitled to a remedy. If so, then it must address whether mandamus was the appropriate remedy and whether it could issue from the Supreme Court in its original jurisdiction. At first glance, this would appear to be a logical and lawyer-like approach to the case. And yet Marshall has been criticized ever since for leaving the question of the Court's jurisdiction, the issue on which Marbury's case would be dismissed, until last.[19] It has long been a precept of Anglo-American jurisprudence that a court's first duty is to determine whether it has jurisdiction and if it does not, to dismiss

---

[14] Sloan & McKean, *supra* note 6, at 149.
[15] William Van Alstyne, *A Critical Guide to* Marbury v. Madison, 1969 Duke L.J. 1, 8.
[16] 5 U.S. 299 (1803).
[17] 14 U.S. 304 (1816).
[18] *Marbury*, 5 U.S. at 154.
[19] *See, e.g.*, Van Alstyne, *supra* note 15, at 7.

the case. By addressing jurisdiction at the end of the opinion, Marshall was able to discuss several other issues that could have been avoided, most significantly the Court's power to review at least some actions by the secretary of state. This aspect of the case provoked Jefferson the most, causing him to assert that Marshall was "traveling out of his case to prescribe what the law would be in a moot case not before the court...[and was] very irregular and very censurable."[20] The manner in which Marshall structured his opinion served his larger purpose however and was almost certainly dictated by the political context of the case. Marshall seemed determined to make the opinion more significant than it needed to be.

Marshall then turned to the first issue identified, whether Marbury had a right to the commission. To modern eyes, this would seem to be the easiest question presented and yet Marshall gave it more attention than any of the other questions raised. He noted that the nominating and confirming power were set forth in different sections of the Constitution from the commissioning power, permitting him to contend that only the former involved presidential discretion.[21] He suggested that the president's signature was not part of the appointment but only evidence of it. And in any event, once signed the appointment was complete and the president's role was finished. Consequently, Marshall separated the president from the case entirely. He could not be accused of interfering with presidential authority or discretion given that the president had done everything that he was required to do before the incidents giving rise to the case occurred. This was an important move by Marshall in that it allowed him to challenge the administration without directly confronting the fairly popular new president himself. Marshall's reasoning on this point clearly reflected the delicate political position in which the Court found itself.

Next, Marshall focused on the "ministerial" duty imposed on the secretary of state by Congress to affix the seal of the United States on the signed commission. Whether the seal was essential to the validity of the appointment or simply evidence of the authenticity of the president's signature, in either event like the signature itself, it had been completed. Thus Marshall was able to focus on the dereliction complained of by Marbury: the failure of Madison to deliver the commission. Having already concluded that the appointment was completed at the very latest when the commission was sealed, the failure to deliver could not be considered part of the discretionary appointment process. As Marshall put it "[t]he transmission of the commission, is a practice directed by convenience but not by law."[22] Anticipating the argument by analogy to the law of deeds that a deed was not valid until signed, sealed, and delivered, Marshall replied that the Constitution seemed to call for a different rule with respect to presidential appointments and the rule with respect to patents was a more apt analogy where delivery was not required. By this point, Marshall had so minimized the significance of delivery that one might ask why the case even needed to be brought. If Marbury was a judge regardless of delivery of the commission, as Marshall seemed to indicate, then why did he even need it? Of course

---

[20] Letter from Thomas Jefferson to Justice William Johnson, June 12, 1823, *supra* note 6 at 447.
[21] *Marbury*, 5 U.S. at 156.
[22] *Id.* at 161.

the answer was that neither Jefferson nor anyone else was prepared to recognize him as a judge absent the commission. Thus delivery did seem to matter quite a bit after all.

In criticizing the opinion 20 years later, Jefferson insisted that as with the law of deeds, the commission did not vest until delivery.[23] But the issue was entirely open when Marshall decided it, and Jefferson had no more authority for his approach than did Marshall.

The final issue as to Marbury's right was whether the failure to deliver the commission should be construed as a revocation of the appointment by the president through the secretary of state. Marshall conceded that were this an appointment at will, the president would indeed be free to dismiss Marbury and the Court would not intervene.[24] But given that Congress had authorized the appointment for a term of five years, Marbury had a vested right in holding the office for that period of time beyond presidential control. Consequently, Marbury was entitled to the commission and the decision to withhold it violated his vested legal right. It was important for Marshall to establish that Marbury had a solid right to the commission before criticizing Jefferson and Madison for declining to deliver it. Difficult questions would be addressed by the Court during the twentieth century regarding the scope of the presidential removal power.[25] Even then, it would not be clear that the president had an unfettered right to remove a judicial officer appointed for a term of years. Marshall's conclusion was defensible if not entirely beyond question.

Marshall labored hard on this aspect of the opinion as had Charles Lee in his argument to the Court. Apparently both feared that it was important to persuade the reader that no attempt was being made to interfere with the president's responsibilities or the secretary of state's discretionary duties. Marshall well understood that the case was politically charged and that it was necessary to tread carefully. This section of the opinion is rarely presented in any detail in contemporary casebooks. Marshall's arguments on Marbury's right to the commission are tight, logical, and quite arguably correct. It should be noted however that Marshall deliberately bypassed two readily available escape hatches— delivery and presidential revocation—which would have permitted him to end the case without confronting other more important constitutional issues. This would seem to indicate that Marshall had every intention of using this great case to advance important ends.

Having established Marbury's right and its violation, Marshall then turned to whether Marbury was entitled to a remedy. Marshall relied heavily on rhetoric to answer this question. He began this section with the proclamation that "[t]he very essence of civil liberty certainly consists in the right of every individual to claim the protection of the laws, whenever he receives an injury."[26] He followed that with the oft-quoted statement that "[t]he government of the United States has been emphatically termed a government of laws, and not of men" but that it would not "deserve this high appellation, if the laws furnish no remedy for the violation of a vested legal right."[27] At that point Marshall

---

[23] Letter of Thomas Jefferson to Justice William Johnson, June 1823, *supra* note 6 at 447-48.

[24] *Marbury,* 5 U.S. at 162.

[25] *Compare* Myers v. United States, 272 U.S. 52 (1926) (senatorial approval of presidential removal of a postmaster was unconstitutional) *with* Humphrey's Executor v. United States, 295 U.S. 602 (1935) (Congress could limit presidential removal of an FTC commissioner to "cause").

[26] *Marbury,* 5 U.S. at 163.

[27] *Id.*

confronted the issue that proved to be most disturbing to the president and Republican critics—could the Court inquire into a breach of duty by a cabinet officer, and if finding such provide, a remedy? He promptly concluded that the Court was not disabled by the nature of the office alone.[28] Rather, whether the Court could examine the claim and provide a remedy depended on the nature of the act in question. Marshall explained that the president possessed certain "political powers" for the exercise of which he was only accountable politically. The Court would not review the exercise of such powers. But if the law imposed a specific duty on a high executive official upon which individual rights depend, a court may provide a judicial remedy if that officer's rights have been violated.

Applying these principles, Marshall reasoned that there could be no judicial remedy for instance for a failure to nominate an individual to a governmental position as the decision would involve purely political discretion. On the other hand, failure to deliver a commission signed and sealed constitutes the breach of a ministerial duty imposed by law and may properly be addressed by a court.

This portion of Marshall's opinion rests more on rhetoric and assertion than on established law. Still most of his argument seems easily defensible. This is the section of the opinion in which he purported to extend judicial authority into the higher realms of the executive branch. He made two separate claims although the first is barely perceptible. At the outset, he implicitly established that a high executive official is subject to the process of the Court. That is, the Court can exert its authority over such an individual. Arguably, the decision by the Jefferson administration not to appear through counsel in *Marbury* was an implicit objection to that principle. In view of this defiance, Marshall may have believed that it was important to establish that the Court's jurisdiction could run to a cabinet officer. And yet when Attorney General Lincoln was requested to answer the Court's interrogatories, he did largely comply. This suggested that though the administration intended to make a statement, it did seek to avoid an outright confrontation. As such, it was not simply the Court that was proceeding cautiously in this supercharged context but the administration as well. Whether the Court had the authority to serve its process on the president himself, a question not presented by *Marbury*, was not judicially settled until the Nixon tapes litigation some 170 years later. Marshall and Jefferson skirmished over that issue a few years after *Marbury* in connection with the Aaron Burr treason trial but avoided definitive resolution of the matter.[29]

The second issue was whether, assuming that judicial process extended to a departmental head, the Court could substantively review that person's actions or lack thereof and order relief if warranted. Marshall attempted to tread a narrow path on this issue distinguishing unreviewable political discretion from legally obligated action affecting individual rights. The distinction was fuzzy and would be difficult to apply in harder cases. That in itself might be reason to resist it as it might well subject cabinet officials to complicated litigation simply to determine whether they were indeed subject to judicial supervision. Moreover, the distinction between cases that affect individual rights and those that do not seems terribly imprecise although its boundaries may have been more obvious in

---

[28] *Id.* at 165.

[29] See JAMES F. SIMON, WHAT KIND OF NATION: THOMAS JEFFERSON, JOHN MARSHALL, AND THE EPIC STRUGGLE TO CREATE A UNITED STATES 220–59 (2002) for a detailed discussion of the Burr case.

the private law domain of the early nineteenth century than they would be in the public law realm of today.

It would appear that Marshall had two goals in this section of the opinion. The first was to convince the reader that Marbury's case was really about private rights rather than public action or policy. The second was to reassure the reader that to the extent that the activity of high governmental officials was implicated, it was only in a minor way that would have no significant impact on their political responsibilities. Thus Marshall was intent on defusing the aspects of the case that might seem to make it noteworthy.

Having concluded that Marbury was entitled to a remedy, Marshall turned his attention to whether mandamus was appropriate. He conceded that directing such a writ to a department head was a matter of some sensitivity. However he disclaimed any intention of "intrud[ing] into the cabinet" or "intermeddl[ing] with the prerogatives of the executive."[30] This was undoubtedly a reply to Republicans in Congress who had charged that Marshall was doing just that.[31] Once again, Marshall emphasized that the Court could not pass judgment on "[q]uestions in their nature political."[32] However, the Court could direct an executive official to perform a duty imposed by law that affected the legal rights of an individual.[33] Madison's duty to deliver Marbury's commission was surely such a case. And because mandamus was intended to require a governmental official to perform a legal duty, it was an appropriate remedy here.

Before concluding the discussion, Marshall acknowledged that mandamus was an extraordinary remedy and was only available where there was no adequate remedy at law. Obviously, a judgment for damages might well seem like an adequate remedy at law precluding the need for mandamus. Marshall acknowledged the possibility but rejected it on the grounds that "the value of a public office...is incapable of being ascertained, and the applicant has a right to the office itself...."[34] This sounds unpersuasive to modern ears. It would seem that a calculation of the salary plus any additional damages would be a perfectly appropriate valuation if not precluded by sovereign immunity. Had Marshall desired to conclude the case without addressing the constitutional question, this would have provided an easy and legally respectable exit. That was not his intention, however. Having been presented with this case, Marshall seemed determined to use it for what it was worth.

That brought Marshall to the final question he had framed at the outset: whether mandamus could issue from the Supreme Court in its original jurisdiction. With no analysis whatsoever, Marshall declared that the Judiciary Act of 1789 gave the Supreme Court original jurisdiction in a case in which a party was seeking a writ of mandamus against a government official. This is arguably the weakest link in Marshall's chain of reasoning. The provision in question certainly does not say that explicitly. Rather, in its first two sentences it sets forth those cases in which the Court has original jurisdiction.[35] Then in

---

[30] *Marbury*, 5 U.S at 170.

[31] The concept of judicial review was criticized by Republicans in Congress during the debate over the bill to Repeal the Circuit Court Act in 1801. 11 ANNALS OF CONG. 178–80 (statement of Senator Breckinridge).

[32] *Marbury*, 5 U.S. at 170.

[33] *Id.*

[34] *Id.* at 173.

[35] Judiciary Act of 1789, ch. 20, § 13, 1 Stat. 73, 80–81.

the next sentence it states that in all other cases specified it shall have appellate jurisdiction, and after a semicolon states that it shall have the power to issue various writs
including mandamus. It would be at least as plausible as Marshall's reading to conclude
that if mandamus creates any jurisdiction in the Court at all it is appellate as the reference to mandamus appears in the same sentence as the grant of appellate jurisdiction.[36]
The most persuasive reading of the provision however is that mandamus, in itself, creates
no jurisdiction at all. Rather, it is simply one of the things that the Court can do if it has
some other basis for jurisdiction.[37]

Marbury's counsel Charles Lee did make the jurisdictional argument that Marshall
adopted, that is, that the statute conferred original jurisdiction in actions for mandamus.[38]
However, he placed more weight on the argument that the case was properly before the
Court in its appellate jurisdiction in that Marbury was appealing from an adverse decision
by the Secretary of State. Marshall quite properly rejected that argument on the grounds
that the natural meaning of *appellate* in a legal context referred to review of a decision of a
lower court, not a public official.[39] Moreover, the broader reading of *appellate* would confer
jurisdiction in every case in which a dissatisfied litigant was "appealing" from an adverse
decision by a public official, extending that reading far beyond any plausible limitation.[40]
Marshall's construction of *appellate* is certainly correct, for the reasons he gave.

The fact that no one before the Court anticipated that a question as to the constitutionality of this provision of the Judiciary Act existed[41] is powerful evidence that Marshall's interpretation of the Act was eccentric. In addition, Marshall's construction of
the Act that brought it into conflict with his construction of Article III runs counter to
the canon of statutory construction that acts of Congress should be interpreted to preserve their constitutionality. This canon is especially strong with respect to acts of the
first Congress given the significant overlap of its membership with the Constitutional
Convention. Eighteen years after *Marbury* in *Cohens v. Virginia*, Marshall, writing for the
Court, relied heavily on the presumption of constitutionality of legislation of the first
Congress in sustaining a provision of the very same Act granting the Court appellate
jurisdiction over state criminal cases presenting questions of federal law.[42] Once again,
Marshall, in Marbury, gave the statute a very strained reading in order to avoid ending
the case in a fairly pedestrian manner. It is difficult to resist the conclusion that Marshall
was determined to reach the issue of constitutionality no matter what.

Interpreting the Judiciary Act was only half of the task required to set up a constitutional conflict. Marshall needed to construe the Article III grants of Supreme Court
jurisdiction as well. Looking at Article III, Marshall concluded that it established an

---

[36] Van Alstyne, *supra* note 15, at 15.

[37] *Id.* at 18. Many commentators support this reading. *See, e.g.*, Akhil Amar, *Marbury, Section 13 and the
Original Jurisdiction of the Supreme Court*, 56 U. CHI. L. REV. 443, 444 (1989); Edward Corwin, Marbury
v. Madison *and the Doctrine of Judicial Review*, 12 MICH. L. REV. 538, 542 (1914); DAVID P. CURRIE, THE
CONSTITUTION IN THE SUPREME COURT: THE FIRST HUNDRED YEARS, 1789–888, 68 (1985).

[38] *Marbury*, 5 U.S. at 148–49.

[39] *Id.* at 175.

[40] *Id.*

[41] SLOAN & MCKEAN, *supra* note 6, at 161–62.

[42] 19 U.S. 264, 420 (1821).

unbreachable division of Supreme Court jurisdiction between the original and the appellate.[43] He argued that were this not the case, the line drawn between original and appellate jurisdiction would be pointless. Suits against public officials were not included among those that could be brought in the original jurisdiction.

Marshall's reading of Article III is more defensible than his reading of the Judiciary Act. Still plausible alternative readings are apparent. In quoting Article III, Marshall failed to cite the language giving Congress the power to make "exceptions and regulations" to the appellate jurisdiction. Under his reading, Congress could only make an exception to the appellate jurisdiction by excluding an item from the Court's jurisdiction entirely as the line between original and appellate was immutable. However, it is at least plausible to read Article III as creating a provisional division of jurisdiction subject to the congressional redistribution of some appellate jurisdiction to original in the future should it see fit.[44] Such a reading, although not required by the text, would hardly render it meaningless. Almost two decades later in *Cohens v. Virginia*, Marshall in fact characterized at least some of his language in *Marbury* construing Article III's jurisdictional division as overly broad dicta.[45] There, he concluded that despite the Article III division, a case that fell within the grant of original jurisdiction could be brought in appellate if there was an independent basis for the appellate jurisdiction, although the most expansive reading of *Marbury* might suggest the contrary.[46] As with Marshall's interpretation of the Judiciary Act, his interpretation of Article III seems designed to produce a conflict between the provisions that need not have existed.

Marshall's interpretation of the Judiciary Act and Article III created a conflict that he seems to have been laboring to achieve. Thus 30 pages into the opinion, Marshall finally arrived at the question that has made *Marbury* one of the most foundational cases in American jurisprudence, that is "the question, whether an act, repugnant to the constitution, can become the law of the land...."[47] Marshall quickly assured the reader that though the "question [is] deeply interesting" its proper resolution is not all that difficult.[48]

It is at this point that Marshall developed his carefully crafted multi-step argument in favor of judicial review of congressional legislation. His thesis proceeded as follows. The people enshrined fundamental and hopefully enduring principles in the Constitution.[49] The government established by the Constitution was to be one of defined and limited powers. To help ensure that those limits were respected "the constitution is written."[50] The Constitution is the superior law and supercedes any legislative act to the contrary. It is the duty of courts in adjudicating cases brought before them to apply all of the relevant law, and in the course of doing so interpret that law where necessary. As Marshall proclaimed "[i]t is emphatically the province and duty of the Judicial department to say what the law is."[51] Resolving conflicts between applicable laws is "the very essence of judicial

---

[43] *Marbury*, 5 U.S. at 174.
[44] Van Alstyne, *supra* note 15, at 31.
[45] 19 U.S. 264, 399–402 (1821).
[46] *Id.* at 405 (1821).
[47] *Marbury*, 5 U.S. at 176.
[48] *Id.*
[49] *Id.*
[50] *Id.*
[51] *Id.* at 177.

duty."[52] If in a case before the Court, an act of Congress should come into conflict with the Constitution, the Court must give the latter precedence over the former. Otherwise there would be no effective check on the legislature and the very purpose of having a written constitution would be "reduce[d] to nothing."[53]

That in a nutshell is Marshall's argument for judicial review. It is a structural argument. He does not rely on text, original understanding, or precedent. The argument is composed of two tightly intertwined themes that nevertheless are in some tension with each other. On the one hand, Marshall maintains that the reason a court must sometimes invalidate an act of Congress is because as an aspect of its duty as a court, charged with deciding cases brought before it, it must simply interpret relevant laws and resolve conflicts between them. Note that Marshall has here treated the Constitution as a law applicable by courts and not simply an aspirational or structural set of principles to be considered if at all within the political process. This is a subtle step in the argument, yet one of great significance. This is a relatively modest justification for judicial review. It does not assume any superior wisdom or institutional role for courts aside from simply behaving as courts ordinarily do in deciding cases. This might suggest that judicial review is to be exercised only occasionally and with restraint.

But that is not all that there is to it. Marshall also emphasized the importance of the written constitution in checking legislative disregard of constitutional limitations. He indicated that absent judicial review, at least in cases properly before the courts, written constitutionalism would fail. This theme of the argument suggests that judicial review has a crucial structural role to play in the enforcement of constitutional limitations. Consequently, the more judicial review, the better. Courts should play an aggressive rather than a restrained role in exercising judicial review.

Both of these themes are present in Marshall's brief for judicial review. One points toward restraint, the other toward activism. They are inseparable pieces of one coherent argument however, and there is the rub. It is a thesis that has given rise to two centuries of debate over the appropriate role of courts in the constitutional system.

Marshall's argument for judicial review of congressional legislation is powerful and has certainly carried the day. It is not beyond criticism however. At the outset, Marshall was quite probably on solid ground in proclaiming that the Constitution should be viewed as imposing legally enforceable limits. That seems to have been a widely shared belief by the time of *Marbury v. Madison*.[54] However, in the context of a dispute with a coequal branch of government, the ultimate question becomes who shall decide whether the limits have been exceeded. Marshall's response was that enforcing such legal limitations is precisely what courts are intended and accustomed to do in appropriate cases. But it could plausibly be argued that the Constitution is qualitatively different from ordinary law and ought not be considered judicially enforceable.[55] Perhaps Marshall assumed too readily that the

---

[52] *Id.* at 178.

[53] *Id.*

[54] Michael McConnell, *The Story of Marbury v. Madison: Making Defeat Look Like Victory, in* CONSTITUTIONAL LAW STORIES 25–26 (Michael E. Dorf ed., 2006); 1 CHARLES WARREN, THE SUPREME COURT IN UNITED STATES HISTORY 263–66 (1922); BICKEL, *supra* note 1, at 15, 104; Corwin, *supra* note 37, at 543–52. See BERNARD SCHWARTZ, A HISTORY OF THE SUPREME COURT 7–10 (1993) for a discussion of pre-*Marbury* state cases recognizing judicial review under state constitutions.

[55] Van Alstyne, *supra* note 15, at 23–24.

interpretation of the Constitution was not significantly different than the interpretation of precedent or legislation. The response of the Jeffersonians, both before and after
Marbury, was that each branch is ultimately responsible for interpreting the Constitution
in good faith within its own sphere of responsibility and that it would violate separation
of powers for the Court to second-guess the constitutional judgments of either the president or the Congress.[56]

Marshall's argument can also be faulted for overstating the necessity of judicial review
as a means of checking the legislature. Although judicial review may well be the most
effective means of keeping Congress within constitutional boundaries, it is not the only
means. With or without judicial review the enforcement of constitutional limitations
could be taken seriously through the political process both within the legislative and electoral realms.[57] A written constitution in a common law system may strongly imply judicial
review but it does not necessarily demand it. Finally, Marshall assumed that the point of
the Constitution and consequently the necessity of judicial review is to check legislative
abuse. But critics of the practice can readily ask who will check the Court given that it is
also a governmental actor presumably capable of exceeding constitutional limitations as
well.[58]

Although Marshall's primary argument in *Marbury* was structural, he did raise several textual arguments near the end of the opinion, although he seemed to indicate that
they were at best incidental. He began by pointing out that Article III vests in the federal
courts jurisdiction over all cases "arising under" the Constitution.[59] Must the Court then
not consider the Constitution itself when it was implicated in a case? Critics have noted
that this argument does not achieve much given that there are cases that "arise under"
that do not involve the constitutionality of an act of Congress.[60] Moreover a jurisdictional
provision such as the "arising under" clause does not necessarily speak to the substantive
law that should govern.[61]

Next Marshall listed several explicit limitations in the Constitution, including a prohibition on taxes on imports, prohibitions on bills of attainder and ex post facto laws,
and a requirement of two witnesses in a prosecution for treason.[62] He asked whether a
court could simply sit silent if Congress were to violate any of these explicit provisions
and a case involving such a law was brought before it. Arguably, Marshall was attempting
to make two points here. First, many portions of the Constitution are in fact the type of
hard law that would be easily enforceable in courts. Second, judicial invalidation would
seem readily warranted were Congress to violate any of these clear prohibitions. The
response to this argument has been that it provides a deceptive portrait of constitutional
litigation given that Congress does not tend to violate such obvious limitations and the

---

[56] BICKEL, *supra* note 1, at 4–5; O'Fallon, *supra* note 5, at 227–29 (for a discussion of the congressional
   debate on this very issue prior to *Marbury*).

[57] Van Alstyne, *supra* note 15, at 18–19.

[58] Congressman Williams made this very argument during the debate on the repeal of the Circuit Court
   Act not long before *Marbury* was litigated. 11 ANNALS OF CONG. 531–33 (1801). See O'Fallon, *supra* note
   5, at 225–41 for a thorough discussion of the debate.

[59] Marbury v. Madison, 5 U.S. 137, 178 (1803).

[60] Van Alstyne, *supra* note 15, at 27.

[61] BICKEL, *supra* note 1, at 5–6.

[62] *Marbury*, 5 U.S. at 179.

vast bulk of constitutional law focuses on the vaguer and more ambiguous provisions of the Constitution over which there is much leeway for reasonable disagreement. It might well be however that Marshall may have assumed that the courts would restrict themselves to bright line violations, considering the distinctions that he had drawn earlier in the opinion between law and politics.[63]

Marshall then noted that the judges are required to take an oath to support the Constitution, and should this not imply that they must apply it in relevant cases?[64] This would seem to be Marshall's weakest argument in that it can readily be turned against his position. Because all public officials, state and federal, are constitutionally required to take a similar oath, it can be argued that the Constitution itself assumes that each will faithfully take account of the constitutional limitations in performing his or her duties and as such there is little need for judicial oversight.[65] Or at the very least there is no reason to conclude that the Court has a special role to play in enforcing constitutional limitations.

Finally Marshall noted that the Constitution is mentioned first in the Supremacy Clause.[66] But this is of slight significance given that the clause is addressed to state court judges and it gives precedence to both the Constitution and federal law.[67] Moreover, the Supremacy Clause applies to laws made "in pursuance to the Constitution," which may simply mean those enacted in the constitutionally prescribed manner or those enacted subsequent to its ratification.[68] Marshall's textual argument gained little ground but it did not need to. His structural argument more than carried the day, and though not flawless remains impressive two centuries later.

THE AFTERMATH

As a result of the decision, Marbury's suit was dismissed. He never received his commission or any other remedy for the right that the Court had found to have been violated by Madison. The fact that he could have sought relief in the Circuit Court for the District of Columbia but failed to do so suggests that he was more interested in scoring points before the Supreme Court than with actually receiving his commission.[69] The case was closely watched by the press and informed public but did not stir up an undue amount of controversy at the time. It was considered important enough however that the complete text of the Court's opinion was published in more than one newspaper.[70] Some attention was deflected by the crisis involving the French and Spanish in New Orleans, which was taking place at the very time that *Marbury* was argued and decided.[71] There was however

---

[63] WILLIAM E.NELSON, *MARBURY V. MADISON: THE ORIGINS AND LEGACY OF JUDICIAL REVIEW* 8, 63 (2000); CHARLES F. HOBSON, THE GREAT CHIEF JUSTICE: JOHN MARSHALL AND THE RULE OF LAW 70 (1996).

[64] *Marbury*, 5 U.S. at 180.

[65] BICKEL, *supra* note 1, at 7–8.

[66] *Marbury*, 5 U.S. at 180.

[67] BICKEL, *supra* note 1, at 8–10.

[68] Van Alstyne, *supra* note 15, at 20–21.

[69] *See* Bloch, *supra* note 10, at 607.

[70] NELSON, *supra* note 63, at 72. See also WARREN, *supra* note 54, at 245–67 for lengthy quotations from the newspaper coverage of the case.

[71] WARREN, *supra* note 54, at 239.

some criticism in the press of Marshall's recognition of judicial review, especially by Littleton writing in the *Virginia Argus* and by "an unlearned layman" writing in the *Washington Federalist*.[72] Interest in the decision was necessarily aroused by the obvious prospect of outright conflict between the president and the Court, which had yet to establish its prestige and place in the constitutional order. Leonard Baker writes that given the press coverage "no one with any public conscience could fail to be aware of it."[73] The failure of the secretary of state to appear through counsel certainly raised the very real possibility that the secretary and president would likewise ignore an adverse judgment, arguably inflicting lasting harm on the Court's credibility.

Madison did not respond and as far as is known never commented on the case at any time during his life.[74] Jefferson said little at the time but resented the decision greatly and criticized it, at least in private correspondence, with some frequency over the remainder of his life.[75] He was quite irritated by what was perhaps Marshall's least controversial conclusion, that is, that Marbury was legally entitled to the commission. Jefferson argued that like a deed, the commission did not take legal effect until delivered.[76] Jefferson also objected to Marshall's dicta to the effect that the Court could exercise at least some oversight over high executive officials such as the secretary of state.[77]

For the most part, Jefferson's dissatisfaction with Marbury and Marshall was expressed in private correspondence; however, a confrontation between the president and the chief justice did arise over a subpoena by the latter to the former seeking evidence in the treason trial of Aaron Burr, with Marshall presiding as a circuit judge.[78] The president asserted what has now become known as executive privilege. After some posturing by each side, a compromise was reached under which some though not all of the requested material was produced.[79] From then on, Jefferson and Marshall managed to stay out of each other's way although the conflict between the two never subsided.

MARBURY AND STUART v. LAIRD

From a standpoint of potential constitutional confrontation, *Marbury* was a case of enormous import. Factually however it was quite insignificant. It truly did not matter then or in the long term whether William Marbury ever became a justice of the peace in the District of Columbia. *Marbury* was decided in a context however in which more important issues were presented to the Court for resolution. The day before the opinion in *Marbury* was announced, Charles Lee, Marbury's counsel, argued the case of *Stuart v. Laird*.[80] That case simply involved an action to collect a debt; however at its heart was the claim that the congressional repeal of the Circuit Court Act in 1802 violated the Constitution. The

---

[72] LEONARD BAKER, JOHN MARSHALL: A LIFE IN LAW 410–11 (1974).

[73] *Id.* at 409.

[74] SLOAN & McKEAN, *supra* note 6, at 167.

[75] *Id.* at 169.

[76] Letter of Thomas Jefferson to William Johnson, June 12, 1823, *supra* note 6 at.

[77] *Id.*

[78] United States v. Burr, 25 F. Case 1 (1807).

[79] SIMON, *supra* note 29, at 242–43.

[80] 5 U.S. 299 (1803).

debt action in question had been adjudicated in one of the newly created circuit courts and then transferred back to the jurisdiction of Supreme Court justices riding circuit following the repeal.[81] Lee argued that Congress had no constitutional right to repeal the Act nor did it have the right to require Supreme Court justices to ride circuit absent explicitly confirming them as circuit judges.[82]

Stuart v. Laird would seem to have been of far greater importance than Marbury v. Madison. By repealing the Circuit Court Act, Congress had effectively deprived of their positions 16 men who had been appointed to life-tenured Article III judgeships. Marshall recused himself from the case considering that he had ruled in the lower court proceedings while riding circuit in Virginia.[83] Despite the apparent gravity of the issues, Justice Patterson upheld the repeal in a cursory four-paragraph opinion, concluding that Congress had the constitutional authority to reorder the lower courts, and the practice of circuit riding had been accepted for too long (all of 13 years) to be challenged as unconstitutional.[84] Apparently, Marshall had tried unsuccessfully to persuade the other justices to strike down the repeal of the Circuit Court Act.[85] The opinion in Marbury was then a small victory by Marshall to compensate for the much larger defeat in Stuart v. Laird.[86]

THE LEGACY OF MARBURY

Marbury is readily viewed as the most important of several Marshall court cases establishing the legitimacy of judicial review in a variety of contexts. Marbury held that the Court had the power to declare an act of Congress unconstitutional. In Martin v. Hunter's Lessee,[87] in an opinion by Justice Story, the Court upheld the constitutionality of section 25 of the Judiciary Act of 1789 providing the Court with appellate jurisdiction over cases raising federal questions from the highest court of a state. A few years later in Cohens v. Virginia,[88] Marshall writing for a unanimous Court confirmed that the same was true for criminal appeals as well. In Fletcher v. Peck,[89] another Marshall opinion, the Court affirmed its power to strike down state legislation as unconstitutional. Martin, Cohens, and Fletcher were arguably easier cases than Marbury as the Supremacy Clause and the need for uniformity re-enforced the need for Supreme Court review where state law or institutions were implicated. Marbury, on the other hand, involved the work product of a coequal branch of government, the Congress, generally approved by another coequal branch, the president. The ability of the Court to exercise judicial review in all of these contexts was vitally important however both to the role of the Court as well as the

---

[81] Id. at 301–02.

[82] Id. at 303–05.

[83] Id. at 307. The opinion notes, "The chief justice, having tried the cause in the court below, declined to give an opinion."

[84] Id. at 309.

[85] O'Fallon, supra note 5, at 239–40.

[86] McConnell, supra note 54, at 31.

[87] 14 U.S. 304 (1816).

[88] 19 U.S. 264 (1821).

[89] 10 U.S. 87 (1810).

operation of the constitutional system. *Marbury* was thus the cornerstone of one of the most important endeavors and accomplishments of the Marshall court.

It has often been noted that once having established the power to invalidate an act of Congress, the Marshall court never again exercised it. Indeed, the next Supreme Court decision striking down an act of Congress was the infamous *Dred Scott* decision 54 years after *Marbury*.[90] Even that assertion must be qualified given that the act in question, the Missouri Compromise, had been largely repealed by the time that Chief Justice Roger Taney declared it unconstitutional. Plainly, for the first half of the nineteenth century, judicial invalidation of congressional legislation was a rarity, although during this period both the Marshall and Taney courts exercised the power of judicial review on several occasions by rejecting constitutional challenges to acts of Congress.[91] That changed with the Civil War and the expansion of federal legislation in the later part of the nineteenth century. Gradually, the Court discovered more conflicts between the Constitution and federal legislation and over a period of time, judicial review as we now understand it developed.

MARBURY AS A "GREAT CASE"

The face-off between the president and the chief justice alone made *Marbury* a great case. Presumably, the case was brought in an attempt to embarrass the president but it had the very real potential to backfire and embarrass the Court. Arguably, the prospect of successful defiance by the president led Marshall to the clever resolution of avoiding such a showdown through the assertion of the power of judicial review. In what is probably the most often quoted assessment of Marshall's strategy, Robert McCloskey wrote that Marbury "is a masterwork of indirection, a brilliant example of Marshall's capacity to sidestep danger while seeming to court it, to advance in one direction while his opponents are looking in another."[92] Consequently "the Court was in the delightful position... of rejecting and assuming power in the same breath...."[93] McCloskey's assessment has been challenged.[94] Marshall's critics, Jefferson in particular, were too shrewd to be fooled or distracted by Marshall's opinion. Nevertheless Marshall deliberately bypassed several plausible and non-controversial means of avoiding the central constitutional issue, as noted above. So it would seem that having been backed into a corner, Marshall took full advantage of the opportunity that presented itself by endorsing judicial review in a case in which the president though not the Congress prevailed. Although it may not be quite as clever as McCloskey suggested, it still appears to be fancy judicial footwork.

As a whole, Marshall's opinion in *Marbury* is subject to many of the same criticisms as most of his major opinions. He relied on bold assertion and rhetorical flourish over precedent and other more conventional legal materials. He often ignored sources of authority

---

[90] Scott v. Sanford, 60 U.S. 393 (1857).

[91] In *Hylton v. United States*, 3 U.S. 171 (1796), decided seven years prior to *Marbury*, in the face of a constitutional challenge the Court upheld a federal law imposing a tax on carriages.

[92] ROBERT G. MCCLOSKEY, THE AMERICAN SUPREME COURT 25 (2nd ed. 1994).

[93] *Id.* at 27.

[94] *See* O'Fallon, *supra* note 5, at 219.

that could bolster his argument. He minimized or wholly ignored cogent counterarguments. Such was the Marshall style. It was not what we would expect of a careful judge today. But he was a master at legal reasoning and writing. Indeed Jefferson once noted that one should never admit anything when arguing with Marshall because his sophistry would twist it to reach his own conclusions.[95] In *Marbury*, Marshall was addressing issues on which there was little if any useful judicial authority. And considering that he was in a rather precarious position politically, it would make sense to proceed with great confidence as if there was no doubt whatsoever as to his conclusions. Even considering that all of Marshall's reasoning was borrowed either from Blackstone's *Commentaries*, Lee's argument, the congressional debate over the Repeal Act, or Hamilton's essay in *Federalist* 78, it is still striking that he could produce the opinion in less than a week.

When *Marbury v. Madison* arrived at Chief Justice Marshall's doorstep, considering the political context, it had the earmarks of a great case. And yet it was a great case that could very readily have been turned into a run-of-the-mill case soon to be forgotten. Instead, Marshall chose to transform it into a far greater case than it really needed to be. As such, *Marbury* is an example of the Court amplifying the significance of the case when it just as easily could have diminished it. *Marbury* was the product of a great and confident justice. Although the Jefferson administration would score a striking victory in *Stuart v. Laird* a few days later, Marshall used *Marbury* to begin his project of elevating the role of the judiciary in American government. Even so, he was able to establish the concept of judicial review by invalidating an obscure jurisdictional provision that no one particularly cared about as opposed to a law of great consequence.[96]

Given that *Marbury v. Madison* is the very cornerstone of the judicial role in constitutional interpretation, it can scarcely be argued that this was a great case that made bad law. Rather it is a highly revered decision. Bernard Schwartz has characterized it as "*the great case in american Constitutional law*."[97] Marshall's biographer Leonard Baker goes so far as to call it "one of civilization's finest hours, one of mankind's greatest achievements."[98] In fact, it was voted the most important Supreme Court decision of all time in a survey of lawyers and judges conducted by the American Bar Association in 1974.[99] Although Marshall's justification for judicial review has been subjected to strenuous academic criticism, the general principle of the opinion has endured with greater vigor than Marshall could ever have intended or even imagined. And yet it could hardly be maintained that but for *Marbury v. Madison*, judicial review of congressional legislation would not exist. Although neither the text nor the original understanding of the Constitution clearly call for it, judicial review was "in the air," as one commentator put it, and its eventual judicial recognition would seem to have been inevitable.[100] Hamilton's essay

---

[95] JEAN EDWARD SMITH, JOHN MARSHALL: DEFINER OF A NATION 12 (1996), noting that the source of this quip comes from a lecture at the Harvard Law School delivered by Joseph Story and captured in the notes of future president Rutherford B. Hayes.

[96] Alfange, *supra* note 11, at 368.

[97] SCHWARTZ, *supra* note 54, at 41.

[98] BAKER, *supra* note 72, at 409.

[99] JETHRO K. LIEBERMAN, MILESTONES! 200 YEARS OF AMERICAN LAW: MILESTONES IN OUR LEGAL HISTORY, at vii (1976).

[100] PAUL BREST, SANFORD V. LEVINSON, JACK M. BALKIN, AKHIL REED AMAR & REVA B. SIEGEL, PROCESSES OF CONSTITUTIONAL DECISION MAKING, CASES AND MATERIALS 125 (5th ed. 2006).

in *Federalist 78* made an a argument not dissimilar to Marshall's justification in *Marbury*. The propriety of judicial review was a central question in the congressional debate on the repeal of the Circuit Court Act a year before the decision in *Marbury*.

As Marshall seems to have been committed to the establishment of the judiciary as a coequal and meaningful branch of government, it is highly probable that if not in *Marbury*, Marshall would have found another case in which to assert the principle that the Court had the authority to invalidate an unconstitutional act of Congress. And yet after *Marbury*, the Marshall court never exercised the power again. It certainly would have been tragic if the principle of judicial review of congressional legislation made its initial appearance in the *Dred Scott* decision instead of *Marbury v. Madison*. That might have cast a cloud over the doctrine not easily removed.

Few today challenge the constitutional propriety of judicial review, period. Rather the contemporary debate rages over whether it should be exercised with restraint or vigor. And the seeds of both judicial restraint and judicial activism may be found in Marshall's opinion in *Marbury*. Does the Court review the constitutionality of congressional action only because of its judicial duty to apply all the relevant law to cases bought before it? Or does it do so because of its essential role of ensuring that Congress remains within constitutional boundaries? The former rationale leans toward judicial restraint. The latter favors a more aggressive judicial role: *activism*. And yet Marshall integrated both justifications into a single argument.[101]

Most constitutional historians believe that by the time of *Marbury*, the institution of judicial review had been widely accepted.[102] The Supreme Court itself although not having invalidated an act of Congress had upheld one, suggesting that it did have the power to engage in constitutional review of congressional legislation. There is little question that the type of judicial review assumed by Marshall and his contemporaries was far more limited than that which has developed over the past two centuries.[103] It is likely that at least as of the time of *Marbury*, invalidation of congressional legislation would be reserved for those cases in which the constitutional error was quite obvious.[104] Moreover, the realm of political discretion immune from judicial review mentioned by Marshall in *Marbury* was almost certainly quite a bit larger than it would be today. Although it is true that Marshall almost certainly would be surprised by the scope and pervasiveness of modern judicial review, he still started the Court down the path that ultimately led to where we are today.

Although *Marbury* is best known for its recognition and exercise of judicial review of congressional legislation, it is responsible for other notable developments as well. Marshall's careful analysis of Marbury's vested right to the commission itself helped enshrine the principle that an individual can in fact have legally enforceable property rights against the government. *Marbury* did not create this principle but did provide meaningful support. It is likely that this portion of the opinion, which is generally ignored by most modern readers, was quite important to Marshall.

---

[101] See G. Edward White, *The Constitutional Journey of* Marbury v. Madison, 80 Va. L. Rev. 1463 (2003) for a careful analysis of the path of *Marbury* and the concept of judicial review from 1803 to the present.

[102] McConnell, *supra* note 54, at 23.

[103] Nelson, *supra* note 63, at 77, 83.

[104] Michael J. Klarman, *How Great Were the "Great" Marshall Court Decisions?*, 87 Va. L. Rev. 1111, 1121 (2001).

Marbury is also responsible for recognizing what came to be understood as the political question doctrine. Marshall went out of his way to acknowledge that there were certain questions involving constitutional issues with respect to executive decision-making that the Court could not address. He purported to draw a distinction between those matters that were political and discretionary and those that were legal. It is not at all clear that he was endorsing a pure political question doctrine under which the Court would refrain from considering certain issues of constitutional law even if it appeared that the executive had misconstrued the Constitution. Rather he seemed to be indicating that where it appeared that the Constitution entrusted the executive with discretion, the Court would not second-guess its exercise. Even so, it is likely that the field of executive discretion contemplated by Marshall would be substantially broader than that which a modern court would find.

Finally, that portion of the *Marbury* opinion to which Jefferson objected as mere dicta has, as Jefferson realized, become quite important. Marshall made a point of establishing that at least in the appropriate case, the Court could issue an order against a cabinet level official. Implicit in this conclusion is the assumption that high executive officials are not immune from legal process. At least with respect to the president, an issue not presented in *Marbury*, that question was not settled until the Nixon tapes cases 170 years later. However the implications of *Marbury* as well as Marshall's subsequent confrontation with Jefferson in the Aaron Burr treason trial case suggested that the president was amenable to legal process. *Marbury* did address the substantive question of whether the Court could exercise supervision over a cabinet officer, at least in the instance of an arguable breach of a legal duty. Marshall of course avoided any direct confrontation by dismissing for lack of jurisdiction. Nevertheless, he made his point to the chagrin of Jefferson. The *Marbury* dicta on this point eventually provided the foundation for judicial supervision of the executive branch and the administrative state.[105] This aspect of *Marbury* effectively precluded the executive branch from successfully asserting that any judicial supervision of its policies and actions was an unconstitutional breach of separation of powers.

From the standpoint of constitutional interpretation, Marshall placed heavy reliance on a structural argument to justify judicial review; that is, he argued from the purpose of the Constitution and the role of courts as legal interpreters to draw the conclusion that judicial review of congressional legislation was warranted. Although this argument has been the subject of much professional criticism, it has still withstood the test of time. The emphasis in *Marbury* on the limitations imposed by a written constitution strongly implies that a textual approach to constitutional interpretation is appropriate.

None of these developments sprung full blown from *Marbury*. Nor would it be fair to assert that Marshall intended or contemplated the use to which *Marbury* has been put in the twentieth century. Like all cases, it was decided within a specific legal context. Still, Marshall wrote an opinion pregnant with possibilities, and it has provided the foundation for much that has come afterward.

Nothing is known as to whatever internal deliberations may have entered into the decision-making process in *Marbury*. Two hundred years of speculation has resulted in virtually every conceivable possibility. Marshall was a crafty tactician cleverly outsmarting

---

[105] Louise Weinberg, *Our* Marbury, 89 Va. L. Rev. 1235, 1404 (2003).

the opposition.[106] Marshall was cowed by the Jeffersonian assault and was simply attempting to save face given the inevitable setback to be delivered shortly thereafter in *Stuart v. Laird*.[107] Marshall was simply a workman-like justice delivering an opinion of no great consequence on the basis of settled legal principles. As Alan Westin put it, in the absence of the discovery of "a crumbling diary or set of letters" that has eluded historians for two centuries, we will never know for certain why Marshall did what he did in *Marbury* given that there is no documentary explanation aside from the opinion itself.[108]

This much is clear: Marshall did indeed fear Jefferson's challenge to the judiciary as well as his basic political philosophy. It is likely that he concluded that the Court had to do or say something in response to what was probably perceived as a war against the judiciary. Marshall was an extraordinarily capable and certainly a confident judge. He preferred to avoid confrontation but at the same time was committed to protecting and over time expanding the prestige and influence of the Court. At the time of *Marbury*, Marshall presided over a court composed of loyal Federalists upon whose support he could depend. Given the operation of the early Marshall court and the short time it took to produce the *Marbury* opinion, it is probable that there was not much internal deliberation. Rather, Marshall wrote the opinion and the other justices concurred, whether or not they read it carefully and agreed with all of it.[109]

The highly charged political context in which *Marbury v. Madison* came to the Court made it a great case upon its arrival. Indeed in the course of the debate in Congress over the repeal of the Circuit Court Act, the *Marbury* action was condemned by some Republicans even before it was argued.[110] *Marbury* scarcely needed to remain a great case however. Marshall had every opportunity to dispose of the case in a manner that would have rendered it insignificant and forgettable. Indeed, it certainly appears that he labored hard to avoid doing just that. Although he could have avoided the constitutional conflict in a variety of ways, his construction of section 13 of the Judiciary Act of 1787 appears to be his least persuasive legal move and the one that most strongly suggests that he was determined to set up the conflict between the Act and Article III no matter what. That implies that John Marshall saw this great case not as a quandary but rather as an opportunity to be embraced and exploited. That is a pattern that would reoccur in other great cases in the future.

---

[106] McCloskey, *supra* note 92, at 25–28.

[107] McConnell, *supra* note 54, at 31.

[108] Alan Westin, Introduction to Charles Beard, The Supreme Court and the Constitution 9 (1962). Dean Alfange used Westin's statement in a persuasive rejection of several revisionist theories of Marbury. Alfange, *supra* note 11 at 329.

[109] *See* G. Edward White, The Marshall Court and Cultural Change 1815–1836 157 (abridged ed. 1991) describing "The Working Life of the Court."

[110] Warren, *supra* note 54, at 232–33.

"*McCulloch v. Maryland* in 1819 is by almost any reckoning the greatest decision John Marshall ever handed down—the one most important to the future of America, most influential in the Court's own doctrinal history, and most revealing of Marshall's unique talent for stately argument."[1]

ROBERT MCCLOSKEY

2

McCulloch v. Maryland

Arguably, *McCulloch v. Maryland*[2] is the greatest of the great cases ever decided by the Supreme Court. It involved a question, the constitutionality of the Bank of the United States, which had been a matter of extreme controversy at the highest levels of government for almost 30 years prior to the decision. The issues giving rise to the litigation were at the center of a national political and economic crisis when the case arrived at the Court's doorstep. *McCulloch*, at least as addressed by the Court, posed the most foundational questions of constitutional law, including the very nature and origin of the nation as well as the appropriate approach to constitutional interpretation. It was argued for nine straight days by some of the finest lawyers ever to appear before the Court. Chief Justice Marshall produced an opinion widely considered to be one of if not the greatest in Supreme Court history.[3] The opinion was criticized so vigorously at the time by Marshall's political opponents that he published pseudonymous essays in the press defending it. Its precedential status was directly challenged by a recalcitrant state and needed to be reaffirmed in a subsequent opinion. Its reasoning was effectively rejected by a subsequent president, ultimately ending the controversy at the center of the case. And the major theoretical premise of the Court's opinion was ultimately settled not by judicial

---

[1] ROBERT G. MCCLOSKEY, THE AMERICAN SUPREME COURT 43 (2d ed. 1994).

[2] 17 U.S. 316 (1819).

[3] MCCLOSKEY, *supra* note 1, at 43; JEAN EDWARD SMITH, JOHN MARSHALL: DEFINER OF A NATION 441 (1996) ("*McCulloch v. Maryland* may be the most important case in the history of the Supreme Court"); CHARLES BLACK, JR., STRUCTURE AND RELATIONSHIP IN CONSTITUTIONAL LAW 15 (1969) ("perhaps the greatest of our constitutional cases"); James Bradley Thayer, *John Marshall, in* JAMES BRADLEY THAYER, OLIVER WENDELL HOLMES, AND FELIX FRANKFURTER ON JOHN MARSHALL 68 (Philip B. Kurland ed., 1967) ("there is nothing so fine as the opinion in *McCulloch v. Maryland*"); Felix Frankfurter, *John Marshall and the Judicial Function*, 69 HARV. L. REV. 217, 219 (1955) ("*McCulloch v. Maryland* is his greatest single judicial performance"); MARK R. KILLENBECK, *MCCULLOCH V. MARYLAND*: SECURING A NATION 7 (2006) (one study ranks *McCulloch* as the most influential decision in Supreme Court history).

decree but rather by the Civil War. After all of that it remains one of the most influential decisions and opinions in American history.

THE BACKGROUND

McCulloch raised the constitutional question of whether the state of Maryland could impose a tax on the paper of a branch of the Bank of the United States operating in Maryland. The very existence of the Bank had been a matter of great constitutional controversy during the early days of the Republic.[4] The Constitutional Convention had rejected a proposal to permit the Congress to create a corporation to build a canal.[5] The First Bank of the United States had been proposed in 1790 during the early days of the Washington administration. The purpose of the Bank was to provide credit to the federal government and the public and to establish a circulating currency.[6] James Madison opposed the proposal in the House of Representatives on the ground that Congress lacked the constitutional power to create a bank.[7] Congress authorized the creation of the Bank nevertheless. When the act authorizing the Bank was presented to President Washington, one of the most famous debates in the history of the executive branch took place. Washington sought the advice of his cabinet as to the legislation's constitutionality. Like Madison in the House, Secretary of State Jefferson argued that Congress lacked the power to create a bank.[8] Secretary of the Treasury Alexander Hamilton disagreed and wrote a classic defense of the Act.[9] Washington asked Madison to prepare a veto message, which he did. Washington agreed with Hamilton however and signed the legislation. The Bank was not, as its name might suggest, a government-owned and managed institution but rather a federally chartered corporation that was largely owned by private investors. Jefferson, though one of the most severe critics of the Bank, as president signed legislation permitting it to establish branch offices.

The charter of the First Bank of the United States expired in 1811. There was a movement to renew the charter, which ultimately failed in Congress. Following the economic dislocations attributable to the War of 1812, Congress created the Second Bank of the United States in 1816. James Madison, then president, initially vetoed the Act on non-constitutional grounds but signed a revised version into law after indicating that he had concluded that its constitutionality had been settled by prior practice.[10] By the

---

[4] *See generally* RICHARD E. ELLIS, AGGRESSIVE NATIONALISM: *MCCULLOCH v. MARYLAND* AND THE FOUNDATION OF FEDERAL AUTHORITY IN THE YOUNG REPUBLIC (2007) and KILLENBECK, *supra* note 3 for a detailed study of *McCulloch* and the Bank crisis.

[5] JAMES MADISON'S NOTES OF DEBATES IN THE FEDERAL CONVENTION OF 1787 638–39 (bicentennial ed. 1987).

[6] ELLIS, *supra* note 4, at 34.

[7] ANNALS OF CONGRESS 1947 (Aug. 9, 1790) (statement of James Madison).

[8] Thomas Jefferson, Opinion on the Constitutionality of the Bill for Establishing a National Bank, Feb. 15, 1791, in 19 Papers of Thomas Jefferson 275 (Julian P. Boyd ed. 1950).

[9] Alexander Hamilton, Opinion on the Constitutionality of an Act to Establish a Bank Feb. 23, 1791, in 8 The Papers of Alexander Hamilton 97 (Harold C. Syrett ed. 1961).

[10] Message of James Madison vetoing the Act Creating the Second Bank of the United States (Jan. 30, 1815), in Compilation of the Messages and Papers of the Presidents, 1789–1897 555 (James F. Richardson ed. 1900).

time that the Second Bank was chartered, over 200 state banks had come into existence as opposed to only three when the First Bank had been chartered.[11] Although the Second Bank was federally chartered, 80 percent of its stock was privately owned. At the time that the *McCulloch* litigation was bought, 35 branch offices of the Bank had been established.

The Second Bank of the United States was by far the largest corporation in the nation at the time.[12] A severe recession followed the creation of the Second Bank. Easy credit for real estate speculation followed by severe credit contraction by the Bank, especially in the western states, played a role in the downturn in the economy.[13] Consequently, the Bank was held responsible by both the public and some state officials for the ensuing recession.[14] The Maryland branch of the Bank was controlled by speculators who manipulated its share prices for their own financial advantage.[15] Many states perceived the Bank as a serious threat to their own state-chartered banks if in fact it was immune from state taxation. Some responded by imposing punitive taxes on the Bank designed to drive it out of their jurisdictions.

The Maryland legislature imposed a 2 percent tax on the paper notes of banks not chartered by the state, the Baltimore branch of the Bank of the United States being the only such entity. In lieu of the tax on the notes, the Bank could pay an annual tax of $15,000, a sizeable but by no means confiscatory sum at the time.[16] The Baltimore branch had lost over 1.5 million dollars and was on the verge of insolvency.[17] McCulloch, the treasurer of the Baltimore branch of the Bank, refused to pay, and an action was brought by John James on his own behalf and on behalf of the state under a Maryland law authorizing a private party to sue to collect the debt and share in the judgment.[18] The Maryland trial court decided the case in favor of the state. The parties agreed to a stipulated set of facts and the decision was quickly affirmed by the Court of Appeals. It is believed that there was collusion between the parties to move the case forward for resolution by the Supreme Court as quickly as possible.[19] Arguably, the political establishment of Maryland favored a decision sustaining the Bank and invalidating the tax.[20] The case was then docketed in the Supreme Court and set for oral argument on an expedited basis. Critics of the decision at the time fairly uniformly charged that the case had been manufactured and rushed to the high court in order to obtain a preemptive decision favorable to the Bank. Whether the Court itself and John Marshall in particular played an active role in setting up the case and moving it along remains a matter of historical speculation.

---

[11] ELLIS, *supra* note 4, at 42.

[12] Bray Hammond, *The Bank Cases, in* QUARRELS THAT HAVE SHAPED THE CONSTITUTION 40 (John A. Garraty ed., 1987).

[13] KILLENBECK, *supra* note 3, at 66.

[14] ELLIS, *supra* note 4, at 62–63.

[15] KILLENBECK, *supra* note 3, at 93.

[16] ELLIS, *supra* note 4 at 68.

[17] Hammond, *supra* note 12 at 45.

[18] McCulloch v. Maryland, 17 U.S. 316, 317 (1819).

[19] ELLIS, *supra* note 4, at 72–73. The governor of Maryland explained to the state legislature that in the court of appeals "a decision in favor of the state was there had by consent." *Id.* at 72.

[20] *Id.* at 69–73.

THE ORAL ARGUMENT

Even assuming that *McCulloch v. Maryland* was in some sense a collusively arranged case, the appearances of counsel before the Court emphasized the significance and gravity of the issues presented. Indeed the Reporter stated that "the court dispensed with its general rule, permitting only two counsel to argue for each party" given that it involves "a question of great public importance, and the sovereign rights of the United States and the state of Maryland."[21] The Bank was represented not simply by Attorney General William Wirt but by Daniel Webster and William Pinkney as well. The state was represented by Joseph Hopkinson, Walter Jones, and Luther Martin. It is certainly arguable that no other case presented to the Court has engaged more distinguished legal talent than *McCulloch*. The argument extended for nine days. This in itself stands as testament to the momentous stature that the case had almost immediately assumed. The public recognized the significance of the case. Justice Joseph Story observed that on the day that the arguments began the small courtroom was "full almost to the point of suffocation, and many went away for lack of room."[22]

Webster, though he had opposed the creation of the Bank in Congress, opened for the Bank proclaiming that the case raised "a question of the utmost magnitude" the mere discussion of which "may most essentially affect the value of a vast amount of private property."[23] He began by addressing the constitutional power of Congress to create the Bank, arguing that past practice and a proper reading of the Constitution resolved the issue in favor of the Bank. Webster proclaimed that state taxation of the Bank was unconstitutional because "[a]n unlimited power to tax involves, necessarily, a power to destroy...."[24]

James Hopkinson representing the state conceded that perhaps Congress had the power to create the Bank in 1791 when no alternative state-chartered banking system existed.[25] However, a federally chartered bank was no longer "necessary" given that so many state banks had since emerged. Next Hopkinson argued that even if creation of the bank was still constitutionally permissible, establishing branches within the states was not constitutionally necessary. Even more important, Hopkinson pressed the argument that the government did not have the constitutional power to establish branches within sovereign states without their consent. But assuming that the branches were lawfully established, the states certainly had the right to tax them, especially as they were largely privately held profit-generating entities. As for potential abuse of the state taxation power, Hopkinson argued that reliance must be placed on "mutual forbearance and discretion."[26] Hopkinson's arguments did not present an outright assault on congressional power but rather offered several carefully crafted reasons for concluding that Maryland's actions were justified. The argument is a sterling example of an attorney attempting to

---

[21] *McCulloch*, 17 U.S. at 317, n.3.

[22] Letter of Joseph Story to Stephen White, March 3, 1819, *in* 2 LIFE AND LETTERS OF JOSEPH STORY 325 (W.W. Story ed., 1851).

[23] *McCulloch*, 17 U.S. at 322.

[24] *Id.* at 327.

[25] *Id.* at 332–33.

[26] *Id.* at 349.

provide the Court with the easiest methods for ruling for his client rather than staking out a more extreme ideological position.

Attorney General Wirt spoke next on behalf of the Bank. Replying to Hopkinson's assertion that the Bank was no longer necessary, Wirt argued that it certainly had proved to be given the financial dislocations experienced in the War of 1812, which had led to its re-establishment.[27] Beyond that, it would be troublesome to make constitutionality turn on ever-changing circumstances. Wirt also contended that the power to establish state branches was necessarily encompassed within the initial power to create the Bank. Turning to the state's power to tax the Bank, like Webster, Wirt argued that such a power could easily be used to interfere with federal authority in violation of the Supremacy Clause.

Walter Jones then appeared for the state. He began by asserting that the questions presented remained open given that they had never been addressed by the Court and that governmental practice should not be viewed as having settled the matters. He then proclaimed that the Constitution originated as a compact between the states rather than emanating directly from "the people of the United States."[28] Unlike Hopkinson, Jones argued at length that Congress did not have the authority either on an implied power theory or based on the Necessary and Proper Clause to establish the Bank. Like Hopkinson, Jones argued that "mutual, confidence, discretion and forbearance" must be relied on to prevent abusive taxation of federal instrumentalities. He concluded with the argument that even if the actual property of the federal government was immune from state taxation, this did not carry over to an essentially private entity such as the Bank.

Luther Martin, a member of the Constitutional Convention and now attorney general of Maryland, was the final advocate for the state. He began by reading from the Federalist Papers and the ratification debates in Virginia and New York to establish that the flexible construction of the Constitution pressed by the attorneys for the Bank was quite inconsistent with the original understanding.[29] Rather, the Tenth Amendment tightly limited both the ends that the federal government could pursue and the means it could employ, and the creation of a corporation could not be justified as either. But assuming that Congress had the power to create the Bank, Martin argued that the state retained the power to tax it, unlike the direct property of the United States such as judicial proceedings or custom houses.

The final attorney to appear on behalf of the United States was William Pinkney. He argued at great length and apparently with great impact as well. Justice Story later indicated that he considered Pinkney's argument in *McCulloch* to be the best argument that he had heard during his tenure on the Court.[30] Pinkney began his "reply" attempting to address a question that he maintained never should have become part of the case to begin with—the power of the Congress to create the Bank—failing to note that at least before the Court it was his co-counsel Webster who first raised the issue. Like Webster, Pinkney argued that the question was settled by prior "legislative, executive and judicial" practice and as such "this practical interpretation had become incorporated into the

---

[27] *Id.* at 354.

[28] *Id.* at 363.

[29] *Id.* at 372.

[30] Letter of Joseph Story to Stephen White, March 3, 1819, *in* 1 LIFE AND LETTERS OF JOSEPH STORY 325 (W.W. Story ed., 1851).

constitution."[31] Relying on original understanding, Pinkney emphasized that the power to create the Bank was supported "by the authors of the constitution themselves."[32]

Pinkney then explained that the Constitution could not specify all of the means of execution of enumerated powers because it would require too much detail and it would be impossible to "foresee the infinite variety of circumstances" that would be presented in the future.[33] He discussed a number of instances in which Congress had legislatively created means that were convenient but hardly essential to the achievement of enumerated ends. Pinkney also argued that though the word "necessary" has both strict and lenient meanings, the latter was clearly the connotation intended in the "Necessary and Proper" Clause.

Pinkney detailed at great length the many ways in which the Bank served and was intertwined with the federal government, probably in part to emphasize its necessity but also to reply to the insistence by the attorneys for that state that it was essentially a private corporation attempting to invoke sovereign privilege. He then turned to what he characterized as the "only difficult question" presented: the power of the states to tax the Bank. Pinkney, like Webster and Wirt, emphasized that recognition of such a power would permit the states to demolish any federal instrumentality, including the army, navy, treasury, or judiciary. Over and over Pinkney emphasized the potentially destructive impact of permitting state taxation of the Bank as well as the impossibility of drawing any workable rule other than complete prohibition.

Finally, Pinkney introduced the argument that there was a significant structural difference between state taxation of federal instrumentalities and federal taxation of state instrumentalities in that the people of the states were represented in Congress but the people of the United States as a whole were not represented in particular state legislatures.

The report of the arguments show that the issues Marshall addressed in his opinion had been thoroughly worked over by the attorneys and that there had also been much discussion of questions that Marshall chose to ignore as well.

THE OPINION

Chief Justice Marshall published his classic opinion in *McCulloch* only three days after the culmination of the oral arguments. He was able to do so no doubt because so many of the core issues had been debated in the public forums as well as the press for almost three decades, and because the extensive oral argument before the Court had been informative and incisive. Marshall borrowed generously from these sources. Moreover, Marshall had discussed some of the issues raised in *McCulloch* in earlier opinions in *United States v. Fisher*[34] and *Bank of the United States v. DeVeaux*.[35] Still much of the greatness of the opinion, especially its organization and rhetorical power, would appear to originate with Marshall's own genius.

---

[31] *McCulloch*, 17 U.S. at 378.
[32] *Id* at 379.
[33] *Id*. at 385.
[34] 6 U.S. 358 (1805).
[35] 9 U.S. 61 (1809).

Marshall began his opinion by taking notice of the great significance of the issues raised and acknowledging "the awful responsibility involved in its decision."[36] He noted that the Court was well aware that its opinion would have great historical significance, as indeed it did. He then declared that "the first question made in the cause is—has congress the power to incorporate a bank?"[37] This was the very question that Pinkney had asserted was scarcely even worthy of consideration. Nevertheless, Marshall devoted the better part of his opinion to it. Recalling the history of the constitutional debates surrounding both the First and Second Banks of the United States, Marshall agreed with counsel for the Bank that it "can scarcely be considered an open question."[38] At this point in his opinion, Marshall made an eloquent case for reliance upon established practice as a significant indicator of constitutionality. He emphasized that there had been considerable financial reliance upon the presumed constitutionality of the Bank for quite some time. To declare the Bank an illegal entity at this point would be quite destabilizing.

Marshall then explained carefully why the legislative conclusions as to the Bank's constitutionality were particularly powerful. He emphasized that the bill authorizing the First Bank of the United States "did not steal upon an unsuspecting legislature, and pass unobserved."[39] Rather "[i]ts principle was completely understood, and was opposed with equal zeal and ability."[40] He declared that greater deference should be accorded congressional legislation when challenged on constitutional grounds where it is clear that Congress understood and debated the issue. He noted that the bill was initially opposed in both the Congress and the cabinet "with as much persevering talent as any measure has ever experienced" but was ultimately enacted having convinced minds "as pure and as intelligent as the country can boast."[41] Here Marshall implicitly makes reference to the opposition of Jefferson and Madison as well as the fact that the Act was signed into law by Washington. Marshall well understood that the Bank was unpopular, as would be his opinion upholding it. He was thus attempting to draw strength from the fact that the First Bank came into existence after the recognized luminaries of the early republic had addressed its constitutionality.

Marshall then pointed out that after the Act chartering the First Bank had expired, financial difficulty convinced even "those who were most prejudiced against the measure of its necessity...."[42] The opposition of the Jeffersonians had been considered and rejected and should carry even less weight now than it had 30 years earlier. This portion of the opinion provides an important precedent for according great weight to actions taken by the political branches shortly after the ratification of the Constitution, presumably as solid evidence of the original understanding even though contested. This is especially true where the political actors had explicitly focused on the constitutional issue. Marshall was well aware that despite the history of the Bank, Jefferson and the Bank's

---

[36] *McCulloch*, 17 U.S. at 400.
[37] *Id*. at 401.
[38] *Id*.
[39] *Id*. at 402.
[40] *Id*.
[41] *Id*.
[42] *Id*.

opponents had scarcely given up the fight, so it was important for him to show that that they had been bested in the political arena not once but twice.

Next Marshall turned to what is perhaps the most foundational argument that the Court could possibly consider: the origin of the United States and the Constitution. He began by noting that counsel for Maryland had espoused the theory that the Constitution emanated not from the people but rather from the states. Walter Jones, one of the three attorneys for Maryland, did begin his argument by endorsing the compact theory of constitutional origin.[43] This was not central to his or the state's position however. As such, Marshall could easily have ignored the issue. Instead, he jumped at the opportunity to make the judicial case for the popular sovereignty theory. He conceded that the conventions called to ratify the Constitution had occurred within the states but asked "where else should they have assembled?"[44] He emphasized that the document ratified by those conventions drew its legitimacy and authority from the people not the state governments. Marshall did concede that the states were not simply innocent bystanders in that they had called the constitutional convention and submitted its draft to the people. Even so, he understated the extent of state responsibility for the Constitution by failing to note that it only became effective when conventions in nine states ratified it regardless of whether a majority of the people of the United States had done so.

The argument over the origin of the Constitution as well as the country was perhaps the most significant foundational constitutional debate of the first half of the nineteenth century. Jefferson and Madison had endorsed the compact theory in the Virginia and Kentucky Resolutions opposing the Alien and Sedition Acts at the turn of the century. The Virginia state courts had relied on the compact theory in resisting Supreme Court appellate review of its decisions in *Martin v. Hunter's Lessee* and *Cohens v. Virginia*. Opponents of internal improvements legislation relied on the compact theory for constitutional support around the time that *McCulloch* was decided. Eventually the compact theory would provide the constitutional foundation for the secession movement culminating in the Civil War. Lincoln would fight the war under the popular sovereignty banner.

Marshall obviously understood that this continuing dispute over constitutional origin was of enormous continuing importance. Consequently, he almost certainly welcomed the opportunity to throw the weight of a unanimous Supreme Court behind popular sovereignty. This was despite the fact that it was at most only tangentially implicated in *McCulloch* and would certainly further inflame the predictable opponents of the decision. Thus on this issue, Marshall went looking for trouble rather than trying to avoid it.

Having had his say on constitutional origins, Marshall then turned to a question closer to the case at hand—the nature of congressional power. He began with recognition that "[t]his government is acknowledged by all, to be one of enumerated powers."[45] He followed however with the propositions that congressional authority was plenary within the scope of an enumerated power, and the exercise of such power was supreme over state law. This was not particularly controversial. He then went to the heart of the argument

---

[43] *Id.* at 363.
[44] *Id.* at 403.
[45] *Id.* at 405.

raised by the Bank's opponents noting that Article I did not explicitly provide a power to create a corporation, much less a bank.

At this point, Marshall found it useful to discuss principles of proper constitutional interpretation, another issue certain to rile the opposition. Marshall began by noting that in contrast to the Articles of Confederation, the Tenth Amendment did not reserve all powers to the states that were not "expressly" delegated to the federal government. But more important, Marshall argued that the Constitution must be recognized as a "great outline."[46] Otherwise it could not have been understood by the people, who after all had been charged with deciding whether to ratify it. Marshall concluded his short but significant exposition on constitutional interpretation with his immortal phrase "we must never forget that it is a *constitution* we are expounding."[47]

It is far from clear what Marshall meant by this quotable phrase. As Robert Dixon noted the line is "wonderfully useful because so semantically meaningless...."[48] At the very least he probably meant that congressional power should be construed flexibly enough to permit the achievement of its purpose. Still the language is malleable enough to permit proponents of a living or evolving constitution approach to argue that it supports a fairly open-ended approach to constitutional interpretation in any context, a construction that does not seem consistent with Marshall's overall constitutional jurisprudence[49] and one that was hardly required by *McCulloch* itself.

Putting these interpretive principles to use, Marshall argued that several of the congressional powers enumerated in Article I, including taxing, spending, borrowing, regulating commerce, the war power, and the power to support armies and navies all involved financial matters for which a banking system would prove useful. Here, Marshall was tracking the argument developed by Hamilton in his famous defense of the Bank of the United States though without attribution. Marshall continued by asserting that the creation of a corporation was a means rather than an end. As such, it would not have been enumerated as a great power but should easily be available as a means of achieving the purposes of the enumerated powers.[50] In another context, Jefferson had earlier characterized this line or reasoning as a "house that jack built argument."[51] Yet despite his reservations, he found it useful as president in constitutionally justifying the Louisiana purchase.[52]

Up to this point, Marshall had justified congressional creation of the Bank with a logical and powerful structural argument. If the text was silent, Marshall's reasoning would still easily carry the day. But as he noted, the Constitution did not leave the matter to "general reasoning."[53] Beyond structure, he had a pertinent textual argument as well—the Necessary and Proper Clause. As Marshall observed, the meaning of that clause had

---

[46] *Id.* at 407.

[47] *Id.*

[48] Robert Dixon, *Reapportionment in the Supreme Court and Congress: Constitutional Struggle for Fair Representation*, 63 MICH. L. REV. 209, 230 (1964).

[49] CHARLES F. HOBSON, THE GREAT CHIEF JUSTICE: JOHN MARSHALL AND THE RULE OF LAW 119 (1996).

[50] 17 U.S. at 407.

[51] Letter of Thomas Jefferson to Robert Livingston, April 30, 1800, *in* 7 WRITINGS OF THOMAS JEFFERSON 446 (Ford ed. 1896) (commenting on a congressional proposal to create a copper mine).

[52] *See* JON MEACHAM, THOMAS JEFFERSON: THE ART OF POWER 389–91 (2012).

[53] McCulloch v. Maryland, 17 U.S. 316, 411 (1819).

been a subject of dispute in the oral argument. Maryland interpreted the clause far more restrictively than did the Bank or Marshall.

As with his structural argument, Marshall's textual reasoning is exemplary. He conceded at the outset that "necessary" was a word with more than one accepted meaning. It could be understood narrowly to mean essential or broadly to mean convenient. Engaging in careful textual analysis, Marshall offered several reasons for concluding that the broader reading was correct. First, he pointed out that the word "necessary" is used elsewhere in the Constitution. In Article I, Section Ten, the text prohibits states from imposing duties on imports or exports except where it may be "absolutely necessary." Relying on the established canon that a word used in one part of a document should be presumed to carry the same meaning in other parts of the document as well unless there is good reason to believe that a different meaning was intended, Marshall argued that "necessary" must mean convenient as otherwise "absolutely necessary" would be redundant.

Next Marshall reasoned that in "a constitution, intended to endure for the ages" limiting Congress to the best possible means would unduly restrict congressional power given the need to meet unforeseeable events. He then set forth several examples of how Congress had in fact exercised the power over time in ways that were certainly convenient but hardly essential. In other words, from the very beginning, Congress and the president had proceeded on the assumption that "necessary" carried the broader meaning.

Marshall then contended that words must be read in context and that the word in question was part of a phrase—"necessary and proper." Reading "proper" to mean appropriate, he reasoned that reading "necessary" to mean essential would create a conflict within the phrase as it would give Congress a choice of means and yet at the same time restrict it to those that were most imperative. This is arguably Marshall's weakest textual argument given that he seems to construe "necessary and proper" to mean essentially the same thing, violating the canon against redundancy. That could have been avoided by reading "proper" to mean "legally" proper, a reading that would neither endorse nor undercut his interpretation of "necessary." Finally, Marshall pointed out that the Necessary and Proper Clause is placed among the powers of Congress rather than the restrictions on those powers. Thus he bolstered his argument with an appeal to the architecture of the Constitution.

Marshall employed four arguments in support of his reading of the text. It is an example of a careful approach to textual interpretation. He made a persuasive case for his reading, emphasizing that a close reading of the Constitution's language is well warranted, and set a standard for textual interpretation.

To determine whether an act of Congress was necessary and proper, Marshall declared "[l]et the end be legitimate, let it be within the scope of the Constitution, and all means which are appropriate, which are plainly adapted to that end, which are not prohibited but consistent with the letter and spirit of the Constitution, are constitutional."[54] He then concluded that the establishment of a nationally chartered bank with branches in the states was clearly a convenient and permissible means of carrying forth congressional Article I powers. Although it caught the attention of the informed public in *McCulloch*, Marshall had in fact set forth the same approach to the Necessary and Proper Clause 14 years earlier in *United States v. Fisher*[55] where he concluded that Congress could grant

---

[54] 17 U.S. at 422.

[55] 6 U.S. 358 (1805).

the United States a preference as a creditor under the Bankruptcy Act. Thus one of the most central and contested issues in the case had long been settled by precedent.

At this point, Marshall had spent 25 pages writing a magisterial opinion on an issue that was simply not at the heart of the case. To be sure, Maryland maintained that Congress lacked the power to create the Bank and would have been delighted had the Court agreed. But unlike some other states such as Ohio, Maryland was not a hard-core opponent of the Bank itself. It almost certainly did not expect the Court to declare the Bank Act unconstitutional. Rather, it maintained that it should have the right to impose a nonabusive tax on the operations of the Bank within the state. It was this issue, which Marshall turned his attention to quite late in the opinion, that mattered most to Maryland.

In addressing the question of whether Maryland could tax the Bank, Marshall initially conceded that the power to raise revenue through taxation was an inherent right of any government, including the states. In reliance on the Supremacy Clause, Marshall reasoned that the power to create implies the power to preserve and that the power to destroy may not be utilized to attack that which Congress has the right to create. He then asserted that the power to tax can be used to destroy. Moreover the only protection against such destructive taxation is the structure of government. Presumably the constituents of a legislature will object if taxation becomes too heavy and abusive. That will provide sufficient protection when Congress taxes the people within the states as they are all represented in Congress. It will not provide protection when the state taxes federal instrumentalities such as the Bank however because the federal government is not represented in the state legislatures. This important structural argument came to be known as the political safeguards of federalism and has influenced constitutional decision-making ever since.[56] Relying on this principle, Marshall concluded that any taxation by the states of a federal instrumentality was constitutionally forbidden. This per se rule relieved courts of the difficult task of determining whether a particular state tax was too destructive.

In response to the argument that the power to tax is the power to destroy, which Webster had pressed in his oral argument, Maryland had responded that the federal government should have confidence in the states not to abuse the power. Marshall rejected Maryland's reliance on "the magic word of *confidence*" however. Returning to the political safeguards argument, he explained that there was no reason a government unrepresented in another's political process should trust the other not to abuse its power of taxation. Relying on an argument raised by Webster, Marshall contended that if a state could tax the banknotes, it could likewise tax the mail, the mint, patent rights, the judicial process, and all other aspects of government. During oral argument, Maryland had responded that unlike the Bank, which was largely a privately held profit-making business, these other entities were all clearly aspects of the government itself. However Marshall rejected this argument on the grounds that no clear distinction could be drawn. The distinction does seem quite clear however, and as such Marshall's dismissal of it seems disingenuous and unpersuasive. Moreover, there was little need to remove the power

---

of state taxation of federal instrumentalities entirely as Congress could readily protect its instrumentalities with statutory immunity if necessary. In addition, the Court could strike down destructive taxes on a case-by-case basis although this might be cumbersome and doctrinally challenging.

Marshall closed the opinion by noting that the decision did not preclude states from imposing non-discriminatory taxes on the real property or the equity of institutions doing business in Maryland such as the Bank as long as it is "in common with other property of the same description throughout the state."[57] Marshall did not say so; however such a non-discriminatory tax would be easily justifiable under his political safeguards argument in that if it became abusive, the citizens of the state as a whole would bear the brunt of it and would have recourse through the political process.

THE AFTERMATH

McCulloch v. Maryland was a case of immense national significance and the fallout continued for well over a decade. Despite the fact that the opinion has come to be regarded as one of if not the greatest in Supreme Court history, it was certainly not well received at the time. As one commentator has noted it "provoked paroxysms of outrage." [58] Despite its length, the opinion was printed in full in several newspapers.[59] The Court had thrown its support behind the Bank, which in itself was politically unpopular especially in the western states. To the critics both the Bank and the Court were considered in the words of Richard Ellis "aggressive, intrusive and coercive."[60] Moreover, critics of the opinion argued that the Court had either created the case or at least moved it forward hastily in order to create an unnecessary precedent supporting the Bank against its political opponents. Thus the Court was accused of manipulating the judicial process to serve political ends. But the most stinging criticisms of the opinion were aimed at the larger themes of Marshall's opinion—the Court's explicit endorsement of the popular sovereignty theory of constitutional origin, its conception of the discretionary nature of congressional power, along with its flexible approach to constitutional meaning. For the defenders of state sovereignty, these aspects of the opinion were more dangerous than Marshall's protection of the Bank. Indeed, some of the critics of the political theory of *McCulloch* were defenders of the Bank. John C. Calhoun, who would become the most outspoken advocate of the compact theory of the Constitution, had been a leading proponent of the Second Bank of the United States in Congress.

First, Marshall's critics recognized that his extended discussion of constitutional origin was largely if not entirely unnecessary to the decision. The constitutionality of the very creation and existence of the Bank was scarcely the central issue in the case. And to the extent that it was implicated, it could readily be sustained without endorsing popular

---

[57] *McCulloch*, 17 U.S. at 436.

[58] SWINDLER, *supra* note 17, at 69. *See also* Hammond, *supra* note 12, at 46 (the decision seemed revolutionary to most people).

[59] I CHARLES WARREN, THE SUPREME COURT IN UNITED STATES HISTORY 511–25 (1922) quoting several examples.

[60] ELLIS, *supra* note 4, at 10–11.

sovereignty. Thus as with Jefferson's criticism of Marshall's opinion in *Marbury*, Marshall was faulted in *McCulloch* for using his case to make controversial pronouncements that could have and should have been avoided. Indeed in a private letter, Madison commented that "the occasion did not call for the general and abstract doctrine interwoven with the decision of the particular case."[61]

But the more serious challenge was to the merits of these pronouncements. Defenders of state sovereignty and those with a far more restricted view of constitutional power than Marshall found his rejection of the compact theory and his endorsement of elasticity in constitutional interpretation appalling. Marshall's critics understood quite correctly that if the vision of the Constitution set forth in *McCulloch* took hold, the concept of a relatively limited national government would ultimately be doomed. So although these aspects of the opinion might have been viewed as an interesting sidebar discussion of political theory, the politically astute understood that the stakes were enormous.

The opinion was subjected to attacks in the press by some of Marshall's long- standing political opponents in Virginia, the heart of states' rights ideology. Writing under the name "Amphictyon," Judge William Brockenbrough challenged Marshall's rejection of the compact theory as well as his generous approach toward congressional power.[62] Marshall was sufficiently troubled by this challenge to publish a response under the name "A friend of the Union." The battle in the press did not end with this exchange however. Marshall's longtime foe and ardent defender of state's rights, Spencer Roane, chief justice of the Virginia Court of Appeals, published four essays under the name "Hampden" challenging Marshall's constitutional vision, arguing that the *McCulloch* opinion was part of a campaign designed to expand the power of the national government at the expense of the states.[63] Marshall responded by publishing nine essays defending *McCulloch* under the name "A Friend of the Constitution." The critics charged that *McCulloch* permitted federal courts to aggrandize power over federal-state relations at the expense of state governments. Marshall replied that the federal courts were impartial agents of the people.

This attempt by a justice to defend a recent decision in the press under a pseudonym is unique in Supreme Court history. It illustrates the momentousness of the *McCulloch* decision. Marshall seemed to recognize that even by the standards of landmark opinions, this was something out of the ordinary. It also seemed to affirm the very charge raised by Marshall's critics, that the decision and opinion represented something more than just an important case, but rather a significant advance in a long- standing political battle. The fact that Marshall was prompted to respond extrajudicially and that his responses were quite defensive suggests that he understood that perhaps he had used the case to push too far and too fast. The debate between Marshall and his worthy opponent Roane remains one of the best exchanges in our constitutional history on the meaning of federalism. Jefferson wrote to Roane praising his attack on *McCulloch* contending that

---

[61] Letter of James Madison to Spencer Roane, September 2, 1819, *in* 8 THE WRITINGS OF JAMES MADISON 448 (1910).

[62] The essays by Brockenbrough and Roane challenging McCulloch as well as Marshall's responses are set forth in GERALD GUNTHER, JOHN MARSHALL'S DEFENSE OF *MCCULLOCH V. MARYLAND* (1969).

[63] Roane had been a supporter of the Bank up to the time of the opinion in *McCulloch*. ELLIS, *supra* note 4, at 117.

Marshall's reasoning made the Constitution "a mere thing of wax in hands of the judiciary, which they can twist and shape into any form they please."[64]

Roane and the Jeffersonians also objected to *McCulloch*'s assumption that it was for the Court to define the scope of federal and state power as opposed to the states themselves. Roane perceived the Court as an institution of the federal government and therefore biased in favor of federal power. Marshall replied that the justices were disinterested interpreters of objective legal principle. Two years after *McCulloch*, Roane published four essays challenging Marshall's opinion in *Cohens v. Virginia* in which Marshall elaborated on the approach to the nation and to the Constitution that he had set forth in *McCulloch*. Roane's sudden death shortly thereafter however terminated the possibility of any further debate between the two.

Apart from the criticism of the opinion and Marshall's response, anger against the Bank and state governmental action against it continued. The Virginia legislature passed a resolution criticizing the decision and recommending that a special court be created to adjudicate federal-state disputes.[65] Perhaps the ultimate hotbed of opposition to the Bank was Ohio. If anything, Ohio's opposition to the Bank intensified after *McCulloch*. Prior to *McCulloch*, the state legislature had passed a law imposing a tax of $50,000 each on the two branches of the Bank operating in the state. When the Bank refused to pay, state officials acting pursuant to explicit authorization in the statute known as the "crowbar law" entered the vaults of the banks and seized $120,000.[66] A federal court enjoined the state from disposing of the seized funds. The Bank of the United States then filed suit in federal court against Thomas Osborn, the Ohio state auditor who had authorized the seizure, and John Harper who had executed it, for return of the funds. The federal district court issued a decision in favor of the Bank. A committee of the Ohio legislature issued a report criticizing the decision in *McCulloch* and asserting that the state was under no obligation to respect it. The state legislature passed an act outlawing the Bank and denying it the use of the state's legal system but permitting it to do business in Ohio and agreeing to return the confiscated funds if the Bank agreed to pay an annual 4 percent tax on its dividends. The seized funds were returned to the Bank; however the case was appealed to the Supreme Court.

Osborn v. Bank of the United States[67] was presented to the Court in 1823 as something of a replay of *McCulloch v. Maryland*. Henry Clay and Daniel Webster defended the Bank before the Supreme Court. Not surprisingly, Marshall issued an opinion for a unanimous Court in favor of the Bank. Most of the opinion was devoted to jurisdictional issues; however he reaffirmed that the state had no constitutional right to impose a targeted tax on the Bank. It is hardly surprising that the Court stood firmly behind its opinion in *McCulloch* but the entire *Osborn* episode emphasized the boldness of McCulloch itself. It is certainly the exception rather than the rule for the Court to have to issue a second opinion explaining to recalcitrant state officials that it really meant what it said in a prior opinion, although the Court had to do just that eight years earlier in *Martin v. Hunter's Lessee*.

---

[64] Letter of Thomas Jefferson to Spencer Roane, Sept. 6, 1819, *in* 10 THE WRITINGS OF THOMAS JEFFERSON 140–43 (1899).

[65] HEBERT A. JOHNSON, THE CHIEF JUSTICESHIP OF JOHN MARSHALL, 1801-1835 75 (1997).

[66] ELLIS, *supra* note 4, at 153.

[67] 22 U.S. 738 (1824).

Neither *McCulloch* nor *Osborn* settled the fate of the Bank of the United States however. In 1828, nine years after the decision in *McCulloch*, Andrew Jackson, a steadfast
opponent of the Bank, was elected President. In July of 1832, Congress re-chartered the
Bank and Jackson vetoed the legislation. Contrary to Marshall in *McCulloch*, he characterized the Bank as a private profit-making institution, and despite *McCulloch*, expressed
doubt as to Congress's constitutional authority to create it.[68] Jackson made it quite clear
that as president he did not consider himself precluded by Supreme Court precedent
from independent review of constitutional issues.[69] Prior to the expiration of the Bank's
charter, Jackson ordered the secretary of the treasury to remove all United States' funds
from the Bank.[70] His first two secretaries of the treasury refused to comply. He removed
both, installed Roger Taney with a recess appointment, and the funds were withdrawn.
This effectively killed the Bank of the United States. It went bankrupt the following year.
The Senate censured Jackson for this action but it proved to be politically popular, and
the House after initially challenging it ultimately endorsed the decision.[71] A few years
later, the House and Senate passed legislation re-chartering the Bank; however President
Tyler, a long-standing critic of the Bank, vetoed it twice.[72] Some vigorous opponents of
McCulloch had actually hoped that the Bank would be re-chartered so that a new legal
challenge could be brought in the hopes of reversing the decision.[73]

McCulloch himself was charged with conspiracy to defraud the investors along with his
partners. He was acquitted and pursued a successful political career, rising to be speaker
of the Maryland House of Representatives and eventually comptroller of the United
States Department of the Treasury.[74]

MCCULLOCH AS A GREAT CASE

McCulloch v. Maryland was certainly a great case but its appearance before the Court was
rather different than many of the other great cases. Often the issues posed by the great
case explode onto the scene and are thrust before a Court that may not be wholly content
with having to decide them. That is not exactly what happened with *McCulloch*, although
it will never be entirely clear what did in fact happen. To be sure, a crisis in several states
was brewing over the policies of the Bank as well as the state's right to tax it either for
legitimate revenue purposes or in a punitive manner designed to drive it out. Antipathy
toward the Bank was more severe in some of the western states such as Ohio and Tennessee than it was in Maryland. At the time of the decision, critics of *McCulloch* insisted
that Maryland and the defenders of the Bank rushed the case forward in order to give
the Court the opportunity to issue an opinion strongly supporting the Bank before much

---

[68] Andrew Jackson's Message Vetoing the Re-authorization of the Second Bank of the United States (July
10, 1832).

[69] *Id.*

[70] ELLIS, *supra* note 4, at 215.

[71] KILLENBECK, *supra* note 3, at 174.

[72] President Tyler's Vetoes of Legislation Re-authorizing the Bank of the United States, August and September 1841, CONG. GLOBE, 27th Cong., 1st Sess. 337–338, 444 (1841).

[73] KILLENBECK, *supra* note 3, at 177.

[74] *Id.* at 187.

action was taken in more antagonistic jurisdictions. According to this narrative, the Marshall court seized the opportunity to vigorously enunciate a very nationalistic exposition of the Constitution. Thus instead of having this crisis forced upon the Court, Marshall welcomed it with open arms. Whatever may have transpired behind the scenes, the case did proceed on an expedited basis. Still Maryland hired three top-flight advocates who defended its actions with great skill and energy.

Marshall did deliver his landmark opinion within three days of the end of the oral argument. However the issue concerning the constitutionality of the Bank and the appropriate approach to congressional power had been explored in great depth since the classic debate between Hamilton and Jefferson in Washington's cabinet. In that sense, Marshall had 30 years, not three days, in which to prepare his opinion. Moreover he sat through nine days of oral argument by some of the most skillful advocates to ever appear before the Court. He quite clearly borrowed heavily from both the arguments of Pinkney and Webster. Thus despite the deceptively short time frame in which the opinion was written, Marshall had all the time that he needed. As such, unlike many great cases there is little reason to believe that time pressure adversely affected the opinion.

McCulloch v. Maryland was decided by a confident Court. It understood that it was sailing into a strong headwind but did not hesitate. Marshall had energetic foes ready to attack but he had powerful allies as well. He had every reason to believe that both he and the Court would easily weather whatever storm the opinion produced. The negative reaction to *McCulloch* and more important Marshall's reaction to that reaction suggest that he may have underestimated the fury of the backlash. In a letter to Justice Story he acknowledged that the opinion had awakened the "sleeping spirit of Virginia, if it ever sleeps."[75] *McCulloch v. Maryland* was not well received at the time but has since come to be considered quite possibly the greatest and most important opinion in Supreme Court history. How did that happen?

To begin with, Marshall went out of his way, arguably far out of his way, to address perhaps the most foundational question in all of American constitutional law: the origin of the United States and its Constitution. Not only was this an issue of the utmost importance, it had been one of the most hotly contested ones in American political theory. In *McCulloch*, Marshall espoused the popular sovereignty theory of origin. He rejected the compact theory that had been endorsed by no less than Jefferson and Madison in the Kentucky and Virginia resolutions. Certainly as of *McCulloch v. Maryland*, the popular sovereignty theory that Justice Story had also endorsed three years earlier in *Martin v. Hunter's Lessee* became the official narrative of the Supreme Court. That scarcely settled the matter however. If anything, Marshall's rejection of the compact theory encouraged its proponents to assert that theory even more vigorously than before, and at least for a period of time quite successfully.

As it turned out, it was simply not the type of issue that could be settled by a Supreme Court decision. Whether Marshall anticipated it at the time of *McCulloch*, and he probably did, the compact theory would become increasingly attractive to southern defenders of slavery despite the fact that one of its most prominent spokesmen, John C. Calhoun, had

---

[75] Letter from John Marshall to Joseph Story (March 24, 1819), *in* 8 PAPERS OF JOHN MARSHALL 280 (1974).

been a solid defender of the Bank of the United States as well. The question of whether Missouri should be admitted as a slave state, which ultimately resulted in the Missouri Compromise, was before the Congress at the very time that *McCulloch* was argued and decided. Proponents of slavery were quite concerned by Marshall's endorsement in *McCulloch* of expansive congressional power.[76] Ultimately, it would take a civil war to settle the question of constitutional origin. The South seceded under the compact theory. Lincoln fought the war under the popular sovereignty theory. One reason this portion of *McCulloch* reads so comfortably today is because Marshall ended up on the right side of history, but that was hardly certain in 1819.

Perhaps the second great achievement of the opinion in *McCulloch* is that it set forth and defended a flexible approach to constitutional interpretation, at least with regard to congressional power. Both with respect to his structural reasoning and his textual analysis of the Necessary and Proper Clause, Marshall forcefully argued for a liberal or expansive reading, summed up in his well-known declaration that "we must never forget that it is a constitution we are expounding."

Justice Frankfurter characterized Marshall's "expounding" statement as "the single most important utterance in the literature of constitutional law—most important because most comprehensive and most comprehending."[77] Frankfurter's statement is frequently quoted because it sounds so elegant and authoritative; however it is every bit as obscure in meaning as the sentence of Marshall's that he was praising. Frankfurter certainly did not believe that Marshall was proclaiming an authority to read the Constitution to mean whatever the expounder believed that it should mean. Six years earlier in a dissenting opinion, he explained that "precisely because 'it is a constitution we are expounding,' we ought not take liberties with it."[78]

Nevertheless Marshall's statement is easily over read as endorsing a free-wheeling evolutionary approach to interpretation that serious Marshall scholars reject as quite inconsistent with his jurisprudential views.[79] Professor Kurland warned that when a court quotes Marshall's expounding language "you can be sure that the court will be throwing the constitutional text, its history, and its structure to the winds in reaching its conclusion."[80]

It should be remembered that Marshall's argument for a generous reading of the Constitution was presented in the specific context of congressional power. In several cases including *McCulloch*, Marshall argued that if the Constitution was to achieve its purposes and avoid the embarrassments of the Articles of Confederation, Congress must be given broad discretion to act. Marshall did not purport to be interpreting congressional power in an idiosyncratic manner but rather in line with the original understanding of its purpose. To be sure, as the oral arguments, as well as the criticism of *McCulloch* illustrate, Marshall's view of the original understanding was scarcely beyond controversy and quite possibly incorrect. Even so, that does not suggest that his approach was disingenuous

---

[76] R. Kent Newmyer, John Marshall and the Heroic Age of the Supreme Court 334 (2001).

[77] Frankfurter, *supra* note 3, at 217.

[78] Nat'l Mut. Ins. Co. v. Tidewater Transfer Co., 337 U.S. 581, 647 (1949) (Frankfurter, J., dissenting).

[79] Hobson, *supra* note 49, at 119.

[80] Philip Kurland, Curia Regis: *Some Comments on the Divine Right of Kings and Courts to Say What the Law Is*, 23 Ariz. L. Rev. 582, 591 (1981).

or willful but rather that it was one perspective on a sharply contested issue. Whether Marshall's expansive approach to judicial interpretation is consistent with constitutional purpose and structure with respect to issues other than congressional authority is a question that Marshall did not need to address in *McCulloch*. It is worth noting that Marshall hardly gave Congress the benefit of the doubt 16 years earlier when deciding *Marbury v. Madison*.

Marshall's liberal approach to the judicial construction of congressional power coupled with a high degree of judicial deference to its exercise has ultimately carried the day although the road has been indirect and bumpy. From the end of the nineteenth century until 1937, the Court interpreted congressional exercises of power, especially under the Commerce Clause, more restrictively than *McCulloch* would have warranted. But that changed dramatically and if anything the Court has shown greater deference to congressional regulation than even *McCulloch* would imply. It is likely that in context, Marshall was less concerned with expanding federal power than in restraining state incursions.

McCulloch is also significant in that as Charles Black has shown in his classic work *Structure and Relationship in Constitutional Law*, perhaps more than any other opinion, it validates structural reasoning, what Marshall refers to as "general reasoning," as a legitimate and powerful method of constitutional interpretation. Marshall relied on three classic structural arguments in *McCulloch*, each of which was served up to him by counsel for the Bank during oral argument. The first structural argument asserted that Congress must be given discretion to choose convenient means for execution of its powers if it is to carry out its constitutional responsibilities. The very structure of the Constitution itself presumed an effective legislative branch. On this point, Marshall had the persuasive textual fallback of the Necessary and Proper Clause. But even in the absence of that clause, the structural argument was more than capable of carrying the day.

The second structural argument was Marshall's thesis as to why a state tax on the Bank was unconstitutional. The power to create implies the power to preserve, and the power to tax is the power to destroy. This argument proceeded from constitutional structure with respect to federalism. It posits that a government in order to exist and be effective must have the power to protect itself and its creations against threatening action by its subunits. Marshall overstated the threat posed, especially in the context of the largely privately owned bank; however this structural argument itself was crucial to the holding.

The final structural argument, which has come to be known as "the political safeguards of federalism," was a further exposition and qualification of the second. Marshall argued that it was permissible for the whole to tax the part but not for the part to tax the whole because the part was politically represented in the whole but not vice versa. As a corollary, Marshall explained that on the other hand, even-handed taxation by the state of an asset such as real property held by both federal instrumentalities and by state citizens was permissible because the equal burden on state citizens would provide a political check against abuse. As Professor Wechsler illustrated in his classic article "The Political Safeguards of Federalism," the political process argument relied upon by Marshall in *McCulloch* has played a significant role in constitutional interpretation ever since and continues to do so to this day.[81]

---

[81] *See* Garcia v. San Antonio Transit Auth., 469 U.S. 528, 551–55 (1985) (Blackmun, J., for the majority), 564–67 (Powell, J., dissenting), 587–88 (O'Connor, J., dissenting).

McCulloch is also noteworthy in that it widely seen as having set a benchmark for judicial craftsmanship. It is generally considered to be Marshall's greatest opinion and quite possibly the greatest opinion in the history of the Court.[82] Even so, it is not without some glaring faults. Marshall's exposition on the origin of the Constitution, which to some extent was the centerpiece of the opinion, was scarcely even pertinent to the decision. The opinion virtually ignored the primary argument raised by the state in its defense: that the Bank was essentially a privately held profit-making entity rather than a significant instrumentality of the federal government. Marshall almost certainly ignored this contention for good reason in that he had no effective response to it, and if accepted it undermined his entire opinion and decision. Moreover, he overstated the risk that was presented to the United States by taxation of the Bank as well as the alternative means available to the government to thwart abusive or destructive taxation.

So how can an opinion that focuses on straw men, ignores the real issue, and overstates the problem possibly be considered great? Indeed Richard Ellis, the author of a recent book on *McCulloch*, characterizes the opinion as "contrived, inadequate and misleading."[83] That is a minority view however. Why is *McCulloch* not considered a very bad opinion, as indeed it was by its critics at the time? The answer is because Marshall did what he did so powerfully and persuasively, and more important that he was ultimately vindicated by history. As Holmes explained "time has been on Marshall's side."[84] To paraphrase Professor Bickel, he bet on the future and won.[85] Marshall took the arguments in favor of his position set forth by Hamilton; other defenders of the Bank; and its advocates before the Court, Webster, Wirt, and Pinkney, and synthesized them into a clear and forthright defense of popular sovereignty, flexibility in interpretation, muscular congressional authority, judicial deference toward that authority along with rigorous textual analysis, a solid endorsement of federal supremacy, and logical structural arguments in the area of federalism. Most of the positions taken by Marshall have not simply survived but rather have become canonical. Despite its obvious flaws, the opinion remains breathtakingly powerful. If anything the flaws enhance its stature as we are forced to admire it in spite of itself.

One fear of great cases is that they will thrust the Court into the center of political disputes that it is incapable of resolving and that will certainly weaken the Court's standing if it should try. *McCulloch* was a case in which the Court, through Marshall, deliberately plunged into the very center of such disputes and produced an opinion whose breadth could only be understood as a political statement. There was a highly charged political debate in progress, and Marshall and the Court delivered an opinion that was certainly intended to stake out a position in that debate. Marshall's opinion in *McCulloch* was supportive of the strong nationalist program favored by Henry Clay. Ordinarily, this would be considered a risky strategy for the Court in that it could significantly injure the Court's

---

[82] *See supra* note 3.

[83] ELLIS, *supra* note 4, at 101.

[84] Oliver Wendell Holmes, John Marshall, remarks delivered on the one hundredth anniversary of when Marshall first took his seat on the Court, Feb. 4, 1901, reprinted in JAMES BRADLEY THAYER, OLIVER WENDELL HOLMES, AND FELIX FRANKFURTER ON JOHN MARSHALL, *supra* note 3, at 129, 133–34.

[85] ALEXANDER M. BICKEL, THE LEAST DANGEROUS BRANCH: THE SUPREME COURT AT THE BAR OF POLITICS 239 (1962).

credibility with the public. And that does seem to have been the case with *McCulloch* given the widespread backlash against the opinion. Kent Newmyer, one of the most insightful Marshall scholars, asserts that the *McCulloch* opinion invigorated the states' rights movement and resulted in "a no-holds-barred debate over the nature of the Court, the Constitution and the federal Union."[86] That led initially to Calhoun's theory of nullification and the Nullification Crisis of 1832. Justice Story's *Commentaries on the Constitution* were written as a defense of the Marshall court against this backlash.[87] The continuing southern outrage against federal authority ultimately resulting in secession was at least to some extent an outgrowth of the fear of a Congress as powerful as that assumed by Marshall in *McCulloch*. As with *Dred Scott* three and one-half decades later, *McCulloch v. Maryland* could scarcely be held responsible for the Civil War. Still there can be little question that it did play a roll in increasing the emerging inter-sectional tensions in the nation. Arguably, the sustained negative reaction against the Court inspired by *McCulloch* was the most severe such event in the nation's history.[88]

To some extent, *McCulloch v. Maryland* was a great case in the sense that it addressed several issues that had been and would continue to be at the center of national controversy. At a general level, the power of Congress, the role of the Court, and the relation between the states and the national government continue to be at the heart of political and constitutional debate almost two centuries later. As one of the first and foremost decisions to address these questions, *McCulloch* could not help but be a great case. The appearance by so many of the legal luminaries of the day, the nine days of oral argument, and the swift and vigorous reaction to the decision confirm that it was understood at the time as something unique.

And yet it would be fair to say that Chief Justice Marshall took what was admittedly a great case and turned it into one of the ultimate great cases. Marshall made the case to be much more than it was, and certainly much more than it needed to be, by directly and forcefully staking out a strong defense of the Bank in particular and federal authority in general. Serious disputes over federal authority were present and more were on the horizon. The Bank was facing far more severe challenges in Ohio than in Maryland, and similar disputes were likely to arise in other states as well. The Court seemed to be in a constant struggle with the Virginia courts over the extent of its appellate jurisdiction. *Martin v. Hunter's Lessee* had been decided three year prior to *McCulloch*, and *Cohens v. Virginia* would be decided two years later. Indeed, Spencer Roane, the most vigorous defender of the Virginia's judicial sovereignty, was also among the harshest critics of *McCulloch*. At the time of *McCulloch*, Congress and President Monroe were engaged in a vigorous constitutional debate over the constitutionality of the Internal Improvements Bill. The Missouri Compromise on slavery in the territories would be enacted the year after *McCulloch* was decided, and the controversy was certainly brewing at the time. It was around then that Jefferson made his famous reference to the issue of slavery in the territories as "the fire-bell in the night."[89] Within a decade the Nullification Crisis would

---

[86] Newmyer, *supra* note 76, at 299.

[87] *Id.* at 384.

[88] Barry Friedman, The Will of the People: How Public Opinion Has Influenced the Supreme Court and Shaped the Meaning of the Constitution 80 (2009).

[89] Letter of Thomas Jefferson to John Holmes, April 22, 1820, *in* XV The Writings of Thomas Jefferson 248, 249 (Library ed. 1904).

arise and the compact theory that Marshall attempted to suppress would take on new political life. In so many ways and on so many fronts, Marshall could not help but see dark clouds gathering over the question of federalism, and almost certainly made *McCulloch* into a truly great case in order to stake out judicial ground as the crises developed. He carried the day in the long run but much less so in his own time.

"It is no exaggeration to say, as did Albert Beveridge, that few events in history have done more to knit the American people into a single nation than [the decision in *Gibbons v. Ogden*]"[1]

JEAN EDWARD SMITH

3

Gibbons v. Ogden

Gibbons v. Ogden[2] was understood to be a great case when it arrived at the Supreme Court in 1824. Specifically it involved one of the most significant commercial issues of the day, whether New York could constitutionally authorize a monopoly on the steamboat passenger trade on the Hudson River between New York and New Jersey. At a more general level, like *McCulloch v. Maryland*, *Gibbons* again presented the Court with a question over the boundaries between federal and state authority, perhaps the most contested constitutional issue of the first half of the nineteenth century. The controversy over the steamboat monopoly had been building for almost 20 years, primarily in the New York courts. It had involved several prominent individuals including Robert Livingston of New York, one of the premier political figures of the founding era, as well as Robert Fulton the developer of the first operational steamboat, although each had died before the case arose. It offered the Court its first opportunity to address the meaning of the Commerce Clause, one of, if not the most important of the Article I congressional powers. As with *McCulloch v. Maryland*, two of the legal giants of the day, Daniel Webster and William Wirt, appeared before the Court, both in opposition to the monopoly. Two equally talented attorneys, Thomas Oakley and Thomas Emmett, appeared on behalf of Ogden and the monopoly. The case was argued for five days and attracted the attention of the public at large. Like *Marbury* and *McCulloch*, *Gibbons* gave Marshall a platform from which he could address several significant issues that were only marginally implicated by the case itself. The decision had an immediate positive impact on the economic development of the country and eventually became the very foundation of the Court's affirmative Commerce Clause jurisprudence. And unlike *McCulloch v. Maryland*, the decision and its result met with widespread public approval.

---

[1] JEAN EDWARD SMITH, JOHN MARSHALL: DEFINER OF A NATION 478 (1996).
[2] 22 U.S. 1 (1824).

45

BACKGROUND

Gibbons centers around one of the most significant economic developments of the early nineteenth century—the steamboat. The steamboat was initially developed in the late eighteenth century by John Fitch and in fact was demonstrated before the delegates to the Constitutional Convention in Philadelphia in 1787 on the Delaware River.[3] In 1798, the New York legislature granted a monopoly on the steamboat trade on the Hudson River on the condition that successful steamboat operation could be demonstrated.[4] In 1807 with the backing of Robert Livingston, a patriarch of New York politics, Robert Fulton successfully demonstrated the operation of the steamboat on the Seine River in Paris.[5] Over the next several years, the New York legislature renewed and extended the monopoly that gave Livingston and his licensees sole authority to operate steamboats on the Hudson River, including the transportation of passengers.[6] At the time, New York claimed complete dominion of the river itself all the way to the New Jersey shore.[7] In retaliation, Connecticut and New Jersey established similar monopolies for the steamboat traffic on their waterways.[8] Fulton obtained a federal patent on his improvements to steamboat technology in 1809.[9] The monopoly was challenged in the New York state courts and Fulton and Livingston defended it successfully in 1811.[10] Over the next decade, the steamboat monopoly spawned an absolutely mind numbing amount of litigation primarily in the New York courts between a variety of parties.[11]

Fulton licensed Ogden, a former governor of New Jersey, to operate steamboats carrying passengers between New York and New Jersey. Operating under a federal license pursuant to the Coasting Act passed by Congress in 1793, Gibbons operated two steamboats carrying passengers between Elizabeth Town, New Jersey, and New York City. Ogden and Gibbons had been partners but disagreements resulted in their becoming competitors.[12] The captain of Gibbons's steamboat, the *Bellona*, was none other than future railroad baron Cornelius Vanderbilt.[13]

Ogden's and Gibbons's relationship continued to deteriorate, leading to physical violence and intimidation between the competing steamboat operators.[14] Gibbons, an extremely wealthy man, became engaged in a serious public quarrel with his son-in-law

---

[3] EDWARD J. RENEHAN, JR., COMMODORE: THE LIFE OF CORNELIUS VANDERBILT 57 (2007).

[4] HERBERT ALAN JOHNSON, *GIBBONS V. OGDEN*: JOHN MARSHALL, STEAMBOATS, AND THE COMMERCE CLAUSE 28 (2010).

[5] George Dangerfield, *The Steamboat Case, in* QUARRELS THAT HAVE SHAPED THE CONSTITUTION 59 (John A. Garraty ed., 1987).

[6] *Id.* at 60.

[7] *Id.* at 63.

[8] JOHNSON, *supra* note 4, at 36.

[9] *Id.* at 27–28.

[10] Livingston v. Van Ingren, 9 Johns 507 (1811).

[11] THOMAS H. COX, *GIBBONS V. OGDEN*, LAW, AND SOCIETY IN THE EARLY REPUBLIC 44–102 (2009) (describing the litigation in great detail).

[12] Dangerfield, *supra* note 5, at 63.

[13] One of the more entertaining and informative descriptions of the origin of *Gibbons v. Ogden* appears in Edward Renehan's *Commodore* (2007), a biography of Vanderbilt.

[14] *See* COX, *supra* note 11, at 93–101 for a detailed account of the personal disputes that led to *Gibbons v. Ogden*.

and daughter, who had accused him of ruining the family reputation through his public philandering. His daughter and his son-in-law, John Trumbull, had attempted to convince him to behave more respectably. Headstrong Gibbons promptly disinherited both. They in turn hired Ogden to defend their financial interest against Gibbons. Gibbons slandered Ogden and challenged him to a duel, which was by then illegal in New Jersey. Ogden sued Gibbons for trespass for proposing an illegal act. The escalation of the disputes between the two ultimately led to the initiation in the New York courts of the great case of *Gibbons v. Ogden.* As Thomas Cox put it "both men would risk their entire fortunes to destroy one another in state and federal courts."[15] Despite the antipathy between the two men, they did continue a business relationship while the case was pending. The highly respected judge and renowned legal treatise author Chancellor Kent sustained the monopoly, which had been upheld in prior litigation, and issued an injunction against Gibbons. In 1819, the decision was affirmed on appeal and then taken to the United States Supreme Court.

ORAL ARGUMENT

Gibbons v. Ogden attracted much public attention and the courtroom was packed to capacity.[16] Daniel Webster opened for Gibbons, arguing vigorously that the power to regulate interstate commerce rested exclusively in Congress.[17] In reflecting back on his argument in *Gibbons*, Webster wrote that Chief Justice Marshall took in his words "as a baby takes in his mother's milk."[18] Moreover he boasted that Marshall's opinion was "little more than a recital of my argument."[19] As will be seen, this was scarcely the case. Webster did raise some fallback arguments but pressed the case for exclusivity most strongly. Thomas Oakley and Thomas Emmet representing Ogden and defending the state-granted monopoly presented nuanced and well-documented arguments in support of the concurrent authority of Congress and the states to regulate interstate commercial activity.[20] William Wirt argued that the New York monopoly was inconsistent with Fulton's patent. He also offered the argument for Gibbons, ultimately accepted by the Court, that assuming that there was concurrent authority to regulate, the state statute was preempted under the Supremacy Clause by the Federal Coasting Act.[21] In summation, Wirt warned that a failure to invalidate the monopoly could lead to civil war among New York, New Jersey, and Connecticut.[22] After five days of argument the case was submitted to the Court.

There has been a dispute among historians as to which of the attorneys had the greatest influence over Marshall's opinion. For quite some time, Webster's contention that he all but dictated Marshall's opinion was given credence. And although it is true that the opinion does track much of Webster's argument, more recent commentators have

---

[15] *Id.* at 63.

[16] Norman R, Williams, Gibbons, 79 N.Y.U. L. Rev. 1398, 1410-11 (2001).

[17] Gibbons v. Ogden, 22 U.S. 1, 5 (1824).

[18] 2 CHARLES WARREN, THE SUPREME COURT IN AMERICAN HISTORY 63 (1922).

[19] *Id.* at 70.

[20] *Gibbons*, 22 U.S. 15–32 (Oakley), 32–60 (Emmett).

[21] *Id.* at 68.

[22] *Id.* at 69.

emphasized the contributions of Oakley, Emmett, and Wirt's arguments to the result as well as the opinion.[23] Indeed preeminent Marshall scholar Herbert Johnson has recently argued that Webster and Wirt were "over confident, ill-prepared and outgunned" by Oakley and Emmet.[24] It took the Court over three weeks to produce the opinion, quite a long time for the Marshall court. This may suggest, as does the opinion itself, that there was a certain degree of disagreement among the justices. Or it may reflect the fact that Marshall had fallen on ice and broken his shoulder following the oral argument.[25]

THE OPINION

Marshall's lengthy opinion for the Court may be divided into three parts—a discussion of the breadth of congressional authority under the Commerce Clause, consideration of whether the congressional power to regulate interstate commerce is exclusive, and the decision of the case itself under the Supremacy Clause.

Marshall began by acknowledging that the New York law had the support of "great names" but that the Court could not simply bow to that authority.[26] Here Marshall was implicitly acknowledging that Chancellor Kent, arguably the most highly respected state court judge and legal commentator in the nation, had upheld the monopoly against challenge more than once. In response to the challenge by counsel for Ogden to the interpretive approach that he had established in *McCulloch*, Marshall took issue with the argument that congressional powers should be "strictly construed."[27] Rather, he argued that the words of the document should be given their natural meaning and should be read in light of their intended purpose. His dispute with the advocates for Ogden turned to a large degree on competing conceptions of that purpose. For Marshall, the predominant purpose of the Commerce Clause was to empower Congress to effectively regulate nationally significant commercial matters. For Ogden and the defenders of state sovereignty, the purpose was to constrain Congress within strict and discernible limits in order to ensure that it did not intrude too deeply into the domain of state governance. As with *McCulloch*, the debate was not so much over interpretive methodology as it was over competing political theories of federalism.

Marshall immediately turned his attention to the text of the Commerce Clause. As he had done with the Necessary and Proper Clause in *McCulloch*, Marshall examined the text word by word. Starting with "commerce," Marshall rejected the argument on behalf of Ogden that it was restricted to commercial exchange excluding navigation. Instead, he concluded that "[c]ommerce, undoubtedly is traffic, but it is something more: it is intercourse."[28] He justified this conclusion by reference to the canon that a general term should not be read as restricted to "one of its significations." That begged the question whether the term "commerce" is general or more specific. One contemporary commentator noted

---

[23] Bernard Schwartz argues that Wirt's approach ultimately prevailed. Bernard Schwartz, A History of the Supreme Court 84-87 (1993), as does Norman Williams, *supra* note 16, at 1443.

[24] Johnson, *supra* note 4, at 8.

[25] *Id.* at 104-05.

[26] *Gibbons*, 22 U.S. at 186.

[27] *Id.* at 188.

[28] *Id.* at 189.

that if "intercourse" fell within the scope of the Commerce Clause, the state fornication laws were unconstitutional.[29]

Marshall then turned to the question of whether commerce included navigation and asserted both on the basis of contemporary and original understanding that clearly it did. He maintained without citing anything specific that it was well understood that vesting Congress with the power to control commercial navigation was one of the primary purposes behind the drafting and ratification of the Constitution itself. As was his style, Marshall did not bother with citing detailed support for this conclusion, despite the fact that Webster had served it up during oral argument.[30] Marshall bolstered his case that commerce includes navigation by noting that the Article I, Section Nine clause prohibiting congressional preference for any specific port seems to assume that Congress has the power to regulate navigation, presumably under the Commerce Clause. Relying on legislative and executive practice as evidence of constitutional meaning, Marshall cited the peacetime embargo as evidence of congressional authority to regulate navigation pursuant to the Commerce Clause. This allowed him to make his point at the expense of his most severe critic, Thomas Jefferson, who as president had been responsible for the embargo. Marshall made a powerful case that commerce includes navigation, based on textual analysis, original understanding, and congressional and executive practice, although this was one of the least controversial issues presented. Marshall was almost certainly correct in concluding that the original understanding of the Commerce Clause comprehended navigation, at least on interstate waters; however his rather vague description of commerce as intercourse probably encompassed more than the original understanding supports, as Justice Thomas and Randy Barnett have recently maintained.[31]

Marshall then turned to the phrase describing the extent of the commerce power "with foreign Nations, and among the several States, and with the Indian tribes." He began by asserting that it is well recognized that Congress has authority over all manners of commerce with foreign nations, and if so the same must be true of the states as well given that the same word—"commerce"—is used with respect to each. Turning to the phrase "among the several States," Marshall engaged in the textual exposition for which *Gibbons* is renowned and that provides the cornerstone for much subsequent exercise of congressional authority. He reasoned that the word "among" "means intermingled with," and as such "commerce among the States, cannot stop at the external boundary line of each State, but may be introduced into the interior."[32] If Marshall was declaring that "among" means within or internal to, that is not at all obvious. It could just as easily mean "between," implying little if any authority to reach beyond state borders.

But just as quickly as Marshall set forth a near limitless definition of "among," he retreated, admitting that it cannot cover "commerce which is completely internal" or "which does not extend to or affect other states."[33] With a summarization that has been quoted by courts ever since, Marshall concluded that congressional authority is limited

---

[29] Dangerfield, *supra* note 5, at 68.

[30] *Gibbons*, 22 U.S. at 6-7.

[31] United States v. Lopez, 514 U.S. 549, 585–87 (1995) (Thomas, J., concurring) (arguing that the original understanding of the term "commerce" was limited to trade and exchange); Randy Barnett, *The Original Meaning of the Commerce Clause* 68 U. Chi. L. Rev. 101 (2001) (confirming Justice Thomas's conclusions).

[32] *Gibbons*, 22 U.S. at 194.

[33] *Id.*

"to that commerce which concerns more states than one...."[34] He followed with a sentence that has assumed great significance in recent Commerce Clause analysis, stating that "[t]he enumeration presupposes something not enumerated...." In other words, the Constitution does not give Congress the authority to regulate all commerce, but only commerce "among the several states." That is, as expansive as the commerce power is, it is not without real boundaries. Marshall summarized the principle by concluding that Congress had the authority to reach "all the external concerns of the nation, and to those internal concerns which affect the States generally; but not to those which are completely within a particular state."[35] With that, Marshall purported to balance the interests in national authority with those of state sovereignty, though it is scarcely the balance that the advocates of the latter would have struck.

Having noted the limits of the power, Marshall again emphasized its expansive potential. He pointed out that the power over foreign commerce must extend to the port of destination even if that lay well within the boundaries of a state. Turning then to commerce among the states, he argued that interstate transactions by nature begin in one state and end in another, and as such must be regulated if at all within the states as opposed to at the "mathematical line" separating them. Although Marshall has justified some internal regulation under the Commerce Clause, it remains in the context of an interstate transaction. There is nothing in his reasoning to validate congressional regulation of activity that is "completely within a particular state" even if it has an impact outside of the state. Indeed his opinion is most easily read as denying congressional power over such activity. As such, Marshall's conception of interstate commerce as expressed in *Gibbons* is considerably narrower than the conception that subsequent courts developed in reliance on *Gibbons*.

Marshall then focused on the third crucial word in the clause: "regulate." Devoting considerably less time to defining that term, he simply concluded that like other Article I powers, it is plenary and can be exercised to the fullest extent. As recognized in *McCulloch v. Maryland*, the primary check against abuse by Congress would be political.

Marshall's textual analysis of the Commerce Clause, which has in turn provided the foundation for congressional exercise of the power ever since, is the aspect of *Gibbons* for which it is best known. It is the section of the opinion that is reproduced in all of the Constitutional Law casebooks. However as with other Marshall opinions such as *McCulloch*, it is not the discussion that went to the heart of the controversy before the Court. Marshall had certainly established that Congress had the power to pass the Coasting Act, a point with which none of the parties to the case would disagree. He had also essentially made the case though not quite explicitly that the Act can be applied to navigation on the Hudson River within the state of New York. This is a point on which the advocates for Ogden joined issue to some extent but it still was not the central controversy in the litigation. Rather most of the oral argument had focused upon whether despite such congressional power, New York could still grant a monopoly over the steamboat trade to Livingston and Fulton. The real issue in *Gibbons* was whether the states had concurrent power with Congress over interstate commerce. Marshall did devote the bulk of his opinion to that issue.

---

[34] *Id.*
[35] *Id.* at 195.

To address that issue, it was necessary to establish that navigation could be commerce, as Marshall had done. He considered the arguments for concurrence raised by Ogden but found that the responses by Gibbons, especially as set forth by Webster, were more persuasive.

Marshall conceded that the states had the power to pass legislation requiring that articles that had moved in interstate commerce could be subjected to inspection after entering the state. However that did not establish concurrent state authority to regulate interstate commerce. Employing a formalistic analysis, Marshall reasoned that inspection laws were applied prior to the entry of items into commerce or after the commercial journey had ceased. Moreover, inspection laws were imposed for a different purpose than commercial regulation: to improve the quality of the items. The same was true with respect to well-accepted quarantine laws. As such they were an aspect of the state's police power rather than concurrent regulation of commerce. To modern ears this aspect of Marshall's opinion seems uncharacteristically strained and formalistic. However it did permit Marshall to recognize a limited concurrent authority in areas where it is already quite well accepted while still maintaining that the congressional power could be essentially exclusive.

Likewise, the 1808 congressional ban on the importation of slaves did not imply that states had a general power to regulate commercial imports, according to Marshall. Rather the Constitution's prohibition against banning the slave trade prior to 1808 was best viewed as a limited exception to congressional control over foreign commerce rather than recognition of general state authority to regulate it. Congressional adoption of state harbor and pilot regulation was only evidence that Congress could control the matter entirely if it so chose.

In summary Marshall seemed to accept Webster's argument that the power to regulate commerce implied a power to leave it unregulated. As such, Congress must have exclusive authority over interstate commerce. As Marshall noted at the end of this section of his opinion "[t]here is great force in this argument, and the Court is not satisfied that it has been refuted."[36] Up to this point, Webster may have been correct in declaring that Marshall had apparently accepted his reasoning completely. But there was more.

Finally, Marshall turned to the Supremacy Clause, the primary issue litigated in the state courts. He noted that Gibbons had obtained a license pursuant to the Coasting Act passed by Congress in 1793. He construed the license to permit its holder to engage in the coasting trade, which would include carrying passengers by steamboat between New Jersey and New York. Consequently, Marshall found Ogden's monopoly enforced by the New York court's injunction to be inconsistent with Gibbons's license under the Coasting Act and thus invalid under the Supremacy Clause. With that, Marshall's lengthy discussion of the exclusive character of the congressional commerce power, Webster's primary argument, was reduced to interesting dicta. Likewise, there was no reason for the Court to consider the additional claim that the New York monopoly was not inconsistent with the Patent Clause. Most scholars find Marshall's interpretation of the Coasting Act unpersuasive in that the licensing provision does not necessarily imply substantive

---

[36] *Id.* at 209.

regulation of commercial navigation.[37] Chancellor Kent had considered and rejected the Coasting Act argument in the lower court proceedings.

Justice Johnson broke with the tradition of the Marshall court by offering a separate concurrence noting that "I feel my duty to the public best discharged, by an effort to maintain my opinions in my own way."[38] No longer would Marshall be the sole spokesperson for the Court in constitutional cases, a practice criticized by his rival Jefferson.[39] Johnson began with a summarization of the interstate commercial difficulties that contributed to the creation of the Constitution.[40] He reasoned that prior to the Constitution the states had complete control over interstate commerce but that control was passed entirely to Congress under the Constitution.[41] He then promptly accepted Webster's argument, reasoning that "since the power to prescribe the limits to the freedom necessarily implies the power to determine what shall remain unrestrained, it follows that the power must be exclusive."[42] Justice Johnson continued at some length to support this conclusion. Thus it was Johnson rather than Marshall who ultimately "recited" Webster's argument.

AFTERMATH

Unlike many of the Marshall court's decisions, *Gibbons v. Ogden* met with great popular approval even at a time when the Court was under severe attack on account of several other decisions.[43] In contrast to *McCulloch v. Maryland* for instance, where the Court validated a powerful and despised institution, in *Gibbons* it struck down a publicly unpopular monopoly. The press was overwhelmingly supportive of the decision with some newspapers publishing it in its entirety.[44] Shortly after the decision, a Connecticut steamer was welcomed into New York harbor by a cheering crowd.[45] The year after *Gibbons* was decided the New York Court of Errors applied its principles to invalidate the monopoly on the Hudson River wholly within the state of New York.[46] Within a few years, the number of steamboats serving New York increased from six to 43 and the cost of a ticket declined dramatically.[47] One of the steamboats plying the Hudson River was named *The Chief Justice John Marshall*.[48] Marshall actually rode a steamboat for the first time when returning to Richmond following the decision in *Gibbons*.[49] Gibbons died two years after the decision was announced. Ogden was bankrupted by the litigation and ended up in debtors' prison.[50]

---

[37] *See* G. EDWARD WHITE, THE MARSHALL COURT AND CULTURAL CHANGE, 1815-1835 578 (1988); Williams, *supra* note 16, at 1399.

[38] *Gibbons*, 22 U.S. at 223.

[39] Letter of Thomas Jefferson to William Johnson, June 12, 1823, *in* 15 WRITINGS OF THOMAS JEFFERSON 439, 451 (Library ed. 1904).

[40] *Gibbons*, 22 U.S. at 223-25.

[41] *Id.* at 226.

[42] *Id.*

[43] WARREN, *supra* note 18, at 72–74.

[44] *Id.*

[45] ARCHIBALD COX, THE COURT AND THE CONSTITUTION 90 (1987).

[46] North River Steamboat Co. v. Livingston, 3 Cow 713 (1825).

[47] COX, *supra* note 45, at 90.

[48] COX, *supra* note 11, at 179.

[49] SMITH, *supra* note 1, at 481.

[50] RENEHAN, *supra* note 3, at 101.

Gibbons v. Ogden has long been recognized as crucial to the expansion of the American economy prior to the Civil War, especially with respect to transportation. It has been credited with creating a favorable climate for investment in westward expansion, including the Erie Canal.[51] Likewise it ensured that there would be free and competitive steamboat traffic on the Mississippi River, especially given that Livingston had acquired a similar monopoly over the steamboat trade in New Orleans. *Gibbons* ensured that similar monopolies would not constrain the railroads, which would be built not long thereafter. Consequently, it was a decision that would be considered great quite apart from its doctrinal impact. Charles Warren declared that Marshall's opinion "was the emancipation proclamation for American commerce."[52]

THE DOCTRINAL IMPACT OF *GIBBONS*

Gibbons v. Ogden is widely considered one of the most significant foundational opinions in all of American constitutional law in that it provided the basis for a muscular conception of congressional authority under the Commerce Clause coupled with relatively extreme judicial deference to the exercise of that authority. Moreover it implicitly recognized the impact of the unexercised or dormant Commerce Clause, a source of much subsequent litigation. Finally in spite of its flirtation with Webster's exclusivity approach, it effectively recognized as Oakley and Emmett had argued that the states did have some concurrent regulatory authority although it did not so characterize it.

Debate continues over whether subsequent courts have read far more into Marshall's understanding of the affirmative Commerce Clause than is warranted. Marshall offered a generous conception of the congressional commerce power to be certain. However he did so in a case in which the activity in question clearly involved commercial activity crossing state lines and in a political environment in which congressional appropriation of funds for the building of roads was constitutionally controversial.

GIBBONS AND THE AFFIRMATIVE COMMERCE CLAUSE

Marshall's interpretation of the affirmative Commerce Clause had no impact on constitutional doctrine for quite some time simply because Congress did not utilize the clause as the basis for aggressive regulation until the latter part of the nineteenth century. When it finally did, the Court for the most part was unreceptive. In *United States v. E.C. Knight*, one of the most significant late nineteenth century affirmative Commerce Clause cases, the Court held that a monopoly controlling 96 percent of the sugar refining industry in the United States was local in nature and therefore did not affect interstate commerce under the Sherman Act.[53] The Court dismissed *Gibbons* as a case involving direct interference or regulation of interstate commerce.[54] In his lengthy and vigorous dissent, Justice Harlan quoted at great length from Marshall's discussion of the affirmative Commerce Clause in

---

[51] WARREN, *supra* note 18, at 76; Williams, *supra* note 16, at 1482–83.
[52] WARREN, *supra* note 18, at 76.
[53] 156 U.S. 1 (1895).
[54] *Id.* at 15–16.

Gibbons.[55] He argued that *Gibbons* and subsequent cases had established that "interstate commerce embraces something more than the mere physical transportation of articles of property, and the vehicles or vessels by which such transportation is effected."

When the Court did give the Commerce Clause a more expansive reading 18 years later in *Houston, East & West Texas Railway v. United States,*[56] it cited *Gibbons* for the proposition that Congress has adequate authority under the Commerce Clause "to meet the varying exigencies that arise, and to protect the national interest by securing the freedom of interstate commercial intercourse from local control." There, the Court upheld an order by the Interstate Commerce Commission requiring Texas to raise its intrastate shipping rates to bring them into parity with interstate rates.

Four year later *in Hammer v. Dagenhart,*[57] where the Court struck down a congressional ban on goods produced by child labor, the Court quoted from *Gibbons* in defense of its conclusion. Referring to *Gibbons* as "the judgment which established the broad power of Congress over interstate commerce," the Court quoted Marshall's language distinguishing inspection and quarantine laws as proof that the present law invaded the domain of the state police powers.[58] Justice Holmes never cited *Gibbons* in his powerful dissent that ultimately prevailed.

In *Carter v. Carter Coal*[59] where the Court rebuffed Commerce Clause–based legislation at the height of the New Deal crisis, the Court quoted some of Marshall's broadest language from *Gibbons* only to give it a restrictive interpretation. A year later in *NLRB v. Jones & Laughlin Steel* the Supreme Court revolutionized Commerce Clause jurisprudence, holding that the National Labor Relations Act could constitutionally be applied to a strike at a local steel mill. Surprisingly, the Court never cited *Gibbons* in its lengthy opinion. Nevertheless the Court's conclusion that a strike at a local steel mill had a substantial effect on commerce must have been influenced by Marshall's spacious construction of the commerce power in *Gibbons.*

Four years later in *United States v. Darby*[60] the Court began to treat *Gibbons* as the case that at the outset had correctly recognized the extreme breadth of the commerce power. *Darby* overruled *Hammer* and upheld the application of the Federal Labor Standards Act to the local manufacture of goods for shipment in interstate commerce. In the process, the Court quoted *Gibbons* for the proposition that "the power of Congress over interstate commerce 'is complete in itself, may be exercised to its utmost extent, and acknowledges no limitations other than are prescribed by the constitution....'"[61]

It was the case of *Wickard v. Filburn* decided in 1942 that re-conceived *Gibbons v. Ogden* as the central foundation of affirmative Commerce Clause analysis. In one of its most expansive applications of the Commerce Clause ever, the Court upheld the application of federal production controls to a relatively small amount of wheat grown and consumed on a farm, on the grounds that the wheat was part of a larger market whose gyrations did

---

[55] *Id.* at 19–21.
[56] 234 U.S. 342, 350 (1914).
[57] 247 U.S. 251 (1918).
[58] *Id.* at 274.
[59] 298 U.S. 238, 298 (1936).
[60] 312 U.S. 100 (1942).
[61] *Id.* at 114, quoting Gibbons v. Ogden, 22 U.S. 1, 196 (1824).

substantially affect interstate commerce.[62] Justice Jackson proclaimed that in *Gibbons* "Chief Justice Marshall described the Federal commerce power with a breadth never yet exceeded."[63] He continued, noting that "he made emphatic the embracing and penetrating nature of this power by warning that effective restraints on its exercise must proceed from political rather than from judicial processes."[64] Jackson then explained how the federal commerce power lay unexercised for most of the nineteenth century, and when it was employed near the end of the century and in the early part of the twentieth century, the Court often took an inappropriately narrow view of it. He observed however that even during this period some cases "called forth broader interpretations of the Commerce Clause destined to supercede the earlier ones, and to bring about a return to the principles first enunciated by Chief Justice Marshall in Gibbons v. Ogden."[65]

So Justice Jackson in *Wickard* created the now-popular narrative that Chief Justice Marshall quite correctly interpreted the affirmative Commerce Clause with extreme liberality; however for the better part of a century Marshall's teachings were ignored, but with the New Deal revolution, *Gibbons* was restored to its rightful place as a foundational opinion. So the story goes. Perhaps the expansive Commerce Clause jurisprudence generated by the New Deal revolution was the logical progression from *Gibbons v. Ogden*. Or perhaps Justice Jackson and the New Deal court employed *Gibbons* as a means of grounding a revolutionary approach to the Commerce Clause in a respected precedent of a far earlier era.

Wickard's reading of *Gibbons* led to the conclusion recognized by Marshall and emphasized by Jackson that the remedy for congressional overreaching under the Commerce Clause is political rather than judicial. From at least 1942 onward, both Congress and the Court operated on that assumption. That is until 1995 when in *United States v. Lopez*,[66] the Court for the first time in almost 60 years invalidated an act of Congress as exceeding its Commerce Clause authority. There, the Court struck down a federal statute that made it a crime to bring a gun into a school zone. The statute was defended on the theory that such conduct necessarily has a substantial effect on interstate commerce either by spreading the costs of crime through interstate insurance markets or by impairing the educational process, resulting in lower economic productivity. Writing for the majority, Chief Justice Rehnquist began his discussion of the commerce power with extensive quotations from *Gibbons v. Ogden*, including Marshall's definition of commerce as intercourse. However he also quoted Marshall's statement that the clause does not reach "that commerce...which is completely internal."[67] Most important however he quoted Marshall's statement that "[c]omprehensive as the word 'among' is it may very properly be restricted to that commerce which concerns more States than one.... The enumeration presupposes something not enumerated, and that something...must be the exclusively internal commerce of a State."[68] Rehnquist took the decision that had "described the Federal commerce power

---

[62] *Wickard v. Filburn*, 317 U.S. 111, 125–30 (1942).
[63] *Id.* at 120.
[64] *Id.*
[65] *Id.* at 122.
[66] 514 U.S. 549 (1995).
[67] *Id.* at 553, quoting Gibbons v. Ogden, 22 U.S. 1, 194–95 (1824).
[68] *Lopez*, 514 U.S. 549.

with a breadth never yet exceeded" and used it to illustrate that indeed the Commerce Clause had real limits, as recognized by Marshall himself. He then walked through the history of the Commerce Clause in the Supreme Court, as had Justice Jackson, but concluded that "even these modern-era precedents which have expanded congressional power under the Commerce Clause confirm that this power is subject to outer limits."[69]

The majority rejected the government's Commerce Clause justifications for a number of reasons, including the fact that the activity in question, carrying a gun into a school zone, was not commercial or economic in nature. Its reading of *Gibbons* as recognizing some limitation on the absolute reach of the commerce power was an important consideration. In rejecting the cost of crime and interference with education theories, the Court noted that neither of these appeared to suggest any limit whatsoever to congressional power. The majority concluded its opinion in *Lopez* by noting that acceptance of the government's argument "would require us to conclude that the Constitution's enumeration of powers does not presuppose something not enumerated, cf Gibbons v. Ogden…and that there never will be a distinction between what is truly national and what is truly local, cf Jones & Laughlin Steel."[70] Thus after decades of serving as a foundation for an expansive reading of the commerce power, in *Lopez* the Court employed *Gibbons* as a precedent for at least some restriction of that clause.

Dissenting in *Lopez*, Justice Breyer cited *Gibbons* for the principle that Congress can "regulate local activities insofar as they significantly affect interstate commerce."[71] Justice Thomas in concurring wrote a lengthy response to Justice Breyer's understanding of *Gibbons*, arguing that it depends upon characterizing "the first 150 years of the Court's case law as a 'wrong turn.'"[72] He argued that the incorrectly expansive reading of *Gibbons* was attributable to a misunderstanding of two statements of Marshall in the case. First, Marshall's statement that the commerce power does not extend to activity that does not "affect other states" hardly means that it empowers Congress to regulate all activity that does.[73] Rather, according to Justice Thomas, Gibbons properly read stood for the proposition that Congress could never regulate the wholly internal commerce of a state regardless of whether it affected interstate commerce. That is a permissible reading of *Gibbons* though hardly the standard reading.

Justice Thomas also maintained that Chief Justice Marshall's statement in *Gibbons* that the Constitution gave the federal government power over "'those internal concerns which affect the States generally'" did not mean that Congress had authority under the Commerce Clause over anything that it considered to be a national matter. Rather Justice Thomas argued that the "substantial effects test is but an innovation of the 20th century."[74] He then provided a discussion of the commerce power up to the New Deal cases to illustrate that the Court had construed the affirmative Commerce Clause as restrictively as he understood it. Thomas made a powerful case for his reading of *Gibbons*. However by the time of *Lopez*, the substantial effects test was too firmly entrenched in the Court's

---

[69] *Id.* at 556–57.
[70] *Id.* at 567.
[71] *Id.* at 616.
[72] *Id.* at 593.
[73] *Id.* at 594–95.
[74] *Id.* at 596.

jurisprudence to be dislodged even if based on a misunderstanding of *Gibbons*. Justice Kennedy's concurrence in *Lopez* emphasizing the need for stability in Commerce Clause jurisprudence was almost certainly intended as a reassurance that no revaluation of Commerce Clause precedent and doctrine as jarring as that proposed by Justice Thomas was on the horizon.

Five years later in *United States v. Morrison*,[75] the Court applied *Lopez* to invalidate Commerce Clause–based legislation providing a civil remedy for gender-motivated acts of violence. Like Justice Breyer in *Lopez*, Justice Souter wrote a lengthy dissent challenging the Court's understanding of Commerce Clause doctrine as it originated in *Gibbons*, arguing that the post New Deal conception of the commerce power was entirely consistent with *Gibbons*.[76] In *Gonzalez v. Raich*,[77] a few years later, the majority upheld the application of federal controlled substance legislation to harvesting, sale, and use of marijuana for medicinal purposes pursuant to a state law without rehashing the debate over the meaning of *Gibbons*.

Arguably, the constraining aspect of *Gibbons* on the commerce power has gained momentum. In the most significant Commerce Clause case in decades, *National Federation of Independent Business v. Sebelius*, the challenge to the constitutionality of the Affordable Health Care Act, Chief Justice Roberts began his opinion rejecting a Commerce Clause justification for the congressional mandate to purchase health insurance by quoting the language from *Gibbons* that "'enumeration presupposes something not enumerated.'"[78] The absence of any workable limiting principle to the government's theory was clearly the reason five justices concluded that the individual mandate could not be justified by the commerce power. The four dissenters, who agreed with Justice Roberts on the Commerce Clause, argued that requiring the purchase of insurance could not be brought within Marshall's definition of "regulate" in *Gibbons*. On the other hand Justice Ginsberg's lengthy opinion attempting to justify the mandate under the Commerce Clause cited *Gibbons* only once for the proposition that the democratic process was the only effective check against congressional abuse of the commerce power.

One hundred and seventy-five years after it was decided *Gibbons* remains the foundational precedent on the scope of the affirmative Commerce Clause, and yet the very essence of the decision is still hotly contested.

THE IMPACT OF *GIBBONS* ON DORMANT COMMERCE CLAUSE DOCTRINE

Gibbons is best known for its impact on affirmative Commerce Clause doctrine but Marshall also spent a significant portion of the opinion discussing the dormant Commerce Clause; that is, did states have any authority to regulate interstate commerce in the absence of congressional regulation, or did the authority to regulate interstate commerce rest exclusively with Congress?. He seemed to agree with Webster that the power to regulate commerce was exclusively federal but found it unnecessary to so hold, basing the

---

[75] 529 U.S. 598 (2000).

[76] *Id.* at 638–45.

[77] 545 U.S. 1 (2005).

[78] 132 S. Ct. 2566, 2577 (2012).

decision instead on federal preemption grounds. In the process however he conceded that the states had significant authority to regulate what might appear to be interstate commerce for police power purpose.

Neither Marshall nor the Court ever carried through with the theory of federal exclusivity over interstate commerce. Three years after *Gibbons*, in *Brown v. Maryland*,[79] Marshall writing for the Court struck down a Maryland law that required persons selling imported goods in Maryland to purchase a license. The Court held that the law violated the clause prohibiting state taxation on imports and exports as well as the Commerce Clause. If anything Marshall's language suggesting federal exclusivity over commerce was even stronger in *Brown* than in *Gibbons*.[80] However, the regulation in question would appear to be inconsistent with the dormant Commerce Clause even assuming a healthy scope for state police power regulation.

Two years later in a brief and cryptic opinion in *Willson v. The Black-Bird Creek Marsh Co.*,[81] after pointing out that the state had authorized the building of a dam across the navigable creek for purposes of protecting the public health, Marshall simply concluded that "under all of the circumstance of the case, [we do not think the Act can] be considered as repugnant to the power to regulate commerce in its dormant state, or as being in conflict with any law passed by congress."[82] Thus despite *Gibbons* and *Brown*, federal power over interstate commerce was not exclusive after all. Dormant Commerce Clause jurisprudence was off and running. *Black Bird Creek* is arguably easily reconciled with *Gibbons* as simply an example of the type of police power regulation that Marshall acknowledged as legitimate in *Gibbons*. However the conclusions in *Black Bird* sound different than those of *Gibbons* in that in the former Marshall seemed to recognize that the state is indeed regulating interstate commerce although for a legitimate purpose, while in the latter he seemed to deny that police power legislation was regulation of commerce, period.

After *Black Bird Creek* however, the understanding that legitimate police power regulation was permissible regulation of interstate commerce took hold and prevails to this day. For a time, the Taney court was unable to gather a majority around any particular approach to the dormant Commerce Clause.[83] Ultimately however, in *Cooley v. Board of Wardens*,[84] a majority of the Court took the position that congressional power was only exclusive where the national needs such as uniformity are paramount, and the states have the power to regulate where local considerations predominate. In the twentieth century, dormant Commerce Clause doctrine became more complex, with different approaches to state legislation based on whether it is challenged as burdensome, discriminatory, or protectionist.[85] The doctrine is at least traced back to *Cooley*; however it is arguably traced back even further to the oral arguments as well as Marshall's opinion in *Gibbons*.

---

[79] 25 U.S. 419 (1827).

[80] *Id.* at 446–47.

[81] 27 U.S. 245 (1829).

[82] *Id.* at 252. The relevant law passed by Congress would have been the very Coasting Act relied on in *Gibbons* given that the vessel, which crashed into the dam, was licensed under that Act like Gibbons's steamboat.

[83] The License Cases, 46 U.S. 504 (1847); The Passenger Cases, 48 U.S. 283 (1849).

[84] 53 U.S. 298, 299 (1851).

[85] *See, e.g.*, Philadelphia v. New Jersey, 437 U.S. 617 (1978); Hunt v. Wash. State Apple Adver Comm'n, 432 U.S. 333 (1977).

GIBBONS AS A GREAT CASE

Gibbons v. Ogden was certainly a great case even by the Holmes definition. It involved a struggle over an economic and political issue of extreme significance and public interest. When it reached the Supreme Court, the eyes of the nation were focused on the Court. The Court clearly understood that it was rendering a decision of both immediate and long-term economic, political, and legal significance. It is hard to know for certain to what extent the "greatness" of the case influenced the opinion. There can be little doubt that the decision on the merits would have been the same whether the case was highly publicized or quite obscure. The decision in favor of Gibbons was very much dictated by two of the most predominant themes in Marshall court jurisprudence: a generous conception of congressional power and a construction of legal rules in such a manner as to support economic expansion.

The context of the case probably had an impact on Marshall's legal analysis however. *Gibbons* is well recognized among constitutional scholars for its ambiguity. Marshall interpreted the Commerce Clause quite expansively but then drew back, recognizing its limits. He spent much of the opinion building the case for congressional exclusivity only to back away and resolve the case on somewhat strained preemption grounds. What accounts for the internal tension of the opinion? Did the "greatness" of the case or the pressurized political context in which it was decided affect the analysis?

Historians have long debated why Marshall wrote the opinion as he did. Marshall's discussion of the affirmative power of Congress under the Commerce Clause would seem to extend beyond what was required by the case. Expansive dicta was of course a defining characteristic of the Marshall opinion so it is not surprising that he indulged in the practice in *Gibbons*. He had before him an important but previously uninterpreted provision of the Constitution, and he could provide it with a liberal construction in a case that would almost certainly be well received. The Court had been under fire since its expansive approach to congressional power five years earlier in *McCulloch v. Maryland.* Arguably, *Gibbons* like *Cohens v. Virginia* is yet another attempt by Marshall to re-enforce the stand that the Court took in *McCulloch* in view of the barrage of criticism directed at it. *Gibbons* may have provided an ideal platform in that Marshall could construe congressional authority expansively in support of an innocuous law, the federal Coasting Act of 1793, and to the detriment of an unpopular state law, the New York steamboat monopoly.

In the same vein, at the time *Gibbons* was decided, Congress was engaged in a heated debate over whether it had the authority to pass internal improvements legislation, most particularly involving road improvements, under the Commerce Clause. President Madison had vetoed an internal improvements bill on constitutional grounds.[86] Marshall's generous reading of congressional power under the clause may well have been intended as signaling that the Court would readily find the Internal Improvements Act constitutional if the issue should arise. Marshall's broad dicta would also be useful to congressional proponents of tariff legislation.[87]

---

[86] Veto Message of President James Monroe, 39 ANNALS OF CONGRESS 1803–05 (1822).

[87] WARREN, *supra* note 18, at 77.

The more intriguing question is why Marshall so forcefully endorsed Webster's congressional exclusivity approach only to change gears near the end of the opinion and decide the case on the basis of federal preemption. Was it a failure of nerve? The Marshall court at the time of *Gibbons* was still near the height of its power. Marshall presided over a solidly Federalist-oriented bench that he could generally count on to back his constitutional opinions.[88] That was beginning to change around the time of *Gibbons* however. Although Marshall still led the Court, it is unlikely that he dominated it to the degree that he once had.[89] Still some of the Marshall court's earlier opinions had provoked a significant backlash, and in the years prior to *Gibbons* at least some members of Congress had proposed various measures to constrain the Court, including court packing, requiring a supermajority to invalidate state or federal legislation, jurisdiction stripping, and the outright repeal of judicial review.[90] Thus as of *Gibbons*, the Court was confident but at the same time had reason to be cautious. Marshall flirted with Webster's exclusive power approach but ultimately blinked. Perhaps the broad dicta coupled with a narrow holding was the compromise required to obtain a near unanimous court, as Herbert Johnson has suggested.[91] Even then, Justice Johnson elected to file a separate concurrence endorsing Webster's approach. Norman Williams has argued that Marshall could have produced a solid majority, perhaps even a unanimous opinion for congressional exclusivity, had he so chosen, but relied on federal preemption in order to shift responsibility to Congress where Marshall believed that it belonged.[92]

Justice (then Professor) Frankfurter argued that Marshall was unable to adequately delineate the boundaries between the federal and state domains in the area of interstate commerce, and as a result shrunk from the task in *Gibbons*.[93] That is a possibility although Marshall's own analysis in *Gibbons* suggests that he had derived a working approach. Marshall purported to agree with Webster's exclusivity approach and yet he made allowance for well-accepted instances of state regulation of commerce by categorizing these examples as legitimate police power regulation. Wirt had argued that there were occasions when the state could regulate interstate commerce at least where the federal interest did not predominate. To a large extent at least, Marshall reached the same result by denying that the state was engaging in regulation of interstate commerce in these instances. Marshall's approach seems unduly formalistic. It does however provide for a compromise between the competing interests. Thus Marshall had a theory, although Frankfurter could be correct in concluding that he was not yet confident that it was sufficiently developed to rely upon.

Yet another possible explanation for Marshall's lengthy consideration of the exclusivity issue is simply that it was the focus of the five-day oral arguments delivered by several highly skilled advocates, and Marshall may have felt some obligation to work through the issues that had dominated the arguments even if they would not ultimately provide the basis for the decision. Marshall may have been disinclined to write an opinion that

---

[88] Williams, *supra* note 16, at 1423–30.

[89] JOHNSON, *supra* note 4, at xii, 107–23.

[90] WARREN, *supra* note 18, at 91; Williams, *supra* note 16, at 1463–71.

[91] JOHNSON, *supra* note 4, at 4.

[92] Williams, *supra* note 16, at 1424–31, 1446–76.

[93] FELIX FRANKFURTER, THE COMMERCE CLAUSE UNDER MARSHALL, TANEY AND WAITE 20–35 (1964).

essentially said "everything that you had to say in your lengthy argument, Mr. Webster, is irrelevant to the decision in this case." Marshall was a gregarious judge who seemed to appreciate and often made great use of the arguments by counsel before the Court. It was quite typical for him to devote much of his opinions to point-by-point consideration of the arguments presented. Webster himself later claimed that Marshall had told him that "he had little to do other than to repeat [my] argument, as that it covered the whole ground."[94] In his opinion in *Gibbons*, Marshall went out of his way to consider and reject most of the arguments that Oakley and Emmett skillfully presented in favor of concurrent authority over commerce. Marshall may have simply concluded that it was an aspect of sound judicial practice to at least work through what counsel considered to be the central issue in the case before rendering a decision on an alternative ground.

No one can know for certain why Marshall wrote the opinion as he did in *Gibbons*. The greatness of the case itself presumably would have provided support for a strong and authoritative opinion considering that for a change Marshall was on the positive side of public opinion. The fact that *Gibbons* was decided in the midst of one of the most sustained political attacks on the Court during its history may well explain the Court's ambivalence.

Gibbons v. Ogden is certainly a great case but few would contend that it made bad law. The economic impact of *Gibbons* has been celebrated ever since. Few, if any, Supreme Court cases are credited with having a more significant and lasting positive impact than *Gibbons v. Ogden*. Although the opinion is ambivalent, Marshall's analysis, particularly his discussion of the meaning of the Commerce Clause, is yet another example of his skill as an interpreter of legal texts. After 190 years, the opinion continues to read well. Likewise, as the foundational case of Commerce Clause jurisprudence, *Gibbons* has had a pervasive effect on the development of constitutional doctrine. Although *Gibbons* may have played a minor role up to the New Deal crisis, it then became the very anchor for the post-1937 judicial approach. Since then, *Gibbons* has provided the basis for both an expansive view of the Commerce Clause as well as some limitations on it. As with *Marbury* and *McCulloch*, Marshall succeeded in transforming a great case into a landmark case.

---

[94] WARREN, *supra* note 18, at 71.

The subject matter of this case "is, even now, heaving the political tides of the country, which has caused enthusiasm to throw her lighted torch into the temples of religion, and the halls of science and learning, whilst the forum of justice, and the village bar-room have equally resounded with discussion.... [I]t has become 'sore as a gangrene' in one region, it is the football of the enthusiast in another."[1]

DEPUTY ATTORNEY GENERAL THOMAS C. HAMBLY OF PENNSYLVANIA ARGUING
PRIGG V. PENNSYLVANIA TO THE UNITED STATES SUPREME COURT

4

Prigg v. Pennsylvania

In *Prigg v. Pennsylvania*,[2] the Court plunged into the red hot national controversy surrounding the obligations of state governments with respect to the rendition of fugitive slaves. The Court confronted the question in a test case essentially arranged by two state legislatures in which the alleged fugitive slave at the center of the issue was all but invisible. A divided Court produced a decision, which like the *Dred Scott* decision a decade and one-half later, attempted to resolve a bitter political controversy but arguably made matters worse. Neither slave nor free states were entirely pleased with the decision. The scholarly New Englander, Justice Joseph Story, who wrote the majority opinion was castigated by fellow northerners. The decision was sufficiently unpopular in several northern states to result in outright defiance by some state legislatures, courts, and executive officials. *Prigg* was a great case that contributed to further national division on the insoluble issue of slavery.

BACKGROUND

Article IV, Section Two, paragraph 3 of the Constitution provided that:

No person held to Service or Labour in one State, under the Laws thereof, escaping into another, shall, in Consequence of any Law or Regulation therein, be discharged from such Service or Labour, but shall be delivered up on Claim of the Party to whom such Service or Labour may be due.

To implement the Fugitive Slave Clause, Congress passed the Fugitive Slave Act of 1793. Under that law, federal and state judges and magistrates were authorized to issue

---

[1] 41 U.S. 539, 572 (1842).

[2] 41 U.S. 539 (1842).

certificates of removal, which permitted an alleged fugitive to be transported out of the state of capture. As the procedures governing recapture and rendition appeared to be a matter of state law, many states addressed the issue legislatively. Pennsylvania passed a Personal Liberty Act in 1826 requiring that a fugitive could not be removed from the state absent the issuance of a certificate of removal following an evidentiary hearing. The person seeking removal was required to provide a detailed statement in support of the claim, and the fugitive was provided with the opportunity to offer evidence in rebuttal. The Act had been the result of a compromise between Pennsylvania and Maryland.[3] Removal without such a certificate would constitute kidnapping.[4]

Margaret Morgan was born a slave to John Ashmore in the state of Maryland. Ashmore treated Margaret and her parents as free but never formally emancipated them. They were not listed as his possessions at his death. In 1832, Margaret married Jerry Morgan and moved with him to Pennsylvania where they had at least one child. In 1837, Ashmore's widow claimed Morgan and her children as slaves and sent Edward Prigg and a few other individuals to Pennsylvania to retrieve her. Prigg obtained an arrest warrant for Morgan from a peace officer in Pennsylvania but failed to obtain a certificate of removal as required by the Fugitive Slave Act of 1793 and by the Pennsylvania Liberty law. Nevertheless, Prigg did return Morgan and her children to Maryland. At a hearing in Maryland, she was found to be a slave in that Ashmore had never consented to her freedom. Apparently, she and her children were sold into slavery, and as one author has observed "disappears from the historical record."[5] Jerry Morgan died tragically in an attempt to obtain his wife and child's freedom.[6] The story ended quickly for the Morgans but was only beginning for Prigg and the Fugitive Slave laws.

Following the removal of Morgan from Pennsylvania, Prigg was charged in Pennsylvania with kidnapping under the Personal Liberty Act. The governor of Pennsylvania requested that Maryland honor the warrants for Prigg's arrest. Many in Maryland were outraged by the charge.[7] The Maryland legislature provided for Prigg's surrender and for the creation of a case that would resolve the question in the United States Supreme Court, a procedure that seems odd to us today.[8] Pennsylvania agreed to this approach. The states further agreed that Prigg would be arrested and then released on his own recognizance with an agreement to abide by a decision of the Supreme Court. The attorney general of Pennsylvania and defense counsel for Prigg would negotiate an agreed statement of facts on which a jury would then render a special verdict. This in turn would be appealed to the Pennsylvania Supreme Court and then to the Supreme Court of the United States.

Among other things, the statement of facts declared that Morgan was Ashmore's slave, that she had escaped to Pennsylvania, that Prigg had obtained a warrant to recapture her in Pennsylvania, and that he had returned her to Maryland without having obtained a

---

[3] Earl M. Maltz, Slavery and the Supreme Court, 1825–1861, at 94 (2009).

[4] The 1826 Act as well as prior Pennsylvania recapture laws was set forth by the Court in *Prigg v Pennsylvania*, 41 U.S. at 544–56.

[5] H. Robert Baker, *Prigg v Pennsylvania*: Slavery, the Supreme Court, and the Ambivalent Constitution 110 (2012).

[6] *Id.* at 112-13.

[7] *Id.* at 114.

[8] *Id.* at 113.

certificate of removal. It noted that one of her children who had also been removed had been born in Pennsylvania.[9] The statement was quite favorable to Maryland's case in that it failed to acknowledge that Morgan had contested the fact that she was actually a slave.

ORAL ARGUMENT

Prigg v. Pennsylvania arrived at the Supreme Court in 1842 at a time when abolitionist activity had led to a powerful backlash from the slave states. The nation was in something of a crisis over slavery, especially efforts by some northern states, most prominently Pennsylvania, to resist the recapture and return of fugitive slaves. Although the Court had decided several cases involving claims of freedom by slaves, *Prigg* was the first case presented to the Court involving the fugitive slave laws. However the Court had decided two cases involving slavery during the previous term. In *Groves v. Slaughter*[10] it had concluded that an amendment to the Mississippi constitution banning the importation of slaves into the state was not self-executing and thus did not invalidate a bill of sale for slaves brought into the state. And in the highly publicized case of *The Amistad*,[11] the Court interpreted a treaty to free a group of alleged slaves who had risen up and killed the captain and much of the crew of the slave ship on which they were being transported. The Court devoted three days to oral argument of *Prigg*. Jonathon Meredith and John Nelson appeared for Maryland on behalf of Edward Prigg. Attorney General Ovid F. Johnson and Deputy Attorney General Thomas C. Hambly appeared for Pennsylvania.

At the outset, Meredith noted that "the case is one of vital interest to the peace and perpetuity of the Union itself."[12] He argued that the Fugitive Slave Clause of Article IV of the Constitution gave the federal government exclusive authority to regulate the rendition of fugitive slaves, and even if it did not, the Fugitive Slave Act of 1793 precluded state legislation. He argued that the constitutional duty of delivery could be defeated if enforcement procedures were left to the states. Moreover the procedures set forth in the Pennsylvania law were more rigorous and hence inconsistent with, and thus preempted by, the federal act.

Representing Pennsylvania, Hambly argued that the passage of the Fugitive Slave Act of 1793 as well as state legislation on rendition was proof that the Fugitive Slave Clause was not understood to be self-executing.[13] He maintained that the text of the Fugitive Slave Clause, especially the use of the term "claim," presumes some procedure for litigation. Hambly maintained that some state procedure was essential to ensure that slave catchers did not seize and carry away freemen. He argued that only the states could create and administer such procedures.

Ovid Johnson noted that the Act of 1826 was the result of negotiation between Pennsylvania and Maryland, but at the time it was considered more favorable to the interests of Maryland. He maintained that the only constitutional restriction on the states was

---

[9] *Id.* at 557.

[10] 40 U.S. 449 (1841).

[11] United States v. Libellants and Claimants of the Schooner Amistad, 40 U.S. 518 (1841).

[12] *Prigg*, 41 U.S. at 559.

[13] *Id.* at 574.

that they could not free fugitives. Johnson argued that a slave catcher could choose to rely on either the Fugitive Slave Act of 1793 or the Pennsylvania Act of 1826, but must abide by the procedures of the Act that he chose.[14] As Prigg relied on the Pennsylvania law he was bound by its requirements.

The argument of John Nelson was not submitted to the reporter.

THE OPINIONS

Justice Story wrote the opinion for the Court, holding that the power to regulate the recapture and return of runaway slaves rested exclusively with the national government, and as such the Pennsylvania law was unconstitutional. At the outset, Story acknowledged the significance of the case, noting that "[f]ew questions which have ever come before this court involve more delicate and important considerations; and few upon which the public at large may be presumed to feel a more profound and pervading interest."[15] He recognized that the purpose of the Fugitive Slave Clause was to prevent non-slaveholding states from "intermedling with, or obstructing, or abolishing the rights of the owners of slaves."[16] Moreover, the Constitution could not have been ratified without the clause.

Story declared that the law of slavery is local in nature. He then stated that the Fugitive Slave Clause in the Constitution "contemplates the existence of a positive, unqualified right on the part of the owner of the slave, which no state law or regulation can in any way qualify, regulate, control or restrain."[17] He maintained that "under... the constitution, the owner of a slave is clothed with entire authority, in every state in the Union, to seize and recapture his slave, whenever he can do it, without any breach of the peace or any illegal violence."[18] This explicitly recognized a right of self-help in the master or his agent. Moreover, it permitted the slave catcher to essentially bring the law of the slave state with him into the free state. Story made no attempt to explain exactly what would constitute a breach of peace or illegal violence.

Focusing on the word "claim" in the clause, Story reasoned that it contemplated some further procedure. As the right of delivery was guaranteed by the Constitution, presumably a national means of effectuating such a delivery must have been contemplated. Story noted that Congress, through the Fugitive Slave Act of 1793, had provided a means for adjudicating the claim of a slaveholder, and such procedure must be considered exclusive. Hence any state regulation of the procedure for claiming an escaped slave would be inconsistent with the federal procedure. Story argued that the rendition power must be considered exclusively national because the duty of recapture was created by the Constitution and demanded uniformity. He noted that it is unimaginable that the slaveholding states would have agreed to permit non-slaveholding states to regulate the procedures of recapture. Story assumed that any state power to regulate rendition would almost certainly be

---

[14] *Id.* at 600.
[15] *Id.* at 610.
[16] *Id.* at 611.
[17] *Id.* at 612.
[18] *Id.* at 613.

used, at least by some states "to destroy the rights of the owner."[19] The states retained the police power to arrest runaway slaves and exclude them from their jurisdictions. Thus the states had the power to act prior to the assertion of a claim by the slave owner. As the federal authority was exclusive, the Pennsylvania Personal Liberty Act was unconstitutional.

Story made a credible argument that the rendition power should be considered to rest exclusively in the national government, but he scarcely established that this was the only permissible reading. Given the need for a workable adjudication and enforcement mechanism, which the federal government seemed logistically incapable of providing, fulfillment of the purpose of the provision would be better effectuated by the recognition of the permissibility of non-obstructionist state procedures as well.

Chief Justice Roger Taney concurred in the opinion of the Court but offered his own opinion in which he argued that only laws impeding the delivery of runaway slaves were preempted by the Constitution and federal law, whereas those that aided the master in recovery were contemplated by the framers and were clearly constitutional. He argued that the phrase "shall be delivered up" in the Fugitive Slave Clause assumes positive action by state authorities. Thus Taney accepted only that aspect of the majority opinion that unambiguously favored the slave owner. Taney's argument for state supplementation was more in accord with achievement of the purpose of the Fugitive Slave Clause as well as principles of federalism than was Storey's opinion for the Court.

Justice Thompson also wrote a concurring opinion agreeing with Taney that only state laws that impeded recapture and delivery were preempted. Like Taney, he argued that in the absence of congressional legislation, state procedures would be necessary and thus could not be preempted by the Constitution itself. Nor was there anything peculiar about the issue to lead to the conclusion that federal exclusivity was essential.

Justice Baldwin concurred in the judgment but dissented from the rationale without explaining why. Justice Wayne wrote a lengthy and complicated opinion agreeing that the right to legislate with respect to delivery of runaway slaves rested exclusively in Congress. He conceded that the text of the Constitution did not preclude state legislation on the subject. However, he argued that given that the purpose of the clause was to protect a type of property "peculiar to some" states from interference by other states, a uniform remedy must be assumed.[20] Justice Wayne feared that state rendition procedures might readily "interpos[e] delays more expenses more costly than the value of the fugitive sought to be reclaimed."[21] He argued that even a law intended to ensure that the claimant in fact owned the slave would be inconsistent with the constitutional clause in that it could result in the discharge of a lawfully held slave. Wayne conceded that states could pass laws to protect free Blacks against being captured and enslaved but could not regulate the rendition of a fugitive. The obvious difficulty with this attempted distinction is that as with Margaret Morgan, the question of whether a free Black was being enslaved or whether a fugitive was being returned could readily be the competing claims in a specific case.

---

[19] *Id.* at 624.
[20] *Id.* at 642.
[21] *Id.* at 643.

Justice Daniel also wrote a concurrence arguing that the majority need not have reached the question of federal exclusivity, but having done so he believed that the rights of the slaveholder would be best protected if the state could also pass legislation aiding the recapture and delivery. Daniel also suggested that Story's police power exception to the prohibition of state regulation could also be abused to the detriment of the slave owner.

Justice McLean wrote a lengthy "concurring" opinion in which he purported to disagree with only one point of the majority opinion, but in fact seemed to disagree with most of it. He did agree that Congress had exclusive authority to develop procedures for the delivery of runaway slaves.[22] Although he agreed with the general assumption of the majority that as a general rule, Congress could not impose duties on state officers, he argued that there was an exception to that rule where the Constitution imposed a specific duty on the state, as was the case with the Fugitive Slave Clause. Consequently, the Act of 1793 could constitutionally require state magistrates to issue certificates of removal. He then argued that pursuant to its police powers, Pennsylvania had the right to require that Prigg comply with state procedures to ensure that no free person was removed without legal authority. Essentially, McLean seemed to argue that although Pennsylvania did not have the authority to interfere with the proper removal of an escaped slave, it did have the power to ensure that the removal was affected through legal process to ensure that a free black person was not enslaved. His reasoning process was complicated and confusing to say the least.

AFTERMATH

The charges against Prigg were dropped given that the Pennsylvania law of 1826 had been declared unconstitutional. Nothing is known as to the fate of Margaret Morgan. It has been assumed that she and her daughter were sold into slavery in the South. The decision was greeted with outrage and contempt by abolitionists in the north. Senator Sumner argued that Congress could ignore the *Prigg* decision.[23] The New Englander Joseph Story who had written the opinion was condemned for collaborating with the forces of slavery. Privately he assured his son that he considered that the impact of the decision would make it more difficult to recapture runaway slaves or to enslave free Blacks as the support of local law was generally necessary to aid in enforcement.[24] To a significant extent, that proved to be the case in states such as Pennsylvania and New York that were solidly opposed to the return of fugitive slaves. Indeed, in the face of *Prigg*, New York enacted a statute rendering recapture more difficult. The difficulty of recapture led to the enactment of a more stringent fugitive slave act by Congress in 1850 as part of a compromise to attempt to diffuse the growing controversy over the slavery issue. The 1850 Act emphasized *Prigg*'s conclusion that any state rendition legislation was void. It re-enforced federal procedures with the authorization of federal commissioners to hear cases. It also

---

[22] *Id.* at 662.

[23] G. EDWARD WHITE, THE AMERICAN JUDICIAL TRADITION: PROFILES OF LEADING AMERICAN JUDGES 77 (1988).

[24] BAKER, *supra* note 5, at 157-58.

required all citizens to aid in the rendition of fugitive slaves. As such, it was a complete anathema to the abolitionist movement. *Prigg* convinced many that the Court was solidly in the hands of the friends of slavery. The decision was unanimous and had been written by a northern scholar who purported to be opposed to slavery. Although the decision seemed to favor the interests of slavery, southerners couldn't help recognize that exclusive federal jurisdiction over the issue of capture was a double-edged sword and could be employed to the disadvantage of slavery interests if control of Congress were to fall into abolitionist hands. That in turn reminded the southerners that the question of slavery in the territories, which the Court would confront 15 years after *Prigg*, was in fact the more decisive question as the continued admission of free territories destined to become free states would eventually shift the congressional balance against slavery.

PRIGG AS A GREAT CASE

Prigg v. Pennsylvania was as much of a test case as has ever been presented to the Court. Although there was clearly a case and controversy in that Prigg faced a criminal trial under the Pennsylvania Act, the case had been arranged by the governments of Maryland and Pennsylvania to resolve the dispute over rendition. As the oral arguments and the opinions acknowledge, the issues at the heart of the case were matters of extreme public controversy. *Prigg* was a great case in the classic sense of the term. The justices well understood that they were confronting an issue on which public passions were inflamed. *Prigg* was only the second case in the history of the Court to that point in which seven justices wrote separate opinions, indicating that they understood it to be both out of the ordinary and troublesome.[25]

There was and remains much speculation as to why Story wrote the opinion that he did. There was certainly no possibility that he could have written an opinion sustaining the Pennsylvania prosecution given that the ultimate decision was unanimously opposed to the state. Story's private explanation that he considered the decision as providing an obstacle to recapture has generally been dismissed as post-hoc rationalization. Rather, the opinion seems consistent with larger themes in Story's jurisprudence. In his *Commentaries on the Constitution*, Story had insisted that the initial compromise on slavery, including the Fugitive Slave Clause as well as the Fugitive Slave Act of 1793, had been essential to the formation of the Union.[26] Story emphasized this in his opinion. In other words, the question of the right to recapture of fugitive slaves was simply not open for debate. It had been settled and any attempt to upset that agreement was likely to destabilize the nation. Perhaps the driving force behind *Prigg*, especially in view of the increasing agitation by the abolitionist movement, was the necessity of protecting the bargain with slavery in order to preserve the Union. Beyond that commitment, Story was the most extreme nationalist to sit on the Court during the first half of the nineteenth century.

---

[25] Paul Finkelman, *Sorting Out* Prigg v. Pennsylvania, 24 RUTGERS L. REV. 605, 606 (1993).

[26] JOSEPH STORY, A FAMILIAR EXPOSITION OF THE CONSTITUTION OF THE UNITED STATES § 411 (1840) (bicentennial ed. 1986). *See also* R. KENT NEWMYER, SUPREME COURT JUSTICE JOSEPH STORY: STATESMAN OF THE OLD REPUBLIC 378 (1985).

A decision that consolidated authority at the federal as opposed to the state level was quite consistent with Story's general constitutional outlook.

Assuming that Story would decide against the Pennsylvania Act, a large and enduring question is why he did not simply strike down the state law as inconsistent with either the federal Fugitive Slave Act or the Fugitive Slave Clause in that it provided more stringent procedures. That certainly would have been the narrowest means of deciding against Pennsylvania. Perhaps Story was inspired by the legacy of Marshall who regularly decided cases broadly, often ignoring narrower alternatives, arguably to have a more significant influence on the future development of the law. Story was a more careful judge than Marshall. In the previous term, he had attempted to defuse the slavery controversy by deciding *The Amistad* on narrow and technical grounds. Why did he not take the same approach in *Prigg*? Arguably, he may not have been able to build a majority to do so given that at least two justices would have gone further by invalidating only those state laws that impeded rendition and not those that aided it. The concurring opinions suggest an extreme skepticism as to the good faith of at least some of the states, such as Pennsylvania, that might pass rendition acts if permitted. At least some of the justices, quite possibly a majority, believed that virtually any state legislation would undermine the rights and efforts of slave owners.

There has been a continuing argument over whether Story even had a majority behind that which he did say given that the reporter does not mention the concurrence of Justices McKinley and Catron.[27] We cannot know for certain. Perhaps like Marshall or even like Taney in *Dred Scott*, Story believed that he could settle a controversial issue by confronting it globally Or perhaps he believed that by attempting to construct a compromise between southern and northern interests reaffirming that right of recapture but relieving northern states of participation, he hoped to defuse the rising tensions surrounding the issue.[28] Whatever the rationale, Story's opinion in *Prigg* is yet one of many examples of a justice taking what was clearly a great case and making it more significant than it needed to be.

Story's opinion has been challenged on other grounds as well. Arguably, he failed to adequately justify federal exclusivity over rendition. Both the sympathizers with slavery such as Taney and its opponents such as McLean argued that some non-impeding state procedure was essential in order to effectuate the federal right given that federal officials were few and far between. Story did not really refute this. He relied on the need for uniformity, but did that outweigh the need for an available and workable procedural framework at the state level—a framework that the federal government would be hard pressed to provide?

Perhaps the most severe challenge to Story's opinion is that it failed to take any account of the interest that the Pennsylvania Act was intended to protect against—the kidnapping of free Blacks by renegade slave catchers. Assuming as Story maintained that the right to recapture runaway slave was indeed a constitutionally protected right that had been and remained essential to the survival of the Union, the state and indeed federal interest in protecting the liberty of free Blacks need not be ignored in order to protect

---

[27] NEWMYER, *supra* note 26, at 374.
[28] MALTZ, *supra* note 3, at 104.

the rights of slave owners. Pennsylvania maintained that its procedures were essential to ensure that these rights were honored as well. Story can be faulted for simply failing to come to grips with this interest. As such, his opinion for the Court appears to cast its lot almost entirely with the interests of slavery.

Story has been criticized as well for largely ignoring the facts of the Morgan rendition that initially gave rise to *Prigg*, especially the fact that Morgan's daughter born in Pennsylvania had a particularly strong argument that she was free. Tragic as it may well be however, the case revolved around Prigg and not Morgan. Her status was relevant if at all only if there was a credible case that she was in fact a free person who had been kidnapped. Unfortunately, the jury had found otherwise and had issued a stipulated statement of facts favorable to Prigg to which the Court was bound.

Story was one of the greatest legal craftsmen in the history of the Court. As was almost always the case, his opinion was tight and forceful, and yet it still seems dictated by considerations beyond the demands of the specific issues before the Court.

Justices Taney and Daniel wrote concurrences arguing that the states had the power to pass legislation in aid of recapture but not that which would impede it. Their sympathies for slave owners were as apparent in *Prigg* in 1842 as they would be in *Dred Scott* 15 years later. Justice McLean who would later dissent in *Dred Scott* was the only justice to draw a distinction between the right to recapture fugitive slaves and the right to protect free Blacks.

To some extent, quite probably to a large extent, the *Prigg* decision and opinion was driven by the growing public controversy surrounding slavery. The case was decided at the time when abolitionist fervor, especially in terms of petitions to Congress, was on the upswing. It was apparent that the Court would be drawn into disputes over slavery issues. As would be the case with *Dred Scott*, the involvement of the Court was not merely happenstance. The political branches clearly looked to the Court for resolution. In *Prigg*, Pennsylvania and Maryland were at loggerheads and determined that the Supreme Court was the ideal forum for resolution of the dispute. As with *Dred Scott*, the justices did not shrink from the challenge but rather embraced it, deciding the case on far broader grounds than necessary. The Court seemed to be of the view that it was up to the task and could indeed diffuse one of the most divisive political controversies in the nation's history to that date. Although the impact was not nearly as disastrous as *Dred Scott*, the controversy was too deep and too political for the Court to settle through constitutional interpretation.

Did *Prigg* make bad law? From a contemporary perspective, it is readily arguable that any decision enhancing the legitimate authority of slavery and slave owners was bad law. Moreover, a decision that placed the primary authority for the protection of slave owners on the federal government was especially bad. Like *Dred Scott*, it led the opponents of slavery to conclude that certainly the Court and perhaps the Constitution as well were devoted to the protection and continuation of slavery. This helped undermine the hope that the slavery issue could be resolved in a peaceful and lawful manner and perhaps it simply could not. However, the justices in *Prigg* did not find themselves in a twentieth century context. Slavery was a fact of life, and the Fugitive Slave Clause was a part of the Constitution—indeed from the perspective of the South, a very crucial part. Moreover, given the composition of the Court, a pro-slavery decision of some sort was simply inevitable. The choice for the Court was between a narrow ruling that would leave the states with some leeway, though with a thumb decidedly on the slavery side of the scale, or a broad ruling that would federalize and hopefully resolve the issue. Justice Story chose the latter approach.

As the Court would learn yet again in *Dred Scott*, slavery was simply too explosive of an issue to be put to rest judicially. The momentousness of the case was emphasized by the attorneys and by the justices themselves. It was apparent that the justices understood that they had been placed in the center of a red-hot national controversy. It is unlikely that the greatness of the case affected the ultimate decision against Pennsylvania. A majority of the justices seemed to be locked into views on slavery and rendition quite apart from the controversy surrounding the case. For Story, who was opposed to slavery, preserving the slavery bargain and, hence, national peace and the Union almost certainly trumped opposition to slavery. It is likely that he was also moved by a desire to write for the majority and perhaps attempt to control the direction of the law to the extent possible. The concurrences reveal that some members of the Court, Taney and Wayne in particular, were scarcely content with Storey's position. It is difficult to see how any result that could possibly have attracted a majority could have done any less damage.

Inadvertently or otherwise, the *Prigg* opinion made it much more difficult to recapture and obtain the return of runaway slaves. This was partially due to the lack of adequate federal enforcement officials and procedures and partially due to the resistance and defiance of certain northern jurisdictions. A decision that does not appear to accomplish what it intended and is met with a significant degree of outright defiance can hardly be considered to have created good law. If in fact Story surreptitiously hoped to create a precedent that would assist the cause of freedom, he succeeded only in the short run. Faced with an increase in runaway slaves as well as the difficulty of achieving rendition, the South demanded and received the enactment of more stringent federal procedures in the Fugitive Slave Act of 1850. That in turn caused even greater resistance and defiance from northern jurisdictions.

A narrower decision would not have resolved the controversy over rendition. Had the Court invalidated the Pennsylvania law as inconsistent with federal law or the Constitution but not reached the issue of federal exclusivity, the problem would not have disappeared. States such as Pennsylvania would have continued to pass laws intended, at the very least, to protect free Blacks against kidnapping and quite possibly to thwart the efforts of fugitive slave rendition as well. These laws would have been challenged and the Court would have been obliged to respond, either considering them on a case-by-case basis or eventually striking them across the board as it did in *Prigg*. McLean's lonely concurrence in *Prigg* bears witness to the reality that there was no chance that the Court would attempt to distinguish state procedures protecting free Blacks from those impeding recapture of fugitives. The majority was too suspicious of states such as Pennsylvania to permit that. *Prigg* was a great case that placed the Court in the position of attempting to resolve a problem that was simply beyond judicial capacity. As a matter of appropriate judicial decision-making, a narrower opinion would have been more desirable, although it is not apparent that it would have led to different political results.

"The Dred Scott decision...remains the most striking instance of the Supreme Court's attempting to play the role of deus ex machina in a setting of national crisis."[1]

DON FEHRENBACHER

5

Scott v. Sanford

AT LEAST IN terms of its political impact, *Scott v. Sanford*, best known as the *Dred Scott Case*, may be the most momentous case in Supreme Court history. It would be an overstatement to claim that it caused the Civil War; however it certainly did contribute to explosive tensions at the time that did lead to the conflict. If as Holmes charged, great cases make bad law, *Scott* was an instance in which such a case made disastrously bad law. The case began as a simple dispute between private parties and escalated into an epic Supreme Court battle played out before an anxious nation. It was argued to the Court twice and resulted in one of the lengthiest sets of opinions in Supreme Court history. Prior to its release, the decision was leaked by a justice to the president-elect for reference in his inaugural address. The chief justice appears to have rewritten his opinion to respond to a dissent after it had been initially read from the bench. It was criticized vigorously by Abraham Lincoln among many others. It was explicitly overruled by the Fourteenth Amendment. It is universally considered the greatest mistake in Supreme Court history. And to this day it is all but impossible to understand with confidence exactly what it held. It was a tragic case but certainly a great case as Holmes used the phrase.

SLAVERY IN THE TERRITORIES

Arguably, the dominant political issue of the first half of the nineteenth century in the United States revolved around the spread of slavery into the territories and then into new states. From the outset, the South well understood that if a sufficient number of

---

[1] DON E. FEHRENBACHER, THE *DRED SCOTT* CASE 5 (1978). Fehrenbacher's 700-page book is the definitive work on the case. Two other significant recent books on the case are EARL M. MALTZ, *DRED SCOTT* AND THE POLITICS OF SLAVERY (2007) and MARK A. GRABER, *DRED SCOTT* AND THE PROBLEM OF CONSTITUTIONAL EVIL (2006).

new states were admitted as free states, eventually the supermajority necessary to amend the Constitution to outlaw slavery, period, would come into existence. At all costs, the southern states were determined to prevent that from occurring. For several decades the question of whether slavery should be permitted in the territories and new states was at the center of the firestorm in the national political process. Initially, the Northwest Ordinance of 1787 banned slavery in territories north of the Ohio River. Eventually, Congress attempted to resolve the issue through the Missouri Compromise of 1820 by which Maine was admitted as a free state, Missouri was admitted without restriction on slavery, and slavery was forever banned in territories north of the 36° 30′ parallel, the southern border of Missouri. The controversy over slavery in the territories was reignited with the addition of Texas as a slave state in 1845 and the acquisition of new territory as a result of the war with Mexico. Pursuant to the Compromise of 1850, California was admitted as a free state, Utah and New Mexico were established as territories where slavery was permissible, and the Fugitive Slave law was strengthened. Finally, in 1854, the Kansas Nebraska Act replaced that portion of the Missouri Compromise banning slavery above the 36° 30′ parallel with Senator Douglas's popular sovereignty principle granting newly admitted states the power to choose for themselves whether slavery would be permitted. That, in turn, led to violent confrontations in Kansas at the very time that the *Dred Scott* Case was argued to the Supreme Court. Greater population growth in northern as opposed to southern states increased the political power of antislavery forces in the House of Representatives, upsetting the initial political balance.

THE BACKGROUND

Dred Scott was a slave owned by Dr. John Emerson, an army doctor who was a resident of Missouri. Emerson had purchased Scott from the Blow family in the early 1830s when they encountered financial difficulties. From 1834 to 1836, Scott accompanied Dr. Emerson to Fort Armstrong, a military post at Rock Island in Illinois, a state that prohibited slavery. Thereafter, from 1836 to 1838, Dr. Emerson and Scott relocated to Fort Snelling in the Upper Louisiana Territory (in present day Minnesota), where slavery was banned by the Missouri Compromise of 1820. Scott married his wife, Harriet, also a slave owned by Dr. Emerson, at Fort Snelling and their daughter, Eliza, was born on a steamer in the Mississippi River in free territory. Scott and his wife and daughter returned with Dr. Emerson to Missouri, a state in which slavery was permitted.

In 1846, following Emerson's death, Scott sued Mrs. Emerson who had inherited Dr. Emerson's estate, for trespass, the legal method by which a slave could attempt to establish his freedom and that of his family, in state court in Missouri. The jury rendered a verdict against Scott for failure to prove that Mrs. Emerson was his purported owner. Thereafter, another suit was filed in state court against all possible owners. In 1850, Scott prevailed in the trial court by proving that under well-established Missouri law, he had become a free man by having resided in a free state or territory. However, the victory was short-lived as the Missouri Supreme Court altered the governing law and held that Scott remained a slave on his return to Missouri. The court noted that "[t]imes are not now as they were when the former decisions were made," declaring that opponents of slavery were engaged in conduct that would result in the "overthrow and destruction of our government."[2] Indeed, in *Rachel v.* Walker,[3] decided by the Missouri Supreme Court in 1836, the court had held that a slave who accompanied an army officer to Fort Snelling, the very same post where Emerson took Scott, could not be re-enslaved on return to Missouri. Scott did not appeal the decision to the United States Supreme Court given that under the Supreme Court's recent decision in *Strader v. Graham*,[4] which bore some similarities to the facts of Scott's case, the Court almost certainly would have held that it was bound by the Missouri Supreme Court's decision and did not have jurisdiction.

In 1853, following the apparent sale of Scott to Sanford, a resident of New York, Scott sued Sanford for trespass in federal district court, relying upon diversity of citizenship for jurisdiction.[5] Pursuant to the Supreme Court's recent decision in *Swift v. Tyson* there was at least a possibility that unlike an appeal from a state court, the Supreme Court might not consider itself bound by state precedent, at least if it seemed somewhat unclear. Sanford entered a plea in abatement arguing that the district court lacked jurisdiction because a slave such as Scott or a descendant of a slave could not qualify as a citizen for purposes of establishing jurisdiction based on diversity of citizenship under Article III of the Constitution. Scott demurred to the plea and the court ruled that it would presume that Scott was a citizen for purposes of jurisdiction though not for other purposes. Sanford then pleaded not guilty to the charge of trespass on the ground that Scott was rightfully a slave and consequently he had the right to restrain him. These common law pleading maneuvers would come to play an important role in the decision by the Supreme Court. The case was submitted to the jury on an agreed statement of facts, the judge instructed the jury that the law favored Sanford, and the jury found for Sanford.

SCOTT IN THE SUPREME COURT

This time Scott chose to appeal the case to the United States Supreme Court. Scott was represented by Montgomery Blair of St. Louis, and Sanford was represented by Senator Geyer of Missouri and former Senator and Attorney General of the United States Reverdy Johnson, a very highly respected advocate. The first oral argument lasted four days. Initially, the case appeared to be a relatively ordinary dispute of slight national significance over whether a slave had obtained his freedom. As such, the press and the public paid it little attention. That changed dramatically however when Reverdy Johnson introduced the argument into the case that the Missouri Compromise, banning slavery in the Upper Louisiana territory, was unconstitutional.[6] Suddenly, the case was understood as presenting the Supreme Court with the most explosive political issue in the nation: the power of

---

[2] Scott v. Emerson, 15 Mo. 576 (1852).

[3] 4 Mo. 350 (1836).

[4] 51 U.S. 82 (1851).

[5] Historians have long debated whether Sanford actually owned Scott or was merely acting as the executor of Emerson's estate. *See* FEHRENBACHER, *supra* note 1, at 270–73.

[6] *Id.* at 288.

Congress to ban or authorize slavery in the territories. The *Washington Star* opined that the *Dred Scott* Case was one of the most important cases ever brought before the Court.[7]

After holding several conferences on the case, the Court set it for re-argument on the questions: (1) was the plea in abatement reviewable by the Court?, and (2) was Scott a citizen for purposes of diversity jurisdiction?. The Court was deeply divided over the common law pleading issue. Four justices believed that Sanford had waived the right to object to Scott's claim of citizenship for diversity jurisdiction purposes by addressing the merits of the case after the trial judge rejected his plea in abatement. Four other justices concluded that in a case arising in federal court, the jurisdictional issue could still be reviewed on appeal. Justice Nelson was undecided; thus re-argument on the procedural and jurisdictional issues was warranted. There has also been some indication that the Court was hesitant to confront the explosive political issue presented by the case during a presidential election year.[8]

Between the first and second oral arguments, violence erupted in Kansas over whether it should be organized as a free or slave state. James Buchanan, a sympathizer of slavery in the territories, had been elected president. By the time of the second oral argument, the press, the political establishment, and the public had become extremely interested in the case. Once again, it was argued over a period of four days. In addition to the two questions posed by the Court itself, the attorneys also debated whether Scott was a free man either as a result of his residence in a free state or in a free territory. The argument of George Curtis (the brother of Justice Curtis) for Scott and that of Reverdy Johnson for Sanford were praised by the press.[9]

The Court was quite divided on the issues following the second argument. Initially, five of the justices did not believe that the plea in abatement challenging jurisdiction, which the trial court had rejected, was properly before the Supreme Court for review. If it was not, then the Court could not reverse the trial court on this point and hold that it did not have jurisdiction to hear the case. Moreover no one had appealed the rejection of the plea in abatement as it favored Scott, the plaintiff, and it was essentially mooted for the defendant Sanford upon prevailing on the merits. So technically, the issue was not presented to the Court. On the other hand, on the merits, five justices, all from the South, believed that the Missouri Compromise was unconstitutional.[10] Justice Nelson changed his mind however and concluded that the Court could consider the jurisdictional issue. He was then designated to write an opinion declaring that as a matter of Missouri law, Scott remained a slave and thus could not be a citizen for jurisdictional purposes.[11] Arguably, because it was believed that the dissenters, especially Justice McLean who harbored political ambitions, would address every issue presented by the case, Justice Wayne persuaded the justices in the majority that Chief Justice Taney should write an opinion addressing every issue as well.[12] There is reason to believe that Wayne, a staunch advocate of the southern position on slavery in the territories, sought a strong declaration by the majority to that effect regardless of what the dissent had to say. In any event, a majority of the justices made the tragic mistake of deciding the case on the

---

[7] *Id.*

[8] *Id.* at 290.

[9] 3 CHARLES WARREN, THE SUPREME COURT IN UNITED STATES HISTORY 9–10 (1922).

[10] FEHRENBACHER, *supra* note 1, at 305–06.

[11] *Id.* at 306.

[12] *Id.* at 309.

broadest and most politically and constitutionally controversial grounds rather than on the narrow and technical grounds that were readily available.

President-elect Buchanan had inquired whether the decision would be released prior to the inauguration.[13] Justices Grier and Catron informed him that the decision would come down soon and that it would invalidate the Missouri Compromise.[14] Buchanan had urged Grier, a justice from the North, to join the opinion so that the majority would not be composed exclusively of justices from slave states. In his inaugural address two days before the decision was released, Buchanan did note that the Court would soon settle the issue of slavery in the territories.[15] The fact that Taney and Buchanan chatted during the inauguration gave rise to rumors, apparently initiated by William Seward, among the opponents of slavery, that some type of conspiracy with respect to the *Dred Scott* Case had been hatched between the president-elect and the Court.[16] Indeed, Lincoln would charge in his "House Divided" speech, without any proof, that the decision was part of a conspiracy hatched by "Stephen (Douglas), Franklin (Pierce), Roger (Taney) and James (Buchanan)."[17]

The decision was announced on March 6, 1857. Taney read his opinion for two hours while Curtis and McLean read their dissents the following day. Taney delayed the release of his opinion for over two months, apparently adding nearly 20 additional pages to respond to the dissents.[18] This led to a dispute between Curtis and Taney resulting in Curtis's resignation from the Court.

THE OPINION

It is difficult if not impossible to determine exactly what the Court held in *Dred Scott* as there were several opinions and the justices were quite unclear as to what extent they concurred with each other's reasoning.

THE TANEY OPINION

The opinion that is ordinarily considered the opinion of the Court is that of Chief Justice Taney although it clearly is not on certain crucial issues. Justices Wayne, Grier, and Daniel explicitly concurred in at least some of the opinion. The first question that Taney addressed, though seemingly a technicality to non-lawyers, had apparently divided the Court sharply. The question was whether Sanford's plea in abatement to jurisdiction had been waived after it had been rejected by the trial court, thus precluding Supreme Court review of the issues.[19]

---

[13] *Id.* at 311–12.

[14] *Id.* at 312, quoting Letter from Justice Grier to James Buchanan, February 23, 1857.

[15] Inaugural Address of James Buchanan, March 4, 1857, *in* IV. MESSAGES AND PAPERS OF THE PRESIDENTS 246 (James D. Richardson ed., 1913).

[16] FEHRENBACHER, *supra* note 1, at 312–13.

[17] Abraham Lincoln, House Divided Speech, Springfield, Illinois, June 16, 1858, *in* II COLLECTED WORKS OF ABRAHAM LINCOLN 461 (Roy P. Basler ed., 1953).

[18] FEHRENBACHER, *supra* note 1, at 316–19.

[19] 60 U.S. 393, 400 (1857).

Taney made a credible argument that the Supreme Court, as a court of limited juris-diction, had the authority to consider jurisdictional challenges at least in a case coming to it from a lower federal as opposed to a state court. He was only able to persuade three other justices including one of the dissenters on this point, however; thus everything that Taney had to say with respect to Scott's lack of citizenship for jurisdictional purpose was the opinion of only three justices and not of the Court.

Having concluded that he could consider the jurisdictional issue, Taney posed the question of whether a Negro whose ancestors had been brought to the country as slaves could become a member of the political community and thus a citizen. The breadth of the question, whether a Negro descended from slaves, as opposed to a slave, could become a citizen, reflected the manner in which Sanford's attorney had framed the issue in the trial court, encouraging, if not necessarily, requiring Taney to do likewise. Taney declared that descendants of slaves had not been considered to be among "the people of the United States" at the time of the framing of the Constitution and as such could not be citizens. He began by drawing a clear distinction between state and national citizenship, conclud-ing that no state had the power to confer United States' citizenship. This was arguably irrelevant given that the question before the Court was whether Scott was a citizen of Missouri. Taney contended that it was crucial to determine whether, at the time that the states broke free from England, slaves or their descendants were considered to be people or citizens of the states in which they resided. He proclaimed that at the time of the Dec-laration of Independence and the framing of the Constitution, Negroes "had no rights which the white man was bound to respect...."[20] He stated that all civilized portions of the white race at the time regarded Negroes as articles of property to be bought and sold. He cited two examples of legislation from Maryland and Massachusetts at the time as evidence that the framers of the Declaration of Independence and the Constitution meant to place "a perpetual and impassable barrier" between the white and black races.[21] Taney argued that the famous clause in the Declaration of Independence "that all men are created equal" could not have been intended to include Negroes given that so many of the signers of the Declaration were slaveholders.

Taney's reliance upon his conception of the original understanding of the status of slaves and their descendants was subjected to withering criticism at the time, especially by Justice Curtis in dissent and ever since. Certainly Taney's reliance on history was so selective as to be disingenuous.[22] Justice Curtis easily demonstrated that even slaves, much less their descendants, did in fact have rights that white men were bound to respect though this did not necessarily make them state citizens. Taney did have support for his position on original understanding, but not as much as he purported to have.[23] He bounced back and forth between whether descendants of slaves could be United States or state citizens without clearly indicating which was dominant.

---

[20] *Id.* at 407.

[21] *Id.* at 409.

[22] FEHRENBACHER, *supra* note 1, at 364; Paul Finkelman, *The Taney Court, in* THE UNITED STATES SUPREME COURT: THE PURSUIT OF JUSTICE 94 (Christopher Tomlins ed., 2005) (Taney's "historical argument was narrow, partisan, and unsophisticated").

[23] GRABER, *supra* note 1, at 46–57; BERNARD SCHWARTZ, A HISTORY OF THE SUPREME COURT 118-21 (1993).

Turning to the Constitution, Taney declared that the ban on the abolition of the slave trade as well as the Fugitive Slave Clause confirmed that the framers had no intention of including what Taney referred to as the "unhappy black race" in either the "people of the United States" or "citizens of the several states."[24] As for those states that had abolished slavery as of the framing of the Constitution, he attributed this to its unsuitability in these states rather than opposition to the concept itself, especially as these states continued to participate in and profit from the slave trade. Citing several examples of laws from states in which slavery had been banned placing restrictions on Negroes, especially with respect to interracial marriage, Taney concluded that the assumption that Blacks were excluded from "the people" under the Constitution was universal.

Again as Justice Curtis illustrated, the conclusions that Taney drew from the text and these historical incidents scarcely followed. Taney took an all-or-nothing approach with respect to the rights of free Blacks, arguing that as there were some restrictions imposed on their rights, then they had no rights whatsoever and could not possibly be citizens. Curtis pointed out the rights of married women and children were even more restricted than those of free Blacks in many states but no one would maintain that the former were disqualified from state or federal citizenship.

Taney maintained that recognition of Blacks as citizens would have entitled them to all other rights afforded by the Constitution, and it was simply beyond the realm of possibility that the southern states would have agreed to such a proposition. He argued that the exclusively federal nature of the naturalization power indicated that a state could not confer rights of citizenship. He also pointed out that the Privileges and Immunities Clause of the Constitution by its terms applied only to "citizens" unlike the similar clause in the Articles of Confederation applicable to "inhabitants" of a state. He attributed this change to a desire to make it as clear as could be that Negroes were not covered.

Taney then asserted that laws passed by Congress shortly after the Constitution was ratified confirmed that the framing generation did not intend to include Blacks. He cited the Naturalization Act of 1790, which confined the naturalization authority to "free white persons." Likewise, the Militia Act of 1792 applied to every "free able-bodied white male citizen." Finally, Taney noted an 1820 Act of Congress that prohibited the employment on any private vessel of the United States of anyone other than a citizen of the United States or persons of color. He also cited an opinion of Attorney General Wirt in 1821 concluding that Negroes could not qualify as citizens of the United States.

Taney conceded that some citizens such as women and minors did not possess all possible rights of citizenship. He also noted that a state could bestow the right to vote on noncitizens, including aliens. However, if Negroes were recognized as state citizens for diversity purposes, then they would also be recognized as such under the Privileges and Immunities Clause of Article IV. It was hardly evident, however, that citizenship for jurisdictional purposes presumed citizenship under Article IV. Indeed, prior to *Dred Scott*, the Court had held that a corporation was a citizen under Article III but not under Article IV.[25] Moreover, contrary to Taney's interpretation, the text of the Privileges and Immunities

---

[24] *Scott*, 60 U.S. at 410-11.

[25] *Compare* Louisville, Cincinnati, and Charleston R. R. Co. v. Letson, 43 U.S. 497 (1844) (a corporation is a citizen for purposes of diversity jurisdiction under Article III) *with* Bank of Augusta v. Earle, 38 U.S. 519 (1839) (a corporation is not a citizen within the Privileges and Immunities Clause of Article IV).

Clause clearly provided that a state need only grant the citizen of another state the same privileges and immunities that it bestowed on its own citizens. This would provide a check against the leveling effect that Taney seemed to fear.

Taney categorically rejected the possibility that changes in attitudes since the adoption of the Constitution could alter its meaning. Rather, he declared that such an approach would transform the Constitution into "the mere reflex of the popular opinion or passion of the day."[26] Summarizing his conclusions to this point Taney stated that:

> The court is of the opinion, that, upon the facts stated in the pleas in abatement, Dred Scott was not a citizen of Missouri within the meaning of the Constitution of the United States, and not entitled as such to sue in its courts; and consequently, that the Circuit Court had no jurisdiction of the case....[27]

One might think that with this declaration Taney was about to conclude his opinion, but in fact he was only getting warmed up. He noted that given the doubts by some of the justices that the plea in abatement was reviewable, Scott's assertion in his filing that he had been a slave would necessarily disqualify him from claiming citizenship unless his travels with Dr. Emerson had changed his status. At the outset of this section of his opinion, Taney addressed the charge that having found no jurisdiction, any further discussion would be mere dicta. He argued that it was the duty of the Court to correct any and all errors that appeared in the lower court's decision. The possible error in question was the circuit court's decision against Scott on the merits as opposed to simply dismissing the case for lack of jurisdiction.

Taney then proceeded to address the question of whether Scott's residence with Emerson in the territory of Upper Louisiana, where slavery was prohibited by the Missouri Compromise of 1820, rendered him a free man. The question he posed was whether Congress had the constitutional authority to enact the Compromise. At the outset, he rejected the most obvious source of such authority, the clause that gives Congress the power "to make all needful rules and regulations respecting the Territory or other property of the United States..." on the rather strange theory that it applied only to that territory belonging to the Union at the time the Constitution was ratified. Presumably, Taney favored this interpretation because it would arguably permit him to distinguish the well-accepted antislavery provision of the Northwest Ordinance from the Missouri Compromise, although not necessarily persuasively. Taney then attempted to justify this bizarre construction of the text at great length, placing some weight on the fact that the text referred to "territory" rather than "territories." He did recognize that if the United States had the authority to acquire new territories it must also have the authority to provide a system of governance there, but only for the equal benefit of the people from all of the states. This was an endorsement of the common property theory of the territories popularized by John C. Calhoun and favored by the southern states. Under this theory, a prohibition of slavery in a territory would discriminate against slaveholders and

---

[26] *Scott*, 60 U.S. at 426.
[27] *Id.* at 427.

therefore not be for the common benefit of all despite the fact that the territories were acquired and held as common property of all Americans.

Taney maintained that territorial governments authorized by Congress must be consistent with constitutional constraints such as those prohibiting the government from establishing religion, abridging freedom of speech, or denying the right of the people to keep and bear arms.[28]

This led Taney to conclude that:

[A]n act of Congress which deprives a citizen of the United States of his liberty or property, merely because either he came himself or brought his property into a particular Territory of the United States, and who had committed no offense against the laws, could hardly be dignified with the name of due process of law.[29]

Taney adopted the southern version of due process that focused on the deprivation of the slave owner's property rather than the northern version that focused on the deprivation of the slave's liberty. By its terms, the Due Process Clause protects persons not citizens. But of course Taney had earlier concluded that the descendants of slaves did not qualify as "the people of the United States." Presumably, states or territories could ban the importation of at least some harmful types of property, the possession of which would be legal in other states. As such, Taney seemed to consider slaves a type of super-protected property.[30]

Taney declared that if the Constitution denies the powers to Congress then "it could not authorize a Territorial Government to exercise them."[31] This was arguably the most politically controversial statement in all of the *Dred Scott* opinion in that it made it clear that no entity of government, including the majority of the population in a territory, possessed the power to prohibit slavery therein. Although this statement was clearly dicta, Lincoln and the opponents of slavery in the territories attacked it with vigor. Presumably once the territory became a state, it could then ban slavery, but it was likely that if the territorial government endorsed slavery, the subsequent state government would do so as well.

Taney then rejected the suggestion that distinctions between property in a slave and any other property, derived from the law of nations, had any impact within the United States.[32] And as the Constitution draws no such distinction, the courts are not permitted to recognize one.

Consequently Taney concluded that:

The act of Congress which prohibited a citizen from holding and owning property of this kind in the territory of the United States north of the line therein mentioned, is not warranted by the Constitution, and is therefore void, and that neither that Dred Scott himself, nor any of his family, were made free by being carried into

---

[28] *Id.* at 450.

[29] *Id.*

[30] MALTZ, *supra* note 1, at 122.

[31] Scott v. Sanford, 60 U.S. 393, 451 (1857).

[32] *Id.*

this territory; even if they had been carried there by the owner, with the intention of becoming a permanent resident.[33]

With this, the Court struck down the first Act of Congress that it had invalidated since *Marbury v. Madison* in 1803. Even so, the Act that it invalidated had been largely repealed by the Kansas-Nebraska Act anyway. Even if Taney was correct that Fifth Amendment due process precluded the emancipation of slaves in the territories, it did not follow that the Missouri Compromise was unconstitutional. Taney could simply have held that emancipation would follow only if Emerson and Scott had been domiciled in the territory, and assignment to a military post did not change the officer's domicile. As such, Scott's status was still governed by Missouri law. Or alternatively the Court could have held that although Scott was conditionally free in the territory, his slave status reattached on return to Missouri. Under either of these theories there would be no need to invalidate the Missouri Compromise. Instead the Court chose to invalidate the Compromise because it very much wanted to do just that.

Turning to Scott's residence with Dr. Emerson in Illinois, Taney held that the issue was controlled by the Court's decision in *Strader v. Graham* where it had held that the status of a slave who had lived with his owner in the free state of Ohio was subject to the law of Kentucky when he was returned there with his owner. Thus in this case, Scott's status would be determined by Missouri law, and the Missouri Supreme Court had previously ruled that he remained a slave.[34] Had Taney chosen to address Scott's residence in Illinois first, he could have applied this principle to the stay in the territory, avoiding any consideration of the constitutionality of the Missouri Compromise. This was the approach taken by Justice Nelson in his concurrence, which initially promised to be the opinion of the Court. Had it remained the majority opinion, it is unlikely that *Dred Scott* would be a great or infamous case.

Taney concluded that Scott was not a citizen of the United States under the Constitution and as such the circuit court had no jurisdiction over his suit; thus the suit should be remanded to the district court with an order that it be dismissed.

JUSTICE WAYNE

Justice Wayne wrote that he concurred entirely and without qualification in Chief Justice Taney's opinion. He mentioned that the case raised questions that had become such a threat to "the peace and harmony of the country" that they required settlement by judicial decision.[35] He did emphasize however that the Court's holding on the Missouri Compromise was not unwarranted dicta because as Chief Justice Taney had maintained, the Supreme Court has the authority to correct errors in a circuit court opinion even where that court had erroneously assumed jurisdiction. It was obvious from the defensive tone of Justice Wayne's opinion that he was stung by the critique of the dissents.

---

[33] *Id.* at 452.

[34] *Id.* at 453.

[35] *Id.* at 455.

JUSTICE NELSON

Justice Nelson wrote a short opinion in which he concluded that Scott's status was properly determined by Missouri law. Justices Wayne and Grier explicitly concurred in the opinion. Otherwise, the law of Illinois would extend to and be binding in Missouri. The laws of Illinois would only attach to Scott if he had established a domicile there. Nelson noted that *Strader v. Graham* had declared that an Act of Congress prohibiting slavery in a territory, in that case the Northwest Ordinance as re-enacted, could have no more force in another state than a law of a different state. The Missouri Supreme Court had settled Scott's status as a slave on his return to Missouri, and the United States Supreme Court was bound by that conclusion. He did not reach the question of the constitutionality of the Missouri Compromise because in his opinion, even if it was constitutional, it would still not control the status of Scott upon his return to Missouri. Nelson did note however that "many of the most eminent statesmen and jurists in the country" had concluded that Congress did not have the authority to enact the Missouri Compromise.[36] Presumably this would have been the opinion for the Court had Justice Wayne not prevailed on Taney to write the broader opinion.

JUSTICE GRIER

Justice Grier stated that he concurred in the opinion of Justice Nelson. He also stated that he concurred in the opinion of the chief justice as to the unconstitutionality of the Missouri Compromise and as to the inability of Scott to sue as a citizen in federal court on the basis of the facts as stated in the opinion.

JUSTICE DANIEL

Justice Daniel began his opinion by noting that never before had the Court considered "questions surpassing in importance those now claiming the consideration of this court."[37] Even more stridently than Taney, Justice Daniel proclaimed that a slave could be regarded only as property and could possess no civil or political rights. He argued that a private person cannot by freeing a slave confer upon him citizenship as only the government can do that. Moreover, a state government lacked the authority to confer United States' citizenship. Residence in Illinois could not control Scott's status once returned to Missouri with his owner. The same would be true with respect to Scott's residence in Upper Louisiana, even assuming the validity of the Missouri Compromise. He argued that the Territories Clause of the Constitution could not be construed to permit the federal government to deprive slave owners of their property as it must regulate all citizens equally. Thus Daniel would find that the circuit court erred in sustaining the demur to the plea in abatement. As such the case should be remanded for dismissal.

---

[36] *Id.* at 464.
[37] *Id.* at 469.

JUSTICE CAMPBELL

Justice Campbell also began his opinion by declaring that he concurred in the opinion of the chief justice. After a very lengthy review of the authority, Campbell declared that the question presented was whether Congress can "determine the condition and *status* of persons who inhabit the Territories?"[38] He argued that the original understanding of the Territories Clause did not assume that Congress had any such power. He reasoned that Congress had no power to regulate the relation between master and slave within a state, and nothing in the Constitution or its structure provided such a power within a territory. Consequently, the Missouri Compromise did not have the effect of changing Scott's status on his return to Missouri. Unlike Taney, Campbell did not address due process.

Given that the record indicated that Scott was a slave and nothing in the evidence suggested otherwise, he was not qualified to sue in federal court, and there was no need to go any farther than to hold that the circuit court did not have jurisdiction over his suit.

JUSTICE CATRON

Justice Catron began his opinion by arguing that Sanford waived his challenge to the court's jurisdiction when he pled to the merits after the court accepted the demurrer to his plea in abatement. As a judge who had imposed the death penalty in the territories pursuant to congressional legislation, Catron considered it too late in the day to question congressional authority to legislate for the territories. He disposed of the argument based on Scott's residence in Illinois briefly noting that as a matter of Illinois law, temporary residence in the state did not free a slave either in Illinois itself or on return to a state in which slavery was legal. Taking the equality of states as a given, Catron argued that Congress could not constitutionally prohibit a slave holder from bringing his slaves into a territory held by the United States for the benefit of citizens of all of the states. He argued that if Congress could prohibit a person from bringing slaves into a territory it could likewise prohibit him from bringing cows, horses or machines.[39] Considering the Missouri Compromise to have violated this structural principle of equality among citizens, as well as the provision of the Treaty ceding the Louisiana Territory to the United States which permitted slavery, Justice Catron found it to be unconstitutional and thus of no use to Scott.

JUSTICE MCLEAN

Justice McLean offered a dissent joined by Justice Curtis. At the outset he maintained that Sanford had waived his objection to jurisdiction. He argued that the fact that Scott was a Negro would not deprive him of the right to sue as a citizen of Missouri since a free

---

[38] *Id.* at 509.
[39] *Id.* at 527.

Negro could bring suit under the diversity of citizenship clause if he was a permanent resident of the state.

He concluded that the Territories Clause clearly gave Congress the power to legislate for the territories. As a matter of national policy, Congress could exercise that power to prohibit slavery in the territories. Counter to the majority, he declared that a "slave is not a mere chattel. He bears the impress of his Maker. . . . "[40] Since slavery was entirely a creature of local law, a slave owner could not hold a person in slavery within a jurisdiction that prohibited it. Justice McLean then discussed several cases in which the Missouri courts had held that when a slaveholder took his slaves into a free state (usually Illinois) or territory and resided there with them for a significant period of time, they may not be re-enslaved upon return to Missouri. Under these cases, Scott would have been completely emancipated by his residence in Illinois and in the Upper Louisiana Territory and would have been legally free from 1838 until the decision of the Missouri Supreme Court in the instant case in 1852. He noted that the Missouri Supreme Court had reversed course only to counter "the excitement against the institution of slavery in free States" and not because it believed that the earlier rule was wrong as a matter of law.[41] By reversing course in Scott v. Emerson, the Missouri Supreme Court effectively enslaved a free person. He noted that the courts of several slave states including South Carolina, Mississippi, Louisiana, Virginia, Kentucky and Maryland had all held that a slave who resides with his master in free territory on a permanent basis is thereby emancipated. Arguably, McLean's dissent was designed to promote his prospects as a Republican Presidential candidate.

JUSTICE CURTIS

Justice Curtis offered a separate dissent. He agreed with Taney that the Court could consider whether it and the Circuit Court had jurisdiction over the case. He noted that Sanford had pleaded that Scott could not be a citizen for diversity of citizenship purposes because he was a Negro descended from slaves. Curtis capitalized on the breadth of this claim, arguing that if, in fact, a Negro descended from slaves could be a citizen, then Scott was entitled to a judgment in his favor. He argued that as of the time of the ratification of the Articles of Confederation, free Negroes were accepted as citizens in New Hampshire, Massachusetts, New York, New Jersey and North Carolina. Under the Articles of Confederation, such free Blacks were entitled to the privileges and immunities of free citizens. Thus he concluded that "every free person born on the soil of a State, who is a citizen by force of its Constitution or laws, is also a citizen of the United States."[42] He noted that South Carolina had attempted unsuccessfully to amend the Articles to protect the privileges and immunities of only free "white" inhabitants indicating that the framers definitely intended to include free Negroes. He argued that in several states, free Blacks were included within the "people" of the United States who ratified the Constitution.

---

[40] *Id.* at 550.

[41] *Id.* at 556.

[42] *Id.* at 576. Despite his powerful dissent in *Dred Scott*, Curtis certainly was not a racial egalitarian. GRABER, *supra* note 1, at 77.

Examining the constitutional structure and text, Curtis concluded that persons born in the several states who as a matter of state law are state citizens are also citizens of the United States. He also argued that the fact that a person was a citizen of a state did not entitle him or her to all of the privileges and immunities of citizens under Article IV. For example, he noted that a naturalized citizen could not run for President and that women and children were not allowed to vote even though they were citizens. Thus states could create citizenship and at the same time place limitations on the rights that it entailed. In any event as Justice Curtis noted, the Article IV Privileges and Immunities Clause guarantees a visiting citizen only the same rights that it extends to its own citizens. Therefore if a state prohibited its own free Negroes from voting, it would not be required to extend the franchise to free Negroes from other states even if they were permitted to vote in their state of residence. Curtis seemed to understate the extent to which free Blacks, who had been recognized as citizens, were still deprived of most significant rights.

Curtis answered the argument that a master would have authority to make a slave a citizen simply by freeing him by noting that the state and not the slave owner would determine the person's "political status."[43] Likewise, he argued that the fact that Congress had chosen to extend the naturalization power only to white aliens has no bearing upon whether Blacks born on American soil can be considered citizens. He also noted that congressional acts denying various rights to free Blacks do tend to assume that such persons could be citizens. For instance an act of Congress prohibiting masters of vessels from importing "any negro" into the country "not being a native, a citizen, or a registered seaman of the United States" clearly assumes that a Negro could be a citizen. He also pointed out that as part of the Missouri Compromise, Congress adopted a provision prohibiting the state from denying privileges and immunities to any citizen of another state, to counteract a provision in the Missouri Constitution requiring its legislature to enact laws prohibiting Negroes or mulattos from settling in the state.

Thus Justice Curtis dissented from the portion of Chief Justice Taney's opinion maintaining that the descendent of a Black slave could never be a citizen. Rather, he concluded that a freeborn Negro was a citizen of the state of residence, was also a citizen of the United States, and could bring suit in federal court under the diversity of citizenship provision. As the plea in abatement did not allege that Scott was not born free in Missouri (although he clearly was not), he was so entitled to sue. There was something of a sleight of hand in Curtis's argument, given that it would not have helped Dred Scott had the pleadings, in fact, acknowledged that he had been born a slave.

He then turned to the Court's ruling on the Missouri Compromise, which he maintained the Court had no authority to consider after having determined that it did not have jurisdiction. Justice Curtis pointed out that under the laws establishing the Wisconsin Territory (what Taney referred to as the upper Louisiana Territory) in which Fort Snelling was located, slavery was forever prohibited. This established that Scott and his family could not be held as slaves while at Fort Snelling with Dr. Emerson. He conceded that it was for Missouri law, as manifested by statute or common law, including principles of international law, to determine whether the law of the Wisconsin Territory controlled Scott's status upon his return to Missouri.

---

[43] *Scott*, 60 U.S. at 585–86.

Turning then to the status of Scott, Justice Curtis reasoned that as an employee of the United States' government while in the Wisconsin Territory, subject entirely to the law of the United States, Dr. Emerson and hence Scott were completely subject to the congressional law prohibiting slavery in that territory. He also argued that Scott's marriage at Fort Snelling with Dr. Emerson's consent also indicated that he was a free man in the territory as the marriage would not be valid in Missouri were he still a slave. Thus from Justice Curtis's perspective, Emerson's consent to Scott's marriage must be viewed as an intention to set him free. Under the circumstances he would not defer to the contrary decision of the Missouri Supreme Court given that the record did not indicate that the Missouri Court knew that Dr. Emerson had intended to return to Missouri or that he had consented to the Scott marriage at Fort Snelling.

Justice Curtis then turned his attention to the question of whether Congress had the power to enact the Missouri Compromise. A thorough review of the enactment of the Territories Clause of Article IV of the Constitution convinced him that contrary to the opinion of Chief Justice Taney, it was not limited to territory held by the United States at the time of ratification. Likewise, the fact that the nation had acquired territory from foreign countries on four occasions by treaty, resulting in the formation of six states, belied the claim that the government had no power to do so. The Territories Clause gave Congress the authority to make "all needful rules and regulations" for the territories, and there was no exception for slavery. As slavery was governed by local law, it must have been understood that Congress had the power to make laws addressing slavery under this power, whether to permit it or prohibit it. Justice Curtis noted that the enactment of the statute banning slavery in the Northwest Territory in 1789 provided evidence that this was the original understanding of the clause. The Act passed the following year accepting territory ceded from North Carolina but prohibiting the abolition of slavery therein was further indication that Congress had the power to address questions of slavery in the territories. He then cited eight instances in which Congress prohibited slavery in the territories along with six in which it permitted it, to show that there was a long and continuous practice with respect to the question.

As far as congressional power to regulate the territories, Justice Curtis observed that there was no difference between him and the Court with respect to the existence of such a power, but rather only in terms of its constitutional source. That brought him to the final question of whether such regulation with respect to slavery was otherwise unconstitutional. He noted that the only ground that the Court suggested for such unconstitutionality was the Due Process Clause of the Fifth Amendment. At the outset, he emphasized that slavery is entirely a creation of local law. As such, there can be no regulation of slavery except by the authority empowered to legislate for a particular jurisdiction, and in the case of the territories that would be the Congress. He maintained that it was highly doubtful that the framers meant through the Due Process Clause to enshrine a principle that a slave owner could bring a slave into a territory where slavery was prohibited, live there with him permanently for a term of years, and then return with him to a state where he would once again be enslaved. Such an interpretation would not simply invalidate the Missouri Compromise but several other acts of Congress, as well as legislation in many slaveholding states that clearly reached a contrary result. Finally, he argued that nothing in the treaty between France and the United States conveying the Louisiana Territory could preclude Congress from abolishing slavery therein. David Currie labeled the Curtis dissent "one of the great masterpieces of constitutional opinion writing."[44]

THE HOLDING?

Perhaps the greatest difficulty presented by the *Dred Scott* opinions is attempting to figure out exactly what the Court held. As incredible as it might seem, it will never be possible to determine this with certainty. All nine justices issued opinions, and the extent to which members of the majority agreed with Chief Justice Taney's opinion or with each other is virtually impossible to tell at least on some issues. Taney certainly purported to write the opinion for the Court but he did not appear to have the votes on at least some significant issues. Seven of the nine justices, all but McLean and Curtis, concluded that Scott remained a slave. The same seven justices held that the stay in Illinois did not render Scott a free man. Six justices with Justice Nelson not joining the majority on this point found that the stay in the Upper Louisiana territory did not free Scott because the Missouri Compromise was unconstitutional. Only two other justices, Wayne and Daniel, joined the first portion of Taney's opinion concluding that an African American descendent of a slave could never qualify as a citizen of a state or of the United States, given that these three were the only members of the majority who believed that the Supreme Court could review the plea in abatement under which the issue had been raised below. Three justices explicitly disagreed with this portion of the opinion and three did not address it. Five members of the Court concluded that there was no jurisdiction because Scott was a slave, but at least one if not two based that conclusion on a review of the merits. Three members of the Court took the extreme position that the descendent of a Negro slave could never be a citizen for any purposes including diversity jurisdiction while three others concluded that Scott could not be a citizen for jurisdictional purposes because he was in fact a slave. Thus there was a clear majority on the jurisdictional issue but it was only achieved by addressing the merits. As such, it is not entirely clear whether the jurisdictional grounds were a holding rendering the discussion of the Missouri Compromise dicta. Commentators continue to disagree as to precisely what the Court held. R. Kent Newmyer has noted that "[r]arely has the Court undertaken so much--but settled so little."[45]

Although both of the primary conclusions of Taney—that a slave or a descendent of a slave was precluded from citizenship, and that the Missouri Compromise was unconstitutional—were devastating blows, the latter was certainly more politically explosive. And yet the latter can hardly be dismissed as dicta as it often has been, given that it had the support of six justices while the former position seemed to have only three. Thus as between Taney's two primary positions, the Court could not have avoided reaching the constitutionality of the Missouri Compromise, at least given the positions that the justices actually took in the case. Of course they could easily have avoided the issue had

---

[44] David P. Currie, The Constitution in the Supreme Court: The First Hundred Years, 1789–1888, at 273 (1986).

[45] R. Kent Newmyer, The Supreme Court under Marshall and Taney 137 (1968).

they exercised the slightest bit of common sense and taken advantage of the many alternatives readily available.

Perhaps the least damaging approach would have been that pursued by Justice Nelson, holding that on return to Missouri, Scott's status was a question of Missouri law and the Missouri Supreme Court had found him to be a slave. In that regard, Scott's sojourns in Illinois and the Minnesota territory with Dr. Emerson who was there on military duty were temporary in nature, and as a matter of Missouri law, at least as most recently declared, had no impact on his status. The Court could have rested on Missouri law either with respect to his status as a citizen of Missouri for jurisdictional purposes or as a substantive matter, even assuming jurisdiction. Or the Court could have held that although the Missouri Compromise did not permit slavery in the Upper Louisiana Territory, it was not intended to have any effect on the status of slaves in the territory with a legal domicile elsewhere.

THE IMPACT OF *DRED SCOTT*

Following the decision, the Blow family purchased the freedom of Scott and his family. Scott died the following year in St. Louis. Sanford had gone insane; he had been committed to a mental institution prior to the issuance of the decision and died two months after it was released.[46] Although it has been asserted that the *Dred Scott* decision caused the Civil War, most historians disagree.[47] It is all but certain that the war would have occurred in any event, and there were certainly many other contributing factors. Still it must be acknowledged that it made a bad situation much worse in a variety of ways. At the outset, one might wonder how the decision contributed to the Civil War insofar as the South seemed to be the big winner in the case, and yet it was the South that seceded from the Union three years later. Perhaps the answer is in Don Fehrenbacher's memorable phrase that the *Dred Scott* decision gave the South "an enormous check that could not be cashed."[48] That is, it suggested that the Court, through its constitutional holding, could protect southern interests in the territories where as a matter of political reality that simply could not be the case. The political balance was simply shifting against the South, significantly strengthening antislavery advocates in the House of Representatives and the electoral college.

Despite the national furor over the decision, David Potter has noted:

Probably no other major judicial decision in history affected the daily lives of as few people as this one. It annulled a law which had, in fact, been repealed three years previously, and denied freedom to slaves in an area where there were no slaves.[49]

The Senate purchased the copyright to the decision and published and distributed 20,000 copies.[50] The *Dred Scott* decision resulted in a furious reaction by the opponents of

---

[46] FEHRENBACHER, *supra* note 1, at 568-69.

[47] *See id.* at 562; MALTZ, *supra* note 1, at 154.

[48] FEHRENBACHER, *supra* note 1, at 450.

[49] DAVID M. POTTER, THE IMPENDING CRISIS: AMERICA BEFORE THE CIVIL WAR, 1848-1861 290 (1976).

[50] CARL BRENT SWISHER, THE TANEY PERIOD, 1836–1864, at 641 (1974).

slavery, strengthening the position of Lincoln and the emerging Republican party as well as rendering political compromise through Stephen Douglas's popular sovereignty approach all the more difficult if not impossible.[51] By constitutionalizing the issue of slavery in the territories, the Court removed the possibility of political compromise in Congress, as difficult as that might have been. As such, the extremes became more entrenched; the middle, to the extent there was one, collapsed. In the debates with Douglas, Lincoln could persuasively argue that if after *Dred Scott* Congress could not constitutionally address slavery in the territories, then how could territorial legislatures, ultimately empowered by Congress, do so either?[52] For Douglas there was no answer that could please both the northern and southern wings of the Democratic party. He quite properly dismissed as dicta the statements by Taney that a territorial legislature could not prohibit slavery and that such a legislature could simply decline to enact positive law supportive of slavery.[53] This enraged southerners who concluded that Douglas was attempting to sabotage the victory they believed they had won in *Dred Scott*. Douglas's inability to appease both the northern and southern wings of the Democratic party, with respect to the Kansas Crisis, caused him far more damage than his position on *Dred Scott*.

Lincoln maintained that the Court did not have the right to settle this overarching political controversy in a single decision, and that it would have little binding effect until reaffirmed by subsequent decisions.[54] During the debates with Senator Douglas, he had suggested that if a slave owner had a constitutional right to bring a slave into the territories, perhaps the Court would extend that protection to the states as well.[55] If so, the *Dred Scott* Case would have made slavery legal nationwide. *Dred Scott* by its own terms did no such thing but Lincoln could effectively argue that that is where it might lead with the aid of a pro-slavery Court.

The *Dred Scott* Case taken to its logical extreme arguably removed the issue from any politically responsive institution. In that sense, the most bitterly contested issue in the country could only be resolved by power rather than politics or law, assuming that at least half of the country was unwilling to abide by the Court's attempted settlement. As such, the decision certainly pushed the nation closer to disunion, and yet other developments including Congress's inability to resolve the conflict over whether Kansas should be admitted as a free or slave state had a far more significant impact on the deterioration of the Union than *Dred Scott*. The division of the Democratic Party and the election of Lincoln resulted in secession, but once again, the crisis in Kansas contributed more to the split in the party than did the Dred Scott Case.[56] With or without *Dred Scott*, it is hard to

---

[51] *See* PAUL FINKELMAN, *DRED SCOTT V SANDFORD: A BRIEF HISTORY WITH DOCUMENTS* 127–68 (1997) for an extensive collection of press responses to the decision. *See also* WARREN, *supra* note 9, at 27–32 for a collection of vigorous press attacks on the decision.

[52] Abraham Lincoln, Second Debate with Stephen Douglas at Freeport, Illinois, August 27, 1858, *in* ABRAHAM LINCOLN SPEECHES AND WRITINGS 1832-1858 537, 541-42 (Don Fehrenbacher ed., 1989). Lincoln asked Douglas, "Can the people of a United States Territory, in any lawful way, against the wishes of any citizen of the United States, exclude slavery from its limits, prior to the formation of a state Constitution?" *Id.*

[53] *Id.*

[54] Inaugural Address of Abraham Lincoln, March 4, 1861, *in* IV. COLLECTED WORKS OF ABRAHAM LINCOLN, *supra* note 17, at 262–71.

[55] III COLLECTED WORKS OF ABRAHAM LINCOLN, *supra* note 17, at 53–54. *See* FEHRENBACHER, *supra* note 1, at 451–52.

[56] FEHRENBACHER, *supra* note 1, at 456–70.

see how the question of slavery in the territories could have been resolved without massive bloodshed. The momentum had been building for over 70 years.

DRED SCOTT AS A GREAT CASE

The conventional wisdom is also that the *Dred Scott* decision had a devastating impact on the reputation of the Court itself. It was the great "self-inflicted wound" as Chief Justice Hughes put it.[57] There is certainly no question that the decision severely tainted the reputation of Taney and his chief justiceship to a degree from which it can never recover, despite significant accomplishments during the two decades preceding *Scott*. The decision was subjected to a withering attack by the antislavery press, which characterized it as "wicked," "atrocious," "deliberately false," "an iniquity," and much more.[58] Much of the abuse was directed at the Court and the justices and not simply the decision. Several northern legislatures passed laws condemning the decision.[59] Mark Graber has made a plausible case, however, that the decision was consistent with the prevailing law at the time and was well received by much of the public.[60] There was no attempt in Congress to alter the Court or its jurisdiction as there had been in the 1820s and would be again in the 1930s.

Dred Scott was decided by a confident, indeed an overconfident Court, and it did not necessarily lose that confidence as a result of the reaction to its decision. Taney died within four years of the decision. The Court was remade by Lincoln, and during the war and reconstruction, it continued to issue significant opinions addressing questions of great moment. If the Court as an institution had lost respect, it regained it quickly enough.

Dred Scott has on occasion been cited as evidence that original understanding as a methodology can lead to terrible results.[61] But that scarcely follows. It is true that Taney relied on his conception of original understanding to reach the conclusion that an African American could never be a citizen, a result that one and all would reject today. But as Justice Curtis demonstrated in dissent, Taney's argument was badly flawed in its selectivity as well as its conclusions. If anything *Dred Scott* simply shows that an otherwise valid methodology can be employed in a disingenuous and partisan manner. That says little if anything about the underlying value of the interpretive method itself.

Doctrinally, the life span of *Dred Scott* was short. Most of Taney's conclusions were repudiated over time. Congress outlawed slavery in the territories in 1862 after the Civil War began, in defiance of the *Dred Scott* opinion. Slavery itself was rejected by the outcome of the Civil War, constitutionally memorialized in the Thirteenth Amendment prohibiting "involuntary servitude." Taney's conclusion that the descendant of a slave could never become a citizen was explicitly rejected by the first sentence of the Fourteenth

---

[57] CHARLES EVANS HUGHES, THE SUPREME COURT OF THE UNITED STATES 50–51 (1928).

[58] WARREN, *supra* note 9, at 27–31.

[59] FEHRENBACHER, *supra* note 1, at 432–33.

[60] GRABER, *supra* note 1, at 1–92.

[61] *See, e.g.*, Christopher L. Eisgruber, *The Story of* Dred Scott: *Originalism's Forgotten Past in* MICHAEL C. DORF, CONSTITUTIONAL LAW STORIES 151 (2004).

Amendment, which provides that "[a]ll persons born or naturalized in the United States, and subject to the jurisdiction thereof, are citizens of the United States and of the state wherein they reside." From that point onward, state citizenship was derived from national citizenship rather than vice versa. Taney's conclusion that constitutional constraints did apply in the territories retained some vitality although it was eventually trimmed down as the nation acquired territories beyond the North American continent.[62]

One aspect of Taney's opinion that did prove to have staying power was the concept of substantive due process, the idea that the Due Process Clause did not simply require a degree of procedural protection before the state could deprive a person of life, liberty, or property, but rather that the state was substantively disabled from implementing certain deprivations. In the case of Dred Scott, the federal government could not leg-islatively deprive a person of his slave simply because he took the slave into a territory in which slavery was prohibited. Taney did not originate the concept of substantive due process. It was arguably derived from the concept of the law of the land in the Magna Carta and had been recognized by the New York Court of Appeals in *Wynehamer v. The People*[63] decided the year prior to *Dred Scott*. Moreover the concept had been employed in congressional debate over slavery as far back as the 1830s.[64] One might have assumed that the concept would perish as a casualty of the repudiation of the *Dred Scott* decision itself. Instead however, in 1876 in the case of *Munn v. Illinois*, the Court recognized sub-stantive due process as applied pursuant to the recently enacted Fourteenth Amend-ment as being a viable constitutional doctrine, and beginning in the late 1880s applied it with vigor in the area of economic legislation for four decades until the constitutional revolution of 1937. After three decades of repose, the Court in the mid-1960s revital-ized the doctrine under the rubric of the right to privacy. Given that economic substan-tive due process has widely been regarded as a wrong turn by the Court, and even the more recent privacy-oriented version has many critics, substantive due process is yet one more doctrinal error often attributed to Taney despite the fact that he simply bor-rowed it.

The *Dred Scott* decision has remained a matter of controversy among constitutional historians and commentators. During the first half of the twentieth century when Taney's reputation as a justice was refurbished, writers including Edward Corwin, Charles Warren, Felix Frankfurter, and Robert McCloskey either defended the decision and opin-ion or at least characterized it as a good faith error in an otherwise distinguished career. More recent commentators including Don Fehrenbacher, Paul Finkelman, and Earl Maltz have been less charitable, emphasizing that the opinions expressed by Taney in *Dred Scott* reflected a racism and southern bias that was present throughout his career but reached a crescendo in this case. Mark Graber accepts that charactercrazation but maintains that Taney's opinion was consistent with and defensible under the existing constitutional

---

[62] In the Insular Cases involving the applicability of constitutional provisions to territories obtained from Spain, the Court in a series of decisions drew a tenuous distinction between incorporated and unincorpo-rated territories. *See* Downes v. Bidwell, 182 U.S. 244 (1901) and Dorr v. United Stars, 195 U.S. 138 (1904).

[63] 13 N.Y. 378 (1856).

[64] John Calhoun argued in 1836 that abolition of slavery in the District of Columbia would deprive a slave owner of his property in violation of the Due Process Clause of the Fifth Amendment. Statement of John Calhoun, CONG. GLOBE, 24th Cong.; 1st Sess. 83 (1836). *See* SCHWARTZ, *supra* note 23, at 117.

doctrine.[65] As the movement toward racial equality progressed in the latter half of the twentieth century, Taney's opinion and the Court's decision became more of an embarrassment than ever. Recently, however, Jack Balkin and Sanford Levinson have noted that the concept of equality, so dominant in contemporary constitutional law, was given an ironic boost in *Dred Scott* by Taney's emphasis on equality between slave and non-slave states with respect to the territories.[66]

By construing the Missouri Compromise as freeing Scott and then invalidating it for having done so, the Court rather deliberately threw a bomb into the existing political culture. *Dred Scott* is the most outstanding example in the Court's history of a great case making bad law, indeed extraordinarily bad law.[67] Justice Holmes almost certainly had *Dred Scott* in mind when he made his famous remarks in his *Northern Securities* dissent. Why did it happen and did it have to happen?

Historians disagree as to why the Court turned what could have been a rather routine case into a political and judicial disaster of the first magnitude. One theory is that it was not completely or even largely the Court's fault. Congress, the political establishment, as well as the parties to the litigation hoped that the Court would resolve the contentious issue of slavery in the territories, and pressed the Court hard to do just that.[68] The correspondence between president-elect Buchanan and several of the justices indicates that some pressure on the Court was coming from the highest of levels. Still, the justices could have resisted that pressure, concluding that it was hardly their role to attempt to settle the divisive political issue. And at least for a while when Justice Nelson was prepared to write a fairly modest opinion for the Court, it seemed that the Court would indeed deflect the controversy. So it was not simply inevitable that the Court would address the Missouri Compromise. The Court rejected that modest approach after Justice Wayne persuaded Chief Justice Taney to write a broadside opinion for the Court. Why did that happen?

One theory, supported by correspondence of Justices Catron and Grier with president-elect Buchanan, is that the majority had reason to believe that the dissenters planned to argue that the Missouri Compromise did in fact free Scott, and the majority was simply unwilling to leave that charge unanswered.[69] But why should that necessarily force the Court's hand? Why would a dissent by two justices overshadow a majority opinion by seven? Were the justices so emotionally committed to the controversy over slavery in the territories that they simply could not bear to have opinions with which they disagreed issued without a response? Given the intensity of the debate on these legal issues and the focus on the Court for answers, perhaps the justices in the majority simply could not allow the dissenters to have the only word on these questions.

It is also possible that Chief Justice Taney as well as Wayne and Daniel felt so strongly about the broader issues discussed in Taney's opinion that they simply could not restrain

---

[65] GRABER, *supra* note 1, at 1–92.

[66] Jack Balkin & Sanford Levinson, *Thirteen Ways of Looking at* Dred Scott, 82 CHI.-KENT L. REV. 49, 83 (2007).

[67] *See* GRABER, *supra* note 1, at 15–16 for a catalogue of scholars condemning *Dred Scott* as the worst Supreme Court decision ever.

[68] *See* FEHRENBACHER, *supra* note 1, at 206–07; GRABER, *supra* note 1, at 35–37.

[69] FEHRENBACHER, *supra* note 1, at 309.

themselves once the opportunity arose. This would be especially true given that they presumably believed that they were on solid legal ground. Taney had in fact written an unpublished paper some 20 years earlier as attorney general making essentially the same arguments with respect to the exclusion of African Americans from citizenship.[70] As the respective positions of the North and South hardened on the slavery-in-the-territories issue during the 1850s, Taney's views hardened as well, and unlike most everyone else, he was in a position to translate southern orthodoxy into constitutional law. By 1857, much of the country was in a state of rage over the territorial issue, especially due to the escalation of violence in Kansas, and unfortunately some of the people who had reached the boiling point happened to sit on the Supreme Court. There is much to be said for this explanation. As Don Fehrenbacher, perhaps the preeminent authority on the case concluded, "the Chief Justice wrote the opinion that he had wanted to write all along."[71]

Or perhaps Taney wanted to attempt to assist president-elect Buchanan, who clearly favored the result that Taney desired to reach. One of the most commonly offered explanations is that Taney and several of the other justices believed, quite erroneously, that they could indeed settle the explosive issue once and for all with a comprehensive constitutional ruling, and indeed one that was in accord with the southern sympathies of a majority of the justices. There is reason to believe that the justices grossly underestimated the backlash that the decision would provoke.[72] Whatever the reasoning, the decision to address the Missouri Compromise proved to be the most egregious error in judgment in Supreme Court history. Taney's opinion itself was unnecessarily provocative, polemical, and to some extent incoherent, and as such it was easily demolished by its opponents. Fehrenbacher characterized Taney's argument "as weak in law, logic, history, and factual accuracy."[73] The obvious deficiencies of Taney's arguments led many to view it as an illegitimate non-judicial act, perhaps a conspiracy among Buchanan, Douglas, and Taney as Lincoln charged. A more measured, less strident opinion attempting to defend the same legal positions such as the one issued by Justice Campbell would not have rendered the *Dred Scott* decision harmless but it might have muted the contemporary attack on the decision at least somewhat. The fact that Taney withheld the opinion initially and revised it to add 19 more pages challenging the arguments made by Curtis in dissent certainly did not help avoid the conclusion that there was something nefarious about what Taney and the majority were doing.

It is also possible, as Mark Graber has maintained, that although *Dred Scott* was a morally indefensible decision, Taney and the majority decided it as they did because constitutional law, as it then existed, supported their conclusions.[74] Graber's argument runs counter to the academic consensus; however, he builds a powerful though hardly a conclusive case. Like Story's opinion in *Prigg v. Pennsylvania*, *Dred Scott* could be viewed as an

---

[70] Unpublished Opinion of Attorney General Roger Taney Defending the Constitutionality of the Negro Seaman's Act, 1832.

[71] FEHRENBACHER, *supra* note 1, at 311; CURRIE, *supra* note 44, at 272 ("[t]he variety of feeble, poorly developed, and unnecessary constitutional arguments suggests, if nothing else, a determination to reach a predetermined conclusion at any price").

[72] SWISHER, *supra* note 50, at 632.

[73] FEHRENBACHER, *supra* note 1, at 384.

[74] GRABER, *supra* note 1, at 20–83.

attempt to preserve the original compromise over slavery that was the glue holding the nation together.[75]

The majority should have recognized that the Constitution lent insufficient support to the argument that the Missouri Compromise was unconstitutional, as evidenced by the thinness of the argument that Taney was able to render for that position. Indeed he never really stated in so many words why that was so, suggesting at most in passing that it violated due process. But more significant, even assuming for the sake of argument that there was a plausible argument that Congress could not prohibit slavery in the territories (and hence render free any slaves who were brought there), Taney and the Court should have recognized that in the context of the politically explosive nature of the issue at the time, a judicial ruling, especially one effectively removing the issue from the political process, could only inflame rather than resolve. If the issue was not technically a political question, it was at least one that a sensible Court would attempt to avoid at all costs. So perhaps the primary lesson of *Dred Scott* is that sometimes, especially in great cases, it is judicious not to decide or at least to decide narrowly even when there is extreme pressure to the contrary. The *Dred Scott* Case could have and easily should have been a historical footnote rather than the most infamous decision in the Court's history.

---

[75] *Id.* at 39.

"It would be difficult to overestimate the consequences which must follow our decision. They will affect the entire business of the country and take hold of the possible continued existence of the government."[1]

JUSTICE STRONG WRITING FOR THE MAJORITY IN THE *LEGAL TENDER CASES*

6

The Legal Tender Cases

⌐⌐_____

THE *LEGAL TENDER* Cases addressed and resolved an issue of extraordinary political, economic, and social importance—whether paper money could be issued as legal tender for the payment of all debts. In *Hepburn v. Griswold*[2] decided in 1869, the Court ruled five to three that Congress could not make paper money legal tender with respect to pre-existing debts. A year later after one justice in the majority resigned and two new justices were appointed, the Court reversed itself in a series of consolidated cases styled the *Legal Tender Cases* and overruled *Hepburn*, holding that Congress was constitutionally authorized to make paper money legal tender for the payment of debts incurred both prior and subsequent to the legislation. Chief Justice Chase, who had been a sturdy advocate of paper money as legal tender as attorney general in the Lincoln administration when the initial legislation was passed, wrote the opinion for the Court invalidating the principle in *Hepburn*. The cases raised an issue as important to the nation as ever considered by the Court. And never in the Court's history has it reversed itself so swiftly on an issue of such significance. The *Legal Tender Cases* (including *Hepburn*) had all the ingredients of a great case.

BACKGROUND

Given that paper currency had circulated prior to the Revolution and had depreciated in value significantly, the framing generation opposed its issuance, period, and would have certainly opposed its authorization as legal tender had the issue been presented.[3] The Constitution contains several provisions that have some bearing on the question of whether Congress could authorize the use of paper money as legal tender for the payment

---

[1] 79 U.S. 457, 529 (1870).
[2] 75 U.S. 603 (1869).
[3] Kenneth Dam, *The Legal Tender Cases*, 1981 SUP. CT. REV. 367, 389 (1981).

of debts. Article I, Section Eight, paragraph 2 authorizes Congress "To borrow money on the credit of the United States." Article 1, Section Eight, paragraph 5 authorizes Congress "To coin Money, regulate the value thereof, and of foreign Coin, and fix the Standard of Weights and Measures." Article I, Section Ten, paragraph 1 declares that "No State shall... coin Money; emit Bills of Credit; make any Thing but gold and silver Coin a Tender in payment of Debts...."

From the very beginning of the nation, Congress declared that only gold and silver would qualify as legal tender, and it set the weight and purity of each to be included in coins. In 1842, Congress diminished the requisite amount of gold to be included by approximately 6 percent in order to recalibrate the relationship between gold and silver. Gold and silver remained the only legally authorized tender until the nation simply ran out of currency to pay its bills during the Civil War. In 1862, Congress passed legislation authorizing the issuance of 150 million dollars' worth of notes, known as greenbacks, which would be made legal tender for the payment of all debts public and private contracted before or after the date of authorization. The greenbacks could also be held by banks as part of their reserves, increasing their solvency and lending capacity.[4] During the course of the war, Congress authorized the issuance of a total of 450 million dollars worth of greenbacks as legal tender. Secretary of the Treasury Salmon Chase was less than enthused about the issuance of greenbacks but concluded that it was necessary under the circumstances.[5] In appointing Chase as chief justice, Lincoln had every reason to be confident that he would uphold the Legal Tender Act if it were challenged.[6] Prior to *Hepburn*, the Court had held that the legislation did not apply to the payment of state taxes or to contracts that explicitly required the payment in bullion.[7]

In early 1863 Congress increased the size of the Supreme Court to 10 justices. Three years later it reduced the size to six justices to prevent President Johnson from appointing a justice. In 1869, it restored the Court to nine justices. At the time of *Hepburn*, the Court had eight members though Justice Grier announced his retirement after *Hepburn* had been argued and officially stepped down two days before the decision was announced. That gave President Grant the opportunity to appoint two new justices as the case was pending. He nominated Massachusetts attorney general Hoar, who was not confirmed by the Senate, and Edward Stanton who died four days after having been nominated. Grant then nominated William Strong of Pennsylvania and Joseph Bradley of New Jersey. Strong was confirmed by the Senate on February 18, 1870 and Bradley on March 21.

The Court had avoided direct challenges to the constitutionality of the Act during the war but such attacks were bound to arise after the war was over. As greenbacks inevitably traded at a discount to their stated value in gold or silver, the Legal Tender Act was supported by debtors and opposed by creditors. By the time *Hepburn* reached the Supreme Court, 15 state courts all controlled by Republican judges had upheld the constitutionality of the Act.[8]

---

[4] *Id.* at 406–08.

[5] Charles Fairman, Reconstruction and Reunion 1864-88, Part One 685 (1971).

[6] William H. Rehnquist, The Supreme Court 241 (1987).

[7] Lane County v. Oregon, 74 U.S. 71 (1869) (Act did not require acceptance of greenbacks for state taxes); Butler v. Horwitz, 74 U.S. 258 (1869) (Act did not require acceptance of greenbacks under a contract requiring payment in specie).

[8] Peter Charles Hoffer, WilliamJames Hull Hoffer & N. E. H. Hull, The Supreme Court: An Essential History 117 (2007).

HEPBURN V.GRISWOLD

The plaintiff in *Hepburn* was the assignee of a note executed prior to the effective date of the Legal Tender Act of 1862. The debtor under the note tendered $12,720, the amount of the principal plus interest, in 1864 in notes issued pursuant to the Act of 1862. The plaintiff refused to accept this as proper payment and sued in the Court of Chancery of Kentucky for payment instead in bullion. The Chancery Court held the notes to be legal tender; however the Kentucky Court of Errors reversed.[9]

The case was appealed to the United States Supreme Court in 1865 but was not argued until December 1868. At the request of the attorney general, given the importance of the case, it was re-argued the following term, giving the United States an opportunity to appear in defense of the Act in what otherwise was a lawsuit between private parties. Benjamin Curtis, the former Supreme Court justice who had written the primary dissent in the *Dred Scott* Case, and Attorney General William Everts defended the Act while Clarkson Potter challenged it. Several other cases raising the same issues were also argued by a total of 15 different attorneys. While *Hepburn* was pending, the Court decided *Lane County v. Oregon* holding that Congress did not require that paper currency was legal tender for the payment of state taxes.[10]

The eight-member Court voted five to three to strike down the Act on November 27, 1869 but apparently also agreed to delay the issuance of an opinion pending the appointment of additional justices. Justice Grier, whose health was failing, may have initially voted to uphold the Act but apparently changed his mind and voted with the majority to invalidate it.[11] There is reason to believe that Grier's mental capacity was in serious decline and he may not have fully understood the vote.[12] Shortly after the vote in *Hepburn*, the other justices suggested that he resign.[13] He announced his resignation December 15 to take effect January 30, 1870. The Court approved the opinion on January 30; Grier resigned on February 5; the Court released the opinion on February 7. At the very time that Chase was reading the opinion, President Grant sent the names of William Strong and Joseph Bradley to the Senate for appointment to the Court.

Chief Justice Chase writing for a five-justice majority (counting Grier) wrote the decision invalidating the Legal Tender Act as applied to debts incurred prior to the passage of the Act.[14] The opinion was relatively short in view of the significance of the case and was more polemical than legal in nature. Initially, the Court flirted with the idea of construing the Act itself as applicable only to debts incurred subsequent to the effective date, but concluded that such an interpretation was not warranted.

Finding no express power to make paper legal tender, Chief Justice Chase inquired whether such action could be considered "necessary and proper" to another expressed power. He summarily dismissed the notion that the Act was a necessary and proper means of exercising the power to coin money or regulate the value of coined money.

---

[9] 75 U.S. 603, 605 (1869).
[10] 74 U.S. 71 (1869).
[11] FAIRMAN, *supra* note 5, at 717-19.
[12] *Id.*
[13] *Id.* at 716-17.
[14] 75 U.S. at 606.

Likewise the Court rejected the contention that the power to issue bills or notes included or implied the right to make them legal tender.

He then focused on the war power, on which the dissents placed the most weight. The Court rejected this justification with the consequential argument that Congress would be able to justify virtually any exercise of power however unwarranted on the ground that it was necessary to the success of the war effort. Moreover, complete deference to Congress on the question of whether the means were sufficiently necessary would grant Congress unlimited power, contrary to the design of the Constitution,

The Court boiled the issue down to whether the government's legitimate power to issue notes implied a power to make them legal tender. It then concluded that making the notes legal tender as opposed to their mere issuance did not further the war effort sufficiently to render the action necessary or proper. Rather, the debasement of the currency caused by the Legal Tender Act canceled out the utility to the war effort or to the exercise of any other explicit congressional power.

Chief Justice Chase quoted the language from *McCulloch v. Maryland* stating that a law must be "consistent with the letter and spirit of the Constitution" to satisfy the Necessary and Proper Clause.[15] This in turn led him to ask whether the legal tender provision was consistent with the spirit of the Constitution. He declared that one of the purposes of the Constitution was to "establish justice" and that the Constitution itself contained an explicit provision prohibiting the states from impairing the obligations of contracts. He then acknowledged that there was no similar prohibition with respect to the federal government. Nevertheless, a law that was not made pursuant to an express power that did in fact impair the obligation of contracts would indeed violate the spirit of the Constitution. The exception for laws passed pursuant to express powers was intended to distinguish the bankruptcy power, under which Congress regularly passed legislation that would impair contractual obligations.

The Court also indicated that the Legal Tender Act would be inconsistent with the spirit of the Takings and Due Process Clauses of the Fifth Amendment as well. Consequently, the Court concluded that a law requiring debts previously contracted to be payable with paper currency was not consistent with the spirit of the Constitution and was thus prohibited by it. At the end of the opinion, the Court noted that Justice Grier, who was still a member of the Court when the case was decided and the opinion was written, believed that the Act did not apply to previously incurred debts but that it was unconstitutional as construed by the other justices in the majority as so applying.

Chief Justice Chase's opinion in *Hepburn* rivals Chief Justice Taney's opinion in *Dred Scott* as an example of an opinion that quite transparently substitutes political for legal argument. The reliance on the "spirit" of the Constitution as a rationale for applying contract clause principles to the federal government was simply at war with the text of the document. The requirement that legal tender must be strictly necessary to the prosecution of the war was completely inconsistent with *McCulloch v. Maryland*, the case on which Chase purported to rely. The majority opinion provided an easy target for the dissents.

Justice Miller dissented, joined by Justices Swayne and Davis. At the outset, the dissent pointed out that although the Constitution explicitly prohibits the states from

---

[15] *Id.* at 622.

making anything but gold and silver a coin in payment of debts, it places no similar limitation on Congress. Justice Miller then argued that the Legal Tender Act was a necessary and proper means for Congress to raise the enormous funds essential to the successful prosecution of the Civil War.[16] Given the deteriorating state of the nation's finances at the time, Miller argued that the issuance of notes alone without the status of legal tender would not have been sufficient.

The dissent dismissed the majority's argument that the legal tender provision violated the spirit of the Constitution by impairing the obligation of contracts, noting that there was no such explicit restraint against the federal government as opposed to the states, and the bankruptcy power showed that Congress had the authority to do just that. Justice Miller was particularly dismissive of the Court's arguments based on the "spirit of the Constitution," declaring that such a principle "is too abstract and intangible for application to courts of justice" and "would authorize this court to enforce theoretical views... or vague notions... of abstract justice."[17]

As long as it was understood as limited to pre-existing contracts, the decision in *Hepburn* was generally not considered particularly harmful.[18] However, the likelihood that the rationale of the Court would apply to subsequent contracts as well did cause concern.[19]

THE *LEGAL TENDER CASES*

As Chief Justice Chase indicated, Justice Grier retired after the case was decided but before the opinion was released. President Grant appointed two new justices, Strong and Bradley, one to replace Grier, and the other pursuant to an Act of Congress expanding the Court again to nine justices. Two months after *Hepburn* was announced, recently appointed attorney general Hoar asked the Court to consider two pending appeals in the *Latham* and *Demming* cases challenging the application of the Legal Tender Act to debt obligations contracted subsequent to the effective date of the Act. The prestigious *American Law Review* (edited by Oliver Wendell Holmes) warned that reconsidering *Hepburn* "would be a terrible blow to the dignity and independence of the profession."[20] However, the Court agreed and set oral argument for April 11, 1870, at which time the justices on the bench engaged in a spirited debate as to whether an order had previously been issued declaring that these two cases would be controlled by the decision in *Hepburn*, with Chief Justice Chase insisting that there had been such an order and Justice Miller declaring that he was unaware of it.[21] A correspondent commented that "'the oldest lawyers practicing there having witnessed nothing like it in their day.'"[22] Chase threatened

---

[16] *Id.* at 632-33.

[17] *Id.* at 638.

[18] 3 CHARLES WARREN, THE SUPREME COURT IN AMERICAN HISTORY 235 (1922).

[19] *Id.* at 237-38.

[20] 5 AM. LAW REV. 366, 367 (1870).

[21] WARREN, *supra* note 18, at 244.

[22] *Id.* (quoting a Washington correspondent).

to file a paper backing up his claim and Miller declared that he would file a paper to the contrary, but neither followed through.[23] The Court postponed the argument and then dismissed the appeals at the request of counsel in the cases. Justice Miller wrote to his brother-in-law complaining that "[t]he Chief Justice has resorted to all the stratagems of the lowest political trickery to prevent [cases reconsidering *Hepburn* from] being heard, and the fight has been bitter in the conference room."[24]

Two weeks later however on April 30, 1870, the Court ordered re-argument in *Knox v. Lee*, which raised the issue of whether the Legal Tender Act could constitutionally be applied to subsequent contracts. The Court consolidated several other pending cases raising the same issue under the heading the *Legal Tender Cases*. At re-argument, neither counsel challenged the constitutionality of the Legal Tender Act as applied. That caused Clarkson Potter who had been the prevailing party in *Hepburn* to seek re-argument on the constitutional issue. The Court granted the request and Attorney General Ackerman appeared to defend the Act.

In May 1, 1871, the three dissenters in *Hepburn* joined by the two newest justices announced that *Knox v. Lee* and *Parker v. Davis* had been affirmed, thereby upholding the constitutionality of the Legal Tender Act and overruling *Hepburn*. The opinions were not issued however until December. Justice Strong, one of the two new appointees, wrote the opinion for the Court. At the outset, he acknowledged that "[i]t would be difficult to overestimate the consequences which must follow our decision" including "the possible continued existence of the government."[25] The Court defined the central issue as "can Congress constitutionally give to Treasury notes the character and qualities of money."[26] As was the case with the majority and dissent in *Hepburn*, the Court recognized that the case would essentially turn on an interpretation of the Necessary and Proper Clause. In determining whether establishing paper as legal tender was necessary and proper to the exercise of the war power, the Court emphasized the dire financial straits in which the nation found itself at the height of the Civil War when the statute was enacted.

The Court cautioned that it was not appropriate for it to consider whether other means would have worked as well, but nevertheless argued that in fact there was no viable alternative.[27] Justice Strong argued that the means (making paper notes legal tender) was clearly adapted to the ends (raising funds to pay the army and navy). Continuing to apply Chief Justice Marshall's test from *McCulloch*, Strong inquired whether the Legal Tender Act was inconsistent with the spirit and letter of the Constitution as the majority had held in *Hepburn*. He disagreed with the dissent's contention that Congress could not constitutionally justify the Legal Tender Act as necessary and proper to the War Power given that monetary matters were more closely related to the coinage power. Strong rejected the *Hepburn* majority's argument that permitting payment of pre-Act debts with paper money violated the "spirit" of the Constitution, by insisting that any contractual

---

[23] Charles Fairman, *Mr. Justice Bradley's Appointment to the Supreme Court and the Legal Tender Cases*, 54 HARV. L. REV. 977, 980 (1941).

[24] Letter from Justice Miller to his brother-in law, April 21, 1870, reproduced in FAIRMAN, *supra* note 5, at 744.

[25] 79 U.S. 457, 529 (1872).

[26] *Id.* at 530.

[27] *Id.* at 541–42.

obligation for future payment implicitly takes account of governmental changes in currency that may have occurred in the interim. In response to the *Hepburn* majority's argument that Congress did not have the power to replace a standard for the currency such as gold, which had intrinsic value, with a standard that did not, mere paper, Strong replied that the United States' government's promise to pay was value enough.

Thus in a relatively short opinion focused almost entirely upon debunking the arguments of the *Hepburn* majority, Justice Strong concluded that the Legal Tender Act was constitutional as applied to the payment of debts contracted both before and after its passage, and consequently *Hepburn* was overruled. It is not surprising that the majority was most concerned with the deficiencies of *Hepburn* as it was after all overruling a major decision that was scarcely over a year old. That presumably required significant justification. In response to the dissent's objection to the overruling of *Hepburn*, the majority noted that *Hepburn* had been decided by a divided court with less than the number of legislatively authorized justices sitting.

Justice Bradley, also one of the newly appointed justices, wrote a concurring opinion that concentrated more on affirmatively defending the constitutionality of the Legal Tender Act than on challenging the reasoning of *Hepburn*. He argued that the Legal Tender Act could readily be sustained as either a necessary and proper means of executing the congressional power to emit bills of credit or to issue treasury notes to provide a proper currency for the country.[28] This was a significant addition to the majority's rationale given that in the future as the Civil War faded into the past, an alternative justification for the Legal Tender Act might prove essential. Emphasizing the financial crisis during the Civil War, he declared that "[t]here are times when the exigencies of the state rightly absorb all subordinate considerations of private interest, convenience or feeling...."[29] Justice Bradley also addressed the issue of stare decisis noting that "[w]here the decision is recent, and is only made by a bare majority of the court, and during a time of public excitement on the subject, when the question has largely entered into the political discussions of the day, I consider it our right and duty to subject it to a further examination...."[30]

Although the majority opinion in the *Legal Tender Cases* was relatively short considering the importance of the issue, the same cannot be said of the dissents. Chief Justice Chase, the author of the *Hepburn* opinion, wrote a lengthy and vigorous dissent. He began by labeling the rapid reversal of *Hepburn* "unprecedented in the history of the court," noting than none of the justices who had originally joined the *Hepburn* opinion had changed their minds.[31] As with the majority, the chief justice also addressed his apparent change of position on the issue from his time as secretary of the treasury to his role as a justice on the Court. He argued that he had initially supported issuance of the notes by the government but had opposed making them legal tender. When it appeared that the bill to issue the notes might fail, he offered an opinion concluding that Congress did have the authority to make the notes legal tender. He had since concluded that "[e]xamination and

---

[28] *Id.* at 560–61.
[29] *Id.* at 565.
[30] *Id.* at 570.
[31] *Id.* at 572.

reflection under more propitious circumstances have satisfied him that this opinion was erroneous and he does not hesitate to declare it."[32]

Chase argued that the case turned on a correct understanding of the Necessary and Proper Clause. He had no problem with the issuance of the notes themselves for payment of the army and navy but believed that the essential question was whether it was a necessary and proper means to the exercise of any legitimate congressional power to make them legal tender for the payment of private debts. He maintained that it was not, given that the fact that the notes were receivable in payment of taxes and debts to the United States was more than sufficient to render them capable of circulation.

Chase returned to the argument of the *Hepburn* majority that making the notes legal tender violated "the spirit, if not the letter of the Constitution" by impairing the obligations of contracts, at least with respect to pre-Act contracts. With respect to post-Act contracts, Chase argued that gold and silver were the universally accepted standard of value throughout the world and that there should be a strong presumption against the substitution of anything else. He finished by quoting Madison, the Federalist Papers, and Webster in opposition to the constitutionality of anything other than gold and silver as the basis of currency. As with his opinion for the Court in *Hepburn*, Chase's dissent in the *Legal Tender Cases* seemed more concerned with questions of policy than of law.

Justice Clifford also published a dissent. He began with the declaration that "[money], in the constitutional sense, means gold and silver fabricated and stamped by the authority of law as the measurement of value, pursuant to power vested in Congress by the Constitution."[33] As such, nothing else could constitutionally serve as a standard of value. He then launched into a lengthy history of the monetary policies of the United States. From this discussion he concluded that "Congress cannot, under any circumstances, make paper promises, of any kind a legal tender in payment of debts."[34] He concluded that *Hepburn* clearly controlled the question of whether paper money could be made legal tender for the payment of previously incurred debts. The result should be the same for subsequently incurred debts as well given that Congress only has the constitutional authority to employ gold or silver as a standard of value. Justice Clifford recited at length the opposition of several important framers to the issuance of paper currency.[35] He argued that permitting the authorization of paper money as legal tender under another congressional power such as the war power would contradict the restriction of Congress to gold and silver under the Coinage and Standard of Value Clause. Webster had made this argument in Congress. Clifford also maintained that the long congressional practice of issuing notes that would not qualify as legal tender was some evidence against the constitutionality of doing so. As for the war power, Clifford argued that various express powers including the power to lay and collect taxes gave Congress more than sufficient means to raise money to conduct the war.

Justice Stephen Field also wrote a lengthy dissent. He began by declaring that neither the arguments of counsel nor the majority cast any doubt on the correctness of *Hepburn*. He observed that "no case has ever been decided by this court since its organization, in

---

[32] *Id.* at 576.
[33] *Id.* at 587.
[34] *Id.* at 599.
[35] *Id.* at 605–09.

which the questions presented were more fully argued or more maturely considered."[36] Like Chief Justice Chase, he stated at the outset that there was no question that Congress could issue the notes and that the only issue was whether it could make them legal tender for private debts.[37]

Turning to the possible sources of congressional authority, Field argued that the power to "borrow money" did not contain a further power to transform the instrument of debt into legal tender acceptable for the payment of other private debts. Field agreed that Chief Justice Marshall's generous construction of the Necessary and Proper Clause in *McCulloch v. Maryland* was the correct approach to its application. However, he concluded that the Legal Tender Act could not satisfy even this lenient standard for measuring congressional power as there was simply no relationship between the congressional need to borrow and the authorization of the notes as legal tender. Rather "[w]ithout the legal tender provisions, the notes would have circulated equally well and answered all the purposes of the government" without having the effect of significantly depreciating the currency used to satisfy private debt.[38] He cautioned that he was not relying on the utility of the measure but rather only on its relationship as a means to a constitutional end.

As for the war power, he declared that the needs of the government could scarcely increase the scope of congressional powers. And with respect to raising money during either peace or war, Congress is limited to the explicitly enumerated powers of "taxation, borrowing, coining and the sale of public property."[39] As a matter of construction, the designation of these specific means negated all others.

Considering the Coinage Clause, Field maintained that the "power to coin money" is simply inconsistent with "the power to make anything but a coin legal tender."[40] And by definition "coins are pieces of metal, of definite weight and value, thus stamped by the national authority."[41] The affirmative grant to make coins legal tender negates the power to make anything else such tender. Justice Field also emphasized that throughout history, virtually all nations had limited currency to precious metals. He also reviewed at some length the opinions of the framing generation limiting legal tender to precious metals.

Putting these considerations together, Justice Field argued that the views of the framers, the natural meaning of the terms, the structure of the Constitution as one of enumerated powers, congressional practice over three quarters of a century, judicial opinions, and the views of statesmen and commentators constituted irrefutable evidence that the Constitution permitted only metallic coins to serve as a standard of value and hence legal tender.

He then argued that the Act impaired the obligation of contracts though conceding that there was no explicit constitutional prohibition against such an impairment by the federal government. Even so, he argued that the very fact that the bankruptcy power was the only enumerated power contemplating the impairment of contractual obligations is

---

[36] *Id.* at 634.
[37] *Id.* at 635.
[38] *Id.* at 647.
[39] *Id.* at 649.
[40] *Id.* at 649.
[41] *Id.*

evidence that Congress did not have such authority in any other context. Permitting Congress "to do anything which it may deem expedient, as a resulting power from the general purposes of government" would effectively change "our government from one of enumerated powers to one resting in the unrestrained will of Congress."[42] In other words, the majority's construction was simply inconsistent with the well-accepted understanding of constitutional structure.

A week after the opinion in the *Legal Tender Cases* was delivered, the Court held in *Trebilcock v. Wilson* that a contract that required payment in "specie" could not be satisfied, over the objection of the creditor, with payment in greenbacks.[43]

JUILLIARD v. GREENMAN–THE FOLLOWUP

Litigation over the legal tender issue did not end with the *Legal Tender Cases* of 1871 however. Given that the majority had relied so heavily on the war power supplemented by the Necessary and Proper Clause to sustain the Legal Tender Act, the question remained whether Congress would have the power to pass legal tender legislation in a peacetime context. By an eight-to-one vote, the Court held that it surely did in *Juilliard v. Greenman* in 1884.[44] Juilliard sued Greenman for failure to pay a debt of $5122 for bales of cotton that had been delivered to Greenman. Greenman replied that he had offered to pay the debt largely with treasury notes designated as legal tender and that Juilliard had refused to accept them. In 1875, Congress passed an Act requiring the secretary of the treasury to pay coin for legal tender notes offered for redemption and to retire such notes from circulation. The purpose of the Act was to curb depreciation of the currency, control inflation, and help return the nation to the gold standard. Three years later, Congress passed an Act prohibiting the further redemption of such notes and requiring that those that had been redeemed be re-circulated. Juilliard challenged the right of Congress to do so. Juilliard was a contrived case designed to test the constitutionality of the Act of 1878.[45]

At the outset, the Court unanimously agreed that the case was indistinguishable from the *Legal Tender Cases* of 1871, and all but Justice Field believed that those cases were correctly decided. The Court examined the discussions in the Constitutional Convention and concluded that they did not establish that the framers were opposed to the issuance of paper money as legal tender. Like Justice Bradley in the *Legal Tender Cases*, Justice Gray, writing for the majority, argued that the powers to coin and to borrow money, broadly construed and bolstered by the Necessary and Proper Clause, permitted Congress to establish either coins or paper as legal tender for the payment of private debts. Whether it is wise for Congress to exercise this power either in war or peace was a political question to be resolved by Congress and not the Court. The Court concluded that the Act of 1878 was valid and that the notes constituted legal tender for the discharge of defendant's debt.

---

[42] *Id.* at 664.

[43] 79 U.S. 687 (1871).

[44] 110 U.S. 421 (1884).

[45] FAIRMAN, *supra* note 5, at 771-72.

Justice Field dissented. At the outset, contrary to the majority, he proclaimed that "if there is anything in the history of the Constitution that can be established with moral certainty, it is that the framers of that instrument intended to prohibit the issuance of legal-tender notes both by the general government and by the states...."[46] He quoted extensively from Daniel Webster's opposition to paper money as legal tender. He reasoned that what had been "a plea of necessity" during the Civil War, now at a time with "a treasury overflowing," has become a "plea of convenience."[47] Field argued that there was simply no connection between the power of the government to borrow on the one hand and the power to declare that its notes constitute legal tender for debts incurred between private parties. Likewise, the power to coin money limits Congress to metallic currency rather than expanding it to paper. Field argued that only money can be constitutionally declared to be legal tender, and "money" as the term is used in the Constitution means precious metals with intrinsic value. Similar to Chase's argument in *Hepburn*, Field argued at length that requiring that paper money be legal tender for the discharge of debts was inconsistent with the spirit as well as the structure of the Constitution. Quite prophetically, he concluded that there was unlikely to be any restraint on "unlimited appropriations by the government for all imaginary schemes for public improvement, if the printing press can furnish the money that is need for them...."[48]

Juilliard decisively ended any further constitutional dispute over legal tender. The Court had moved from a close division on the issue to near unanimity. Only Justice Field, the most rigorous critic of paper money as legal tender, refused to yield an inch.

HEPBURN AND THE *LEGAL TENDER CASES* AS GREAT CASES

Although for many students of constitutional law, *Hepburn* and the *Legal Tender Cases* are largely a historical curiosity, they were certainly cases of utmost importance at the time and are indeed a part of the foundation of the modern national and world economies. It is difficult to imagine our economy without paper money as legal tender, and yet but for the *Legal Tender Cases* or some subsequent opinion reaching the same result, we would presumably be paying our debts and making our purchases primarily with gold or silver coins or at least with private bank notes. Thus the significance of the decisions is difficult to overstate.

The momentousness of the issues did not seem to deter a majority from initially invalidating an Act of extreme national significance and then reversing itself in less than two years. Indeed, the greatness of the cases probably contributed to both decisions. It seems clear from Chase's opinion for the Court in *Hepburn* that he and the other justices in the majority were convinced that the continued authorization of paper money as legal tender would do substantial harm to the nation through the depreciation of the currency. Likewise the majority that reversed *Hepburn* believed just as strongly that failure to do so would have devastating financial consequences.

---

[46] 110 U.S. at 451.

[47] *Id.* at 458.

[48] *Id.* at 470.

Hepburn and the *Legal Tender Cases* evoked a significant response by the press and public but to a large extent the response was dictated by ideology and self-interest. Debtors favored paper as legal tender. Creditors did not. Republicans favored the Act and its validation. Democrats did not. Nationalists favored the *Legal Tender Cases*. The defenders of limited government preferred *Hepburn*. According to Charles Warren "most thoughtful men believed that the evils [of legal tender] outweighed the benefits."[49]

There was also disagreement over which was worse for the nation—an ideologically based decision in *Hepburn* that was quite probably inconsistent with the demands of the bustling post–Civil War economy or an arguably politically driven near instantaneous reversal. Critics battled over which was more harmful to the long-term reputation of the Court.[50] Chief Justice Charles Evans Hughes famously characterized the *Legal Tender Cases* as one of the three great self-inflicted wounds in the history of the Court; however he did not base this conclusion on the fact that *Hepburn* had invalidated the Act.[51] Rather, he argued that "the reopening of the case was a serious mistake and the overruling in such a short time by one vote, of the previous decision shook popular respect for the Court."[52]

Although *Hepburn* had been lingering in the Supreme Court for over four years, Chase seemed to push it forward once it had been argued in order to preempt a different result once two new justices took their seats. Given the central role that Chase had played in the enactment of the Legal Tender Act, it can be questioned whether he should have participated in the case at all despite the fact that he obviously was not biased in favor of the Act. In his dissent in the *Legal Tender Cases*, he attempted to explain away his role in the passage of the Legal Tender Act, but the explanation does not seem particularly convincing. It is scarcely the only case in which a justice has reversed course from a position he had taken in a different public capacity; however it is quite possibly the most remarkable such instance. It is unusual in that in *Hepburn* and in his *Legal Tender Cases* dissent, Chase not only argued that the law was clearly unconstitutional but that it was terrible economic policy as well. Perhaps both questions appeared quite different while in the midst of the economic chaos of the Civil War.

The fact that the majority in *Hepburn* driven by Chase relied on the vote of Grier, who appeared to have been mentally confused, and pressed the case forward to avoid consideration by the Court at full strength, which would almost certainly have been sympathetic to the Act, cast an immediate pall over the decision. It seems that Grier did in fact vote to invalidate the Act. Still the sequence of events suggests a Court operating in an injudicious manner. It appeared to many contemporary observers as it does now to be an instance, not unlike *Dred Scott*, in which a chief justice and some of the other justices were intent on achieving a specific result and were more than prepared to do whatever was necessary to get there. As such, *Hepburn* is scarcely one of the Court's finest hours. The fact that the decision-making process was flawed in *Hepburn* quite obviously contributed to the willingness of the newly reconstituted Court to reconsider the issue decided by Hepburn almost immediately. The feud that had developed between Chase and Miller

---

[49] WARREN, *supra* note 18, at 221.

[50] *Id.* at 240–50 for a collection of press commentary pro and con.

[51] CHARLES EVANS HUGHES, THE SUPREME COURT OF THE UNITED STATES 51–52 (1928).

[52] *Id.* at 52.

in the wake of *Hepburn* almost certainly added to the momentum to reconsider the decision. Under the circumstances, with the addition of two new justices, a majority of the Court simply did not consider the issue of legal tender, even with respect to pre-existing contracts, definitively settled despite *Hepburn*.

From the standpoint of precedent and stare decisis, the cases are unique. Never has the Court overruled such an important case so rapidly. Nor has it done so as a result of the appointment of two new justices, especially given that one of the two was the result of expansion of the size of the Court (although only to restore the Court to its prior size of nine justices). Given that the crucial fifth vote to reverse was attributable to the congressional addition of another justice, it was asserted at the time that Grant had packed the Court to achieve a specific result.[53] However, that is hardly accurate given that the restoration of the Court to nine justices was in the works before the *Hepburn* decision was announced. Still it would seem likely that in filling the two vacancies that immediately presented themselves as *Hepburn* was being decided, President Grant would certainly take advantage of the opportunity to nominate justices favorably disposed to paper money as legal tender, especially as several cases raising the question of its legality, at least for subsequently incurred debts, were already on the Court's docket. Indeed as Charles Warren has noted, Grant would have been hard-pressed to find Republican nominees who were not disposed to reconsider *Hepburn*.[54] Still, the swift reversal of *Hepburn* was at the very least a pleasant surprise for the president.

At the time, it was alleged that Grant had obtained an assurance from at least Bradley that he would vote to reverse *Hepburn*. If so, it would have been unethical for both in that the nominee would essentially be compromising his objectivity in exchange for a seat on the Court. Given that Grant sent the nominations of Strong and Bradley to the Senate at the very moment when the *Hepburn* decision was being announced, he would have to have had advance notice of the decision. Apparently Chase leaked the result in *Hepburn* to the secretary of the treasury two weeks before the opinion was released in view of the possibility that the decision would cause fiscal disruption.[55] Charles Warren asserted that Grant would not have known of the outcome before the decision was announced, which seems unlikely if his secretary of the treasury had been informed.[56] But even assuming that Grant had been informed of the result in *Hepburn* in advance, Charles Fairman has argued strenuously and at great length that Bradley and Strong were men of great integrity and neither would have given Grant a pledge to vote a certain way with respect to any case.[57] Considering the sequence of events, the consensus among historians is that Grant did not obtain pre-commitments from either appointee but rather simply appointed justices whom he believed would support his views of the Constitution, as most presidents do. The opportunity to alter both the size and direction of the Court combined with the immediate decision to reconsider such a precedent fueled speculation that something improper had occurred. The fact that the decision to reconsider *Hepburn* came within six

---

[53] WARREN, *supra* note 18, at 248 (quoting press charges to that effect).

[54] *Id.* at 240.

[55] Fairman, *supra* note 23, at 979.

[56] WARREN, *supra* note 18, at 239.

[57] Charles Fairman, *Mr. Justice Bradley's Appointment to the Supreme Court and the Legal Tender Cases* II, 54 HARV. L. REV. 1128 (1941).

weeks of the confirmation of Bradley created the appearance that the new majority could scarcely wait to reverse course.

The momentousness of the issues also contributed to the majority's willingness to revisit the case almost immediately. Indeed, Justice Strong began his majority opinion by stressing the devastating effect that invalidation of the Act would have on the nation and the economy.[58] And at the end of his opinion, in an attempt to justify the rapid reversal of *Hepburn*, Strong pointed to the fact that the case had not been decided by a full Court, but also emphasized that it was appropriate to reconsider a decision that was of "the most vital importance to the government and the public at large."[59] Justice Bradley was even more explicit in explaining that the "greatness" of the case was justification for reconsideration. He noted that "[w]here the decision is recent, and is only made by a bare majority of the court, and during a time of public excitement on the subject, when the question has largely entered into the political discussions of the day, I consider it our right and duty to subject it to a further examination...."[60] Moreover he was "so convinced that" *Hepburn* "was erroneous and prejudicial to the rights, interests and safety of the general government" that he had "no hesitation in reviewing and overruling it."[61] Thus for Justice Bradley the book simply could not be closed on an issue of this character by one decision, especially a decision of somewhat questionable legitimacy. That was of course the same approach that Lincoln had taken with respect to the *Dred Scott* Case. For the majority in the *Legal Tender Cases* the greatness of the case seemed to be a solid justification for what the justices perceived as a need to correct a very unfortunate error.

It isn't easy to evaluate the opinions in *Hepburn* and the *Legal Tender Cases* from the perspective of an integrated economy in which it is all but impossible to imagine our world without paper money as legal tender. From the world we know, *Hepburn* can readily appear to be a reactionary decision even in its own time. That view is certainly re-enforced by the weakness of Chase's opinion for the majority, which was more concerned with the economics of the matter than with the law. The fact that Chase seemed intent on pushing the case forward before Grant could add justices likely to disagree also casts a pall over *Hepburn*. The dissents in *Hepburn* as well as the majority opinion in the *Legal Tender Cases* simply demolished Chase's crabbed view of the Necessary and Proper Clause that had so forcefully been rejected by Marshall in *McCulloch*. Just as the outcome of the Civil War ensured that Marshall's popular sovereignty theory expounded in *McCulloch* was accepted as the true understanding of constitutional origin, so the *Legal Tender Cases* ensured that his generous view of the Necessary and Proper Clause would prevail. Had Chase's opinion in *Hepburn* remained the law of the land, *McCulloch* would scarcely be the foundational case it has become, although it is difficult to imagine that the *Hepburn* analysis could have survived into the mid-twentieth century in any event. Likewise, Chase's "spirit of the Constitution" argument, though borrowed to some extent from Marshall in *McCulloch*, seems strange and threatening if constitutional text matters. Once again the dissent tore it apart.

---

[58] *Legal Tender Cases*, 79 U.S. 457, 529 (1870).
[59] *Id.* at 554.
[60] *Id.* at 570.
[61] *Id.*

Justice Field, probably the keenest legal mind on the Court at the time, wrote the most thorough challenge to the constitutionality of the Legal Tender Act in either of the cases. He provided a stronger argument than Chase that making the notes legal tender was not necessary and proper given that they would circulate effectively as payment for government debts. Moreover, the taxing and borrowing powers and the power to sell government property gave Congress ample means to finance the war. Even so, a fair reading of *McCulloch* would suggest that the question of necessity was almost always for Congress rather than the Court to determine. Field and Clifford had an answer to that argument however. Although the Necessary and Proper Clause should be construed spaciously in the absence of other constitutional constraints, it should not be construed so broadly as to undermine other enumerated powers. Clifford argued that the Coinage Clause, properly understood, limited legal tender to precious metals. If Congress could use the war powers boosted by the Necessary and Proper Clause to make paper legal tender, then the explicit limits of this enumerated power would be evaded. Likewise, Field argued that the clear enumeration of three specific powers by which Congress could raise revenue negated other alternatives. As such, the Necessary and Proper Clause should not be employed as a means of deviating from the constitutional text and structure. The clause is not a constitutional wild card but rather must be interpreted within the context of the document as a whole. Perhaps these arguments are not sufficiently powerful to overcome the force of *McCulloch* in the context of a civil war but they do reveal that there was a better case against the constitutionality of the Act than had been set forth by Chase.

The dissenters in the *Legal Tender Cases* argued that the framers of the Constitution were adamantly opposed to the issuance of paper money, period, and that the concept of paper money as legal tender would have been an anathema to them. A powerful case can be made that paper money as legal tender is contrary to the original understanding of the Constitution.[62] However James B. Thayer argued,[63] as had the Court in *Juilliard*, that the Convention had left the issue open. The dissenters emphasized the original understanding but did not seem to suggest that it was conclusive. For an originalist justice however, presumably it would be. That in turn raises the question of whether the Court should ignore a clear showing of original understanding on account of public necessity. The justices in the dissent essentially dodged this question by arguing that even at the height of the Civil War, there was no public necessity to employ paper currency as legal tender in view of other viable alternatives. But what if there was not? Should the demands of the Civil War take precedence over constitutional limitations? Possibly. After the war was concluded, should the demand for a more efficient monetary system in a world quite different than that known to the framers justify the Court in ignoring the original understanding? For a dedicated originalist, almost certainly not. Constitutional amendment though difficult would be the proper answer. For a proponent of a living or evolving constitution approach, presumably the Court would be warranted in ignoring the original understanding under these circumstances and indeed would be subject to harsh criticism if it did not. *Hepburn* and the *Legal Tender Cases* arguably presented a test for original

---

[62] Dam, *supra* note 3, at 389; BERNARD SCHWARTZ, A HISTORY OF THE SUPREME COURT 156 (1994).
[63] James B. Thayer, *Legal Tender*, 1 HARV. L. REV. 73 (1887).

understanding as a methodology. Is the original understanding simply one of many relevant considerations, as even the dissenting justices seemed to believe, or is it the touchstone for constitutionality, as a modern originalist might argue?

Hepburn and the *Legal Tender Cases* certainly were appropriate cases for the Court to decide. They raised significant questions that were crucial to the operation of the commercial system. Similar to *Dred Scott*, the cases presented a political and economic issue on which the nation was deeply divided. The issuance of greenbacks as legal tender was a recent development born of the necessities of the war and quite inconsistent with the nation's financial traditions. The peacetime continuation of paper money as legal tender raised serious economic questions, but the public was divided as to whether soft money would have a positive or negative impact on the financial future of the nation. In such a context, the Court should have tread cautiously in an attempt to ensure that it did not stray from the domain of law into that of economics and policy. Clearly the majority did not do that. That hardly means that the Court should have avoided the issue, as in fact it did during the Civil War and for a few years thereafter, nor that it necessarily was required to uphold the Act. There were in fact significant legal arguments as to its unconstitutionality. However the Court should have stuck with traditional legal arguments, applied the precedent faithfully, shown at least some deference to the existing legislative judgments, and made sure to proceed in an unassailable judicious manner. Unfortunately, Chief Justice Chase and the majority did none of these. Consequently, the Court issued an opinion that was readily perceived as a transparent attempt to achieve a political result. But instead of achieving that end, the Court simply paved the way to near immediate reversal.

Had the Court waited a few years to reconsider *Hepburn*, a decision to reverse would not have seemed quite so political. The Court does reverse prior decisions from time to time. But considering that the question of the constitutionality of the Act with respect to subsequent contracts remained open, and the answer to that question was of great significance to the economy, arguably the Court needed to speak sooner rather than later. As *Hepburn* created the uncertainty over the constitutionality of the Legal Tender Act, it can be blamed for the precipitous reconsideration. It is understandable that if a majority of the Court believed that the previous majority had made an extreme error of constitutional interpretation with serious ramifications for the economy of the nation, the ordinary respect for stare decisis must yield. But the Court had to realize that such a reversal of course was scarcely cost free.

Did the cases make bad law? In a strictly doctrinal sense, Chase's opinion in *Hepburn* certainly did in that it grossly misinterpreted the Necessary and Proper Clause as expounded by Marshall in *McCulloch* and injected an unmanageable "spirit of the Constitution" approach into the jurisprudence. On the other hand a more respectable constitutional justification for the result could have been offered as Field and Clifford showed in their *Legal Tender Cases* dissents. Regardless of whether the prohibition of paper money as legal tender had a credible constitutional rationale, it is difficult to believe that the principle could have survived into the mid-twentieth century. Either the Court would have eventually reversed course as the near unanimous opinion in *Juillard* suggests was likely or the Constitution would have been amended, probably during the Progressive Era. That does not mean that Field was wrong as a matter of constitutional interpretation. But it certainly means that his principles, however well-grounded in the text and original understanding, could not have endured. In that sense, in the long term at least, even a well-reasoned opinion in *Hepburn* would have eventually made bad law.

To some extent, *Hepburn* and the *Legal Tender Cases* suggest that the Court was not nearly as humbled by the *Dred Scott* decision delivered only 13 years earlier as has been alleged. Indeed both *Hepburn* and the *Legal Tender Cases* suggest that the Court was not simply confident but downright arrogant. The justices were quite prepared to take center stage in resolving a question of extreme political and economic controversy and consequence. Perhaps nothing would have served the Court better at this point than a healthy dose of humility. But to a large extent the very concept of a great case is dependent on a confident Court to hear and decide it. Some have argued that *Dred Scott*, *Hepburn*, and the *Legal Tender Cases* adversely affected the Court's standing with the public. If so, these cases did not necessarily dampen the Court's confidence. On the very day that the opinions in the *Legal Tender Cases* were released, the Court began to hear oral arguments in the *Slaughter-House Cases*, one of the greatest cases of all.

"No questions so far-reaching and pervading in their consequences, so profoundly interesting to the people of this country, and so important in their bearing upon the relations
of the United States, and of the several States to each other and to the citizens of the
States and of the United States, have been before this court during the official life of any
of its present members."[1]

JUSTICE MILLER WRITING FOR THE MAJORITY IN THE *SLAUGHTER-HOUSE CASES*

7

The *Slaughter-House Cases*

UNLIKE MOST GREAT cases, the factual dispute that gave rise to the *Slaughter-House
Cases*, whether a group of butchers in New Orleans could ply their trade only at one particular state-sanctioned slaughterhouse in the city, did not provoke significant public
interest at the time.[2] And yet each of the justices who wrote opinions in the case commented on how this was one of the most significant cases ever presented to the Court. If
the public did not recognize that this was a case of monumental significance, the justices
certainly did. It was in fact the first case in which the Court would construe the substantive guarantees of the Fourteenth Amendment, the constitutional centerpiece of Reconstruction. The justices well understood that their decision would have a major impact
on the constitutional law and the nation itself for the indefinite future as indeed it did.

THE BACKGROUND

The three consolidated cases that assumed the official name the *Slaughter-House Cases*
involved challenges to a recent Louisiana law that created a single central slaughterhouse
in New Orleans operated by a private corporation, which all butchers were required to
use.[3] There is no question that the city had been suffering serious health problems as the
result of unregulated slaughterhouses dumping their waste into the Mississippi River
above the city's water supply.[4] There were approximately 150 separate slaughterhouses in

---

[1] 83 U.S. 36, 67 (1873).

[2] BERNARD SCHWARTZ, A HISTORY OF THE SUPREME COURT 158–59 (1993).

[3] 83 U.S. at 58–59. Robert McCloskey refers to it as "a 'carpetbag' legislature." ROBERT G. MCCLOSKEY, THE
AMERICAN SUPREME COURT 78 (2d ed. 1994). One case was brought by butchers challenging the legislation.
Another was brought by the state defending it. A third was brought by the beneficiaries of the monopoly
attempting to exclude other butchers from the slaughterhouse business. 83 U.S. at 85 (Field, J., dissenting).

[4] RONALD M. LABBE & JONATHAN LURIE, THE *SLAUGHTER-HOUSE CASES*: REGULATION, RECONSTRUCTION,
AND THE FOURTEENTH AMENDMENT 12–24 (2005).

the city at the time that the Act was passed.[5] Under the Act, a large slaughterhouse would be constructed south of the city to be operated by the Crescent City Live-Stock Landing and Slaughterhouse Company.[6] The Act provided that all members of the company had the "exclusive" privilege of using the facility for a period of 25 years. All other butchers could use this facility on payment of a fee; however they could not open or operate their own slaughterhouses.[7] It was alleged that bribery of members of the legislature and the press led to the passage of the Act although that has never been proven.[8] The Act was unpopular at least in part because it was the product of a state legislature created during Reconstruction with substantial membership of African Americans.[9]

The Act was challenged by several butchers who were not a part of the Crescent City Company. The butchers hired former Supreme Court justice John Campbell, one of the leading appellate advocates in the nation, to represent them. Campbell charged that the Act had created a monopoly excluding the butchers from their chosen trade and that this was inconsistent with both the common law and the Constitution. Extensive litigation in the local courts ensued. At one point there were over 200 lawsuits pending and over 500 separate injunctions from several different courts in place, many in direct conflict with each other.[10] It appeared that the cases would end when the Louisiana Supreme Court rejected the butchers' challenges to the Act. That changed, however, when Justice Joseph P. Bradley writing for the federal circuit court struck down the Act as a violation of the Fourteenth Amendment. Even then, a compromise between the company and most of the butchers might have ended the litigation but for the fact that several individual butchers determined to go forward with the challenges, which by then were pending before the United States Supreme Court. Although the Act in question appeared to be an ordinary example of police power legislation, the butchers based their challenge on the substantive provisions of the Fourteenth Amendment ratified only four years earlier. As such, the case presented the Court with its first significant opportunity to construe the amendment, which was the crowning achievement of the Reconstruction Congress.

The case was argued in 1872 and again in 1873 because, as the Court noted, one justice (Justice Nelson) missed the initial argument due to illness, and the Court was split four to four. Justice Nelson resigned between the arguments and was replaced by Justice Ward Hunt, who after the second argument broke the tie. The Court granted four hours to each side for argument, twice the normal time generally allotted, given the importance of the case. Its apparent magnitude was enhanced by the fact that the butchers were represented before the Court by former justice Campbell. According to the reporter, Justice Campbell "gave a vivid and very interesting account of the conditions and grievances of the lower orders in various countries of Europe, especially in France...."[11] Indeed Justice Campbell provided a lengthy and detailed history of oppression through monopoly in

---

[5] *Id.* at 26.

[6] *Id.* at 57.

[7] *Id.* at 59–60.

[8] *Id.* at 54. *See also* Michael Les Benedict, *The Slaughter-House Cases, in* THE OXFORD COMPANION TO THE SUPREME COURT OF THE UNITED STATES 789 (Kermit L. Hall ed., 1992).

[9] LABBE & LURIE, *supra* note 4, at 6.

[10] *Id.* at 78.

[11] *Id.* at 45.

France, Scotland, and England before ever turning his attention to the Fourteenth Amendment. According to Robert McCloskey "[t]he Court was visibly shaken by [Justice Campbell's] brilliant improvisation" turning the Reconstruction Amendments into a charter of free market capitalism.[12] Matthew Carpenter, a former senator who was one of the draftsmen of the Fourteenth Amendment, appeared on behalf of Louisiana in defense of the Act.

JUSTICE MILLER'S OPINION

Before addressing the challenges based on the Reconstruction Amendments, Justice Samuel Miller, writing for a five-justice majority, noted quite correctly that the plaintiffs were not prohibited from plying their trade as butchers but must do so in the defendant's slaughterhouse. In that regard, the deprivation was nowhere near as extreme as Justice Campbell and the dissents portrayed it. Miller observed that through the "police power," states have the right to regulate businesses such as slaughterhouses, which pose definite risks to the public health.

Miller then dismissed the argument that the monopoly violated the Thirteenth Amendment prohibition of involuntary servitude, noting that the Amendment was concerned with human slavery not with common law servitudes on property. The Court devoted the remainder of its opinion to the Fourteenth Amendment. The second sentence of the first section of the amendment sets forth three substantive guarantees of protection against state governments. It protects any person against deprivation of life, liberty, or property without due process of law. It prohibits the state from denying any person within its jurisdiction equal protection of the laws. As a direct result of the Court's decision in The *Slaughter-House Cases*, these two provisions have loomed very large in constitutional jurisprudence over the past 100 years. But there is every reason to believe that the framers of the Fourteenth Amendment intended the first substantive guarantee, which prohibited any state from making or enforcing any law that abridged the Privileges or Immunities of citizens of the United States, to be the primary vehicle for the enforcement of civil rights against state governmental abridgment.[13] This would seem to be confirmed by the fact that both the majority and the dissents discussed the Privileges or Immunities Clause at great length but dismissed the due process and equal protection arguments as all but irrelevant.

Justice Miller explained that it was crucial for the Court to come to grips with the purpose of the Reconstruction Amendments. Characterizing the events that resulted in the passage of the Amendment as "almost too recent to be called history, but which are familiar to us all," he concluded that "the one pervading purpose" of the amendments was freedom of "the slave race" as well as the establishment of security and protection of freedmen from oppression.[14] This was unquestionably correct; however it immediately placed the contentions of the butchers at a disadvantage as they were not former slaves nor were they the subject of racial discrimination or oppression. Justice Miller conceded as he must that the language of the Fourteenth Amendment was general and not limited

---

[12] McCloskey, *supra* note 3, at 79.

[13] *See* Schwartz, *supra* note 2, at 159.

[14] *Slaughter-House Cases*, 83 U.S. 36, 71 (1872).

to racial subjugation. However in construing the amendment, it was still necessary to be guided by its purpose. For Justice Miller and the majority, although the purpose did not necessarily displace the text, it went a long way toward explaining it.

To understand the Privileges or Immunities Clause, Miller initially focused on the first sentence of Section One of the amendment, which provides that "[a]ll persons born or naturalized in the United States, and subject to the jurisdiction thereof, are citizens of the United States and of the State wherein they reside." He noted that the primary purpose of this sentence was to overrule the *Dred Scott* Case[15] in which Chief Justice Taney had declared that an African American could never be a citizen of a state or of the United States. But for purposes of the *Slaughter-House Cases*, the significance of this sentence was that it seemed to recognize two types of constitutionally protected citizenship—that of the state and that of the nation. This was crucial to the majority because the substantive guarantee in the next sentence spoke only to "Privileges or Immunities of citizens of the United States." Given this distinction, the Court focused on those rights that were inherent in federal as opposed to state citizenship. Miller's distinction between state and federal citizenship has been heavily criticized by commentators as unsupported by the text or the original understanding.[16]

But in order to come to grips with the meaning of the privileges or immunities of United States' citizenship, Miller first attempted to discern the content of the privileges and immunities of state citizenship. He noted that the concept of privileges or immunities of state citizenship initially appeared in the Articles of Confederation. The clause was then placed in Article IV of the original Constitution. The early definitive construction of that provision was rendered by Justice Bushrod Washington riding circuit in the District of Pennsylvania in the case of *Corfield v. Coryell*.[17] Justice Miller quoted (though somewhat inaccurately and incompletely) from Justice Washington's opinion where he had declared that privileges and immunities of state citizenship include those rights that are fundamental, such as acquiring and possessing property and pursuing and obtaining happiness.[18] Miller explained that Article IV by its terms was not intended to create these rights but rather to ensure that to the extent that a state extended them to its own citizens, it must extend them to visitors from other states as well.

He then observed that prior to the passage of the Fourteenth Amendment, no one would have suggested that the protection of these basic civil rights was dependent upon the federal government rather than the states. That in turn brought the Court to the central issue of the case. As the right that the butchers were asserting, the right to pursue their common calling, would seem to be the type of fundamental right easily

---

[15] Scott v. Sanford, 60 U.S. 393 (1857).

[16] *See, e.g.*, John Harrison, *Reconstructing the Privileges and Immunities Clause*, 101 YALE L.J. 1385, 1415 (1992).

[17] 4 Washington's Circuit Court 371.

[18] *Slaughter-House Cases*, 83 U.S. at 76. Justice Bradley, dissenting, pointed out that Justice Miller misquoted *Coryell* as referring to the privileges or immunities "of" the several states rather than "in" the several states, which to Justice Bradley bore substantive implications. *Id.* at 116–17. In describing the rights that Justice Washington deemed to be fundamental, Justice Miller also omitted the reference to "the enjoyment of life and liberty" that arguably covered the conduct in issue in this case. *See* Kevin Newsom, *Setting Incorporation Straight: A Reinterpretation of the Slaughter-House Cases*, 109 YALE L.J. 643, 673 (2000).

encompassed within the *Corfield* definition, should the Fourteenth Amendment be read as having been "intended to bring within the power of Congress the entire domain of civil rights heretofore belonging exclusively to the States?"[19] Was the Fourteenth Amendment intended to "radically [change] the whole theory of the relations of the State and Federal governments to each other and of both of these governments to the people"?[20] The very statement of the issue explains why the Court understood that it was confronting a great case. Essentially it was being asked to rule on the central meaning of Reconstruction, if not the Civil War itself, and in a manner that would almost certainly have a profound impact on the nation's constitutional future.

Placing decisive reliance upon the possible consequences of endorsing the butchers' conception of privileges or immunities, the majority concluded that such a result could not have been intended by either Congress or the states that ratified the Fourteenth Amendment. From Justice Miller's perspective, if the butchers were correct, then Congress would be responsible for protecting the basic rights of citizens and could significantly restrict the ways in which state legislatures could regulate matters traditionally within their domains. Indeed such an approach would "constitute this court a perpetual censor upon all legislation of the States [and] on the civil rights of their own citizens...."[21] The majority conceded that an argument "drawn from consequences" "is not always the most conclusive."[22]

However when "these consequences are so serious, so far-reaching and pervading, so great a departure from the structure and spirit of our institutions; when the effect is to fetter and degrade the State governments by subjecting them to the control of Congress, in the exercise of powers heretofore universally conceded to them of the most ordinary and fundamental character; when in fact it radically changes the whole theory of the relations of the State and Federal governments to each other and of both of these governments to the people," then such an interpretation must be rejected as incorrect.[23]

Forgetting everything else in the opinion, this lengthy conclusion as to the radical nature of the plaintiffs' theory is without question the very essence of the Court's decision in the *Slaughter-House Cases*. The Court was invited by former justice Campbell, on behalf of the petitioners, to proclaim that the Fourteenth Amendment had indeed significantly altered American federalism. The majority simply could not accept that conclusion.[24]

Up to that point, the Court had not addressed the content of the privileges or immunities of United States' citizenship. Rather, it had considered the nature of the plaintiffs' claim and concluded that they were asserting instead a privilege or immunity of state citizenship. Lest it be accused of deciding that there were no privileges or immunities of United States' citizenship, however, the Court attempted to acknowledge some. It

---

[19] *Slaughter-House Cases*, 83 U.S. at 77.

[20] *Id.* at 78.

[21] *Id.*

[22] *Id.*

[23] *Id.*

[24] Relying on the recent history of the passage of the Fourteenth Amendment which Justice Miller had referred to, William Nelson has argued that Miller and the majority simply had to know that this conclusion was just flat wrong. WILLIAM E, NELSON, THE FOURTEENTH AMENDMENT: FROM POLITICAL PRINCIPLE TO JUDICIAL DOCTRINE 163 (1988).

declared that such privileges include the right to come to the seat of government, to seek its protection, to do business with its offices, to access its seaports and courts, to demand its protection on the high seas, to peaceably assemble, to employ the right of habeas corpus, to use the navigable waters, and to rely on rights secured by treaties. None of these rights, however, were useful to the butchers in their challenge. Consequently the Court concluded "the rights claimed by these plaintiffs... are not privileges and immunities of citizens of the United States...."[25]

Next the Court responded briefly to the due process argument raised by the plaintiffs but dismissed it, noting that "under no construction" of that clause could the alleged monopoly created by the Louisiana legislature be considered a deprivation of property. As for equal protection, the Court doubted that it would ever be applied to anything other than racial discrimination given that that was so clearly its purpose. Having thus rejected all of the plaintiffs' arguments, the Court affirmed the judgment of the Supreme Court of Louisiana.

JUSTICE FIELD'S DISSENT

The *Slaughter-House Cases* rejected an expansive interpretation of the Fourteenth Amendment and effectively deprived the Privileges or Immunities Clause of any significance. The case was decided by a five-to-four vote however over vigorous dissents. The lengthiest dissent joined by all of the dissenting justices was filed by Justice Field. As with the majority, Field emphasized that "[t]he question presented is... one of the gravest importance, not merely to the parties here, but to the whole country."[26] That question was whether the Reconstruction Amendments "protect the citizens of the United States against the deprivation of their common rights by State legislation."[27] At the outset, Justice Field contended that the police power simply did not justify prohibiting the plaintiffs from opening their own slaughterhouse in the same area as the defendants. He was more disposed toward the Thirteenth Amendment involuntary servitude argument than was the majority; however after discussing it briefly he moved on to the Fourteenth Amendment privileges or immunities question that was plainly at the heart of the case.

Justice Field agreed with the Court that the Fourteenth Amendment was not intended to "confer any new privileges or immunities upon citizens."[28] However he disagreed completely as to the type of pre-existing privileges that the clause did protect. He pointed out quite effectively that if the clause protected only the type of rights suggested by the majority, then "it was a vain and idle enactment, which accomplished nothing" as virtually all of the rights listed by the Court were already explicitly or implicitly protected by the Constitution.[29] If, however, "the amendment refers to the natural and inalienable rights which belong to all citizens, the inhibition has a profound significance and consequence."[30] This was a powerful argument; however, reliance on natural rights also raised

---

[25] *Slaughter-House Cases*, 83 U.S. at 80.
[26] *Id.* at 89.
[27] *Id.*
[28] *Id.* at 96.
[29] *Id.*
[30] *Id.*

the specter of undefined and limitless coverage. The Fourteenth Amendment with the Privileges or Immunities Clause at its core was understood to be extraordinarily significant. In the words of Justice Field it "excited Congress and the people on its passage."[31] It seems intuitively correct that the majority's narrow interpretation of the clause and of the amendment would hardly justify such enthusiasm.

Instead, Justice Field suggested that the type of rights specified in the Civil Rights Act of 1866, including the right to contract, sue, and hold property, were the type of rights that would qualify as privileges or immunities as a recognized purpose of the Fourteenth Amendment was to provide a constitutional basis for the protection of these rights against state infringement. These were the "civil" rights that states had traditionally protected. If so limited, the privileges or immunities would be given a defined yet significant meaning. However Field made it clear that the Civil Rights Act merely catalogued "some of the rights" encompassed by the Privileges or Immunities Clause, and most important, it did not refer to the right involved in this particular case, the right to pursue a common calling. So something more was needed.

Field quoted the same language from *Corfield v. Coryell* as had Justice Miller but drew a very different conclusion. Miller had used this language characterizing "the right to acquire and possess property of every kind, and to pursue and obtain happiness" as privileges and immunities of state citizenship under Article IV as proof that these fundamental civil rights had been and remained within the domain of state as opposed to federal protection.[32] Justice Field agreed that as of the time of *Corfield* prior to Reconstruction, these were privileges and immunities of state citizenship. Relying on a statement by Senator Trumbull during the debates on the Civil Rights Act, Field argued that the type of privileges and immunities mentioned in *Corfield* were the very sort to be protected as privileges of United States' citizenship. Thus for Justice Miller, Corfield was evidence of what remained within the state domain while for Justice Field it was evidence of what the Fourteenth Amendment had included in the federal domain.

Field believed that the purpose of the Privileges or Immunities Clause of the Fourteenth Amendment was to provide a citizen of a state protection against infringement of fundamental civil rights (such as those claimed by the butchers) by his or her own state just as the Privileges and Immunities Clause of Article IV extends protection of these rights to a citizen of another state against infringement by a state in which he or she is temporarily present. As such, the Privileges or Immunities Clause filled a constitutional gap. Prior to the amendment, a citizen from another state was protected against deprivation of a right by a state in which he was temporarily present whereas a citizen of that very state had no federal constitutional protection against deprivation of that very same right by his or her own state. For Field and the dissenters, the Fourteenth Amendment was intended to address and resolve this anomaly.

From Justice Miller's perspective however there was no gap or anomaly. Even Justice Field admitted that Article IV did not create rights but only offered constitutional protection to the out-of-state citizen of those rights that the state had provided to its own citizens. Thus for Justice Miller and the majority, the state already provided all of the

---

[31] *Id.*
[32] *Id.* at 76.

protection that the in-state citizen was entitled to under state law. As state law did not necessarily protect out-of-state citizens, Article IV had been necessary to fill that gap. However there was no gap to be filled with respect to in-state citizens as state law was sufficient. Justice Field disagreed. He seemed to believe that either state law might sometimes fail to protect basic rights that were worthy of protection, or that even if it did, in a given case, perhaps such as this one, it would not be adequately enforced by state courts. Consequently, a constitutional backstop was needed, and that is exactly what the Fourteenth Amendment was intended to provide. As he put it, the Fourteenth Amendment placed the privileges or immunities of United States' citizenship "under the guardianship of the National authority."[33] He maintained that the "equality of right" to pursue "ordinary avocations of life" is "the distinguishing privilege of citizens of the United States."[34] The Constitution was not creating a new privilege or immunity but simply recognizing one that was deeply embedded in the nation's history, tradition, and common law. In conclusion, he lamented the majority's unwillingness to protect "the right of free labor, one of the most sacred and imprescriptible rights of man."[35] The language throughout Justice Field's opinion emphasizing the importance of equality with respect to the pursuit of trade and free labor clearly builds upon the Jacksonian antipathy to class-based legislation as well as the abolitionist free labor movement, both of which had become powerful cultural forces prior to the Civil War and remained so thereafter.[36] These were themes that Field would champion throughout his lengthy career on the Court. If Justice Miller and the majority had reason to fear that opening up the Privileges or Immunities Clause would vest the federal government with pervasive authority over state regulation, Justice Field did not give the majority any reason to believe that such a fear was unwarranted.

JUSTICE BRADLEY'S DISSENT

Justice Bradley also filed a dissenting opinion. He had actually decided a constitutional challenge to this monopoly in favor of the butchers two years earlier while riding circuit.[37] Like Miller and Field, Bradley also recognized the significance of the case, noting that the question of whether the right to pursue a common calling was a privilege or immunity of a citizen of the United States is "of vast importance, and lies at the very foundation of our government."[38] Like Field, Bradley relied heavily on what he perceived to be the strong historical basis of the right in issue. He characterized the rights as those of "citizens of any free government."[39] Given that the people "inherited certain traditionary rights and privileges from their ancestors, citizenship means something."[40] He argued that the privileges or immunities of United States' citizens were greatly expanded by the Fourteenth

---

[33] *Id.* at 101.

[34] *Id.* at 109–10.

[35] *Id.* at 110.

[36] *See* JEFFREY ROSEN, THE MOST DEMOCRATIC BRANCH: HOW THE COURTS SERVE AMERICA 48 (2006).

[37] Live-Stock Dealers & Butchers Ass'n v. Crescent City Live-Stock Landing & Slaughterhouse Co., 15 F. Cas. 649 (C.C.D. La. 1870).

[38] *Slaughter-House Cases*, 83 U.S. at 112.

[39] *Id.* at 114.

[40] *Id.*

Amendment in that it effectively incorporated much if not all of the Bill of Rights against the states. But even were that not the case, the right to pursue a trade or calling would be protected based on historical tradition.

Justice Bradley concluded that the Act did not qualify as a legitimate police power regulation, characterizing the requirement that a butcher slaughter his animals in someone else's slaughterhouse and pay a fee to do so as "onerous, unreasonable, arbitrary, and unjust."[41] The state could regulate a trade such as the operation of a slaughterhouse but it could not prohibit a qualified person from engaging in that calling. He impugned the law as "one of those arbitrary and unjust laws made in the interest of a few scheming individuals...."[42] As such, the slaughterhouse monopoly violated the Privileges or Immunities Clause of the Fourteenth Amendment, which was intended to protect against state infringement of "the fundamental rights of the citizens."[43] But unlike Field, Bradley also found that the Act violated the Fourteenth Amendment Due Process Clause as well in that the "right of choice [of employment] is a portion of their liberty" and "their occupations is their property."[44] The reference to due process was brief but it is important. Justice Bradley was relying on the concept of substantive due process first introduced into Supreme Court constitutional jurisprudence by Chief Justice Taney in the *Dred Scott* Case. In other words, he was claiming that there are certain aspects of liberty or property that the state simply does not have the right to infringe regardless of the procedural protection that may have preceded the decision. Though *Dred Scott* was discredited and indeed overruled by the first sentence of the Fourteenth Amendment, Justice Bradley effectively rescued one of its most controversial doctrinal concepts and planted it in the post-Reconstruction jurisprudence of the Court, even if only in a dissent. The privileges or immunities theory on which both Justices Field and Bradley placed such heavy reliance would never gain judicial acceptance; however the substantive due process argument that was simply noted in passing would come to dominate constitutional jurisprudence for decades.

Justice Bradley also declared that the law in issue deprived citizens of equal protection of the laws without any further elaboration. Given the persistent emphasis that both Justice Field and Bradley had placed on equality throughout their opinions, it seems unusual that neither attempted to build a cogent argument around the Equal Protection Clause. Perhaps this well illustrates the extent to which all of the justices understood that it was the Privileges or Immunities Clause that was intended by the framers to be the true centerpiece of the Fourteenth Amendment. Alternatively, perhaps the dissenters accepted the majority's conclusion that the Equal Protection Clause though general in its language was all but exclusively aimed at racial discrimination. Justice Bradley did explicitly note that the language of the Amendment was not limited to race; however he did not explicitly refer to the Equal Protection Clause in that regard.

Justice Bradley explained that "the mischief to be remedied [by the Amendment] was not merely slavery and its incidents and consequences; but that spirit of insubordination

---

[41] *Id.* at 119.
[42] *Id.* at 120.
[43] *Id.* at 122.
[44] *Id.*

and disloyalty to the National government which had troubled the country for so many years in some of the States...."[45] This observation was significant in two respects. It did reply to the majority's conclusion that the Equal Protection Clause, if not the amendment as a whole, was aimed overwhelmingly at racial oppression and discrimination. But beyond that, Justice Bradley explained that quite contrary to the majority's understanding, the Fourteenth Amendment was indeed intended to significantly change the nature of existing governmental relations in that it was "an attempt to give voice to the strong National yearning" for safety and the full protection of rights throughout the country.[46] It did represent a radical change in the federal structure.

Finally, in the last two paragraphs of his dissent, Bradley addressed what seemed to be the ultimate concerns that had led the majority to deny protection. He referred to the "great fears expressed" that his interpretation would lead to enactments by Congress interfering with the internal affairs of the states and thus "abolishing the State governments in everything but name."[47] He also noted the majority's fear that it would cause the federal courts to engage in "supervision of State tribunals on every subject of judicial inquiry...."[48] He concluded that neither of these threats was serious. There would be little need for congressional legislation in that the amendment would largely "execute itself." Likewise, privileges or immunities "would soon become so far defined as to cause but a slight accumulation of business in the Federal courts."[49] Moreover establishing the true meaning of the amendment would "prevent its frequent violation."[50]

Justice Bradley's counterarguments here are at best wishful thinking. Once Congress did become drawn into the protection of civil rights under the Fourteenth Amendment, nearly a century after the decision in the *Slaughter-House Cases*, it did in fact enact multiple and voluminous statutes regulating state conduct. And the Due Process and Equal Protection Clauses have given rise to tens of thousands of federal court cases in the century and one-half since the decision. Likewise, the intense resistance to civil rights enforcement encountered by the federal courts in the mid-twentieth century after the decision in *Brown v. Board of Education* gives lie to the claim that states would simply fall into line and obey.

Perhaps recognizing the weakness of these responses, Bradley declared that if litigation did arise, then Congress could simply "supply the remedy by increasing [the] number and efficiency" of the federal courts.[51] But ultimately Justice Bradley concluded his opinion by declaring that "[t]he argument from inconvenience," which was essentially the primary reason for the majority's decision, "ought not to have a very controlling influence in questions of this sort."[52] Basically, an extraordinarily significant constitutional provision should not be effectively nullified out of fear of adverse consequences.

---

[45] *Id.* at 123.

[46] *Id.*

[47] *Id.*

[48] *Id.*

[49] *Id.* at 124.

[50] *Id.*

[51] *Id.*

[52] *Id.* William Nelson has argued that Justice Bradley read the framers' purpose in expanding federal power more broadly than the legislative history of its passage warranted, just as Justice Miller read it more narrowly. NELSON, *supra* note 24, at 164.

JUSTICE SWAYNE'S DISSENT

Justice Swayne wrote a short dissent. Taking direct issue with the majority's primary conclusion, he argued that the Reconstruction Amendments did constitute a major restructuring of the federal system, a conclusion that the majority had found implausible. Rather these amendments "mark an important epoch in the constitutional history of the country" and "rise to the dignity of a new Magna Charta."[53]

Turning his attention to the provisions of the Fourteenth Amendment at issue, Justice Swayne did grossly overstate the clarity of the language in question. He wrote that:

Its language is intelligible and direct. Nothing can be more transparent. Every word employed has an established signification. There is no room for construction. There is nothing to construe. Elaboration may obscure, but cannot make clearer, the intent and purpose sought to be carried out.[54]

Contrary to this claim, a persuasive case has been made that the substantive provisions of the amendment were deliberately written at a high level of generality so that persons with very different conceptions of its meaning could accept it.[55] Like Justice Bradley, Swayne maintained that both the Privileges or Immunities and the Due Process Clause protected the rights claimed by the butchers.[56]

He also flatly rejected the majority's conclusion that the framers and ratifiers could not possibly have meant to significantly alter the basic structure of the federal system. To that he responded that "[t]he prejudices and apprehension as to the central government which prevailed when the Constitution was adopted were dispelled by the light of experience."[57] Instead "[t]he public mind became satisfied that there was less danger of tyranny in the head than of anarchy and tyranny in the members."[58] Finally, Justice Swayne was highly critical of the distinction that the majority had drawn between the rights of state and national citizenship, which he argued turned the amendment from "bread into a stone."[59] The final sentence of Justice Swayne's dissent lamented the potential adverse impact of the decision, hoping that "the consequences to follow may prove less serious and far-reaching than the minority fear they will be."[60]

THE AFTERMATH

Despite the Supreme Court's decision, the battle over the Crescent City slaughterhouse was still not over, even at the Court itself. Following the end of Reconstruction in 1876, Democrats regained control of the Louisiana legislature and drafted a new constitution

---

[53] *Slaughter-House Cases*, 83 U.S. at 125.

[54] *Id.* at 126.

[55] NELSON, *supra* note 24, at 110–47; MCCLOSKEY, *supra* note 3, at 78–79.

[56] *Slaughter-House Cases*, 83 U.S. at 125-26.

[57] *Id.* at 128.

[58] *Id.*

[59] *Id.* at 129.

[60] *Id.* at 130.

banning government-created monopolies and specifically repealing the Act creating the central slaughterhouse in New Orleans.[61] That in turn led to further litigation. The Louisiana Supreme Court upheld the repeal against a claim that it violated the clause prohibiting the state from impairing the obligations of a contract.[62] On the other hand, the federal circuit court in Louisiana invalidated the repeal on the grounds that it was not warranted by the police power. In *Butchers Benevolent Ass'n v. Crescent City Live Stock Co.*, the Supreme Court unanimously reversed the circuit court, holding that the state did not have the power to contract away the police power and that the repeal was valid.[63] Justices Field and Bradley wrote special concurrences maintaining as they had in their *Slaughter-House Cases* dissent that the original Act creating the company was and remained unconstitutional.[64] Nevertheless, even without the statutory guarantee of exclusivity, the slaughterhouse at the center of the controversy remained in operation for another 40 years even though the Crescent City Co. itself soon dissolved.

Like the Court, the nation was divided with respect to the appropriate coverage of the Fourteenth Amendment. As such, the Court's decision was both praised as a wise exposition of well-recognized principles of federalism and attacked as an attempt to cancel out the results of the Civil War and Reconstruction.[65] On balance however, it was well received by the press, including the Republican press.[66] The debate would continue for the next century and a half, although over time, the critics of the decision would gain the upper hand.

THE *SLAUGHTER-HOUSE CASES* AND CONSTITUTIONAL DOCTRINE

The *Slaughter-House Cases* appeared from the outset to be a potential landmark case—that is, a case of monumental importance to the development of the law—and indeed it turned out to be just that. Along with other cases decided in the latter half of the nineteenth century, especially *The Civil Rights Cases* and *Plessy v. Ferguson*, the *Slaughter-House Cases* significantly diluted the protection otherwise provided by the recently enacted Fourteenth Amendment just as the dissenters charged that it would. Most important, the decision eliminated for all practical purposes the Privileges or Immunities Clause as a viable constitutional provision despite the fact that it was quite arguably intended to be the very heart of civil rights protection against the states from Reconstruction onward. Despite reading the Fourteenth Amendment narrowly however, all of the justices assumed that it was legitimately a part of the Constitution, as Bruce Ackerman has noted.[67] This implicit validation was not inconsequential given the controversy over the fact that the states which had seceded were coerced into ratifying the amendment as the

---

[61] LABBE & LURIE, *supra* note 4, at 164–65.

[62] Crescent City Live Stock Landing & Slaughterhouse Co. v. City of New Orleans, 33 La Ann. 934 (1881).

[63] 111 U.S. 746 (1884).

[64] *Id.* at 760 (Bradley, J., concurring), 766 (Field, J., concurring).

[65] 3 CHARLES WARREN, THE SUPREME COURT IN UNITED STATES HISTORY 263–69 (1922) (collecting contemporaneous opinion pro and con).

[66] BARRY FRIEDMAN, THE WILL OF THE PEOPLE: HOW PUBLIC OPINION HAS INFLUENCED THE SUPREME COURT AND SHAPED THE MEANING OF THE CONSTITUTION 147 (2009).

[67] BRUCE ACKERMAN, WE THE PEOPLE, VOLUME 2: TRANSFORMATIONS 245 (1998).

price of complete re-inclusion.[68] Some historians have argued, however, that the Court in 1873 could scarcely be expected to foresee all that would occur over the next 50 years, especially with respect to race relations in the South.[69] There is no reason to assume bad faith on the part of the majority and as such, it is unfair to judge the Court too harshly as a matter of hindsight. That said, the dissenters did predict that the decision would have severe adverse consequences for the nation.

THE MEANING OF PRIVILEGES OR IMMUNITIES

The majority almost certainly took too crabbed of a view of the impact of the Fourteenth Amendment in general and of the Privileges or Immunities Clause in particular.[70] The counter interpretations set forth by the dissenters were for the most part equally implausible. The majority chose a reading of the amendment that was too narrow as opposed to an alternative lacking meaningful limitations. Over the long run, especially from the Warren court on, the Supreme Court's explication of the Fourteenth Amendment as a whole, but certainly not the Privileges or Immunities Clause in particular, has confirmed that amendment deserved a more spacious reading than Justice Miller provided. However with but a few limited exceptions, the Privileges or Immunities Clause has remained a dead letter in the Constitution despite the fact that legal scholars have over a lengthy period of time pleaded for its rediscovery and revival.[71] As Robert McCloskey observed however, Justice Miller's approach made it possible for Fourteenth Amendment principles to evolve incrementally "by slow 'Burkean' accretions rather than by a single great mutation."[72]

Although the vast majority of constitutional scholars have concluded that the *Slaughter-House Cases* majority misunderstood the scope and meaning of the Privileges or Immunities Clause, they disagree among themselves as to the correct interpretation. In addition to the majority's claim that it was intended to provide protection to certain structurally oriented rights of national citizenship, it has also been maintained that its purpose was to incorporate the Bill of Rights against the states.[73] Another reading favored

---

[68] *Id.*

[69] CHARLES FAIRMAN, RECONSTRUCTION AND REUNION 1864-1888 1343 (1971).

[70] *See, e.g.,* NELSON, *supra* note 24, at 63–64; DAVID P. CURRIE, THE CONSTITUTION IN THE SUPREME COURT: THE FIRST HUNDRED YEARS, 1789-1888 342–51 (1985); AKHIL REED AMAR, THE BILL OF RIGHTS: CREATION AND RECONSTRUCTION 211–13 (1998); SCHWARTZ, *supra* note 2, at 159–60; MICHAEL KENT CURTIS, NO STATE SHALL ABRIDGE: THE FOURTEENTH AMENDMENT AND THE BILL OF RIGHTS (1986); Harrison, *supra* note 16, at 1486–88 (1992); Richard Aynes, *On Misreading John Bingham and the Fourteenth Amendment*, 103 YALE L.J. 57 (1993).

[71] *See* JOHN HART ELY, DEMOCRACY AND DISTRUST: A THEORY OF JUDICIAL REVIEW 28–30 (1980); Newsom, *supra* note 18; AMAR, *supra* note 70.

[72] MCCLOSKEY, *supra* note 3, at 80.]

[73] Adamson v. California, 332 U.S. 46, 71–72 (1946) (Black, J., dissenting); Duncan v. Louisiana, 391 U.S. 145, 166 (1968) (Black, J., concurring); Aynes, *supra* note 70, at 103: AMAR, *supra* note 70 (for a nuanced theory of incorporation of some rights); CURTIS, *supra* note 70 (for the argument that it incorporated the Bill of Rights and protected other fundamental rights as well); Newsom, *supra* note 18, at 643 (for the argument that Justice Miller's opinion properly read is not inconsistent with incorporation through the Privileges or Immunities Clause).

by at least a few influential commentators is that the clause was intended to constitutionalize the provisions of the Civil Rights Act of 1866 prohibiting racial discrimination
with respect to certain specified civil rights that the state might choose to recognize.[74]
Under this reading the clause would not recognize rights in an absolute sense but rather
protect those civil rights that states chose to recognize against denial on the basis of race,
much as the Privileges and Immunities Clause of Article IV would protect them against
denial on the basis of out-of-state citizenship. Others would interpret this clause as in
fact protecting these rights against state infringement regardless of discrimination.[75] Yet
another possibility is to construe the clause as protecting all rights deemed fundamental as defined by *Corfield v. Coryell*, a case on which the framers of the amendment had
arguably relied.[76] Still another construction is that the clause vests either Congress or the
courts or both with the authority to define otherwise unenumerated substantive rights
as privileges or immunities of national citizenship.[77] And yet another understanding is
simply to provide vague moralistic rhetoric acceptable to persons with different views as
to what the amendment was intended to accomplish.[78] Alexander Bickel noted that the
clause appears in the Fourteenth Amendment simply because Senator Bingham "liked
the sound of it."[79] The congressional debates at the time of the framing of the amendment provide at least some support for each of these approaches but furnish undeniable
proof to only the most vigorous advocates of a particular theory. This caused Judge Bork
to conclude that the clause is the equivalent of an inkblot on the parchment, incapable
of meaningful understanding.[80] This disagreement over the proper understanding of the
clause may to some extent explain why with but one significant exception, it has been
largely ignored by the Court. It also helps to explain why in the recent important case
of *McDonald v. City of Chicago*,[81] the justices rebuffed the plaintiff's attempt to encourage the Court to revisit the Privileges or Immunities Clause and essentially overrule the
Slaughter-House Cases.

THE RISE OF SUBSTANTIVE DUE PROCESS

Perhaps one of the most direct consequences of the diminishment of the Privileges or
Immunities Clause by the *Slaughter-House Cases* Court was, over time, to force the other
two clauses of sentence two to play a much larger role than might otherwise have been the
case. This development was foreshadowed by two of the three Slaughterhouse dissents.
Both Justice Bradley and Justice Swayne maintained that in addition to the Privileges or

---

[74] CURRIE, *supra* note 70, at 346–50; Harrison, *supra* note 16.
[75] RAOUL BERGER, GOVERNMENT BY JUDICIARY: THE TRANSFORMATION OF THE FOURTEENTH AMEND-
MENT (1977).
[76] Philip B. Kurland, *The Privileges or Immunities Clause: "Its Hour Come Round at Last"?*, 1972 WASH.
U. L.Q. 405.
[77] ELY, *supra* note 71, at 28–30; MCCLOSKEY, *supra* note 3, at 78 (at least "arguable that Fourteenth Amendment was a kind of license for the Court to proceed at will within broad limits").
[78] NELSON, *supra* note 24, at 52.
[79] ALEXANDER M. BICKEL, THE MORALITY OF CONSENT 44 (1975).
[80] ROBERT H. BORK, THE TEMPTING OF AMERICA: THE POLITICAL SEDUCTION OF THE LAW 166 (1990).
[81] 130 S. Ct. 3020, 3028–29 (2010).

Immunities Clause, the Louisiana law violated the Due Process Clause as well. Neither dissent developed a reasoned or coherent argument for substantive due process protection. Both mentioned it largely in passing, clearly indicating that Privileges or Immunities was easily the stronger ground of decision. Importantly however, rather than attempting to destroy any basis for a due process theory in a context such as this, the majority simply dismissed it as irrelevant. Consequently, unlike Privileges or Immunities, it lay there fallow for a few years but fully capable of revival when the time was right.

That time came more quickly than may have been expected when in *Munn v. Illinois*,[82] only four years later, a majority of the Court endorsed substantive due process as a legitimate theory for challenging state imposition of maximum rates for grain storage facilities, even though it ultimately found no violation of the doctrine in that case. Over the next two decades, the Court continued to consider substantive due process arguments in business regulation cases until in 1897, in *Allgeyer v. Louisiana*, it employed the doctrine to invalidate a state law prohibiting out-of-state insurance companies from issuing policies with respect to in-state property.[83] With *Allgeyer*, the era of economic substantive due process was off and running and would continue for the next 40 years. *Lochner v. New York*, decided in 1906, came to represent the basic judicial approach during this time period.[84] In this era, the Court would invalidate over 200 state laws under the due process theory although it would uphold the validity of as many.[85] This approach came to an end when the Court rejected its basic tenets in *Nebbia v. New York*[86] in 1934 and *West Coast Hotel v. Parrish*[87] in 1937. From that point forward, the Court exhibited a highly deferential approach to business regulation under the Constitution.

It is probable that had the Court recognized a vigorous Privileges or Immunities Clause in the *Slaughter-House Cases*, it would have employed it to reach essentially the same results over the next 60 years that it did under substantive due process. Indeed for Justices Bradley and Swayne, the two theories largely overlapped. Even so, privileges or immunities, which on its face appears to be oriented toward the protection of substantive rights, would seem to be a more logical doctrine for addressing these issues than due process, which at least literally appears to be concerned with the provision of procedural protection. Perhaps the results would not have been different but arguably the analysis would have been more coherent.

Another area in which the recognition of a potent Privileges or Immunities Clause may have mattered was the incorporation of the Bill of Rights against the states. It has long been argued based on legislative history that one of the central purposes of the framers of the Fourteenth Amendment was to incorporate some or all of the provisions of the Bill of Rights, previously applicable only to the federal government, to the states as well. Justice Bradley so argued in his *Slaughter-House Cases* dissent.[88] Again there is no way of

---

[82] 94 U.S. 113 (1877). *See* NELSON, *supra* note 24, at 165–76 for a cogent analysis of the Court's doctrinal journey from the *Slaughter-House Cases* to Munn v. Illinois.

[83] 165 U.S. 578 (1897).

[84] 198 U.S. 45 (1906).

[85] GEOFFREY R. STONE, LOUIS M. SEIDMAN, CASS R. SUNSTEIN, PAMELA S. KARLAN & MARK V. TUSHNET, CONSTITUTIONAL LAW 749 (6th ed. 2009).

[86] 291 U.S. 502 (1934).

[87] 300 U.S. 379 (1937).

[88] 83 U.S. 36, 118 (1872).

knowing whether a more vigorous Privileges or Immunities Clause would have changed the results in the incorporation cases. Over a period of 70 years, the Court ultimately did apply most significant provisions of the Bill or Rights to the states, relying on the Due Process Clause instead. Justice Black alone maintained that the Privileges or Immunities Clause would provide a more textually sensible approach to incorporation.[89] Still the question of whether it was appropriate judicially to apply various Bill of Rights provisions against the states most likely would have been fought out case by case over several decades, as in fact it was regardless of which textual provision the Court employed.

A more muscular Privileges or Immunities Clause may have mattered at least somewhat in the development of the right to privacy that the Court has grounded in substantive due process. Although the substantive due process doctrine was essentially discredited as of 1937 and lay dormant for 30 years, it was reinvigorated in 1965 in *Griswold v. Connecticut*[90] and provided the constitutional basis for the right to privacy decisions leading to *Roe v. Wade* and beyond. These decisions would have been intensely controversial under any constitutional theory. The question of whether it is appropriate for the Court to recognize unenumerated rights would still loom large. At the very least however, it could be argued that the Privileges or Immunities Clause provides a somewhat more explicit invitation for the judicial recognition of such rights than due process liberty. Had the dissenters in the *Slaughter-House Cases* prevailed, the case that judicial recognition of such rights is illegitimate might be weaker, although the argument that it is imprudent and still inconsistent with the original understanding of the clause would remain.

EQUAL PROTECTION DOCTRINE

Just as the early demise of privileges or immunities as a viable constitutional theory led to the eventual development of substantive due process, the implosion of substantive due process resulted in the flowering of vigorous equal protection doctrine. The equal protection approach, which remains the Court's most significant doctrinal device for the protection of civil rights against various forms of discrimination, covers much, though not necessarily all, of the same ground as would a fully developed privileges or immunities approach. The Court's concern with racial discrimination resulting in the characterization of race as a suspect classification could readily have been deduced as a substantive privilege or ommunity of United States' citizenship. Likewise, its recognition of certain fundamental interests under the Equal Protection Clause such as the right to travel could more comfortably have been recognized as privileges or immunities as in fact the Court has recently done. Protection of the right to vote as a fundamental interest under a privileges or immunities rationale would be difficult to justify however as a matter of original understanding as there is substantial evidence that the framers did not mean to cover political rights.[91] As with the privacy cases, a privileges or immunities approach would not have removed the essential question of the appropriate judicial role; however it arguably would have been more faithful to the text and in some instances the original

---

[89] Adamson v. California, 332 U.S. 46, 71–72 (1946) (Black, J., dissenting).
[90] 381 U.S. 479 (1965).
[91] *See* Harrison, *supra* note 16, at 1438–40.

understanding of the Fourteenth Amendment, and may have held out the promise of a more coherent doctrinal framework. On the other hand, as Alexander Bickel observed, it may be fortunate that the Court has relied primarily on equal protection and due process instead of privileges or immunities as the protection of the former clauses is extended to "persons" whereas that latter speaks in terms of the privileges or immunities of "citizens."[92] As Bickel put it, *Dred Scott* illustrated that "it always will be easier to think of someone as a noncitizen, than to decide he is a nonperson...."[93]

THE *SLAUGHTER-HOUSE CASES* AND RACE

The *Slaughter-House Cases* may also be thought of as eventually having had some impact on the Court's concern with racial discrimination under the Fourteenth Amendment. The case itself did not involve a claim of racial discrimination, which did cause the Court to suggest that the butchers' case had little to do with the central purpose of the Fourteenth Amendment—establishing "the protection of the newly-made freemen and citizen from the oppressions...."[94] Five years later in *Strauder v. West Virginia*, the Court quoted and reaffirmed that language from the *Slaughter-House Cases*.[95] However it ignored the centrality of racial discrimination to the core of the Fourteenth Amendment some 20 years later in *Plessy v. Ferguson*[96] where it upheld a Louisiana statute requiring racial segregation in railroad cars. One-half century later in *Brown v. Board of Education* when the Court implicitly overruled *Plessy*, it explained that "[i]n the first cases in this Court construing the Fourteenth Amendment, decided shortly after its adoption, the Court interpreted it as proscribing all state imposed discriminations against the Negro race" citing the *Slaughter-House Cases* and quoting *Strauder*.[97] It then noted that "[t]he doctrine of 'separate but equal' did not make its appearance in this court until 1896 in the case of Plessy v. Ferguson...."[98] In other words, the *Slaughter-House Cases* and *Strauder* nearly contemporaneous with the ratification of the Fourteenth Amendment correctly understood its central principle and *Plessy* misconstrued it. The *Brown* Court may have read the Slaughterhouse dicta for more than it was worth, especially given that the case did not involve racial discrimination; however it did prove useful to the Court in its attempt to argue that it was *Plessy* and not *Brown* that misunderstood the purpose of the Fourteenth Amendment.

A REVIVAL OF PRIVILEGES OR IMMUNITIES?

In *Saenz v. Roe*,[99] one of the Court's more recent right-to-travel cases, Justice Stevens, writing for the majority, did rely on the Privileges or Immunities Clause to best explain

---

[92] BICKEL, *supra* note 79, at 53.
[93] *Id.*
[94] *Slaughter-House Cases*, 83 U.S. at 71.
[95] 100 U.S. 303, 305 (1879).
[96] 163 U.S. 36 (1896).
[97] 347 U.S. 483, 490 (1954).
[98] *Id.* at 491.
[99] 526 U.S. 489, 504 (1999).

at least some of the right-to-travel decisions. Indeed, he quoted from both Justice Miller's opinion for the Court as well as Justice Bradley's dissent for the proposition that the clause protects the right of newly arrived citizens to enjoy the same privileges or immunities as long-standing citizens of the state.[100] Consequently, the California law limiting new residents of the state to the same level of public assistance benefits provided by their former state of residence during their first year in California violated the clause. Justice Stevens maintained that this interpretation was squarely within the contours set forth by the majority in the *Slaughter-House Cases*.

Chief Justice Rehnquist dissenting pointed out that in the 130-year period since the *Slaughter-House Cases* were decided, the Court had invalidated only one state law under the Privileges or Immunities Clause, and that case had been subsequently overruled. He found the Court's reliance on the Privileges or Immunities Clause both surprising and inappropriate in a case that he believed involved a standard objective durational residency requirement.

Justice Thomas also dissented, arguing that the Privileges or Immunities Clause should be interpreted on the basis of original understanding. He noted that legal scholars seem to agree that the majority in the *Slaughter-House Cases* certainly misinterpreted the clause, but otherwise are in disagreement as to its proper meaning.[101] Tracing its historical origin, Justice Thomas concluded that the framers of the Fourteenth Amendment were heavily influenced by Justice Washington's opinion in *Corfield v. Coryell* and had intended to protect only fundamental rights under the Privileges or Immunities Clause. All of the justices in the *Slaughter-House Cases* seemed to agree with this conclusion in principle but disagreed as to what those rights were, at least in the Fourteenth Amendment context. Justice Thomas remarked that he would be open to re-evaluating the meaning of the Privileges or Immunities Clause in the appropriate case. However he noted that given that the marginalization of the clause had arguably driven the Court to read the Due Process and Equal Protection Clauses more broadly than warranted by the original understanding, the Court should "also consider whether the Clause should displace rather than augment" those clauses.[102]

The real test for a potential revitalization of the Privileges or Immunities Clause came before the Court in *McDonald v. City of Chicago*.[103] Two years earlier in *District of Columbia v. Heller*,[104] the Court had held that the Second Amendment, properly understood, created a fundamental right to possess a working firearm. McDonald raised the question of whether the right was incorporated against the states by the Fourteenth Amendment. The attorneys for the petitioner built their case around the long-neglected Privileges or Immunities Clause, inviting the Court to revisit it and overrule the *Slaughter-House Cases*. A four-justice plurality politely declined the invitation, concluding that it had developed its incorporation doctrine pursuant to the Due Process Clause and there was significant conflict of opinion regarding the original understanding of the Privileges or Immunities Clause.[105] Justice Thomas, concurring, would have relied on the Privileges or Immunities

---

[100] *Id.* at 502–04.
[101] *Id.* at 523 citing many of the leading works in a footnote.
[102] *Id.* at 528.
[103] 130 S. Ct. 3020 (2010).
[104] 554 U.S. 570 (2008).
[105] *McDonald*, 130 S. Ct. at 3030–31.

Clause.[106] He argued that at the very least, the framing generation meant to incorporate against the states all expressly enumerated rights such as the right to keep and bear arms. Consequently, the original understanding of the Privileges or Immunities Clause was quite a bit clearer than that of the dubious doctrine of substantive due process. In any event, *McDonald* demonstrated that at least for the foreseeable future, any attempt to convince the Court to reconsider the Privileges or Immunities Clause is futile. Justice Miller's opinion is secure.

THE *SLAUGHTER-HOUSE CASES* AS A GREAT CASE

Although the justices did not find themselves at the vortex of public interest in deciding The *Slaughter-House Cases*, there is no question that they understood that they were deciding a case of monumental constitutional importance, as all admitted in their opinions. In that sense whatever hydraulic pressure existed in the decision-making process was internally rather than externally imposed. Three of the four justices who issued opinions in the case, Miller, Field, and Bradley, were first-rate lawyers, and the former two were among the great justices in the history of the Court. Thus from a standpoint of legal ability, the Slaughterhouse Court was up to the task before it. Sitting in the wake of the Civil War, the Court had decided several cases of great national significance, including quite recently the *Legal Tender Cases*. Indeed in the three-year period preceding the *Slaughter-House Cases* the Court had invalidated six acts of Congress, more than it had invalidated in the previous 84 years.[107] Thus the Slaughterhouse Court was a confident Court led by strong-willed and talented justices who would not have been affected by public interest or pressure even had there been any. Rather, it was a Court that was prepared to address issues of great constitutional moment and resolve them as it believed best, with little concern for the specifics of the case and with great regard for perceived long-term consequences.

As with many great cases, the crucial issues that made them great could easily have been avoided. The majority took the position that nothing in the Fourteenth Amendment was relevant to the resolution of the case. Given that the amendment was primarily concerned with establishing the protection of the civil rights of recently freed slaves in the South, it could have left the initial interpretation of the amendment to a case more closely aligned with its purpose, such as *Strauder v. West Virginia*, in order to avoid being misled by an unhelpful factual context.

Justice Miller could have declared, as indeed he did, that the Act was well within the state's police powers, and contrary to the charges of the dissent, that it simply did not exclude the butchers from their profession; consequently the Fourteenth Amendment was not implicated. Had he done no more, the *Slaughter-House Cases* would not be famous. This would have left the powerful and inevitable dissents of Field and Bradley unanswered; however they could be dealt with in the future in a more appropriate case.

Likewise, Justices Field, Bradley, and Swayne did not need to write their vigorous dissents in this particular case. The Act in question simply did not deprive the butchers of

---

[106] *Id.* at 3063.
[107] WARREN, *supra* note 65, at 255.

their livelihood. If anything it made it easier for them to ply their trade in that they were guaranteed access to the same slaughterhouse that every other butcher in New Orleans would be using. The defendants pointed this out in their briefs, and the dissenting justices were certainly acute enough to understand it.

The *Slaughter-House Cases* became a great case not because it was inevitable given the circumstances but rather because the justices on both sides of the issue wanted it to be "the" great case confronting the recently enacted Fourteenth Amendment. And yet but for the briefs and arguments of Justice Campbell thrusting the Fourteenth Amendment into the center of a dispute in which it was scarcely implicated, the *Slaughter-House Cases* would probably be no more than a historical footnote. Once Campbell pushed the recent amendment to the center of the dispute, the justices seemed eager to take the bait and attempt to define its significance. Miller and the majority seemed to be driven by the fear that a vigorous construction of the amendment would upset the traditional balance between state and federal authority and would cut far too deeply into the ability of the state to regulate local affairs. These fears were almost certainly magnified by the open-ended character of Campbell's and Field's approach. For fear of cutting too deeply into state autonomy however, Miller chose the other extreme of unduly limiting the scope and vitality of the Privileges or Immunities Clause. As Bradley noted, it must mean something, and yet under Miller's reading it meant almost nothing, which simply could not be right.

On the other hand Campbell and the dissenters, for the most part, failed to offer a sufficient limiting principle to avoid the federal intrusion that Miller seemed to fear. Their reliance on natural law and common law may have suggested that they believed that the amendment did grant the federal government authority over rather ordinary activities. The application of the amendment to the police power–backed regulation in the *Slaughter-House Cases* must have encouraged the belief that once released, the amendment was capable of nationalizing virtually everything. Although Justice Millers's concerns may have been overblown, in the context of the case, they were certainly understandable.

The dissenters on the other hand were equally committed to the project of putting some teeth into the Fourteenth Amendment, especially the Privileges or Immunities Clause. To a large extent, they almost certainly believed that Congress had in fact intended for the amendment to cut deeply into traditional conceptions of federalism, given the destabilization caused by the war as well as the southern backlash against Reconstruction. Beyond that however, Justice Field was clearly committed to a constitutional ideology based to some extent on Jacksonian anti-class bias, free labor principles, and free market capitalism. The *Slaughter-House Cases* presented Field with the opportunity, building on Campbell's arguments, to anchor that approach to the Fourteenth Amendment, and he would continue to develop it throughout his long career on the Court.

Like many great cases, the *Slaughter-House Cases* presented the Court with the opportunity to decide a great case or an ordinary case. Given all of the circumstances surrounding the matter however, perhaps it was all but inevitable that the justices would choose the former.

Did the *Slaughter-House Cases* make bad law? For most commentators, the question is hardly worth posing. The answer would be a resounding yes. In *McDonald*, Justice Alito quoted from a Brief of Constitutional Scholars, which asserted that "'an overwhelming consensus among leading constitutional scholars' claim that 'the opinion is egregiously wrong.'"[108] However writing in 1922, Charles Warren declared that "Justice Miller's opinion has justly been regarded as one of the glorious landmarks of American law."[109] Given that Miller's opinion minimized the significance of what was arguably intended to be the central provision of the Fourteenth Amendment, the Privileges or Immunities Clause, it could be and often has been argued that the *Slaughter-House Cases* did indeed make bad law. But on the other hand, despite the relentless criticism that has been directed at the case, as a judicial matter it has withstood the test of time. One hundred forty years after it was decided, the case is still accepted by the Court as a valid precedent. When faced with a well-developed frontal assault on the decision recently in *McDonald v. City of Chicago*, the Court showed no interest at all (with the exception of Justice Thomas) in revisiting the holding. If the case was as wrongheaded as its critics maintain, it is at least a little puzzling that the Court itself has chosen to leave it undisturbed for so long. Perhaps the explanation lies in the fact that it has been able to largely accomplish what it believes the Privileges or Immunities Clause was designed for through overly generous constructions of due process and equal protection. Any attempt to turn back the clock and revive the Privileges or Immunities Clause would either destabilize settled doctrine in other areas or would accomplish very little at this point. Alternatively, perhaps Judge Bork was on to something with his inkblot comment. Although expositors of the Privileges or Immunities Clause argue with extreme passion that their own interpretation of the clause is clearly correct, the inability of them to reach agreement among themselves may have simply convinced the justices that any attempt to define the true meaning of the provision is little more than a pit of quicksand. So if the *Slaughter-House Cases* did make bad law, it is bad law that we have learned to live with.

---

[108] *Id.* at 303.
[109] WARREN, *supra* note 65, at 268.

"IT WAS A GREAT CASE—great beyond the awareness of the participants."[1]

CHARLES FAIRMAN

8

The Civil Rights Cases

THE SUPREME COURT'S decision in 1883 in five consolidated cases known as *The Civil Rights Cases* was a significant event. It was a test case involving the constitutionality of the Civil Rights Act of 1875, the final achievement of the Reconstruction Congress. And by an eight-to-one vote of Supreme Court the Act failed the test. Perhaps even more than the *Slaughter-House Cases, The Civil Rights Cases* were the ultimate judicial rejection of a generous view of the constitutional and statutory work product of the short-lived but aggressive Reconstruction Congress. The practical result of the case, making it all but impossible for the federal government to prohibit racial discrimination in the private sphere, would prevail for 80 years. The doctrinal foundation of the case, that congressional legislation under the Enforcement Clause of the Fourteenth Amendment is limited to state action, remains valid even now. The lone voice in opposition was the first of many great constitutional dissents of Justice John Marshall Harlan. *The Civil Rights Cases* were recognized as a great case at the time and remain so today.

BACKGROUND

Following the conclusion of the Civil War, the Reconstruction Congress, which sat from approximately 1865 to 1876, passed three constitutional amendments and extensive legislation to provide protection for the recently freed slaves and to guarantee some degree of legal protection for all persons against oppression by the states. The Thirteenth Amendment prohibited slavery, or involuntary servitude, to use its precise language. The Fifteenth Amendment prohibited denial of the right to vote on the basis of race. However the Fourteenth Amendment, which prohibited a state from abridging the privileges or immunities of a United States' citizen; or depriving any person of life, liberty, or property without due process of law; or denying any person equal protection of the laws, was

---

[1] CHARLES FAIRMAN, RECONSTRUCTION AND REUNION 1864–1888, PART TWO 586 (1987).

certainly the centerpiece of civil rights protection against the states. Section Five of the amendment gave Congress the power to enforce the provisions of the amendment with appropriate legislation.

Congress enacted several important pieces of civil rights legislation during the Reconstruction Era, much of which still survives. The last and in many ways one of the most important of these statutes was the Civil Rights Act of 1875, which provided protection against racial discrimination in many significant private enterprises including common carriers, hotels and restaurants, and places of entertainment. The Act had been a project that Senator Sumner had pressed unsuccessfully during Reconstruction and the ultimate momentum for its passage was to a large extent a tribute to his efforts. At the time of its passage, even some of its supporters expressed grave doubts as to its constitutionality.[2] Reconstruction collapsed shortly after the Act was passed with the election of 1876. Even before that however a backlash against Reconstruction and the products of the Reconstruction Congress had been growing in both the South and the North.[3]

Among much of the country, the Civil Rights Act of 1875 was not well received. Prior to *The Civil Rights Cases*, the Supreme Court had taken a grudging approach to some of the civil rights legislation passed by the Reconstruction Congress, especially to the extent that it attempted to reach private conduct. *United States v Cruickshank*[4] affirmed the dismissal of an indictment of several members of a mob that had attacked and killed a large number of African Americans, on the ground that there could be no violation of equal protection or due process as there was no allegation of any action by the state. Then in the 1883 term prior to the decision in *The Civil Rights Cases*, in *United States v Harris*[5] the Court invalidated sections of the Ku Klux Klan Act that seemed to permit prosecution of private persons for denying another person civil rights absent any allegation of state participation or failure by the state to protect the individuals. These decisions as well as others exhibited hostility by the Court toward a liberal reading of either the civil rights statutes or the Reconstruction Amendments. It was in this context that the four lawsuits involving criminal charges against defendants for excluding African Americans from institutions covered by the Act and a fifth involving an attempt to recover damages for such an exclusion were brought before the Court.

The *Ryan* and *Singleton* cases from California and New York respectively involved refusal to admit African Americans to theaters.[6] The *Nichols* case from Missouri involved refusal by a hotel whereas the *Stanley* case from Kansas was based on denial of service by a restaurant.[7] The *Robinson* case from Tennessee involved refusal by a railroad to allow an African-American woman to sit in the parlor car.[8] Alan Westin has suggested that perhaps as many as 100 similar cases were litigated under the Civil Rights Act.[9] The *Ryan*

---

[2] Bernard Schwartz, A History of the Supreme Court 167 (1993).

[3] Peter Charles Hoffer, Williamjames Hull Hoffer & N. E. H. Hull, The Supreme Court An Essential History 137–38 (2007).

[4] 92 U.S. 542 (1876).

[5] 106 U.S. 629 (1883).

[6] 109 U.S. 3, 4 (1883).

[7] Id.

[8] Id.

[9] Alan Westin, *The Case of the Prejudiced Doorman, in* Quarrels That Have Shaped the Constitution 146 (John Garraty ed. 1987).

and *Stanley* cases were docketed in the Court as early as 1876 and remained there for six years prior to decision. The Court simply passed over the cases year after year. *The Civil Rights Cases* were unique among great cases in that they were decided on the briefs without benefit of oral argument.[10]

THE OPINION

Justice Bradley writing for the majority spent little time on the facts, concluding that all five cases turned on the same constitutional issue: whether Congress had the power to prohibit private discrimination.[11] He quoted the relevant provisions of the Act and summarized them as declaring that with respect to public conveyances, accommodations, theaters, and places of public amusement, persons of different color or race are entitled to the same treatment as white persons, with violations to be enforced by criminal penalties.

Recognizing that the Act could be sustained if at all by reliance on the enforcement sections of the Fourteenth or Thirteenth Amendments, Justice Bradley turned to the key substantive provisions set forth in Section One, sentence two of the Fourteenth Amendment—the Privileges or Immunities, Due Process and Equal Protection Clauses—and noted that each was explicitly aimed at deprivations by the state, or "state action" as he put it. He asserted that Section Five was aimed at enforcing these substantive prohibitions of state law or actions and "this is the whole of it."[12] Like the majority opinion in the *Slaughter-House Cases* from which he had dissented, Justice Bradley expressed a concern that Congress had not been authorized to "create a code of municipal law for the regulation of private rights."[13] He indicated without elaboration that the proper understanding of the scope of the amendment had been discussed by the Court in the prior decisions of *United States v. Cruickshank, Virginia v. Rives*, and *Ex parte Virginia*.

Bradley cited the Contract Clause by way of analogy, which focused on impairment of contracts by the state and not by private parties. Repeating the concern for state regulatory autonomy, he explained that authorizing Congress to reach private conduct "would be to make congress take the place of the state legislatures and supercede them."[14] Recognizing that perhaps the amendment granted Congress some leeway to provide a remedy where a state neglected its obligations to protect the civil rights of persons within its jurisdiction, Bradley noted that the Act "applies equally to cases arising in states which have the justest laws respecting personal rights of citizens."[15]

In a straightforward fashion, the Court declared that the "wrongful act of an individual, unsupported by any [state] authority, is simply a private wrong, or a crime of that individual."[16] Referring to the acknowledged purpose of the Fourteenth Amendment,

---

[10] FAIRMAN, *supra* note 1, at 556–57.
[11] *The Civil Rights Cases*, 109 U.S. at 10–11.
[12] *Id.* at 11.
[13] *Id.*
[14] *Id.* at 13.
[15] *Id.* at 14.
[16] *Id.* at 17.

Justice Bradley noted that it was the "abrogation and denial of rights, for which the state alone were or could be responsible" that was "the great seminal and fundamental wrong which was intended to be remedied."[17] That would seem to suggest that a state failure to protect civil rights could constitute a violation of the Fourteenth Amendment. But the Court concluded that the Act in question was "not corrective legislation; it is primary and direct. . . ."[18] That is, it did not focus on any failure or denial by the states.

The Court qualified its holding in a number of ways. It assumed for the sake of argument that equal access to the facilities covered by the Act was a privilege that could not be denied by the states. That is, had the states sanctioned the discrimination, there presumably would have been a constitutional violation. Nor did the Court address the plenary authority of Congress to prohibit private discrimination in the District of Columbia or the territories. Finally, it reserved the question of whether Congress could prohibit private discrimination in public conveyances under the Commerce Clause.

The Court then turned to the Thirteenth Amendment as a possible source of authority for the legislation. It recognized that unlike the Fourteenth Amendment, which focused on state action, the Thirteenth abolishing involuntary servitude was "primary and direct."[19] That is, it applied to conduct by individuals as well as the state. However unlike the Fourteenth Amendment, the Thirteenth was concerned only with slavery and its badges and incidents, and not with discrimination based on race or class. Justice Bradley reasoned that racial discrimination with respect to the type of facilities covered by the Act was widespread with respect to free African Americans prior to the demise of slavery and as such was legally distinct from slavery itself. Consequently, "[i]t would be running the slavery argument into the ground to make it apply to every act of discrimination. . ."[20] Then in a frequently quoted statement that seems both naive and callous, Justice Bradley wrote that "[w]hen a man has emerged from slavery, and by the aid of beneficent legislation has shaken off the inseparable concomitants of that state, there must be some stage in the progress of his elevation when he takes the rank of a mere citizen, and ceases to be the special favorite of the laws."[21]

Coming fewer than 20 years after the conclusion of the Civil War and at a time when the backlash against the protection of recently freed slaves was on the rise in both the South and the North, this statement would seem to be a gratuitous slap at the cause of racial reconciliation. Despite the fact that it acknowledged that the Fourteenth Amendment could provide greater protection against racial discrimination though only with respect to state action, the statements near the end of the Court's Thirteenth Amendment discussion could certainly be taken as a declaration that the Court was not favorably disposed toward claims for assistance from African Americans, period, and that is certainly how the African-American community understood the opinion. This was especially true given that the opinion was joined by eight justices, including two who had dissented in the *Slaughter-House Cases*.

Finding no constitutional basis for its authorization, the Court invalidated the Act.

---

[17] *Id.* at 18.
[18] *Id.* at 19.
[19] *Id.*
[20] *Id.* at 24.
[21] *Id.* at 25.

JUSTICE HARLAN'S DISSENT

Justice Harlan, a southerner and former slave owner, wrote the sole dissent using the very pen and inkwell employed by Chief Justice Taney to write the *Dred Scott* opinion.[22] It was destined to become one of the great dissents in Supreme Court history. Harlan went straight to the heart of the problem with the Court's approach in the very first sentence of his dissent, arguing that the approach was "too narrow and artificial."[23] The Court had failed to construe the Act so as to effectuate the intent of the framers. Before turning his attention to the Act itself, he quoted at length from congressional legislation passed to aid slave owners as well as the Court's own generous interpretation of such legislation and the Constitution favoring slave owners in cases such as *Prigg v. Pennsylvania*, *Ableman v. Booth*, and *Scott v. Sanford*. Harlan found it sad and ironic that the Court had construed congressional power so broadly in favor of slavery and now construed it so narrowly in support of freedom.

As a source of congressional authority, Harlan initially turned to the Thirteenth Amendment. He argued that the Enforcement Clause of that amendment, which did proscribe private discrimination, had been utilized to justify the enactment of the Civil Rights Act of 1866.[24] Contrary to the majority's skepticism, Justice Harlan maintained that the 1866 Act was clearly constitutional without the additional support of the Fourteenth Amendment. Although he acknowledged that the Thirteenth Amendment did not provide Congress with the authority to legislate with respect to all civil rights, it definitely permitted it to prohibit racial discrimination, which was essentially the very foundation of slavery. In making this argument, Justice Harlan seemed to have unduly minimized the constitutional doubts that existed in Congress as to whether the Civil Rights Act of 1866 really could have been constitutionally authorized by the Thirteenth Amendment alone.[25] Certainly the serious concerns over that issue were a primary motivation behind the enactment of the Fourteenth Amendment.

In order to establish that racial discrimination in the facilities covered by the 1875 Act was within the scope of the Thirteenth Amendment, Harlan quoted at some length from Supreme Court and state court opinions declaring that railroads, inns, and places of public amusement were business with a public or quasi-public character either because of the significance of the service provided and the tradition of a duty to serve all guests, or because of governmental subsidization or licensing. His point was that racial exclusion in institutions of this significance was closely akin to the disabilities of slavery itself.

Justice Harlan then turned to the Fourteenth Amendment. In order to avoid the Court's state action limitation, he focused on the first sentence of Section One of the amendment, which declares "All persons born or naturalized in the United States, and subject to the jurisdiction thereof, are citizens of the United States and of the State wherein they reside." The acknowledged purpose of this sentence was to overrule the holding of the *Dred Scott* Case that a former slave or descendant of a slave could never be a citizen of either a state or the nation. But Justice Harlan argued that the concept of

---

[22] WESTIN, *supra* note 9, at 152–53.

[23] *The Civil Rights Cases*, 109 U.S. at 26.

[24] *Id.* at 35.

[25] John Harrison, *Reconstructing the Privileges or Immunities Clause*, 101 YALE L.J. 1385, 1403–04 (1992).

citizenship embodied in this sentence had substance beyond that purpose. In a nutshell, he argued that the Article IV Privileges and Immunities Clause protected out-of-state citizens against discrimination with respect to fundamental rights when they are present in another state. Under that provision, a state could not deny civil rights to an out-of-state Black citizen that it granted to an in-state white citizen. And if the state could not discriminate on the basis of race against a Black citizen from another state, then surely it could not discriminate on the basis of race against its own state citizen. The argument was similar to that set forth by the *Slaughter-House Cases* dissents of Field and Bradley 11 years earlier. However as with the *Slaughter-House* dissents, this argument unduly minimized the degree to which the rights protected by Article IV were relative as opposed to absolute in nature. But more significant, the argument had been rejected by the Court in the *Slaughter-House Cases*, and the two primary dissenters who endorsed that argument there clearly rejected it here.

Justice Harlan's argument is overly complicated and clumsy, involving several logical leaps. The point however was to render the state action obstacle irrelevant. His contention was that under Section Five, Congress may "enforce 'the *provisions of this article:*' not simply those of a prohibitive character."[26] In other words, by enforcing Section One citizenship, it can reach primary conduct regardless of state action. This is an appealing argument. It would have been far cleaner and simpler had Justice Harlan merely argued that Congress had the right to flesh out the concept of state or national citizenship as embodied in the first sentence of the Fourteenth Amendment without taking a the complex detour through Article IV. Despite its appeal, such an approach would be inconsistent with Justice Miller's opinion in the *Slaughter-House Cases* in that it seemed to limit sentence one to the reversal of the *Dred Scott* opinion. Moreover, as Miller had construed the privileges or immunities of national citizenship under sentence two of the amendment quite narrowly, there would be no reason to believe that a majority of the Court would be charitably disposed to a spacious interpretation of sentence one citizenship as that would pose the same threat to state autonomy. Harlan's argument may seem to be an intriguing and clever method of avoiding the state action barrier; in retrospect however it had no chance of acceptance by even one other justice at the time.

Justice Harlan returned forcefully to the point that he had made earlier in the opinion, that the Court should construe the concept of liberty at least as generously to protect the liberty of freemen as it had previously done to secure the rights of slaveholders. From a rhetorical standpoint, this was a powerful argument. Likewise, Harlan argued that because sentence two of Section One already prohibited unequal treatment by the state, the Enforcement Clause would be rendered meaningless if Congress could not use it to go further and reach private discrimination. That hardly follows however. Given the generality of the substantive guarantees of the Fourteenth Amendment, Congress could accomplish a great deal by simply providing detailed enforcement mechanisms under Section Five if only against state action, as indeed it has.

In response to the Court's federalism-based concern that permitting Congress to reach private discrimination would invade the domain of the states and allow Congress to create a municipal code, Harlan responded that the right to be free from racial discrimination

---

[26] 109 U.S. at 46.

was a newly created national right and as such never was part of the state police power to begin with.

Up to this point, Justice Harlan had offered two theories to avoid the state action hurdle entirely. But he was more than willing to argue that "[t]here has been adverse state action within the fourteenth amendment."[27] Harkening back to his earlier discussion of how the state was implicated in the particular institutions covered by the Act, he maintained that "railroad corporations, keepers of the inns, and managers of places of public amusement are agents of the state because amenable, in respect to their public duties and functions, to public regulations."[28] This proved to be the genesis of what would later become the public function theory of state action although the Court would never take it to the extreme suggested by Harlan in *The Civil Rights Cases*.

Justice Harlan agreed that Congress could not prohibit discrimination in the social sphere but maintained that the rights in question were legal, not social. He did not suggest that Congress had the power to prohibit all racial discrimination but rather only that in which "a corporation or individual wielding the power under state authority for the public benefit or the public convenience" and was denying a civil right.[29] Harlan's conception of civil rights was much closer to that of our own than to that of the latter part of the nineteenth century where the domain of civil rights tended to be limited to the type of rights set forth in the Civil Rights Act of 1866, such as the right to contract, the right to hold property, the right to bring a lawsuit, and the right to testify in court. It did not include the right to travel in an unsegregated railroad car, as the Court indicated 13 years later over another vigorous dissent by Justice Harlan in *Plessy v Ferguson*.[30]

With respect to the *Robinson* case involving a railway, Justice Harlan maintained that the Act could readily be sustained under the Commerce Clause even though Congress had not explicitly relied upon it.[31] He noted that in *Hall v. De Cuir*, the Court had recently invalidated a Louisiana law prohibiting discrimination in transportation on the ground that it interfered with the regulation of interstate commerce. If the state could not prohibit discrimination in interstate commerce, then presumably Congress could. This aspect of Justice Harlan's opinion would prove quite prophetic in that the Commerce Clause would indeed serve as the foundation for the Civil Rights Act of 1964 extending anti-discrimination protection far beyond the limits of the 1875 Act.

Justice Harlan closed his opinion with a response to the Court's declaration that it was time to end special legal favoritism for African Americans. He replied that it "was scarcely just to say that the colored race has been the special favorite of the law."[32] Rather, Congress had simply attempted to "secure and protect rights belonging to them as free men and citizens; nothing more."[33]

---

[27] *Id.* at 58.
[28] *Id.* at 55.
[29] *Id.* at 59.
[30] 163 U.S. 537 (1896).
[31] *Civil Rights Cases*, 109 U.S. at 60.
[32] *Id.* at 61.
[33] *Id.*

IMPACT OF THE DECISION

The Civil Rights Cases was a significant setback for legal protection against racial discrimination. It invalidated one of the crowning achievements of the Reconstruction Congress. Congressional protection against discrimination in the private sphere would be delayed for 80 years. It must be acknowledged that the Act was unpopular and generally not enforced at the time. Press coverage of the decision was overwhelmingly favorable.[34] Indeed much of the press coverage of the decision argued that it was not a significant setback for civil rights in that the Act was generally ignored even before the Court invalidated it.[35] Nevertheless had it remained on the books, it almost certainly would have been enforced in the future as the civil rights movement developed. At a civil rights rally shortly after the decision was announced, Frederick Douglass criticized it "more in sorrow than in anger" but maintained that "[w]e have been as a class, grievously wounded, wounded in the house of our friends. . . ."[36] Addressing the argument that the decision was unimportant in that the Act had rarely been enforced, Douglass declared that even so the Act "was a banner on the outer wall of American liberty, a noble moral standard, uplifted for education of the American people."[37] The decision was not a break with precedent. It was indeed foreshadowed by prior decisions such as *Reese, Cruickshank*, and *Harris*. But none of those decisions had the immense societal impact of *The Civil Rights Cases*. The question of racial discrimination in the facilities covered by the Act resonated throughout the country, and as such the case was understood by the press and public to be quite important.

Despite the fact that a major piece of legislation had been struck down, the Court's opinion was quite in step with the mood of the nation.[38] Much of the editorial comment declared that Congress had exceeded its constitutional limits in passing the Act.[39] A consistent theme of the commentary was that it was futile to attempt to legislate social relations, viewing access to the institutions in question as social rather than civil rights, a theme that the Court would emphasize 13 years later when it decided *Plessy v. Ferguson*.[40] Indeed the crowd at the Atlanta Opera House cheered loudly when the decision was announced.[41] Likewise, Justice Harlan's dissent, which has grown in stature over time, was not highly regarded when released.[42] Ordinarily when the Court invalidates an important and relatively recent Act of Congress, the decision can be viewed as a significant challenge

---

[34] BARRY FRIEDMAN, THE WILL OF THE PEOPLE: HOW PUBLIC OPINION HAS INFLUENCED THE. SUPREME COURT AND SHAPED THE MEANING OF THE CONSTITUTION 149 (2009) (quoting THE NATION and THE PHILADELPHIA NORTH AMERICAN); LAWRENCE GOLDSTONE, INHERENTLY UNEQUAL: THE BETRAYAL OF EQUAL RIGHTS BY THE SUPREME COURT, 1865-1903 128 (2011) (quoting favorable reports in the NEW YORK TIMES, BROOKLYN DAILY EAGLE, HARPERS and the ATLANTA CONSTITUTION).

[35] FAIRMAN, *supra* note 1, at 568–82.

[36] Speech of Frederick Douglass at the Civil Rights Mass-Meeting held at Lincoln Hall. October 22, 1883, *reprinted in* FAIRMAN, *supra* note 1, at 583–85.

[37] *Id.* at 585.

[38] WESTIN, *supra* note 9, at 150.

[39] FAIRMAN, *supra* note 1, at 569–82 (for an extensive collection of editorial comment on the decision).

[40] *Id.*

[41] WESTIN, *supra* note 9, at 150.]

[42] JEFFREY ROSEN, THE SUPREME COURT: THE PERSONALITIES AND RIVALRIES THAT DEFINED AMERICA 97 (2006).

by the one branch to the other. But Congress had changed during the eight-year period between the passage of the Act and the Court's invalidation of it. The Reconstruction Era was over, and there was no chance that the Congress in place at the time of *The Civil Rights Cases* decision would have passed the Act. Consequently the decision was less a slap in the face of Congress than a recognition of the new political realities.

THE CIVIL RIGHTS CASES AS A GREAT CASE

The Civil Rights Cases was a great case in the sense that it involved an issue of significant societal interest and importance and raised a constitutional issue of the first magnitude. In deciding the case however, the Court was not operating in the type of pressure cooker atmosphere that is usually present when a great case is presented. With the exception of Justice Harlan, who appeared to be an outlier on the issue of racial discrimination, Justice Bradley worked within both a judicial and societal consensus. In that sense *The Civil Rights Cases* was relatively easy for the Court despite the fact that some of the cases had lingered on its docket for six years prior to decision.

However great a setback the case may have been for the anti-discrimination cause, was the decision correct, or at least arguably so? Doctrinally, *The Civil Rights Cases* are best known for having firmly embedded the state action doctrine in Fourteenth Amendment jurisprudence. This was not the first decision to recognize the necessity of state action but it was certainly the most prominent early embodiment of it. On their face, the three substantive guarantees of the second sentence of the Fourteenth Amendment are explicitly aimed at denial by the state. Thus a denial of privileges or immunities, equal protection. or due process would seem to assume some state action or at least state responsibility. So the most well-known holding of *The Civil Rights Cases*, the necessity of state action, was almost certainly correct with perhaps one important qualification.

Virtually all of the Reconstruction Amendments and legislation were written in response to the failure of state governments in the South to protect the rights of freedmen. As a matter of original understanding, it could certainly be argued that a clear failure by the state to protect the equal rights of African Americans against discriminatory treatment constituted a violation of equal protection. That is, state inaction could sometimes suffice. That is not to take the radical view that the state is responsible for everything that occurs within its jurisdiction. Such a complete collapse of the public/private distinction could not possibly be reconciled with the dominant views of the Reconstruction Congress, which certainly intended to reserve a significant degree of state autonomy. But at least if it were proven that a state deliberately failed to prevent serious racially based abuses (beyond mere private discrimination), then arguably the Fourteenth Amendment would apply. Such a scenario of state indifference toward race-based tyranny was not implicated by the facts of *The Civil Rights Cases* however. Indeed much of the commentary on the case at the time assumed that the invalidation of the Act was inconsequential given that the states themselves would provide more than adequate protection for civil rights.[43] In retrospect, that would seem naive but it does appear to be a widely held belief at the time.

---

[43] *See* FAIRMAN, *supra* note 1, at 569–82.

Recently in *United States v. Morrison*, the Court has cast doubt on whether Congress can reach private conduct under Section Five of the Fourteenth Amendment on the theory that the state has failed to provide adequate protection.[44] In *Morrison*, the Court considered the constitutionality of a statute that created a federal private cause of action against private individuals responsible for gender-motivated violence, on the ground that Congress had found that many states had failed to adequately investigate and prosecute gender-based crimes. The Court held however that Section Five of the Fourteenth Amendment did not permit Congress to punish private actors absent any allegation of state participation. It essentially concluded that to affirm the statute based on Section Five authority would effectively overrule *The Civil Rights Cases*, which it was not inclined to do given that all of the justices who participated in that decision had personal knowledge of the circumstances giving rise to the passage of the Fourteenth Amendment.[45] Even assuming that there was bias in the state criminal justice systems resulting in a lack of enforcement, the Court declared that the remedy provided by Congress made no attempt to correct such state inaction. As such, it fell beyond what *The Civil Rights Cases* had suggested was permissible. *Morrison* casts grave doubt on whether Congress could ever provide a remedy against private discrimination on a failure of state enforcement theory even if such an approach had not been absolutely foreclosed by *The Civil Rights Cases*.

Quite apart from legislation based on a finding of a state failure to protect civil rights, Harlan argued that the Section Five Enforcement Clause provided Congress with the power to pass legislation prohibiting private discrimination, period, just as the Necessary and Proper Clause authorizes Congress to legislate beyond the literal limitations of other congressional heads of authority. Such an approach was defensible though scarcely inevitable. However at some point, as the Supreme Court has recognized in *City of Boerne v. Flores*, Congress moves beyond enforcement of Fourteenth Amendment rights to the unwarranted creation of rights.[46] Was congressional coverage of private discrimination simply acceptable enforcement or was it an unjustifiable extension of the coverage of the amendment? In 1966, at the very height of the Warren court, six justices in dicta in *United States v. Guest* suggested that Congress did have the power under Section Five of the amendment to reach acts of private discrimination.[47] The Court never followed through on that suggestion however. In *United States v. Morrison*, the Court rejected the *Guest* dicta as being quite inconsistent with *The Civil Rights Cases*. Thus the argument of Harlan was rejected in 1883 and again in 2000 by a majority of the Court.

Assuming that state action is required for an equal protection violation, was Justice Harlan correct in arguing that it could readily be found with respect to the facilities in question? Should the Court have concluded that common carriers, inns, and places of public amusement were state actors in that they were performing a public function? Justice Harlan made a decent case that considering the long-established obligation of common carriers and inns to accept all unobjectionable guests as well as the pervasive degree of regulation and subsidization of the former, both should be considered state actors at least with respect to claims of racial discrimination. As he conceded, the case for covering

---

[44] 529 U.S. 598 (2000).
[45] *Id.* at 621–24.
[46] 521 U.S. 507 (1997).
[47] 383 U.S. 745 (1966).

places of public amusement must rest upon state licensing and was not nearly as compelling. Justice Harlan provided a plausible legal argument for saving the Act at least with respect to railroads and hotels, but even that was out of step with late nineteenth century conceptions of the relationship between the public and private spheres.

The Court did not take that argument seriously in *The Civil Rights Cases*. Some 60 years later in *Marsh v. Alabama*,[48] it would adopt the public function doctrine in the context of a company town There it held that a privately owned town that performed all of the functions of an ordinary town and that appeared to the public to be such a town was effectively a state actor. As such, it could not prohibit persons from exercising their First Amendment rights on the streets even though they were technically on private property. More recently the Court has narrowed the public function doctrine to apply only to those private activities that have been traditionally and (almost) exclusively performed by the state itself, greatly limiting the scope of the doctrine.[49] At no point has the Court ever applied the public function concept with the vigor suggested by Justice Harlan in *The Civil Rights Cases*.

Both the majority and Justice Harlan spent more time addressing congressional enforcement power under the Thirteenth than under the Fourteenth Amendment. As the Thirteenth Amendment does not require state action, the issue was whether Congress could consider private racial discrimination, at least in the private facilities in question, a badge or incident of slavery. Justice Harlan made a forceful case that Congress could so conclude; however the majority declined to find a sufficiently close connection between the two. It seemed particularly concerned, as it was in the *Slaughter-House Cases*, that such a result would cut too deeply into the legitimate domain of state regulation.

This aspect of *The Civil Rights Cases* has been modified however. In 1968 in *Jones v. Alfred Mayer*, the Court held that section 1982 derived from the Civil Rights Act of 1866 and passed pursuant to the Thirteenth Amendment prohibited private persons from discriminating on the basis of race with respect to the sale of real estate.[50] The Court concluded that its reading was consistent with *The Civil Rights Cases* given that Congress could reasonably have concluded that racial discrimination with respect to the sale of real property was indeed a vestige and incident of slavery.[51] The second Justice Harlan dissented, arguing that the Court had misinterpreted the statute.[52] The Court reaffirmed this approach in *Runyon v. McCrary* in which it held that section 1981, also derived from the Civil Rights Act of 1866, constitutionally authorized a suit against a private school that refused on account of race to enter into a contract to admit a black child.[53] Justice White dissented and Justices Powell and Stevens concurred based on the precedential value of *Jones* even though both believed that the courts in both *Jones* and *Runyon* were misinterpreting the legislation. Thus as to the power of Congress under the Thirteenth Amendment to attack private racial discrimination, the first Justice Harlan's approach at least with respect to recognized civil rights, largely prevailed although it would take

---

[48] 326 U.S. 501 (1946).
[49] *See, e.g.*, Jackson v. Metro. Edison, 419 U.S. 345 (1974); Flagg Brothers v. Brooks, 436 U.S. 149 (1978).
[50] 392 U.S. 409 (1968).
[51] *Id.* at 440–43.
[52] *Id.* at 449-50.
[53] 427 U.S. 160 (1976).

over 80 years. Although it is all but certain that *The Civil Rights Cases* majority would have disagreed with the decisions in *Alfred Mayer* and *Runyon*, they are at least arguably distinguishable in that the rights involved in the latter cases would clearly have been recognized as "civil" rights in 1883 whereas the rights protected by the 1875 Act were not.

The final issue raised by the case, if only tangentially, was the power of Congress under the Commerce Clause to prohibit discrimination in the private sphere. The majority acknowledged the possibility but did not reach the issue as Congress had not explicitly relied on the commerce power. Justice Harlan replied that it was well established that Congress need not identify a source of constitutional authority in order to employ it. He would have sustained application of the Act to common carriers under the commerce power. Given that Congress had not legislated extensively under the Commerce Clause as of 1883 when the case was decided, and that the Court would not construe the power generously for another 50 years, even Justice Harlan was not prepared to extend the Commerce Clause to inns and places of amusement. Even in the late nineteenth century, the Commerce Clause would have been a promising source of authority for the prohibition of discrimination on interstate transportation but certainly not with respect to the other facilities covered by the Act.

Although the Commerce Clause was a minor consideration in *The Civil Rights Cases*, it loomed large when in the Civil Rights Act of 1964, Congress extended protection against racial discrimination deeply into the private sector. By the time that Congress was debating the Civil Rights Act of 1964, the Court had begun to erode the state action hurdle somewhat, at least in cases involving racial discrimination; however *The Civil Rights Cases* remained the controlling precedent. The Court had yet to revive the enforcement power under the Thirteenth Amendment. Given the expansive and deferential approach that the Court had taken toward congressional exercise of the Commerce Clause since 1937, that easily appeared to be the safest approach for attacking private discrimination. Consequently, Congress passed a broad prohibition against racial discrimination in various businesses that are in or affect interstate commerce. Once again, Justice Harlan was vindicated as Congress went far beyond what he would have conceived as supportable by the Commerce Clause nearly a century earlier. The Supreme Court readily upheld the application of the Act to hotels in *Heart of Atlanta Motel v. United States*[54] and to restaurants in *Katzenbach v. McClung*.[55] Justice Harlan's grandson, by then a Supreme Court justice, joined the majority in both cases.

Did *The Civil Rights Cases* make bad law? That would depend on one's perspective. From the standpoint of effective enforcement of civil rights over the next century, probably so. The state action doctrine did make it difficult if not nearly impossible to challenge racial discrimination in the private sphere. On the other hand in view of the extent to which the Jim Crow racial caste system became embodied in the fabric of much of society over the next 75 years, it is doubtful that either the 1875 Act or the potential for more expansive congressional enforcement authority would have made much if any difference. Still as Frederic Douglass proclaimed, the Act could have served as a "noble moral standard" pointing toward the future, even if unenforced.

---

[54] 379 U.S. 241 (1964).
[55] 379 U.S. 294 (1964)

Even assuming that a contrary decision may have led to far more desirable societal outcomes, the Court's insistence on state action as a predicate for a substantive Fourteenth Amendment violation is in accord with the most defensible reading of the text and the original understanding. The Court did not create the state action doctrine out of thin air. Not only does the Amendment itself focus on deprivations by the state but it is clear that such deprivations were a primary concern for the Reconstruction Congress. Many of the radical republicans would have agreed wholeheartedly with Justice Harlan's analysis. But as William Nelson has shown, perhaps the overarching goal of the Reconstruction Congress in enacting the Fourteenth Amendment was to provide for the protection of recognized "civil" rights, those embodied in the Civil Rights Act of 1866, without cutting too deeply into state autonomy as it had traditionally existed.[56] Arguably, congressional legislation aimed specifically at correcting pervasive state failures to protect against the denial of civil rights by private parties would have been consistent with the original understanding of the Fourteenth Amendment. But as *The Civil Rights Cases* held, that is not what the 1875 Act did. And even such a statute may have cut more deeply into state autonomy than would have been acceptable to the post-Reconstruction generation. Although Harlan began his dissent with the argument that the majority had taken an unduly constrained view of the original understanding of the Fourteenth Amendment, and although there was definitely some truth in the charge, Harlan's own conception of the amendment's scope if clearly stated would never have made it out of Congress.

The *Slaughter-House Cases* majority opinion set forth an interpretation of the Fourteenth Amendment that was almost certainly incorrect but that nevertheless has endured for 140 years. The majority in *The Civil Rights Cases* presented an interpretation of the Fourteenth Amendment that was not beyond challenge but was largely consistent with the text and original understanding, and for the most part has also withstood the test of time. At the same time the Court's interpretation of the congressional enforcement power under the Thirteenth Amendment was unduly narrow and has been modified by the Court.

The Civil Rights Cases was a great case but not a hard case for the Court at the time. The public had lost enthusiasm for the civil rights agenda of the Reconstruction Congress, which probably never had widespread public support to begin with. The extension of protection against discrimination in certain areas of the private sector seemed to exemplify overreaching by Congress at the expense of the states. This popular feeling was consistent with the importance of maintaining a clear public/private distinction as a key element of late nineteenth century jurisprudence. The text of the Fourteenth Amendment made the rejection of the plaintiffs' Fourteenth Amendment arguments relatively easy for the Court. Justice Harlan in dissent illustrated that there were alternative interpretations of both amendments that were possibly more consistent with the original understanding and certainly more likely to promote the cause of freedom. Although his approach has been heralded by subsequent generations, in 1883 he was a relatively isolated if not eccentric voice. *The Civil Rights Cases* illustrate that often the results in even great cases are dictated by the larger social context in which they are decided.

---

[56] WILLIAM E. NELSON, THE FOURTEENTH AMENDMENT: FROM POLITICAL PRINCIPLE TO JUDICIAL DOCTRINE 114 (1988).

"I do not believe that any member of this court ever has sat or ever will sit or hear and decide a case the consequences of which will be so far-reaching as this...."[1]

ORAL ARGUMENT OF JOSEPH CHOATE ON BEHALF OF CHARLES POLLACK

9

Pollack v. Farmers' Loan & Trust Co.

IN TWO LENGTHY decisions in the same case issued six weeks apart in 1895, the Court invalidated the recently enacted federal income tax. Consequently, Congress was effectively deprived of the ability to enact such a tax until the Sixteenth Amendment was ratified 18 years later. The case was at the center of an extremely bitter controversy over both the constitutionality and wisdom of such a law, provoking overheated rhetoric by the justices on both sides of the issue. In context, it was viewed as part of a developing trend by the Court to throw its weight firmly behind wealth and privilege and to create constitutional obstacles to progressive legislation. This appraisal was magnified by the fact that the Income Tax decisions were rendered during the same term that the Court in *United States v. E.C. Knight Co.*[2] held that the Sherman Antitrust Act could not constitutionally be applied to a trust that controlled over 90 percent of sugar refining in the United States. And even more controversially, immediately prior to the Income Tax decisions, in *In re Debs* the Court upheld the issuance of an injunction against a labor strike of the Pullman Company.[3] The specific legal issues in *Pollack* may have seemed technical and arcane; however at the heart of the case was one of the primary partisan issues of the time, and that was certainly appreciated by both the justices and the public at large.

---

[1] Pollack v. Farmers' Loan & Trust Co., 157 U.S. 429, 553 (1895) (oral argument of Joseph Choate on behalf of Charles Pollack).

[2] 156 U.S. 1 (1895).

[3] 158 U.S. 564 (1895).

BACKGROUND

There are several clauses in the Constitution that bear on congressional authority to tax income from a variety of sources. Article I. Section Eight, paragraph 1 declares that:

> Congress shall have the Power To lay and collect Taxes, Duties, Imposts and Excises, to pay the Debts and provide for the common Defence and general Welfare of the United States; but all Duties, Imposts and Excises shall be uniform throughout the United States.

In addition Article I, Section Nine, paragraph 4 provides that:

> No Capitation, or other direct, Tax shall be laid, unless in Proportion to the Census or Enumeration herein before directed to be taken.

Finally Article I, Section Two, paragraph 3 states that:

> Representatives and direct Taxes shall be apportioned among the several States which may be included within the Union, according to their respective Numbers, which shall be determined by adding to the whole number of free Persons, including those bound to Service for a Term of Years, and excluding Indians not taxed, three fifths of all other Persons.

Thus the original Constitution seemed to divide the types of taxes that Congress can enact into two or possibly three separate categories—direct taxes and "duties, imposts and excises," which apparently are indirect taxes or perhaps a third category that are neither direct nor duties, imposts, and excises. Each category had its own qualification. Direct taxes had to be apportioned by population among the states. In other words, the amount of a direct tax imposed on the citizens of New York divided by the number of citizens must be the same as the amount of the tax imposed on the citizens of Texas divided by its number of citizens. Indirect taxes on the other hand must be uniform throughout the nation—that is the rate in New York must be the same as the rate in Texas. If there were other taxes that fell into neither category, then presumably neither the requirement of apportionment nor uniformity would apply. It has been consistently acknowledged by the justices that the reason for the apportionment limitation with respect to direct taxes was to assure the southern states that Congress could not impose oppressive taxation on either the land or slaves in the South given that the southern states had an abundance of both but an otherwise small population. As such, this provision arguably served little if any purpose after the Civil War. As Article I, Section Two, paragraph 4 indicates, the Constitution ties both representation and direct taxation to population. This appears to have been part of a compromise granting the slave states 3/5 representation for each slave in return for which each slave would count for 3/5 in computing a state's apportioned share of direct taxes. Given that Congress would place little reliance on direct taxes prior to the Civil War, the South definitely got the better deal.

The obvious question raised by these provisions is how does a court determine whether a tax is direct or indirect. During the Constitutional Convention when these clauses were under discussion, Rufus King asked that very question, and the records indicate there was no reply.[4] It was not long however before the Supreme Court was called upon to address that question in *Hylton v. United States*,[5] one of it's most significant early cases. That case involved a refusal to pay a tax on carriages by a man who purported to own "125 chariots" all "for private use and not to let out to hire."[6] As a member of Congress, James Madison had argued that the tax was in fact a direct tax and therefore unconstitutional because unapportioned.[7] The four justices who heard the case, three of whom had been members of the Constitutional Convention, issued seriatim opinions but each concluded that the tax was an excise or indirect tax and as such need not be apportioned among the states based on population. Each of the justices indicated albeit in dicta that the obvious examples of direct taxes under the Constitution were capitation (or head taxes) and taxes on land.[8]

Throughout the nineteenth century, Congress relied primarily on tariffs on imports to fund the government. Direct apportioned taxes on lands, improvements, and slaves were enacted in 1798, 1813, and 1815.[9] A tax on real estate and income was imposed as a matter of national necessity during the Civil War.[10] That tax ceased to exist following the war. After the war the Court upheld various taxes without apportionment by population, including taxes imposed on the dividends issued by insurance companies,[11] state bank notes,[12] and the succession of estates.[13] Most significant, in *Springer v. United States*,[14] the Court upheld the income tax passed during the Civil War, concluding, as in the prior cases, that the only direct taxes were capitation and taxes on land.

Against this background, Congress in 1894 passed the Act invalidated in *Pollack*. The law imposed a tax of 2 percent on personal income above $4,000, which would exclude 98 percent of the public. There was no exemption for corporations; however savings and loans, building and loans, and mutual insurance companies were exempted from the tax entirely. The tax was not adopted as a result of any significant revenue needs given that the government was running a revenue surplus.[15] Rather, it was attributable to reaction by southern and western states against high tariffs as well as part of the progressive agenda to redistribute wealth.[16] Support in Congress for the tax came almost entirely from the

---

[4] NOTES OF DEBATES IN THE FEDERAL CONVENTION OF 1787 REPORTED BY JAMES MADISON 494 (Bicentennial ed. 1987).

[5] 3 U.S. 171 (1796).

[6] *Id.* at 171.

[7] 4 ANNALS OF CONG. 730 (1794). The majority in *Pollack I* quoted Madison's statement at 157 U.S. 429, 569 (1895).

[8] Hylton v. United States, 3 U.S. 171, 175 (Chase, J.), 176 (Patterson, J.), 183 (Iredell, J.).

[9] *Pollack*, 157 U.S. at 572–73.

[10] Act of August 6, 1861, 12 Stat. 294 c.45.

[11] Pacific Ins. Co v. Soule, 74 U.S. 433 (1868).

[12] Veazie Bank v. Fenno, 75 U.S. 533 (1869).

[13] Scholey v. Rew, 90 U.S. 331 (1874).

[14] 102 U.S. 586 (1880).

[15] OWEN M. FISS, TROUBLED BEGINNINGS OF THE MODERN STATE, 1888–1910 78–80 (1993).

[16] *Id.*

poorer states, and virtually all of the opposition came from the wealthier states.[17] The debate in Congress and in the press over the Act was extremely bitter.[18] The tax would fall largely on individuals and corporations located in the northeastern states.

The Act prohibited a taxpayer suit against the government to enjoin the enforcement of the tax. Consequently, Pollack, a stockholder of the Farmer's Loan and Trust, filed suit against the company to preclude it from paying the tax on income derived from its real estate holdings and on its securities, on the ground that the tax was an unconstitutional unapportioned direct tax. He also argued that the tax as applied to the income from municipal bonds was an unconstitutional tax on the instrumentalities of state and local governments. Finally, he argued that if the tax was indirect, the various exemptions rendered it nonuniform, in violation of the Constitution. The case was dismissed by the federal district court and an appeal was taken to the United States Supreme Court.

ORAL ARGUMENT

Several of the leading lawyers of the day appeared before the Court and were permitted to argue over a period of five days. In his Holmes Devise volume, Owen Fiss notes that the *Pollack* case was "a great ceremonial occasion for the Court."[19] Attorney General Richard Olney defended that Act vigorously. He argued that the Court would have to disregard five precedents in order to invalidate the tax, and as a matter of policy and fairness, the government had the right to enact a progressive income tax.[20] James Carter representing the Continental Trust Company provided a careful response to the legal arguments raised against the tax. He also defended it as a matter of policy, chastising the challengers for attempting to "prevent a slight burden being lifted from the shoulders of the poor, who have borne it so long, and placed upon the shoulders of the rich who have been comparatively exempt!"[21] Carter cautioned the Court to defer to Congress, declaring that it would be inappropriate for the Court to substitute its judgement for that of "sixty millions of people" on an issue that forms "the subject of public discussion, array[s] class against class, and become[s] the turning points in our general elections."[22] Carter's forceful defense of the Act by one of the taxpayers subject to it suggests that the cases were not simply contrived.

The final attorney to appear for Pollack was one of the leading lawyers of the time, Joseph Choate. He began his argument with an oft-quoted declaration that the Act in question is "communistic in its purposes and tendencies, and is defended here upon principles as communistic, socialistic—what shall I call them—populistic as ever have been addressed to any political assembly in the world."[23] Moreover if the Court did not halt

---

[17] WILLARD KING, MELVILLE WESTON FULLER-CHIEF JUSTICE OF THE UNITED STATES 1888–1910, at 193 (1950).

[18] Linda Przybyszewski, *The Fuller Court (1888-1910)*, *in* THE UNITED STATES SUPREME COURT: THE PURSUIT OF JUSTICE 153 (Christopher Tomlins ed., 2005).

[19] FISS, *supra* note 15, at 75.

[20] 157 U.S. 429, 509 (1895).

[21] *Id.* at 520.

[22] *Id.* at 531.

[23] *Id.* at 532.

"this communistic march" now, there would never be another principled opportunity.[24] After this rather bombastic opening, Choate proceeded to lay out a carefully crafted legal challenge to the Act, attempting to distinguish all of the troublesome precedents. He concluded however with a response to Carter's plea for deference that "if it be true that a mighty army of sixty million citizens is likely to be incensed by this decision," the Court must "not hesitate in executing that power [to invalidate unconstitutional laws] no matter what the threatened consequences of popular or populistic wrath may be."[25]

The case was initially heard by only eight justices as Justice Jackson was ill. The Court issued an opinion invalidating the tax with respect to income derived from real estate and splitting four to four as to whether it was a direct tax as applied to other income. The decision was leaked in advance to a reporter from the *Chicago Tribune*, quite possibly by Justice Harlan.[26]

POLLACK I

At the very beginning of his opinion, recognizing that the Court was almost certainly headed into a firestorm of controversy, Chief Justice Melville Fuller quoted at length from *Marbury v. Madison*, emphasizing that it was the duty of the Court to invalidate laws that were in conflict with the Constitution.[27] After setting forth the facts, Fuller, writing for the majority, engaged in a very lengthy review of the original understanding of the taxing provisions of the Constitution. He noted that the framers were quite familiar with the economic theorists of their day including Turgot and Adam Smith. He then described the compromise at the Constitutional Convention that led to the adoption of the direct tax apportionment provision. Fuller emphasized at length that the framers seemed to agree that Congress would be able to impose very few direct taxes.

Turning to the legislative history of the tax on carriages upheld in *Hylton*, the Court quoted several members of Congress as well as Albert Gallatin for the principle expounded by Adam Smith that a tax was direct if it could not be passed on to someone else. Chief Justice Fuller declared that *Hylton* should only be understood as holding that the tax on carriages was a tax on expenses rather than on income, and as such was indirect, and that the justices did not purport to lay down a controlling rule distinguishing direct from indirect taxes. With this brief discussion, Fuller attempted to distinguish the government's foundational precedent.[28]

From this historical discussion, the chief justice concluded that the distinction between direct and indirect taxation "was well understood by the framers," a proposition that he had scarcely proven and for which there was substantial evidence to the contrary. Moreover, he declared that under state systems of taxation "all taxes on real estate or personal

---

[24] *Id.* at 533.

[25] *Id.* at 553.

[26] Jeffrey Rosen, The Supreme Court: The Personalities and Rivalries that Defined America 108 (2006).

[27] 157 U.S. 429, 554 (1895).

[28] *See* Calvin Johnson, *Apportionment of Direct Taxes: The Foul-Up in the Core of the Constitution*, 7 Wm. & Mary Bill Rts. J. 1 (1999) for an extensive argument that *Hylton*'s understanding of direct taxes was correct and *Pollack*'s was wrong.

property or the rents or income thereof were regarded as direct taxes,"[29] which even if true was of slight relevance to whether that was a correct interpretation of the constitutional language.

Fuller then turned his attention to the precedents that the dissents claimed were indistinguishable from the case before the Court. The majority read each of these cases narrowly however, distinguishing them from the recently adopted income tax, on the ground that the Court in each case had held that the taxes in issue were duties or excises and therefore indirect. The Court conceded that of all of the post–Civil War cases, *Springer v. United States*[30] was the case on which the dissents placed the greatest weight. There, the Court had rejected an attempt to invalidate the sale of a piece of real estate by the United States for failure of the owner to pay income taxes imposed during the Civil War. Chief Justice Fuller distinguished *Springer* on the ground that inspection of the original record indicated that the taxes in question were attributable to the defendant's income as an attorney as opposed to rents from the property and as such was not on point with Pollack.

The crux of Chief Justice Fuller's opinion was simply that it was well settled that a tax on land was a direct tax that must be apportioned, and that a tax on the rents or income from land was indistinguishable from a tax on the land itself. The Court offered little in the way of justification for this conclusion despite the fact that quite obviously the land itself and the income from the land are two distinct entities. Fuller maintained that federal taxation on real or personal property was intended to be the rare exception rather than the rule, and if the Court were to permit the government to do indirectly what it could not do directly it would effectively extinguish "one of the bulwarks of private rights and private property."[31] Although the Court attributed this desire to protect private property to the framers, it certainly suggests that the justices themselves were troubled by what they perceived as a legislative assault on private property.

All of the justice agreed that a tax on the income from municipal bonds violated the principle that the federal government may not constitutionally impose a tax on an instrumentality of a state. Chief Justice Fuller reported that the Court was divided four to four on three other issues: (1) whether other provisions of the Act were severable, (2) whether the tax on income from personal property was direct, and (3) whether any indirect taxes under the Act were uniform.[32]

Justice Field wrote a lengthy concurrence. Like the majority, he emphasized that the clause distinguishing direct from indirect taxes was a compromise that was indeed essential to the very creation of the Constitution, under which direct taxes, especially on land, would be apportioned on the basis of population, and in return coastal states would relinquish the authority to tax imports. Field suggested that some of the Court's precedents, especially *Springer*, might have defined the concept of direct taxation incorrectly, but in any event they were clearly distinguishable from a tax on rents. He proclaimed that it had been recognized in England for centuries and in the United States since colonial days that

---

[29] *Pollack*, 157 U.S. at 573-74.
[30] 102 U.S. 586 (1881).
[31] *Pollack*, 157 U.S. at 583. *See* Johnson, *supra* note 28, at 36–37 for the argument that the framers did not intend to protect wealth or property by making direct taxation difficult if not impossible.
[32] *Pollack*, 157 U.S. at 586.

taxes on land or on the income from land were a direct tax and that an argument to the contrary was simply a rejection of well-established principle.

Proceeding beyond the opinion of Chief Justice Fuller, Field also argued that even if the taxes were viewed as indirect, they would violate the principle of uniformity due to the exemptions of certain businesses as well as the exemption of personal income of less than $4000. In the process, he rejected the conventional view that all that was required was geographical uniformity, that is, that the tax applied the same rate to the object taxed from one state to the next. He argued that so much of the law was unconstitutional that it should be invalidated in its entirety. More explicitly than Fuller, Justice Field expressed his concern that if the law was allowed to stand

> [t]he present assault on capital is but the beginning. It will be the stepping stone to others, larger and more sweeping, till our political contests will become a war of the poor against the rich,—a war constantly growing in intensity and bitterness.[33]

Although it may seem that this was merely an ideological concern, Justice Field made it clear that he believed that such class warfare was precisely what the Apportionment and Uniformity Clauses were intended to curb.

Justice White wrote the primary dissent in the first *Pollack* case. He began by noting that although he did not generally favor lengthy dissents, he concluded that one was warranted in this instance given that the Court's opinion was so inconsistent with established precedent. At the outset, he maintained that the lawsuit should be dismissed as precluded by the statute prohibiting actions to enjoin the collection of a tax.

Justice White began by noting that it was pointless to consider the definition of direct taxes attributable to pre-constitutional economic theorists such as Adam Smith, as the meaning of the concept had been definitively settled by the *Hylton* case as well as almost a century of subsequent legislation and precedent. He argued that in sustaining the carriage tax in *Hylton*, the Court clearly rejected the economists' conception of direct (as any tax whose incidence could not readily be transferred). He maintained that the opinions of the justices in *Hylton* made it plain that only a capitation or a tax on land could be considered direct within the constitutional meaning. Indeed, this definition of direct tax "has become a part of the hornbook of American constitutional interpretation, has been taught as elementary in all the law schools. . . ."[34] White then devoted several pages to quotations in support of this definition from leading treatise writers including Kent, Storey, Cooley, and Miller.

Justice White then worked through the relevant Supreme Court precedents in painstaking detail for the purpose of showing that it was well established that taxes on income of virtually any type had been regarded as indirect.[35] He emphasized that these cases had limited direct taxation to capitation and taxes on land itself.

Summarizing this lengthy discussion, Justice White declared that the "economic construction" of direct tax favored by the majority "was repudiated by the framers themselves,

---

[33] *Id.* at 607.
[34] *Id.* at 620.
[35] *Id.* at 626–36.

and has been time and time again rejected by this court" and the framers "settled the question which the court now virtually unsettles."[36] Given that income taxes in general have been recognized as indirect, it should not matter that the tax is imposed on the income from land. Rather to be direct, the tax must be levied on the land itself. And he argued that the tax in question was not even properly viewed as a tax on rents from land but rather simply a tax on income that would include rents. White argued that if the tax on inheritance, including inheritance of land, upheld by the Court in *Scholey v. Rew*, was indirect, then the same must be true of a tax on income including rents from land.

Finally Justice White chastised the majority for ignoring its prior precedents and making light of stare decisis. He declared that if:

> [t]he permanency of [the Court's] conclusions is to depend upon the personal opinions of those who, from time to time make up its membership, it will inevitably become a theater of political strife, and its action will be without coherence or consistency.[37]

Thus the majority argued that the nation would be subjected to political strife if the income tax was not invalidated, and the dissent argued that the Court would be subjected to such strife if precedent was ignored and it was struck down.

Justice White agreed with the majority that the federal government could not tax the interest on municipal bonds.

Justice Harlan offered a short dissenting opinion.

In the initial *Pollack* opinion, Chief Justice Fuller wrote for the majority with respect to the unconstitutionality of the income tax as applied to rents and income from land and municipal bonds. Justice Jackson was ill and had not participated in the decision however, and as a result the Court split four to four as to the constitutionality of the tax as applied to the income from various other sources. Consequently, re-argument was ordered and an additional opinion was issued six weeks later. Justice Jackson recovered, or was pressured by the dissenters to "recover" or to resign without a pension.[38] Jackson voted to uphold the tax and died shortly after the decision was handed down. Apparently one of the justices who had originally voted to uphold the Act with respect to other income switched sides as the Court still invalidated the Act in all other circumstances by a vote of 5-4. As the opinion in *Pollack I* had not indicated how the justices had voted in the 4-4 split, the identity of the justice who changed his mind in *Pollack*, assuming that there was one, is considered one of the great mysteries in the history of the Court.[39] Some have identified Justice Shiras as the likely switch but have not been able to prove it conclusively.[40] Others have argued that it may have been either Justice Brewer or Gray.[41] Another theory is that Fuller tabulated the votes in *Pollack I* incorrectly, perhaps

---

[36] *Id.* at 636.

[37] *Id.* at 651.

[38] *See* KING, *supra* note 17, at 207–18.

[39] FISS, *supra* note 15, at 77; BERNARD SCHWARTZ, A HISTORY OF THE SUPREME COURT 185 (1993).

[40] MORRIS ERNST, THE GREAT REVERSALS 79 (1973).

[41] KING, *supra* note 17, at 219–20.

deliberately recording an abstention as a vote to sustain in order to avoid invalidating the entire Act by a 4-3 vote.[42]

Charles Evans Hughes later considered *Pollack* to be one of the Court's three significant self-inflicted wounds, not because of the decision to invalidate the income tax, which he believed raised a "difficult constitutional question," but rather due to the apparent vote switching between *Pollack I* and *II* that cast the Court in an unfavorable light for years to come.[43]

POLLACK II

In the second *Pollack* opinion, the majority, again speaking through Chief Justice Fuller, held that a tax on income from any form of personal property, including income derived from stocks and bonds, was also a direct tax and therefore unconstitutional if not apportioned. At the outset, presumably in response to the dissents in both the first and second *Pollack* cases, the majority distinguished *Hylton* on the grounds that the tax on carriages was considered indirect because it was an excise tax on consumption.[44] As such, it simply identified one specific type of indirect tax but said nothing of significance as to what would qualify as a direct tax. The majority further attempted to minimize the significance of the case by observing that "it was badly reported."[45]

The majority concluded that if a tax on the income from real property was direct, as *Pollack I* had held, then there was simply no basis for distinguishing a tax on the income from personal property. Of course under the reasoning of *Pollack I*, there was indeed such a basis given that the first opinion was largely based on the argument that a tax on real property was conceded by all to be a direct tax and a tax on the rent or income from real property was effectively the same thing. As there was little if any support for the conclusion that a tax on personal property was direct, then the analogy broke down. But that did not seem to bother the majority.

In response to the dissents' argument that the tax was simply on income earned by the taxpayer and the source of the income was irrelevant, the Court argued that such a principle would presumably sustain the tax on income from municipal bonds as well, which all members of the Court had concluded was unconstitutional in the prior *Pollack* opinion.

The Court noted that the efficiency and convenience of the income tax was of no significance to the constitutional issue.[46] Likewise, the fact that a broad-based income tax could lead to a reduction in tariffs was also a political matter irrelevant to the constitutional issue. Having concluded that the tax on the income from real or personal property was unconstitutional, the majority further held that the remainder of the statute, including the imposition of the tax on wages, was invalid as well because it was quite unclear that Congress would have enacted the statute absent those provisions.

---

[42] FISS, *supra* note 15, at 77.

[43] CHARLES EVANS HUGHES, THE SUPREME COURT OF THE UNITED STATES 53–54 (1928).

[44] Pollack v. Farmers' Loan & Trust Co., 157 U.S. 429, 625 (1895).

[45] *Id.* at 626.

[46] *Id.* at 634.

Justice Harlan wrote a lengthy dissent covering much of the same ground as Justice White had done in his dissent to *Pollack I*. Apparently he delivered it with extreme anger, prompting *The Nation* to characterize it as " 'the most violent political tirade ever heard in a court of last resort' "[47] although it certainly does not read that way. Just as Justice Field had charged that there would not have been a Constitution absent the compromise on direct and indirect taxes, Justice Harlan suggested that there would not have been a Constitution had the framers adopted the Court's conception of a direct tax. Like Justice White, Justice Harlan maintained that every argument and piece of evidence relied upon by the majority had been carefully considered and rejected by the Court in previous cases.

Justice Harlan then engaged in a very lengthy review of both the legislation and precedent, including a seven-page review of the *Hylton* case. This review convinced him that based on the reasoning of *Hylton*, direct taxation was limited to taxes on real property and slaves, and both the Congress and the Court had proceeded on that assumption ever since. Although Madison as a member of Congress had argued that the tax on carriages was a direct tax in need of apportionment, the Court in *Hylton* rejected that view, and as president, Madison signed several laws that imposed apportioned taxes on income of one type or another.

Harlan argued that as a practical matter, the Court had rendered it impossible for the Congress to tax income given that apportionment would be very difficult and grossly unfair as the tax rate imposed on income in less populous states would greatly exceed that in more heavily populated states (a point that had been made by Justices Chase and Patterson in *Hylton*). He expressed fear that under the Court's approach, the nation would be unable to raise sufficient revenue during a war or other crisis. Moreover, the Court's approach would favor those whose income is derived from investment rather than labor. Referring to the oral argument of Mr. Choate urging the Court to "protect the just rights of property against socialism," Harlan replied that that was a policy question committed to Congress and not the Court. Even so, he pointed out that the tax could hardly be considered "an assault by the poor upon the rich" given that so many associations with accumulated capital had been exempted from the tax." Rather the effect of the decision was to give investment property favorable protection under the Constitution. Justice Harlan also rejected the Court's conclusions as to severability. He characterized the decision as a "disaster to the country" and opined that "the American people cannot too soon amend their constitution."[48]

Justice Brown also offered a dissenting opinion. He argued that the primary purpose of the apportionment rule for direct taxes was to prevent oppressive taxes from being imposed on slaves, and as that was no longer an issue, the provision should be construed narrowly. He noted that aside from capitation taxes, the framers probably intended to include taxes on real estate as direct given that such taxes were the primary means of financing state governments. He also argued that the provision simply does not apply to taxes such as income taxes that cannot be fairly and efficiently apportioned. Justice Brown also argued that this was an area in which stare decisis should prevail, noting that "[e]ven 'a century of error' may be less pregnant with evil to the state than a long-deferred

---

[47] SCHWARTZ, *supra* note 39, at 185.
[48] *Pollack*, 157 U.S. at 673, 685.

discovery of the truth."[49] In response to the majority, Justice Brown argued that although a tax on rents was a tax on land, it was not a direct tax on the land.

With respect to the Court's criticism of income taxes in general, Justice Brown noted that "[i]f men who have an income or property beyond their pressing needs are not the ones to pay taxes, it is difficult to say who are...."[50] Brown maintained that "[r]espect for the constitution will not be inspired by a narrow and technical construction which shall limit or impair the necessary powers of congress."[51] He declared that the decision "approaches the proportions of a national calamity" that might well be "the first step toward the submergence of the liberties of the people in a sordid despotism of wealth."[52]

Justice Jackson, who had not participated in the initial *Pollack* decision, also issued a dissent. As with the other dissenters, he argued that a tax that could not be fairly apportioned by definition could not be a direct tax. He characterized the decision as "the most disastrous blow ever struck at the constitutional power of Congress."[53]

Justice White submitted a short dissent. He pointed out inconsistencies in the majority's arguments and also chastised the Court for giving "invested wealth" favorable status under the Constitution. He opined that the majority had placed the government of the United States in "the paralyzed condition which existed under the Confederation...."

White had been promoted to Chief Justice when the Sixteenth Amendment overruling the primary holding of *Pollack* was ratified.

AFTERMATH

As the dissenters predicted, *Pollack* was indeed the end of the income tax until the Constitution was amended two decades later. *Pollack* (*I* and *II*) was one of three highly controversial cases decided by the Court in 1895. In *United States v. E.C. Knight*, the Court held that the Sherman Antitrust Act could not be applied to a sugar monopoly controlling 96 percent of the sugar refining in the nation, on the ground that sugar refining took place locally and thus was beyond the scope of the Commerce Clause. And in *In re Debs*, the Court upheld an injunction against a labor strike of the Pullman Company in Chicago. All three cases were attacked on the grounds that the Court was throwing its weight behind wealth and capital and against the public and the working man. Of the three cases, *Pollack* was arguably most vulnerable to challenge given that it seemed to be inconsistent with established precedent, and the switched vote between *Pollack I* and *II* suggested that something out of the ordinary had taken place within the Court. Moreover statements in the opinions of justices on both sides of the issue suggested that ideological as opposed to legal considerations may have played a role.

The establishment press praised the decisions, with *The Nation* noting that Harlan had "'expounded the Marx gospel from the Bench.'"[54] The following year in the 1896 presidential

---

[49] *Id.* at 690.

[50] *Id.* at 694.

[51] *Id.*

[52] *Id.*

[53] *Id.* at 706.

[54] Barry Friedman, The Will of the People: How Public Opinion has Influenced the Supreme Court and Shaped the Meaning of the Constitution 175 (2009).

election, the Democratic candidate, William Jennings Bryan, campaigned vigorously against the Court on the basis of these decisions but was defeated by William McKinley in a landslide.[55] Despite *Pollack*, within the next two decades the Court did sustain both a corporate income tax and an inheritance tax.[56] *Pollack* was an important precedent near the beginning of the so-called *Lochner* era in which the Court often invalidated economically and socially progressive legislation under a variety of constitutional theories. There was an attempt in Congress to challenge *Pollack* legislatively by passing a statute all but identical to the one invalidated by the Court.[57] President Taft disagreed and urged that the decision be reversed by constitutional amendment.[58] Unlike most of the other *Lochner* era decisions however that did in fact happen. The Sixteenth Amendment ratified in 1913 reads:

> The Congress shall have the power to lay and collect taxes on incomes, from whatever source derived, without apportionment among the several States, and without regard to any census or enumeration.

This was a relatively narrow amendment aimed at the specific holding of *Pollack* itself. It did not remove the principle that aside from income taxes, direct taxes (whatever they may be, but certainly capitation taxes as specified in the Constitution and presumably taxes on land as well) must be apportioned among the states. Thus it is still possible that the difficult question of whether a tax is direct can arise as well as whether all conceivable taxes are either direct taxes or "duties, imposts or excises," or whether there is a third category of taxes authorized by Article I that falls into neither category.[59] Following the ratification of the Sixteenth Amendment, the Court rejected a substantive due process–based challenge to the new income tax.[60] The holding of the Court in *Pollack* that the interest on state bonds was constitutionally exempt from federal taxation was explicitly overruled by the Court in *South Carolina v. Baker* in 1988.[61] Although *Pollack* may now seem like something of a historical footnote, its meaning as well as that of the Sixteenth Amendment would become quite pertinent were the Congress to decide to adopt a value-added or consumption tax.[62]

POLLACK AS A GREAT CASE

The big question, whether or not the income tax was constitutional, was obviously an issue of great public moment. The legal answers to that question however were quite

---

[55] PETER HOFFER, WILLIAMJAMES HOFFER & N. E. H. HULL, THE SUPREME COURT: AN ESSENTIAL HISTORY 173–74 (2007).

[56] Knowlton v. Moore, 178 U.S. 41 (1900) (upholding the estate tax); Flint v. Stone Tracy Co., 220 U.S. 107 (1911) (sustaining the corporate income tax).

[57] ALPHEUS THOMAS MASON, THE SUPREME COURT FROM TAFT TO BURGER 19–20 (1979).

[58] *Id.* at 21–22.

[59] *See* Bruce Ackerman, *Taxation and the Constitution*, 99 COLUM. L. REV. 1 (1999).

[60] Brushaber v. Union Pac. R. Co., 240 U.S. 1 (1916).

[61] 485 U.S. 505 (1988).

[62] *See* Ackerman, *supra* note 59; Johnson, *supra* note 28; Erik M Jensen, *The "Apportionment of Direct Taxes": Are Consumption Taxes Constitutional?*, 97 COLUM. L. REV. 2334 (1997).

technical and arcane. Owen Fiss has noted in his volume of the *Holmes Devise History of the Supreme Court* that the majority's rationale for rejection of the tax, that it was direct and unapportioned, seemed "beside the point" to a nation engaged in a heated debate over the propriety and fairness of a tax on the income of the very wealthy.[63] Both the majority and some of the dissents explored the original understanding of the taxing clauses. There was dispute as to whether the framers had a clear understanding of what was meant by a direct tax. In a nutshell, the majority argued that prior to the Constitutional Convention, Adam Smith and others had set forth the theory that a tax was direct as long as the incidence of the tax could not readily be transferred and that the framers, most especially James Madison, understood and accepted that definition. The dissents replied that it was not at all clear that the framers adopted that definition, but even if they did the Court definitively rejected it early on in *Hylton*, concluding instead that only capitation taxes and taxes on land itself could be considered direct. As Madison as a member of Congress had argued that the tax on carriages was direct, that simply proves that the Court in *Hylton*, composed of three other participants in the Constitutional Convention, disagreed with Madison's understanding. As *Hylton* was the very foundation of the dissents' argument, the majority minimized it by reading it narrowly, dismissing the *Hylton* justices' definition of a direct tax as mere dicta, on the grounds that it simply held that a carriage tax was an excise or indirect tax and was not required to opine on what otherwise would be a direct tax. The majority's treatment of *Hylton* was narrow though at least plausible.

The dissent's primary argument however was based on long-standing precedent and practice. It was not simply that *Hylton* had rejected the majority's interpretation of direct tax but that the *Hylton* view had been consistently relied upon by Congress, the Court, and the commentators for 100 years. Until *Pollack*, the *Hylton* view had clearly carried the day. The majority attempted to distinguish every case and piece of legislation that the dissents relied upon, but the weight of the authority was simply too great to ignore. The dissenters made a near irrefutable case that contrary to the majority view, the law had long been settled, and that the majority's opinion was indeed one of the most extreme rejections of stare decisis in the Court's history.

The impracticality of apportioning an income tax also played a role in the analysis as it had in *Hylton*. For the dissents, this was proof that considering a tax on income to be a direct tax must be incorrect in that it would effectively negate the possibility of income taxation. But the majority replied that that was precisely the point in that the framers did not want Congress to rely on income taxation and consequently rendered it nearly impossible.

So why did the majority reject what would appear to be a well-settled approach to the question? Was it as the dissenters and the critics in the press and academia charged—nothing more that sympathy for accumulated wealth?[64] Certainly Choate as counsel for Pollack had defined the issue as the last chance to stand firm against a communistic advance. Rarely if ever had the Court been exhorted more vigorously, by a highly respected member of the bar, to decide a case essentially on ideological grounds, though he did offer

---

[63] FISS, *supra* note 15, at 98.
[64] *See, e.g.,* ROBERT G. MCCLOSKEY, THE AMERICAN SUPREME COURT 94 (1994).

doctrinal means to effectuate such a decision. Chief Justice Fuller did not respond explicitly to this argument; however Justice Field did seem to embrace it, characterizing the tax as a form of aggression against the wealthy. The dissenters especially Justice Harlan appeared equally sympathetic to the class warfare appeals made by the defenders of the tax. In the words of one of his biographers, Harlan had a "loathing for those who accumulated capital," "joined in the general condemnation of inherited wealth," and believed that "unprecedented industrial growth" was "the result of corruption and dishonesty."[65]

Was *Pollack* ultimately the result of an ideological struggle on the Court in which one economic faction had one more vote than the other? Perhaps, especially when placed in its historical context of several other decisions of a similar nature. Even so, it should be remembered that the justices then and now viewed the Constitution itself, quite properly to a large extent, as embodying many ideological commitments, one of which as Field proclaimed was a commitment to the protection of private property. As such, it is not necessarily easy to determine where law turns into mere ideology or economics. If the issue had been presented to the Court on a blank slate, perhaps the dissent's approach could be characterized as being as political as the majority's. But the dissent's ace in the hole was a century of solid precedent. Thus all the dissent needed to do was follow the established law whereas the majority needed to uproot it.

Quite apart from constitutional doctrine, *Pollack* raised a crucial institutional question as well: When and to what extent, should the Court defer to the work product of Congress? Both James Carter and Joseph Choate brought the oral arguments to the Court to a climax by focusing on that question. For Carter, the Court should defer to the will of the majority, at least on an issue that stirred up passions and created division along political lines. A decision invalidating the majoritarian will could only be perceived as political rather than legal. For Choate, invoking John Marshall, the Court's role was to apply the Constitution regardless of the circumstances and let the chips fall where they may. On the one hand there is much to be said for the position that economic policy is largely beyond the judicial domain, absent clear constitutional constraints. On the other hand, the majority believed that the very point of the limitations on the congressional power to tax was to prevent numerical majorities from confiscating the wealth of the minority through the taxing power. As such, this was precisely the type of case in which it was incumbent on the Court to reject congressional legislation. At least in the area of taxation, the Court backpedaled and grew far more deferential to Congress not long after *Pollack* was decided. With respect to other regulation of economic matters however, the Court would follow Choate's lead and intervene with some frequency for another 40 years until the New Deal revolution of 1937.

Pollack was clearly a great case. It involved a question of extreme public importance and visibility. It arose at a time when the issue was at the very center of intense political disagreement. Both sides argued to the Court that a decision contrary to their position would be cataclysmic. If the justices were not swayed by these pleas, at least some appeared to be sympathetic to them. The opinions themselves seem to suggest that the ideological predispositions of the justices played at least some role in the decisions. Two opinions were issued within six weeks with reason to believe that at least one justice may

---

[65] Linda Przybyszewski, The Republic according to John Marshall Harlan 173–75 (1999).

have changed his views in the process. The decisions were highly controversial and were in fact condemned in the presidential platform of the Democratic Party the following year. As with *Dred Scott*, the decisions were eventually reversed by constitutional amendment. When Holmes made his famous quip about great cases and bad law some nine years later, surely he had *Pollack* in mind. And for good reason. It was a great case that did make bad law. It was bad in the sense that it was almost certainly wrong as a matter of precedent and from the standpoint of the appropriate institutional role of the Court. The case for extending the concept of direct taxation beyond head and land taxes was at best strained. Considering the difficulty of achieving the supermajority necessary to pass a constitutional amendment, a case that is overturned by such an amendment within two decades of its decision must almost certainly have constituted bad law.

It is certainly possible that some of the justices were swayed by the "greatness" of the case. The presumptive switch of one justice between *Pollack I* and *II* has raised questions as to the decision-making process, although it is not uncommon for the outcome of a case in the Supreme Court to be altered because a justice has changed his mind after the initial argument or conference. In the context of this controversial decision however, the specter that something out of the ordinary had occurred bolstered the critics of the case. The vigor of the dissents also doubtlessly contributed to some of the public disrespect for the majority opinion. The tone of some of the oral argument as well as that of some of the opinions suggests that ideological considerations were at least present. Again, this is not unique in Supreme Court history, but these political considerations seemed to be closer to the surface in *Pollack* than usual. As is true of most "great cases," *Pollack* was decided by a strong willed and confident Court. It seemed to charge into the teeth of settled precedent without trepidation. Perhaps the furor caused by the enactment of the income tax law a year earlier emboldened the Court to take a stand despite the fact that it could easily anticipate severe political and professional criticism. The Court's decisions the same term in *E.C. Knight* and *In re Debs* also provoked a strong public reaction. However, each of those cases were decided by 8-1 rather than 5-4 margins and in neither was the Court faced with the precedential hurdles that it encountered in *Pollack*. *Pollack* along with *Debs* and *E.C. Knight* suggests that this was a Court prepared to follow its own lights and damn the consequences. The greatness of the *Pollack* cases certainly provided the Court with the opportunity to make bad law. It provided a hyper-charged atmosphere that seems to have permeated the Court itself. Even so, *Pollack* was decided by a confident and capable Court that may simply have taken full advantage of the opportunity that this great case presented.

When the decision in NLRB v. Jones & Laughlin Steel was announced "[t]he silent intake of spectators' breaths all but caused a vacuum in the courtroom."[1]

ASSOCIATED PRESS REPORT

10

NLRB v. Jones & Laughlin Steel Corp.

THE DECISION IN *NLRB v. Jones & Laughlin Steel Corp.*[2] was the pivotal point in the famous judicial revolution of 1937. The case was decided at the very time that the Senate was considering President Franklin Delano Roosevelt's plan to pack the Court. The nation was still in the midst of the Great Depression. In the previous two terms, the Court had invalidated several federal statutes intended to address the economic crisis.[3] The president was explicitly challenging the Court as an obstructionist institution. The attorneys for the federal government were asking the Court to significantly alter its method of analyzing questions of congressional authority, especially under the Commerce Clause. The case and its companions raised a challenge to the constitutionality of the National Labor Relations Act (the Wagner Act), the most significant piece of labor relations legislation ever passed by Congress. Arguably, the Court has never decided a case in a more pressurized atmosphere. Following the decision, constitutional law would move in a very different direction.

DUAL FEDERALISM AND THE COMMERCE CLAUSE

The year 1937 was unquestionably a crucial turning point in American constitutional law especially with respect to the Court's approach to issues of federal and state power over economic matters. The story of the developments leading to the decisions in 1937

---

[1] RICHARD C. CORTNER, THE *JONES & LAUGHLIN* CASE 160 (1976).
[2] 301 U.S. 1 (1937).
[3] Carter v. Carter Coal Co., 298 U.S. 238 (1936) (invalidating the Bituminous Coal Conservation Act of 1935); United States v. Butler, 297 U.S. 1 (1936) (invalidating a portion of the Agricultural Adjustment Act of 1933); R.R. Retirement Bd. v. Alton, 295 U.S. 330 (1935) (invalidating the Railroad Retirement Act of 1934); A.L.A. Schechter Poultry Corp. v. United States, 295 U.S. 495 (1935) (invalidating the application of the National Industrial Recovery Act to a wholesale poultry business).

has been told at great length elsewhere;[4] however a brief summary is in order to place the *Jones & Laughlin* case in context. As discussed in a previous chapter, Chief Justice Marshall construed congressional power under the Commerce Clause broadly, although how broadly remains a matter of controversy even today. Congress did not employ the commerce power as a basis for economic regulation until the latter part of the nineteenth century. When it did, the Court tended to construe the reach of that power restrictively although there were significant exceptions. During the late nineteenth and early twentieth century, the Court analyzed federal power questions through the lens of dual federalism. The Court perceived a clear division between federal and state authority with little room for overlap. Areas such as manufacturing, agriculture, mining, and retail sales were local in nature and hence beyond the power of the federal government to reach regardless of the size, scope, or impact of these activities. Consequently activity that clearly exerted a significant impact on interstate commerce was often beyond congressional control.

SUBSTANTIVE DUE PROCESS

Viewed in isolation it might appear that the Court was simply concerned with the proper allocation of regulatory power in the federal system—that is, the areas beyond congressional control could be regulated but by the states. However when the states attempted to regulate economic activity during the early part of the twentieth century, they were often thwarted by the doctrine of substantive due process. The doctrine maintained that state governments were precluded from regulating private economic activity through the imposition of maximum hour, minimum wage, and other economic and labor regulation because to do so would violate the right of contract implicit in the concept of liberty protected by Fourteenth Amendment due process.

The concept of substantive due process had initially been introduced in Chief Justice Taney's opinion in the *Dred Scott* Case, carried forward by Justice Bradley's dissent in the *Slaughter-House Cases*, recognized but not relied upon in *Munn v. Illinois*,[5] and finally adopted by the Court in *Allgeyer v. Louisiana*.[6] The classic statement of the doctrine along with vigorous challenges in the dissents came in *Lochner v. New York* in 1905.[7] It remained the exception rather than the rule until it was applied with great force and regularity by the Court in the 1920s and early 1930s. Combining the restrictive approach to the Commerce Clause with the substantive due process liberty of contract, a significant amount of democratically supported social welfare legislation was essentially beyond the control of either federal or state government.

As the Depression deepened, judicial invalidation of federal and state relief legislation moved the nation toward a constitutional crisis. Substantive due process doctrine began to crumble earlier than did the restrictive approach to the Commerce Clause. In 1934 in

---

[4] *See, e.g.*, Jeff Shesol, Supreme Power: Franklin Roosevelt vs. The Supreme Court (2010); Barry Cushman, Rethinking the New Deal Court: The Structure of a Constitutional Revolution (1998).

[5] 94 U.S.113 (1876).

[6] 165 U.S. 578 (1897).

[7] 198 U.S. 45 (1905).

Nebbia v. New York,[8] the Court upheld against a substantive due process challenge a state law imposing minimum price controls on the retail sale of milk. In the process, it rejected the long-standing principle that the state only had freedom to regulate those businesses "affected with the public interest." Instead, the Court concluded that any business worthy of state regulation was by definition affected with the public interest, draining the concept of any doctrinal significance. Justice McReynolds and the other three hard core advocates of substantive due process well understood that this was the beginning of the end of that doctrine and wrote a vigorous dissent in protest. Instead of collapsing however as might have been expected, substantive due process showed itself very much alive when in *Morehead v. New York ex rel. Tiplado*[9] in 1936, the Court employed that doctrine to invalidate a New York law setting a minimum wage for women. That decision coming at the end of the Court's term provoked more public and press criticism than perhaps any other decision during this tumultuous period.[10]

THE COURT AND THE NEW DEAL

Following his election in 1932, President Roosevelt encouraged a solid Democratic Congress to pass a flurry of measures intended to help lift the nation out of the Great Depression. Many of these were ill thought out, especially with respect to constitutional issues.[11] The National Industrial Recovery Act (NIRA) was the centerpiece of the early New Deal. It required businesses and labor groups to enact detailed codes governing most aspects of operation. Businesses generally regarded these codes as clumsy and overly intrusive. The Court's approach to federal legislation at this point was quite threatening. In *Railroad Retirement Board v. Alton Railroad* in 1935, the Court invalidated a congressional attempt to establish a retirement and pension system for railroad workers.[12] The same year in *Panama Refining v. Ryan*, the Court invalidated provisions of the NIRA as unlawfully delegating legislative authority to the president.[13] Relying on dual federalism principles, in 1936 the Court struck down an agricultural subsidy program promulgated under the Spending Clause in *United States v. Butler*.[14]

Fearing that the Court might invalidate the NIRA, the government managed to delay a challenge to the Act before the Supreme Court until shortly before it was due to expire. That challenge finally came in *A.L.A. Schechter Poultry Corp v. United States* where the Court unanimously invalidated the "live poultry Codes" promulgated under the NIRA as applied to a wholesale poultry slaughterhouse reselling chicken only in New York.[15] Writing for the Court, Chief Justice Hughes rejected a Commerce Clause justification on the ground that the chickens had come to New York before Schechter acted on them, and held as well that the Act delegated unconstrained legislative authority to the president. In the

---

[8] 291 U.S. 502 (1934).
[9] 298 U.S. 857 (1936).
[10] SHESOL, *supra* note 4, at 222-24.
[11] *Id.* at 43-44.
[12] 295 U.S. 330 (1935).
[13] 293 U.S. 388 (1935).
[14] 297 U.S. 1 (1936).
[15] 295 U.S. 495 (1935).

process, Hughes cautioned that "[e]xtraordinary conditions do not create or enlarge constitutional power."[16] *Schechter* was not a case of great national significance in that it only involved the activity of a relatively small in-state wholesaler under an Act that was set to expire anyway. The president reacted to *Schecter* by declaring that the Commerce Clause had been adopted at a time when the country was still in the horse-and-buggy era.[17] This was perceived as a somewhat intemperate criticism of the Court.

Carter v. Carter Coal[18] was another matter entirely however. There the Court invalidated the Bituminous Coal Act of 1935, which gave industry boards the right to regulate economic and labor conditions in the coal industry, including the promulgation of minimum prices. The Court recognized that the coal industry was a crucial national industry with a long history of volatile labor conditions and that labor disruptions in the industry could have a significant impact on the economy. Nevertheless, applying the formalistic analysis that it had developed over the years, it concluded by a 6-3 majority that mining was a local activity, and any effects on interstate commerce, no matter how great they might be, were nevertheless indirect. Relying on *Schechter*, the Court unanimously invalidated the provisions of the codes governing labor relations as an unconstitutional delegation of legislative power, in this instance to private groups. Justice Cardozo, dissenting with respect to the Commerce Clause, emphasized the very real and serious impact that instability in the coal industry posed for the national economy. Rejecting the majority's formalistic analysis, Cardozo argued that "a great principle of constitutional law is not susceptible of comprehensive statement in an adjective."[19] Justice Stone characterized the 1936 term as "the most disastrous" in the Court's history.[20] Robert McCloskey noted that in 1935 and 1936, the Court "waged what is surely the most ambitious dragon-fight in its long and checkered history."[21]

THE COURT PACKING PLAN

President Roosevelt won an overwhelming victory in the election of 1936 as did the Democratic Party in both houses of Congress. Shortly after the inauguration on February 5, 1937, he unveiled his "court packing" proposal. Under the plan, an additional justice or federal judge would be appointed for every judge or justice who had served for 10 years and had not retired within six months of reaching the age of 70. Implementation of the plan would result in the appointment of four additional Supreme Court justices, which would prove more than sufficient to swing the already closely divided Supreme Court easily in Roosevelt's direction. Initially, Roosevelt defended the proposal on the grounds of judicial efficiency, maintaining that the older justices were not keeping current with their workload. When this was criticized as disingenuous however, he openly argued that

---

[16] *Id.* at 528.

[17] Frank Freidel, *The Sick Chicken Case, in* QUARRELS THAT HAVE SHAPED THE CONSTITUTION 233, 251 (John A. Garraty ed., 1987).

[18] 298 U.S. 238 (1936).

[19] *Id.* at 327.

[20] ALPHEUS THOMAS MASON, THE SUPREME COURT FROM TAFT TO BURGER 96 (1979).

[21] ROBERT G. MCCLOSKEY, THE AMERICAN SUPREME COURT 110 (2d ed. 1994).

the goal of the proposal was to change the direction of the Court, which he viewed as obstructing efforts to revive the national economy.[22] After the plan was announced, the press was nearly unanimous in its condemnation.[23] Justice Jackson would later declare that the court packing plan was equivalent to "throwing a stone through a cathedral window."[24]

Democratic Party opposition to the proposal began to mount. In response to a request from Senate Judiciary Committee Chairman Burton Wheeler, Chief Justice Hughes provided a letter showing statistically that the Court was keeping abreast with its caseload and arguing that the appointment of additional justices would slow the Court down.[25] The chief justice's letter increased the political opposition to the proposal and almost certainly played a crucial role in its eventual defeat.[26] Representative Hatton Sumners of Texas, Chairman of the House Judiciary Committee, led the opposition to the plan declaring "Boys, here's where I cash in my chips."[27]

THE FALL OF SUBSTANTIVE DUE PROCESS

West Coast Hotel v. Parrish[28] marked the end of the era of economic substantive due process. Decided in the spring of the 1936–1937 term, it can also be considered the beginning of the judicial revolution of 1937. *West Coast Hotel* was notable given that it upheld a state law establishing a minimum wage for women despite the fact that the Court had invalidated such a law only nine months earlier in *Morehead*. The membership of the Court had not changed. Only Justice Roberts's shift from the *Morehead* majority to the *West Coast Hotel* majority made the difference.

Chief Justice Hughes, writing for the majority, attempted to construct an opinion that for the most part suggested that nothing much had changed and that the result was driven by well-established precedent. He contended that in *Morehead* the Court had not been asked to reconsider *Adkins*, which had invalidated the minimum wage law for women in 1923. Most important there was no difference of significance between minimum wage legislation and maximum hour legislation, which had long been sustained. Despite the majority's attempt to portray its decision as a logical progression from precedent, it made it quite clear that the era of substantive due process was over. It explicitly rejected the previous assumption that there was something constitutionally special about freedom of contract. In addition, the state could quite properly take account of inequality of bargaining power in the labor market. Moreover, it also emphasized that the state had a legitimate interest in regulating employee-employer relations in such a way as to minimize the social welfare burden shouldered by the state. With the removal of these pillars, economic substantive due process simply collapsed. Justice Sutherland's dissent for the four remaining defenders of the doctrine accused the Court of amending

---

[22] Roosevelt announced this change of direction in a speech at the Mayflower Hotel on March 4, 1937.

[23] SHESOL, *supra* note 4, at 305.

[24] Oral History of Justice Jackson quoted in *id.* at 503.

[25] WILLIAM H. REHNQUIST, THE SUPREME COURT 227–28 (1987).

[26] *Id.*

[27] *Id.* at 220.

[28] 300 U.S. 379 (1937).

the Constitution in response to the economic turmoil of the Depression. It also defended the distinction that had been drawn between maximum hour and minimum wage legislation.

Justice Roberts shift between *Moorhead* and *West Coast Hotel* (as well as between *Carter Coal* and *Jones & Laughlin Steel* two weeks later) was famously characterized as the "switch in time that saved nine."[29] The implication was that he had been intimidated by the court packing plan that had been announced several weeks before the opinion was issued. Justice Roberts maintained based on internal records of the deliberations that he had cast his vote in the case, which had been argued in December 1936, well before the plan was announced on February 5, 1937. At that time, Justice Stone was ill and did not participate in the conference. The Court held back the decision to avoid affirming by a 4-4 vote. The opinion was actually finished shortly after the court packing plan had been announced; however its publication was withheld to avoid the appearance that it was simply capitulation to the threat.[30] Of course, widespread public opinion was that this was exactly what had happened. Historians and commentators have long debated whether and to what extent either knowledge of the specific plan or of the likelihood that Roosevelt intended to propose some type of action to influence the Court may have been a factor.[31] Various proposals to limit the Court legislatively or by constitutional amendment had been floated by both the White House and Democrats in Congress for two years prior to the release of the court packing plan. At the behest of Justice Frankfurter, Justice Roberts later wrote a memo, to be published after his death, explaining that the decision in *West Coast Hotel* had been reached prior to the announcement of the court packing plan. Frankfurter published the memo several years later.[32] Roberts's recollection of some of the facts has been challenged.[33] A full answer to whether this had any impact on the Court's decision-making will never be known. It seems likely however that the pressurized political and economic climate in which *West Coast Hotel* was decided significantly influenced Justice Roberts, who was not known as a justice of firm convictions in any event.[34] As important as *West Coast Hotel* was doctrinally, it pales in significance when compared to *NLRB v. Jones & Laughlin Steel* decided seven weeks later.

NLRB v. JONES & LAUGHLIN STEEL

The National Labor Relations Act (NLRA), the most important piece of labor legislation passed at the time and even to this date, was enacted in 1935 before the Court invalidated the Bituminous Coal Conservation Act in *Carter v. Carter Coal*. The Act provided protection for collective bargaining in businesses engaged in or affecting interstate commerce.

---

[29] No one seems to know who was responsible for the famous quip. SHESOL, *supra* note 4, at 434.

[30] CUSHMAN, *supra* note 4, at 18.

[31] *See, e.g.*, Robert L. Stern, *The Commerce Clause and the National Economy, 1933–1946, Part One*, 59 HARV. L. REV. 645, 681–82 (1946) (lawyers at the time believed that the court packing plan had influenced the decisions); CUSHMAN, *supra* note 4, at 32 (there is no direct evidence that the justices were influenced by the court packing plan).

[32] Felix Frankfurter, *Mr. Justice Roberts*, 104 U. PA. L. REV. 311 (1955).

[33] SHESOL, *supra* note 4, at 413–14.

[34] *Id.* at 122.

In its early enforcement proceedings, the Labor Board proceeded cautiously, focusing either on companies that were clearly engaged in interstate commerce such as bus and telegraph or on industrial giants such as the steel industry.[35] After *Carter Coal* however, it appeared that local activities in even the largest and most economically significant industries would not fall within the scope of the commerce power. The labor relations provisions of the Act were substantially the same as those invalidated in *Carter Coal*.[36]

The incidents giving rise to *NLRB v. Jones & Laughlin Steel Corp.* arose in the context of a labor dispute at the steel works in Alquippa, Pennsylvania, a classic company town. Union organizers were fired in a discriminatory manner, and a complaint was filed with the Board.[37] The Board held for the employees; however, the Court of Appeals reversed on the ground that the Board did not have the constitutional authority to regulate disputes at the production stage.[38] In its brief, the government emphasized the significant vertical integration of the company in an attempt to portray it as operating at an intermediate point within the stream of commerce like the packing plant in *Swift Packing Co v. United States*, thereby distinguishing it from *Carter Coal*. The case was set for argument with other NLRA cases, including a small clothing manufacturer, a trailer company, and the Associated Press. A case involving the Railway Labor Act was also set for argument with the NLRA cases. Together the five cases were argued over a four-day period before a crowded courtroom.

The oral argument took place only five days after the announcement of the court packing plan. There was a consensus that the Court would invalidate the Act in reliance on *Carter Coal*.[39] The government was represented by Solicitor General (and future justice) Stanley Reed along with future federal judges Charles Fahey and Charles Wyzanski. Celebrated Supreme Court advocate John W. Davis appeared on behalf of the Associated Press in one of the companion cases to *Jones & Laughlin Steel*. Several violent labor strikes occurred while the case was under consideration by the Court.[40] Two weeks before the decision in *Jones & Laughlin* was announced, the Court handed down its opinion in *West Coast Hotel v. Parish* signaling the end of economic substantive due process. By the time the *Jones & Laughlin* decision was announced, the court packing plan was effectively doomed despite the fact that Roosevelt would continue to fight for it even after the Court had essentially capitulated.[41]

The Court announced its opinion in *Jones & Laughlin Steel* on April 12, 1937, two months after the oral argument. The opinion is reported at 301 U.S. 1. Supreme Court historian Bernard Schwartz viewed 301 U.S. as the crucial turning point in the constitutional jurisprudence of the twentieth century.[42]

---

[35] STERN, *supra* note 31, at 675.

[36] *Id.* at 676.

[37] ARCHIBALD COX, THE SUPREME COURT AND THE CONSTITUTION 156–60 (1987) Cox provides a detailed discussion of the events leading to the lawsuit.

[38] 83 F.2d 998 (5th Cir. 1936).

[39] SHESOL, *supra* note 4, at 421–22.

[40] STERN, *supra* note 31, at 678.

[41] CUSHMAN, *supra* note 4, at 20. *See* SHESOL, *supra* note 4, at 435–500 for a discussion of how Roosevelt continued to press for the court packing plan against the advice of almost everyone around him.

[42] BERNARD SCHWARTZ, A HISTORY OF THE SUPREME COURT 236 (1993).

Chief Justice Hughes wrote for the five-member majority. After summarizing the relevant provisions of the NLRA, he turned to the nature of the defendant's business as described by the Labor Board. Hughes explained that the company was the fourth largest producer of steel in the United States. It owned iron ore, limestone, and coal mines; steamships; barges; a railroad; warehouses; fabricating shops; distribution centers; and sales offices across the country. Quoting the Board, he noted that the plants in Pittsburgh and Alquippa "'might be likened to the heart of a self-contained, highly integrated body [that] draw[s] in the raw materials from Michigan, Minnesota, West Virginia, Pennsylvania...through arteries...controlled by the respondent...transform the materials and then pump them out to all parts of the nation....'"[43] He then explained that the company employed 33,000 ore miners, 44,000 coal miners, 4,000 in limestone quarries, 16,000 in manufacturing coke, 343,000 in manufacturing steel, and 83,000 in transporting the product. This factual recitation certainly suggested that the Court was prepared to follow the government's lead and conclude that the company was operating in the stream of commerce, a conclusion that could easily be supported by established case law. Hughes did not rest on the continuous stream theory however.

At the outset, the chief justice recognized that there remained a crucial distinction between activity that affected interstate commerce and that which was purely local. He focused on the jurisdictional provision of the NLRA that extended Board authority to activity "burdening or obstructing commerce or the free flow of commerce." In concluding that Congress had the authority to regulate labor relations within a state where a labor dispute might burden the flow of interstate commerce, Hughes relied on two railway labor cases, including one argued along with *Jones & Laughlin* and decided two days earlier along with dicta from *Schechter*, which had of course rejected the government's Commerce Clause argument. Although not wholly inapposite, it was rather weak precedent for the proposition.

Hughes explained that the company rested its argument on the proposition that manufacturing is not commerce, citing several cases including *Schechter* and *Carter Coal*. He explicitly declined to rely on the government's "stream of commerce" argument. Instead citing dicta from earlier decisions, he proclaimed that under the Commerce Clause, Congress may protect interstate commerce and promote its growth no matter what the source of the activity that threatens it. Intrastate activity could be regulated if there was a "close and substantial relation to interstate commerce."[44] He conceded however that Congress could not reach effects that were so indirect and remote as to destroy the distinction between national and local.

Hughes attempted to distinguish prior precedent to the contrary. Most significant were the two most recent cases, *Schechter* and *Carter Coal*. *Schechter* was fairly easily set aside as a case involving a highly remote effect. *Carter Coal*, which was directly on point, was distinguished on the grounds that the codes were invalidated as unlawful delegations of legislative authority and as violative of due process. Be that as it may, the Court in *Carter Coal* had also clearly and forcefully held that the application of the codes to the

---

[43] 301 U.S. 1, 27 (1937).

[44] *Id.* at 37.

coal mining industry exceeded the commerce power. The *Jones & Laughlin* Court simply ignored that crucial aspect of the opinion.

Turning to the case at hand, the chief justice explained that "it is idle to say that [a labor dispute in the industry] would be indirect and remote."[45] Rather "it would be immediate and might be catastrophic."[46] This was undeniably true but it was equally true of the even more rancorous coal industry. Without mentioning *Carter Coal* by name, the Court clearly rejected its mode of analysis proclaiming that the question of direct and indirect effects cannot be determined in an intellectual vacuum and "that interference with... commerce must be appraised by a judgment that does not ignore actual experience."[47] With that pronouncement, the Court had finally accepted the government's approach to the Commerce Clause emphasizing economic reality over legal constructs. With that conclusion, constitutional law had changed significantly and forever.

Applying this analysis, Hughes noted that "the steel industry is one of the great basic industries of the United States," and the fact that there had not been significant labor turmoil in the industry in recent years did not prevent Congress and the Board from protecting against the threat. The majority then concluded that Congress could rationally proceed on the assumption that uninhibited collective bargaining would promote labor peace, which would in turn protect interstate commerce. It reversed the Court of Appeals and upheld the action of the Board.

In the companion case of *NLRB v. Freuhauf Trailer Co.* involving a relatively small Michigan company that bought materials and sold its finished products in interstate commerce, the Court simply stated the facts and concluded that the principles set forth in *Jones & Laughlin Steel* "are applicable here."[48] In *NLRB v. Friedman-Harry Marks Clothing* involving a small manufacturer of clothing that bought materials and sold its products in interstate commerce, the majority stated that the objections raised to the Board's jurisdiction "were without merit" "for the reasons stated in our opinion" in *Jones & Laughlin Steel*.[49] Thus despite the emphasis on the enormous size and vertical integration of the steel company, the companion cases established absent any further analysis that even the smallest of businesses could readily be found to affect commerce under the NLRA if it bought raw materials or shipped finished goods across state lines. As such, the Court had gone much further than simply reversing *Carter Coal*. The Commerce Clause holding of *Schechter* was rejected as well.

Justice McReynolds wrote a dissent for the famous "four horsemen" of laissez faire constitutional doctrine. He took issue with the decision in *Jones & Laughlin Steel* as well as the other three NLRA cases decided along with it. At the very outset, the dissent charged that the decisions were in conflict with the recent opinions in *Schechter* and *Carter Coal*, the latter rendered only nine months earlier. Unlike the majority, which not surprisingly had focused primarily on *Jones & Laughlin Steel*, the largest of the three companies, Justice McReynolds chose to focus on the clothing company, the smallest of the three. Unlike the steel company, Justice McReynolds noted that if the company were shut down, the

---

[45] *Id.* at 41.

[46] *Id.*

[47] *Id.* at 41–42.

[48] 301 U.S. 49, 57 (1937).

[49] 301 U.S. 58, 75 (1937).

effect on interstate commerce would be negligible.[50] Under the rationale of *Carter Coal* he argued that the dismissal of 10 men by the clothing company could have only an indirect and remote impact on interstate commerce. McReynolds set forth a lengthy parade of horribles asking whether all manners of local activity could now be regulated if the business in question bought or sold products in interstate commerce. Subsequent cases would confirm that the answer was clearly yes. Justice McReynolds must have realized that his dissent in *Jones & Laughlin* was truly the last gasp of dual federalism.

Following the decision in *Jones & Laughlin Steel*, negotiations began between the company and the union, but then broke down. A strike was called and a new contract was signed shortly thereafter.[51]

THE IMPACT OF *JONES & LAUGHLIN STEEL*

NLRB v. Jones & Laughlin Steel was one of the crucial turning points in American constitutional law. By upholding the constitutionality of the NLRA, it ushered in a new era of collective bargaining in labor relations. That in itself was of great significance. However the impact of the decision went far beyond the specific legislation before the Court. It was a crucial step in the rejection of dual federalism and the substitution of an expansive and economically realistic approach to the Commerce Clause as well as strong judicial deference to its congressional exercise.

Despite its revolutionary nature, the opinion itself was low key in its approach. It did not claim to be taking the law in a new direction. Rather it purported to build incrementally on established precedent while distinguishing a few arguably troublesome cases. It did not explicitly overrule any prior decision despite the fact, as the dissent maintained, the conflict with prior cases, especially *Carter Coal* decided only nine months earlier, was stark and unavoidable.

The stability of law and precedent was extraordinarily important to Chief Justice Hughes. Especially in view of the court packing plan, which had been announced a few days before *Jones & Laughlin Steel* was argued and remained on the table though mortally wounded at the time the opinion was issued, it was crucial that Hughes write an opinion that did not appear to break sharply with the past while in fact doing just that. Hughes, brilliant jurist that he was, produced a remarkable synthesis of existing precedent, suggesting that this revolutionary decision was nothing more than a logical progression from established principle. The attempt by Hughes to distinguish *Carter Coal* as merely a delegation and due process decision was hardly persuasive. The Commerce Clause holding had been quite clear. But that was apparently the price of a change of direction.

Although *Jones & Laughlin* relied on an affecting-commerce theory, it could readily have been rationalized under stream-of-commerce doctrine established in *Swift* and *Stafford*. As such neither the facts of the steel case nor of the companion trailer and clothing cases presented the Court with the more challenging issue of applying the affects theory where there was no interstate movement of goods or materials.

---

[50] *Id.* at 87.
[51] CORTNER, *supra* note 1, at 168.

Following *Jones & Laughlin Steel*, the Court upheld several applications of the Commerce Clause. Two cases in particular stand out as doctrinally significant. In *United States v. Darby*[52] decided in 1941, the Court upheld the application of the minimum wage, maximum hour, and record keeping requirements of the Federal Labor Standards Act to a local lumber manufacturer who intended to ship the finished product in interstate commerce. By the time of *Darby*, Roosevelt had substantially remade the Court with justices favorably disposed to federal economic legislation, having replaced all four of the *Jones & Laughlin* dissenters. The unanimous Court upheld the application of the labor standards to local production both as a means of prohibiting shipment of non-complying goods in interstate commerce and as a means of preventing unfair competition in interstate commerce.

The Court in *Darby* took a far bolder and more expansive approach to the commerce power than had the *Jones & Laughlin* Court. *Darby* cited *Gibbons v. Ogden* as having taken a broad view of the Commerce Clause at the outset unlike *Jones & Laughlin*, which made no mention of *Gibbons* at all. Also unlike *Jones & Laughlin*, *Darby* acknowledged the inconsistency of the Court's present approach to the Commerce Clause with the reasoning of *Carter Coal* and stated that so far as it was inconsistent with the conclusions reached in the instant case "its doctrine is limited in principle by the decision under the Sherman Act and the National Labor Relations Act, which we have cited and which we follow."[53] Thus as of *Darby*, the Court was prepared to admit that it had changed course in *Jones & Laughlin* albeit with the suggestion that *Carter Coal* had been the anomalous decision. *Darby* also cut to the very core of the dual federalism doctrine in dismissing the Tenth Amendment as "but a truism that all is retained which has not been surrendered."[54]

The third crucial decision solidifying the Court's post-1937 approach to the Commerce Clause was *Wickard v. Filburn*.[55] There, the Court upheld government-imposed quotas on the amount of wheat that could be grown and consumed on a farm, as a means of helping to stabilize prices in the extremely volatile wheat market. Unlike either *Jones & Laughlin* or *Darby* where the federal government had regulated the local production of goods that were clearly destined for interstate shipment, *Wickard* involved the application of the effect on commerce theory to the local production of goods, which by definition were not intended for interstate shipment. As such, a rationale upholding the regulation would inevitably be more expansive than what had preceded it—and so it was. The Court's opinion was written by Justice Jackson, who had recently been appointed to the Court and who as attorney general had argued the *Darby* case the year before. Even more than in *Darby*, Justice Jackson grounded the Court's approach to the commerce power on *Gibbons v. Ogden*, which he noted "described [that] power with a breadth never yet exceeded."[56] Thus *Wickard* established the narrative that Marshall had at the outset understood the commerce power as being extraordinarily broad, and thus it was subsequent narrowing decisions such as *E.C. Knight, Hammer v. Dagenhart*, and *Carter Coal* that had misunderstood the true scope of the Commerce Clause. As such, the contemporary

---

[52] 312 U.S. 100 (1941).
[53] *Id.* at 123.
[54] *Id.* at 124.
[55] 317 U.S. 111 (1942).
[56] *Id.* at 120.

Court was interpreting the Constitution conservatively, not radically, by returning to the original and correct meaning.

Jones & Laughlin Steel had turned the Court away from the formalistic analysis of *Carter Coal* toward the more economically realistic approach favored by the government. In *Wickard*, however, Justice Jackson hammered home that message with a vengeance. He explained that "questions of the power of Congress are not to be decided by a reference to any formula which would give controlling force to nomenclature such as 'production' and 'indirect' and foreclose consideration of the actual effects of the activity in question upon interstate commerce."[57] Applying this approach, the unanimous Court upheld the regulation of wheat grown for home consumption on the theory that in the aggregate, such wheat could impact the interstate market either by decreasing demand or altering supply in the event of an increase in market price. With *Wickard*, the Court's expansive reading of the commerce power with extreme deference to Congress was complete and would prevail unchallenged for the next 53 years until the Court would rein it in slightly in *United States v. Lopez*.[58] As it happened, it was *Wickard v. Filburn*, not *Gibbons v. Ogden*, that "described the federal commerce power with a breadth never yet exceeded."

NLRB v. *JONES & LAUGHLIN STEEL* AS A GREAT CASE

NLRB v. Jones & Laughlin Steel was certainly a great case in the sense that it was one of the crucial pivotal points in American constitutional law. It upheld legislation that is the very foundation of American labor law. It launched the modern era of congressional power doctrine, essentially redefining federalism. But it was also very much a great case in the sense of bringing a significant constitutional issue to the Court in a highly pressurized atmosphere. Indeed, one could argue that in view of the presence of the court packing plan it was one of the most pressurized contexts that the Court had ever encountered.

Ever since *West Coast Hotel* and *Jones & Laughlin Steel* were decided, commentators have speculated over whether President Roosevelt intimidated the Court into changing its direction by announcing and pressing the court packing plan. David Currie declared the "the price of judicial independence was the death of our federal system."[59] *West Coast Hotel* was the initial case in which the Court rejected recently decided precedent. Contemporary commentators were convinced that Justice Roberts had been bullied into changing his views. The record does establish that the decision in conference was reached well before the court packing plan was announced. Thus Justice Roberts "shift in time to save nine" would not appear to be a direct response to Roosevelt's threat. It was after all Justice Roberts who authored the *Nebbia* decision three years earlier that had begun to weaken the foundations of economic substantive due process.

Both Justice Roberts and Chief Justice Hughes, the two swing votes on the Court at this time, seemed to lack a clear constitutional grounding, bouncing from one camp to the other in a seemingly random manner. Even their fellow justices had a difficult time

---

[57] *Id.*

[58] 514 U.S. 549 (1995).

[59] DAVID P. CURRIE, THE CONSTITUTION IN THE SUPREME COURT: THE SECOND CENTURY, 1888–1986 236 (1990).

understanding their jurisprudential frameworks. Apparently, it was extremely important to Hughes to at least appear to be deciding the cases consistently with precedent, especially to protect the Court as an institution against charges that it was deciding cases on the basis of politics or ideology. This was usually possible given that accumulated precedent pointed in different directions, as it generally does. Hughes and Roberts were both highly skilled judges capable of manipulating legal doctrine to serve their ends. Prior to *Jones & Laughlin Steel*, Hughes and Roberts had tended to decide cases, especially those favoring the government, on the narrowest of grounds, which failed to remove doubt as to the constitutionality of much of the recent New Deal legislation. In *Jones & Laughlin Steel* and its companion cases, Hughes went out of his way to avoid the narrower stream-of-commerce ground served up by the government and instead relied upon the much broader effects on commerce theory. Moreover, the chief justice resisted any temptation to distinguish the large industry steel case from the two small business companion cases. In effect, the Court was announcing that it was essentially prepared to end the turmoil that had revolved around it for the past two years.

Perhaps the Court was troubled by the momentum to curb its authority in some manner, even if not by the court packing plan specifically. Or maybe it simply concluded that the headwind for more aggressive regulation of the economy was simply too strong to continue to resist, especially after the Democratic landslide in the 1936 elections. Or maybe Hughes and Roberts recognized that with four more years in office, President Roosevelt would inevitably be able to replace one or more justices through retirement. If so, to preserve some appearance of objectivity and stability perhaps it was better for the Court to change directions before new justices arrived. Or perhaps the justices concluded that the ongoing conflict among the president, Congress, and the Court was simply causing too much long-term institutional damage to the Court. Likewise, the persistence of the Depression as well as its resistence to governmental efforts up to that point may have convinced the justices that it was constitutionally proper to accord the government even more leeway. No one will ever know for certain. But as a practical matter, in *Jones & Laughlin Steel* and *West Coast Hotel*, Chief Justices Hughes and Justice Roberts essentially raised the white flag.

Careful attempts have been made to explain the decisions largely if not wholly in legitimate doctrinal terms.[60] That is, the Court should be taken at its word and the legal distinctions that it provided should be accepted. Certainly, the Court's own doctrinal explanations should not be dismissed as window dressing. Legal concepts do in fact matter to judges. However, purely doctrinal explanations seem inadequate to explain the significant and abrupt shifts of direction that did occur.

Whether or not political pressure played a role in the decision of *West Coast Hotel*, *Jones & Laughlin* is a different matter. It was argued shortly after the court packing plan was announced, although by the time the opinion was issued the plan had effectively been defeated. Arguably, *West Coast Hotel* marked the end of aggressive judicial review of economic legislation be it state or federal. If so, then it was the crucial decision and *Jones & Laughlin* was anticlimactic. But that is hardly self-evident. Certainly from the

---

[60] *See, e.g.,* CUSHMAN, *supra* note 4.

perspective of the president and Congress, federal regulation of the economy was far more crucial than state regulation. That after all was what the New Deal was all about.

Moreover, the issues were scarcely the same. It would be quite possible to reject the concept of economic substantive due process with a highly protected liberty of contract for the reasons set forth by Justice Holmes and Harlan in their *Lochner* dissents and still accept dual federalism with its narrower conception of congressional power. Indeed, loosening the restraints on state economic regulation would temper though not eliminate the need for stronger federal regulation. As such *West Coast Hotel* neither determined the result in *Jones & Laughlin* nor rendered it any less important.

It is likely that *Jones & Laughlin Steel* is an example of a highly pressurized social and political context exerting some pull on the direction of the law. But it is unlikely that it was pressure brought to bear by the litigation in this specific case, important though it was, than by the progression of multiple related cases over a period of years coupled with a highly charged political atmosphere in which a direct challenge to the Court was but one factor.

If *NLRB v. Jones & Laughlin Steel* is a great case as Holmes used the term, it did not make bad law. By most accounts it made very good law. The Court adopted an approach to the Commerce Clause that was both more in line with its original purpose and certainly more consistent with contemporary necessities. It was defensible as a matter of precedential development though hardly consistent with everything that had come before. It went a long way toward defusing a serious constitutional crisis. It validated a crucial piece of federal regulation. It began the transition of the Court from economic regulator to civil libertarian guardian.[61]

That is not to say that every expansive construction of the commerce power that has followed is wholly attributable to *Jones & Laughlin Steel*. The opinion was relatively low key and modest. Whether *Wickard v. Filburn* was rightly or wrongly reasoned, it is at most a permissible and not an inevitable consequence of *Jones & Laughlin Steel*. *Jones & Laughlin* was certainly correct in adopting a more economically realistic approach to Commerce Clause analysis. Decisions such as *Carter Coal* were properly condemned as wooden and obstructionist. That scarcely should mean that the Court must accord Congress complete deference when it regulates pursuant to the commerce power. The decision in the NLRA cases was somewhat disingenuous. The Court chose a relatively easy case involving a massive vertically integrated steel company as the showcase for its doctrinal shift, but then buried the magnitude of that shift in the much smaller-scale companion cases. Any close student of the Court would understand the true significance of the decision, and yet the Court chose to conceal it, at least to some degree.

NLRB v. Jones & Laughlin Steel does mark one of the great changes of direction in constitutional jurisprudence. It did occur in a great case, and there is good reason to believe that the political context of the case played a significant role in the Court's shift in direction. But at least in retrospect, it would seem that the changes ushered in by *Jones & Laughlin Steel* would have occurred in any event. The Court's formalistic jurisprudence had fallen out of favor. The era of dual federalism was coming to a close. President Roosevelt would

---

[61] The theoretical grounding for such a shift was set forth by Justice Stone the following year in the famous footnote four of United States v. Carolene Products, 304 U.S. 144, 152 n. 4 (1938).

have the opportunity to mold the Court to his liking through retirements soon enough. As such, although *Jones & Laughlin* was the occasion for the change of direction, it was bound to occur with or without a great case.

The decision in *NLRB v. Jones & Laughlin Steel* will however stand as a significant constitutional landmark, never to be free of speculation and controversy as to the factors that led to its outcome.

> "Everything conspired to make Dennis a great moment... And the Court responded to it as a great case.... But in the end Dennis does not prove to be a great case...."
> HARRY KALVEN[1]

11

Dennis v. United States

In his concurring opinion *in Dennis v. United States*, Justice Felix Frankfurter quoted the famous dictum from Holmes that "great cases, like hard cases make bad law...." He then declared "[t]his is such a case."[2] And so it was. *Dennis* was the most politically explosive criminal appeal to ever come before the Supreme Court. It involved a First Amendment challenge to the convictions under the Smith Act of the officers and organizers of the Communist Party of the United States. The defendants had been indicted for organizing the Communist Party with the intent that at some point in the future, it be employed to violently overthrow the government of the United States. They were convicted after a six-month unruly trial that the defendants used to a large extent to publicize their cause. The trial and appeal occurred in the midst of the post–World War II Red Scare and as such was of extreme public interest and concern. In order to decide the case, the justices found it necessary to take judicial notice of the state of world affairs especially with respect to the advances of communism, questions ordinarily well beyond the realm of judicial consideration. Given the hysteria over the internal communist threat at the time, the Court may have had little choice but to uphold the convictions. In doing so, it seemed to halt if not retard the development of greater judicial protection of seditious speech only to quietly undo the damage a few years later as the fear subsided. *Dennis* may very well be an example of the kind of great case about which Holmes was correct. As Harry Kalven notes, *Dennis* did not remain a landmark case in terms of its continuing doctrinal impact; however it was certainly a great case as it was presented to and decided by the Court.

---

[1] HARRY KALVEN, JR., A WORTHY TRADITION: FREEDOM OF SPEECH IN AMERICA 190 (1988).
[2] 341 U.S. 494, 528 (1951).

SEDITIOUS SPEECH AND THE FIRST AMENDMENT

Appreciation of the *Dennis* case requires some understanding of the history of seditious speech and the First Amendment. All of the justices on the Supreme Court as well as the Court of Appeals perceived *Dennis* as part of a long line of Supreme Court precedent exploring the extent to which the First Amendment protects speech that is perceived as harmful to the structure or existence of the government or to the war efforts of the nation. As the justices in *Dennis* recognized, the Court's freedom of speech jurisprudence actually began in 1919 in a seditious speech case—*Schenck v. United States*.[3] In a brief opinion, the Court speaking through Justice Holmes upheld the conviction of Schenk who had distributed pamphlets criticizing the draft and the war effort during World War I. The case is famous because Holmes introduced the "clear and present danger" test as a device for determining when speech critical of the war effort forfeits First Amendment protection. In *Schenck* and subsequent cases at the time, the Court applied the test consistently to uphold convictions and reject the First Amendment defense.[4]

Abrams v. United States,[5] decided the following year, involved a prosecution under an amendment to the Espionage Act that specifically targeded speech critical of the American war effort. In *Abrams*, Holmes dissented and introduced the marketplace of ideas theory into freedom of speech jurisprudence as an explanation of the need for vigorous protection of unpopular and seemingly threatening ideas and opinions.

Several years later in *Gitlow v. New York*,[6] the Court upheld a conviction under a state criminal syndicalism statute making it a crime to advocate the overthrow of the United States' government. The Court held that the defendant was not entitled to an individual assessment of whether his speech or actions constituted a clear and present danger when the legislature had determined as part of the statute that the action in question necessarily posed a clear and present danger as a matter of law. Justice Holmes again dissented, maintaining that the First Amendment required the government to prove a clear and present danger in the individual case. Two years later in *Whitney v. California*,[7] the Court sustained a similar conviction. Justice Brandeis, joined by Justice Holmes, offered a concurrence of rhetorical brilliance, providing perhaps the most comprehensive statement of freedom of speech theory ever offered in a Supreme Court opinion. Brandeis attempted to shore up the doctrine to provide greater protection for speech by requiring that the speech in question incite unlawful action, that the occurrence of the danger be imminent, and that the harm be of great magnitude. The Holmes-Brandeis approach to the First Amendment was applauded by scholars and commentators but would not prevail on the Court itself for quite sometime. In the 1940s in non-seditious speech cases such as the labor picketing case of *Thornhill v. Alabama*,[8] the Court, though not necessarily by a solid majority, began to move toward the Brandeis and Holmes approach from *Gitlow* and *Whitney*.

---

[3] 249 U.S. 47 (1919).
[4] *See, e.g.*, Frohwerk v. United States, 249 U.S. 204 (1919); *Debs v. United States*, 249 U.S. 211 (1919).
[5] 250 U.S. 616 (1919).
[6] 268 U.S. 652 (1925).
[7] 274 U.S. 357 (1927).
[8] 310 U.S. 88 (1940).

THE *DENNIS* LITIGATION

Following the end of World War II, the public became very concerned about the threat of communism both abroad and at home. Several incidents stoked these fears. The Soviet Union behaved very aggressively in eastern Europe in contravention of the Yalta Accord. North Korea invaded South Korea and the United States committed troops in aid of the latter. In response to concern about internal communist infiltration, Congress passed the Taft-Hartley Act over President Truman's veto prohibiting communists from belonging to labor unions certified by the NLRB. The House Un-American Activities Committee (HUAC) commenced hearings to expose communist sympathizers in government. The president announced the "Truman Doctrine" under which the nation would oppose Soviet aggression anywhere in the world where it posed a threat to freedom. Truman also signed an executive order authorizing loyalty investigations of federal employees and job applicants. Under federal and state law over four and one-half million government employees and contractors were investigated for potential subversive activity between 1947 and 1953.[9]

It was in this atmosphere that Eugene Dennis and ten other officers of the Communist Party of the United States (CPUS) were indicted for conspiring to violate sections 2 and 3 of the Smith Act of 1940. The Act was passed as a rider to the Alien Registration Act and attracted little attention at the time.[10] Section 2 of the Smith Act made it unlawful:

(1) to knowingly or willfully advocate, abet, advise, or teach the duty, necessity, desirability, or propriety of overthrowing or destroying any government in the United States by force or violence, or by the assassination of any officers of any such government;

(2) with an intent to cause the overthrow or destruction of any government in the United States, to print, publish, edit, issue, circulate sell, distribute or publicly display any written or printed matter advocating advising, or teaching the duty, necessity, desirability, or propriety of overthrowing or destroying any government in the United States by force or violence;

(3) to organize or help to organize any society group or assembly of persons who teach, advocate or encourage the overthrow or destruction of any government in the United States by force or violence; or to be or become a member of, or affiliate with, any such group, or assembly of persons, knowing the purposes thereof.

Section 3 of the Act made it unlawful to attempt or conspire to commit any of the offenses prohibited.

As all of the judges and justices who wrote opinions acknowledged, the defendants were not charged with actually attempting to overthrow the United States' government. Rather, they were indicted for conspiring to organize the Communist Party of the United

---

[9] GEOFFREY R. STONE, PERILOUS TIMES: FREE SPEECH IN WARTIME: FROM THE SEDITION ACT OF 1798 TO THE WAR ON TERRORISM 348 (2004).

[10] THOMAS IRWIN EMERSON, THE SYSTEM OF FREEDOM OF EXPRESSION 110 (1970).

States, a group that taught and advocated such overthrow, and for conspiring to knowingly and willfully advocate such overthrow.[11]

The prosecution was essentially an attempt to destroy the Communist Party of the
United States by convicting and imprisoning all of its leaders. The prosecution resulted
in one of the most raucous and unwieldy trials in American history, lasting six months
with a record of 16,000 pages. Indeed, it was one of the longest criminal trial in American
history.[12] During the trial, all of the defense attorneys were held in contempt of court and
their convictions were later sustained by the Supreme Court.[13] All of the defendants in
Dennis were convicted.

THE COURT OF APPEALS

The defendants appealed their convictions to the Court of Appeals for the Second Circuit.
Judge Learned Hand wrote a lengthy opinion affirming the convictions and rejecting
all of the arguments raised, most of which the Supreme Court would not consider. The
central issue was whether the Smith Act, making it a crime to conspire to take any of the
prohibited actions with the intent that they ultimately result in the violent overthrow
of the United States' government, violated the First Amendment. Judge Hand devoted
several pages to what he characterized as a "wearisome analysis" of the relevant Supreme
Court precedent, starting with *Schenck*.[14] This led Hand to conclude that "the phrase 'clear
and present danger,' is not a slogan or shibboleth to be applied as though it carried its
own meaning; but that it involves in every case a comparison between interests which are
to be appraised qualitatively."[15] This in turn led Hand to attempt to reduce the inquiry to
something of an algebraic formula. He declared that:

> In each case they must ask whether the gravity of the "evil," discounted by its
> improbability, justifies such invasion of free speech as is necessary to avoid the
> danger.[16]

Hand cautioned that the case before the Court must be distinguished from "the bitter
outcast vent[ing] his venom."[17] Rather, the Communist Party had "thousands of adherents," was "rigidly and ruthlessly disciplined," and "[t]he violent capture of all existing governments is one article of [its] creed."[18] Thus the question before the Court was
reduced to "how long a government, having discovered such a conspiracy, must wait."[19] Or
"[w]hen does the conspiracy become a 'present danger'?"[20]

---

[11] 341 U.S. 494, 496 (1951).
[12] STONE, *supra* note 9, at 396.
[13] Sacher v. United States, 343 U.S. 1 (1952).
[14] 183 F. 2d 201, 207–12 (2d Cir. 1950).
[15] *Id.* at 212.
[16] *Id.*
[17] *Id.*
[18] *Id.*
[19] *Id.* at 213.
[20] *Id.*

In order to determine how imminent the danger was in the summer of 1948 when the indictment was issued, Judge Hand declared that the court needed to take account of "our position in the world at that time."[21] After discussing the recent advances of communism on the world stage, he declared "[w]e hold that it is a danger 'clear and present.'"[22] The court further held that the Act was constitutional as represented in the trial judge's charge to the jury and that the evidence was sufficient to support the jury verdict against the defendants. Finally, the court agreed that the trial court was correct in concluding that the question of whether there was in fact a clear and present danger was a question of law for the court rather than a question of fact for the jury. The court of appeals then devoted the largest portion of its opinion to the rejection of the defendants' challenges to the selection of the jury and conduct of the trial.

Judge Chase wrote a short concurring opinion noting that because the Smith Act was closely modeled after the New York statute sustained in *Gitlow*, nothing beyond citation to *Gitlow* was needed to uphold the Smith Act.

THE SUPREME COURT

The defendants appealed their convictions to the Supreme Court, which granted review on a limited basis. It agreed to consider whether the Smith Act on its face or as applied violated the First Amendment or was unduly vague in violation of the First and Fifth Amendments. The Court would not however consider the sufficiency of the evidence in the case.

With respect to the public fear of communism, matters had changed for the worse since the defendants were indicted and convicted in 1948. China had fallen to the communists. Russia had detonated an atomic bomb. North Korea had invaded South Korea. Whittaker Chambers had alleged that Alger Hiss was a Soviet spy. And Senator Joseph McCarthy had proclaimed that he had a list of over 200 communists in the Department of State. The "Red Scare" was reaching a fever pitch. While the Court was deliberating, the Communist Party threatened demonstrations and the ABA called for disbarment of the defendants' attorneys.[23]

Chief Justice Vinson announced the judgment of the Court affirming the Second Circuit in a plurality opinion joined by Justices Reed, Burton, and Minton. Justice Clark did not participate in the decision because he had been attorney general when the indictments were issued. Vinson began by confirming that a conviction under the Act required proof of specific intent to overthrow the government by force, even though the trial judge had so charged the jury and the defendants hardly disagreed. He next declared that there was no "right to revolution" in a democracy. Vinson then stated that contrary to the assertion of the defendants, the statute as properly construed by the trial judge, punished only advocacy of violent overthrow and not "peaceful studies and discussions or teaching. . . ." As with Judge Hand below, Chief Justice Vinson found it useful to work

---

[21] *Id.*

[22] *Id.*

[23] JAMES F. SIMON, THE ANTAGONISTS: HUGO BLACK, FELIX FRANKFURTER AND CIVIL LIBERTIES IN MODERN AMERICA 199 (1989).

through the Court's seditious speech precedent, starting with *Schenck*. He concluded that neither Holmes nor Brandeis "ever envisioned" that the clear and present danger test "should be crystalized into a rigid rule to be applied inflexibly without regard to the circumstances of each case...."[24]

The plurality concluded that protecting against the violent overthrow of the government was not simply a substantial interest but rather "the ultimate value of any society."[25] When faced with a conspiracy to overthrow the government at some point in the future, Vinson, like Judge Hand, declared that the government need not wait until "the putsch is about to be executed" before it may intervene.[26] He recognized that even if an attempt at violent overthrow was destined to fail, it still posed serious physical and political damage that the government had the right to prevent. The plurality noted that the classic Holmes and Brandeis dissents arguing that speech could be prohibited only where the danger to the state interest was imminent were written with respect to "isolated events" and did not contemplate slowly developing organized movements such as the one in issue. Consequently, the chief justice quoted and adopted Judge Hand's formula whereby the gravity of the evil was discounted by its improbability as the appropriate focus of a case such as this one.

Like the trial court and court of appeals, the plurality concluded that a clear and present danger did in fact exist considering among other things the "highly organized conspiracy, with rigidly disciplined members subject to call...coupled with the inflammable nature of world conditions [and] similar uprisings in other countries...."[27] Chief Justice Vinson also affirmed the conclusion that the issue of clear and present danger was one of law rather than fact.

Critics challenged the plurality's approach. Noted First Amendment scholar Thomas Emerson declared that the Hand/Vinson alteration of the clear and present danger test all but eliminated "clear," subordinated "present," and overemphasized the "danger."[28] Noting that the plurality did not quote any of the statements that the defendants made, Harry Kalven pointed out that Vinson had shifted the focus from the danger presented by the speech to that presented by the speakers.[29] There was no question that the plurality's approach diminished whatever protection the clear and present danger standard had offered to potentially subversive speech. On the other hand, as the plurality and Justice Jackson maintained, the clear and present danger standard was not well designed for addressing the type of stealthy subversion presented by the Communist Party and as such needed to be adjusted.

Justice Frankfurter contributed a lengthy concurring opinion. Near the outset, he recognized that "[f]ew questions of comparable import have come before this Court in recent years."[30] One of Frankfurter's primary points was that it was futile to attempt to resolve a case of this complexity through application of a legal formula such as clear and

---

[24] 341 U.S. at 507.
[25] *Id.* at 509.
[26] *Id.*
[27] *Id.* at 511.
[28] EMERSON, *supra* note 10, at 114.
[29] KALVEN, *supra* note 1, at 194, 198.
[30] 341 U.S. at 518.

present danger. Rather the question must be resolved by "weighing of the competing interests."[31] Later in the opinion he wrote "[i]t does an ill service to [Justice Holmes] the author of the most quoted judicial phrases regarding freedom of speech, to make him the victim of a tendency which he fought all his life, whereby phrases are made to do service for critical analysis by being turned into dogma."[32] Obviously disappointed with Judge Hand's formula and the plurality's endorsement of it, Frankfurter proclaimed that the problem could not be solved by "announcing dogmas too inflexible for the non-Euclidian problems to be solved" and that the issues "are not subject to quantitative ascertainment."[33] The difficulty of balancing the competing interests in a case of this complexity led Frankfurter to the primary point of his concurrence, which was that the judiciary simply did not have the capacity to evaluate and balance the interests. Rather that was a job for Congress. The Court should accept the balance that Congress struck as long as it was rational.[34]

Then in an attempt to come to grips with the relevant legal principles, Justice Frankfurter engaged in a lengthy and rather tedious discussion of the Court's free speech precedent, at the end of which he announced that "I must leave to others the ungrateful task of trying to reconcile all these decisions."[35] Although he disagreed with the conclusion that a serious danger was presented by the facts of *Gitlow*, he did assert that pursuant to the principle of that case Congress could clearly have found such a danger posed by the communist conspiracy.

In assessing the reasonableness of the congressional conclusion, Justice Frankfurter maintained that the Court could look beyond the trial record and take judicial notice of world conditions where "Communist doctrines...are in the ascendency" in nations hostile to the United States.[36] In contrast to the dissents, Justice Frankfurter would not have the "validity of legislation depend on judicial reading of events still in the womb of time," a task well beyond the competence of judges.[37]

Critics of the Frankfurter approach pointed out that it was difficult if not impossible for him to successfully argue that on the one hand *Gitlow*'s conclusion that the courts must defer to a legislative finding that a particular type of speech constitutes clear and present danger as a matter of law is incorrect and yet give heavy if not conclusive deference to legislative findings in the present case.[38] This was one of many cases in which Frankfurter called for an interest-balancing approach for resolving First Amendment issues, although in this case he maintained that the balancing process was best left to the legislature, resulting in near complete judicial deference. As a practical matter, the Hand/Vinson approach was also a balancing test with a somewhat greater role for the judiciary. Under that approach, and arguably under Frankfurter's as well, it would be the district court's finding of clear and present danger as a matter of law as opposed to the

---

[31] *Id.* at 525.
[32] *Id.* at 543.
[33] *Id.* at 525.
[34] *Id.*
[35] *Id.* at 539.
[36] *Id.* at 547.
[37] *Id.* at 551.
[38] EMERSON, *supra* note 10, at 117; KALVEN, *supra* note 1, at 208.

prior legislative conclusion that would carry the greatest weight. If so, this would be an intermediate step between the approaches of Holmes and Brandeis where the presence of clear and present danger was a question of fact presumably for the jury and the *Gitlow* majority, which held that it was a question that had been taken off the table entirely by the legislature.

Justice Jackson also offered a concurrence without joining the plurality opinion. He began by noting that the statute in question was modeled on legislation aimed at the very different threat posed by anarchists in the early part of the twentieth century. As with several of the other justices, he described the organizations and workings of the Communist Party, noting that it is "a relatively small party whose strength is in selected, dedicated, indoctrinated and rigidly disciplined members."[39] He declared that the party was unlikely to attempt to resort to violence against an existing government "until it is about ready to fall of its own weight."[40] He also detailed the success of the party in both Russia and Czechoslovakia.

Turning to First Amendment doctrine, Justice Jackson explained that the clear and present danger test was an appropriate device for application to the problems in which it originated, "hot headed speech on a street corner," but was not useful with respect to a slow-moving deliberate conspiracy such as that posed by the Communist Party. He argued that the test was inadequate in the present context given that it would require the Court to attempt to forecast unforeseeable events in the distant future. For Justice Jackson, the key to the case was the fact that the defendants were indicted for conspiracy. In his characteristic rhetorical fashion, he declared that "[t]he Constitution does not make conspiracy a civil right;"[41] rather, "conspiracy may be an evil in itself."[42] Relying on antitrust cases, he noted that it was not necessary to prove an overt act in furtherance of the conspiracy. He concluded that the law of conspiracy was an essential means for the government to deal with the threat from organizations such as the Communist Party.

Unlike the other justices in the majority, Jackson seemed to understand that the law of conspiracy was at the very heart of the government's case. It was arguably the glue that held it together. Still he almost certainly gave the fact of conspiracy itself more weight than it should bear if freedom of speech is to receive protection in the context of group action.

Justice Black dissented. He understood the opinions of the justices in the majority as a repudiation of the clear and present danger test, a test that he did not believe went far enough in protecting freedom of speech. Black joined issue with Frankfurter's and Vinson's balancing approach, arguing that it was inconsistent with the absolute protection of speech provided by the First Amendment. Like Justice Douglas, he also objected to the trial court's conclusion that the existence of clear and present danger was a question of law rather than of fact.

From Justice Douglas's perspective in dissent, the defendants were indicted and convicted for conspiring to teach standard communist doctrine, an activity that he considered squarely within the protection of the First Amendment. Contrary to Justice Jackson,

---

[39] 341 U.S. at 564.
[40] *Id.* at 565.
[41] *Id.* at 572.
[42] *Id.* at 573.

he did not believe that under the law of conspiracy, speech could take the place of action. He argued that the issue of clear and present danger was for the jury and that there was no evidence in the record from which the jury could find that such a danger existed. Although Justice Douglas acknowledged that world communism was a force to be taken seriously, the Communist Party of the United States posed no threat as it had been thoroughly discredited in the marketplace of ideas.

AFTERMATH

The decision met with general approval in the press including the *New York Times* and *Washington Post*.[43] The *Dennis* defendants remained in prison. Over the next six years over 200 more members and officers of the Communist Party were indicted under the Smith Act with more than 100 convicted.[44] During this period, the Court continued to uphold federal and state laws regulating and punishing subversive activity, including loyalty oaths, public employee membership in subversive organizations, professional license suspensions, and deportations.[45] In the term following *Dennis*, the Court wrestled at length with whether to hear an appeal in the Rosenbergs' treason case.[46] The Court declined to hear the case, and the Rosenbergs were executed, The Court did a near about-face, however, in 1957, when it decided *Yates v. United States*.[47] By then, the membership of the Court had changed considerably. There the Court reversed the Smith Act convictions of several members of the Communist Party not by explicitly overruling *Dennis* on constitutional grounds but rather through a tight construction of the statutory language.[48] Writing for a 6-1 majority, Justice Harlan declared that in view of potential First Amendment difficulties, the Smith Act should not be read as authorizing the punishment of persons for merely advocating the overthrow of the government at some point in the future. Rather, for there to be a violation, the speaker had to urge the listener to take action now. Justice Harlan drew a distinction between express advocacy of unlawful conduct and advocacy of abstract doctrine. Not only did the Court order the reversal of the convictions but concluded that there was no possibility that the defendants could be convicted on the trial record under a correct understanding of the Act. There is also no possibility that the *Dennis* defendants could have been convicted under the *Yates* Court's reading of the Act. *Yates* effectively put an end to Smith Act prosecutions.[49] *Yates* was

---

[43] STONE, *supra* note 9, at 411.

[44] *Id.*

[45] Garner Bd. v. Public Works, 341 U.S. 716 (1951) (upholding loyalty oath) (decided same day as *Dennis*); Adler v. Bd. of Educ., 342 U.S. 485 (1952) (upholding ban on members of subversive organizations from employment as public school teachers); Harisaides v. Shaughnessey, 342 U.S. 580 (1952) (upholding deportation of long-term resident noncitizen for Communist Party membership); Shaughnessy v. United States, 345 U.S. 206 (1953) (upholding authority of attorney general to imprison alien with no formal charges).

[46] Melvin I. Urofsky, Division and Discord: The Supreme Court Under Stone and Vinson, 1941-1953 178–83 (1997).

[47] 354 U.S. 298 (1957).

[48] *Id.* at 310-12.

[49] STONE, *supra* note 9, at 414–15.

essentially a complete repudiation of *Dennis*. The Court elaborated on *Yates* thereafter in *Scales v. United States* where it did sustain a conviction under the membership provision of the Smith Act.[50]

In the decade following *Dennis*, the Court decided several cases on a variety of grounds limiting the ability of the government to punish subversive activities.[51] The *Dennis* approach to seditious speech has been the subject of scathing academic criticism.[52] The Korean War had ended, Joseph McCarthy had been rejected, and perhaps most important, four justices who had been in the majority in *Dennis* had been replaced. Still, it was a stunning reversal in such a short period of time. Arguably, the public and the political process were not yet prepared for such a change of direction by the Court. The day on which several decisions were announced limiting the government's ability to prosecute or investigate subversive activity was characterized as "Red Monday." Congress responded with an effort to strip some of the Court's jurisdiction, which came surprisingly close to adoption.[53] Thereafter the Court trimmed its sails somewhat, taking a more sympathetic approach to government attempts to curb subversive activity.[54] Eventually some 18 years after *Dennis*, in *Brandenburg v. Ohio*,[55] the Court combined an emphasis on imminent danger with a requirement of incitement by the speaker to create a highly speech-protective approach to the question of seditious speech.

DENNIS AS A GREAT CASE

Justice Frankfurter noted that *Dennis* was the type of case that Holmes had in mind with his great cases dictum. And it is arguably a clear example of Holmes's prediction that great cases are likely to make bad law on account of the hydraulic pressure brought to bear on the justices. Although public and academic opinion was somewhat divided at the time,[56] the verdict of history has been harsh. As Chief Justice Vinson acknowledged, the Court had been moving, albeit by fits and starts, in the direction of a fairly protective clear and present danger approach propounded decades earlier in the opinions of Holmes and Brandeis. However in *Dennis*, a case where it really mattered, the Court pulled back and substituted the watered-down balancing approach devised by Judge Hand. One of

---

[50] 367 U.S. 290 (1961).

[51] Watkins v. United States, 354 U.S. 178 (1957) (limiting the ability of HUAC to obtain information); Sweezy v. New Hampshire, 354 U.S. 234 (1957) (limiting state investigative authority); Service v. Dulles, 354 U.S. 363 (1957) (limiting ability to dismiss employees on loyalty grounds); Kent v. Dulles, 357 U.S. 116 (1958) (statute does not authorize denial of passport based on political beliefs); Aptheker v. Sec'y of State, 378 U.S. 500 (1964) (invalidating denial of passport to a member of the Communist Party).

[52] *See, e.g.*, KALVEN, *supra* note 1, at 198–99; 208, 210; EMERSON, *supra* note 10, at 114–121; STONE, *supra* note 9, at 408–11.

[53] BARRY FRIEDMAN, THE WILL OF THE PEOPLE: HOW PUBLIC OPINION HAS INFLUENCED THE SUPREME COURT AND SHAPED THE MEANING OF THE CONSTITUTION 253–54 (2009).

[54] *Id.* at 254–58. *See* Barenblatt v. United States, 360 U.S. 109 (1959) (upholding contempt citation for failing to answer congressional questions pertaining to Communist Party membership); Communist Party v. Subversive Activities Control Bd., 367 U.S. 1 (1961) (upholding requirement that communist action organizations register with the attorney general).

[55] 395 U.S. 444 (1969).

[56] STONE, *supra* note 9, at 411.

the great ironies of the case was that three decades earlier, Judge Hand had argued both on and off the bench for an incitement approach that he deemed to be more protective than clear and present danger.[57] From a purely doctrinal standpoint, *Dennis* was quite properly viewed as a fairly extreme setback for freedom of speech, though one that would be corrected within the decade. By emphasizing the gravity of the evil, the Hand balancing approach permitted the government to prohibit speech that is far removed from a potential violent overthrow of government, and as such prohibits speech where alternative methods of protection would likely be available.

Dennis is also quite properly faulted for permitting speech and activity to be criminalized that is little more than discussion or advocacy of subversive activity, at least in the context of a nebulous conspiracy. This does not simply expose misguided but essentially harmless individuals to criminal prosecution but through the inevitable chilling effect it casts a pall over radical speech, period. Justice Frankfurter explicitly recognized this in his concurrence but simply concluded that it was an unfortunate byproduct of the government's need to protect national security.

Is *Dennis* glaring proof of an instance in which the Court was incapable of deciding the case in a principled manner in the context of an extreme public crisis? Perhaps so. However just as it may have been difficult for the Court to grapple with the legal issues at the height of Cold War hysteria, so it may be difficult as well to fairly assess the Court's performance at the time once the crisis has passed. The six justices in the majority certainly seemed to believe that the communist movement in the United States did indeed present a serious threat to national security. In retrospect, the extent of the threat seems greatly exaggerated. And yet files revealed since the fall of the Soviet Union indicate that the American Communist Party was subjected to the control of the Soviet communists and that at least some of the leaders of the Party had engaged in espionage activities for the Soviet Union.[58] That does not prove that it was a severe threat to national survival but it does suggest that it was worthy of serious concern. The justices who voted to affirm the convictions seemed to believe that the threat was real and serious, that the Court was ill-equipped to assess the likelihood that the harm would in fact occur, and perhaps most important, that the existing legal doctrine in the form of the clear and present danger test was wholly inadequate to resolve the issue. Despite widespread condemnation of the *Dennis* Court's approach by constitutional scholars, Eric Posner and Adrian Vermeule have recently argued that the Court's response to a serious threat that it was in no position to adequately evaluate was both rational and inevitable.[59] Moreover, they maintain that in the event that a similar crisis were to recur even today, courts would respond in the same manner.

In retrospect it seems that the justices at the government's urging grossly overestimated the threat of the Communist Party of the United States. It would seem that Justice Douglas's assessment was closer to the mark when he wrote that the American communists

---

[57] *See* Masses Publ'g Co. v. Patton, 244 F. 535 (S.D.N.Y. 1917), rev'd, 246 F. 24 (2d. Cir. 1917); Gerald Gunther, *Learned Hand and the Origins of Modern First Amendment Doctrine: Some Fragments of History*, 27 STAN. L. REV. 719 (1975).

[58] STONE, *supra* note 9, at 409–10.

[59] ERIC A. POSNER & ADRIAN VERMEULE, TERROR IN THE BALANCE: SECURITY, LIBERTY, AND THE COURTS 128-29, 233-34 (2007).

"are miserable merchants of unwanted ideas; their wares remain unsold."[60] One theory of the *Dennis* decision is that the justices were simply caught up in or at least heavily influenced by the same hysteria over the internal communist threat that was prevalent in the nation at large, and were incapable under the circumstances of providing the "sober second thought" that is generally expected of the judiciary.[61] As such, they accepted the government's assessment of the threat posed by the defendants uncritically. It was only after the crisis had passed that the Court could evaluate the circumstances more clearly. One need not conclude that the justices were swept up in a state of public hysteria to recognize that at the time of *Dennis*, given recent events both at home and abroad, intelligent and rational judges and justices however progressive they might otherwise be saw the internal threat posed by the Communist Party as extremely serious. William Wiecek has detailed how justices such as Harlan Fiske Stone and Frank Murphy, as well as the members of the *Dennis* majority were unwilling to give communists the benefit of the doubt.[62] As such, the justices largely shared the general public mindset among the educated class at the time regarding communism. Presumably, Justice Black was unwilling to sacrifice vigorous protection of freedom of speech regardless of the severity of the threat. Justice Douglas was sufficiently eccentric as to be beyond the pale of consensus opinion.

It seems unlikely that the judges and justices who heard the *Dennis* case were simply stampeded by public panic. The Second Circuit panel that affirmed the conviction was a distinguished one consisting of Learned Hand, Swan, and Chase. Hand is generally considered the greatest circuit judge in the history of the nation, and he had been a defender of freedom of speech during a period of national crisis when First Amendment jurisprudence was in its infancy. Hand did indicate in private correspondence that he did not believe the *Dennis* defendants presented much of a threat but was required to apply the law as he understood it.[63] Justices Jackson and Frankfurter were among the greatest justices to ever sit on the Court. Although both tended to be deferential to government, Frankfurter had a distinguished civil liberties record as a lawyer and law professor and Jackson had shown no fear of adverse public reaction in his classic opinion in *West Virginia Board of Education v. Barnette*, the Jehovah's Witness flag salute case. The recitation in the plurality opinion of the insidious nature of communism as well as its recent triumphs on the world stage does suggest that the justices took the threat seriously. That does not mean however that they had lost all ability to consider the matter judiciously.

Perhaps the better explanation of *Dennis* is that offered by Justice Frankfurter and to some extent, Justice Jackson. That is, *Dennis* presented the Court with the challenge of resolving a question that it simply did not have the capacity to resolve. The justices had no means of determining whether the threat posed by the Communist Party was as serious as the government maintained that it was. If in fact it was, then it did need to be halted. If not, then punishing the defendants would be a setback for freedom of speech and civil liberties. As the risk was serious and the Court did not have the tools to resolve

---

[60] 341 U.S. 494, 589 (1951).

[61] STONE, *supra* note 9, at 410.

[62] William Wiecek, *The Legal Foundations of Domestic Anti-Communism: The Background of* Dennis v. United States, 2001 SUP. CT. REV. 375, 429–33 (2001).

[63] Letter from Learned Hand to Elliot Richardson, February 29, 1951, *quoted in* GERALD GUNTHER, LEARNED HAND: THE MAN AND THE JUDGE 604–05 (1994).

the central issue, it had little choice but to defer to the government. Such an approach was bolstered by the fact that all of the justices in the *Dennis* majority tended to be deferential toward the government as a matter of judicial philosophy. The *Dennis* majority consisted of a former attorney general (Jackson), a solicitor general (Reed), a secretary of the treasury (Vinson), two senators (Burton and Minton), and a high level presidential advisor (Frankfurter). As such, the justices could be expected to appreciate the government's perspective. Although it should be noted that the dissenting justices had served as senator (Black) and chairman of the SEC (Douglas), it should also be noted that the year after *Dennis*, three members of the *Dennis* majority rejected the national security arguments of the president in *Youngstown*, the steel seizure case. Thus, it is scarcely necessary to assume that the justices were swept up in a mindless panic over the communist threat. It is much more likely that they simply concluded that in view of the complexity of the issue, the gravity of the risk, and the imperviousness of the questions to judicial evaluation, deference was the best and quite possibly the only reasonable course of action.

Hindsight would suggest that Justice Douglas evaluated the threat posed by the communists far more accurately than did the majority. However it could be argued that we can never know how serious of a threat the communists may have posed given that the Smith Act convictions affirmed in *Dennis* and in subsequent cases essentially destroyed any possibility of success. Even so, the historical record suggests that there is little likelihood that the American Communist Party could have posed a significant threat to the stability of the government even if left wholly undisturbed.

Yet another perspective on *Dennis* might suggest that at least some of the justices in the *Dennis* majority may have agreed with Douglas that there was little likelihood of serious threat to the nation, but considering the extent of the public panic over the communist threat that existed at the time, the Court simply could not intervene on behalf of the defendants without doing serious damage to its institutional reputation. Reversing the convictions of the leadership of the Communist Party in 1951 would almost certainly have whipped up a hurricane of criticism toward the Court, possibly even leading to threats of impeachment. At some level, at least some of the justices in the majority may have concluded that the time simply was not right to stand firmly behind the First Amendment. The following year in *Youngstown*, public opinion was running very solidly against the government and as such there was no judicial risk in rejecting Truman's seizure of the steel mills. The emasculation of the Smith Act in *Yates* six years after *Dennis* may suggest that the Court simply waited until the crisis had subsided to reassert itself. Even then, the Court was subjected to significant political pushback. Although it must be acknowledged that the membership of the Court had changed quite significantly in the interim and that it is rather unlikely that most of the *Dennis* majority would have concurred in *Yates*, although Frankfurter and Burton did. The change in the Court's composition provides a better explanation for the change of direction than strategic behavior. But that in itself does not undermine the theory that the *Dennis* Court may have drawn back from vigorous commitment to the First Amendment at least to some extent to protect the Court as an institution.

If *Dennis* was in part the result of strategic behavior by the Court, it was not without costs. The development of vigorous free speech doctrine suffered a setback at least for a while. Although *Yates* undercut the Smith Act, it did so through statutory interpretation, leaving the First Amendment analysis in place until it was discarded by *Brandenburg* a decade later. In addition, over 100 persons were convicted and imprisoned under the

Smith Act in the years following *Dennis*. If *Dennis* incorrectly applied the First Amendment, as both the justices and commentators later concluded, most of these convictions were quite improper. On the other hand, considering that the Court would rebuff the president's seizure of the steel mills the following year and decide *Brown v. Board of Education* three years after *Dennis*, this was a time in its history in which the Court's preservation of its reputation and credibility with the public was of the utmost importance. The failure to challenge the government's prosecution of Communist Party officials at the height of the McCarthy era may have been a more than worthwhile sacrifice.

Yet another interpretation of the *Dennis* Court's approach is that it simply does not need any explanation. It was not the result of fear of communists, inability to assess the threat, or unwillingness to risk the Court's moral capital. Rather the plurality simply believed that the Hand balancing approach to the clear and present danger standard was the best way of addressing the issue of subversive speech, especially as employed by a group such as the Communist Party but arguably in other contexts as well. Although defenders of freedom of speech might consider this a serious setback in the movement toward a more speech-protective approach, which it certainly was, the Court may simply have believed that it was the best reconciliation of the competing interests. As such the retrenchment from the prior movement toward a more progressive standard as well as the subsequent return to that direction can each be explained by changes in Court personal.[64] In the late 1930s and early 1940s, a majority of the justices took a more libertarian approach to freedom of speech. With retirements and replacements, a majority of the justices leaned more toward the government during the late 1940s and early 1950s. With a significant turnover in justices, a solid majority from the mid-1950s on took a more libertarian approach to freedom of speech than ever before.

The failure of the Court to protect freedom of speech in the initial Red Scare during and following World War II as well as the subsequent failure in *Dennis* has caused many First Amendment scholars to argue that it is important for the Court to erect strong doctrinal fortifications around freedom of speech that are capable of withstanding the pressure during what Vince Blasi has characterized as "pathological periods."[65] Recently however, Eric Posner and Adrian Vermeule have disagreed with the conventional view among First Amendment scholars, arguing that under the circumstances *Dennis* was correctly decided given that the Court quite properly recognized that it simply did not have the institutional capability to resolve the complex issues at the heart of the case.[66] They dismissed the pathological perspective as "a mishmash of imprecise ideas" and concluded that no doctrinal bulwark that the Court could design would be capable of withstanding the pressure to defer to the government during national security emergencies.[67]

Dennis v. United States was scarcely the Court's finest hour. But in its historical context, the decision is certainly understandable. Arguably, it is a case that tends to confirm Justice Holmes's dictum. If so it does so with the qualification that "Great cases... make bad law," at least for awhile.

---

[64] KALVEN, *supra* note 1, at 187.
[65] Vince Blasi, *The Pathological Perspective and the First Amendment*, 85 COLUM. L REV. 449 (1985).
[66] POSNER & VERMEULE, *supra* note 59, at 128–29, 233–34.
[67] *Id.* at 233–34.

"Youngstown is an example of a political *cause celebre* in constitutional law, an exception to the detached atmosphere and sense of isolation from public strife in which most cases–even many which decide the largest principles of constitutional law–are normally adjudicated."[1]

ALAN WESTIN

12

Youngstown Sheet & Tube Co. v. Sawyer

Youngstown Sheet & Tube Co. v. Sawyer[2] is the very model of the great case. The Court assumed center stage in a heated dispute between the president of the United States and the nation's largest steel companies (and as a practical matter Congress as well) in the midst of the Korean War. Initially, an attorney for the government and the president himself made unprecedented claims of executive authority, which were sharply rejected by the press and public. The litigation proceeded with extreme haste resulting in a landmark decision of the Court less than two months after the crisis arose. The Court's rejection of the president's seizure of the steel mills constituted quite arguably the most significant judicial rebuke of executive action to that date. The decision featuring seven separate opinions stands as the Court's most important, though ambiguous, judicial exposition on the issue of separation of powers.

THE BACKGROUND

The labor agreement between the nations' steel manufacturers and the unions expired as of December 31, 1951. Attempts to reach a new agreement were constrained by post–World War II federal regulatory authorities. The federal Wage Stabilization Board was prepared to authorize an increase in wages; however the Office of Price Stabilization would not accept an increase in prices. The companies would not agree to the former absent the latter. The union threatened a strike, and the companies prepared to close down the plants.

At the time, the country was entrenched in the war in Korea, which had ground to something of a stalemate. Public support for the war had declined.[3] Fearing that a steel

---

[1] ALAN F. WESTIN, THE ANATOMY OF A CONSTITUTIONAL LAW CASE 176 (1958).
[2] 343 U.S. 579 (1952).
[3] MAEVA MARCUS, TRUMAN AND THE STEEL SEIZURE CASE: THE LIMITS OF PRESIDENTIAL POWER 31–34 (1994).

strike would adversely interfere with the war effort, on April 8, 1952, President Truman announced to the nation in a radio address that he had directed Secretary of Commerce Sawyer to seize the steel companies and to continue their operation.[4] Under the order, the companies rather than the government itself would continue to operate the mills. In his statement, Truman declared that a "work stoppage would immediately imperil our national defense... and would add to the continuing danger of our soldiers, sailors and airmen engaged in combat in the field."[5] Allegedly, Chief Justice Fred Vinson, a confidant of Truman, had assured the president that he had proper legal grounds to seize the steel companies.[6] Truman declined to invoke the Taft-Hartley Act, which would have required the appointment of a board of inquiry and quite possibly a petition to enjoin the strike for an 80-day cooling off period. The Act had been passed over Truman's veto. As the president was a friend of labor, the Taft-Hartley option was politically unattractive to him. A large segment of the public tended to believe that Truman was motivated by a desire to resolve a labor dispute as opposed to preventing a military emergency.[7]

The following day, Truman sent a message to Congress explaining that he had taken the action in question "with the greatest reluctance."[8] He stated that he did not believe "immediate congressional action to be essential" but "would cooperate in developing any legislative proposals which Congress may wish to consider."[9] Congress failed to respond. He sent a second message to Congress 12 days later.[10] At a press conference, Truman was asked whether he believed that he could seize the press in a state of emergency, and he seemed to indicate that he believed that he could.[11] Shortly thereafter, he denied that he had suggested that he could constitutionally seize the press.[12] During this period, several bills to impeach President Truman were introduced in the House of Representatives.[13]

On April 9, 1952, the day after Truman's address, the steel companies unsuccessfully sought a temporary restraining order against the seizure from federal district judge Alexander Holtzoff.[14] Two weeks later a hearing on the steel companies' motion for a preliminary injunction was held before federal district judge David Pine. The U.S. Steel Company sought an injunction not against the seizure, but rather against any escalation of wages during the course of the seizure; however, Bethlehem Steel sought to enjoin the seizure itself. As Bruce Bromley, attorney for Bethlehem Steel put it at the hearing, "our position is the whole hog."[15] Judge Pine pressed the government hard on the source of the

---

[4] Radio Address of President Truman, April 8, 1952, United States Presidents, Public Papers 1952–53 at 246–50.

[5] Id.

[6] MELVIN I. UROFSKY, DIVISION AND DISCORD: THE SUPREME COURT UNDER STONE AND VINSON, 1941-1953 209 (1997).

[7] Neal Devins & Louis Fisher, The Steel Seizure Case: One of a Kind?, 19 CONST. COMM. 63, 67 (2002).

[8] President Truman's Message to Congress, CONG. REC., Apr. 9, 1952, at 3962.

[9] Id.

[10] Message from President Truman to Congress, CONG. REC., Apr. 21, 1952 at 4192.

[11] MARCUS, supra note 3, at 100.

[12] Id.

[13] WESTIN, supra note 1, at 66.

[14] The argument on the motion and the opinion is quoted in part in WESTIN, supra note 1, at 26–43.

[15] Transcript of Proceedings partially reproduced in WESTIN, supra note 1, at 56.

president's constitutional authority to seize the steel mills.[16] In response, Holmes Baldridge from the Department of Justice asserted that the president was not bound by constitutional limitations when acting in a national emergency and that his actions were not subject to judicial review.[17] He argued that the ballot box and impeachment were the only check on the president's emergency powers. Judge Pine rejected the claim as wholly unwarranted and granted a preliminary injunction against the seizure.[18] The government's claim of unbridled authority was criticized vigorously in the press, causing the president to disavow the position and the Department of Justice to file a clarification.[19] Given the procedural posture of the case, the government had not had time to develop a full record with respect to the state of emergency that it had claimed as justification for its order. Press coverage overwhelmingly opposed Truman, perhaps by as much as 95 percent.[20]

The government sought a stay in the court of appeals and filed a petition asking the Supreme Court to grant certiorari immediately, bypassing appellate review. Youngstown Sheet & Tube filed a similar petition with the Court. The day after the injunction was issued, the Court of Appeals granted a stay for 48 hours while Supreme Court review was sought.[21] Meanwhile a federally supervised negotiated settlement between the companies and unions had essentially been reached; however once the companies learned of the stay, they abandoned the negotiations, concluding that they had little to lose and much to gain by seeking Supreme Court review.[22] On May 3, 1952, the Court granted the petition for certiorari, scheduling oral arguments for May 9 and 10.

The parties worked around the clock to file lengthy briefs in five days.[23] The Court extended the time for oral argument to two and one-half hours per party given the significance of the case. The renowned Supreme Court advocate John W. Davis, appearing for the steel company, took only half of his allotted time.[24] The Court permitted him to present his argument with only a couple of questions from the bench.[25] He made a point of quoting the statements by Assistant Attorney General Baldridge in the district court that the president had unlimited power, though conceding that they had been disclaimed.[26] Solicitor General Phillip Pearlman, representing the government, took his full time allotment and was bombarded with questions by the Court for most of his argument. Arthur Goldberg appearing as amicus represented the unions.[27] It was in the government's best interest to persuade the Court that an injunction was unwarranted as a

---

[16] Youngstown Sheet & Tube v. Sawyer, Hearing before Judge Pine, on Apr. 25, 1952, reprinted in part in WESTIN, *supra* note 1, at 62–65.

[17] *Id.* at 62.

[18] 103 F. Supp. 569 (D.D.C. 1952).

[19] MARCUS, *supra* note 3, at 125–26.

[20] WESTIN, *supra* note 1, at 73.

[21] 197 F. 2d 582 (D.C. Cir. 1952).

[22] MARCUS, *supra* note 3. at 147–48.

[23] *Id.* at 149.

[24] David C. Frederick, *Advocacy before the Supreme Court: 1791 to the Present, in* THE UNITED STATES SUPREME COURT: THE PURSUIT OF JUSTICE 389 (Christopher Tomlins ed., 2005).

[25] Transcript of Oral Argument 879 in 48 LANDMARK BRIEFS AND ARGUMENTS OF THE SUPREME COURT OF THE UNITED STATES: CONSTITUTIONAL LAW (Philip B. Kurland & Gerhard Casper eds., 1975).

[26] *Id.* at 895.

[27] *Id.* at 963.

matter of established equitable principle. It had failed to steer the district judge in that direction however. And the High Court was also interested primarily in the constitutional issues. Arguably, *Youngstown* presented the Court with a dispute between the president and Congress over separation of powers in which Congress was not directly represented.[28] All nine justices had been appointed by either Franklin D. Roosevelt or Harry Truman, and all had prior experience in either the executive or legislative branches of government.

The Court met in conference for four hours and voted 6-3 to uphold the injunction.[29] The justices, especially those in the majority, staked out positions quite similar to those that they would take in their opinions. Justice Black as the senior justice in the majority assigned the opinion of the Court to himself. Given the pressure to release a decision quickly there was little attempt to iron out differences through the circulation of drafts. Instead seven of the nine justices filed opinions. The opinions were announced on June 2, 1952, three weeks after the case had been argued, and less than two months after the crisis had begun with President Truman's order.

There were ample and quite respectable means by which the Court could have avoided reaching the constitutional merits of the case. At the outset it hardly needed to hear the case at all before the court of appeals had ruled on the merits. Professor Freund of Harvard argued that the Court should have remanded the matter to the district court for further fact findings on the state of the emergency as well as potential damages to the steel companies.[30] Or the Court could have found that the equitable prerequisites for the issuance of an injunction had not been met, as the solicitor general had urged in his brief and oral argument. Finally, the Court could have avoided the merits by dismissing the case as a political question. But the Court was not at all interested in avoiding a decision on the merits.

JUSTICE BLACK'S OPINION FOR THE COURT

Justice Black authored the opinion of the Court, joined by Justices Douglas, Frankfurter, Jackson, and Burton. The opinion was short and doctrinaire. Initially Black rejected the government's argument that the case should be disposed of under the law of equity, declaring that the district court was correct in concluding that the steel companies would suffer irreparable harm and that there was no adequate remedy at law.[31] He also explained that there was no statutory authorization for the seizure, noting that an amendment to the Taft-Hartley Act permitting such emergency seizures had been rejected.

The Department of Justice raised four sources of constitutional authority for the president's action: (1) the introductory clause of Article II vesting executive authority in the president, (2) the clause in Article II granting the president the responsibility to see that the laws are faithfully executed, (3) the Article II commander in chief power, and

---

[28] Paul Kauper, *The Steel Seizure Case: Congress, the President and the Supreme Court*, 51 MICH. L. REV. 141, 155 (1952).

[29] THE SUPREME COURT IN CONFERENCE (1949–1985): THE PRIVATE DISCUSSIONS BEHIND NEARLY 300 SUPREME COURT DECISIONS 172–82 (Del Dickson ed., 2001).

[30] Paul Freund, *Foreword, The Year of the Steel Seizure Case, Supreme Court, 1951 Term*, 66 HARV. L. REV. 89 (1952).

[31] 343 U.S. 579, 585 (1952).

(4) inherent authority to protect the nation in emergencies. Justice Black dismissed all four in a fairly cursory manner. With respect to the first two, Black concluded that the president's action was not executive in nature. He gave the commander in chief argument, arguably the strongest of the four, the most attention. Still he concluded that commander in chief authority diminished greatly outside of the actual "theater of war."[32] With regard to labor relations that might impact the war effort, Black proclaimed that the president must rely on Congress for assistance.[33] Black barely acknowledged the inherent authority argument and concluded that prior instances of presidential action were quite irrelevant to the constitutional question.

Ultimately, Justice Black concluded that the oresident's action was legislative in nature and as such was beyond his constitutional authority. Black made it clear, however, that Congress could have authorized the seizure. His approach, joined by a majority of the justices, has been criticized as formalistic and simplistic. It certainly lacked the nuance of some of the other opinions. It seems inadequate both in light of the significance of the issues before the Court and the alternative analysis of both Justices Jackson and Frankfurter. It did not seem to give sufficient consideration to the detailed arguments of either side. It provided no guidance at all for the resolution of future disputes. It brushed aside dozens of historical analogs as if they were all but nonexistent. It declined to acknowledge the detailed counterarguments raised by the dissents, particularly with respect to statutory authorization. As disappointing and anticlimactic as the Black opinion was however, it is difficult to quarrel with its straightforward conclusion. As Justices Frankfurter and Jackson demonstrated, pages of careful analysis ultimately led to the same place: the President's action was too legislative in nature and unauthorized by Congress.

JUSTICE JACKSON'S CONCURRING OPINION

Justice Jackson wrote an eloquent and lengthy concurring opinion that upstaged Justice Black's opinion for the majority and has carried the day with subsequent courts. Jackson was one of the most skillful writers to ever serve on the Court, and he offered a concurring opinion that eclipsed the majority. From the outset, Justice Jackson had been thrust into the center of the dispute given that as attorney general he had written a memo justifying a similar unauthorized seizure by President Roosevelt during World War II.[34] Both in the district court and before the Supreme Court, the government had placed heavy reliance on the Jackson memo. Part of the impetus for Justice Jackson's concurrence seems to have been to distinguish his earlier position from the decision of the Court. By the same token, John W. Davis, representing the steel companies, also had to distinguish a brief he had filed some 40 years earlier as solicitor general arguing for broad inherent presidential emergency powers.[35]

Recognizing at the outset that great cases could produce bad law, Justice Jackson warned against the tendency "to emphasize transient results upon policies" at the

---

[32] *Id.* at 587.
[33] *Id.*
[34] The memo was quoted in the Brief of the Steel Companies.
[35] Marcus, *supra* note 3, at 169.

expense of "enduring consequence upon the balanced power structure of our Republic."[36] He dismissed originalist arguments at the outset, observing that sources on each side "largely cancel each other"...as "[a] Hamilton may be matched against a Madison."[37] More contemporaneous opinion was likewise unhelpful in that "Professor Taft is counterbalanced by Theodore Roosevelt."[38] Judicial precedents were not helpful in that they tended to deal "with the largest questions in the most narrow way."[39] Nor could the questions be resolved by focusing on "isolated clauses or even single Articles [of the Constitutional text] torn from context."[40] So at the very outset of his opinion, Justice Jackson swept away original understanding, precedent, and text, arguably the three most conventional tools of constitutional analysis, as being useless in this context.

Instead, Jackson developed an analytical approach derived from constitutional structure. After explaining that the relationship between the president and Congress involved "separateness but interdependence, autonomy but reciprocity," he set forth his now famous tri-part framework for assessing separation-of-powers disputes.[41] Jackson maintained that the president's authority was at its greatest when explicitly or implicitly supported by Congress as such a situation assumed all of the authority that the federal government possessed. Presidential power was less secure when exercised in the absence of congressional approval or disapproval, although in this "zone of twilight," the president might well possess concurrent authority with Congress. Finally, presidential power was at its "lowest ebb" when employed in the face of congressional disapproval as it must be based on that constitutional authority Congress could not diminish.[42] Justice Jackson conceded that these groupings were "over-simplified."[43] Nevertheless they have been appealing to subsequent courts.

Justice Jackson then turned to the application of this analytical framework to the case at hand. He readily dismissed category one as he did not believe there was any statutory authorization. Category two was inapplicable given that Jackson believed that Congress had in fact disapproved of executive seizure of property by failing to authorize it in any of the recent statutes addressing response to emergencies. One obvious difficulty with the Jackson approach is that it is often difficult to determine whether Congress did in fact intend to preclude presidential action. That was particularly true in a case such as *Youngstown* in which Congress did not enact legislation prohibiting a presidential seizure but rather simply provided an alternative procedure. The question remains whether Congress intended Taft-Hartly to be the only means of confronting the crisis or simply one possibility. In analyzing the case under category three, Jackson discussed the government's four sources of constitutional authority in greater detail than did any other justice.

---

[36] *Youngstown*, 343 U.S. at 634.

[37] *Id.* at 635, n.1.

[38] *Id.*

[39] *Id.* at 635.

[40] *Id.*

[41] *Id.* at 635-36.

[42] *Id.* at 637.

[43] *Id.* at 635.

In response to the argument that the Vesting Clause of Article II granted all exercisable executive authority to the president, Jackson replied that this would undermine further enumeration of power in Article II and would be quite inconsistent with the constitutional design of limited power. Thus the better reading was that the vesting clauses allocated power as between the branches but did not create authority.

The Commander in Chief Clause was the government's most serious textual argument. Justice Jackson responded to it in some detail and with his capacity for the quotable phrase. He made the strong rejoinder that it was the constitutional duty of Congress not the president to supply the armed forces. Allowing the president "to do anything, anywhere, that can be done with an army or navy," would run counter to the American constitutional tradition of limited power and would effectively make the president "Commander-in-Chief of the country, its industries and its inhabitants."[44]

He disposed of the government's reliance on the president's textual responsibility to see that the laws were faithfully executed with the reply that this obligation was qualified by the requirement of due process.

The final source of authority, which Jackson devoted the most attention to, was the claim of inherent presidential emergency power derived from necessity and past practice. This claim was of special interest to Justice Jackson considering that the Department of Justice had placed much reliance on a memo that he had written as attorney general justifying President Roosevelt's seizure of the North American Aircraft Company during World War II. Jackson argued that that incident was distinguishable from the steel seizure case on several grounds, and moreover it did not set a precedent that a court was bound to follow. His primary concern with an inherent authority argument however was that it was dangerous to democracy and difficult to limit. He feared that "emergency powers would tend to kindle emergencies."[45]

Moreover, inherent executive power was scarcely necessary given the haste with which Congress could act in an emergency. Jackson also observed that given the power and prestige of the modern president with the aid of mass media and as head of a political party, inherent authority was hardly essential to effective administration. The president under the Constitution was not above the law. He ended his opinion with a warning that "only Congress itself can prevent power from slipping through its fingers."[46]

Justice Jackson's concurrence was the most powerful of the seven opinions written. From a rhetorical standpoint it was a classic with one memorable phrase following upon another. His tri-part analysis of separation-of-powers disputes offered the reader something tangible to grasp in this overly nebulous field. The Jackson opinion seemed to recognize greater nuance and complexity than did most of the other opinions. Finally, it drew some of its moral authority from the very fact that Jackson himself had been one of the foremost defenders of executive authority in the area of foreign relations as President Roosevelt's attorney general.

---

[44] *Id.* at 642, 644.
[45] *Id.* at 650.
[46] *Id.* at 654.

JUSTICE BURTON'S CONCURRENCE

Justice Burton wrote a short concurrence. He explained that under the Taft-Hartley Act, Congress had authorized a procedure for dealing with labor disputes that could have a serious impact on the nation and its interests. The procedure called for appointment of a board of inquiry and a 60-day cooling off period followed by another 20 days for a secret ballot election. Moreover the legislative history indicated that Congress had declined to permit seizure of facilities absent additional congressional authorization. The president chose not to follow the congressionally mandated procedures. Burton concluded that Truman had no inherent authority or any authority as commander in chief to seize the plants in absence of specific congressional authorization; hence his actions were unconstitutional. Burton's opinion was as brief and straightforward as Justice Black's though somewhat different in emphasis.

JUSTICE CLARK'S CONCURRENCE

Justice Clark, also a former attorney general, wrote a short opinion concurring in the judgment though not the opinion of the Court. He began by citing Chief Justice Marshall's opinion in *Little v. Barreme*[47] where the Court invalidated for failure to comply with congressional directives a presidentially ordered seizure of a vessel. Unlike Justices Black and Jackson, Justice Clark conceded that based on custom, precedent, and necessity, the president did have inherent authority to seize private property in a national emergency. However when Congress provided procedures to govern such an emergency, the president was bound to follow them. As the president failed to abide by the procedures of the Taft-Hartley Act, the Defense Production Act of 1950, or the Selective Service Act of 1948, his actions were not constitutionally permissible. Justice Clark gave the president more leeway than the other justices in the majority but nothing that would save him in this case.

JUSTICE DOUGLAS'S CONCURRENCE

Justice Douglas wrote a short concurrence in which he endorsed Justice Black's conclusion that the president had engaged in unconstitutional legislative activity. He offered a symmetrical explanation for the division of authority, noting that the seizure constituted a taking within the Fifth Amendment and as only Congress could appropriate funds for just compensation, it should have the sole authority to authorize the initial taking as well. Justice Douglas's opinion was as formalistic as that of Justice Black. It added little of significance.

---

[47] 2 U.S. 170 (1804).

JUSTICE FRANKFURTER'S CONCURRENCE

Justice Frankfurter wrote a concurrence that was long-winded but significant. At the outset, he explicitly declared that "the principle of separation of powers seem to me more complicated and flexible than...appear from what Mr. Justice Black has written."[48] He recognized that there was pressure in a case such as this to attempt to decide too much in that "constitutional questions seem to exercise a mesmeric influence over the popular mind."[49] He cautioned against indulging that preference. Like Justices Burton and Clark, Justice Frankfurter examined the existing legislation, particularly Taft-Hartley, and concluded that the legislative history established that Congress clearly meant to deny the president seizure authority, absent specific authorization.

Justice Frankfurter's major contribution to constitutional analysis in *Youngstown* stems from his recognition that long-standing custom could place a gloss on the constitutional text.[50] Such a gloss should not be readily inferred, however. Rather there would need to be "a systematic, unbroken, executive practice, long pursued to the knowledge of the Congress and never before questioned...."[51] Applying this standard to the instant case, Justice Frankfurter found no support for such a gloss. In a lengthy appendix, he catalogued every incident in American history that might be relevant. He concluded however that only three pre–World War II seizures by President Roosevelt were pertinent and that these were insufficient to establish a long-standing gloss on executive power.

Much of Frankfurter's concurrence seems verbose and beside the point. However, his recognition that congressionally accepted executive practice can matter is important. Like Justice Jackson, Frankfurter articulated a vision of separation of powers that was more realistic than that suggested by Black. It is an area in which the overwhelming number of disputes are settled without resort to law and adjudication. As such, there is an accretion of custom and understanding that must be taken into account. Frankfurter's articulation of this corner of constitutional law in *Youngstown* renders his opinion an essential piece of the constitutional understanding of this area.

CHIEF JUSTICE VINSON'S DISSENT

Chief Justice Vinson wrote the sole dissent joined by Justices Reed and Minton. He made a fairly powerful case for the legality of the president's action. He began by arguing that "these are extraordinary times" with the nation facing a "terrifying global conflict."[52] He cited statistics suggesting that a work stoppage would indeed create a crisis with respect to the supply of steel needed to support the war effort. He then quoted the president's executive order directing the seizure as well as his initial message to Congress in full to establish the president's basis for acting along with his articulated pledge to abide by congressional directives. The largest segment of the dissent consisted of a 15-page review

---

[48] 343 U.S. at 589.

[49] *Id.* at 594.

[50] *Id.* at 610.

[51] *Id.*

[52] *Id.* at 668.

of the emergency actions by presidents from Washington to Truman. He quoted at great length from John W. Davis's brief as solicitor general in the Midwest Oil case defending presidential authority to withdraw federally owned land from private sale despite congressional authorization of such sale. He then quoted at length from Justice Jackson's defense, as attorney general, of President Roosevelt's seizure of the North American Aircraft Company. Justice Frankfurter's lengthy appendix was a point-by-point response to Chief Justice Vinson's historical review. Contrary to Frankfurter's conclusions, Vinson argued that history was filled with examples of presidents taking sufficiently analogous action absent statutory authorization.

The essence of Chief Justice Vinson's argument was that the president had the authority in an emergency to preserve the status quo until Congress could act without specific statutory authorization. He likened the president's action to the judicial grant of a stay in the course of litigation.[53] Vinson seemed to derive this authority from the Article II directive to "take care that the laws were faithfully Executed" as interpreted by John Marshall in the House of Representatives in 1800 and endorsed by subsequent Supreme Court precedents.[54] The chief justice argued for a more muscular conception of the presidency than the majority quoting Hamilton's dictum as to the necessity of "[e]nergy in the Executive" and lamenting the Court's "messenger-boy" conception of the president.[55] Suggesting that perhaps the majority was intimidated by the political context of the case, the chief justice closed with the remark that "[a] sturdy judiciary should not be swayed by the unpleasantness or unpopularity of necessary executive action. . . ."[56]

The six justices in the majority provided several reasons for rejecting the president's action. Chief Justice Vinson provided a different perspective on the case, and demonstrated that an opinion could be written providing a plausible legal justification for the seizures as long as past executive practice was taken into account and as long as these historical examples were considered more pertinent to the instant case than either Justices Jackson or Frankfurter considered them to be.

AFTERMATH

The Court's decision was widely applauded by the press.[57] Following the decision, President Truman ordered Secretary Sawyer to return possession of the mills to the companies. The union then went on strike. Once again Truman declined to invoke the procedures of the Taft-Hartley Act. The strike lasted for 53 days, but contrary to the claims of the government during the litigation, no steel shortage materialized. A new contract was eventually signed after Truman threatened to seize the mills pursuant to the Selective Service Act. Apparently it was the demand for a union shop as opposed to a wage increase that had caused the steel companies to resist a settlement.[58]

---

[53] *Id.* at 703.
[54] *Id.* at 684, 702.
[55] *Id.* at 682, 708.
[56] *Id.* at 709.
[57] Devins & Fisher, *supra* note 7, at 70.
[58] MARCUS, *supra* note 3, at 253.

YOUNGSTOWN AS A GREAT CASE

Youngstown would seem to embody all of the characteristics of the great case. It involved emergency action taken by the president in a wartime crisis. It was the focus of intense public attention. It raised important cutting edge constitutional issues. It was litigated on an extremely expedited basis by some of the great advocates of the day. Is there reason to believe that these factors had a significant impact on the decision or the opinions themselves?

In an often-cited article published shortly after the case was decided, Professor Corwin suggested that *Youngstown* was an "example of... [a] frame of mind in which the Court is occasionally maneuvered by the public context of the case before it."[59] The publicity and public attention to the case almost certainly played a role in the Court's decision to hear the case on an expedited basis. It is less clear however that it influenced the resulting decision itself. Some commentators believe that the decision was heavily influenced, and indeed the case may well have been lost as a result of the recklessly broad position taken by the government attorney, Holmes Baldridge, in the district court.[60] One White House aide characterized the government's position before the district court as "the legal blunder of the century."[61] A legal argument that the president was almost immediately forced to disavow could scarcely be helpful. Chief Justice Rehnquist began his book on the Supreme Court with a detailed account of the *Youngstown* case through the eyes of a law clerk who had just gone to work for Justice Jackson as the case began to unfold. He concluded that "speaking as one who was on the scene at the time, I don't think that [the government's initial argument] could be erased from anyone's mind... [and] it undoubtedly had an effect on how the case was finally decided by the Supreme Court."[62] Whether it had a decisive effect cannot be known but it certainly cast the government's position in a bad light.

Although the government's argument for unchecked presidential emergency power was presented only in the district court, it was arguably attributable to the pressurized nature of the proceedings. President Truman issued his order seizing the steel mills on the evening of April 8, 1952. The initial request for an injunction by the steel companies occurred later that very evening. The crucial hearing before Judge Pine took place two weeks later on April 24. This was an especially rapid time frame for major constitutional litigation. Arguably because of the pace, the government did not have time to think through its position thoroughly. When Judge Pine pressed Assistant Attorney General Baldridge hard on its theory of presidential authority, he blundered into serious difficulty given that he had preferred to stick to the issue of whether an injunction was warranted by equitable principles. However, Judge Pine seemed intent on focusing on the larger question of presidential authority. Indeed, William Harbaugh has argued that Judge Pine was prepared to slam the president's claim regardless of Baldrige's argument.[63]

---

[59] Edward S. Corwin, *The Steel Seizure Case: A Judicial Brick without Straw*, 53 COLUM. L. REV. 53, 64 (1953).

[60] *See, e.g.*, WILLIAM H. REHNQUIST, THE SUPREME COURT: HOW IT WAS, HOW IT IS 95–96 (1987); MARCUS, *supra* note 3, at 111.

[61] MARCUS, *supra* note 3, at 124-25.

[62] REHNQUIST, *supra* note 60, at 95–96.

[63] William Harbaugh, *The Steel Seizure Reconsidered*, 87 YALE L.J. 1272, 1278–79 (1977) (reviewing MARCUS, *supra* note 3).

Apparently, the seeming need for haste that surrounded all of the proceedings was responsible for the fact that the Court was faced with resolving the case at all. While the petitions for certiorari were pending, a settlement agreement was all but reached. The companies walked away from the agreement however on learning that the Supreme Court had agreed to hear the case on an expedited basis. Had the case proceeded in a less pressurized manner, it most likely would have been resolved outside of court and the entire incident would be but a historical footnote.

Aside from the fact of the government's initial argument in the district court, there is little reason to believe that the pressurized nature of the case had an impact on the outcome itself. Despite the speed with which it progressed, the parties were able to provide extensive, well-developed briefs in a short period of time. The restraint shown by the Court toward John W. Davis during oral argument coupled with the barrage of critical questioning aimed at Solicitor General Perlman suggests that the die was cast in advance of conference. Chief Justice Rehnquist has noted that "[t]his was a case that unfurled in the newspapers before the eyes of the justices long before any papers were filed in the Supreme Court."[64] He speculated that "the tide of public opinion suddenly began to run against the government [and had] a considerable influence on the Court."[65] Chief Justice Vinson charged as much in his dissent.[66] Perhaps so. Rehnquist was there, on the inside, if only as a law clerk. Though he did not participate in researching or drafting Justice Jackson's concurring opinion, he was in a position to apprehend the mood of the Court. At the very least, the Court understood that it was almost certain that the public, the press, and the legal elites would be supportive of a decision invalidating the seizure.

It is likely however that the decision was driven primarily by the constitutional views of the justices on the issues quite apart from the haste of the proceedings and publicity surrounding the case. At least four of the justices in the majority—Black, Douglas, Jackson, and Frankfurter—were brilliant, strong willed, confident, and inclined to have well-developed views on questions of federal power. None could be considered indecisive or easily influenced. Indeed the notes of the conference on the case indicate that virtually all of the justices expressed opinions very close to those subsequently stated in their opinions.[67]

The emergency nature of the situation was presumably the government's ace in the hole but it was scarcely enough, especially as there is evidence that the justices had reason to believe that the threat to the war effort was nowhere near as serious as the government maintained. Chief Justice Rehnquist did assume that the case would have been decided in favor of the government during World War II.[68] That seems plausible. Although the Korean War was a serious undertaking costing thousands of American lives, the intensity of the threat pales next to the Second World War. Commentary on *Youngstown* generally notes that the war effort itself was not going well by the time the case arose. Moreover, the fact that it was an undeclared war, characterized by the president as "a police action." probably undercut the administration's position somewhat.[69] By the time of *Youngstown*,

---

[64] REHNQUIST, *supra* note 60, at 95.

[65] *Id.*

[66] 343 U.S. 579, 710 (1952).

[67] THE SUPREME COURT IN CONFERENCE, *supra* note 29, at 172–82.

[68] REHNQUIST, *supra* note 60, at 97.

[69] MARCUS, *supra* note 3, at 259.

President Truman had dismissed General MacArthur and public support for the war effort, especially so closely after the end of World War II, had diminished significantly.[70]

It is likely that the wide berth that President Roosevelt was given by the courts during World War II contributed to the judicial desire to reign in executive authority once circumstances were less severe. Arguably, the Court could not and would not have restrained a popular commander in chief in the midst of a war that threatened the continuing existence of the free world. But the justices in the majority, especially Justice Jackson, who as attorney general had been one of Roosevelt's strongest defenders, expressed great discomfort with ever expanding presidential power. It is also likely that the justices were eager to limit the broad dicta of *United States v. Curtiss-Wright Exporting Co.*[71] decided 18 years earlier, which had suggested that the president possessed inherent and unlimited authority to act in the area of foreign affairs. Though *Curtiss-Wright* was not directly on point as *Youngstown* was not really a foreign affairs case, there can be little question that the *Youngstown* majority was quite uncomfortable with the deferential attitude that the *Curtiss-Wright* Court had shown toward the president. As such, *Youngstown* presented the majority of the justices with what they perceived as a much-needed opportunity to begin to restore the appropriate constitutional balance. If so, perhaps a majority of the Court welcomed the opportunity that the case provided. The fact that the issue was presented in the context of an alleged wartime emergency made the judicial message all the more powerful.

Even if the pressurized nature of the *Youngstown* litigation did not dictate the result, it probably did have an impact on the nature of the opinions. Only three weeks elapsed between the oral argument and the publication of the opinions. The issues were factually complicated especially with respect to the possible application of congressional statutes and review of 150 years' worth of historical incidents. The fact that Justice Jackson could produce a classic opinion and that Justice Frankfurter and Chief Justice Vinson could produce such lengthy and detailed opinions in such an abbreviated time period is quite impressive.

Still *Youngstown* is quite unusual in that the four justices who joined Justice Black's opinion for the Court each filed their own concurrence, three of which clearly did not accept much of Black's reasoning. Justice Clark concurred in the judgment but could not join the opinion at all. Not surprisingly this unusual situation of a majority opinion that does not truly represent the views of anywhere close to a majority of the justices has been attributed to the lack of time to achieve greater consensus.[72] Apparently, the justices prepared their individual opinions with insufficient opportunity for circulation and response.[73] There must have been some time however given that the opinions of Frankfurter and Vinson are somewhat responsive to each other on the relevance of historical exercises of presidential power.

But there is no question that the justices did not have the time to iron out differences and establish more common ground. Presumably, the justices believed that an opinion of "the Court" was essential in a case in which emergency action ordered by the president

---

[70] REHNQUIST, *supra* note 60, at 96–97.
[71] 299 U.S. 304 (1936).
[72] REHNQUIST, *supra* note 60, at 92.
[73] *Id.*

during a wartime crisis is rejected. The justices would have appeared weak and ineffective had they been unable to even attempt to speak with a voice styled as the Court. But considering the very real differences of opinion between the justices in the majority, their high level of self-confidence, and the antipathy that several of them held for each other, it is likely that some of their differences would not have been resolved had they an entire court term in which to proceed. There were significant disagreements between strong willed justices with deeply held views. Justice Jackson saw the need for recognition of interdependence between the president and Congress. Justice Black did not. Justice Frankfurter believed that historical custom and practice was important. Justice Black dismissed it as irrelevant. Justice Clark believed that the president possessed inherent emergency powers. Justices Black, Douglas, and Jackson disagreed. It is not obvious that a real consensus could have developed as long as Justice Black was writing the majority opinion.

The difficulty of achieving consensus was probably aggravated by the bad blood that existed between Justice Black on the one hand and Justices Jackson and Frankfurter on the other. In discussing the *Youngstown* case in his book, Chief Justice Rehnquist devotes several pages to the origin of the feud between these justices seven years earlier.[74] From Rehnquist's perspective as a law clerk, serious personality conflicts continued to affect the behavior of the justices. Considering the legitimate differences between these justices in terms of legal reasoning in the case, personal animosity could only complicate any effort toward agreement. Perhaps a coherent majority opinion could only have been prepared by someone other than Black, Douglas, Jackson, or Frankfurter. Still, *Youngstown* can be cited along with the Pentagon Papers, *United States v. Nixon*, and *Bush v. Gore* as a warning of the dangers that are posed by preparing opinions without adequate time for a reconciliation of conflicting views.

Justice Frankfurter stated that the "differences in attitude" toward the separation-of-powers principle "may be merely differences in emphasis and nuance"; however "they can hardly be reflected by a single opinion for the Court."[75] Consequently "[i]ndividual expression of views in reaching a common result is therefore important."[76] There was much wisdom in this observation. The readers of Supreme Court opinions are far better served by the elegant concurrences of Frankfurter and Jackson than they would be by a more cohesive but pedestrian opinion for the Court.

Youngstown certainly has become a major precedent, indeed probably the Court's most significant precedent in the area of separation of powers. The case represents one of the most notable judicial challenges to presidential authority, especially in a wartime emergency context in Supreme Court history. As with *Marbury v. Madison*, the president himself was not the subject of judicial process; rather it was his delegate in the person of a Cabinet officer. Despite the fact that the style of the case is *Youngstown Sheet & Tube v. Sawyer* and not *Youngstown Sheet & Tube v. Truman*, all of the justices analyzed the issues as if the president, not the secretary of commerce, was the respondent, as he was as a practical matter. As such, *Youngstown* is an important predecessor to *United States*

---

[74] *Id.* at 65–69.
[75] 343 U.S. 579, 868 (1952).
[76] *Id.*

v. Nixon and *Clinton v. Jones* where the president was indeed the formal target of the litigation. Thus *Youngstown* is an essential precedent in bringing the president into the judicial orbit. As with Marshall's dicta in *Marbury v. Madison*, it symbolizes the central constitutional principle that we are a government of "of laws not of men" or that "no man is above the law."

Youngstown may also be viewed as an important precedent in attempting to recalibrate the balance of power between Congress and the president, especially in the area of war powers.[77] Presidential power grew exponentially during World War II. In the prewar case of *United States v. Curtiss-Wright Exporting Co.*,[78] the Court took an expansive view of inherent presidential authority with respect to foreign affairs. *Youngstown*, though not a foreign affairs case, emphasized the central role of Congress, even in the context of military emergencies. In so doing, it purported to check assertions of inherent presidential authority somewhat though not with great clarity given the split among the justices. Arguably only Justices Black and Douglas, and more ambiguously Justice Jackson, rejected the concept of inherent presidential authority to meet emergencies. The other four justices who joined the majority recognized some such authority whether textually or structurally based, albeit with the understanding that Congress had the authority to either channel it or preclude it entirely.

Given the variety of opinions offered in *Youngstown*, the case does not establish much as a matter of precedent. It does however set forth several interpretive approaches that continue to play a significant role in the area of separation of powers. Justice Black's formalistic approach has been subject to criticism, but a not dissimilar formalism continues to play a significant role in separation-of-powers jurisprudence with the decisions in *INS v. Chadha*[79] and *Bowshers v. Synar*[80] as more recent illustrations.

Justice Frankfurter's opinion recognized the importance of established custom and practice in the area of separation-of-powers analysis. The overwhelming majority of separation-of-powers issues are resolved through accommodation rather than litigation. Consequently the structures and practices that the executive and legislative branches settle on in this area are of great importance and may well place a gloss on the text as Frankfurter recognized. Frankfurter's standard for determining whether congressional acceptance of executive practice is of constitutional significance is exacting and difficult to satisfy. Nevertheless it constitutes a distinctive contribution to constitutional interpretation. Though they drew different conclusions Chief Justice Vinson and Justice Burton emphasized the need to examine congressional action carefully in order to determine whether constitutional law was even implicated.

As noted above, Justice Jackson's concurrence in *Youngstown* stole the show. As Dean Koh put it, the Jackson opinion has become "the lodestar" of separation of powers analysis.[81] Perhaps this is because it makes good sense. Perhaps it is because it provides a doctrinal construct that has at least some substance to it. In any event, in relying upon

---

[77] HAROLD HONGJU KOH, THE NATIONAL SECURITY CONSTITUTION: SHARING POWER AFTER THE IRAN-CONTRA AFFAIR 136 (1990).

[78] 299 U.S. 304 (1936).

[79] 462 U.S. 919 (1983).

[80] 478 U.S. 714 (1986).

[81] KOH, *supra* note 77, at 105.

Youngstown, courts often treat the Jackson opinion as if it was the majority opinion for all practical purposes. One of the most prominent examples of the influence of the Jackson concurrence is the case of *Dames & Moore v. Regan*.[82] There, the question was whether as a condition of obtaining release of American hostages held in Iran, the president had the authority to nullify attachments of and to suspend claims against Iranian assets in the United States. The Court unanimously upheld the authority of the president to do both. The opinion was written by Chief Justice Rehnquist, who as noted earlier had clerked for Justice Jackson during the term that *Youngstown* was decided. Rehnquist quoted extensively from Justice Jackson and relied on his tri-part analysis to resolve the case after briefly referring to Justice Black's opinion. The Court was able to find specific congressional authorization for the presidential nullification of the attachments. With respect to the suspension of claims however, it would seem that the Court misapplied the Jacksonian analysis. After admitting that there was no congressional statute on point, Rehnquist pointed to statutes that granted suspension authority in other contexts and presumed that Congress meant that the same should apply in this situation as well.[83] Consequently, the Court found implicit authorization, thus treating this as a category one case within the Jacksonian analysis. At most however, the circumstances suggested a category two situation in which Congress was silent. In noting that analogous legislation should give rise to an inference of approval "[a]t least where there is no contrary indication of legislative intent," the Court seemed to place on Congress an affirmative obligation to object.[84] This seems difficult to square with Justice Jackson's analysis in *Youngstown*.

The prominence of the Jackson concurrence was emphasized recently in *Medellin v. Texas*[85] where the Court held that a memorandum of the president did not require a Texas court to reconsider a Mexican national's death sentence on account of a treaty violation. Writing for the majority, Chief Justice Roberts, who had served as a law clerk to Justice Rehnquist when *Dames-Moore* was decided, proclaimed that "Justice Jackson's familiar tripartite scheme provides the accepted framework for evaluating executive action in this area."[86] The Court concluded that by definition, a non–self-executing treaty presumes that the Senate has not consented to direct presidential enforcement; hence the case falls into Justice Jackson's third category.

One criticism of *Youngstown*, especially shortly after it was decided, was that it provided little in the way of useful law or guidance in that the justices in the majority failed to agree on much if anything in terms of legal doctrine. Although there is much truth in this critique, the consequences are not necessarily that severe given that separation-of-powers cases are not litigated with great regularity and when they are, the factual divergence from one case to the next render them poor candidates for resolution through established doctrine in any event. Moreover as Paul Kauper noted in the wake of *Youngstown*, there was actually more agreement among the justices than meets the eye.[87] Despite the fact that Black's opinion was presented as the opinion of the Court, arguably seven of the

---

[82] 453 U.S. 654 (1981).

[83] *Id.* at 677–80.

[84] *Id.* at 678.

[85] 552 U.S. 491 (2008).

[86] *Id.* at 524.

[87] Kauper, *supra* note 28, at 174–78.

nine justices rejected its rigid analysis. Absent explicit or implicit congressional disapproval these seven, combining the concurring and dissenting justices with the exception of Douglas, would be inclined to permit some degree of presidential emergency action. As such, the long-term impact of *Youngstown* would seem to be to empower rather than constrain the president with the caveat that Congress would generally have the power of restraint either before or after the presidential activity occurs.

Early critics of the *Youngstown* opinions grossly underestimated the attractiveness and staying power of the Jackson concurrence as well. Although it would be an overstatement to describe it as setting forth a doctrinal test, it certainly does provide a useful approach or framework for thinking about separation-of-powers issue. In hard cases, reasonable judges will disagree as to where the analysis leads, as indeed they did in *Youngstown* itself.

Youngstown made neither good nor bad law in a strict doctrinal sense. It did provide an attractive and lasting approach to separation-of-powers issues through the Jackson concurrence. Justice Frankfurter's concurrence also made a significant contribution to constitutional analysis. Moreover the case established that the Court has a role to play in policing the boundaries in separation-of-powers disputes if it so chooses. It also made it clear that although the president has some leeway to meet emergencies, Congress can usually channel or preclude presidential action if it so decides. Neither the Court nor Congress has consistently attempted to constrain the president especially in the area of foreign affairs, but that is scarcely to fault *Youngstown*. *Youngstown* was a great case to be sure. If it did not make good law in a strict doctrinal sense, it certainly did establish some solid principles of constitutional analysis. That in itself is a major accomplishment.

"As we Justices marched into the courtroom on that day, there was a tenseness that I have not seen equaled before or since.... When the word 'unanimous' was spoken, a wave of emotion swept the room."[1]

EARL WARREN

13

Brown v. Board of Education

Brown v. Board of Education is simply the greatest of the great cases. In *Brown*, the Court declared that the racial segregation of public schools, which at that time existed in a significant portion of the country, was unconstitutional. There were two separate *Brown* decisions culminating from five consolidated cases argued three times over a four-year period. Among the advocates to appear were Thurgood Marshall and John W. Davis, arguably the two greatest lawyers of the twentieth century. With the *Brown* decision, the Court became engaged in and committed to a process of momentous legal and social change that was already developing outside of the courts through the civil rights movement. *Brown* placed the Court in direct confrontation with a relatively widespread and entrenched resistance movement determined to test and retest the judicial will. The Court clearly recognized that the decision in these cases was quite unlike anything it had ever confronted before.

BACKGROUND

Segregated public schooling was well entrenched in the United States even prior to the Civil War. A pervasive system of racial segregation in virtually all public and private

---

[1] EARL WARREN, THE MEMOIRS OF CHIEF JUSTICE EARL WARREN 3 (1977). The scholarship on *Brown* is overwhelming and continues to accumulate. The definitive history of the cases is RICHARD KLUGER, SIMPLE JUSTICE: THE HISTORY OF *BROWN V. BOARD OF EDUCATION* AND BLACK AMERICA'S STRUGGLE FOR EQUALITY (1975). Also especially helpful in understanding the intricacies of the litigation and the Court's decision-making process are MARK V. TUSHNET, MAKING CIVIL RIGHTS LAW: THURGOOD MARSHALL AND THE SUPREME COURT, 1956-1961 (1994) and BERNARD SCHWARTZ, SUPER CHIEF: EARL WARREN AND HIS SUPREME COURT—A JUDICIAL BIOGRAPHY (1983). Also useful are JAMES T. PATTERSON, *BROWN V. BOARD OF EDUCATION*: A CIVIL RIGHTS MILESTONE AND ITS TROUBLED LEGACY (2001) and ROBERT J. COTTROL, RAYMOND T. DIAMOND & LELAND B. WARE, *BROWN V. BOARD OF EDUCATION*: CASTE, CULTURE, AND THE CONSTITUTION (2003). For an extensive discussion of the larger impact of Brown, see MARTHA MINOW, IN *BROWN'S* WAKE: LEGACIES OF AMERICA'S EDUCATIONAL LANDMARK (2010).

institutions, which came to be known as Jim Crow, swept through the South in the later part of the nineteenth century.[2] The Supreme Court gave its constitutional blessing to racial segregation in 1896 in *Plessy v. Ferguson*[3] where it upheld a Louisiana law mandating separate but equal railroad cars for whites and blacks. The Court relied in part on the fact that the very Congress that had drafted the Fourteenth Amendment had also provided for racially segregated schools in the District of Columbia. Justice John Marshall Harlan wrote a vigorous dissent proclaiming that "there is no caste here. Our Constitution is color blind. . . ."[4] Over the next several decades the proponents of racial segregation placed great weight on *Plessy*.

During the first third of the twentieth century, the Court addressed questions of racial discrimination occasionally, sometimes invalidating them and sometimes not but never in a systematic manner.[5] Between 1938 and 1950, the Court struck down racial segregation in graduate and professional schools in four cases, finding in each that the facilities or program either constituted a complete exclusion based on race or though separate was not equal. In *Missouri ex rel. Gaines v. Canada*,[6] the Court struck down Missouri's practice of sending black students to law school in Illinois to avoid integrating the University of Missouri Law School. In *McLaurin v. Oklahoma State Regents*,[7] the Court prohibited the University of Oklahoma Department of Education from requiring a black student to sit in a separate section of the classroom and lunchroom. On the same day, in *Sweatt v. Painter*,[8] the Court held that a separate black law school established across from the Texas Capitol was scarcely equal to the law school at the University of Texas. Significantly, the Court in *Sweat* explained that even if the facilities had been equalized the intangibles including reputation of faculty, alumni contacts, and prestige and traditions certainly had not been. The United States, as amicus curie, asked the Court to reconsider and reject *Plessy*; however, the Court declined to do so.

At the very time that *McLaurin* and *Sweatt* were before the Court, the NAACP was engaged in legal challenges to racial segregation in public elementary and secondary schools in several jurisdictions. In cases challenging school segregation in Topeka, Kansas, Clarendon County, South Carolina, Prince Edward County, Virginia, and the District of Columbia, the lower courts held that a separate but equal system was constitutional, that the black schools had not been or were not substantially equal but that they had

---

[2] C. Vann Woodward, The Strange Case of Jim Crow (3d ed. 1974); Michael J. Klarman, From Jim Crow to Civil Rights: The Supreme Court and the Struggle for Racial Equality (2004).

[3] 163 U.S. 537 (1896).

[4] *Id.* at 559.

[5] Gong Lum v. Rice, 275 U.S. 78 (1927) (state could require a student of Chinese ancestry to attend a segregated school for African Americans); Buchanan v. Warley, 245 U.S. 60 (1917) (statute prohibiting whites or blacks from living on a block where the majority of houses were inhabited by members of the other race violates the Fourteenth Amendment); McCabe v. Atchison, Topeka & Santa Fe Ry, 235 U.S. 151 (1914) (rejecting state refusal to require sleeping and dining cars for African Americans on the ground that there was insufficient demand); Berea Coll. v. Kentucky, 211 U.S. 45 (1908) (affirming a conviction of a college for permitting whites and blacks to receive instruction together on the ground that a corporation does not have all the rights of an individual).

[6] 305 U.S. 337 (1938).

[7] 339 U.S. 637 (1950).

[8] 339 U.S. 629 (1950).

been or were in the process of being equalized.[9] The district court in *Brown*, the Kansas case, did make a specific fact-finding that segregated education harmed black students. The courts in Delaware, however, finding substantial inequality ordered the admission of the black student plaintiffs to white schools. During the 1952 term, all five cases were consolidated before the United States Supreme Court under the style of *Brown v. Board of Education*. The five cases were set for oral argument in December 1952.

The Department of Justice was not invited to appear in the oral arguments; however it did submit a lengthy amicus brief written primarily by Philip Elman concluding that racial segregation in schools did in fact violate the Fourteenth Amendment and proposing a gradual approach toward implementing the remedy. Elman had clerked for Justice Frankfurter 10 years earlier and Frankfurter referred to him as "a law clerk for life."[10] According to Elman, he and Frankfurter were in continual contact discussing the case while *Brown* was pending before the Court, which would seem to constitute a serious breach of ethics.

FIRST ROUND OF ARGUMENTS

All five cases were argued over the course of three days. Leading off in the *Brown* case, Robert Carter, arguing for the plaintiffs, did attack *Plessy* head on, calling for its rejection.[11] The Topeka School Board declined to appear; however the state of Kansas defended its statute, which permitted but did not require large cities such as Topeka to segregate its schools. Perhaps the most significant of the arguments came in the South Carolina case *Briggs v. Elliot* pitting Thurgood Marshall for the plaintiffs against renowned Supreme Court advocate John W. Davis. Marshall argued that the Fourteenth Amendment properly understood prohibited all state-sponsored discrimination, including segregated public schooling.[12] He emphasized that there was no legitimate state purpose behind segregation; rather it was simply based on racism.[13] Davis argued that the original understanding of the Fourteenth Amendment clearly did not ban school segregation and that the Court's precedents from *Plessy* on recognized its constitutionality.[14] During the argument in the Virginia case, the justices began to focus on the nature of the remedy that the Court might issue.[15]

Shortly after oral argument the Court met in conference to discuss the cases but refrained from taking a formal vote.[16] Information about the discussions in this conference are based on the notes left by Justices Burton and Jackson. Chief Justice Vinson

---

[9] The cases were: Brown v. Board of Education (Kansas); Briggs v. Elliot (South Carolina); Davis v. Cnty. Sch. Bd. (Virginia); Gebhart v. Belton (Delaware); Bolling v. Sharpe (District of Columbia).

[10] Philip Elman, *The Solicitor General's Office, Justice Frankfurter and Civil Rights Litigation, 1946–1960: An Oral History*, 100 HARV. L. REV. 817 (1987).

[11] ARGUMENT: THE ORAL ARGUMENTS IN *BROWN V. BOARD OF EDUCATION OF TOPEKA*, 1952–55 12 (Leon Friedman ed., 1970).

[12] *Id.* at 37, 42-43.

[13] *Id.* at 45.

[14] *Id.* at 55–56.

[15] *Id.* at 106–07.

[16] THE SUPREME COURT IN CONFERENCE (1940–1985): THE PRIVATE DISCUSSIONS BEHIND NEARLY 300 SUPREME COURT DECISIONS 646-54 (Del Dickson ed., 2001).

worried that the Court's decision could lead to "the complete abolition of the public school system in the south."[17] Justice Black was prepared to invalidate segregation but with the understanding that "it will mean trouble."[18] Justice Reed argued that "the states should be left to work out the problem for themselves." He concluded that "I uphold segregation as constitutional."[19] Frankfurter argued vigorously for setting the cases for re-argument.[20] Douglas stated that the question was simple—that racial discrimination was unconstitutional.[21] Jackson declared that neither the text, original understanding nor precedent rendered segregation unconstitutional but that it would disappear in time.[22] Burton stated that "segregation violates equal protection" but he would give the states "plenty of time."[23] Clark seemed to favor invalidation but with a substantial amount of time for compliance.[24] Minton declared that "segregation is per se unconstitutional."[25]

In a memo written in 1954, the day *Brown I* was announced, Douglas claimed that had the case been decided in 1952, it would have been a 5-4 decision upholding school segregation.[26] That seems unduly pessimistic in view of the conference notes. Justice Frankfurter played an important role in the Court's deliberations. From the outset, he maintained that if the Court was to invalidate racial segregation in schools it must do so in a unanimous opinion, given the likelihood of vigorous opposition.[27] During the conference and throughout the spring, the Court was divided as to the result with probably four or five justices committed to rejecting segregation, at least one favoring upholding it, and three or four leaning toward invalidation but only if implementation of the decree was extremely gradual.

SECOND ROUND OF ARGUMENTS

Primarily as a result of the division on the Court, the justices followed Justice Frankfurter's suggestion to set the five cases for re-argument the following term. Frankfurter argued that the newly elected Eisenhower administration deserved the opportunity to take a position on the litigation given that it would be primarily responsible for enforcement of the decisions.[28] From Frankfurter's standpoint, delay would increase the opportunity to achieve unanimity and to reconcile a decision invalidating school segregation with the state of existing law, an extreme concern for both Justices Frankfurter and Jackson.[29] In ordering re-argument the Court asked the parties to address several specific

---

[17] *Id.* at 647.
[18] *Id.* at 648.
[19] *Id.* at 649.
[20] *Id.* at 650–51.
[21] *Id.* at 652.
[22] *Id.* at 652-53.
[23] *Id.* at 653.
[24] *Id.*
[25] *Id.*
[26] *Id.* at 660–61.
[27] KLUGER, *supra* note 1, at 599.
[28] COTTROL ET AL., *supra* note 1, at 166.
[29] TUSHNET, *supra* note 1, at 215.

questions that had been proposed by Frankfurter, including the significance of the original understanding of the Fourteenth Amendment on the question of school segregation, the respective powers of Congress and the Court to address school segregation, and the appropriate remedial framework. The Court also asked the solicitor general to file a brief addressing the questions.

Prior to the second round of arguments, the parties spent most of their time researching and addressing the question of original understanding. Of particular concern was the significance of the Civil Rights Act of 1866. Initially the Act contained language prohibiting racial discrimination with respect to "civil rights and immunities," which arguably was understood as banning racially segregated schools.[30] This proved to be too controversial however and was omitted prior to passage. In view of doubts as to whether Congress had the constitutional power under the Thirteenth Amendment to pass the 1866 Act, Congress enacted the Fourteenth Amendment in 1868. Among other things, the amendment was intended to provide such authority and quite probably constitutionalize the substance of the 1866 Act through the Privileges or Immunities Clause.[31] The inference thus arose that if the 1866 was not intended to reach racially segregated schooling, then neither was the Fourteenth Amendment. Moreover, the very Congress that drafted and approved the Fourteenth Amendment also funded racially segregated schools in the District of Columbia. Both sides spent the summer conferring with Reconstruction Era historians in order to develop arguments that would interpret the historical materials most favorably toward their positions.

After exhaustive consideration of the historical materials, the NAACP argued that the Reconstruction Amendments, in their totality, stood for the principle that any state-mandated racial segregation was unconstitutional.[32] Moreover, a speech by Representative Bingham urging the removal of the "civil rights" language from the 1866 Act suggested that a constitutional amendment was necessary to provide a basis for such an anti-discrimination principle. Consequently, the enactment of the Fourteenth Amendment should be understood as encompassing the broad principle, including a ban on school segregation, that Bingham believed could not constitutionally be accomplished through mere legislation.[33] Marshall believed, quite correctly, that he needed only to achieve a draw on the original understanding to win the case.[34]

The southern states responded by arguing that there was no support in either the framing debates or ratifying conventions of the Fourteenth Amendment for the prohibition of school segregation.[35] Rather, the purpose of the Fourteenth Amendment was merely to constitutionalize the Civil Rights Act of 1866 from which language that would have prohibited racially segregated schools had been deliberately omitted. The states emphasized that at the time of the ratification of the amendment, 27 of 34 states, including many northern states, required racially segregated schools.

---

[30] Alexander M. Bickel, *The Original Understanding and the Segregation Decision*, 69 HARV. L. REV. 1, 57 (1955). KLUGER, *supra* note 1, at 627–29, 640.

[31] Bickel, *supra* note 30, at 57-58.

[32] TUSHNET, *supra* note 1, at 199.

[33] KLUGER, *supra* note 1, at 641.

[34] *Id.* at 619.

[35] *Id.* at 647–49.

The Department of Justice filed an extensive brief concluding that there was insufficient discussion of segregated schooling during the debates on the Fourteenth Amendment to support the conclusion that it was intended to prohibit school segregation. However, the amendment was written in broad enough language to permit future courts to invalidate segregation. Still, unlike the earlier government brief, the second one did not argue that segregated schooling was necessarily unconstitutional.

Independent research was done by the Court itself on the original understanding. Before the cases were set for re-argument, Justice Frankfurter directed his law clerk, Alexander Bickel, to conduct a thorough review of the original understanding of the Fourteenth Amendment with respect to school segregation. Bickel produced a memo that Frankfurter circulated to the other justices. Bickel found the history too inconclusive to support the position of either side to the litigation. A few years later, Bickel revised his research and published it in the *Harvard Law Review*.[36] It remains one of the most thorough studies of the subject.

Between the first and second round of oral arguments, Chief Justice Vinson died and was replaced by California governor Earl Warren. There is a consensus among scholars that the achievement of unanimity by the Court would not have been possible absent Warren's leadership.

The second round of oral arguments in the desegregation cases took place December 7–9, 1953. *Briggs v. Elliot* featuring both Thurgood Marshall and John W. Davis was the first case argued. For the plaintiffs, Spottswood Robinson began by attempting to confront the original understanding of the Fourteenth Amendment. He tried to make the case that the Amendment embodied a broad anti-discrimination principle that could and did prohibit segregated education.[37] Marshall followed but his argument became bogged down in quibbles with Justices Reed and Frankfurter over the correct interpretation of the Court's precedents.[38] John W. Davis, making the last of his 250 arguments to the Court, maintained that the legislative history of the amendment clearly showed that it was not intended to prohibit segregated education.[39] Near the end of his argument, Davis asked whether the gains that had been made in equalizing segregated schools in the south should be "thrown away on some fancied question of racial prestige?"[40] The Court permitted Davis to proceed almost without interruption. Davis's argument is generally considered the most eloquent and powerful of all of the many oral arguments delivered in the desegregation cases; however it was destined to be rejected by a unanimous Court.[41]

In rebuttal, in response to Davis's statement that the only thing the Negro plaintiffs were after was prestige, Marshall replied that is "[e]xactly correct… the Negro has been trying to get… the same status as anybody else regardless of race."[42] He also repeated the observation that he had made in the first argument that black and white children in the South played together before and after school and thus were only separated during

---

[36] Bickel, *supra* note 30.
[37] ARGUMENT, *supra* note 11, at 191.
[38] *Id.* at 195–206.
[39] *Id.* at 207.
[40] *Id.* at 216.
[41] KLUGER, *supra* note 1, at 671.
[42] ARGUMENT, *supra* note 11, at 236.

school.[43] He further argued that there was no basis for the racial segregation in schools other than the belief the Negroes were inferior to whites.[44] Finally, Marshall declared that the plaintiffs seemed to have more faith that the people of the South would comply with the law than the states themselves had.[45] Marshall's rebuttal was his most powerful argument in the *Brown* cases, perhaps to some extent because he was not interrupted by the justices nearly as much.

J.Lee Rankin from the solicitor general's office argued on behalf of the government. Although he maintained that the legislative history of the Fourteenth Amendment was too ambiguous to support either side, the United States believed that school segregation violated the principle of racial equality embodied in the Fourteenth Amendment.[46] This went beyond the position that the government had taken in its brief. Much of Rankin's argument focused on the question of the remedy. He introduced the concept of "deliberate speed" for the first time in the *Brown* litigation, making reference on another occasion to the need for "diligent speed" in enforcement.[47]

None of the other arguments spread out over three days contributed much new information to what the Court had already heard.

DELIBERATIONS

The Court's first conference following the second round of arguments took place in December. At the outset, Chief Justice Warren agreed with Marshal's argument that segregated education could only be sustained on the belief the Negroes were inferior.[48] He concluded that "we should abolish, in a tolerant way, the practice of segregation in the public schools."[49] Consequently, he was prepared to reject racial segregation in schools. Black was not present but sent word that he would vote to end segregation.[50] Reed stated that segregation was not based on Negro inferiority but rather "racial differences."[51] Frankfurter equivocated noting that segregation was not inconsistent with the original understanding but that the Court needs to be capable of recognizing that times change.[52] Douglas agreed with Warren.[53] Jackson explained that the challenge was "to make a judicial basis for a congenial political conclusion," which he was prepared to do.[54] Burton was prepared to invalidate segregation.[55] Clark would invalidate if we "permit different handling in different places."[56] Minton was also prepared to strike it down.[57] It appears that all

---

[43] *Id.* at 239.

[44] *Id.*

[45] *Id.* at 237.

[46] *Id.* at 250.

[47] *Id.* at 253, 256.

[48] THE SUPREME COURT IN CONFERENCE, *supra* note 17, at 654.

[49] *Id.* at 655.

[50] *Id.*

[51] *Id.* at 656.

[52] *Id.* at 657.

[53] *Id.* at 658.

[54] *Id.*

[55] *Id.*

[56] *Id.* at 659.

[57] *Id.* at 660.

of the justices but Reed were prepared to agree with Warren; however both Frankfurter and Jackson were troubled by the lack of legal support for such a decision.[58] Indeed Jackson seemed only willing to support it if it was characterized as a political rather than a legal act.[59]

The Court met again in conference to discuss the desegregation cases in January. Frankfurter's notes are the only record of this conference. Although it had not yet voted to reject school segregation, the justices turned their attention to the nature of the remedy in the all but certain event that it would rule for the plaintiffs. Justice Black favored sending the cases back to the district courts with no guidance while Frankfurter would send them back with some direction.[60] In a memo, Frankfurter picked up on the concept of "deliberate speed" mentioned by Rankin during oral argument. He pressed the case for a gradualist approach toward implementing the remedy, which he later credited Philip Elman with introducing in one of the government's brief.[61] Jackson apparently began to draft a concurring opinion but was unable to complete it due to a heart attack.

A third conference for which there are no notes apparently took place in February or March, at which time there probably was a vote.[62] In his *Memoirs*, Warren declared that the Court was unanimous as of the first conference vote in February and that there was never any mention of dissent.[63] Most historical accounts of the decision-making process suggest otherwise however. Earl Warren, who had been appointed by Eisenhower with a recess appointment, was finally confirmed by the Senate on March 1, 1954, at a point at which he was already preparing the opinion in *Brown v. Board of Education*. Warren had finished a draft of the opinion in April but did not circulate it until May 7. Warren brought the opinion to Jackson in the hospital where he approved of it. Apparently, Reed was still considering dissenting. Warren met with him and said, "Stan, you're all by yourself in this now. You've got to decide whether it's really the best thing for the country."[64] Reed agreed to join the opinion. The opinion was officially approved at a conference on May 15.

THE OPINION IN *BROWN I*

On May 17, 1954, the Court released its unanimous opinion written by Chief Justice Warren invalidating under the Equal Protection Clause of the Fourteenth Amendment racially segregated public schools. Justice Jackson returned to the bench from the hospital for the delivery of the opinion by Warren. Despite having asked the parties to address the original understanding of the Fourteenth Amendment, the Court immediately dismissed it as "inconclusive."[65] Warren acknowledged that some of the proponents believed that the amendment banned school segregation, some clearly did not, and it was

---

[58] *Id.* at 660–61.

[59] *Id.*

[60] Tushnet, *supra* note 1, at 221–22.

[61] Cottrol et al., *supra* note 1, at 170-71 (quoting a letter from Felix Frankfurter).

[62] Schwartz, *supra* note 1, at 94.

[63] Warren, *supra* note 1, at 2, 285.

[64] Kluger, *supra* note 1, at 698.

[65] 347 U.S. 483, 489 (1954).

impossible to determine what others believed. This was the approach taken by both the Bickel memo and the government's brief.

Chief Justice Warren explained that public education was not well developed in the North and all but nonexistent in the South at the time of Reconstruction. Consequently, the framers views on the constitutionality of segregated schooling were of limited utility in assessing the issue almost a century later when education had become "perhaps the most important function of state and local governments" and the key to success in life.[66]

The Court was faced not only with potentially troublesome original understanding but with difficult precedent as well in *Plessy v. Ferguson*, which had constitutionally blessed separate but equal in the transportation context, as well as *Gong Lum v. Rice*,[67] which had arguably recognized its validity in the area of public education. Warren attempted to undermine *Plessy* in three ways: by arguing that it had been wrong on the law, that it had been undermined by subsequent precedent, and that it had been wrong on the facts. First Warren argued that the *Slaughter-House Cases* and *Strauder v. West Virginia*, decided within a decade of the passage of the Fourteenth Amendment, correctly understood the amendment as establishing a relatively broad anti-discrimination principle. The separate but equal doctrine did not appear until 30 years after the ratification of the Fourteenth Amendment, suggesting at least that the early cases had properly understood the true scope of the amendment and *Plessy* had been misguided. This was a point that Marshall had pressed vigorously in both his brief and oral argument.

Likewise, the graduate school cases, especially the most recent ones, *McLaurin* and *Sweatt*, had significantly undermined *Plessy*. Again, this was an argument that Marshall had emphasized. Later in the opinion, Warren cited sociological data for the proposition that segregation, by stigmatizing black children, caused real harm, implicitly suggesting that the contrary conclusion in *Plessy* that segregation did not denote inferiority was factually wrong. Thus without condemning *Plessy* explicitly, Warren strongly implied that it was not worthy of respect as a precedent.

Having dealt with original understanding and adverse precedent, Warren acknowledged that unlike the graduate school cases, the cases before the Court were based on findings of substantial equalization or at least significant progress in that direction. Consequently, they could not be resolved on the basis of the separate but equal doctrine but instead were premised on a direct challenge to that doctrine. Warren framed the issue to be decided as whether "segregation of children in public schools solely on the basis of race, even though physical facilities and other 'tangible' factors may be equal, deprive children of the minority group of equal educational opportunities?"[68] He concluded that "it does."[69]

Warren cited *Sweatt* for the principle that the inequality of intangible factors is significant and *McLaurin* for the proposition that physical separation undermines the student's ability to learn. He then explained that these "considerations apply with added force to children in grade and high schools."[70] This led to the central premise of the Court's rationale—that separation of students because of race "generates a feeling of inferiority as to

---

[66] *Id.* at 493.
[67] Gong Lum v. Rice, 275 U.S. 78 (1927).
[68] *Brown*, 347 U.S. at 493.
[69] *Id.*
[70] *Id.*

their status in the community that may affect their hearts and minds in a way unlikely ever to be undone."[71] Warren quoted a fact-finding by the district court in Kansas for the proposition that such separation was likely to have an adverse impact on black children in the educational process, and noted that the Delaware court had reached a similar conclusion. He then dropped the controversial footnote citing sociological studies to discredit the contrary conclusions of *Plessy*.[72] The Court declared that separate facilities were inherently unequal. The plaintiffs had won; however, rather than ordering relief, the Court scheduled yet one more round of oral arguments to address the question of the appropriate remedy.

The Court did separate *Bolling v. Sharp*, the District of Columbia case, out from the four state cases for the obvious reason that the Fourteenth Amendment did not apply to the federal government. As such, the Court faced particular doctrinal difficulties in *Bolling*. At the outset, Warren acknowledged that unlike the Fourteenth Amendment, the Fifth Amendment does not contain an Equal Protection Clause.[73] He explained however that both equal protection and due process, at least at a generalized level, were concerned with fairness, and as such an equality principle was to some extent inherent in due process. He cautioned that the Fifth Amendment equality principle was not necessarily identical to that of the Fourteenth Amendment but in fact it has turned out to be in practice. The opinion in *Bolling* was somewhat more traditionally doctrinal than in *Brown*. Citing its prior decision in *Korematsu v. United States*, the Court concluded that racial classifications must be scrutinized with care as they are constitutionally suspect. The Court had not alluded to a specific standard of review in *Brown*. Moreover the *Bolling* Court declared that there was simply no constitutionally legitimate purpose for racial segregation in public schools. Warren had not quite said that in the more sensitive context of the southern state desegregation cases. The Court acknowledged that its decision was largely driven by necessity, explaining that it would be "unthinkable" that segregation would be prohibited in the states yet permissible in the District of Columbia. It well understood that such a result would be devastating to its credibility.

Warren found it necessary under the circumstances to construct a somewhat awkward rationale under Fifth Amendment due process in order to reach this result. The theory was awkward because the Fourteenth Amendment also contained a Due Process Clause, and if due process included an equality principle then the Equal Protection Clause would appear to be redundant. Moreover, for 60 years, the Due Process Clause of the Fifth Amendment coexisted with slavery, so at least as a matter of original understanding it could scarcely be read as prohibiting segregated schools.

ASSESSING THE *BROWN I* OPINION

As great cases go, the opinion in *Brown* was quite unusual. As Warren had noted in his cover memo delivering the opinion to the other justices: "'it was short, readable by the lay public, non-rhetorical, unemotional and above all non-accusatory.'"[74] It was also rather

---

[71] *Id.* at 494.

[72] *Id.* at 494–95.

[73] 347 U.S. 497, 499 (1954).

[74] KLUGER, *supra* note 1, at 696.

vague in terms of its rationale. The opinions in most "great cases" are quite different. There are obvious reasons the *Brown* opinion was so written. The Court understood that it needed to seek the cooperation of a large swath of the general public, including school boards, law enforcement officials, and parents if its decision was to be successfully implemented. Justice Black had repeatedly warned his colleagues that there would be extreme resistance in the South. Consequently, the Court was speaking to a far broader audience than is ordinarily the case. As such, the opinion needed to be short enough to encourage publication in daily newspapers and written in a style accessible to non-lawyers.[75] Accordingly, the *Brown* opinion is far less doctrinal or legalistic than most Supreme Court opinions. Likewise, it goes out of its way to be low key, avoiding explicit condemnation of racial segregation. It did not even directly overrule *Plessy*. The general absence of legal explication is to some extent attributable to the desire of providing the Court's critics the smallest target possible. The generality and ambiguity of the decision must be considered a consequence of the Court's perceived need for unanimity, which inevitably demands compromise. Frankfurter and Jackson in particular were very troubled with the difficulty of producing an opinion that was well grounded legally. It is not apparent that this bothered any of the other justices however.

The opinion is less than clear as to its rationale. Reading it in isolation, it could be interpreted as holding that segregated schools are unconstitutional because of the importance of education in modern society and the adverse impact that racial segregation has on the educational achievement of black students. In other words, the principle was limited to the educational context. But subsequent per curiam opinions striking down racial segregation in all public facilities indicated that the principle of Brown was hardly limited to education.[76] Drawing to some extent on the companion case of *Bolling v. Sharp*, arguably the best reading of Brown is that publicly sponsored racial segregation is unconstitutional because it stigmatizes the victims causing real constitutional harm, and in addition it has no constitutionally legitimate purpose.

THIRD ROUND OF ARGUMENTS

In scheduling the third round of oral arguments in *Brown*, the Court directed the parties to focus on the question of remedy, which in fact had already been discussed at some length during the second round of arguments. In particular, questions four and five that the Court had addressed to the parties prior to the second round were at the heart of the arguments in the third round as well. In its order, the Court had asked the parties to explain whether it should require that the plaintiff children "forthwith be admitted to schools of their choice" or whether in the exercise of equity powers "an effective gradual adjustment" should be mandated.[77] Second, it asked the parties to recommend whether the Court itself should issue a detailed decree, whether it should refer the cases

---

[75] WARREN, *supra* note 1, at 3.

[76] Gayle v. Browder, 352 U.S. 903 (1956) (buses); Holmes v. City of Atlanta, 350 U.S. 879 (1955) (public golf courses); Mayor of Baltimore v. Dawson, 350 U.S. 877 (1955) (public beaches); Johnson v. Virginia, 373 U.S. 61 (1963) (courtroom seating); Turner v. City of Memphis, 369 U.S. 350 (1962) (public restaurants).

[77] *Brown*, 347 U.S. at 496 n. 13.

to a master for further findings, or whether it should remand the cases back to the district courts with orders to frame appropriate decrees. Once again, the parties huddled to devise responses to the Court's expressed concerns.

Prior to the re-argument, Justice Jackson died of a heart attack and was replaced by Justice Harlan, the great grandson of the famous dissenter in *Plessy*. As a result, the argument was delayed until April 1955 to ensure that the Court was at full strength. John W. Davis had left the case and had passed away shortly before the third round of arguments. Moreover, the Topeka School Board voted to end segregation, and significant desegregation occurred in the District of Columbia prior to the argument on the appropriate remedy.[78] In the oral argument on the remedy, the states pressed for an indeterminate amount of time to begin compliance. Emery Rodgers in *Briggs*, the South Carolina case, infuriated Chief Justice Warren by refusing to acknowledge that the state would comply with the Court's decree.[79] A brief filed by several state attorneys general from segregating states warned the Court that an order to end racial segregation might also end public education in the South. The plaintiffs argued for a decree requiring fairly immediate desegregation, giving the states no more than a year to adjust. Marshall argued that only Negroes were asked to wait before their constitutional rights would be enforced.[80] The Department of Justice submitted a brief, personally approved by the president, arguing for gradualism and flexibility in implementation.[81] President Eisenhower actually contributed a paragraph to the brief expressing some understanding of the difficulties to be encountered by the southern states.[82] To some extent, the solicitor general's brief was the result of the back channel communication between Justice Frankfurter and Philip Elman building on the briefs previously filed.[83] The plaintiffs objected to the United States' government's unwillingness to support a forthwith decree.

Apparently Chief Justice Warren and the Court had decided upon a remand and a gradualist approach even before the oral arguments on remedy and indeed even before the initial *Brown* opinion was written.[84] At the conference on April 16, 1955, Warren argued for a decree that said a bit more than what the Court ultimately produced. He concluded that "we should give the district courts as much latitude as we can and as much support as we can."[85] Justice Black anticipated extreme resistance and would limit immediate relief to the named plaintiffs.[86] Justice Reed supported a narrow opinion.[87] Like Reed, Frankfurter argued that the suits were class actions and could not be limited to the named plaintiffs.[88] Justice Douglas agreed with Black that the opinion should be limited to the named plaintiffs.[89] Justice Burton favored enjoining school segregation "as rapidly

---

[78] Tushnet, *supra* note 1, at 218.
[79] Argument, *supra* note 11, at 413–14.
[80] *Id.* at 525.
[81] Tushnet, *supra* note 1, at 223.
[82] *Id.*; Elman, *supra* note 10, at 842.
[83] Elman, *supra* note 10, at 828, 841–42.
[84] Schwartz, *supra* note 1, at 91–93; Kluger, *supra* note 1, at 736.
[85] The Supreme Court in Conference, *supra* note 17, at 665.
[86] *Id.* at 665-66.
[87] *Id.* at 666.
[88] *Id.* at 667.
[89] *Id.*

as possible."[90] Clark expressed concern as to the difficulty of implementing a decree.[91] Like several of the other justices, Minton warned against issuing "a futile decree that we cannot enforce."[92] Harlan, like most of the other justices, emphasized the importance of unanimity.[93] There was general agreement on the Court that the opinion should be brief and should remand to the district courts for further proceedings. Warren prepared the opinion on the remedy.

THE OPINION IN *BROWN II*

Six weeks after the arguments, the Court issued a short opinion in what became known as *Brown II*. Citing variations in local conditions, the Court chose to remand the cases to the district courts for the implementation of specific decrees.[94] It declared that the lower courts should be guided by equitable principles, and take account of legitimate logistical difficulties, but should certainly not permit delay out of mere disagreement. Warren indicated that the local school districts must make a "prompt and reasonable start" to desegregation. The Court ordered the district courts to do whatever was necessary in order "to admit to public schools on a racially nondiscriminatory basis with all deliberate speed the parties to these cases."[95] The phrase "all deliberate speed" was apparently not intended to provide a doctrinal test although it eventually became such. Justice Frankfurter liked the phrase and had lobbied hard for its inclusion in the opinion. It had initially appeared in an opinion written by Justice Holmes who seemed to believe that it was derived from English Chancery practice.[96] However, a diligent search by Frankfurter and others could find no trace of the phrase in English jurisprudence.[97] Ultimately, the consensus is that Holmes may have remembered the phrase from an English poem by Francis Thompson titled the "Hounds of Heaven" that contains the phrase "deliberate speed, majestic instancy."

ASSESSING THE OPINION IN *BROWN II*

There are many explanations for the Court's choice of gradualism and remand. Perhaps foremost among them is the strong possibility suggested by internal court memoranda that gradualism with respect to relief was simply the price of unanimity in *Brown I*. That is, some justices would only join the Court's opinion on the unconstitutionality of segregation on the understanding that the South would be given adequate time to adjust. There is every reason to believe that unanimity could not have been achieved absent a commitment to gradualism, and as a practical matter the agreement on the remedial approach

---

[90] *Id.* at 668.
[91] *Id.*
[92] *Id.*
[93] *Id.*
[94] 349 U.S. 294, 299 (1955).
[95] *Id.* at 301.
[96] Virginia v. West Virginia, 222 U.S. 17, 20 (1918).
[97] SCHWARTZ, *supra* note 1, at 122.

preceded the issuance of the opinion in *Brown I*. The value of consideration by judges closer to the school districts either due to familiarity or contextual differences is sensible and almost certainly played a role in the decision. The justices apparently believed that there would be somewhat less resistance to an otherwise unpopular decree imposed by a respected local figure than by a distant tribunal. There is also the likelihood that the Court did not know what to expect in terms of resistance, logistical difficulty, or workable remedial orders. Consequently, remand for further proceedings would provide an opportunity to find out what would work and what would not. In view of the resistance that did eventually materialize as well as the long delay before meaningful desegregation was achieved, it has been contended that perhaps more could have been accomplished had the Court acted more decisively in *Brown II*.[98] No one can know for certain; however, in view of the hard fought resistance that did occur, this seems unlikely. Warren later noted that "[t]he Court expected some resistance from the South. But I doubt that any of us expected as much as we got."[99]

THE REACTION TO THE *BROWN* OPINIONS

Not surprisingly, the *Brown* decisions were the subject of massive coverage by the press. The decision was well received in the African-American community.[100] Initially, the segregated south appeared to be in a state of shock. A violent counter-reaction did not occur immediately. But it was soon in coming. The official declaration of resistance to segregation came in the Southern Manifesto early in 1956 in which 96 members of the House and Senate condemned *Brown* and pledged to use all lawful means to obtain its reversal.[101] Moreover, President Eisenhower never publicly endorsed the decision, raising serious questions regarding the extent to which executive support might be forthcoming.[102] Chief Justice Warren clearly resented the lack of followup by the president.[103] Many southern legislatures passed laws designed to obstruct any attempts at desegregation.[104] Throughout the late 1950s and early 1960s, resistance to school desegregation was the dominant political opinion in the Deep South.[105] Many southern political leaders exploited racial fears for political gain.[106] Fear of desegregation increased the power of the Ku Klux Klan and White Citizens Councils in the South.[107] Some efforts at desegregation were met with violence and riots.[108] Resistance, defiance, and violence would continue well into the 1960s. Few desegregation suits were filed in the Deep South prior to the early 1960s.[109] Federal judges in desegregation cases were sometimes subjected

---

[98] KLUGER, *supra* note 1, at 752–53; PATTERSON, *supra* note 1, at 113–14.

[99] WARREN, *supra* note 1, at 290.

[100] COTTROL ET AL., *supra* note 1, at 185.

[101] 102 CONG. REC. H3948, 4004 (Mar. 12, 1956).

[102] KLUGER, *supra* note 1, at 753.

[103] WARREN, *supra* note 1, at 289–90.

[104] COTTROL ET AL., *supra* note 1, at 190; PATTERSON, *supra* note 1, at 99–100.

[105] PATTERSON, *supra* note 1, at 90.

[106] KLARMAN, *supra* note 2, at 382–421.

[107] *Id.* at 424.

[108] PATTERSON, *supra* note 1, at 105-12.

[109] KLARMAN, *supra* note 2, at 353.

to harassment and intimidation tactics.[110] Thus to some extent at least, the *Brown* decisions halted or even reversed some of the racial progress that was being made, especially in the Deep South.[111] Six years after *Brown II*, massive civil rights demonstrations, sit-ins, marches, and freedom rides burst onto the scene in the South. The relationship between the *Brown* litigation and the nonviolent protest movement is a matter of debate among historians. There is no question that the attempts by southern officials and mobs to violently suppress the civil rights movement garnered national public support for its efforts and goals.

DOCTRINAL FOLLOWUP

As the Court almost certainly well understood, when it decided *Brown*, it was embarking upon a long hard struggle to realize its promise. For most of the next decade, the Court left desegregation to the lower courts. That encouraged delay and further litigation. Some federal district courts in the South took the position articulated in the remand of *Briggs v. Elliot* that *Brown* only mandated the end of segregation imposed by law, not voluntary segregation.[112]

In 1958 in *Cooper v. Aaron*, the Supreme Court did declare forcefully that Governor Faubus of Arkansas had no constitutional authority to defy a lower court order to desegregate Central High School in Little Rock.[113] In *Griffin County v. School Board*,[114] decided in 1964, the Court held that Prince Edwards County, one of the original districts before the Court in the *Brown* litigation, could not avoid a desegregation order by simply closing its public schools. Finally in 1968, in *Green v. County School Board*,[115] 13 years after *Brown II*, the Court lost all patience with dilatory tactics and made it quite clear that the era of "all deliberate speed" had come to an end. In an opinion by Justice Brennan, the Court declared that a district that was operating legally segregated schools as of the date of *Brown* was under a constitutional obligation to eliminate racial segregation "root and branch" and replace it with a unitary school system—and would not be free of federal judicial supervision until it had done so.[116] This arguably clarified the meaning of *Brown* 14 years after it was decided, reading it as imposing an affirmative duty to integrate as opposed to a mere duty to stop segregating.

In the 10-year period following *Brown*, little desegregation occurred in the South.[117] Following the passage of the Civil Rights Act of 1964 however, detailed desegregation guidelines developed by the Department of Health Education, and Welfare as conditions for the receipt of federal funding seemed to have a very positive effect.[118] Three year later in *Swann*

---

[110] *Id.* at 356.

[111] *Id.* at 392.

[112] Patterson, *supra* note 1, at 86, 96.

[113] 358 U.S. 1 (1958).

[114] 377 U.S. 218 (1964).

[115] 391 U.S. 430 (1968).

[116] *Id.* at 437.

[117] Gerald N. Rosenburg, The Hollow Hope: Can Courts Bring About Social Change? 49-57 (1991).

[118] *Id.* at 46–57.

v. Charlotte Mecklenberg School District, the Court approved of several devices for achieving desegregation, especially in large urban school districts with significant residential segregation.[119] Among the methods endorsed were bussing, the redrawing of district lines, and the creation of magnet schools Three years later in *Keyes v. School District Number 1, Denver*,[120] the Court created a series of legal presumptions that allowed plaintiffs who proved intentional segregation in a substantial portion of a school district with significant residential segregation but no legally mandated segregation as of the time of *Brown* to nevertheless obtain a district-wide desegregation order. From that point onward with a few exceptions, the Court left most desegregation litigation in the hands of the lower courts. By the year 2000 almost 50 years after *Brown*, most district courts still exercising continuing jurisdiction in desegregation litigation concluded that they had done virtually all that they could do even if they could not achieve much integration on account of white flight to the suburbs. As a result, the injunctions were dissolved and federal court supervision ended.

BROWN AS A GREAT CASE

Brown v. Board of Education was a great case in every respect. It placed before the Court one of the most troubling questions in American history and constitutional law. It was argued to the Court by several of the finest advocates of the era, three times over three days on each occasion. The ultimate decisions were among the greatest landmarks of American constitutional law. The momentousness of the issues had a profound impact on the decision and opinions. The Court understood that in overturning what was in essence the social and legal foundation of a significant portion of the nation, it would be subjected to a counterattack more vigorous than it had experienced since the *Dred Scott* opinion a century earlier. As such, the opinion needed to be legally defensible, though not legalistic, in spite of the fact that it was not supported by and was arguably in conflict with the original understanding of the Fourteenth Amendment as well as some long-standing precedent. That led to a special round of oral arguments directed specifically at these most troublesome issues and an opinion that largely ducked them. *Brown* was also the very unusual case in which most of the justices understood that unanimity was essential in order to dissuade defiance. Chief Justice Warren and Justice Frankfurter labored hard internally to achieve such unanimity despite the predilection of some of the justices to concur or dissent. It is widely accepted that the joint efforts of the experienced judge and scholar and the new chief with a valuable political background and an overpowering sense of justice largely made *Brown* the great case that it became and remains. There is controversy over the importance of Frankfurter's role, especially after Warren arrived.[121] The Frankfurter-Warren partnership did dissolve however not long after *Brown* was decided, largely due to Frankfurter's overbearing and intrusive manner.[122]

---

[119] 402 U.S. 1 (1971).

[120] 413 U.S. 189 (1973).

[121] G. EDWARD WHITE, EARL WARREN: A PUBLIC LIFE 168 (1982) (arguing that Frankfurter's role has been overestimated). See also Cottrol, ET AL, *supra* note 1, at 170.

[122] WHITE, *supra* note 121, at 183.

Like any case, *Brown* was a product of its times. The NAACP had been focusing on the elimination of racial segregation in public schools for decades but it well understood that it would be dangerous to bring a direct challenge to the Court before it was prepared to decide it favorably. Even when the cases were presented there remained some concern within the organization that the time might not yet be ripe. Many factors beyond the Court conspired in the plaintiffs' favor. The experience of black service personnel during World War II undermined racial isolation. The fear that communist nations would use racial discrimination in the United States against its interest in developing countries became a serious concern. President Truman's integration of the armed forces and the integration of major league baseball contributed momentum. The increasing political power of Blacks in the North made desegregation an important political issue. The development of a civil rights culture especially among Blacks quite apart from school desegregation litigation also contributed. As such, *Brown* was a part of a much larger social context.

Brown was a great case in the classic sense. The opinion was dictated by the pressurized circumstances. Unlike many great cases however, it was decided over a leisurely period of time rather than in great haste. The low key non-doctrinal nature of the opinion was almost certainly driven by the need to make it accessible to a broad-based lay audience as well as the need to render it as unprovocative as possible under the circumstances. It is difficult to recall any other opinion in which the Court was so concerned with unnecessarily provoking a backlash. Writing a short non-legalistic opinion came with a cost in terms of clarity and guidance. The Court did not offer much in the way of an applicable legal rationale for subsequent decision-makers. The ambiguous nature of the opinion may also have been driven by an inability to reach agreement among the justices as well as an inability to predict future needs. There is every reason to believe that the justices were aware that they could not accurately foresee what obstacles with respect to effective integration might be presented and consequently did not want to foreclose their options.

Brown has been subjected to intense criticism not only by those who hated the decision but by those who loved it as well. The Court has been criticized for understating the significance of the original understanding. As a practical matter, an attempt to discuss the original understanding in any detail would have destroyed any hope of unanimity, which many of the justices considered essential. It seems unlikely that any opinion could have convinced Jackson, Reed, Clark, or Frankfurter that the decision was in fact consistent with the understanding of the framers of the Fourteenth Amendment. There was simply too much evidence to the contrary. The argument provided by the Bickel memo and the government brief that the original understanding was inconclusive provided a means by which those justices who really cared about that issue could reconcile it with the decision. Given the necessity of keeping the opinion short and nontechnical, the Court could not develop this point in any detail. Consequently, the opinion reads as though the Court is taking a cavalier and dismissive approach to the original understanding. But the argument that the original understanding was inconclusive was not simply a ruse. The best assessment of the evidence is that Bickel and the government were correct—the original understanding was indeed inconclusive with respect to the issue before the Court. This was especially true considering that the framers were not focusing on the question of the constitutionality of school segregation to any extent if at all.[123] On the one hand, it would be difficult if not impossible to argue that there was an understanding at the time that the amendment was adopted that it prohibited segregated public school education. The NAACP did not seriously argue to the contrary. Rather the counter-argument was that the framing generation meant to embody within the amendment a broader principle of racial equality capable at least at some point in the future of eliminating all state-based racial discrimination, including school segregation. That was essentially the NAACP position. It is certainly arguable, and over time in light of *Brown* it has become the consensus understanding.

Brown has presented a challenge to original understanding as an interpretive methodology. As *Brown v. Board of Education* is without question one of the paradigm cases of constitutional law, if *Brown* is in fact inconsistent with the original understanding, then arguably there is some question as to the viability of originalism as an appropriate methodology.[124] As a result, opponents of originalism have been inclined to argue that *Brown* cannot be reconciled with the original understanding while defenders of originalism have argued that it can for the most part, adopting the broad principle argument of the NAACP.[125]

Brown was also criticized vigorously for reliance on social science data in that such data is readily subject to challenge, reinterpretation, and refutation. In addition, a reliance on social science would seem to undercut the moral force of the constitutional anti-discrimination principle that should be the true foundation of the opinion. Most specifically, the Court was attacked even by its supporters for the inclusion of footnote 11 citing various social science works, including the experiments of Kenneth Clark that were of questionable validity.[126] Justices Black and Clark later wrote that they had unsuccessfully urged Warren to omit the footnote.[127] Bernard Schwartz argues quite persuasively that had they in fact done so, Warren certainly would have complied.[128] Warren later maintained that the references to social science, particularly footnote 11, were not intended to serve as the foundation for the decision but rather only to refute the observation of the *Plessy* Court that segregation caused no harm to black people.[129] In retrospect, this seems like a sensible explanation although he could have been clearer in the opinion. In fact, the concept of stigma did seem to play a crucial role in the Court's explanation as to why segregation was unconstitutional. As Warren clearly wanted to avoid provoking

---

[123] Bickel, *supra* note 30, at 7; WILLIAM E. NELSON, THE FOURTEENTH AMENDMENT: FROM POLITICAL PRINCIPLE TO JUDICIAL DOCTRINE 9, 187 (1988).

[124] ROBERT H. BORK, THE TEMPTING OF AMERICA: THE POLITICAL SEDUCTION OF THE LAW 77–78 (1990).

[125] COTTROL ET AL., *supra* note 1, at 232-33. *Compare* BORK, *supra* note 124, at 74-84 (*Brown* is consistent with the primary anti-discrimination principle of the original understanding); ARCHIBALD COX, THE COURT AND THE CONSTITUTION 260 (1986) (*Brown* is consistent with the more general goals of the framers); Michael McConnell, *Originalism and the Desegregation Decisions*, 81 VA. L. REV. 947 (1995) (*Brown* is consistent with the understanding of the framers), *with* Michael Klarman, Brown, *Originalism and Constitutional Theory: A Response to Professor McConnell*, 81 VA. L. REV. 1881 (1995) (*Brown* is not consistent with original understanding); RAOUL BERGER, GOVERNMENT BY JUDICIARY: THE TRANSFORMATION OF THE FOURTEENTH AMENDMENT 243–45 (1977) (*Brown* is inconsistent with the original understanding).

[126] *See, e.g.*, Edmund Cahn, *Jurisprudence*, 30 N.Y.U. L. REV. 150 (1955).

[127] SCHWARTZ, *supra* note 1, at 108.

[128] *Id.*

[129] KLUGER, *supra* note 1, at 706.

the South no more than necessary, he could not say that the reason school segregation was unconstitutional was because it was based on an illegitimate purpose, pure racism, although he came closer to saying that in *Bolling* than in *Brown*. That was of course the reason he gave during the very first conference on *Brown* for his conclusion that segregation must be rejected. What he found necessary to say instead was that segregation caused real harm even assuming that the states that practiced it were unaware of that fact and had not intended to inflict it. Thus the concept of stigma was a polite way of avoiding indicting southern school districts as racists. It would have been better had the Court simply declared without any attempt at empirical justification that segregation was stigmatizing. In retrospect the controversy over social science data was overblown.

Perhaps the third major criticism of the *Brown* opinions was the adoption of the gradualist approach embodied in the concept of "all deliberate speed." One critique of this approach conceded by Philip Elman, who is acknowledged as the progenitor of gradualism, is that "[i]t was entirely unprincipled. Just plain wrong as a matter of constitutional law."[130] Elman went on to defend the approach however as simply essential to the achievement of unanimity, which in turn was under the circumstances more important than constitutional principle.[131] Effective school desegregation took a long time. It is likely that no one on the Court other than Justice Black fully understood that the process would continue for decades. Critics have argued as did the NAACP at the time that had the Court chosen immediacy over gradualism, there would have been a greater chance for compliance. Instead, the concept of all deliberate speed invited challenge and delay, suggesting that the Court was timid. At the outset it simply must be acknowledged that the debate is completely hypothetical in that there was simply no possibility that even a bare majority of the Court, much less a unanimous Court, would demand immediate desegregation. Whether an order to desegregate immediately would have resulted in more effective compliance is a matter of speculation. The South was sufficiently outraged by the decision that it was likely to resist any order. Arguably, successful defiance of an order to desegregate immediately would have undermined the perception of the Court's authority even more than the gradualistic approach. No one can know for certain. Elman argued that the delay in desegregation was more attributable to lack of followup by the Court itself than as a result of the concept of "all deliberate speed." Moreover President Eisenhower was ambivalent about providing executive support for desegregation, as the Court was well aware. Under the circumstances, it is likely that regardless of the strategy pursued by the Court, the South needed at least a decade to blow off steam, given the radical change to its culture required by desegregation. Perhaps compliance could have been pressed somewhat more quickly but not much.

Brown is an example of a case in which under extremely pressurized circumstances, the Court confronted a very difficult and controversial issue that had quite legitimately been brought before it. The Court decided the case decisively yet humbly. The tentative nature of the *Brown* opinions was among their greatest strengths. Retrospective critiques of the *Brown* Court's failure to say more inevitably undervalue the enormity of the task of desegregation facing the Court as well as the difficulty of building and holding a majority.

---

[130] Elman, *supra* note 17, at 827.
[131] *Id.*

Brown v. Board of Education was simply the Supreme Court's finest hour. Although the opinion did not make a great deal of law in the doctrinal sense in that it was only the first step in a lengthy journey, the law that it did make, measured in terms of the societal results to which it contributed, was very good law indeed.

The decision in *Brown* had many consequences. It certainly led to a judicial crusade to enforce the Court's mandate and end state-sponsored school segregation. The litigation would continue for decades. It would prove more successful in the South and in rural areas than in the North and urban areas. By instructing the lower courts to assume continuing jurisdiction until desegregation was achieved, *Brown* encouraged litigants to undertake other instances of institutional reform litigation as well challenging allegedly unconstitutional conditions in prisons, state hospitals, and other facilities. *Brown* also had the consequence, almost certainly unintended by the Court, of encouraging individuals distressed by the inability to resolve intractable social problems through the political process to turn to litigation. To some extent, it may have emboldened federal judges to respond to these challenges with a vigor that they would not have considered prior to *Brown*. Although the Court had been moving in that direction prior to *Brown*, the case helped to bring the Equal Protection Clause to the very forefront of constitutional law. *Brown* along with the nonviolent protest movement of Dr. Martin Luther King, Jr., which was proceeding on a parallel track, propelled the civil rights movement to the center of the nation's political agenda.

If *Brown* led to a more aggressive role by federal courts when faced with litigation seeking significant political and social change, it led as well along with other Warren Court precedents to a counterattack on vigorous judicial review. One of the nation's leading constitutional scholars, Hebert Wechsler of Columbia, expressed misgivings as to the opinion and decision itself, or at least the direction in which it was arguably taking the Court.[132] The Supreme Court of the early 1950s was not shy. Within a period of four years it decided the great cases of *United States v. Dennis, Youngstown Sheet & Tube v. Sawyer*, and *Brown v. Board of Education*. It was *Brown* however that initiated the era of the Warren Court and placed the Court in the center of political debate to an extent that had not been the case since the mid-1930s. *Brown v. Board of Education* was not simply a great case but rather a seismic event in the Court's and the nation's history. To the extent that the parties and justices could perhaps only dimly appreciate at the time, the public understanding of the Court and the Court's understanding of itself would be forever changed.

---

[132] Herbert Wechsler, *Toward Neutral Principles of Constitutional Law*, 73 HARV. L. REV. 1, 31–35 (1959).

"I think that reapportionment... is perhaps the most important issue we have had before the Supreme Court."[1]

EARL WARREN

14

The Reapportionment Cases

In his memoirs, Chief Justice Warren wrote that he believed that *Baker v. Carr* and the subsequent reapportionment cases were of greater significance than *Brown v. Board of Education*.[2] There was a consensus among scholars and commentators that the Reapportionment Cases were a "startling," "bold," and dramatic move by the Court.[3] As Archibald Cox who argued the cases as solicitor general observed, "the Court went extraordinarily far in breaking away from established practices with little apparent support in conventional sources of law."[4] Ultimately, the decisions significantly altered the political balance in virtually every elected body in the country other than the United States' Senate. The dissenters also appreciated the significance of the cases. Justices Frankfurter and Harlan considered these to be among the most catastrophically bad decisions ever rendered by the Court. Unlike many great cases, the Reapportionment Cases did not arouse great popular excitement although they did result in a significant though temporary political backlash. The legalistic issues presented, especially in *Baker v. Carr*, were hardly of the nature to interest non-lawyers. However, the political and legal world certainly understood that something momentous was developing when the Court agreed to address the question of legislative reapportionment. And even more important the justices fully understood that they were in the process of deciding truly great cases with profound ramifications for the nation.

---

[1] Interview with Chief Justice Earl Warren on June 25, 1969, quoted in BERNARD SCHWARTZ & STEPHAN LESHER, INSIDE THE WARREN COURT 1953–1969, at 184 (1983).
[2] EARL WARREN, THE MEMOIRS OF CHIEF JUSTICE EARL WARREN 306 (1977); See generally RICHARD C. CORTNER, THE APPORTIONMENT CASES (1970).
[3] ROBERT G. McCLOSKEY, THE AMERICAN SUPREME COURT 162 (rev. ed. Sanford Levinson 1994) (*Baker* represented "a bold departure for the Court"); MARTIN J. HORWITZ, THE WARREN COURT AND THE PURSUIT OF JUSTICE 84 (1998) (*Reynolds* was a dramatic reinterpretation of equal protection).
[4] ARCHIBALD COX, THE COURT AND THE CONSTITUTION 303 (1987).

BACKGROUND

It would be fair to say that the history of the United States, indeed the history of the world, has been one of continual urbanization. Over time, as people relocated from rural to urban areas and then to the suburbs, electoral districts that may have initially been apportioned at least to some extent on the basis of population equality became increasingly malapportioned. This in turn allowed rural areas to exert disproportionate political influence in legislative bodies. Consequently, rural-dominated legislatures often exhibited little interest in addressing urban issues. In many instances, despite statutory mandates requiring decennial reapportionment, state legislatures refused to reapportion themselves for several decades. This was quite understandable as politicians are disinclined to apportion themselves out of power or even worse out of office entirely. Lacking an effective political remedy in most states, it is not surprising that persons and groups disadvantaged by malapportionment turned to the courts.

During the early part of the twentieth century, the Supreme Court confronted a couple of malapportionment challenges on one ground or another without deciding much. Then in 1946 in *Colegrove v. Green*,[5] the Court was confronted with a claim that the gross malapportionment of Illinois congressional districts violated the clause in Article IV of the Constitution under which the United States guarantees each state a republican form of government. With only seven justices participating, a 4-3 majority dismissed the claim.[6] Writing for a three-justice plurality, Justice Frankfurter essentially concluded that the case presented a non-justiciable example of the political question doctrine. In the process he proclaimed that "[c]ourts ought not enter this political thicket."[7] Justice Rutledge created a majority with a concurring opinion in which he concluded that the case was justiciable but that the Court should dismiss for want of equity. Justice Black writing for three justices in dissent argued that the case was justiciable and that the Court should invalidate the Illinois congressional apportionment under the Equal Protection and Privileges or Immunities Clauses of the Fourteenth Amendment. Justice Black would have required substantial population equality in apportionment. Despite the fact that a majority of the justices had agreed that reapportionment challenges did not present a political question, because of Justice Frankfurter's opinion, *Colegrove* came to stand for the principle that such challenges were in fact non-justiciable. In the 15-year period between *Colegrove* and *Baker*, the Court disposed of several reapportionment cases on the basis of *Colegrove*.[8]

---

[5] 328 U.S. 549 (1946).

[6] Justice Stone died before the case was decided, and Justice Jackson was prosecuting the Nuremberg cases in Germany.

[7] *Colegrove*, 328 U.S. at 556.

[8] Cook v. Fortson, 329 U.S. 675 (1946) (challenge to Georgia unit system); South v. Peters, 339 U.S. 276 (1950) (challenge to Georgia county unit system); Cox v. Peters. 342 U.S. 936 (1952) (challenge to Georgia county unit system); Colgrove v. Barrett, 330 U.S. 804 (1947) (challenge to Illinois congressional reapportionment); Remmey v. Smith, 342 U.S. 916 (1952) (challenge to Pennsylvania apportionment); Anderson v. Jordan, 343 U.S. 913 (1952) (challenge to California apportionment).

BAKER v. CARR

Finally, in 1960 in *Baker v. Carr*, the Court agreed to entertain a head-on challenge to *Colegrove* and the principle that challenges to malapportionment, at least as based on the Equal Protection Clause, were non-justiciable political questions. *Baker* involved a challenge to the apportionment of the Tennessee legislature. Under the state constitution, the legislature was required to be apportioned on a population equality basis.[9] This requirement had been ignored in practice, and the legislature had not in fact been reapportioned since 1901. Consequently, it was grossly malapportioned from a population-based standpoint. The question presented in *Baker* was whether a challenge to this situation based on the Equal Protection Clause presented a non-justiciable political question. A three-judge federal district court dismissed the case as non-justiciable. Solicitor General Archibald Cox pressed the Supreme Court to hear the case on the merits.

The case was initially argued to the Court on April 19 and 20, 1961. Much of the argument focused on whether *Colegrove v. Green* was distinguishable. The challengers emphasized that litigation appeared to be the only avenue for reform in Tennessee given the legislature's refusal to reapportion and the absence of an initiative and referendum alternative in the state. Solicitor General Cox urged the Court to determine that it had subject matter jurisdiction, and that the case was justiciable, and then simply to remand for further proceedings without reaching the merits of the equal protection claim.

At the first conference following the oral argument, four justices (Warren, Black, Douglas, and Brennan) favored reversing the decision to dismiss, four justices (Frankfurter, Whittaker, Clark, and Harlan) were prepared to affirm and Justice Stewart indicated that he was not yet prepared to decide.[10] Justices Frankfurter and Harlan criticized Solicitor General Cox as "irresponsible" and "reckless" for pressing the case for judicial intervention.[11] At the conference the following week, Justice Stewart characterized the case as "as important of a case as our school desegregation case."[12] As he was of the view that under the precedents "we can go either way" and as "[i]t will establish a big precedent if we go in and let the federal courts supervise these affairs," he suggested that "the case be put down for rehearing," which it was.[13]

Following the second round of oral arguments, the Court met once again in conference to discuss the case. Chief Justice Warren, adopting the position of the solicitor general, stated that the Court should conclude that the federal courts can hear the case and remand for further proceedings. Justice Black was prepared to reverse on the basis of his dissent in *Colegrove*.[14] Relying on a memo that he had circulated, Justice Frankfurter urged affirmance, asserting that judicial intervention would present a danger "to our whole system."[15] Justice Douglas favored intervention whereas Clark favored dismissal.[16] Justice Harlan, who believed

---

[9] 369 U.S. 186, 189 (1962).

[10] THE SUPREME COURT IN CONFERENCE (1940–1985): THE PRIVATE DISCUSSIONS BEHIND NEARLY 300 SUPREME COURT DECISIONS 845–47 (Del Dickson ed., 2001).

[11] *Id.* at 845–46.

[12] *Id.* at 847.

[13] *Id.*

[14] *Id.* at 847–48.

[15] *Id.* at 848.

[16] *Id.*

that this was one of the most important cases to ever come before the Court, argued vigorously that no constitutional right was violated and that the Court should stay out.[17] Justice Brennan favored reversal and remand for further proceedings.[18] Justice Whittaker would have affirmed the dismissal, noting there was jurisdiction but no right to be enforced.[19] So as with the initial conference it all came down to Justice Stewart. He broke the tie concluding that there was standing and jurisdiction and that the political question doctrine was not implicated.[20] However he explicitly rejected a population-based equality approach, suggesting that perhaps the plaintiffs could establish on remand that the plan was simply arbitrary and capricious.[21] He indicated that his views were closest to those of Justice Brennan.[22]

To ensure that Justice Stewart remained with the majority, Chief Justice Warren assigned the opinion to Brennan.[23] Justice Clark changed his mind and decided to favor reversal on the merits.[24] At that point, there were six votes to reverse and five willing to address the merits; however Justice Brennan chose to honor his prior commitment to Justice Stewart to limit the opinion to jurisdiction and justiciablity.[25] As Bernard Schwartz has noted, had Clark committed to the majority before Stewart, the Court would almost certainly have reached the merits in *Baker* but would have applied the one person/ one vote approach to only one house of a bicameral legislature, contrary to what it ultimately did in *Reynolds v. Simms*.[26] Justice Whittaker, who had initially voted with the dissent, became ill before the decision was announced and did not participate.

THE OPINION IN *BAKER v. CARR*

The Court's opinion in *Baker v. Carr* was published on March 26, 1962, and immediately it was recognized as a landmark decision. Justice Brennan offered a 48-page opinion for the majority concluding that there was jurisdiction, that the plaintiffs did have standing, and that the case did not present a non-justiciable political question. The bulk of the opinion was devoted to a detailed analysis and synthesis of the political question precedent. It is one of the most impressive examples of precedential analysis in the Court's history. He concluded that most political question cases implicate the separation of powers.[27] He then explained that the precedent identifies six factors that may indicate that a case presents a political question. Perhaps the two most decisive would be a textual commitment to another branch of government or the lack of judicially manageable standards. The other four seemingly related prudential considerations included the need for a non-judicial policy determination, a showing of lack of respect for another branch of

---

[17] *Id.* at 849.
[18] *Id.*
[19] *Id.* at 850.
[20] *Id.*
[21] *Id.*
[22] *Id.* at 851.
[23] BERNARD SCHWARTZ, DECISION: HOW THE SUPREME COURT DECIDES CASES 222 (1996).
[24] *Id.* at 223.
[25] *Id.*
[26] *Id.* at 224.
[27] *Id.* at 217.

government, an unusual need for adherence to a previously rendered political decision, or embarrassment due to multiple pronouncements from different branches.

Brennan analyzed the landmark Taney Court case of *Luther v. Borden* in some detail given that it arguably stood for the principle that all Guarantee Clause claims were non-justiciable. He concluded that the only one of the identified political question characteristics relevant to reapportionment was the possible lack of judicially manageable standards. Although that might well explain the non-justiciability of a Guarantee Clause challenge to malapportionment as in *Colegrove*, it had no relevance to this case as "[j]udicial standards under the Equal Protection Clause are well developed and familiar."[28] Consequently, the Court reversed and remanded for further proceedings.

Justice Clark, who had initially leaned toward non-justiciability, wrote an opinion concurring in the judgment in which he was prepared to reach the merits and invalidate the Tennessee apportionment as wholly irrational, characterizing it as a "crazy quilt."[29]

Justice Stewart, who at least for a while had been the crucial vote to the decision and remained the crucial vote to Justice Brennan's opinion, wrote a brief concurrence emphasizing the narrowness of the holding, asserting that it certainly had not adopted a principle of political equality in apportionment.

Justice Frankfurter, the author of the *Colegrove* plurality, was quite obviously incensed by the decision in *Baker* and offered a dissent even longer than Justice Brennan's majority opinion. At the outset, he declared that the decision "may well impair the Court's position as the ultimate organ of the 'Supreme Law of the Land.'"[30] This was a dire prophecy but Justice Frankfurter no doubt believed it. He answered Justice Brennan's analysis of the precedent with his own counter-analysis. Contrary to Justice Brennan, Frankfurter concluded that the lack of judicially manageable standards was not attributable to the nature of the constitutional provision invoked, the Guarantee Clause, but rather by the nature of the underlying factual issue itself—reapportionment.

Frankfurter's main point was that the Court could not rationally address the issue of justiciabiltiy without having first concluded that there was in fact some definable constitutional benchmark for measuring whether a legislative body was sufficiently malapportioned as to support a constitutional challenge. He assumed that the majority's benchmark must be approximate population equality (what eventually came to be known as one person/one vote) and devoted a significant portion of his opinion to an attempt to demonstrate that this had never been the accepted standard in Great Britain, the colonies, the early Union, the states at the time of ratification of the Fourteenth Amendment, or contemporary America.

This was Justice Frankfurter's last significant opinion before suffering a debilitating stroke, one of his most impressive dissents, and in the words of David Currie the loss of "his greatest battle."[31] *Baker v. Carr* is a landmark opinion not simply because of the impressive majority opinion of Justice Brennan but because of the classic dissent of Justice Frankfurter as well.

---

[28] *Id.* at 226.

[29] *Id.* at 254.

[30] *Id.* at 267.

[31] DAVID P. CURRIE, THE CONSTITUTION IN THE SUPREME COURT: THE SECOND CENTURY 1888–1986, at 412 (1990).

Justice Harlan, who would carry Justice Frankfurter's crusade forward, also wrote a dissenting opinion. He declared that "what lies at the core of this controversy is a difference of opinion as to the function of representative government."[32] For Justice Harlan, that was a controversy that the federal courts had no business attempting to resolve. Rather than rest on the political question doctrine, Harlan concluded that the plaintiffs had failed to allege a constitutional violation, given that the Constitution did not adopt a particular theory of representation. Like Frankfurter, Harlan believed that the decision was mischievous and could result in significant harm to the Court's reputation.

Baker v. Carr certainly encouraged judicial challenges to malapportionment, which were already well underway. Over 40 such challenges appeared during the next few years. Considering that the Court had studiously avoided the merits in *Baker*, it was inevitable that it would soon be called upon to provide further guidance to the lower courts. Indeed the gist of Justice Clark's separate concurrence had been that it was irresponsible for the Court not to have done so at the time.

TOWARD ONE PERSON/ONE VOTE

A year after *Baker*, the Court decided its next reapportionment case—*Gray v. Sanders*.[33] The case is notable in that it was the first and only oral argument by Attorney General Robert Kennedy. *Gray* presented an equal protection challenge to Georgia's county unit system for tabulating votes in statewide primaries under which the winner of the popular vote in various counties would receive the same number of votes in the primary even though the counties themselves had vastly different populations.[34] The impact was to dilute the voting power of urban counties.

In a relatively short opinion, Justice Douglas rejected Georgia's analogy to the electoral college as an inapposite historical incident. Instead, the Court concluded that "all who participate in an election are to have an equal vote...wherever their home may be in that geographical unit."[35] Douglas concluded the opinion noting that "[t]he conception of political equality from the Declaration of Independence, to Lincoln's Gettysburg Address, to the Fifteenth, Seventeenth, and Nineteenth Amendments can mean only one thing— one person, one vote."[36] With that, the famous reapportionment formula was introduced into constitutional law. The majority and the brief concurrence of Justice Clark emphasized that the case did not address legislative apportionment but the reader could wonder why it would be treated differently given the breadth of the majority's principle. Justice Harlan wrote a short opinion defending the rationality of a decision to accord differential political power to different regions of a state, as Georgia had attempted to do.

In February 1964, the Court released its opinion in *Wesberry v. Sanders*, another case from Georgia.[37] Unlike the six other reapportionment cases that the Court would decide

---

32 *Baker*, 369 U.S. at 333.
33 372 U.S. 368 (1963).
34 *Id.* at 370–71.
35 *Id.* at 379.
36 *Id.* at 381.
37 376 U.S. 1 (1964).

during the 1963–64 term, *Wesberry* involved the apportionment of congressional rather than state legislative districts and as such was governed by Article I, Section Two rather than the Equal Protection Clause. In an opinion by Justice Black, the Court held that the language in Article I declaring that "Representatives Be chosen 'by the People of the several states'" meant that as nearly as practicable, one person's vote must be worth as much as that of another. He attempted to base this conclusion on the legislative history from the Constitutional Convention. Quoting a statement of Madison in *Federalist 57* that "'[t]he electors [of the Federal representatives] are to be the great body of the people of the United States,'" he concluded that "[r]eaders surely could have fairly taken this to mean 'one person one vote'" quoting *Gray v. Sanders.*[38]

Justice Harlan dissented, demonstrating beyond question that the framers of the Constitution had no intention of imposing anything like a one person/one vote requirement on the states in congressional districting. As he put it, "they did not surreptitiously slip [such a] belief into the Constitution in the phrase 'by the People' to be discovered 175 years later like a Shakespearean anagram."[39] He pointed out that the decision would invalidate over 90 percent of existing congressional districts. Harlan concluded his opinion with the observation that "[t]he Constitution does not confer on the Court blanket authority to step into every situation where the political branch may be thought to have fallen short."[40]

Justice Clark agreed with Justice Harlan with respect to Article I but would have remanded for consideration of the application of the Equal Protection Clause. Justice Stewart agreed with Justice Harlan except for the implication that reapportionment challenges were not justiciable.

REYNOLDS V. SIMMS

In a sense, *Baker, Gray*, and *Wesberry* were simply a prologue to *Reynolds v. Simms* and the other five companion cases decided along with it. *Baker* only purported to address justiciability. *Gray* considered a unique Georgia rule in primary elections. *Wesberry* involved congressional elections under Article I. But *Reynolds* presented the big issue deferred in *Baker*: does gross malapportionment of one or both houses of a state legislature violate the Equal Protection Clause, and if so what standard will be applied by the Court? The malapportionment of the Alabama legislature was similar to that of Tennessee in that there had been had been no reapportionment in several decades.[41] In litigation that was pending before a three-judge district court when *Baker* was decided, the district court invalidated the existing apportionment plans for both houses and gave the legislature an opportunity to reapportion itself. The legislature adopted two plans (one a fallback), neither of which the district court found acceptable. Consequently it imposed its own provisional plan for the next election. The appeal in *Reynolds* raised the question of whether the original Alabama apportionment, either of the two legislative plans or the district court's provisional plan, satisfied the Constitution.

---

[38] *Id.* at 18.
[39] *Id.* at 27.
[40] *Id.* at 48.
[41] 377 U.S. 533, 540 (1964).

Reynolds involved three consolidated suits from Alabama so seven attorneys appeared to argue the matter before the Court. Representing appellant Reynolds, W. McLean Pitts engaged in a bombastic assault on *Baker v. Carr*, time and again asking the Court to over-rule it.[42] He concluded his presentation with the declaration that if the district court opin-ion was allowed to stand then "there is no longer a sovereign state."[43] Pitts was followed by Richmond Flowers, attorney general of Alabama, who struck quite a different tone, conceding that the original apportionment was unconstitutional, the Alabama constitu-tion prevented fair apportionment, and consequently the Court should affirm the dis-trict court.[44] Thus, the primary spokesman for the state was essentially siding with the plaintiffs. Charles Morgan, representing the plaintiffs, urged the Court to go beyond the order of the district court and impose the one person/one vote standard on both houses.[45]

Solicitor General Cox argued as amicus and far and away made the most cogent and useful arguments in the case. Senior officials at the Department of Justice had pressed Cox hard to argue for one person/one vote; however he believed that it was not legally warranted or appropriate and refused to do so.[46] Instead, he argued for a case-by-case rationality approach. He contended that the deliberate malapportionment of the Ala-bama senate did not violate Justice Clark's "crazy quilt" principle from *Baker* as it was not irrational to give every county a senator and then distribute additional senators on the basis of population.[47] He noted that a state should be allowed to deviate from population equality to some extent in the apportionment of one house if it has adhered to it in the other.[48] He argued that some deviation from pure population equality in one house would be acceptable if it did not go "too far."[49] On the other hand, the apportionment of the Alabama senate was unconstitutionally arbitrary in that it subordinated equality to too great an extent to otherwise permissible objectives. The Court also heard substantial oral argument in the companion cases from New York, Delaware, Maryland, and Virginia, and five months later in the case from Colorado.

When the justices first met to discuss the Reapportionment Cases, the conference was interrupted by the news that President Kennedy had been shot.[50] Initially, the justices seemed to have agreed with Solicitor General Cox's position that it would be sufficient if one house was apportioned on a population basis with greater leeway for the other house.[51] That had been the California system that Warren had supported as governor.[52] Warren assigned the opinion to himself in order to take the public criticism that he fully expected to follow, especially from California.[53] He soon concluded however that he could

---

[42] Oral Argument in Reynolds v. Simms at 58 Landmark Briefs and Arguments of the Supreme Court of the United States: Constitutional Law 979, 984–86 (Philip B. Kurland & Gerhard Casper eds., 1975).

[43] *Id.* at 990.

[44] *Id.* at 995.

[45] *Id.* at 1000.

[46] Cox, *supra* note 4, at 298-300.

[47] Oral Argument in Reynolds v. Simms, *supra* note 42, at 1027.

[48] *Id.* at 1029.

[49] *Id.* at 1030.

[50] Schwartz, *supra* note 23, at 105.

[51] *Id.*

[52] Earl Warren, The Memoirs of Chief Justice Earl Warren 309 (1977).

[53] *Id.* at 310.

not justify restricting the one person/one vote principle to only one house and explained to Justice Brennan that contrary to the agreement in conference, he would like to extend it to both.[54] He was able without much difficulty to persuade the other justices in the majority of the need for a broader opinion.[55]

THE OPINION IN *REYNOLDS V. SIMMS*

The opinion in *Reynolds v. Simms* was released on June 15, 1964. It served as the lead opinion for all six of the Reapportionment Cases. In reciting the facts, Chief Justice Warren noted that "[n]o effective political remedy to obtain relief against the alleged malapportionment of the Alabama Legislature appears to have been available."[56] To the *Reynolds* majority, the fact that entrenched legislators were highly unlikely to apportion themselves out of office seemed to be a factor justifying judicial intervention.

Relying on cases primarily concerned with denial or dilution of the vote based on race, Warren proclaimed that "[t]he right to vote. . . is of the essence of a democratic society. . . and the right of suffrage can be denied [as effectively] by a debasement or dilution of the weight of a citizen's vote."[57] Although this sounded fair and just, in view of the long history of malapportionment in the United States, it could not be said to have been an uncontestable statement of constitutional law at that point. Chief Justice Warren then engaged in discussion of the prior reapportionment precedents *Baker, Gray*, and *Wesberry*. He noted that *Gray* and *Wesberry* had adopted population equality as a standard and, though they were clearly distinguishable, they created a presumption that population should govern unless there is some good reason to the contrary. *Gray* and *Wesberry* had been decided with the explicit notation that of course they were distinguishable from the yet-to-be- decided legislative reapportionment cases. But not surprisingly they proved not to be particularly distinguishable after all.

Chief Justice Warren well understood that the essential case for permitting at least somewhat malapportioned legislatures was based on the thesis that more sparsely populated areas such as farming or mining regions of the state could be given greater representation than their population would otherwise warrant in order to ensure that they would not simply be overwhelmed by the political power of urban areas. Warren understood the theory because he had endorsed it as governor. The core of his opinion in *Reynolds* was designed to reject that theory.

Warren began by emphasizing that the right to vote is "individual and personal in nature."[58] This was obviously designed to undermine any claim that discrete regions should be entitled to political protection. He indicated that because the right to vote is fundamental, any infringement of the right must be subject to strict judicial review. Then came the most famous line from Reynolds quoted in almost every discussion of the case: "Legislators represent people, not trees or acres. Legislators are elected by voters

---

[54] SCHWARTZ, *supra* note 23, at 105.

[55] *Id.*

[56] 377 U.S. at 553.

[57] *Id.* at 556.

[58] *Id.* at 561.

not farms or cities or economic interests."[59] Replying directly to this statement, Justice Harlan, dissenting, observed that "people are not ciphers and that legislators can represent their electors only by speaking for their interests—economic, social, political—many of which do reflect the place where the electors live."[60]

Warren's next move was to argue by way of analogy. He asserted that it would be clearly unconstitutional to explicitly give the votes of some citizens greater weight than those of others, although he cited no authority for this claim. If the state could not do so directly then surely it could not do so indirectly through malapportionment. Stating the generalized political philosophy at the core of the decision, Warren proclaimed that "each and every citizen has an inalienable right to full and effective participation in the political processes of his State's legislative bodies," which means that "each citizen have an equally effective voice in the election of members of his state legislature."[61] Consequently, "a majority of the people of a State [should be able to] elect a majority of the legislators."[62] This was a clear statement of the egalitarian or majoritarian philosophy driving the decision.

Turning to equal protection, Warren then declared:

> The concept of equal protection has been traditionally viewed as requiring the uniform treatment of persons standing in the same relationship to the government action... challenged. With respect to the allocation of legislative representation, all voters, as citizens of a State, stand in the same relation regardless of where they live.[63]

These two sentences were truly the core of the reapportionment decisions. If the declaration in the second sentence is correct as a matter of constitutional law, then one person/one vote follows almost as a matter of course, as the Court held in the next paragraph. But the critics of the decision argued that Warren had failed to demonstrate that in fact all voters were similarly situated regardless of where they lived. Warren relied on relatively abstract pronouncements that majoritarianism was demanded by the very concept of equal protection, but made no attempt to respond to Justice Harlan's powerful demonstration that both the original understanding and consistent traditions of the nation were very much to the contrary.

Warren promptly declared that the population equality principle applied to both houses of a bicameral state legislature. The argument for permitting deliberate malapportionment of one branch relied to some extent on the "federal analogy," noting that while the framers required the House of Representatives to be apportioned on the basis of population, each state was entitled to two senators regardless of its population. The Court rejected the analogy however. It pointed out that the apportionment of the Senate

---

[59] Professor Schwartz indicated that these famous lines were drafted by Warren's law clerk, Francis X. Beytagh. Warren read the lines and "got a kick out of it." SCHWARTZ, *supra* note 23, at 105–106 (quoting Francis X. Beytagh who later became a distinguished professor of law at Notre Dame).

[60] *Reynolds*, 377 U.S. at 623–24.

[61] *Id.* at 565.

[62] *Id.* at 567.

[63] *Id.* at 565.

was the result of a compromise that broke the deadlock in the Constitutional Convention, permitting formerly sovereign states to retain equality in one legislative branch. Unlike that situation, political subdivisions of states were never sovereign entities. Warren also noted that in the very year that the Constitution was adopted, Congress through the Northwest Ordinance required that both houses of territorial legislatures be apportioned on the basis of population, indicating that the framing generation did not believe that the federal analogy extended to the states. Warren noted that legislatures could still create divergent constituencies for the two legislative houses by varying the size of the electoral districts. The Court's confident rejection of any allowance for deviation from population-based apportionment in at least one house was striking given that a majority of the Court had agreed to just such a principle initially in conference.

Turning to the specifics of reapportionment, the Court indicated that a state could attempt to honor existing political boundaries as long as it did not vary too significantly from population and that it need not adhere to population equality quite so rigorously with respect to state as opposed to congressional districting. The Court declared that decennial apportionment would be appropriate though not necessarily constitutionally required. It upheld the reapportionment ordered by the three-judge district court below.

Justice Clark concurred in the judgment but not the opinion of the Court, indicating that he believed that it was inappropriate for the Court to impose a specific standard on the lower courts and that he was partial to application of the federal analogy.

Justice Harlan wrote a lengthy dissent. He argued that the text and original understanding of the Fourteenth Amendment as well as the subsequent history of legislative apportionment in the country demonstrated that there was no legitimate constitutional basis for the Court's approach. With respect to the text, Harlan pointed out that Section Two of the Fourteenth Amendment provides that the constitutional remedy for denial of the right to vote is the diminishment of congressional representation of the offending state. He argued that this was intended to be the sole constitutional remedy for infringement of the right to vote under the Fourteenth Amendment. A lengthy review of the history of the drafting and ratification of the Fourteenth Amendment convinced Harlan that the framing generation had not understood the amendment as restricting state control over apportionment. He also maintained that from the ratification of the Fourteenth Amendment in 1868 to the present, malapportionment of state legislatures had been the well-accepted practice.

Justice Harlan closed his opinion with a vigorous challenge to the legitimacy of the Court's venture into the area of legislative apportionment. He understood the decision as a significant break with the jurisprudential understandings up to that time, characterizing it as "a radical alteration in the relationship between States and the Federal Government, more particularly the Federal Judiciary."[64] Harlan scolded the majority for proceeding on the assumption that for "every major social ill in this country [the Court] can find its cure in some constitutional 'principle' and that this Court should 'take the lead' in promoting reform when other branches of government fail to act."[65] From Harlan's perspective, the Court was simply amending the Constitution. The majority made no attempt to answer Harlan's critique.

---

[64] *Id.* at 624.

[65] *Id.*

The cases from New York, Delaware, Virginia, and Maryland were readily disposed of in boilerplate opinions citing *Reynolds*. The *Lucas* case from Colorado was different from the others however. It had been argued several months after the initial five cases, and it raised some very distinct issues. Unlike *Reynolds* and its other companion cases, the malapportionment of the Colorado legislature was recent, deliberate, and approved by a majority of the state's voters in every county in the state in a referendum. In 1962 by a 2 to 1 margin, the voters of Colorado approved an amendment to the state constitution that retained a significant degree of malapportionment in the state senate. Colorado is a state of very distinct geographic and economic regions, including urban areas, farming, ranching, mining and the tourist trade. The plan was designed to provide sparsely populated regions with some protection against domination by the urban areas along the front range of the Rocky Mountains. Nevertheless, the Court held that *Reynolds* controlled and invalidated the plan. The Court rejected each of the factors that arguably distinguished *Lucas* from *Reynolds*. It did not matter that the citizens of the state had a political remedy to avoid legislative gridlock and in fact had used it.[66] Nor did it matter that the plan was approved by an overwhelming majority statewide as long as one individual citizen objected to the dilution of his vote. As such, the Court took an aggressively individualistic approach to reapportionment and equal protection. It concluded that the attempt to give greater representation to certain geographic, topographical, economic regions, or interests could not justify the extent of disparity from population equality.

Justice Harlan's dissent in *Reynolds* applied to *Lucas* as well. Justice Clark, who concurred in *Reynolds*, issued a dissenting opinion in *Lucas*. He relied on the fact that the citizens of Colorado had enacted a rational apportionment plan through the exercise of initiative and referendum. Finally, he concluded that deliberate and reasonable variance from population equality in one house should be acceptable as long as the other house was in fact apportioned on a population basis. Justice Stewart, joined by Justice Clark, wrote a dissenting opinion in *Lucas* that was also applicable to the New York case. Stewart agreed with Harlan's demonstration that the majority's approach was not supported by history, tradition, or precedent.[67] Like Harlan, he accused the majority of imposing its own conception of wise political theory on the nation. As such, the Court had simply chosen one of several acceptable theories of representation. He explained that "[r]epresentative government is a process of accommodating group interests through democratic institutional arrangements."[68] For Justice Stewart, it was quite rational and certainly constitutional for Colorado to take into account the various geographic and economic interests in the state in apportioning its senate. Justice Stewart would uphold a reapportionment plan that was rational and did not systematically frustrate the will of the majority. In applying this standard, he explained how Colorado consisted of several very different geographic and economic regions, given its mountainous terrain. He also concluded that the New York plan providing minimum representation to every county was also rational given the state's interest in ensuring that New York City did not completely dominate the state legislature.[69] The dissents of Clark and Stewart in *Lucas* indicated that the Court

---

[66] 377 U.S. 713, 736 (1964).
[67] *Id.* at 745-46.
[68] *Id.* at 749.
[69] *Id.* at 762–63.

was not as overwhelmingly behind one person/one vote as the 8-1 decision in *Reynolds* might have suggested.

A week after issuing its opinion in *Reynolds*, the Court remanded cases from Connecticut, Florida, Illinois, Iowa, Oklahoma, Ohio, and Washington.

AFTERMATH AND IMPACT

Baker v. Carr was a revolutionary decision in that it opened the door to judicial consideration of legislative reapportionment. As such, it was an error of catastrophic proportions to proponents of judicial restraint, most typified by Justice Frankfurter. One need not accept Chief Justice Warren's assertion that the Reapportionment Cases were the most significant decisions of the Warren Court to agree that they did have an enormous impact on the nation. In the years after *Reynolds*, the Court extended the holdings to virtually all elective offices with policy-making authority.[70] Obviously, radically changing the apportionment of virtually every elective body in the country down to the county level had extreme consequences. It shifted political power away from rural to urban and perhaps even more decidedly to suburban areas. The reformers who had spearheaded the reapportionment litigation apparently hoped that it would result in more progressive legislation.[71] Studies indicate that it did not produce such a shift.[72] Still it did shift political power from some groups to others. It did make it easier for legislatures to engage in outright political gerrymandering, given that geographic and established political boundaries could no longer play a significant role.[73]

Unlike *Brown*, the one person/one vote principle was implemented quickly and without much resistance. Within four years, virtually all states were in compliance with *Reynolds*.[74] As the Reapportionment Cases did not involve issues that seemed to directly touch the lives of people on a daily basis, the public was not overly aware of the decisions.[75] But to the extent that the public was familiar with the decisions, it tended to be supportive of them.[76] This was almost certainly attributable to the apparent fairness of the Court's principle. One person/one vote reflects a democratic ideal deeply embedded in American culture. Majority rule was probably the way in which most clubs and organizations to which Americans belonged carried on their affairs. As such, it would seem to be an eminently fair way to structure a legislative body as well even though it had been the rare exception rather than the rule throughout most of American history. Moreover, the administrative ease of the one person/one vote rule avoided the protracted court battles of school integration. Thus it would not seem that the judicial branch was continually embroiled in public policy in this area.

---

[70] Avery v. Midland Cnty. Texas, 390 U.S. 474 (1968) (county commissioners court); Hadley v. Junior College District of Metropolitan Kansas City, 397 U.S. 50 (1970) (junior college district).

[71] GERALD N. ROSENBERG, THE HOLLOW HOPE: CAN COURTS BRING ABOUT SOCIAL CHANGE? 295-96 (1991).

[72] *Id.* at 297.

[73] LUCAS A. POWE, JR., THE WARREN COURT AND AMERICAN POLITICS 269 (2000).

[74] ROSENBERG, *supra* note 71, at 295.

[75] *Id.* at 299.

[76] *Id.*

The political elites were nowhere near as accepting of the reapportionment decisions as the public at large however. In fact, they attempted to resist them at least for a while. The House of Representatives passed a bill to strip the Court of jurisdiction in reapportionment cases; however it died as the result of a filibuster in the Senate.[77] Congress did express its anger at the Court by denying Supreme Court justices the $3000 pay raise that it granted to all other federal judges.[78] Meanwhile 32 of the necessary 34 states voted to call a constitutional convention to consider an amendment that would create a Court of the Union composed of the chief justices of the 50 states, which would have the authority to overrule Supreme Court decisions involving federal-state relations.[79]

The decision was subjected to withering professional criticism as well by many who were generally supportive of the Court. Indeed Professor Auerbach, a staunch defender of the decision, conceded that "[n]o case in modern memory has evoked so much controversy with respect to the scope of judicial review."[80] The attacks followed the lead of Justices Frankfurter and Harlan questioning whether the Court should have intervened at all and critiquing the inadequate reasoning of the decisions.[81] Archibald Cox, who had coordinated the reapportionment challenges as solicitor general but had taken a cautious approach before the Court, was disappointed with the Court's emphasis on numerical equality.[82] Professors Bickel and Wechsler, two of the most eminent constitutional scholars in the nation, feared that the Court would encounter severe difficulties implementing one person one vote.[83] They were soon proven to be quite wrong.

Justices Frankfurter and Harlan sincerely believed that the Reapportionment Cases would cast the Court into the same type of disrepute as decisions such as *Lochner v. New York* had. That was hardly the case. In fact, it was not long before the Reapportionment Cases were being described as the Warren Court's greatest success.[84] This was attributable to the fact that the decisions were implemented quickly without further contentious litigation, and even more so because the one person/one vote standard, however tenuous in terms of any constitutional pedigree, resonated with the public. Moreover under the Court's approach most people were better off.

---

[77] POWE, *supra* note 73, at 252.

[78] *Id.* at 254.

[79] COX, *supra* note 4, at 301; EARL WARREN, *supra* note 52, at 311.

[80] Carl Auerbach, *The Reapportionment Cases: One Person One Vote-One Vote One Value*, 1964 SUP. CT. REV. 1, 2.

[81] *See* ALEXANDER M. BICKEL, THE LEAST DANGEROUS BRANCH: THE SUPREME COURT AT THE BAR OF POLITICS 192–93 (1962). See also MARTIN M. SHAPIRO, LAW AND POLITICS IN THE SUPREME COURT: NEW APPROACHES TO POLITICAL JURISPRUDENCE 173–252 (1964) for a sophisticated analysis of the reapportionment question, concluding that the Court was correct in intervening but mistaken in adopting one person/one vote.

[82] POWE, *supra* note 73, at 252.

[83] ALEXANDER M. BICKEL, THE SUPREME COURT AND THE IDEA OF PROGRESS 174–75 (1968); HERBERT WECHSLER, THE NATIONALIZATION OF CIVIL LIBERTIES AND CIVIL RIGHTS 25 (1968). *See also* BARRY FRIEDMAN, THE WILL OF THE PEOPLE: HOW PUBLIC OPINION HAS INFLUENCED THE SUPREME COURT AND SHAPED THE MEANING OF THE CONSTITUTION 269 (2009) (quoting an interview with Bickel).

[84] Robert McKay, *Reapportionment: A Success Story of the Warren Court*, 67 MICH. L. REV. 223 (1968).

THE REAPPORTIONMENT CASES AS GREAT CASES

Unlike most great cases, the Reapportionment Cases did not attract much attention from the general public. Although the cases had the potential of having a significant impact on most Americans, they dealt with relatively technical issues that did not appear on the public radar as did the school prayer decisions that the Court was handing down at virtually the same time. However, the political and legal elites well understood the importance of these cases and so did the justices. When *Baker v. Carr* was argued, Justices Frankfurter and Harlan knew that the decision would not simply have a major political impact but could very easily be a turning point in the Court's approach to its own role. Fearing that the Court was about to commit to a path of aggressive review of legislative action far beyond the field of apportionment and to employ interpretive methodology far more open-ended than it generally had in the past, Frankfurter and Harlan opposed with extreme vigor consideration of the case on the merits. At least initially, they had company. Justices Whittiker and Clark shared their concerns and Justice Stewart was too conflicted to decide so the case was set for re-argument. Following re-argument, however, Stewart opted for intervention, Clark eventually agreed, and Whittiker took ill and could not participate. Thus in a matter of months the Court went from a state of equal division to a solid majority for entry into the "political thicket." Arguably, the extreme degree of malapportionment coupled with the lack of a viable political remedy made the difference for Stewart and Clark. Nor can the persuasive abilities of Chief Justice Warren and Justice Brennan be minimized. Brennan's scholarly opinion for the Court did not necessarily indicate the sea change that had occurred on the Court; however, the dissents of Justices Frankfurter and Harlan made it clear that something momentous, and from their perspective, quite terrible had happened.

As of *Baker*, there was still the possibility that when the Court reached the merits of apportionment it might proceed cautiously. It appears that there was neither a majority for a strict population-based approach nor in any event an application of such an approach to both houses of a bicameral legislature. That possibility vanished however with the health-based retirements of Justices Frankfurter and Whittaker not long after the *Baker* decision was announced. The replacement of Whittaker with Justice White provided a somewhat mercurial vote; however the replacement of Frankfurter with Arthur Goldberg created a fairly dependable majority for expansion of the judicial role.

By the time the Reapportionment Cases arrived on the Court's doorstep in 1964, it was virtually certain that it would invalidate at least some reapportionment plans but it was not at all clear to what extent. For several of the justices, *Baker* and *Reynolds* were not simply great cases but hard cases as well. In *Baker*, the newest justice, Potter Stewart, had a difficult time deciding and vacillated between the Brennan and Frankfurter camps. Justice Clark also had difficulty making up his mind. The final 6-2 decision with two concurring opinions and Justice Whittaker dropping out due to poor health did not fully reveal the concerns within the Court.

Reynolds v. Simms was also a more difficult decision than might appear from the lop-sided 8-1 vote. The limited concurrences of Clark and Stewart combined with their dissents in *Lucas* indicated that not all of the majority was comfortable with Warren's approach. Even Warren himself, along with most of the rest of the majority, had initially been attracted to a more deferential approach that would have permitted the states to deviate from population equality with respect to one house of the legislature. Warren had endorsed this solution but was unable to satisfy himself that it could be justified. The source of his difficulty is not entirely clear. Solicitor General Cox had made a very well-reasoned argument for just such an approach, and Justice Stewart demonstrated in his dissent in *Lucas* that the distinction could easily be defended. Apparently, Warren was so wedded to the majoritarian principle as the foundation of his decision that he could see no basis for compromise. In retrospect, it can be argued that allowing more discretion with respect to the apportionment of one legislative house would have undermined the simplicity of the remedial approach by embroiling courts in the question of how far is too far, as acknowledged in the solicitor general's oral argument. But there is no indication that the line-drawing quandary led Warren to the across-the-board population equality standard. *Reynolds v. Simms* ended up as an aggressive and doctrinaire opinion; however, it very easily could have been more nuanced.

As Justices Frankfurter and Harlan recognized at the time of *Baker*, the reapportionment decisions would be a watershed in terms of aggressive judicial review. Indeed, the *New York Times* characterized *Reynolds* as the farthest-reaching exercise of judicial review since *Marbury v. Madison*.[85] *Brown v. Board of Education* was a bold decision, but there was no question that the Fourteenth Amendment spoke to the issue of racial discrimination. There was no serious argument that the issue itself was beyond judicial competence. But that had been the received wisdom with respect to reapportionment prior to *Baker*. Moreover, judicial intervention was likely to restructure the political landscape nationwide. The issue of reapportionment could only be engaged by a bold and confident Court that had come into existence at least as of *Reynolds* in 1964. The dissenting justices and much of the political establishment and academic community viewed the reapportionment decisions, at least at the time, as reckless and unwise. However Warren and at least a bare majority of the Court in *Reynolds* seemed to have no qualms about conquering new ground or about any potential political pushback. The 1964 reapportionment cases were decided by a confident majority convinced that it would carry the day despite predictable opposition. And it did, perhaps more easily than it expected.

Baker and *Reynolds* marked the demise of the Frankfurter school of judicial restraint, which had often prevailed during the Vinson years on the Court although it had been fighting a rear guard action against aggressive judicial action ever since Warren had joined the Court in 1953. The self-confident Court that decided *Reynolds* would exist for less than a decade. But it would be a period of great and largely enduring judicial activity. The Reapportionment Cases, especially *Reynolds v. Simms*, illustrate that the legal and societal momentousness of a case may have little if any impact on a Court that has a secure conception of its institutional role.

Were the Reapportionment Cases great cases that made bad law? That turns to a large extent on what is meant by bad law. The Brennan opinion in *Baker* significantly sharpened the analysis of the political question doctrine, which was in a state of disarray at the time. Given the ad hoc character of the doctrine, it was not as easily categorized as either Brennan or Frankfurter would have it. The framework that Brennan provided however

[85] N.Y. Times, June 16, 1964, at 38.

was sensible and has endured, although the political question doctrine has receded in importance to some extent as a result of *Baker*. Thus from the standpoint of constitutional doctrine, *Baker* is a great case that made a very positive contribution to the state of the law, especially given that it survived the challenge of Justice Frankfurter's incisive dissent.

From a purely doctrinal standpoint however, the case for *Reynolds* is much weaker. Justice Warren simply failed to explain why population equality is the constitutionally required standard, in the face of devastating arguments to the contrary by Frankfurter and Harlan along with the hesitancy of Solicitor General Cox. Warren argued that similarly situated persons must be treated the same but wholly failed to explain why persons living in different regions of a state are constitutionally similar. It is perhaps the most prominent example in all of constitutional law of the Court assuming its conclusion or arguing by way of tautology. As Warren biographer and former law clerk G. Edward White noted, at least to his critics, Warren "substituted homilies for doctrinal analysis."[86] Thus from a standpoint of traditional legal reasoning, *Reynolds v. Simms* made very bad law indeed.

However, doctrinal purity is scarcely the only way to evaluate an opinion. Arguably, *Reynolds* is an example of what Philip Bobbit has characterized as an ethical argument.[87] That is, the Court identified a principle that is deeply embedded in the American ethos, in this case majoritarian rule, even though it is not readily derived from conventional legal sources including text, original understanding, tradition, or precedent. Alexander Bickel, a severe critic of the reapportionment decisions, argued that the Court should not manufacture principles as it had done in *Reynolds* as they are generally unlikely to be durable.[88] Whether he was correct as a general matter, Bickel was clearly too pessimistic about the durability of *Reynolds* and its principles. Bickel and Cox have argued that if the Court devises a constitutional principle, it needs to be one that is already embedded in the nation's culture, or at least one that the nation will soon accept.[89] Chief Justice Warren succeeded in doing just that in *Reynolds*. Unlike other prescient opinions, the Court did not have to wait for decades for vindication. Rather, Warren seized on a principle of political equality that already resonated within the American ethos. All he had to do was to announce it and it would gain acceptance by all but the political class adversely affected and the legal academics who understood that it had little if any traditional legal pedigree. But for the population at large it was essentially axiomatic. The ease of application shielded the Court from getting stuck in "the political thicket." Moreover, one person/one vote was readily susceptible to legislative application in that there could be a near infinite number of ways in which a person with a map and a calculator could achieve compliance. As such, the courts could limit their involvement and supervision. Thus from the standpoint of popular acceptance and institutional entrenchment within the constitutional system, *Reynolds* would seem to have made very good law.

Given the degree to which one person/one vote has become embedded in our constitutional system, the doctrinal critique of *Reynolds* may seem nothing less than cranky

---

[86] G. Edward White, Earl Warren A Public Life 239 (1982).
[87] Philip Bobbitt, Constitutional Fate: Theory of the Constitution 220–21 (1982).
[88] Bickel, *supra* note 83, at 173–78.
[89] Bickel, *supra* note 81, at 239; Cox, *supra* note 4, at 304.

and pedantic. But it should not be ignored for at least two reasons. First, there is a solid argument that even assuming that as a general rule one person/one vote was a constitutionally defensible rule, the Court applied it in entirely too doctrinaire of a manner, as is illustrated by *Lucas*. It is one thing for the Court to upset the egregious malapportionment in *Reynolds*, especially given that there was no viable alternative for reform. It is quite another matter however to strike down the slight degree of malapportionment recently approved by a solid and widespread majority of the Colorado voters in *Lucas* for quite rational reasons. Unlike the result in *Reynolds, Lucas* seems dogmatic in the worst sense. The obvious reply is that the introduction of any discretion would drag the courts into the complicated slippery slope problem of deciding how much is too much. Perhaps so, but as Justice Holmes once noted, where to draw the line is "the question in pretty much everything worth arguing in the law...."[90] At some point, ease of administration must yield to competing values.

The other problem with the *Reynolds* approach, which deeply troubled Harlan in his dissent, is that if the Court decides a major case such as *Reynolds* without offering traditionally accepted legal justification and proves to be successful, that will inevitably encourage litigants to bring additional cases of tenuous validity, which the Court in turn may be emboldened to decide. Every future case that is on the fringe of what might be considered conventional constitutional interpretation will not turn out to be as successful as *Reynolds v. Simms*. And even if it did, it would be institutionally troublesome for the Court to attempt to provide a judicial remedy for every social ill that is brought before it when text, original understanding, precedent, and doctrine for resolving the issue are lacking. Thus in a sense *Reynolds v. Simms* may be seen as a logical predecessor of *Roe v. Wade* even though by then Warren was gone.

It is likely that most constitutional commentators today would conclude that the Reapportionment Cases were great cases that made very good law without qualification. Some qualification is in order however. Despite the spectacular success of the reapportionment decisions, the doctrinal weakness of *Reynolds*, indeed the sense that the majority was not particularly concerned with making a legally solid defense of its decision, suggests that the Court blazed a trail that should rarely be followed.

---

[90] Irwin v. Gavit, 268 U.S. 161, 168 (1925).

"[T]he Court compelled by the political realities of the case to decide in favor of the *Times*, yet equally compelled to seek high ground in justifying its result wrote an opinion that may prove to be the best and most important it has ever produced in the realm of freedom of speech."[1]

HARRY KALVEN

15

New York Times v. Sullivan

New York Times v. Sullivan easily qualifies as a great case from several perspectives. It revolutionized First Amendment jurisprudence, subjecting libel law to constitutional oversight for the first time ever. In the process it provided the Court's most significant theoretical understanding of freedom of speech ever offered before or since. It was a crucial decision to the civil rights movement, preventing defamation plaintiffs and state court juries from silencing critical commentary on resistance to the movement. It protected the *New York Times* and other national media from a legal threat that arguably could have driven them into bankruptcy. When presented to the Court, the case was understood as one of monumental significance. The Court issued an opinion that more than lived up to these expectations.

BACKGROUND

New York Times v. Sullivan arose at the very height of the civil rights struggle in the South. The Court had declared racially segregated schools unconstitutional in *Brown v. Board of Education* in 1954 and had ordered that desegregation proceed with all deliberate speed the following year. The boycott of segregated buses in Montgomery, Alabama, began in December 1955. The Supreme Court ordered desegregation of the buses the following year in *Gayle v. Browder*. In 1956, Judge Jones, who would try the *Sullivan* case, ordered the NAACP to produce a list of its Alabama membership. The organization refused, took

---

[1] Harry Kalven, *New York Times Case: A Note on the "Central Meaning" of the First Amendment*, 1964 SUP. CT. REV. 191, 194 (1964). Professor Kalven's article provides the definitive legal analysis of the opinion. Two useful books have been devoted to the case: ANTHONY LEWIS, MAKE NO LAW: THE SULLIVAN CASE AND THE FIRST AMENDMENT (1991) focuses primarily on the First Amendment aspects of the case. KERMIT L. HALL & MELVIN I. UROFSKY, *NEW YORK TIMES V. SULLIVAN*: CIVIL RIGHTS, LIBEL LAW, AND THE FREE PRESS (2011) calls attention to the civil rights context of the decision. Also quite useful is BERNARD SCHWARTZ, SUPER CHIEF (1983) for a detailed discussion of the drafting of the opinion.

the matter to the United States Supreme Court, and won an important victory in the landmark case of *NAACP v. Alabama*[2] recognizing that the First Amendment right of association precluded such an attempt to compel disclosure. On account of resistance from the Alabama Supreme Court, the NAACP was forced to appeal to the United States Supreme Court on two more occasions to obtain enforcement of its victory.

The student-led lunch counter sit-in movement began in North Carolina in February 1960. The sit-ins quickly spread to Montgomery, resulting in the events at the heart of *New York Times v. Sullivan*. Thirty-five students from Alabama State College were arrested for attempting to desegregate the lunch counter in the basement of the Montgomery County Courthouse.[3] Governor Patterson demanded that they be expelled. Eight hundred students marched to the state capital to protest, where they were beaten by members of the Ku Klux Klan while the police looked on.[4] No one was arrested or punished for the attack. Earlier in the year, Dr. Martin Luther King, Jr. had been charged with income tax evasion and perjury with respect to his Alabama tax returns. It was in this context that the advertisement at the heart of *New York Times v. Sullivan* was written and published.

In March 1960, a group of civil rights leaders including Bayard Rustin and A. Philip Randolph published a full-page advertisement in the *New York Times* titled "Heed Their Rising Voices."[5] The purpose of the ad was to raise funds for the movement. The ad described several instances of mistreatment of civil rights activists by local authorities in Montgomery, Alabama. It alleged that student protestors were expelled from Alabama State College for peaceful protest, and were prohibited from re-registering; that truck-loads of armed police ringed the campus; and that the student dining hall was padlocked "to starve them into submission." The ad also asserted that "again and again Southern vio-lators have answered Dr. King's peaceful protest with intimidation and violence," bomb-ing his home, assaulting his person, and having him arrested several times. It alleged that those supporting civil rights were being met with "an unprecedented wave of terror."

Shortly thereafter, Montgomery Commissioner L.B. Sullivan sent a letter to the *New York Times* demanding a retraction, as he was required to do under state law prior to filing a libel action.[6] The *Times* responded by stating that it was puzzled as to why he believed that the ad referred to him as he was not mentioned by name.[7] Sullivan then filed a suit for defamation against the *Times* as well as the four civil rights leaders whose names had appeared on the ad. Joinder of the four Alabama preachers prevented the *Times* from removing the suit to federal court as it precluded complete diversity of citi-zenship. Sullivan sought $500,000 in damages against the *Times*.

In the state court, the defense that the *Times* pressed the hardest was lack of personal jurisdiction. The trial court found however that the *Times* had a sufficient presence in Alabama as a result of its employment of a stringer to occasionally file reports, its solici-tation of advertising from Alabama businesses, and its circulation of 390 daily and 2,500 weekend editions in the state.[8]

---

[2] 357 U.S. 449 (1958).

[3] HALL & UROFSKY, *supra* note 1, at 14.

[4] *Id.*

[5] New York Times v. Sullivan, 376 U.S. 254, 256–57 (1963). The ad is reproduced in the opinion.

[6] *NAACP*, 357 U.S. at 261.

[7] *Id.*

[8] New York Times Co. v. Sullivan, 144 So. 2d 25, 29–31 (Ala. 1962).

Sullivan argued that because he was a commissioner with oversight of the police, readers of the ad would conclude that he was responsible for their alleged misconduct. In such a suit under Alabama law, given that the statements were "libelous per se," falsity, malice, and general damages to reputation were presumed. To prevail on a defense of truth or fair comment, the defendant would need to show that the statements were true in all of their particulars. As such, the law was extraordinarily favorable to the plaintiff. There were relatively minor inaccuracies in the story. The police amassed near the campus but did not ring it. The dining hall was never padlocked shut. There was no attempt to starve the students. And Dr. King was arrested four times not seven. The jury readily found in favor of Sullivan both against the *Times* and against the individual defendants, who claimed that they had not consented to the inclusion of their names in the ad. The jury awarded $500,000 damages against the *Times*.

The Alabama Supreme Court affirmed the verdict. It concluded that there was personal jurisdiction, the statements were libelous per se, and the statements were "of and concerning" the plaintiff; that is, readers would attribute the defamatory statements regarding police misconduct to him.[9] In one sentence it rejected the claim that the First Amendment had any application to a libel case. The court also indicated that the Fourteenth Amendment was not implicated as it was concerned with state rather than private action. Finally, the Alabama Supreme Court rejected the *Times* request to mitigate the damage award in view of the fact that at the time of publication, the *Times* own files contained information indicating that some of the allegations in the advertisement were incorrect.

A $500,000 verdict in 1964 dollars was extremely threatening to the *Times*. Even more troubling was the fact that several other defamation suits had been filed against the *Times* in Alabama seeking similarly large damage awards. Were the *Times* to lose all of these cases, it could suffer total damages of well over three million dollars.[10] At the very least, the *Times* would almost certainly have been forced to curtail its coverage of the civil rights movement in the South simply as a matter of self-preservation. At the worst, a series of such verdicts might well have driven the paper out of business. An appeal to the Supreme Court was a matter of the utmost importance to the *Times*.

As the *Sullivan* case proceeded through the courts, the civil rights struggle in Alabama and throughout the South continued to heat up. In the spring of 1961, freedom riders who came to the South on buses were savagely beaten. Governor Wallace blocked the admission of two black students to the University of Alabama, leading to riots and violence. In the spring of 1963, Dr. King led a series of boycotts and demonstrations and was arrested in Birmingham, Alabama, resulting in his famous "Letter from the Birmingham Jail." While Dr. King was in jail, Director of Public Safety Bull Connor had the police blast demonstrators, including many children, with high pressure fire hoses and loosed police dogs on them. This was covered extensively on national television. In late August, Dr. King delivered his famous "I Have a Dream" speech at the civil rights march on Washington. A month later, four black school girls were killed by a bomb placed in a

[9] *Id.* at 29–40.
[10] HALL & UROFSKY, *supra* note 1, at 33.

Birmingham church. The civil rights context of *New York Times v. Sullivan* was far more pervasive and intense then might appear from the opinion itself.

BRIEFING AND ARGUMENT

The *Times* was well aware that it faced formidable obstacles in having the judgment reversed. First, libel was indeed a relatively harsh strict liability tort, as the Alabama Supreme Court recognized. Although there is no question that the Alabama jury used the cause of action to severely punish an unwelcome outside voice, it was able to do so within the legitimate confines of existing legal doctrine. Moreover, the Alabama Supreme Court was also correct in its cursory conclusion that at least so far, the First Amendment had never been construed to place any limitations on the law of libel. Thus as a doctrinal matter, the verdict against the *Times* was both frightening and unexceptional. As Roland Nachman, Sullivan's attorney later put it, the Supreme Court would have "'to change one hundred years or more of libel law'" in order for Sullivan to lose.[11] Faced with this, the *Times* hired Professor Herbert Wechsler of the Columbia University Law School, arguably the most highly regarded constitutional scholar of the day, to represent it.

Wechsler's task was to frame an argument that had at least a chance of convincing the Court that the verdict against the *Times* must be reversed. To do this he would need to develop a theory to explain why the well-accepted exclusion of libel from First Amendment coverage was incorrect, at least with respect to the facts of this case. The key for Wechsler was that this was not a run-of-the-mill private libel action. Rather, this was a case in which a public official who had not been named or even referenced in the allegedly libelous publication had obtained a crushingly large verdict on account of criticism of governmental policies and practices in an ad that had been incorrect in some relatively minor respects. As such, the case appeared to award substantial damages for criticism of the government itself. This was a serious matter, but under existing doctrine could it be framed as a constitutional violation?

After researching and thinking through the case at great length, Professor Wechsler produced what must be considered one of the great briefs in Supreme Court history. It would not be difficult to argue that the verdict in the *Sullivan* case was dangerously inconsistent with First Amendment policy. But Professor Wechsler needed something more. He needed to show that the assumption that defamation was beyond the scope of the First Amendment had always been wrong even if it had been accepted for over 170 years. To counter the state's powerful argument of precedent and tradition, Wechsler turned to history as well. He explained that an award of substantial damages to a public official on account of somewhat inaccurate criticism of government conduct (without explicitly referencing the official) was analogous to prosecution for seditious libel, a practice that had occurred in the early days of the Republic but had rather quickly been discredited as wholly inconsistent with freedom of speech in a democracy. Wechsler proceeded to review the Alien and Sedition Act prosecutions of the Adams administration along with

---

[11] Lucas A. Powe, Jr., The Warren Court and American Politics 307 (2000).

Madison's trenchant criticism of these tactics and then drew the parallel between these 160-year-old criminal prosecutions and the libel verdict in *Sullivan*.[12]

When Wechsler argued the case for the *Times*, the justices were largely concerned with the facts and record and with whether there were any limiting principles to the argument. Still Wechsler attempted to remind the justices of the Sedition Act analogy and Madison's disapproval of the Sedition Act prosecutions as often as he could. Acknowledging that so far defamatory speech had been considered outside of the scope of the First Amendment, he argued that until recently the same could be said of contempt proceedings based on criticism of a court as well as obscenity, and yet when faced with these cases, the Court brought both into the First Amendment domain.[13] Following the argument in the *Times* case, the case involving the verdicts against the individual defendants was argued to the Court as well. I. H. Wachtell, attorney for the Alabama preachers, stressed the civil rights aspect of the case.

New York Times v. Sullivan was not a difficult case for the Court in terms of the ultimate result. There was no possibility that the Court would permit such a large verdict against the *Times* to stand considering the limited proof of meaningful falsity or actual damage to reputation, as well as the obvious fact that the action was essentially an attempt to silence media criticism of southern resistance to the civil rights movement. Reversal, quite possibly unanimous reversal, was probably a foregone conclusion. As such *New York Times v. Sullivan* was not a hard case in terms of the result. But doctrinally the case did present difficult questions given that libel had been excluded from First Amendment coverage up to that point. The tone of the oral argument suggested that the Court was likely to decide the case on narrow factually oriented grounds. Perhaps the easiest such ground would be a holding that as a constitutional matter, on the record, the jury could not reasonably conclude that the statements in question were "of and concerning" the plaintiff Sullivan. But in order to do even that, the Court would need to explain why the First Amendment had any application to libel at all, even in the extreme case.

DECISION AND OPINION

In conference all nine justice agreed that the verdict should be overturned.[14] They expressed concern about the tenuous relation of the charges to the plaintiff, the slight degree to which the allegations might have been false or even defamatory, and the fact that the jury had almost certainly used libel law to punish unpopular commentary. Most of the justices believed that a clear distinction should be drawn between libel regarding public affairs or officials and purely private defamation. Most believed that the case should be decided in such a way as to preclude a retrial, for fear that a local jury might reach the same result even under new constitutional guidelines.

---

[12] Brief of Petitioner in New York Times v. Sullivan, at 41–50.

[13] Oral Argument of Herbert Wechsler in New York Times v. Sullivan, *in* 58 LANDMARK BRIEFS AND ARGU-MENTS OF THE SUPREME COURT OF THE UNITED STATES: CONSTITUTIONAL LAW 697 (Philip B. Kurland & Gerhard Casper eds., 1975).

[14] THE SUPREME COURT IN CONFERENCE (1940–1985): THE PRIVATE DISCUSSIONS BEHIND NEARLY 300 SUPREME COURT DECISIONS 379–81 (Del Dickson ed., 2001).

Justice Brennan was assigned the opinion and went through eight drafts before achieving the final version. Despite the fact that there was unanimous agreement that the verdict must be reversed, Brennan struggled to produce an opinion that would command a majority of the justices. The most troubling issue for a few of the justices was not the doctrinal or theoretical basis for the decision but rather whether the Court could or should analyze the evidence and preclude a retrial. Justice Harlan was troubled by this question and did not agree to join the Brennan opinion until a day before it was announced.

The decision would certainly be significant considering that it would necessarily extend some degree of constitutional protection into the area of defamation along with the civil rights implications of the case. But there was no reason to believe that it would produce the classic First Amendment opinion that Justice Brennan delivered. The opinion was issued on March 9, 1964, approximately two months after oral argument, and applied to both the case against the *Times* as well as that against the individual defendants. Anthony Lewis reporting for the New York Times declared that "it had the sense of a great occasion when the decision was read."[15]

Justice Brennan announced at the outset that the Court was required to decide for the first time whether the First Amendment limited "a State's power to award damages in a libel action brought by a public official against critics of his official conduct."[16] He then devoted seven pages to a description of the facts and proceedings below. Turning to the merits, Brennan announced that the judgments against both the *Times* and the individual petitioners must be reversed "for failure to provide the safeguards for freedom of speech and of the press that are required by the First and Fourteenth Amendments in a libel action brought by a public official against critics of his official conduct."[17] He also declared that "the evidence presented in this case is constitutionally insufficient to support the judgment for respondent."[18]

Initially, the Court dismissed the argument that the First Amendment, as applied through the Fourteenth, was inapplicable for lack of state action, pointing out that the judgment against the petitioners was rendered in a state court applying state law. Nor was the material in question excluded from First Amendment protection because it was a paid advertisement given that it addressed a matter of public concern.

Brennan then turned to the central obstacle presented to the Court: whether as dicta in prior cases had suggested, libel was beyond the scope of the First Amendment. After briefly considering the relevant precedents, he distinguished them on the ground that none involved the imposition of liability "upon expression critical of the official conduct of public officials."[19] He proclaimed that "libel can claim no talismanic immunity from constitutional limitations."[20]

Over the next 11 pages, Justice Brennan developed a multi-step argument to explain why libel of public officials was not excluded from First Amendment protection. First, he explained that in our democracy there is "a profound national commitment to the

---

[15] Lewis, *supra* note 1, at 141.
[16] 376 U.S. at 256.
[17] *Id.* at 264.
[18] *Id.* at 265.
[19] *Id.* at 268.
[20] *Id.* at 269.

principle that debate on public issues should be uninhibited, robust, and wide-open and that it may well include vehement, caustic, and sometimes unpleasantly sharp attacks on government and public officials."[21] This statement would be quoted with great frequency in subsequent First Amendment cases. Second, quoting at length from Madison, Brennan then proclaimed that "[a]uthoritative interpretations of the First Amendment guarantees have consistently refused to recognize an exception for any test of truth...."[22] This was because "erroneous statement is inevitable in free debate, and... it must be protected if the freedoms of expression are to have the 'breathing space' that they 'need....'"[23] Likewise "[i]njury to official reputation... affords no more warrant for repressing speech...."[24] Third, the ultimate proof of the validity of these principles according to Justice Brennan was the historical rejection of the Alien and Sedition Act under which several individuals had in fact been fined and imprisoned for publishing "false, scandalous and malicious" criticisms of the government or of certain high government officials.[25] He noted that the Act and the prosecutions were condemned by Madison and Jefferson, the fines were repaid and those convicted were pardoned. He explained that "[a]lthough the Sedition Act was never tested in this Court, the attack upon its validity has carried the day in the court of history."[26] The final step in the argument was to assert that in terms of potential chilling effect on speech, massive libel judgments could be as harmful if not worse than the criminal prosecutions under the Alien and Sedition Act, especially in view of the absence of procedural protections in the civil context that would apply in a criminal case.

This carefully developed thesis with multiple citations to precedent as well as Madison, Jefferson, Mill, and Milton did not simply assert that a libel case by a public official was covered by the First Amendment but explained logically and persuasively why that must be so. It is one of the classic arguments in all of Supreme Court jurisprudence. It was without question inspired by and indeed closely tracks Herbert Wechsler's brief. In order to counter the argument that there was over 100 years of precedent against providing First Amendment protection to libelous statements, Wechsler and Brennan reached back to the very beginning of the country to retrieve a powerful counter-argument. The original understanding of freedom of speech required prohibition of the use of libel law to punish criticism of the government rather than per se exclusion of libelous statements from First Amendment protection.

As the discussions in conference indicated, most of the justices including Justice Brennan were not prepared to subject private libel verdicts to First Amendment scrutiny, at least not yet. Nor were they inclined to strip public officials of all protection against defamation. Consequently, Brennan needed to create a standard for providing significant First Amendment protection while at the same time allowing some scope for the protection of reputation of libeled public servants. He resolved this by proclaiming that a public official is prohibited "from recovering damages for a defamatory falsehood relating to his official conduct unless he proves that the statement was made with 'actual malice'—that

---

[21] *Id.* at 270.

[22] *Id.* at 271.

[23] *Id.* at 271–72.

[24] *Id.* at 272.

[25] *Id.* at 273–74

[26] *Id.* at 276.

is, with knowledge that it was false or with reckless disregard of whether it was false or not."[27] It was harder for Justice Brennan to provide constitutional justification for this standard as he was essentially creating out of whole cloth a test designed to reconcile the competing interests, though weighted heavily in favor of the defendant and free speech. Basically he borrowed a convenient standard from state law cases. As a matter of fairness, Brennan argued that the citizen should have at least a qualified privilege against a libel claim by a public official as the public official enjoys an absolute privilege against such a claim filed by a private citizen.

The Court then turned to the case at hand and concluded that the verdict must be vacated as it was not clear whether the jury had applied an actual malice standard. Anticipating a possible retrial, the Court also held that the evidence produced at trial against the *Times* and the individual defendants could not as a matter of law satisfy the actual malice standard. In so doing, it indicated that it was appropriate in a case implicating freedom of speech for the Court to engage in an independent review of the evidence to ensure that it established actual malice with "convincing clarity."

Beyond that, the Court also held that as a matter of constitutional law, the allegations in question simply could not be considered "of and concerning" the plaintiff. Justice Brennan noted that the advertisement made no reference at all to the plaintiff by name or position. The Alabama Supreme Court based its conclusion that the statements referred to the plaintiff exclusively on his official position as commissioner with some responsibility for the police. The Court found this insufficient as a matter of law in that a libel action brought by a public official based solely on allegations directed at a government institution or government practices would be essentially the same as the seditious libel approach that the Court had definitively rejected. Permitting such an action would allow public officials through libel actions to chill if not entirely suppress criticism of government policy or practice. With that the Court reversed.

Justices Black and Douglas joined the opinion of the Court but added a concurring opinion. They would have provided an absolute privilege against libel actions involving "criticism of the way public officials do their public duty."[28] Justice Black explicitly recognized that the libel actions filed against the *New York Times* were almost certainly intended to deter it from shining a light on southern resistence to racial integration. He also maintained that it was unlikely that the majority's actual malice standard would have prevented the Alabama jury and courts from reaching the same decisions as they had. Black concluded that there was simply no room under the First Amendment for libel actions by public officials regarding their public responsibilities in a representative democracy.

Justice Goldberg joined by Justice Douglas offered an opinion concurring in the result. Like Justice Black, Justice Goldberg would find an absolute privilege to criticize official conduct in the First Amendment.[29] Also like Black, he believed that libel actions based on government conduct were simply inconsistent with democracy. Despite the fact that Brennan's opinion for the Court was a radical break with precedent, the concurring

---

[27] *Id.* at 279–80.
[28] *Id.* at 295.
[29] *Id.* at 298.

justices were not concerned that it went too far. but instead argued that it did not go far enough.

Considering that *New York Times v. Sullivan* constituted the greatest victory that the press had ever achieved before the Supreme Court, it is not surprising that the press was ecstatic in its praise of the decision. Lucas Powe notes "[t]he press, having found a champion, was in love," and as a result it was blinded to the fact that *Sullivan* was driven primarily by the racial component.[30] He was correct in understanding that but for the racial component, the case would never have been brought, much less ended up in the Supreme Court. But certainly as a matter of theory and doctrine, *Sullivan* fits much more comfortably into First Amendment jurisprudence.

DOCTRINAL DEVELOPMENT

This ended the libel litigation in the south against the *Times*. There was no attempt to retry the case.[31] The other cases against the *Times* and against CBS were dismissed as well. *New York Times v. Sullivan* was only the beginning of the Court's efforts to reconcile the law of libel with the First Amendment. Over the next decade, the Court revisited the issues on several occasions to expand and clarify the doctrine. In *St. Amant v. Thompson*,[32] it indicated that "the reckless disregard" element of the actual malice standard entailed proof of subjective awareness that the statement might be false rather than merely objective gross negligence. In *Rosenblatt v. Baer*,[33] the Court defined a public official for purpose of the *Times* rule as a government employee with substantial responsibility over government affairs, in that case the manager of a government-owned ski resort. Then in *Monitor Patriot v. Roy*,[34] it extended the holding to political candidates as well.

In the companion cases of *Curtis Publishing Co v. Butts*[35] and *Associated Press v. Walker*,[36] the Court struggled with the standard applicable to defamation litigation brought by public figure plaintiffs, without deciding much. Then, in *Rosenbloom v. Metromedia*,[37] a plurality of the Court in an opinion written by Justice Brennan extended the coverage of the *Times* actual malice rule beyond public officials to private plaintiffs as well if the defamatory statement touched on a "matter of public concern." Three years later however in a lengthy and comprehensive opinion in *Gertz v. Robert Welch, Inc.*,[38] a majority of the Court rejected the matter of public concern approach and concluded that the distinction between public and private figure plaintiffs was indeed the appropriate focus. The Court did require that even a private figure defamation plaintiff establish fault by the publisher with respect to falsity; however, it permitted the states to require proof of negligence

---

[30] POWE, *supra* note 11, at 309. *See also* ROBERT G. MCCLOSKEY, THE AMERICAN SUPREME COURT 152 (revised by Sanford Levinson 1994) (few decisions ever received as much editorial support).

[31] LEWIS, *supra* note 1, at 160–61.

[32] 390 U.S. 727 (1968).

[33] 383 U.S. 75, 85 (1966).

[34] 401 U.S. 265 (1971).

[35] 318 U.S. 130 (1967).

[36] 388 U.S. 130 (1967).

[37] 403 U.S. 29 (1971).

[38] 418 U.S. 323 (1974).

rather than actual malice in such a case. In addition, it held that absent proof of actual malice, a plaintiff could not recover general or punitive damages. A plaintiff must also establish actual injury be it to reputation or emotional distress. Finally in *Philadelphia Newspapers v. Hepps*,[39] the Court held that the First Amendment required that proof of falsity was part of the plaintiff's case rather than the common law rule establishing truth as an affirmative defense. Within 10 years of the *Sullivan* decision, the Court had brought most of the law of libel into the domain of the First Amendment. Moreover, the combination of *Sullivan* and *Gertz* brought a large degree of stability to the area. Although many were not pleased with the balance struck by the Court, it has prevailed without serious challenge for 40 years.

New York Times v. Sullivan is the most thorough statement of free speech theory to ever appear in a majority opinion of the Supreme Court. Without denigrating the majesterial quality of the opinion, it should be noted that this still may not be saying much in that the Court rarely develops a theoretical foundation for its doctrine. As such, *Sullivan* was and remains particularly exciting for free speech scholars. Harry Kalven, one of the foremost students of the First Amendment ever, kicked off the celebration of the case with his classic article "New York Times Case: A Note on the 'Central Meaning' of the First Amendment."[40] Kalven appreciated the groundbreaking character of Brennan's opinion but read too much into it in suggesting that the prohibition of seditious libel was destined to be the key concept in free speech jurisprudence. As important as it was in context, the extension of First Amendment protection has simply become too expansive to be adequately understood through any single lens. Brennan's statement that freedom of speech must be "uninhibited, robust and wide-open" certainly captures the spirit that has characterized most of the Court's free speech jurisprudence ever since. Noted speech scholar Lee Bollinger has stated that *Sullivan* "provided the major modern context for defining the underlying meaning of the First Amendment."[41] *New York Times v. Sullivan* did not create the Court's libertarian approach to freedom of speech. It was already on the march when *Sullivan* was decided to a large degree on account of opinions written by Justice Brennan. But *Sullivan* provided both the foundation and the momentum for the further expansion of the First Amendment that is still occurring almost 50 years later. As crucial as *Sullivan* was in bolstering First Amendment values, Thomas Emerson, Kalven's equal as a First Amendment scholar, argued that it did not go far enough, agreeing with Black, Douglas, and Goldberg that an absolute privilege was warranted.[42] Academic praise for the decision has been pervasive, with Richard Epstein most forcefully stating the contrarian view that the Court, mesmerized by the peculiar features of the case, cut far too deeply into the common law of defamation.[43]

---

[39] 475 U.S. 767 (1986).

[40] Kalven, *supra* note 1.

[41] LEE C. BOLLINGER, IMAGES OF A FREE PRESS 5 (1991). *See also* Mary-Rose Papandrea, *New York Times v. Sullivan in* FIRST AMENDMENT STORIES 230 (2012) (it "is likely the most important First Amendment case that the Court has ever decided").

[42] THOMAS IRWIN EMERSON, THE SYSTEM OF FREEDOM OF EXPRESSION 529–30 (1970).

[43] Richard Epstein, *Was* New York Times v. Sullivan *Wrong?*, 53 U. CHI. L. REV. 192 (1986).

NEW YORK TIMES v. SULLIVAN AS A GREAT CASE

Did the greatness of *New York Times v. Sullivan* make a difference? Given the Court's expansion of First Amendment coverage to previously excluded types of speech such as obscenity prior to *Sullivan*, it is almost certain that had the *Sullivan* case not come along, the Court would have eventually applied constitutional limitations to the law of defamation. If not in *Sullivan*, then in some later case, quite possibly the *Butts* and *Walker* cases decided three years later. Even so, the context of the *Sullivan* case with a crushing damage verdict against the *New York Times* almost certainly in retaliation for its coverage of the civil rights movement made the need for resolution by the Court unavoidable. In addition, the potential threat posed by unchecked libel law was brought home to the Court by the context of the *Times* case to a degree that probably would not have resulted from a more typical defamation case. The *Sullivan* facts almost certainly made it easier for the Court to achieve unanimity as to the result. Perhaps the greatest value in the Court first confronting the relationship between defamation and freedom of speech in the dramatic context of the *Sullivan* case was the availability of the Sedition Act analogy. The most formidable legal obstacle faced by the *Times* was the absence of free speech limitations on the law of libel during the first 170 years of our constitutional existence, coupled with several instances in dicta in which the Court had proclaimed that the First Amendment had no application to defamation. Ultimately, the Court could have proclaimed either that it had simply never confronted the issue on the merits before or that the evolution of free speech doctrine had altered old assumptions. Instead however, the context of the *Times* case with a public official unmentioned in the allegedly defamatory publication obtaining a massive damage award for an advertisement critical of governmental policy, made the Sedition Act analogy compelling. This allowed the Court to make a powerful argument that its decision was not at odds with but rather wholly consistent with the original understanding of the First Amendment.

But that by itself probably would not have been enough. The argument was presented to the Court in the masterful brief by Professor Wechsler as counsel for the *Times*. The analogy would hardly have been obvious to most appellate lawyers or for that matter to most of the justices. It was apparently brought to Wechsler's attention by his co-counsel Marvin Frankel.[44] Had *Sullivan* not been the great case it was with the country's most influential newspaper facing the prospect of a series of ruinous judgments, it is unlikely that Professor Wechsler would have been brought into the case and more than likely the classic argument would never have appeared in either the briefs or the opinion.

But *New York Times v. Sullivan*'s status as a great case may have contributed even more to First Amendment jurisprudence. Most of the time, the Supreme Court does not address the larger theoretical questions implicated by constitutional law. Rather it leaves those inquiries to the academics. The Court understands that its primary responsibility is to decide the case before it based on the relevant law. *New York Times v. Sullivan* was an exception to standard practice. There Justice Brennan wrote a classic opinion that at least to some extent attempted to come to grips with as he put it "the central meaning of the First Amendment."[45] In a nutshell, he argued that the core principle underlying freedom

---

[44] Lewis, *supra* note 1, at 106.
[45] 376 U.S. 252, 273 (1963).

of speech was the encouragement of uninhibited debate on public issues and affairs. He built this argument through reliance on statements from several of the Supreme Court's leading free speech decisions. including Justice Brandeis's concurrence in *Whitney v. California, Bridges v. California,* and *Terminello v. City of Chicago.* Brennan also quoted extensively from James Madison. He capped the argument with the analogy to the Sedition Act. The result was along with the famous Holmes dissent in *Abrams v. United States* and the Brandeis concurrence in *Whitney v. California* one of the most eloquent expositions of free speech theory to ever appear in the United States Reports. Brennan seized the opportunity presented by a great case to write a great opinion. It was recognized and celebrated immediately, most prominently by renowned First Amendment scholar Harry Kalven in his article "The *New York Times* Case: A Note on the Central Meaning of the First Amendment."[46] Professor Kalven recognized that the opinion seemed to emphasize the "Meiklejohn Theory" of the First Amendment; that is, that speech regarding government and public affairs is truly at the core of the guarantee and as such is protected to an extraordinary degree. Professor Kalven reported that Professor Meiklejohn himself had characterized the publication of the *Sullivan* opinion as cause for "dancing in the street."[47] Justice Brennan confirmed the following year that this interpretation of the opinion was well warranted when he delivered the Alexander Meiklejohn lecture at Brandeis University titled "The Supreme Court and the Meiklejohn Interpretation of the First Amendment."[48]

It has been argued that the peculiar context that made *Sullivan* a great case may have caused the Court to attempt to constitutionalize a large swath of defamation law in an extremely atypical lawsuit.[49] The ordinary libel case scarcely involves an effort by a segregationist community to stifle criticism and muzzle the national media. Although vindictive and retaliatory actions do occur, the normal plaintiff is simply an individual who has been the subject of arguable defamatory falsehoods by the press. Unlike in *Sullivan,* in most instances, the plaintiff will have been explicitly identified in the publication. Thus had the Court confronted the question in a more typical libel action, it may have been more difficult to justify the demanding actual malice standard. Moreover absent the fear that a vindictive southern jury would disregard the new constitutional standards on remand, there would have been no need to impose the clear and convincing evidence standard or to review the sufficiency of the evidence de novo. Even in the context of *Sullivan,* the review of the evidence was clearly the most controversial aspect of the case within the Court and appeared capable of preventing Brennan from building a majority, at least for a while. It is difficult to imagine that the Court could have or would have pursued this approach had the first case it confronted been more typical. Thus it can be argued that *Sullivan* was a great case that induced the Court to make inappropriate if not necessarily bad law.

Although *Sullivan* created the analytical framework, there was still a great deal of work to be done. If in fact the approach of the Court in *Sullivan* was not the best method for reconciling defamation and the First Amendment, then there would be ample opportunities

---

[46] 1964 SUP. CT. REV. 191.
[47] Kalven, *supra* note 1, at 221 n.125.
[48] The lecture was published in the HARVARD LAW REVIEW, 79 Harv. L. Rev. 1 (1965).
[49] Epstein, *supra* note 43, at 787.

for the Court in the future to extend *Sullivan* or to retreat from it. In the years to come, it did both. Consistent with the seditious libel justification of *Sullivan*, in cases involving public official plaintiffs, the Court arguably strengthened the protection provided by *Sullivan* by extending it to relatively low level officials and candidates for public office, and by defining actual malice as a difficult to prove subjective scienter-based standard. Within three years of *Sullivan* in the companion cases of *Butts* and *Walker*, it became apparent that the Court was seriously divided over the extension of the *Sullivan* principles to defamation actions involving private plaintiffs. When the plaintiff was no longer a government official, the analogy to seditious libel, perhaps Justice Brennan's strong suit, broke down. The case for constitutional protection was no longer quite so close to the "central meaning" of the First Amendment. For the next several years, the Court was unable to reach agreement as to the proper approach. Finally, in *Gertz v. Robert Welch, Inc.*, with five new members of the Court since *Sullivan*, a bare majority, over the vigorous dissent of Justice Brennan, focused analysis on the status of the private figure plaintiff as opposed to the nature of the issue. This brought a halt to the continuing expansion of the *Sullivan* approach, shifting its direction in the process. It produced a result however that was probably closer to where the Court may have come out had it first addressed the question of the constitutional protection of defamatory speech in a case that was not as dramatic as *Sullivan*.

There is an academic consensus, especially among speech scholars, that *New York Times v. Sullivan* made very good law. There can be quibbles with respect to whether the Court went far enough or too far on specific points. There is room for argument that the Court may have been wiser to concentrate on limiting damages instead of or in addition to curbing liability. Likewise, the difficulty of proving actual malice increases the cost of litigation. Nor does the *Sullivan* framework provide for a simple and inexpensive correction of media errors. The basic principle that speakers are constitutionally entitled to a high degree of protection in criticizing the government and that they cannot be held liable by an unnamed public official for general criticism of governmental operations are quite properly seen as essential to the basic functioning of what Thomas Emerson would call a system of free expression. The principle that federal appellate courts will closely examine the evidence to ensure that the constitutional limitations have been satisfied is also of great importance. Although there has been concern that the stringent standards of *Sullivan* might deter good people from public service, result in unremedied destruction of reputation, and permit the spread of false and defamatory allegations to the detriment of the marketplace of ideas, most commentators would agree that the societal benefits justify the costs. As such, although *Sullivan* may not have made perfect law, it made very good law and certainly durable law. Some in the press have maintained that absent *New York Times v. Sullivan*, the type of investigative reporting that led to some extent to the revelation of the coverup of the Watergate break-in would not have been possible under the threat of strict liability defamation actions.[50]

New York Times v. Sullivan definitely came to the Court as a great case. At the very height of the civil rights struggle, southern plaintiffs and juries threatened to drive the nation's most prominent newspaper not simply out of the South but out of business as

---

[50] LEWIS, *supra* note 1, at 115.

well. Herbert Wechsler, a renowned legal scholar, appeared for the *Times*. Although the table was set for a great case, the opinion hardly needed to live up to the occasion. There were so many ways in which the Court could have readily disposed of the case favorable to the *Times* without saying anything particularly memorable. But the case was presented to a confident and relatively unified Court at least with respect to free speech and civil rights issues. The case was assigned to Justice Brennan, who had the inclination as well as the doctrinal and theoretical skills to write a landmark opinion, not to mention the blueprint provided by Wechsler. Moreover, Brennan had the patience and the political skills to start with two other justices and ultimately bring five more on board. Like Chief Justice Marshall, Brennan was able to use the opportunity presented by a great case to create a landmark case. *Sullivan* illustrates that the prominence of the great case can at least on occasion inspire the Court to reach new heights.

"If *Miranda* is not the most controversial decision by the Warren Court, it is close enough, and it is the most controversial criminal procedure decision hands down...."[1]
LUCAS POWE

16

Miranda v. Arizona

⌢———————————————————————————————————————

Miranda v. Arizona[2] was as politically explosive as any case that the Warren court ever decided. A major project of the Warren court was to reform criminal procedure, especially at the state level, through constitutional law. That project was realized in literally dozens of decisions but none did so as ambitiously or evoked the public and political fury as *Miranda*. Indeed, *Miranda* became Exhibit A in the challenge to the Court's judicial activism and seemed to play a significant role in both the political and judicial realignment that would follow the Warren Court years. When the Court set *Miranda* and its three companion cases for argument in the spring of 1966, it well understood that it was confronting a great case. The five-member majority staked out new constitutional ground without hesitation despite a ferocious challenge by the four dissenting justices. Over the next three decades, a new majority would consistently chip away at the decision though declining to overrule it outright. *Miranda* survived though not necessarily as the majority had intended, and the cost to the Court was not insignificant.

BACKGROUND

At the time of the *Miranda* decision in 1966, the Supreme Court had confronted for over 70 years in dozens of cases the question of whether out-of-court confessions obtained by some degree of pressure were admissible in criminal trials. Although the Court had placed some reliance on the Fifth Amendment Privilege against Self-Incrimination,[3] it had largely determined the voluntariness and hence the admissibility of confessions pursuant to a totality of the circumstances approach derived from the Due Process Clauses of the Fourteenth

---

[1] LUCAS A. POWE, JR., THE WARREN COURT AND AMERICAN POLITICS 394 (2000).

[2] 384 U.S. 436 (1966). LIVA BAKER, *MIRANDA*: CRIME, LAW AND POLITICS (1983) provides a sweeping and detailed examination of the case and its political impact.

[3] The Court had placed reliance on the privilege in the early case of Bram v. United States, 168 U.S. 532 (1897).

Amendment.[4] This fact-specific approach resulted in a large measure of unpredictability. It also resulted in the admission of many confessions produced with a fair amount of pressure or trickery. Many of the more egregious confession cases involved black defendants, often but not exclusively in southern jurisdictions. In cases from the 1930s such as *Brown v. Mississippi*[5] and *Chambers v. Florida*,[6] the Court had been confronted with interrogation techniques involving extreme brutality. By the 1960s, the methods of interrogation were more civilized but still dependent on the exertion of pressure on the suspect.

Prior to *Miranda*, the Court had issued landmark criminal procedure decisions such as *Gideon v. Wainwright*,[7] extending the right to the assistance of counsel to all indigent defendants charged with felonies, and *Mapp v. Ohio*,[8] extending to state criminal trials the rule excluding evidence obtained pursuant to a search conducted in violation of the Fourth Amendment. *Gideon* changed the law in only a handful of outlying states. *Mapp* was quite unpopular with law enforcement. Still, restricting the use of confessions by criminal suspects was another matter entirely.

In 1964, in an unusually muddled opinion in *Escobedo v. Illinois*,[9] the Court held that the Sixth Amendment precluded the admission into evidence of a confession made after the defendant had requested to speak with his attorney and the state had denied the request. The majority listed several factors that had influenced its decision without making any attempt to devise a bright-line rule. As such, the case gave rise to an extraordinary amount of litigation, with most courts interpreting it very narrowly while others read it as cutting very deeply into the ability of the police to interrogate a suspect in custody. *Escobedo* suggested to some that the Court was preparing to reform the constitutional law of confessions and gave rise to a significant amount of activity in the legal profession designed to attempt to address the issue perhaps before the Court could.[10] Several highly respected appellate judges, including Lumbard and Friendly of the Second Circuit, Schaefer of the Illinois Supreme Court, and Traynor of the California Supreme Court, warned against any further expansion of *Escobedo*.[11] At the time that the Court convened to begin the 1965 term, well over 100 *Escobedo* cases were pending for review. From those, the Court selected four cases to consolidate for consideration of the question of whether confessions obtained during custodial interrogation should be admissible in evidence and one further case to consider whether the Court's decision should apply retroactively.

THE CASES

Four cases were consolidated for oral argument on the confession issue at the end of February and beginning of March 1966. In *Miranda v. Arizona*, the defendant had confessed to kidnapping and rape after a two-hour interrogation in a police station after

---

[4] Justice Harlan cited 30 such due process confession cases in his dissent. *Miranda*, 384 U.S., at 507–09.
[5] 297 U.S. 278 (1936).
[6] 399 U.S. 309 (1936).
[7] 372 U.S. 335 (1963).
[8] 367 U.S. 643 (1961).
[9] 378 U.S. 478 (1964).
[10] BAKER, *supra* note 2 at 158.
[11] *Id.*

having been confronted by the victim who identified him. Although the victim was not certain that she could identify Miranda, when she confronted him at the station, he identified her, declaring "that's the girl."[12] In *Vignera v. New York*, the defendant was taken to the police station for questioning with respect to a robbery, where he confessed orally and then signed a written confession later at another police station. In *Westover v. United States*, the defendant was picked up and interrogated by the Kansas police in connection with a robbery. He denied the charges, and was then turned over to the FBI who interrogated him at the police station with respect to a robbery in California to which he confessed. In *California v. Stewart*, the defendant was arrested in connection with several robberies, and after interrogation over a period of nine days admitted participation in one of the robberies, resulting in charges of robbery, rape, and murder for which he was sentenced to death. The records did not indicate that any of the suspects had been warned of their rights prior to interrogation nor was there any indication that any of them had been subjected to physical abuse during interrogation.

ORAL ARGUMENT

One of the primary points of discussion in the argument of the four cases was the meaning of *Escobedo*.[13] Counsel for Miranda had approached the case as a Sixth Amendment Right to Counsel rather than a Fifth Amendment Privilege against Self-Incrimination case. Looking at it as a Sixth Amendment case, a central question was: When specifically did that right attach? Did the right to counsel come into play when the investigation began to "focus" on the accused, as the *Escobedo* opinion had suggested, and if so, when did that occur?[14] The Court and the attorneys during the three days of oral argument also debated the constitutional source of any limitation on the custodial interrogation of suspects. There was discussion of whether judicial supervision of confessions produced during police interrogation could be derived from the Fifth Amendment Privilege against Self-Incrimination, the Sixth Amendment Right to Counsel, or from the Fifth and Fourteenth Amendment Due Process Clauses.[15] The Court and the lawyers were especially interested in the role of attorneys in the context of custodial interrogation. Did *Escobedo* turn on the fact that the suspect had actually requested to speak with his attorney? Was there a right to have counsel present during police interrogation as a matter of course?[16] Was there a right to

---

[12] *Id.* at 13.

[13] Gordon Ringer, Deputy Attorney General of California. In Oral Argument Transcript in California v. Stewart, 63 LANDMARK BRIEFS AND ARGUMENTS OF THE SUPREME COURT OF THE UNITED STATES: CONSTITUTIONAL LAW at 939 (Philip B. Kurland & Gerhard Casper eds., 1975).

[14] As Justice Stewart noted during the argument of Miranda v. Arizona, "I don't understand the magic in this phrase of 'focusing.'" Oral Argument Transcript in Miranda v. Arizona, *supra* note 13, at 851.

[15] In *Miranda*, Justice White asked counsel for the defendant "I'm just trying to find out if you claim that his Fifth Amendment rights have been violated." Oral Argument Transcript, *supra* note 13, at 854.

[16] Telford Taylor for New York in Vignera v. New York in Oral Argument Transcript, *supra* note 13, at 867 ("The Fifth Amendment cannot, and should not be read as requiring counsel to be present at the time the confession is taken").

have counsel appointed for indigents before any formal proceedings had commenced?[17] Was custodial interrogation a "critical stage" under Sixth Amendment jurisprudence, invoking the right to counsel? In *Escobedo*, the Court had ventured into uncharted waters and the *Miranda* oral arguments wrestled with many of the unanswered questions.

Justice Black played a significant role in the arguments. He staked out the position that custodial interrogation was inherently compulsive within the meaning of the Fifth Amendment and as such, a statement taken without a knowing and intelligent waiver was necessarily inadmissible in evidence.[18] He suggested that the Fifth Amendment might well be read to prohibit any "pre-trial proceedings" when the suspect "was in the possession of the State."[19] Attorneys for the states and the federal government responded by defending the traditional totality of the circumstances approach on the issue of compulsion, under which the absence of warnings or of an attorney would not necessarily prohibit the admission of a confession into evidence.[20] That was a complete anathema to Justice Black in that it was reminiscent of the approach that the Court had previously rejected with respect to the right to counsel.[21] The attorneys for the state maintained that all custodial interrogation was not necessarily inherently coercive and that at least some defendants understood their rights and were more than capable of making informed decisions.[22]

Victor Earle, the attorney for the petitioner Vignera, suggested that the police should be required to warn the suspect of his rights prior to interrogation, and cited the warnings recently adopted by the chief of police of the District of Columbia as an example, which were essentially the same as those that would be adopted by the Court.[23] Justices Stewart, Fortas, and White then questioned him in some detail about the effect of these warnings as well as the requirements for a valid waiver.[24]

The attorneys for the states emphasized that confessions were often essential to the prosecution of some very serious crimes[25] and that any competent criminal defense attorney would instruct his client not to speak with the police, thereby terminating the interrogation process.[26] Consequently, a balance needed to be struck between the rights

---

[17] Solicitor General Thurgood Marshall argued that the government was under no obligation to appoint counsel for indigents prior to the commencement of formal proceedings. Oral Argument Transcript in Westover v. United States, *supra* note 13, at 916–17.

[18] *See* Oral Argument Transcript in Miranda v. Arizona, *supra* note 13, at 898. In *California v. Stewart*, Justice Black asked counsel when "they take him down to a little police room by himself, and they interrogate him about whether he's guilty. Does that not spell compulsion to you?" Oral Argument Transcript, *supra* note 13, at 954.

[19] Justice Black in Miranda v. Arizona, Oral Argument Transcript, *supra* note 13, at 864.

[20] Gary Nelson for the State of Arizona argued for a totality of the circumstances approach in *Miranda*. Oral Argument Transcript, *supra* note 13, at 859.

[21] During the argument on *Vignera*, Justice Black declared that the Court was simply incapable of deciding all of these confession cases on a case-by-case basis. Oral Argument Transcript, *supra* note 13, at 893-94.

[22] Deputy Attorney General Gordon Ringer in California v. Stewart, *supra* note 13, at 967.

[23] Oral Argument Transcript in Miranda v. Arizona, *supra* note 13, at 885-86.

[24] *Id.* at 886–89.

[25] In *California v. Stewart Deputy*, Attorney Gordon Ringer noted that "We are dealing in this type case with an unwitnessed homicide, where there are no fingerprints, no technical leads, no magnetic evidence, no specific evidence of any kind–and there are certain kinds of crimes which can only be solved by asking questions." Oral Argument Transcript, *supra* note 13, at 965.

[26] Gary Nelson for the State of Arizona in Miranda v. Arizona, Oral Argument Transcript, *supra* note 13, at 862 (once an attorney is brought in "interrogation would immediately stop"); William Siegal for the

of the suspect and the needs of law enforcement and the community. More than one of the state's attorneys attempted to remind the Court that the police were not bad guys attempting to extract confessions through the third degree.[27] The attorney for the defendant in *Westover* replied that the attorneys for the states were simply conjuring up "hobgoblins to frighten the Court."[28] Justice Fortas noted that the Constitution required respect for the rights of the accused even if that interfered with the conviction of criminals. Chief Justice Warren, who would play the major role in writing the *Miranda* opinion, did not participate nearly as much in the oral arguments as several of the other justices although he did ask "Do we have an investigatory stage in this country? I didn't know we could arrest people for investigation."[29] The oral arguments highlighted the degree of confusion that existed with respect to custodial interrogation but did not clearly telegraph the approach that the Court was destined to take. Columbia Law professor Telford Taylor on behalf of New York urged the Court to move slowly, allowing the states to attempt to resolve the custodial interrogation problem.[30] The ACLU, which did not participate in oral argument, produced an amicus brief written primarily by law professor Anthony Amsterdam, which brought to the Court's attention the various techniques of pressure and trickery recommended by various police interrogation manuals. This was destined to be more influential than any of the other briefs or oral arguments.

CONFERENCE AND DECISION

At the conference following the arguments, Chief Justice Warren argued for an approach that would preclude the admission of confessions that resulted from custodial interrogation in the absence of detailed warnings. He indicated that the opinion could rest on either the Fifth Amendment Privilege against Self-Incrimination or the Sixth Amendment Right to the Assistance of Counsel.[31] Warren was particularly impressed by the fact that the FBI delivered warnings prior to interrogation and yet still seemed to be highly effective.[32] Justice Black appeared to go even further, arguing for a ban on custodial interrogation entirely. Justice Douglas favored a Sixth Amendment rationale while Brennan favored the Fifth, though with an emphasis on arrest rather than custodial interrogation. Justice Clark seemed to concur though not fully. Justice Harlan argued that Warren's approach was quite inconsistent with history and precedent. Justices Stewart and White

---

State of New York in Vignera v. New York, Oral Argument Transcript, *supra* note 13, at 903–04 (every lawyer will tell their client " 'Button Your Lip' or 'Don't Talk' or 'Shut Up' ").

[27] Williams Siegal for the State of New York noted that "there has been too much talk of the police on one side and the defendant on the other and not enough reference to the rights of the community." Oral Argument Transcript in Vignera v. New York, *supra* note 13, at 895.

[28] F. Conger Fawcett for the petitioner Westover, Oral Argument Transcript in Westover v. United States, *supra* note 13, at 910.

[29] Oral Argument Transcript in Vignera v. New York, *supra* note 13, at 900.

[30] Transcript of Oral Argument in Miranda v. Arizona, *supra* note 13, at 868.

[31] THE SUPREME COURT IN CONFERENCE (1940–1985): THE PRIVATE DISCUSSIONS BEHIND NEARLY 300 SUPREME COURT DECISIONS 515 (Del Dickson ed., 2001).

[32] BERNARD SCHWARTZ, SUPER CHIEF: EARL WARREN AND HIS SUPREME COURT—A JUDICIAL BIOGRAPHY 589 (1983).

agreed with Harlan, and Justice Fortas agreed with Warren. As with *Brown* and *Reynolds*, Warren assigned the opinion to himself and set about drafting it. Justice Clark moved to the dissent camp. Warren circulated the opinion to Justice Brennan, who found it too doctrinaire and urged Warren to declare that the state could well devise alternatives to the delivery of the warnings.[33] Warren agreed and did so. Aside from that, the battle lines were hardened with no realistic room for movement among the justices.

THE MAJORITY OPINION

Two and one-half months after the oral arguments, Chief Justice Warren produced a 60- page opinion for the majority that went far beyond the resolution of the cases before the Court and announced a detailed set of rules for addressing the admissibility of confessions obtained through custodial interrogation. It ranks as one of the most "legislative" seeming decisions ever issued by the Court. Contrary to ordinary practice where the justices only summarize their opinions, Warren spent over an hour reading his entire opinion from the bench.

He began with a discussion of the recent *Escobedo* decision and then set forth a summary of the rules that the majority would impose on custodial interrogation. He explained that in the absence of other effective safeguards, before any questioning can occur, a person taken into police custody must be advised (1) that he has a right to remain silent, (2) that any statement he makes may be used in evidence against him, (3) that he has the right to have an attorney present, and (4) that if he cannot afford an attorney one will be appointed.[34] The rights mentioned can be waived by the suspect if the waiver is voluntary and intelligent, but the state has the burden of proving that such a waiver has occurred. Moreover, all questioning must cease if the suspect indicates that he desires to speak with an attorney or that he does not wish to be questioned further. The announcement of this detailed set of requirements near the very beginning of the opinion created the impression that the Court was engaged in rule-making rather than typical adjudication, a point that the dissents and critics would emphasize.

Chief Justice Warren then turned his attention to the nature of police interrogation. He observed that in the past there had been instances of extreme physical brutality during the course of interrogation but noted that the pressure employed by the police at the present tended to be of a psychological nature.[35] Noting that there is little information as to what occurs during police interrogations, Warren devoted several pages of the opinion to a summary of techniques suggested by several contemporary police interrogation manuals. He concluded that the interrogators are advised to express certainty in the guilt of the suspect, to be relentless in the questioning, and to use a variety of tricks and tactics to undermine the suspect's resistance. The ultimate point of this discussion was to make the case that custodial interrogation as practiced by the police, even without physical intimidation, was effectively the same as the legal compulsion that the Privilege against Self-Incrimination had traditionally been understood to prohibit. This was the crucial

---

[33] *Id.* at 590.
[34] 384 U.S. 436, 444 (1966).
[35] *Id.* at 445–48.

move in Warren's legal argument given that as the dissents would establish, the privilege had not been extended beyond formal legal compulsion. Ironically, the Court's reliance on an interrogation manual written by Professors Inbau and Reid substantially increased its sales, leading to publication of a new edition.[36]

Turning to the history of the privilege, Warren concluded quoting Wigmore that it was intended "to maintain a 'fair state-individual balance.'"[37] This is in accord with the "dignity and integrity of its citizens...."[38] Warren argued that the nature of custodial interrogation was to impose pressure that in turn would inhibit rational judgment by the suspect. Presence of an attorney or the prescribed warnings would counteract that pressure.

Warren indicated that Congress or the states could devise alternative means of dispelling the inherent pressure of custodial interrogation. This suggested but certainly did not say that the warnings were not mandated by the Fifth Amendment but were rather a judicially created device to protect the privilege in an atmosphere dominated by the police. Warren then explained the purpose of each of the warnings at some length. He emphasized that the issuance of the warnings was an "absolute prerequisite to interrogation" and that no amount of circumstantial evidence of the suspect's preexisting knowledge of his rights could substitute for the delivery of the warnings. Warren emphasized that an intelligent and voluntary waiver must be proven and cannot be presumed from the very fact of a confession. He also noted that the rules adopted by the Court would not preclude general on-the-scene questioning of citizens nor voluntary statements made to the police in the absence of custodial interrogation.

Warren then turned his attention to perhaps the most powerful argument raised by the critics of its approach—the cost to law enforcement and society in general. His initial argument was simply that the protection of constitutional rights takes precedence over the non-constitutional interest in the detection and prosecution of crime, quoting from the famous Brandeis dissent in *Olmstead v. United States*. Warren emphasized that the FBI has followed a similar procedure of delivering warnings prior to interrogation without apparent detriment. The majority also pointed to the adoption of a similar approach in England, Scotland, India, and Ceylon.

Finally, Warren addressed that facts of the four specific cases before it and concluded that all four confessions were inadmissible; consequently all four convictions must be vacated.

If the Court was to attempt to constitutionally reform the confession process, its approach was more moderate than many possible alternatives. As Justice Black had suggested during oral argument, the Court could have banned custodial interrogation, period, prior to arraignment, though there was no possibility that a majority of the justices would have agreed to such an approach. Or the Court might have prohibited custodial interrogation unless a lawyer was present, which would have effectively precluded the practice entirely. Once again, there is little chance that a majority would have adopted that option. Or the Court could have required that all interrogations must be videotaped

---

[36] FRED P. GRAHAM, THE SELF-INFLICTED WOUND 315-16 (1971).
[37] *Id.* at 460, quoting 8 WIGMORE, EVIDENCE 317 (McNaughten rev. ed. 1961).
[38] *Miranda*, 384 U.S. at 460.

as some commentators had urged. It does not appear that such an option was discussed, and given the various circumstances in which interrogation occurs, it would seem impracticable. The Court's warnings-and-waiver approach seemed to be designed to at least preserve the possibility of effective custodial interrogation although with greater restriction than had been the case prior to *Miranda*. Although the Court was determined to attempt to curb the abuses of custodial interrogation in a judicially efficient manner, it did seem to accept the utility of the practice as a given.

Justice Clark wrote a short opinion dissenting with respect to three of the cases and concurring with respect to the fourth. His opinion was less deferential to the majority than his remarks in the conference would have suggested. At the outset, he declared that "I am unable to join the majority because its opinion goes too far on too little, while my dissenting brethren do not go quite far enough."[39] Clark dismissed the relevance of the "police manuals" cited by Warren given that they were not shown to be actual manuals employed by any actual police department.[40] This kicked an important pillar out from underneath the majority's case. He also argued that the practices of the FBI and the foreign nations cited by the majority were readily distinguishable. Clark objected to the Court's adoption of a set of doctrinaire rules absent any experience as to how they might work in practice, which of course was one of the primary critiques of *Miranda*. Consequently, like the other dissenters, Clark would continue to employ the due process totality of the circumstances approach. Other than emphasizing the state's burden of proving an intelligent and voluntary waiver in the absence of the delivery of the warnings, Justice Clark did not really explain why he did not believe that the dissents went "far enough." Clark was quite troubled by a statement in Warren's majority opinion criticizing the police, and returned to his chambers and inserted an additional sentence in his already published opinion replying to Warren.[41]

Justice Harlan wrote the primary dissent. Given that Chief Justice Warren was no match for Justice Harlan as either a writer or scholar, as in *Reynolds v. Simms* two years earlier, the Harlan dissent reads far more powerfully than the Warren opinion for the Court. He began by charging that the majority's "voluntariness with a vengeance" was essentially designed to all but entirely curtail the use of confessions in criminal trials. He then engaged in a lengthy review of the precedent intended to show that throughout the Court's history, the Due Process Clause rather than the Fifth Amendment had been the primary and indeed the constitutionally appropriate device for assessing the admissibility of extrajudicial confessions.[42] He maintained that the traditional due process totality of the circumstances approach took account of both the significant factual variations from one case to the next and the legitimate needs of law enforcement and society.[43]

Harlan conceded that a credible legal argument could be made to expand the coverage of the Fifth Amendment Privilege to cover custodial interrogation.[44] Nevertheless the components of such an argument were deeply flawed. Rather, the majority was simply

---

[39] *Id.* at 499.

[40] *Id.*

[41] BAKER, *supra* note 2, at 172.

[42] *Miranda*, 384 U.S. at 506–10.

[43] *Id.* at 508–09.

[44] *Id.* at 511.

wrong in assuming that pressure on the suspect violates the privilege or that knowledge of the underlying right is essential to its waiver. Harlan emphasized that it was well settled that the type of compulsion covered by the Privilege against Self-incrimination was legal as opposed to psychological compulsion. As such, the Court was drawing its principles instead from Sixth Amendment right-to-counsel cases that in fact had no relevance to extrajudicial settings to which they had never been applied except for *Escobedo*. He accused the majority of engaging in what Judge Friendly had characterized as the "'domino method of constitutional adjudication...wherein every explanatory statement in a previous opinion is made the basis for extension to a wholly different situation.'"[45]

Justice Harlan then challenged the Court's approach on policy grounds. He argued that confessions are a valuable tool of law enforcement and that some degree of pressure on the suspect in the course of obtaining a confession is both inherent and permissible. He believed that the warnings required by the Court were most probably a "minor obstruction" to the obtaining of confessions. However the waiver rules had the potential to "end interrogation" entirely. The need for confessions in order to solve crimes was simply too significant to permit the Court's "hazardous experimentation."[46] Unlike some of the Court's previous alterations to constitutional criminal procedure, Justice Harlan pointed out that law enforcement as a whole was vigorously opposed to the majority's approach here. He also explained that neither the FBI nor the countries relied on by the majority leaned as far in favor of the suspect as did the Court. Applying the traditional due process analysis to the cases before the Court, Harlan would find all of the confessions admissible.

Justice White also produced a dissenting opinion. He argued that there was no support in the text, history, or precedent of the Fifth Amendment for the Court's extension of the privilege to custodial interrogation.[47] White wondered how a waiver could ever be considered voluntary if, as the majority believed, custodial interrogation is inherently coercive.[48] He believed that ultimately the Court had concluded that "evidence from the accused should not be used against him in any way, whether compelled or not."[49] The Court's talk of human dignity seemed to overlook the dignity of the victims of crime, according to Justice White.[50] To be blunt "[i]n some unknown number of cases the Court's rule will return a killer, a rapist or other criminal to the streets...to repeat his crime [giving rise to] a loss in human dignity."[51]

In the companion case of *Johnson v. New Jersey*,[52] the Court held that *Miranda* was only retroactive to a limited extent. Aside from the defendants in the four cases before the Court, it would only apply to those cases in which the trial began after the announcement of the decision. This at least protected the Court against the charge that previously convicted killers and rapists would be released on account of the decision. Ernesto Miranda

---

[45] *Id.* at 514.
[46] *Id.* at 517.
[47] *Id.* at 527–28.
[48] *Id.* at 536.
[49] *Id.* at 538.
[50] *Id.* at 539.
[51] *Id.* at 542.
[52] 384 U.S. 719 (1966).

was retried without the confession he had made to the police but with a confession that he had later made to his girlfriend at the time. He was convicted, the conviction was upheld by the Arizona Supreme Court, and the United States Supreme Court denied certiorari. He served time in prison. After he was released he sold autographed copies of *Miranda* warnings cards for $1.50. In 1976, he was stabbed to death in a bar over a gambling debt. The suspect in his murder, who was not convicted, was given *Miranda* warnings.[53]

THE REACTION

Few decisions of the Court have been as widely castigated in the political process as *Miranda*.[54] It became the poster child for the challenge to judicial activism, which to some extent led to the election of President Nixon on a law and order platform two years later. Professional critics echoed Justices Harlan's and White's argument that the decision was a revolutionary change in the law with little if any legal support. The dissents were quoted regularly by the critics. The popular slogan of *Miranda*'s critics was that it would "handcuff the police" and lead to the release of dangerous criminals, including murders and rapists as Justice White had predicted. Senator Sam Ervin of North Carolina proclaimed that "[e]nough has been done for those who murder, rape and rob....It is time to do something for those who do not wish to be murdered, raped or robbed."[55] Senator McClellan held hearings in which the *Miranda* decision was criticized vigorously by witnesses.[56] The *Miranda* opinion was issued at a time when violent crime was on the increase, perhaps to some extent due to the coming of age of the post–World War II baby boom generation. The public backlash against *Miranda* increased significantly when several confessed murders were released in its wake.[57] The release of dangerous and violent criminals due to legal technicalities including *Miranda* violations became a consistent theme for television and movie dramas, most particularly Clint Eastwood's popular Dirty Harry movies. *Miranda* infiltrated the public consciousness to a degree that perhaps no other Supreme Court decision had—and not in a favorable manner.

Chief Justice Warren's indication in *Miranda* that governments might well be able to create alternative procedures to take the place of the warnings in protecting the privilege gave rise to the theory that the warnings were not constitutionally required but were rather simply one judicially crafted prophylactic device for protecting the privilege: what Professor Henry Monaghan later characterized as "constitutional common law."[58] Acting on the assumption that the Constitution did not strictly require the warnings, as part of the Omnibus Crime Act of 1968 Congress included a provision that at least in federal court, the warnings were only one of many factors to consider in judging the voluntariness of a confession under a traditional totality of the circumstances approach.[59] As this

---

[53] BAKER, *supra* note 2, at 408–09.
[54] ED CRAY, CHIEF JUSTICE: A BIOGRAPHY OF EARL WARREN 46–61 (1997) (quoting attacks by Senators Byrd and Ervin); BARRY FRIEDMAN, THE WILL OF THE PEOPLE: HOW PUBLIC OPINION HAS INFLUENCED THE SUPREME COURT AND SHAPED THE MEANING OF THE CONSTITUTION 274–76 (2009).
[55] BAKER, *supra* note 2, at 201.
[56] *Id.* at 205.
[57] GRAHAM, *supra* note 36, at 184-86.
[58] Henry Monaghan, *Foreword –Constitutional Common Law*, 89 HARV. L. REV. 1 (1975).
[59] 18 U.S.C. 3501 (1968).

legislation did not substitute any other procedure for the warnings but rather attempted to return the law to its state before *Miranda* was decided, it was understood as a flat-out challenge to the *Miranda* decision itself and as such was ignored by the Department of Justice until eventually invalidated three decades later.

Seizing on law and order as a central theme in his 1968 campaign for president, Richard Nixon was explicitly critical of *Miranda* promising to appoint judges and justices who would support the peace forces rather than the criminal forces.[60] Nixon was elected and very quickly had the opportunity to act on his campaign promise. During his first year in office, Earl Warren resigned and Abe Fortas was forced to step down due to allegations of financial improprieties and conflicts of interest. Nixon appointed Warren Burger of the District of Columbia Court of Appeals, perhaps *Miranda*'s harshest judicial critic, to replace Warren. Eighth Circuit Judge Harry Blackmun was chosen to replace Fortas. At the end of the 1970–1971 term, both Justice Black, a supporter of *Miranda* and Justice Harlan, its harshest critic on the Court, resigned due to failing health. They were replaced by Lewis Powell, an outspoken critic of *Miranda* and William Rehnquist a staunch conservative destined to be one of the Court's most persistent foes of the case. So within five years of the *Miranda* decision, the Court had swung from a 5-4 majority in favor of *Miranda* to perhaps a 7-2 majority opposed to its basic premises though not prepared to overrule it.

Over the next three decades, the Court would decide over 30 cases in which it was called on to interpret some aspect of *Miranda*. Most of the time it would reject challenges to overturn convictions based on *Miranda* violations, often cutting down the scope of the decision in the process. The Burger Court's first opportunity to challenge *Miranda* came in *Harris v. New York*[61] decided in 1971. There over a vigorous dissent of Justice Brennan, the majority in an opinion written by Chief Justice Burger held that a confession inadmissible on the question of guilt due to failure to comply with *Miranda* could nevertheless be admitted for impeaching the defendant's testimony. This was seen as a major blow to *Miranda* by its supporters.[62] Three years later in *Michigan v. Tucker*, Justice Rehnquist writing for the majority explicitly endorsed the position that *Miranda* warnings were prophylactic in nature rather than constitutionally prescribed.[63] This critique went to the very foundation of the legitimacy of the decision itself. The Court turned away a direct challenge to overrule *Miranda* however two years later in *Brewer v. Williams*[64] where a police officer had cajoled a mentally disturbed suspect to lead him to the body of a child he had murdered after having spoken with counsel and having expressed an unwillingness to talk to police at that time. The Court dodged the *Miranda* issue, reversing the conviction as a violation of the Sixth Amendment Right to Counsel.

Finally in *United States v. Dickerson*,[65] decided 34 years after *Miranda*, the Court by a 7-2 margin struck down section 3501, the 1968 Congressional challenge to *Miranda*,

---

[60] BAKER, *supra* note 2, at 211, 224-25.

[61] 401 U.S. 222 (1971).

[62] Alan Dershowitz & John Hart Ely, Harris v. New York: *Some Anxious Observations on the Candor and Logic of the Emerging Nixon Majority*, 80 YALE L.J. 1198 (1971).

[63] 417 U.S. 433, 444 (1974).

[64] 430 U.S. 387, 397 (1977).

[65] 530 U.S. 428 (2000).

concluding that the requirement of the warnings was constitutionally based after all and, as such, Congress did not have the power to alter or ignore them. Chief Justice Rehnquist, perhaps *Miranda*'s most persistent critic on the Court, wrote the opinion rejecting the challenge. He acknowledged that "Miranda has become embedded in routine police practice to the point where the warnings have become part of our national culture."[66] *Miranda* was here to stay. Justice Scalia wrote a spirited dissent quoting from case after case in which the Court had stated that the *Miranda* warnings were prophylactic rules designed to protect the privilege, but were not constitutionally required themselves. He argued that either *Miranda* was not constitutionally based and as such was illegitimate and should be overruled, or the many cases that had carved out exceptions to *Miranda* were unsupportable and should be rejected—but it simply was not logically possible to accept both. Nevertheless, that is what the Court did.

MIRANDA AS A GREAT CASE

When the Court set oral argument in the four cases to be decided as *Miranda v. Arizona*, it clearly understood that it was embarking on a path that would embroil it in the center of a national controversy. It simply had to understand that the prospect of releasing a confessed murderer because the officer had failed to deliver the requisite warnings in a timely manner would excite extreme anger on the part of the general public and law enforcement and might well lead to a backlash against the Court, as in fact it did. Indeed, law enforcement officials and politicians were already quite upset by *Escobedo* even before *Miranda* was argued and decided. There is little indication that the potential controversial nature of the decision mattered to the justices in the majority. Two years earlier, the Court had issued the even more radical decision in *Reynolds v. Simms* and the Reapportionment Cases without significant resistance, at least with respect to enforcement. However the Court was still embroiled in defiance of *Brown v. Board of Education* and there was a serious backlash against the Court's school prayer decisions a few years prior to *Miranda*. There is every indication that at the very least Warren, Black, and Douglas were prepared to do what they considered to be right constitutionally regardless of the consequences to the Court itself. None of the three appeared to care much if at all whether they produced a legally defensible explanation for their decision.[67] Black was driven by his textually derived absolutes. Brennan was the superb doctrinalist of the Warren Court and almost certainly would have been capable of producing a much tighter opinion; however he did not seem to play a significant role in crafting the opinion. Rather as Justice Fortas noted the opinion was all Warren's doing.[68]

Arguably many of the Warren Court's criminal procedure decisions, especially *Miranda*, were driven by concern about the mistreatment of black suspects by the police, especially in the South, as well as the extent to which the poor were at a significant disadvantage in the criminal process. By the time of *Miranda*, the Warren Court had issued many decisions that significantly altered constitutional criminal procedure. Some such as *Gideon*

---

[66] *Id.* at 443.
[67] POWE, *supra* note 1, at 303–04.
[68] SCHWARTZ, DECISION 108 (1996).

v. Wainwright extending the right to counsel to indigents in all felony cases were well received. Others such as *Mapp v. Ohio* excluding evidence in state proceedings that was seized or discovered in violation of the Fourth Amendment were the subject of harsh criticism. Still, the Court had weathered the storm. Arguably it looked at *Miranda* and confessions as simply more ground to be conquered. As with most great cases, *Miranda* was decided by a confident majority though a sharply divided Court. It is likely that the *Miranda* majority was all but certain that its decision was intuitively and constitutionally correct, and that over time it would be publicly accepted. Internal accounts suggest that the *Miranda* decision was driven by Chief Justice Warren. He entered the oral arguments and the conference with a clear idea of what needed to be done, and four other justices fell into line. Warren's sense of confidence in his own moral instincts made *Miranda* a relatively easy case for him and the majority despite the trenchant critique by Justice Harlan in dissent. The fact that Warren was a former prosecutor and state attorney general may have carried some weight on the Court. *Miranda* is an example of an instance in which the Court did not simply accept the responsibility of a great case but instead welcomed it as an opportunity, much as Marshall had done with *McCulloch v. Maryland*.

One view of *Miranda*'s seeming lack of concern with the controversy and backlash that the decision was likely to provoke is that the majority was simply overconfident if not arrogant. Although the Court had severe critics to be certain, it also had some passionate admirers in both academia and the press who rather persistently challenged it to slay even more dragons. Perhaps the justices believed that the majority's agenda would prevail as long as the best, the brightest, and the most articulate stood with it. Fred Graham labeled the Court's approach in *Miranda* as an act of "benevolent authoritarianism."[69]

Alternatively, perhaps the justices simply did not care whether there was a political backlash against the Court's decision. Certainly some of them probably believed that it was the Court's responsibility to interpret the Constitution as it believed that it should be interpreted and let the chips fall where they may. Traditionally, there has been a widespread belief that the justices are concerned with the Court's "moral capital" and tend to behave in a cautious and strategic manner when it appears to be threatened. For the most part, that would not seem to capture the spirit of the justices in the *Miranda* majority. The Court did resist the temptation of going even further by either banning all custodial interrogation or requiring the presence of an attorney, which would have inevitably led to that result.

The failure of the *Miranda* majority to trim its sails and decide the cases in a more fact-oriented manner, developing its standards incrementally over time as opposed to announcing them all at once, opened the Court to the quite plausible charge that it was legislating from the bench. This played into the hands of the Court's critics who could not only simply object to the result but could charge that the Court had not arrived at it in a judicially appropriate manner either. *Miranda* more than any other decision made the Court itself a political issue. Perhaps the Court did not see that coming. Perhaps it would not have made any difference to the decision or opinion if it had. Still, as the title of one book on the Warren Court's criminal procedure decisions suggested, employing a famous phrase of Chief Justice Hughes, it was a "self-inflicted wound."[70] With or without

---

[69] GRAHAM, *supra* note 36, at 157.
[70] *Id.*

Miranda, Richard Nixon probably would have won the presidential election of 1968. Moreover, given the health of the justices and the ethical issues pertaining to Justice Fortas, Nixon almost certainly would have had the opportunity to appoint four justices in a relatively short period of time. And there is no reason to believe that he would not have used that opportunity to appoint justices dedicated to changing the direction that the Court had taken under Chief Justice Warren in most areas. Although *Miranda* was certainly exploited by the Court's critics in the political process, it is far from clear that it had a significant impact on the future of the Court.

From a purely legal standpoint, the Court's decision to largely replace the traditional totality of the circumstances voluntariness analysis with the bright-line approach of the warnings could be defended as at least an attempt to make it easier for both police officers to act with some confidence and for courts to resolve questions regarding the admissibility of confessions in a more predictable manner. By definition, a totality of the circumstances approach is uncertain and manipulable, whereas if the warnings were properly delivered and a waiver was obtained, the confession would be admissible. As this was an issue that would arise repeatedly and often in a context where informed legal judgment might be absent, there was much to be said for an easy-to-apply bright-line approach. In that regard, the Court could believe that to some extent it was doing the police a favor, making their job easier rather than harder. The fact that post-*Miranda* empirical surveys indicated that the delivery of the warnings do not tend to impede the ability of the police to obtain confessions nearly as much as the critics of *Miranda* had assumed may confirm that on the whole, the police are better off with *Miranda* than without it.[71] Some confessions that might otherwise be obtained doubtlessly have been lost however. And the Court at the time could not necessarily anticipate that the warnings would not hamper the police as much as they claimed. At least some of the reason *Miranda* has not had as severe an impact on law enforcement as predicted is probably due to the degree to which the Court narrowed and qualified it in subsequent cases, an approach that the *Miranda* majority itself almost certainly would not have endorsed. However it appears that the warnings have largely failed to limit the ability of the police to obtain confessions considering that the police often minimize their significance through a monotone delivery, suspects frequently feel a psychological need to talk. and many suspects either do not understand or misunderstand the substance of the warnings.[72]

Beyond judicial efficiency however, the Court may well have concluded that a bright-line rule was essential to prevent the police from lying about the nature of interrogation in order to prevail under the voluntariness approach. If the question of what occurred during the course of custodial interrogation turned into a swearing match between the police and the suspect, the police had a decided advantage before most judges and juries. Of course the warnings would not provide a complete cure-all. Justice Harlan noted in his *Miranda* dissent that if in fact the police would lie about the nature of the interrogation itself, they would just as readily lie about the delivery of the warnings or circumstances of waiver. Still the majority may have considered this a step in the right direction.

---

[71] GERALD N. ROSENBERG, THE HOLLOW HOPE: CAN COURTS BRING ABOUT SOCIAL CHANGE? 324–29 (1991) (discussing several empirical studies that indicate *Miranda* had little if any impact on the ability of police to obtain confessions). *See also* BAKER, *supra* note 2, at 178–82 (accord).

[72] *Id.*

Whether or not *Miranda* was a great case that made good or bad law, it was certainly a great case that made a lot of law. One of the most defensible criticisms of the *Miranda* decision is that the extent to which it laid down a series of prospective rules extending well beyond the necessities of the four cases before that Court was profoundly non-judicial in nature. Indeed, the four cases seemed to be a mere sideshow in *Miranda*, simply an excuse for judicial rule-making but scarcely relevant to the opinion itself. Miranda is almost certainly the most extreme instance in the Court's history of "legislating from the bench." There is nothing quite like it before or since. As such, if *Miranda* did not make bad law, it did provide a sterling example of how courts ought not to proceed. The prospective rule-oriented nature of the opinion was certainly inconsistent with the common law decision-making process that the Court follows even in constitutional cases. The majority obviously understood this and simply did not care despite the fact that the Court was opening itself to significant professional criticism even from many of its staunchest supporters. It would have created greater uncertainty and probably would have led to more reversed convictions had the Court chosen to develop the *Miranda* warnings and all of the subsidiary rules on a case-by-case basis. So the value of judicial efficiency as well as predictability can be cited in defense of the Court's approach. But it certainly would have appeared more judicial in nature had the Court followed that method.

Did *Miranda* make good law? Over 50 years after the decision was handed down, that question is still open for debate. As the Court recognized in *Dickerson, Miranda* did make enduring law. The *Miranda* warnings are solidly entrenched in our legal culture and are unlikely to disappear. Chief Justice Warren believed that the warnings were an embodiment of basic fairness. They are perhaps more defensible as an element of due process than of the Privilege against Self-Incrimination. Warren may not have been able to make a persuasive case that the warnings were essential to protect the privilege. As with *Reynolds v. Simms*, Harlan had the stronger argument from a purely legal standpoint. However it is probable that a large segment of the population would conclude that we are better off with the warnings than without them. To some extent this may be influenced by the fact that the cost to law enforcement and society has not been anywhere nearly as severe as the dissenters and critics had predicted. If it had been, it is unlikely that the warnings would have survived.

The key to the endurance of *Miranda* may well be that law enforcement was able to adjust to the warnings quite readily. Arguably, the warnings provide far too little protection to the suspect. The police may rattle off the warnings in a monotone and then go about their business of serious and effective interrogation. The ability of the suspect to waive the warnings without having first spoken to an attorney has also been identified as a weak point from the suspect's perspective. If police custody by its very nature is equivalent to compulsion, the foundation on which *Miranda* was constructed, then how can a waiver be voluntary? But if a suspect cannot waive the right to silence without first speaking with an attorney, then custodial interrogation essentially vanishes. As such *Miranda* is best understood as an uneasy compromise with the realities of effective law enforcement. Something was needed to provide a degree of protection to the suspect (the warnings) but not something that would effectively end custodial interrogation (the presence of counsel). *Miranda* is definitely the type of case that can only be evaluated in the long run. Shortly after the case was decided, and perhaps for more than a decade afterward, a substantial segment of the Court's commentators would have suggested that the Court made a major mistake by attempting to go too far, too fast without sufficient legal support. As such, *Miranda* was a mistake. But taking the long view, *Miranda* weathered the storm and has endured but with the crucial qualification that it has endured as cut back over and over again by subsequent cases. The Warren Court, careless and oblivious as it may have been, won its bet with the future but quite possibly only because the Burger and Rehnquist Courts reduced Miranda to a *decision* with which law enforcement and society at large could live.

Miranda is evidence that the Court can if it chooses create a great case where one might not otherwise exist and proceed boldly to alter existing law. Although the Court may ultimately carry the day, the institutional costs may not be insignificant.

"[T]his was no ordinary 'civil action' or 'litigation.' It was an extravaganza, a mixture of law, politics and journalism that had always been bound for the Supreme Court."[1]

FLOYD ABRAMS, COUNSEL FOR THE *NEW YORK TIMES* IN THE PENTAGON PAPERS CASE

17

The Pentagon Papers Case

New York Times v. United States, the Pentagon Papers Case, is the very paradigm of the great case. The *New York Times* and *Washington Post* received unauthorized copies of the Defense Department's classified internal history of the escalation of the Vietnam War. The newspapers decided to publish the documents. The government rushed into federal district courts requesting that the publication be enjoined. It was successful in one case but not in the other. The Supreme Court heard and decided the case on an extremely expedited basis. The case pitted two of the most prominent newspapers in the country against the United States' government. It involved a controversy of great public and political interest. It was argued by two of the most prominent legal authorities in the nation and proceeded with unprecedented speed. It raised a crucial and largely undecided issue of First Amendment law—the legitimacy of injunctive prior restraint against the press. It resulted in a fractured opinion with little precedential value. It turned out to be a crucial event in the progression toward the Watergate burglary and the eventual resignation of President Nixon.

BACKGROUND

The controversy at the heart of the Pentagon Papers Case began when Daniel Ellsberg, a Rand Corporation defense analyst who had become disenchanted with the United States' war effort in Vietnam, made illicit copies of the Pentagon Papers and leaked them to the *New York Times* and *Washington Post*. Two separate sets of documents were involved. The first was a 47-volume "History of United States Decision Making Process on Vietnam

---

[1] Floyd Abrams, Speaking Freely:Trials of the First Amendment 36 (2005). The Pentagon Papers is the subject of two very useful books: David Rudenstine, The Day the Presses Stopped: A History of the Pentagon Papers Case (1996), and Sanford J. Ungar, The Papers & the Papers: An Account of the Legal and Political Battle Over the Pentagon Papers (1975).

Policy" prepared by historians for the Department of Defense, covering the time period 1946–1968. The second was a single volume entitled "Command and Control Study of the Gulf of Tonkin Incident." The Pentagon Papers contained a documentary history of the war from the perspective of the Department of Defense accompanied by interpretive essays. They did not contain documents or materials from the White House. It had been commissioned by Secretary of Defense McNamara presumably for purposes of preserving a relatively complete record of the decision-making process. Only 15 copies of the study were made, and very few people were aware of its existence. The *Times* published summaries and excerpts from these studies on June 12, 13, and 14, 1971. Ellsberg had initially been a strong proponent of United States' policy in Vietnam but over time had become a vigorous and passionate critic of the war and apparently hoped that publication of the "Pentagon Papers" would help turn the tide of public opinion even further against the war.[2]

Anticipating litigation, the *Times* hired renowned constitutional law expert and Yale Law professor Alexander Bickel to represent it after the paper's long-standing counsel claimed a conflict of interest. Both the *Times* and the *Washington Post*, which also published excerpts from the Papers, thought long and hard before deciding to publish, fearing that they could very well be exposing themselves to potential criminal liability under the Espionage Act. Outside counsel for both newspapers attempted to dissuade the newspapers from going forward. Initially President Nixon, who first learned of the existence of the Pentagon Papers when the *New York Times* began publication, seemed unconcerned about the publication.[3] The Pentagon Papers dealt only with decisions made by prior administrations and contained no discussion of the efforts of the Nixon administration. Within a day however, National Security Advisor Henry Kissinger convinced Nixon that it was crucial that he oppose further publication.[4]

The matter was referred to the Department of Justice, which recommended filing suit in federal district court for the Southern District of New York seeking to have further publication enjoined and to have some of the documents in the possession of the newspaper returned to the government. Initially Judge Gurfein, sitting in his very first case as a judge, granted the government's request for a temporary restraining order against further publication until the matter could be properly adjudicated. Gurfein considered arguments from the parties and heard testimony from government officials in camera. The government declined to produce specific references to the Pentagon Papers that would result in harm to national security, arguing instead that an injunction was warranted if it established that the material was properly classified. On June 19, 1971, Judge Gurfein dissolved the temporary restraining order and denied the government's motion for a preliminary injunction, concluding that it had failed to prove that further publication would result in a serious breach of national security.[5] He did find that the government was acting out of a good faith concern for protecting national security and not out of a desire to suppress criticism or the disclosure of embarrassing information. Likewise, he found that the *Times* was acting in a good faith effort to serve the public right to know.

---

[2] Rudenstine, *supra* note 1, at 33–47.
[3] *Id.* at 66–67.
[4] *Id.* at 72–74.
[5] United States v. New York Times, 328 F. Supp. 324 (S.D.N.Y 1971).

The government appealed immediately to the Court of Appeals for the Second Circuit, which heard argument en banc on June 22, 1971. Over the objections of the *Times*, the government submitted an appendix with specific citations to items in the Pentagon Papers that it maintained threatened national security interests if disclosed.[6] Some of the judges on the Court of Appeals, especially Judge Friendly, were very unreceptive to Bickel's arguments for the *Times*. In a 5-3 decision, the court remanded to the district court the following day with directions to consider whether the publication of the specific documents cited by the government might cause "grave and immediate danger to the security of the United States."[7] The court entered a stay prohibiting the *Times* from publishing any of the items specifically identified by the government as presenting a threat to the national security.

At the same time, the government sued the *Washington Post* in federal district court in the District of Columbia seeking the same relief as it was seeking against the *New York Times*. Judge Gesell also found that the government had failed to prove that publication would cause irreparable harm to national security. The government prevailed upon Solicitor General Erwin Griswold, who had not been involved in the case up to that point, to argue the appeal. The D.C. Circuit, sitting en banc, affirmed the district court.[8] Two days later, the court denied a motion by the government for a rehearing in view of the intervening decision by the Second Circuit but reaffirmed its earlier decision.[9] Judges MacKinnon and Wilkey dissented, arguing that the case should be remanded to the district court for more particularized findings of fact.

Several other newspapers received copies of at least some of the material in the Pentagon Papers. The Department of Justice obtained injunctions prohibiting further publication against both the *Boston Globe* and the *St. Louis Post Dispatch* whereas other newspapers remained free to publish the material.

ORAL ARGUMENT

The Supreme Court granted a writ of certiorari in both cases two days after the Second Circuit decision and a day after the denial of the rehearing in the District of Columbia Circuit. Quite incredibly, oral argument before the Court was held the following day, June 26, 1971. Because the material in question was classified as top secret, the parties filed both open and closed briefs. The closed briefs discussed specific items in the Pentagon Papers that allegedly threatened national security. The Court denied the government's motion to conduct part of the oral argument in camera.[10] Solicitor general and former dean of the Harvard Law School Erwin Griswold represented the United States. Professor Bickel argued on behalf of the *New York Times*. William Glendon represented the *Washington Post*.

---

[6] RUDENSTINE, *supra* note 1, at 220.
[7] United States v. New York Times, 444 F.2d 544 (2d Cir. 1971).
[8] United States v. Washington Post Co., 446 F.2d 1327 (D.C. Cir. 1971).
[9] *Id.* at 1331.
[10] RUDENSTINE, *supra* note 1, at 283–84.

Solicitor General Griswold, seeking a remand for further proceedings in the district courts, emphasized the extreme haste with which the case had proceeded. He noted that the briefs for the newspapers had been served on him 15 minutes prior to the commencement of the oral argument, and he had not had an opportunity to look at them.[11] He indicated that he had spent the entire day before conferring with officials of the State and Defense Departments and the National Security Agency in an attempt to learn what the most damaging revelations in the Pentagon Papers were and then prepared the closed brief that evening. Griswold declared that the government's position was that the documents in question should not be published because they posed a "grave and immediate danger to the Security of the United States." Justice Stewart responded that as counsel for the newspapers appeared to accept that standard, the case boiled down to a factual question as to whether the government had shown, primarily through the 10 examples cited in its closed brief, that such a threat existed. The justices pressed the solicitor general as to how such a grave and immediate threat might occur. He could not say that publication of the documents would result in the death of troops; however he did urge that it could interfere with the negotiation of a peace agreement in Vietnam or with the negotiation of the Strategic Arms Limitation Treaty.[12]

Griswold conceded that his argument did not rest on the fact that the documents were top secret or that they had been obtained without permission from the government; however these factors provided a relevant context.[13] Rather, the crux of the government's position was that publication would cause grave and immediate harm. In his rebuttal, the solicitor general directly challenged Justice Black's absolutist reading of the First Amendment, stating that:

You say that "no law" means "no law" and that should be obvious.

And I can only say, Mr. Justice, that to me, it is equally obvious that "no law" does not mean "no law."[14]

Professor Bickel, on behalf of the *Times*, pressed the argument that the government had simply failed to prove that the nation would suffer grave and immediate damage if the material was published. He conceded that a prior restraint of the press might be warranted if it could be shown that a substantial number of American soldiers would die as a direct and immediate result of the publication, but the government had made no such showing in this case. He also emphasized that it was important that Congress had not authorized the executive branch to seek an injunction under these circumstance.[15] Bickel had placed far greater emphasis on this separation-of-powers argument than on the First Amendment prior restraint challenge throughout the litigation although he seemed to recognize that the Supreme Court was far more interested in the latter. Justice Stewart posed a hypothetical to Bickel under which publication would definitely result in the death of 100 troops. Bickel conceded that under those extreme circumstances "my inclinations of humanity overcome the somewhat more abstract devotion to the First

---

[11] 71 Landmark Briefs and Arguments of the Supreme Court of the United States: Constitutional Law 217 (Philip B. Kurland & Gerhard Casper eds., 1975).

[12] *Id.* at 228–30.

[13] *Id.* at 227.

[14] *Id.* at 257.

[15] *Id.* at 232–33.

Amendment. . . ."[16] Despite the wisdom of Bickel's concession as an advocate attempting to win a case, the ACLU filed a post-argument brief disavowing it.[17]

William Glendon representing the *Washington Post* argued that the government's burden was extremely high and it had clearly failed to meet it.

THE OPINIONS OF THE JUSTICES

The justices retired to study the record and then met in conference. Justice Douglas's notes from the conference indicate that the views expressed by the justices during the conference were substantially similar to those taken in their individual opinions.[18] Five justices were prepared to hold for the newspapers, three for the government, and Stewart who later went with the majority was undecided. The Court issued its opinions four days later on June 30, 1971. The opinion of the Court was a two-paragraph per curium that simply stated that the burden for establishing a prior restraint[19] was heavy, the government had failed to meet the burden, and the decision of the Second Circuit was reversed and the D.C. Circuit affirmed. All nine of the justices issued separate opinions.

JUSTICE BLACK

Justice Black, the senior justice on the Court and a self-proclaimed First Amendment absolutist, in an opinion joined by Justice Douglas, took the most uncompromising approach. He began his opinion by proclaiming that he believed that the decision of the Second Circuit should have been reversed without oral argument and "that every moment's continuance of the injunctions. . . amounts to a flagrant, indefensible, and continuing violation of the First Amendment."[20] Black maintained that the language, original understanding, and purpose of the First Amendment was to prohibit the government from interfering with the ability of the press to inform the people. He scolded Solicitor General Griswold for arguing that there was a national security exception to this principle. The tone of Justice Black's opinion was both strident and angry and critical of the Vietnam War. This was the last opinion that Black wrote as he would retire as a result of ill health prior to the commencement of the next term.

JUSTICE DOUGLAS

Justice Douglas agreed with Justice Black that there is "no room for government restraint on the press."[21] He devoted most of his opinion to reaffirming Judge Gurfein's analysis

---

[16] *Id.* at 240.

[17] Abrams, *supra* note 1, at 43.

[18] The Supreme Court in Conference (1940–1985): The Private Discussions Behind Nearly 300 Supreme Court Decisions 369–72 (Del Dickinson ed., 2001).

[19] 403 U.S. 713, 723–24 (1971).

[20] *Id.* at 715.

[21] *Id.* at 720.

that the only statute that the government cited in support of its actions was concerned with espionage (providing a specific type of classified information to the nation's enemies) and not with publication by the press. Both the language and legislative history of the provision supported this reading. He then closed his opinion with a firm rejection of the government's argument that it possessed "inherent power" to prohibit publication in defense of national security. He proclaimed that "[s]ecrecy in government is fundamentally anti-democratic, perpetuating bureaucratic errors."[22]

JUSTICE BRENNAN

Justice Brennan wrote a short concurrence only slightly less demanding than the approach of Justice Black. He noted that though it was understandable that the lower courts issued temporary injunctions against publication in order to preserve the status quo during the course of the litigation, such relief nevertheless violated the First Amendment in view of the government's failure to establish an imminent threat. Citing dicta from the 1931 decision in *Near v. Minnesota*, the most relevant decision on prior restraint of the press, Justice Brennan conceded that an injunction might be warranted if the government established that publication would "inevitably, directly, and immediately cause the occurrence of an event kindred to imperiling the safety of a transport already at sea...."[23] Brennan acknowledged that perhaps there was more room for such a prior restraint in peacetime in the nuclear age. Still his "inevitably, directly and immediately" standard would appear to be more stringent than the "grave and immediate" standard derived from *Near*. As a practical matter, prior restraint under the Brennan standard would be almost as impossible to obtain as it would be under Justice Black's absolute prohibition.

JUSTICE STEWART

In an opinion joined by Justice White, Justice Stewart offered perhaps the most nuanced approach set forth by any of the justices. Most of his opinion consisted of advice to the executive branch. He acknowledged that secrecy was essential to national security and foreign relations. However, he maintained that only the executive, perhaps with some assistance from Congress, could maintain such secrecy. In order to do so, the executive must be quite circumspect with respect to its decisions to classify. He explained that "when everything is classified, then nothing is classified, and the system becomes one to be disregarded by the cynical or the careless, and to be manipulated by those intent on self-protection or self-promotion."[24] By engaging in "maximum possible disclosure," the executive will bolster its own credibility.[25] Given the extent of executive power in this area, a vigorous and unrestrained press was essential to ensure an informed public. As such, the courts could rarely aid the executive in maintaining secrecy once the press

---

[22] *Id.* at 724.

[23] *Id.* at 726-27.

[24] *Id.* at 729.

[25] *Id.*

obtained information. Although Justice Stewart believed that the executive was correct in arguing that the nation would suffer harm if at least some of the material was published, it was not the "direct, immediate and irreparable" harm necessary to support prior restraint by injunction. Justice Stewart's opinion was brief but contained a considerable amount of wisdom.

JUSTICE WHITE

Justice White, joined by Justice Stewart, submitted an opinion emphasizing that although it was extraordinarily difficult for the government to obtain a prior restraint against publication, subsequent criminal punishment for violation of an applicable statute remained an option. Justice White began his opinion by conceding that he believed that publication of the documents in question "will do substantial damage to public interests."[26] However the United States had not satisfied the heavy burden necessary to obtain a prior restraint. White also questioned the propriety of the "grave and irreparable damage" standard relied upon by the government. He maintained that the standard was too nebulous to provide any guidance. He feared that in a case such as the Pentagon Papers in which the relevant documents were sealed, lower courts, the press, the executive branch, and the public would be unable to determine what showing was necessary to justify a prior restraint. White then spent several pages reviewing possibly relevant criminal statutes. He explicitly disagreed with Judge Gurfein's conclusion that the government must prove intent to injure the United States under section 793 of the criminal code. Justice White clearly meant to fire a warning shot across the bow of potential leakers as well as news organizations, and perhaps even to encourage the executive branch to institute criminal prosecutions in this case (which in fact it did).

JUSTICE MARSHALL

Unlike the other justices, Justice Marshall largely ignored the First Amendment issue, and taking a cue from the arguments of Professor Bickel focused instead on separation of powers. As he put it, "the ultimate issue" is "whether this Court or the Congress has the power to make law."[27] Building on *Youngstown Sheet & Tube v. Sawyer*, Marshall argued that given that Congress had declined to give the executive branch the power to seek an injunction under the facts of this case "[i]t is not for this Court to fling itself into every breach perceived by some Government official. . . ."[28]

---

[26] *Id.* at 731.
[27] *Id.* at 741.
[28] *Id.* at 747.

CHIEF JUSTICE BURGER

Chief Justice Burger dissented, criticizing the *New York Times* quite harshly for creating the pressurized context in which the case was inevitably litigated. He maintained that there was little difference among the justices regarding the standards for reviewing a prior restraint. Picking up an argument made by the solicitor general, he declared that the "imperative [of] the effective functioning of a complex modern government" must also be taken into account.[29] Because of the haste with which the litigation had proceeded, the chief justice proclaimed "[w]e do not know the facts" of this case.[30] He pointed out that time and again during oral argument counsel were unable to answer questions about the state of the record because of the pace of the litigation. Burger placed the blame for the unwarranted haste with which the case was decided squarely on the shoulders of the *New York Times*. He noted that the *Times* had spent three months analyzing the documents and preparing its stories, but now the public's right to know "must be vindicated instanter."[31] Moreover, he declared that the duty to return stolen property to its rightful owners "rests on taxi drivers, Justices and the New York Times."[32] In reference to the paper's reason for refusing to show the government the documents in question, he found it especially ironic that the "Times…asserts a right to guard the secrecy of its sources while denying that the Government of the United States has that power."[33] There was no mistaking the frustration and anger that the chief justice felt at both the way in which the litigation had unfolded as well as the underlying conduct of the *Times*.

JUSTICE HARLAN

Justice Harlan added a dissent joined by Chief Justice Burger and Justice Blackmun. Harlan began his dissent by quoting Justice Holmes famous dictum "Great Cases, like hard cases make bad law…" from the *Northern Securities* dissent. He complained about the fact that the Court had been "almost irresponsibly feverish" in its handling of the case, describing the unusual pace of the litigation in some detail.[34] Turning to the merits, Harlan asserted that the speed of the litigation had precluded the Court from considering most of the crucial issues raised, including the government's authority to bring suit, the scope of the prior restraint doctrine in this context, the question whether the harm caused by the very breach of security would justify injunctive relief, the question whether the disclosure would imperil national security, the degree of deference that should be accorded the executive branch, and the question whether the newspapers should be required to return the documents.

Justice Harlan's primary disagreement with the Court however was with the appropriate scope of review. He argued that in matters of foreign policy and national security,

---

[29] *Id.* at 748.
[30] *Id.*
[31] *Id.* at 750.
[32] *Id.* at 751.
[33] *Id.* at 751 n.2.
[34] *Id.* at 753.

the Court lacked the "'aptitude, facilities and responsibility'" to second-guess the executive branch.[35] Consequently, "the scope of review must be exceedingly narrow." He would require the courts to review the material to ensure that the subject matter does in fact lie within the proper scope of the foreign relations power. In addition, he would insist that the head of the relevant executive department, whether the secretary of state or defense, verify after examining the documents in question that their disclosure would indeed "irreparably impair the national security."[36] That would be the extent of the judicial role.

JUSTICE BLACKMUN

Like Justice Harlan whose opinion he joined, Justice Blackmun also began his dissent with the "great cases" quotation from Holmes. He also criticized the frantic pace with which the case had been litigated, concluding that due to the time pressure, the briefs, the oral arguments, and the judicial opinions had been inadequate. He would have remanded for further litigation "free of pressure and panic and sensationalism."[37] Blackmun closed his opinion with the somber warning that like Judge Wilkey he had reason to believe based on his review of the few documents in the record that publication could well result in the "'death of soldiers [and] the destruction of alliances'" as well as "prolongation of the war and of further delay in the freeing of United States prisoners."[38]

AFTERMATH

Following the decision, both papers and several others as well continued to publish excerpts from the Pentagon Papers. Bantam Publishing came out with a best-selling abbreviated version of the Pentagon Papers. The items that the government was most concerned about were not published. Neither newspaper had the four-volume Diplomatic History of the War that was almost certainly the most sensitive, so it was not published. The consensus is that the publication of the Pentagon Papers did not cause serious damage to the nation. Even Solicitor General Griswold so concluded.[39] Considering President Nixon's legendary hatred of the press as well as the subsequent events culminating in Watergate, many believe that the attempt to enjoin the publication of the Pentagon Papers was nothing more than an attempt by the Nixon administration using national security as a pretext to strike out at and to intimidate the press. In a careful study, David Rudenstine has argued that the case did begin with legitimate national security concerns, and the attorneys and experts who participated in the litigation did believe that there was a legitimate national security threat.[40] Much of this concern was driven by a fear that a leak of this proportion would necessarily undermine trust in the nation by foreign

---

[35] *Id.* at 758 quoting Justice Jackson concurring in Chicago & Southern Air Lines, Inc. v. Waterman Steamship Corp., 333 U.S. 103, 111 (1948).

[36] 403 U.S. at 757.

[37] *Id.* at 762.

[38] *Id.* at 762–63.

[39] Erwin Griswold, *No Harm Was Done*, N.Y. TIMES, June 30, 1991, § 4 at 15.

[40] RUDENSTINE, *supra* note 1, at 8–11.

actors as opposed to a concern that specific revelations in the Pentagon Papers would inflict damage. That was an untenable position to pursue during the litigation however in that it would cut too deeply into the ability of the press to publish any leaked information pertaining to war or foreign relations. Rather, it was incumbent on the government to establish that specific items in the Pentagon Papers that might be disclosed could pose a grave and irreparable threat to national security. Initially, in the district courts, the government was simply not inclined to even attempt to offer such proof. When at the appellate and Supreme Court level it recognized that it would have to make a case based on specific material within the Pentagon Papers, it was unable to do so.

Once it was established that Daniel Ellsberg had leaked the Pentagon Papers, he was immediately indicted and arrested. Along with a colleague Anthony Russo he was ultimately charged with stealing, concealing, obtaining, retaining, and conveying classified documents. The indictments were dismissed however due to gross government misconduct after it was revealed that the administration had engaged in unauthorized wiretapping of Ellsburg.

The publication of the Pentagon Papers actually led to another Supreme Court decision as well. At the very time that the Pentagon Papers litigation was in progress, Ellsburg delivered a set of the papers to Senator Mike Gravel of Alaska. Senator Gravel, then an opponent of the continuation of the war, called a special session of the Subcommittee on Building and Grounds of which he was chairman, read from the Pentagon Papers, and inserted them into the official record.[41] He was the only senator in attendance at the meeting.[42] He also arranged to have the Pentagon Papers published by the Beacon Press of Boston. A grand jury investigating the leak called Leonard Rodberg, a legislative assistant of Gravel's as well as an officer of the M.I.T. Press to whom the Papers had been offered for publication.[43] Senator Gravel intervened with a motion to quash the subpoena on the ground that it violated the congressional Speech and Debate Privilege. The federal district and appellate courts granted partial relief.[44] The Supreme Court held that the Speech and Debate Privilege protected a congressional aide to the extent that the senator would have been protected while engaging in the same activity.[45] The privilege would not protect the private publication of the Pentagon Papers however. Consequently, the senator's aide could be questioned before the grand jury with respect to the arrangements for republication of the papers as well as with respect to how they were initially acquired by the senator. Four justices dissented in part.

THE PENTAGON PAPERS, NIXON, AND WATERGATE

Arguably, the most profound impact of the Pentagon Papers publication if not the Supreme Court decision itself was a series of events culminating in the Watergate break-in, another "great case" *United States v. Nixon*, and the resignation of the president. Despite the fact

---

[41] UNGAR, *supra* note 1, at 262.
[42] *Id.*
[43] Gravel v. United States, 408 U.S. 606, 608 (1972).
[44] *Id.* at 610–11.
[45] *Id.* at 622.

that the material published in the Pentagon Papers did not cover decision-making by the Nixon administration, President Nixon was extremely disturbed by the very fact of the leak.[46] He feared that similar leaks could severely damage existing arms control talks with the Soviet Union as well as the negotiations regarding the president's planned trip to China.[47] Moreover, Nixon had been informed that a copy of the Pentagon Papers had been leaked to the Soviet embassy even before it was leaked to the *Times*, although this has never been confirmed.[48] Nixon was especially troubled that a dedicated supporter of the Vietnam War such as Daniel Ellsburg could change his perspective so drastically.[49]

Consequently, the president made it clear to his top advisors that such national security leaks must be eliminated.[50] Several of the president's aides, including John Erlichman, Egil Krough, Herb Klein, and William Safire believe that Nixon's anger over the Pentagon Papers leak was the event that started the train of events culminating in Watergate.[51] To discover and plug the leaks, the "Plumbers Unit" was created within the White House.[52] It authorized its operatives to break into the office of Dr. Fielding, Ellsburg's psychiatrist, in search of information that could either explain his recent change of mind or be used to discredit his antiwar activities.[53] The break-in, supervised by G. Gordon Liddy and authorized by John Erlichman, one of the president's closest advisors, and possibly by the president, occurred and nothing of interest was discovered.[54]

The break-in to Ellsburg's psychiatrist office launched the White House down the path that culminated in the break-in of the Democratic National Committee headquarters at the Watergate seven months later. The Watergate break-in was also led by Liddy. When the Watergate break-in was foiled, Nixon and his advisors concluded that a cover-up was the only viable option. Arguably, Nixon and his advisors were as concerned with preventing disclosure of White House authorization of the Fielding break-in as that of the Watergate. Given the paranoia of the Nixon administration, it is certainly possible that had there been no break-ins to the offices of Ellsburg's psychiatrist or the Democratic headquarters some other executive misdeed would have led to its demise. But as it happened it was the president's severe overreaction to the Pentagon Papers leak, fomented by Kissinger, that set the fatal chain of events in motion. Nixon was distressed by the leak itself rather than the Supreme Court's decision to permit publication. There is little reason to believe that the White House would have moderated its response even if the Court had sustained the injunction. John Erlichman, Egil Krough, Charles Colson, and Gordon Liddy were convicted and sent to prison for their participation in the break-in to Dr. Fielding's office. The file cabinet that was damaged during the break-in is now prominently displayed in the Smithsonian Institute's National Museum of American History.

---

[46] Egil "Bud" Krough, Integrity: Good People, Bad Choices, and Life Lessons from the White House 43-51 (2007), Rudenstine, *supra* note 1, at 327, 345.

[47] Rudenstine, *supra* note 1, at 327.

[48] Krough, *supra* note 46, at 41.

[49] *Id.*

[50] Rudenstine, *supra* note 1, at 343–44.

[51] *Id.* at 344.

[52] See Krough, *supra* note 46, at 31-52, for an inside account of the creation of the Plumber's Unit and the subsequent break-in.

[53] *Id.* at 66.

[54] *Id.* at 74–75.

THE PENTAGON PAPERS AND THE LAW OF PRIOR RESTRAINT

The publication of the Pentagon Papers was an historic victory for freedom of the press. Archibald Cox has noted that the documents such as these could have been published in no other country in the world.[55] Given the justices' inability to produce an opinion for the Court with respect to prior restraint, the Pentagon Papers case did little to advance doctrinal clarity. The cost to the system from this failure was not significant however considering that it had already been recognized that prior restraint by injunction was highly disfavored, and attempts to obtain such injunctions were quite rare. It has long been accepted that an aversion to prior restraint, which had been a common device employed by the Crown under the English press licensing laws during the seventeenth century, was a primary reason for the existence of the speech and press clauses of the First Amendment.[56] In *Patterson v. Colorado*, the Court's very first freedom of speech case, Justice Holmes suggested in dicta that the primary purpose of the First Amendment was to prohibit prior restraint.[57] Shortly thereafter in *Schenck v. United States*, he conceded that the scope of the amendment extended beyond prior restraint to subsequent punishment as well.[58]

Prior to the Pentagon Papers Case, *Near v. Minnesota*[59] was the leading (and virtually the only) case on prior restraint by injunction although the statute in issue was quite peculiar. Near was the publisher of a newspaper that charged that gangsters engaged in extensive criminal activities in Minneapolis and that the chief of police and mayor declined to enforce the laws against them. As a result of a suit brought by the local district attorney, Near was enjoined from further publication under a statute that permitted such an injunction against a "malicious, scandalous or defamatory newspaper." The Supreme Court reversed. Quoting Blackstone and Madison, it emphasized that prohibition of prior restraint was a primary purpose of the First Amendment. The Court did explain however that the prohibition against prior restraint was not absolute. It declared that it would be permissible in a wartime situation to prohibit the "publication of the sailing dates of transports or the number and location of troops."[60] It also indicated that prior restraint would be warranted against obscenity or incitement to violence.

One of the few prior restraint cases decided by the Court prior to the Pentagon Papers occurred only a month earlier when the Court reversed an injunction against distribution of pamphlets in *Organization for a Better Austin v. Keefe*.[61] There Justice Burger writing for the Court cited *Near* and declared that a community organization could not be enjoined from distributing leaflets protesting a relator's alleged "block-busting" tactics. The Court cited the decision in its per curiam opinion in the Pentagon Papers Case.

Nebraska Press v. Stuart[62] is the only significant prior restraint case decided by the Court since the Pentagon Papers Case. There, the Court unanimously disapproved of

---

[55] Archibald Cox, The Court and the Constitution 227 (1987).
[56] Leonard W. Levy, Emergence of a Free Press (1985).
[57] 205 U.S. 454, 462 (1907).
[58] 249 U.S. 47, 51 (1919).
[59] 283 U.S. 697 (1931).
[60] *Id.* at 716.
[61] 402 U.S. 415 (1971).
[62] 427 U.S. 539 (1976).

an injunction entered by a state court in a sensational murder case in a small town in Nebraska, which prohibed the press from publishing a confession and other incriminating evidence, most of which had been presented in open court, until a jury was empaneled. The Court declined to hear the case on an expedited basis and the injunction had expired long before the case reached the High Court. Writing for the majority, Chief Justice Burger emphasized the heavy presumption against prior restraints as recognized in the Pentagon Papers Case but proceeded to invalidate the injunction pursuant to the relatively lenient balancing test employed in *Dennis v. United States*. Justice Brennan, in an opinion joined by Justices Stewart and Marshall, concurred in the judgment but not the opinion of the Court. If Chief Justice Burger, a dissenter in the Pentagon Papers Case, minimized its significance in the *Nebraska Press* case, Justice Brennan seemed to read it for more than it was worth. He read the Pentagon Papers Case as erecting an "almost insuperable presumption against the constitutionality of prior restraints."[63] He argued that the Court had determined that the "military security" example of the Near "troop ship" caliber was the only exception to the per se rule against prior restraint, and even that "exception was to be construed very, very narrowly." Perhaps the presumption against prior restraint is that strong. But the Pentagon Papers Case did not nor could not so hold given that no such fact situation was before the Court. Despite the dicta in the various opinions, the Court simply concluded that the government had failed to meet its burden on the facts before the Court.

The case of the *United States v. The Progressive, Inc.* [64] litigated in federal district court in 1979 illustrated that the Pentagon Papers Case had not necessarily precluded the issuance of a prior restraint against the press in all circumstances. There, the district court did enjoin the *Progressive* from publishing an article explaining how a hydrogen bomb was created based primarily, though not exclusively, on public domain material. Recognizing that this would be the first such injunction issued against the press if sustained, the district court nevertheless concluded that the prior restraint was warranted considering that the material in the article could aid a medium-sized nation in developing a hydrogen bomb, which might in turn result in nuclear annihilation. As such, the Court concluded that the "grave, direct, immediate and irreparable harm" standard proposed by two justices in the Pentagon Papers Case was satisfied. The court explicitly distinguished the Pentagon Papers Case on the grounds that the threat to national security in this case was far more substantial, and that the government did have explicit statutory authority for the injunction pursuant to the Atomic Energy Act. The government abandoned defense of the injunction on appeal however after other media sources published the material in question.

In *Snepp v. United States*,[65] the Court upheld the imposition of a constructive trust on the profits from a book written by a former CIA agent without obtaining prepublication review from the government. *Snepp* was not a pure prior restraint case however given that the Court relied on the fact that Snepp had breached his agreement to submit the manuscript for review prior to publication.

---

[63] *Id.* at 594.
[64] 467 F. Supp. 990 (1979).
[65] 444 U.S. 507 (1980).

The Pentagon Papers case emphasized the stringency of the presumption against prior restraints but did little to clarify the appropriate doctrinal standard unless Justice Stewart's opinion is generally accepted as the lowest common denominator and hence controlling.

The Pentagon Papers case did not make very much law, considering the inability of the justices to build a coherent majority. It did re-enforce the principle that prior restraint against the press would rarely, if ever, be acceptable. If it is law, it is almost certainly good law.

THE PENTAGON PAPERS AS A GREAT CASE

Nixon's initial instinct was correct. The publication should have been ignored. The case should never have been brought. The presumption against prior restraint was sufficiently powerful to render a government victory unlikely. The government quickly discovered that there was little that it could point to in the Pentagon Papers capable of convincing the Court that an injunction was warranted. There was no chance that the argument that such a massive leak would inhibit future diplomacy could possibly succeed. The litigation itself focused attention on the government's inability to protect classified information, and a solid defeat in the Supreme Court would tend to encourage future leaks and publications of classified material. Even if the government chose to proceed initially, it would have been wise to concede after its defeat in the district courts. It is likely however that the government was encouraged by the harsh attitude that the Second Circuit took toward Professor Bickel and his arguments.

As both Justices Harlan and Blackmun maintained, the Pentagon Papers Case certainly seemed to fit the description of the "great case" offered by Holmes in which "the immediate interests exercise a kind of hydraulic pressure," presumably resulting in the creation of "bad law."[66] Rarely has the Court decided a case with more such hydraulic pressure at work. Indeed the time pressure that the Court essentially imposed upon itself was so intense that the Court's diverse opinions were likely to have limited precedential value. There certainly was a clear majority to the effect that there is an especially heavy presumption against prior restraint of the news by judicial injunction. That much was understood prior to the decision. However the application of the principle to classified material, the publication of which was at least alleged to endanger national security and significant foreign policy objectives, drove the point home with unique authority. After the decision, the strength of the presumption could scarcely be doubted.

The inability of the justices to produce a single opinion for the Court was almost certainly the result of the intense time pressure. There was not even an attempt to unify around an opinion for the Court. Five justices clearly believed that the government had failed to meet the heavy burden. They seemed to disagree as to the weight of the burden, with Justices Black and Douglas contending that the First Amendment banned prior restraint by injunction against the press per se, Justice Brennan suggesting that the government must show that publication would "inevitably, directly and immediately" result

---

[66] Northern Sec., Co. v. United States, 193 U.S. 197, 400–02 (1904) (Holmes, J., dissenting).

in harm equivalent to the sinking of a troop ship, and Justice Stewart and White requiring proof of "direct, immediate and irreparable damage." With more time it is possible if not probable that the justices could have coalesced around a single articulated standard. Even if Justice Black held out for an absolutist approach, it is likely that Justice Marshall, who only addressed the issue of governmental authority to seek an injunction, could have been persuaded to endorse a standard governing prior restraint. Thus additional time for interchange and dialogue among the justices would likely have resulted in a strong plurality if not majority opinion on the significant doctrinal issue. If so, that would have been an improvement. As it was however, the Court sent out a strong message that rarely if ever could a prior restraint against the press be justified. Doctrinally, Justice Stewart's concurrence seemed to provide the lowest common denominator among the justices with regard to an articulated standard.

There is no reason to believe that additional time would have changed the result in the case however. It appears fairly clear that the government was able to identify the most potentially harmful documents, and six justices simply did not believe that their publication would result in the type of serious harm required by the prior restraint doctrine. In that sense, the pressure and sensationalism was most likely irrelevant to the decision of the case as such.

Like several other great cases that were litigated with extreme haste, the Pentagon Papers Case certainly illustrates that it is difficult if not impossible for the Court to produce a coherent and persuasive majority opinion with little time for reflection or discussion. That is hardly surprising. Indeed it would be surprising if it could. It could be argued that even under normal circumstances, the Court does not have adequate time to do its job properly.[67]

The dissents blamed the newspapers for creating the "frenzied" pace by insisting that any delay whatsoever constituted an egregious violation of the First Amendment despite the fact that the material in question was of a historical nature and the *Times* had spent three months analyzing it prior to publication. It was not within the power of the newspapers however to set the judicial calendar. Clearly the Court could have slowed the litigation down had it so chosen. Justices Black, Douglas, and Brennan believed that any delay contributed to the constitutional violation. It is likely that on the record, Justices Stewart and White concluded that there were insufficient grounds for believing that a more deliberate pace would help the government prove its case. Justice Harlan in particular made a solid argument for proceeding in a more judicious manner but his opinion was also premised on a narrower scope of review than expounded by the justices in the majority. It is difficult to believe that significant harm to the public understanding or to the First Amendment would have resulted had the Court permitted slightly more extensive factual development in the lower courts, a more reasonable briefing and argument schedule, and more time to draft its opinions. The process and resulting opinions would arguably have been better served had the litigation taken a month rather than a week. As the case came to the Court at the very end of its term, any further delay would almost certainly have resulted in putting the case over three and one-half months to the beginning of the October 1971, which in fact four justices had favored initially.[68] For the majority however,

---

[67] *See* Henry Hart, *Foreword: The Time Chart of the Justices*, 73 Harv. L. Rev. 84 (1959).

[68] Rudenstine, *supra* note 1, at 263.

that was not an option. The warp speed pace with which the case was litigated seemed to suggest that the Court was being buffeted by forces beyond its control, which simply was not the case.

The decision-making process surely suffered from the time pressure under which the attorneys labored. Solicitor General Griswold had been brought into the case late and had little time to acquaint himself with the voluminous record. Because of the massive nature of the Pentagon Papers (over 7000 pages) and the secrecy surrounding much of the material, it was difficult for the attorneys to digest the record in the manner that would normally be expected from top-flight appellate lawyers. The government attorneys were unaware of exactly what materials the newspapers possessed. The newspapers' attorneys were unclear as to what items in the Pentagon Papers most troubled the government. So both sides were essentially fencing in the dark.

Despite his well-deserved reputation as a constitutional scholar, this was the first time that Professor Bickel had ever been involved in litigation. He seemed to struggle before both the Second Circuit and the Supreme Court, although given the nature of the case, perhaps a more experienced advocate would have had trouble as well. His extreme emphasis on separation of powers, which ultimately attracted only the vote of Justice Marshall, seems strange in a case that virtually everyone else considered to be governed by the First Amendment. Bickel did understand that it was crucial to win the vote of either Justice Stewart or Justice White in order to prevail and that neither would be sympathetic to an absolutist approach. It is likely however that the *Times* prevailed not because of the doctrinal position taken by Bickel but rather because the government simply failed to convince the Court that there was anything in the Pentagon Papers that would cause grave and immediate harm to national security. Had it been able to so, there is a substantial chance that the case would have gone the other way. Solicitor General Griswold was a very experienced Supreme Court advocate; however, he would be the first to concede that this was not one of his strongest performances. There was no way in which it could be considering the limited time he had to prepare. If the Supreme Court's decision and opinions in the Pentagon Papers can be faulted it is less because it was a great case than because it was a hasty case.

"Many constitutional decisions have had more immediate direct effects on American society than Roe v. Wade. None except the Dred Scott case has aroused as intense popular emotion. Few have raised more profound questions concerning the role of the Supreme Court of the United States in American government."

ARCHIBALD COX[1]

18

Roe and Casey

As Archibald Cox observed, with the exception of *Dred Scott*, no other case in the history of the Supreme Court has been as controversial as *Roe v. Wade*.[2] It has divided the nation for 40 years. Its supporters consider it a decision of the utmost significance. Its opponents view it as one of the most unprincipled and illegitimate decisions in the history of the Court. The struggle over the future of *Roe* has infected Supreme Court confirmation hearings as well as presidential elections. Several cases have been brought in an attempt to have it overruled or narrowed. Finally, in *Planned Parenthood of Pennsylvania v. Casey*,[3] the Court came very close to overruling *Roe* and reaffirmed it only in a significantly modified form.

Roe was a troubling case from the outset. The justices struggled with it after the initial oral argument and decided it only after hearing re-argument the following year. Any case in which a serious challenge to *Roe* is mounted becomes a media spectacle. *Roe*, at least as modified by *Casey*, may now be well entrenched in the Court's constitutional jurisprudence; however, the challenges continue and a cloud that it cast over the Court is likely to remain.

---

[1] ARCHIBALD COX, THE COURT AND THE CONSTITUTION 322 (1987). Several books have been written about *Roe v Wade*. The most comprehensive is DAVID J. GARROW, LIBERTY AND SEXUALITY: THE RIGHT TO PRIVACY AND THE MAKING OF ROE V. WADE (1994). Two other detailed narratives about the case and its antecedents are N. E. H. HULL & PETER CHARLES HOFFER, ROE V. WADE: THE ABORTION RIGHTS CONTROVERSY IN AMERICAN HISTORY (rev. ed. 2010) and MARIAN FAUX, ROE V. WADE: THE UNTOLD STORY OF THE LANDMARK SUPREME COURT DECISION THAT MADE ABORTION LEGAL (1988).

[2] 410 U.S. 113 (1973).

[3] 505 U. S. 833 (1992).

LEGAL BACKGROUND

The origin of the legal challenge to restrictive abortion laws can be traced at least as far back as three Supreme Court cases challenging a Connecticut law that made it a crime for married couples to use contraceptives for purposes of contraception and for physicians to prescribe contraceptives for them. The Court dismissed the first challenge in 1943 in *Tileston v. Ullman*[4] on the ground that the physician plaintiffs did not have standing to litigate the rights of their patients. Eighteen years later in *Poe v. Ullman*, the Court dismissed yet another challenge to the law.[5] In a plurality opinion, Justice Frankfurter affirmed dismissal of the challenge for lack of ripeness. Justice Harlan however wrote an extremely influential dissenting opinion arguing that the law violated the substantive component of the Due Process Clause of the Fourteenth Amendment.[6]

Finally, four years later in *Griswold v. Connecticut*,[7] the Court addressed the merits of the law and declared it unconstitutional. Justice Douglas wrote the opinion for the Court. In an attempt to avoid the taint of substantive due process, which had fallen out of judicial favor following the constitutional revolution of 1937, Douglas derived a right of privacy from the emanations and penumbras of several provisions of the Bill of Rights. Justice Goldberg, concurring, seconded the suggestion of Justice Douglas that the Ninth Amendment was relevant to the recognition of unenumerated constitutional rights. Justice Harlan wrote a concurring opinion incorporating by reference his dissent in *Poe v. Ullman*. Unlike Douglas, Harlan was prepared to rest his opinion squarely upon substantive due process liberty. He argued that substantive due process analysis remained legitimate despite the rejection of *Lochner v. New York*. Properly understood, due process required the Court to strike a balance between "respect for liberty of the individual" and "the demands of organized society."[8] The imposition of judicial value preferences, which so concerned Justice Holmes in his *Lochner* dissent, could be avoided according to Harlan as long as the Court relied upon history and tradition for objective guidance in defining protected aspects of liberty under the Due Process Clause. Justice Black, in a powerful dissent, would have none of it. He argued that the Court was indeed making the same mistake as in *Lochner* by preferring one specific aspect of liberty, in this case privacy.

All of the justices who joined the majority opinion in *Griswold* limited its holding to interference with sexual intimacy in the marital relationship. That limitation did not survive long however. In 1972 in another contraception case, *Eisenstadt v. Baird*,[9] the Court struck down a Massachusetts law that prohibited distribution of contraceptives to unmarried persons. Writing for a four-justice majority of the seven justices who heard the case, Justice Brennan proclaimed that the right of privacy attached to the individual and not simply the married couple.

---

[4] 318 U. S 44 (1943).
[5] 367 U.S. 497 (1961).
[6] *Id.* at 539–55.
[7] 381 U.S. 479 (1965).
[8] Poe v. Ullman, 367 U.S. 497, 542 (1961) (Harlan, J., concurring).
[9] 405 U.S. 438 (1972).

THE *ROE* LITIGATION

Roe v. Wade began when two recent graduates of the University of Texas Law School, Linda Coffee and Sarah Weddington, decided to challenge the constitutionality of the Texas abortion law that proscribed all abortions unless necessary to save the life of the mother.[10] After searching for a plaintiff for quite some time, the two attorneys filed suit on behalf of a married couple (the Does), who alleged that they feared that a pregnancy would be injurious to Mary Doe's health and desired to have the option of abortion in the event of pregnancy. They also filed suit on behalf of a single woman who had become pregnant named Norma McCorvey, who was identified during the litigation as Jane Roe. James Halford, a physician who had been indicted for performing abortions in order to provide proper care to his patients, intervened as a plaintiff.

The case was heard by a three-judge district court consisting of Fifth Circuit Judge Irving R. Goldberg and federal district Judges Sarah T. Hughes and William Taylor. The Court issued a short per curiam opinion invalidating the Texas abortion statute on grounds of over breadth and vagueness.[11] The court accepted the plaintiffs' argument that the constitutional right in issue was derived from the Ninth Amendment, quoting from Justice Goldberg's opinion in *Griswold*. It acknowledged that the state might well have a compelling interest in prohibiting abortions after "quickening"; however the statute was not narrowly tailored to serve that interest considering that it prohibited all abortions. As a criminal statute was involved, the court declined to grant an injunction against further enforcement, entering a declaratory judgment instead. The plaintiffs appealed to the Supreme Court from the denial of injunctive relief. District Attorney Henry Wade announced that he would continue to prosecute abortion cases in Dallas County though it had never been a high priority for his office. Jane Roe gave birth not long after the district court decision.

At the time that *Roe* was being litigated in Texas, a challenge was brought as well to the Georgia statute restricting abortions. Unlike the Texas statute, the Georgia statute was based on the recent proposals of the American Law Institute's Model Penal Code and was not nearly as harsh as the nineteenth-century Texas statute. *Doe* was also heard before a three-judge district court, which invalidated all of the provisions except one requiring that abortions be performed in a hospital and be approved by a panel of three doctors. The plaintiffs appealed to the Supreme Court from the district court's decision upholding that provision.

ROE IN THE SUPREME COURT

After the district court decision in *Roe*, the Supreme Court upheld the District of Columbia abortion statute against a vagueness challenge in *United States v. Vuitch*.[12] In his concurring and dissenting opinion, Justice Douglas noted that abortion law cases are among the "most inflammatory" to reach the Court.[13] By the time *Roe* and *Doe* were docketed

---

[10] FAUX, *supra* note 1, at 39–42.
[11] 314 F. Supp. 1217, 1225 (D.C. Tex. 1970).
[12] 402 U.S. 62 (1971).
[13] *Id.* at 79.

with the Court, several other challenges to state abortion laws had also made their way to the Court. Five federal courts had sustained state abortion laws while four had invalidated them.

Roe attracted considerable public attention, especially among supporters of abortion reform. Forty-two amicus briefs were filed in support of Jane Roe. Prior to the oral argument in *Roe*, Justices Harlan and Black retired leaving only seven justices on the Court. Nevertheless the case was argued on December 13, 1971. The arguments were not as illuminating as one might have hoped for in a case of this magnitude. Sarah Weddington spent much of her time detailing the problems presented by an unwanted pregnancy and very little on the constitutional basis of the right that she was claiming.[14] Under questioning from Justice White, she conceded that it was her position that the state had no legal right to protect the fetus at any point during the pregnancy.[15] Much of her argument was consumed by the Court's interest in the technical legal issue of why an injunction was appropriate in the case.[16]

Jay Floyd, arguing for the state, spent the first part of his argument attacking the plaintiff's standing to litigate and arguing that the case was moot because Jane Roe was no longer pregnant.[17] Justice Marshall pressed Floyd on the nature of the state interest behind the statute. Relying on a recent case decided by the Texas Court of Criminal Appeals, Floyd stated that the interest was the protection of fetal life.[18] He was forced to concede however that the original purpose of the statute enacted in 1859 was protection of the life and health of the mother.[19] Just as Weddington took the somewhat extreme position that Texas had no legitimate interest in protecting the life of the fetus at any point during the pregnancy, Floyd defended the other extreme, that Texas could choose to protect the fetus from the very moment of conception.[20] The argument in *Doe* focused primarily on the technicalities of the provision at issue.

At the conference on December 16, 1971, it appeared that there were five solid votes to affirm the district court (Douglas, Brennan, Stewart, Marshall, and Blackmun). Douglas and Brennan seemed to favor invalidation of the statute on the basis of vagueness.[21] Stewart, Marshall, and Blackmun indicated that the state should be able to protect fetal life at some point during the pregnancy.[22] Douglas quickly drafted an opinion that he circulated only to Justice Brennan. It would eventually become the basis of his concurring opinion in *Doe*. Chief Justice Burger assigned the case to Justice Blackmun as though he was in the majority even though he had seemed to indicate that he was prepared to uphold the statute.[23] Douglas was quite troubled by Burger's action and threatened to

---

[14] Transcript of First Oral Argument in Roe v Wade, *in* 75 LANDMARK BRIEFS AND ARGUMENTS OF THE SUPREME COURT OF THE UNITED STATES: CONSTITUTIONAL LAW 786–88 (Philip B. Kurland & Gerhard Casper eds., 1975).

[15] *Id.* at 790.

[16] *Id.* at 791–94.

[17] *Id.* 798–800.

[18] *Id.* at 802.

[19] *Id.* at 802-03.

[20] *Id.* at 803.

[21] THE SUPREME COURT IN CONFERENCE (1940–1985): THE PRIVATE DISCUSSIONS BEHIND NEARLY 300 SUPREME COURT DECISIONS 806–07 (Del Dickson ed., 2001).

[22] *Id.* at 807.

[23] GARROW, *supra* note 1, at 532–34.

publish a memo criticizing it. He was talked out of releasing the memo; however it was leaked to the *Washington Post* and published.[24]

Justice Blackmun labored throughout the year on the opinion. He produced a draft in May affirming the district court on the grounds of vagueness.[25] When Justice White responded with a vigorous dissent, Blackmun withdrew the opinion and asked to be allowed to work on it over the summer. Particularly because Justices Powell and Rehnquist had not been appointed in time to participate in the oral arguments of *Roe* and *Doe*, the Court voted to set the case for re-argument in the fall, but did not ask the parties to address any specific issues. Blackmun worked on the draft throughout the summer at the Mayo Clinic. After circulating the new draft, Justice Brennan sent Blackmun a memo with extensive suggestions.

At the second oral argument in November 1972, Sarah Weddington explained that Dallas District Attorney Henry Wade had taken the position that the state was not bound by the declaratory judgment and therefore the antiabortion statute could still be enforced.[26] Consequently an injunction was necessary. After repeated questioning from Justice White, she admitted that if the Court decided that the fetus was a person within the Fourteenth Amendment she "would have a difficult case."[27]

Robert Flowers argued on behalf of the state. The justices wanted to know on what basis they could decide that a fetus was a person from the moment of conception as the state maintained.[28] He was forced to concede that the Fourteenth Amendment refers to "any person, born or naturalized in the United States."[29] He was also forced to acknowledge that historically the law had presumed that personhood commenced with live birth.[30] He could not produce medical testimony establishing that personhood began at conception.[31] Noting that during the pregnancy, the fetus does become quite developed, he argued that there is no basis for a court to draw a line between life and non-life.[32] The Court turned his argument against him, suggesting that if a fetus was a person from conception then the legislature could not permit abortion in exceptional cases, including to save the life of the mother.[33] He also had to concede that initially, the Texas statute seemed to be concerned with the dangers of the abortion procedure to the mother.[34]

In rebuttal, Weddington used Flowers's argument that a court could not draw a line between non-life and life during the pregnancy to support her argument that the line had to be drawn at live birth.[35] As was the case with the state's insistence on conception as the only place to draw the line, Weddington's contention that live birth was the only defensible alternative also seemed to give pause to some of the justices concerned with

[24] *Id.* at 554–58.
[25] *Id.* at 548.
[26] LANDMARK BRIEFS AND ARGUMENTS OF THE SUPREME COURT, *supra* note 14, at 808–09.
[27] *Id.* at 817.
[28] *Id.* at 818–19.
[29] *Id.* at 819.
[30] *Id.* at 824.
[31] *Id.* at 827.
[32] *Id.*
[33] *Id.*
[34] *Id.* at 829.
[35] *Id.* at 830.

finding some means of compromising the competing interests. For as monumental of a case as *Roe v. Wade* was, the oral arguments of neither side were particularly helpful, but the arguments by the state were exceptionally poor. One can at least wonder whether it would have made any difference at all if the state had been represented by well-prepared counsel. Probably not with respect to the decision itself given that at least five justices seemed to be locked in on the result. However, one would hope that a stronger brief and argument could have persuaded the Court to produce a more nuanced and better reasoned opinion.

At the conference after the second oral argument, the vote was 7-2 in favor of striking down the Texas law, with Justices White and Rehnquist prepared to dissent.[36] There seemed to be agreement to rely on the Fourteenth rather than the Ninth Amendment. Over the summer, Justice Blackmun had rewritten his draft opinion shifting the legal basis from vagueness to the right to privacy.[37] He chose the end of the first trimester as the point at which the state interest in regulation could commence.[38] Justice Powell convinced Blackmun to make *Roe* rather than *Doe* the lead case. Powell and Marshall persuaded him to make viability rather than the end of the first trimester the point at which the state's interest in protecting fetal life commences.[39] Justice Stewart convinced Blackmun to add a section to the opinion explaining that the fetus was not a "person" within the Fourteenth Amendment.[40] Justices Burger and Stewart prepared concurring opinions, and White and Rehnquist offered short dissents.

THE OPINION

Finally the opinion in *Roe* was announced on February 26, 1973. It has become one of the most severely criticized opinions in Supreme Court history. It starts out defensively, seeming to realize that the Court was walking into a firestorm. Blackmun wrote that "[w]e forthwith acknowledge our awareness of the sensitive and emotional nature of the abortion controversy, of the vigorous opposing views, even among physicians, and of the deep and seemingly absolute convictions that the subject inspires."[41] He then invoked Justice Holmes dicta from his *Lochner* dissent, "'[The Constitution] is made for people of fundamentally different views....'"[42] After reviewing the facts of the case, Blackmun concluded that Jane Roe and Dr. Halford both had standing to litigate.

The next section of Justice Blackmun's opinion consisted of an 18-page history of abortion regulation from ancient times to the present, including the approaches of the American Medical Association. Blackmun attempted to show that for most of recorded history, abortion regulation was not nearly as strict as at present, and until relatively recently the regulation that did exist was primarily concerned with protecting the health

---

[36] THE SUPREME COURT IN CONFERENCE, *supra* note 21, at 810–12.
[37] BERNARD SCHWARTZ, DECISION: HOW THE SUPREME COURT DECIDES CASES 235 (1996).
[38] *Id.*
[39] THE SUPREME COURT IN CONFERENCE, *supra* note 21, at 811 n. 37.
[40] FAUX, *supra* note 1, at 303.
[41] 410 U.S. 113, 116 (1973).
[42] *Id.* at 117.

of the mother as opposed to the life of the fetus. He never clearly indicated the purpose of this lengthy historical review. Perhaps he was attempting to show that there was no long-standing tradition of protecting fetal life, in an attempt to appeal to the tradition-based analysis expounded by Justice Harlan in his *Poe* dissent. If so, that would have been a hard case to make given that his research revealed that for the past 100 years most states had banned abortion or regulated it quite heavily. In view of this, it would have been impossible to argue that there had been a solid tradition in Anglo-American law of liberty to obtain an abortion.

Turning to the state interests in regulating or prohibiting abortion, Blackmun noted that abortion was no longer as hazardous as it once was but conceded that the state had an interest in protecting the health of the woman at least at "a late stage of pregnancy." He explained that the state also asserted an interest in protecting potential life from the point of conception on.

At that point, Blackmun turned to the legal issues. He began by providing a lengthy string citation to all of the Court's privacy autonomy cases, much as the appellants had done in their briefs and oral argument. He then concluded that "[t]his right to privacy, whether it be founded in the Fourteenth Amendment's concept of personal liberty and restrictions on state action, as we feel it is, or, as the District Court determined, in the Ninth Amendment's reservation of rights to the people, is broad enough to encompass a woman's decision whether or not to terminate her pregnancy."[43] Justice Blackmun simply cited a group of loosely related cases and then asserted that they covered the abortion right, without any attempt to explain what principle if any tied these cases together or why that principle did in fact apply to abortion. Not surprisingly, the paucity of legal analysis on this crucial point became the subject of scathing criticism in the law reviews.[44] As Justice Powell had urged, Justice Blackmun did set the Ninth Amendment aside and rested the case on Fourteenth Amendment due process liberty.

Perhaps to indicate why the privacy right was implicated, Justice Blackmun summarized the adverse impact that could flow from an unwanted pregnancy, much as Sarah Weddington had done in her brief and oral argument. He then made a point of rejecting the arguments that a woman has a wholly unrestricted right to seek an abortion at any point during the pregnancy or that a person has a right to do whatever he or she chooses with his or her own body. This reflected the view that Blackmun had maintained throughout that there needed to be a balancing of interests in the case.

Blackmun then turned to the issue that had been most dominating during oral argument—whether the fetus is a "person" within the Fourteenth Amendment. He conceded, as had the appellants during oral argument, that if the fetus was a constitutional person, then the case for an abortion right "collapses."[45] Relying on intra-textual analysis, Blackmun explained that the term "person" was used in several instances in the Constitution and in none of them did it seem to cover the unborn. The reasonable inference was that it was not understood to apply to the yet to be born under the Fourteenth Amendment either. This was a solid example of textual analysis and one of the better arguments that

---

[43] *Id.* at 153.

[44] *See, e.g.,* John Hart Ely, *The Wages of Crying Wolf: A Comment on* Roe v Wade, 82 YALE L.J. 920 (1973).

[45] *Roe*, 410 U.S. at 156.

Blackmun was able to make in *Roe*. Still it could be noted that given that the Court was taking an evolving approach to Fourteenth Amendment "liberty," which almost certainly did not include abortion when the amendment was ratified in 1868, why could the concept of "person" not evolve over time as well?

Turning to the state's side of the balance, Blackmun acknowledged that "at some point" the interests in the health of the mother or potential human life become "significantly involved."[46] It is here that Justice Blackmun sailed into particularly rough waters. He noted that Texas maintained that life begins at conception. However as "those trained in the respective disciples of medicine, philosophy, and theology are unable to arrive at any consensus, the judiciary, at this point in the development of man's knowledge, is not in a position to speculate as to the answer."[47] The choice of terminology was inaccurate. There is no question that a fetus is a form of life. The real question was whether it is a human being. By acknowledging that the judiciary could not decide what was, in fact, an unavoidable question, Justice Blackmun all but gave away his case at this point. The position of Texas was that it does not matter whether the judiciary can decide it because we can and have.

Blackmun noted that there has been a wide divergence of thinking on the subject of when life begins with some support for conception, quickening, viability and live birth. Given the disagreement, Texas may not "by adopting one theory of life...override the rights of the pregnant woman that are at stake."[48] But why not? Someone must adopt a theory of life in order to resolve the case, that is, to determine whether Jane Roe is entitled to an abortion.

At that point, Blackmun veered back to the state interest in the woman's health and proclaimed that after the first trimester, the state could regulate abortion to protect the health of the mother because that is the point at which the mortality rate from abortion begins to exceed that from childbirth. The Court would later recognize that this was a non sequitur, and indeed the state should be able to regulate abortion even in the first trimester to make it even safer.[49]

Justice Blackmun then returned to the state interest in potential life and simply proclaimed that it became compelling at viability: "This is so because the fetus then presumably has the capability of meaningful life outside of the mother's womb."[50] In the memorable words of John Hart Ely, the Court mistook "a definition for a syllogism."[51] The emphasis on viability might suggest that Justice Blackmun understood the right as a right not to be pregnant as opposed to a right not to be a mother. A few paragraphs earlier, he had asserted that neither the Court nor Texas could determine when life began, given that there were at least four plausible possibilities. But someone had to decide something in order to resolve the case so Blackmun returned to the issue and decided when "potential life began." But no one was fooled. He had set a trap from which he could not logically extricate himself. He had been forced to do exactly what at some level he understood that he could not do, at least as a matter of reasonable constitutional analysis.

---

[46] *Id.* at 159.
[47] *Id.*
[48] *Id.* at 162.
[49] *Planned Parenthood of Se. Pa. v. Casey*, 505 U.S. 833, 846, 872, 878 (1992).
[50] *Roe*, 410 U.S. at 163.
[51] Ely, *supra* note 44, at 923.

This was the crux of *Roe v. Wade*. This was where the opinion collapsed of its own weight. In defense of Justice Blackmun, it could be argued that the Court balances interests and draws arbitrary lines with great frequency in constitutional law, so what was so extraordinary about this instance? Justice Blackmun had answered that question himself when he acknowledged earlier that the "judiciary, at this point in its knowledge is not in a position to speculate as to [when life begins]." And the reason was because the question was metaphysical in nature. Changing the question from life to potential life did not render it any less spiritual. It could also be argued that the Court simply had to draw a line somewhere beyond conception to prevent Texas from overriding the woman's right to privacy. Indeed, Justice Blackmun said as much. But that simply suggests that the Court was mistaken to have recognized such a right to begin with as it would be unable to define it in a principled manner.

Blackmun then broke the analysis down into the trimester framework, providing that the state had no authority to regulate during the first trimester; had the power to regulate to protect the woman's health in the second trimester; and had the authority to prohibit abortions entirely in the third trimester, at least after the point of viability, as long as there was an exception to protect the life and health of the mother. Justice Stewart had warned that this analysis would subject the Court to criticism on the grounds that it was too technical and legislative, which of course it did.[52]

Justice Stewart wrote a short concurrence in which he made peace with the right to privacy and substantive due process after having objected to that approach in his *Griswold* dissent.[53]

In view of the controversial nature of the *Roe* decision, the dissents were surprisingly short. In one of his first opinions since joining the Court, Justice Rehnquist questioned whether the concept of privacy made sense in the context of abortion considering that the doctor, a third party, was necessarily involved. He also chided Justice Blackmun for quoting the Holmes dissent in *Lochner*, arguing, as so many critics of *Roe* would maintain, that it was more reminiscent of the majority opinion in that case. Rehnquist also emphasized the extent to which the decision was inconsistent with the laws of a majority of the states both as of the time of the passage of the Fourteenth Amendment and at the present.

Justice White's dissent was short but caustic. He asserted that the Court had placed the "convenience, whim or caprice" of the pregnant woman above the state's interest in protecting the life of the fetus.[54] Moreover, the Court did this "[a]s an exercise of raw judicial power" without any support in the language or history of the Constitution.[55] Consequently, the Court should have left the issue to "the people and the political process."[56] White would later characterize *Roe* as "the only illegitimate decision the Court rendered during my tenure."[57]

The companion case to *Roe*, *Doe v. Bolton*[58] involved a challenge to the more modern abortion statute based on the Model Penal Code. The questions raised in *Doe* were more technical

[52] James F. Simon, The Center Holds: The Power Struggle Inside the Rehnquist Court 114 (1995).

[53] *Roe*, 410 U.S. at 167.

[54] *Id.* at 221.

[55] *Id.* at 221–22.

[56] *Id.* at 222.

[57] Dennis Hutchinson, The Man Who Once Was Whizzer White: A Portrait of Justice Byron R. White 368 (1998).

[58] 410 U.S. 179 (1972).

or procedural than those presented in *Roe*. The Court invalidated several provisions of the Georgia statute however, including requirements that abortions be performed in accredited hospitals, that abortions be approved by hospital committees, that abortions be approved by two doctors, and that women seeking an abortion in Georgia reside in the state. Justice Blackmun, again writing for the majority, concluded that these requirements imposed a burden on the woman seeking an abortion and did not serve sufficient state interests.

Justice Douglas wrote a rambling concurrence discussing different aspects of the right to privacy. Chief Justice Burger also offered a short concurrence.

REACTION

The immediate press and public reaction to *Roe* was stifled by the fact that former president Lyndon Johnson died the day *Roe* was announced. However the pro-abortion movement was quick to praise the decision while antiabortion forces condemned it. Academic criticism of the decision was severe. One of the earliest, most devastating and influential critiques of *Roe* came from John Hart Ely of the Yale Law School. The year after *Roe*, he published an article castigating Justice Blackmun's opinion line for line.[59] In his most frequently quoted statement, he declared that *Roe* "is bad because, it is bad constitutional law, or rather because it is not constitutional law and gives almost no sense of an obligation to try to be."[60] Thus Ely set the tone for the critique that *Roe* was not simply a poorly reasoned decision but rather an illegitimate one, a point that Justice White had expressed in his dissenting opinion. Academic criticism continued over the next two decades. Judge Robert Bork wrote that "there is not one line of explanation. Not one sentence that qualifies as legal argument."[61] Judge Henry Friendly wrote that *Roe* "failed to articulate a defensible principle."[62] Gerald Gunther, perhaps the most highly regarded constitutional scholar of the day, wrote, "I have not found a satisfying rationale to justify *Roe* on the basis of modes of interpretation I find legitimate."[63] Harvard law professor and former solicitor general Archibald Cox wrote that the decision "ran contrary to the prevailing moral code [and] lacked support in conventional sources of law."[64] Guido Calabresi, the dean of the Yale Law School, characterized *Roe* as "offensive" and a "disaster" in that it declared that the values of persons who disagreed with abortion were simply beyond the scope of the Constitution.[65] Professor and later judge Noonan declared that Roe "floated without mooring in the Constitution."[66] Richard Fallon of Harvard Law School wrote that "it is puzzling, disappointing, almost embarrassing to read."[67] Mark Tushnet of the

---

[59] Ely, *supra* note 44.

[60] *Id.* at 947.

[61] ROBERT H. BORK, THE TEMPTING OF AMERICA: THE POLITICAL SEDUCTION OF THE LAW 112 (1990).

[62] Henry Friendly, *The Courts and Social Policy: Substance and Procedure*, 33 U. MIAMI L. REV. 21, 33 (1978).

[63] Gerald Gunther, *Some Reflections on the Judicial Role: Distinctions Roots and Prospects*, 1979 WASH. U. Q. 817, 820 (1979).

[64] COX, *supra* note 1, at 334.

[65] GUIDO CALABRESI, IDEALS, BELIEFS, ATTITUDES, AND THE LAW: PRIVATE LAW PERSPECTIVES ON A PUBLIC LAW PROBLEM 93–97 (1985).

[66] JOHN T. NOONAN, JR., A PRIVATE CHOICE: ABORTION IN AMERICA IN THE SEVENTIES 22 (1979).

[67] RICHARD H. FALLON, JR., IMPLEMENTING THE CONSTITUTION 62 (2001).

Georgetown Law School, who as Justice Marshall's law clerk had urged the justices to focus on viability, characterized *Roe* as akin to a new art form: "the totally unreasoned judicial opinion."[68] Justice Powell later stated that "the abortion opinions were the worst opinions I ever joined.'"[69] This is simply a smattering of the academic criticism of *Roe*. The decision had its defenders to be certain. Still, one would be hard-pressed to identify any Supreme Court decision aside from *Dred Scott* subjected to more trenchant criticism from the very elite of the legal profession, many of whom favored liberalized abortion laws. This criticism took a toll convincing many that *Roe* was a singularly indefensible decision as a matter of constitutional doctrine. In response defenders of *Roe* labored hard to justify the decision as constitutionally legitimate.[70]

THE JUDICIAL RESPONSE

The opponents of *Roe*, especially the Roman Catholic Church, rallied to oppose and undermine the decision. Marches both in support and opposition to the decision became a regular occurrence outside of the Court. Several states, especially Missouri and Pennsylvania, were quick to challenge *Roe* by enacting legislation that was almost certainly inconsistent with the substance of the opinion. With the exception of state funding of abortion, the Court stood strongly behind *Roe*, invalidating most of the legislation that came before it. In *Maher v. Roe*, Justice Powell wrote that the funding restriction should be constitutional as long as it did not "unduly burden" the woman's right to choose abortion.[71] Justice O'Connor would later pick up upon this approach. Over time however with new appointments to the Court, the majority supporting *Roe* shrank from 7 to 2 down to 5 to 4, and then by 1989 it appeared that a majority of the Court might be prepared to overrule *Roe* as the Department of Justice had been urging. The two original *Roe* dissenters, Chief Justice Rehnquist and Justice White, remained on the Court. They were joined by Justice Scalia, who definitely favored rejecting *Roe*, and Justice O'Connor and Kennedy, who seemed to lean in that direction. It was then that the Court considered Missouri's latest abortion regulation statute in *Webster v. Reproductive Health Services*,[72] a case many believed would be the end of *Roe*. Because of the possibility that *Roe* might be overruled, a record of 78 amicus briefs were filed in *Webster*.[73] Former solicitor general Charles Fried appearing for the United States as Amicus Curia did urge the Court to overrule *Roe*. A majority of the Court was unwilling to do so however.

Rather Chief Justice Rehnquist wrote an opinion concluding that the provisions of the statute were not inconsistent with *Roe*. Writing for only himself, White, and Scalia, Rehnquist argued that the standard of review for evaluating laws restricting abortion should be dropped from the demanding strict scrutiny standard to the lenient rational basis approach. Such a change would indeed be equivalent to a complete rejection

---

[68] Mark V. Tushnet, Red, White, and Blue: A Critical Analysis of Constitutional Law 54 (1988).

[69] John C. Jeffries, Jr., Justice Lewis F. Powell, Jr. 341 (1994).

[70] *Id.* at 363–64 (discussing the many attempts by Professor Tribe to justify *Roe*).

[71] 432 U.S. 464, 473 (1977).

[72] 492 U.S. 490 (1989).

[73] Simon, *supra* note 52, at 127-28.

of *Roe*. Justice O'Connor, concurring, seemed to be responsible for the Court's failure to confront *Roe* directly.[74] Justice Scalia wrote a scathing concurring opinion critical of O'Connor's cautious approach, declaring that the Court had simply postponed the day of reckoning for *Roe*. Justice Blackmun wrote an anguished dissent recognizing that the *Roe* decision was no longer secure and would be challenged again in the future. The constant attacks on *Roe* and on Blackmun's opinion had apparently caused Justice Blackmun to become increasingly angry, resentful, and defensive, sometimes resulting in unexpected emotional outbursts.[75]

PLANNED PARENTHOOD v. CASEY

Three years later, another direct challenge to *Roe* came in the case of *Planned Parenthood of Pennsylvania v. Casey*.[76] This time the Court made it clear that it was prepared to hear argument on the question of whether *Roe* should be overruled. Once again the United States, through Solicitor General Starr, asked the Court to overrule *Roe*. The litigation involved challenges to five provisions of the recent Pennsylvania statute, some of which were similar to laws that had previously been rejected by the Court. The Act provided for informed consent prior to abortion. To achieve that end, the woman was required to consider information presented by the state 24 hours before the abortion was performed. A minor could not obtain an abortion absent informed consent by one parent, although a judicial bypass procedure was available. Spousal notification was required before an abortion could be performed. The Act also imposed certain reporting requirements on abortion providers. The district court invalidated all of the provisions while the Court of Appeals for the Third Circuit reversed, upholding all but the spousal notification require-ment. Between *Webster* and *Casey*, Justice Brennan had retired and had been replaced by Justice David Souter, and Justice Marshall had retired and had been replaced by Justice Clarence Thomas. Although it was unclear exactly how the new justices would vote in an abortion case, it seemed likely that they would be less sympathetic toward *Roe* than the justices they had replaced. As of *Casey*, the only three justices remaining on the Court who had participated in the *Roe* decision itself were its author Justice Blackmun and the two dissenters, Chief Justice Rehnquist and Justice White. There was every reason to believe that *Roe* would meet its most severe challenge yet. The supporters of *Roe* had largely resigned themselves to the fact that it was likely to be overruled.

Recognizing that the Pennsylvania statute was intended to be inconsistent with *Roe* and subsequent precedent, thereby presenting the Court with another opportunity to overrule *Roe*, Katherine Kolbert, representing the challengers to the law, insisted that the Court simply had to consider whether *Roe* should be overruled. Despite several attempts by the justices during oral argument to steer her toward an evaluation of the individual provisions of the Act, she continued to maintain that the case simply boiled down to an up or down verdict on *Roe* itself.[77] Solicitor General Starr argued that the Court should

---

[74] *Webster*, 492 U.S. at 522.
[75] Jeffries, *supra* note 69, at 368–70.
[76] 505 U.S. 833 (1992).
[77] Oral Argument Transcript, *supra* note 14, at 1196, 1199–2000.

adopt the rational basis standard proposed by Chief Justice Rehnquist in *Webster*, effectively overruling *Roe*.[78] To the consternation of some of the justices however, he declined to elaborate on how that standard might play out with respect to various future regulations.[79] He did assert that under such a standard, all of the provisions of the Pennsylvania statute would be upheld.

At the conference, it appeared that Chief Justice Rehnquist had five votes to reject *Roe*. He began to write an opinion that would replace *Roe's* strict standard of review with a lenient rational basis test. Apparently, Justice Kennedy was troubled by the prospect of overruling *Roe*.

At some point during the process of drafting the opinions, Justices O'Connor and Souter convinced Justice Kennedy to join an opinion significantly modifying but ultimately saving at least the core of *Roe v. Wade*.[80] Each of these justices drafted one portion of what became the Joint Opinion of the three. Neither Chief Justice Rehnquist nor Justice Scalia could persuade Kennedy to abandon the Joint Opinion and concur in the Rehnquist opinion rejecting *Roe*. By most accounts, the Court came very close to overruling *Roe* in *Casey*.

THE *CASEY* OPINIONS

When the decision was announced, each of the members of the three justices' Joint Opinion read that portion for which he or she was responsible. The first portion written by Justice Kennedy boiled the essence of *Roe* down to three principles. First, a woman has the right to choose to have an abortion prior to viability of the fetus. Second, the state may prohibit abortion after viability as long as there is an exception to protect the life and health of the woman. Third, the state has an interest in protecting maternal health and fetal life throughout the pregnancy.

In section II of the Joint Opinion joined by a majority of the Court, Justice Kennedy confirmed that substantive due process was a legitimate constitutional doctrine and quoted extensively from Justice Harlan's *Poe v. Ullman* opinion, indicating that its tradition-based balancing approach was the appropriate focus of such analysis. The Joint Opinion then made an attempt to explain why the abortion decision was included as a fundamental aspect of protected liberty in substantially more detail than had Justice Blackmun in *Roe*. The Joint Opinion characterized the decision whether to bear a child as one of "the most intimate and personal choices a person can make in a lifetime, choices central to personal dignity and autonomy."[81] Continuing in a vein that has been criticized as perhaps too mystical, the Opinion maintained that the decision involved "the right to define one's own concept of existence, of meaning, of the universe, and of the mystery of human life."[82] It then concluded:

---

[78] *Id.* at 1214.

[79] *Id.* at 1215, 1218.

[80] SIMON, *supra* note 52, at 163.

[81] 505 U.S. at 851.

[82] *Id.*

[the woman's] suffering is too intimate and personal for the State to insist, without more, upon its own vision of the woman's role, however dominant that vision has been in the course of our history and our culture. The destiny of the woman must be shaped to a large extent on her own conception of her spiritual imperatives and her place in society.[83]

The Opinion argued that protection for the abortion decision was derived quite readily from the Court's previous privacy decisions, including *Griswold v. Connecticut.* Although perhaps a bit too lyrical, the Joint Opinion's explanation of why the abortion decision was a highly protected aspect of liberty was certainly a significant improvement over Justice Blackmun's treatment of the issue in *Roe.*

Section III of the opinion, written and read by Justice Souter and also joined by a majority, provided arguably the Court's most in-depth consideration of the role of precedent and stare decisis in the Court's history. Recognizing that adherence to precedent is the rule and rejection the rare exception, the Court explained that there are four factors that must be considered to determine whether a precedent should be overruled. Before deciding to overrule, the Court should consider whether the doctrine of the case has been unworkable, whether there exists a reliance interest, whether the doctrine has been abandoned, and whether facts have changed undermining the initial decision.

Turning to the application of these criteria to *Roe,* the Joint Opinion quickly concluded that there was nothing unworkable about *Roe,* despite the fact that later in the opinion it would reject its trimester framework. As for the reliance interests, it had to concede that the case was not as strong as it would be in the commercial area given that the abortion decision is often "an unplanned response to the consequences of unplanned activity."[84] The opinion argued however that there was indeed a reliance interest in that over the past two decades since *Roe,* people have organized their lives, at least to some extent, around the availability of the means to terminate pregnancy if necessary. This seemed rather speculative and unpersuasive. There was perhaps a different type of reliance interest that may have been at work: that is, the very reliance upon the existence of the right created by *Roe* as a symbolic matter. Supporters of *Roe* had been inclined to say that if the Court overruled *Roe* it would be the first time that the Court had recognized and then taken away a constitutional right. That certainly was not true as the demise of *Lochner* would indicate. But there was something to the argument in that for millions of people, including most who would never have occasion to take advantage of the decision, it represented a very significant legal and social advance. As such, the clock could never be turned back to the way it was before *Roe.* The very existence of *Roe* as an iconic decision altered the shape of the culture. And in that sense there was a real if not necessarily specific reliance interest at stake. As one volume on *Roe* has put it, the decision had developed "social *stare decisis.*"[85]

The Joint Opinion also concluded that the essence of *Roe,* the protection of the woman's liberty interest, had not been abandoned, and if there had been any alteration in

---

[83] *Id.* at 852.
[84] *Id.* at 856.
[85] HULL & HOFFER, *supra* note 1, at 227.

thinking on the issue, it was only with respect to some degree of increased protection for the life of the fetus. As for the final factor, factual change, the Joint Opinion conceded that there have been some changes since *Roe*, especially with respect to the timing of viability; however it insisted that these changes did not undermine the woman's liberty interest but rather simply enhanced the state's interest in protecting the fetus. Applying these four factors, the Joint Opinion concluded that there was no basis for overruling *Roe*.

Rather than rest entirely on these four factors, the Joint Opinion then embarked on a misguided attempt to distinguish *Roe* from *Lochner* and *Plessy v. Ferguson* on the basis of changed circumstances. Relying on a short quote from a book by Justice Jackson, the Opinion argued that the *Lochner* doctrine had been rejected because the Court had realized that a laissez-faire approach to the economy had been insufficient. In fact, the demise of *Lochner* is more accurately explained by the Court's recognition that Justice Holmes was correct in maintaining that there simply was no highly protected liberty of contract, as Chief Justice Rehnquist noted in dissent.

The Joint Opinion made the same argument with respect to the overruling of *Plessy v. Ferguson* by *Brown v. Board of Education*. The Court attributed the change from *Plessy* to *Brown* on factual change in that the *Plessy* Court had failed to understand that segregation was stigmatizing while the *Brown* Court thought otherwise. This did not appreciate the degree to which *Brown* represented a significant alteration of legal principle, a fact that the Joint Opinion itself conceded, noting that "we think Plessy was wrong the day it was decided."[86] The Joint Opinion's discussion of the overruling of *Lochner* and *Plessy* was strained and embarrassing and certainly did not strengthen the opinion.

The justices joining the Joint Opinion were still obviously troubled by the stare decisis question so they continued to discuss it, arguing that the Court's standing with the public would be diminished by a decision to overrule *Roe*. To develop this argument, the Opinion delved into an area rarely discussed by the justices—the basis of the Court's legitimacy as an institution. It made the well-accepted point that the Court's power is based upon the public perception that it decides constitutional questions on the basis of principles derived from the Constitution and not on the basis of political or social compromise. In context, this was a remarkable argument to make in defense of *Roe* given that from the very outset, the case against *Roe* had been that there was absolutely no principled basis for the decision. Recall that Justice White dissenting in *Roe* declared that the Court "announced a new constitutional right...with scarcely any reason or authority for its action" and that it was nothing more than "a raw exercise of judicial power."[87] A solid majority of the academic commentary on *Roe* accepted Justice White's assessment. As such, it was difficult to believe that the Opinion would argue that adherence to principle was a persuasive argument for standing behind *Roe* as opposed to rejecting it.

The Joint Opinion then made a rather extraordinary argument. It maintained that occasionally, the Court will decide a case that "calls the contending sides of a national controversy to end their division by accepting a common mandate rooted in the Constitution."[88] The Opinion failed to explain why it believed that bringing an end to contentious

---

[86] 505 U.S. at 863.
[87] Roe v. Wade, 410 U.S. 113, 222 (1973).
[88] *Casey*, 505 U.S. at 867.

national controversies was part of the Court's legitimate role. It cited *Brown v. Board of Education* as an example of such a case, but as Justice Scalia argued in dissent, *Dred Scott* would have been a better example of that type of thinking. In any event, as the contrast between *Dred Scott* and *Brown* emphasizes, the Court can successfully arbitrate such controversies, if and only if it can persuade a substantial majority of the public that it is correct. It is hardly enough that the Court has spoken. The Opinion argued that overruling under pressure would break the bond with those who had accepted the prior decision. In dissent, Justice Scalia pointed out that in fact *Roe* had made the controversy over abortion even more divisive by nationalizing it and by eliminating the possibility of political compromise.

The Joint Opinion acknowledged that the pressure both to overrule and to retain *Roe* was more intense than ever, but overruling at this point would undermine the Court's legitimacy and the nation's commitment to the rule of law. The Joint Opinion's section on stare decisis was long and highly defensive in tone. It did not speak with a self-confident voice.

Part IV. of the Joint Opinion, written and read by Justice O'Connor, which detailed the adjustments that needed to be made to *Roe*'s analytic framework, was not joined by anyone other than Kennedy and Souter. The Opinion confirmed the woman's right to choose abortion up to the point of viability both as a matter of stare decisis and because it considered it the only workable line. It rejected the trimester framework, which it "did not consider to be part of the essential holding of Roe."[89] Indeed, the Court found rigid enforcement of the trimester approach inconsistent with the balance that it believed that *Roe* had struck between the pregnant woman's right to an abortion and the state's interest in the protection of fetal life. This was particularly true to the extent that the trimester framework limited the state's ability to provide the woman with information regarding the choice prior to viability. Instead, the Joint Opinion declared that state regulation would interfere with the woman's right to an abortion only when it imposed an undue burden, an approach that Justice O'Connor had long favored. According to the Opinion, regulation would create an undue burden if it placed a substantial obstacle in the woman's ability to choose to have an abortion. As such, the woman's right "was to make the ultimate decision, not a right to be insulated from all others in doing so."[90] Consequently, the state may attempt to persuade her to choose childbirth over abortion as long as it does not place a substantial obstacle in her path.

Part V. the Joint Opinion also written by Justice O'Connor, turned to the statutory provisions at issue in the case. In section V-A joined by a majority, the Joint Opinion held that the statutory definition of medical emergency did not impose an undue burden. In part V-B in which only Kennedy and Souter joined, the Joint Opinion upheld the informed consent provisions of the Pennsylvania statute, which required that 24 hours before the abortion procedure, the woman be advised of the nature of the procedure; potential health risks; the approximate gestational age of the fetus; and the availability of information regarding assistance for childbirth, child support obligations, and adoption alternatives. In so doing, the Court overruled two prior decisions, *Akron I* and

---

[89] *Id.* at 872.
[90] *Id.* at 878.

Thornburgh, which had reached a contrary result. In part V-C, a majority of the Court concluded that the spousal notification requirement did impose an undue burden in view of statistics indicating a large degree of spousal abuse.[91] In part V-D, a majority of the Court affirmed the informed consent procedure for minors as consistent with prior decisions on the issue. In V-E, a majority upheld the abortion provider reporting requirements except for those pertaining to spousal notice. As a result, most of the provisions of the Pennsylvania statute survived undue burden analysis.

Justice Stevens wrote a concurring and dissenting opinion objecting to the Joint Opinion's increased solicitude for state protection of fetal life and arguing that the informed consent provisions were inconsistent with existing precedent.

Justice Blackmun wrote an anguished concurrence and dissent. He began his opinion by lamenting that with the Court's recent abortion decisions, many believed that darkness would fall, but now with the Joint Opinion "the flame has grown bright."[92] No one can accuse Justice Blackmun of being an effective literary stylist to be sure. He argued vigorously that *Roe* was correct in its entirety, the Pennsylvania statute should be invalidated in its entirety under the strict standard of review, and efforts of Chief Justice Rehnquist to overrule *Roe* would undermine the Court and the rule of law.

Chief Justice Rehnquist joined by Justices White, Scalia, and Thomas, offered a lengthy dissent, some of which he had hoped would have been a majority opinion overruling *Roe*. He argued that neither history and tradition nor prior due process precedent supported the decision to consider the right to abortion fundamental, and thus the strict standard of review should be replaced not with the Joint Opinion's undue burden standard, but rather with the rational basis standard as he had contended in *Webster*. He noted that the Joint Opinion failed to declare that *Roe* was correct when decided. He charged that the Joint Opinion's alteration of *Roe* caused it to exist "the way a storefront on a western movie set exists: a mere facade to give the illusion of reality."[93]

Chief Justice Rehnquist argued that the Joint Opinion was quite wrong in maintaining that the Court's reputation would be tarnished if it overruled *Roe* under pressure from its opponents as an equal amount of pressure was being brought to bear by those favoring its retention. Rather, the appropriate course was to ignore the pressure one way or the other. The fact that people had grown accustomed to *Roe* was not a sufficient reason to preserve it if it had been wrongly decided to begin with. He found all elements of the statute to be rationally related to legitimate state purposes.[94]

Justice Scalia also dissented. Going to the heart of *Roe* itself, he argued that it was inevitably wrong in that it unavoidably concluded that a fetus was not a human life, a decision that the Court was incapable of making. He summed up the Joint Opinion's application of the undue burden standard as maintaining that the state could pursue the interest in protecting fetal life "only so long as it was not too successful."[95] He characterized the Joint Opinion's stare decisis analysis as a "keep-what-you-want-and-thr ow-away-the-rest" approach.[96] He wondered why the trimester framework was not part of

---

[91] *Id.* at 888–98.
[92] *Id.* at 922.
[93] *Id.* at 954.
[94] *Id.* at 966–79.
[95] *Id.* at 992.
[96] *Id.* at 993.

the central holding of *Roe*. Justice Scalia observed that it was frightening that the Court would stand behind a decision that it otherwise might overrule simply to prove that it would not be intimidated by public disapproval.

As for the protests for and against *Roe*, Justice Scalia laid the blame for that phenomenon at the Court's door. He reasoned that once the public recognizes that the Court is deciding cases such as *Roe* by applying value judgments rather than legal principles "then the people should demonstrate, to protest that we do not implement *their* values instead of *ours*."[97] He declared that "[w]e should get out of this area where we have no right to be."[98] Justice Scalia concluded that *Roe* was similar to *Dred Scott* in that it constitutionalized a political dispute, rendering it alterable only by Supreme Court reversal or constitutional amendment.

AFTERMATH

With the exception of partial birth abortion, *Casey* largely settled the legal issues regarding abortion, at least for a while. The partial birth abortion cases do highlight the meaning of *Casey* however. In *Stenberg v. Carhart*,[99] the Court by a 5-4 majority invalidated a Nebraska statute prohibiting partial birth abortion, a process involving the destruction of the fetus at a point where it has partially entered the birth canal. The Court held that the statute was unconstitutional in that the definition of the procedures covered was unduly vague and because it failed to provide an exception to protect the health of the mother. The case is particularly noteworthy with respect to Justice Kennedy's vigorous dissent. Kennedy had been the crucial vote to save *Roe* in *Casey*. With the replacement of Justice White with Justice Ginsburg, he was no longer the fifth vote for *Roe*. In his *Stenberg* dissent, Justice Kennedy made it clear that he believed that the Court had now repudiated the compromise in *Casey* that had saved *Roe* in a modified form. In particular he noted that *Casey* had recognized a state interest in the life of the fetus throughout the pregnancy, along with a modification of the standard of review from strict scrutiny to undue burden. The unstated premise of Justice Kennedy's opinion was that he would not have voted with the majority in *Casey* had he understood that it would be interpreted as it was in *Stenberg*.

But with the replacement of Justice O'Connor with Justice Alito, Justice Kennedy was once again the crucial fifth vote on abortion. When a federal law banning partial birth abortion without an exception for the health of the mother came before the Court in *Gonzales v. Carhart*, Justice Kennedy wrote an opinion for the 5-4 majority sustaining it.[100] His majority opinion in *Gonzales* reads much like his dissent in *Stenberg*. Thus Justice Kennedy's perception of the proper understanding of *Casey* ultimately carried the day.

More recently several states have passed laws that would seem to be inconsistent with *Roe* even as modified in *Casey*.[101] As with the laws in both *Webster* and *Casey*, these state

---

[97] *Id.* at 1001.

[98] *Id.* at 1002.

[99] 530 U.S. 914 (2000).

[100] 550 U.S. 124 (2007).

[101] Federal district courts have enjoined the enforcement of abortion regulations recently passed by the Arkansas and North Dakota legislatures. Edwards v. Beck (E.D. Ark. May 23, 2013) (granting preliminary

laws would appear to be intended, at least in part, to force a direct challenge to the continued vitality of *Roe*. If one of these laws is sustained by the lower courts, it is almost certain that yet another "great case" regarding abortion will be presented to the Court.

ROE AND CASEY AS GREAT CASES

Roe v. Wade is arguably the most controversial decision in Supreme Court history aside from the *Dred Scott* Case. Forty years after *Roe* was decided, even as modified by *Casey*, it remains a flashpoint for vigorous disagreement. The justices understood at the time that the decision would be controversial. Justice Blackmun says as much at the outset of his opinion. But it is highly unlikely that they recognized how deep and entrenched the firestorm over *Roe* would be. Despite the probability of resistance, *Roe* was decided by a confident Court. Once having voted to invalidate the abortion laws of Texas and Georgia in its initial conference, the majority never seemed to waiver despite the fact that it took over a year to produce an opinion. As the author of the majority opinion, and over time the most ardent defender of *Roe*, Justice Blackmun bore the brunt of the criticism for the decision. And yet of all the members of the majority, he seemed to have been the most troubled by the decision initially. The inability of Justice Blackmun to produce a minimally persuasive opinion after expending so much time and effort should have alerted the other justices to the fact that they were preparing to sail into a hurricane. A significantly stronger legal opinion would not have dissolved the controversy over *Roe* as it went to the very legitimacy of deciding the case at all. But a more cogent opinion in *Roe* would have made the decision appear at least somewhat more legal and less arbitrary. As with *Dred Scott*, the incoherence and overall substandard quality of the opinion's legal craftsmanship provided an easy target for its critics.

Why was the *Roe* opinion so poorly reasoned? Why did seven justices sign on to an opinion that could be so easily discredited, even by those who sympathized with the outcome? It should be obvious that Justice Blackmun simply did not have the skills as a legal craftsman to produce a minimally competent defense of the decision despite laboring for over a year. As inadequate as the *Roe* opinion is, apparently Blackmun's first draft, which was demolished by Justice White's critique, was far worse. When Blackmun produced a new draft the following year that ultimately became the basis for the *Roe* opinion, the other members of the majority were eager to praise it and relatively quick to concur. Surely they understood that it remained a terribly weak opinion. A master legal craftsman such as Brennan could certainly have produced a remarkably better opinion. Brennan did make extensive suggestions to Blackmun, some of which were accepted, but in the end, the substance of *Roe* remained Blackmun's product. Apparently, the other justices sensed that writing *Roe* had placed Blackmun under extreme stress. He had become quite defensive and possessive about the opinion, especially given that his background as

---

injunction); MKB Mgmt. Corp. v. Burdick (D. N.D. July 22, 2013) (granting preliminary injunction). The Arkansas law prohibited abortions after the twelfth week of pregnancy while the North Dakota law banned them after the sixth week. Texas recently passed a law that would require doctors performing abortions to have hospital admission privileges. The law was enjoined by a federal district court however the injunction was stayed by the Fifth Circuit Court of Appeals.

counsel for the Mayo Clinic had convinced him that he was uniquely qualified to write it. Under other circumstances, a more collaborative effort may have been welcomed, but not in *Roe*. It would appear that the other justices simply understood that in order to produce an opinion at all, they would essentially have to live with whatever Blackmun produced. Given the agonizingly slow pace at which Blackmun worked, especially on this case, it is likely that the rest of the majority was grateful, at last, to have something. There is no reason to believe that the decision and opinion in *Roe* could have been written in a manner that did not result in extreme controversy, but at least some of the criticism could have been averted if someone other than Justice Blackmun had written the opinion.

If as *Roe*'s harshest critics charge, the inevitable flaw in the decision is the inability of the Court as a matter of constitutional law to justify defining when the state's interest in protecting life or potential life outweighs the woman's interest in obtaining an abortion, the opinion and the oral arguments would seem to suggest that the justices simply failed to understand how significant this difficulty was. If as Justices White and Scalia have charged, the Court had no business deciding *Roe*, it was because the question at the center of *Roe* was qualitatively different than virtually every other case that the Court had decided. But at the time of *Roe*, no one on the Court other than Justice White and possibly Justice Rehnquist seemed to recognize this. The failure of the Court, if there was one, to fully appreciate the arguably non-judicial nature of the case cannot be attributed to the fact that *Roe* was a great case. There was certainly momentum pushing the abortion issue toward the Court as lawsuits were being brought nationwide challenging state abortion laws. But the very greatness of the case in the sense that it presented the Court with a question of extreme national controversy also produced several amicus briefs warning the Court against proceeding.

Roe is a prime example of the difficulty engendered by the jurisdictional statutes that existed at the time the case was decided. If a constitutional challenge was brought to a state statute, a three-judge district court consisting of two district and one appellate judge would be impaneled. If the three-judge court enjoined enforcement of the state law, the state would have the right to a direct appeal to the Supreme Court. If the court invalidated the law but declined to enjoin its enforcement, as happened in *Roe*, the challengers could appeal the denial of injunctive relief, as in fact they did. The state cross appealed. This forced the Court to consider many cutting edge issues before there was an opportunity for the lower courts to work through the legal issues over an extended period of time, providing the Supreme Court with more useful factual and legal information. *Roe* may be an example of a case that appeared on the Court's doorstep too quickly. The Court might have benefited from more thorough consideration in the lower courts. The opinion of the three-judge district court in *Roe* itself was too cursory to be helpful. There were some state court decisions to be sure, but a wider array of lower court federal precedent may have alerted the Court to the intractability of the litigation. Within a decade after *Roe*, the three-judge court procedure was replaced with jurisdictional provisions providing the Court with near complete control over its own docket.

Sometimes, great cases result in thorough and informative briefing and argument by highly skilled advocates, and sometimes, as was the case with *Roe*, they do not. None of the advocates in *Roe* were experienced at the Supreme Court level. None of them seemed to grasp that the Court was searching for a compromise of competing interests, as difficult as that may have been in this case. The arguments for *Roe* were mediocre at best. Those for the state were atrocious. It is unlikely that better advocacy would have changed the result but perhaps it would have contributed at least to a marginally better opinion.

The ease with which the Court was willing to enter the abortion fray is arguably the inevitable result of the path that the Court had taken during the Warren Court era, tackling school segregation, reapportionment, criminal procedure, school prayer, and the death penalty. It had rejected Justice Harlan's warning that the Constitution was not a panacea for every social ill. There can be little question that the justices who voted to strike down the abortion laws of Texas and Georgia found them to be harsh, punitive, and quite wrongheaded. For some members of the Court, perhaps that was sufficient. The constitutionality of restrictive abortion laws may well have seemed no different than other reactionary laws that the Court had addressed over the past two decades. The fact that abortion by definition involved the termination of at least a potential life in being did not seem to distinguish the issue significantly for the justices in the *Roe* majority or for that matter for the two unanimous three-judge district courts that had also invalidated the laws. Arguably by 1971, many, if not most federal judges, perceived themselves as heroic agents of social change. If so, restrictive abortion laws were simply the next dragon to be slain.

It is unlikely that the Court anticipated the severe criticism it received from highly respected academics, many of whom were quite sympathetic to its civil liberties jurisprudence. If the Court was disappointed with these stinging rebukes, it did not flinch as a result. For over 20 years after *Roe*, the Court defended the decision vigorously. *Roe* might suggest that even when the justices have some reason to believe that they may have made a very serious error, at least as long as they have some constituency of support, they are more than willing to resist both public and professional criticism and pressure. For Justice Blackmun, defending *Roe* became an intensely emotional personal crusade, as his dissents in *Webster* and *Casey* reveal. The irony is that Blackmun, who was arguably the most reluctant member of the *Roe* majority, became the living embodiment of the decision and its most strident champion.

Did *Roe v. Wade* make bad law? One hesitates to even pose the question. To its critics, it made the worst law of any decision of the past 100 years. To its supporters, the law it made is among the greatest triumphs in the Court's constitutional history. It certainly produced an opinion that was hard, if not impossible, to defend. Both the trimester framework and many of the specific applications have been overturned by justices who were at least somewhat sympathetic to what they deemed its core values. Its standard of review has been reduced significantly from strict scrutiny to undue burden. Abortion remains widely available. However its opponents have been encouraged to continue the enactment of legislative challenges. It has survived an explicit challenge before the Court, but it has been modified significantly in the process. It seems to be entrenched in the public consciousness. But it remains a polarizing issue in elections and in Supreme Court confirmation hearings. Can a decision that has remained so publicly controversial after 40 years be said to have produced good law in any ordinary sense of the phrase?

Roe was an unusual great case in that it in turn gave rise to another great case when the Court finally did agree to reconsider it in *Casey*. It is unusual though not entirely unprecedented for the Court to explicitly reconsider the correctness of a major decision that has become fairly entrenched. To some extent, the very fact that the Court did revisit *Roe* in *Casey* is testament to the fact that the critics of *Roe* both on and off the Court attacked the decision as not simply wrongly decided, but rather as a wholly illegitimate exercise of judicial power. Of course the primary reason the Court was willing to reconsider *Roe* in *Casey* was because the opponents of *Roe* on the Court were relatively confident that they finally had the votes to overrule it—and they almost did. The failure to muster a majority to overrule *Roe* despite the fact that Justices Kennedy and O'Connor had clearly expressed misgivings as to the correctness of the decision is evidence of the power of the Court through its decisions to reshape the world around it. As controversial as *Roe* was, it certainly had a large and loyal contingent of supporters. *Roe v. Wade* was not just another case. For many Americans, it was one of their most cherished decisions. The members of the Joint Opinion understood that in 1992 the Court could not return the legal landscape to where it stood in 1973. *Roe* whether rightly or wrongly decided had forever altered the constitutional universe. The price of overruling would be steep indeed, not simply because a large segment of the population would be disappointed with the result but rather because so many would view the Court as having removed a crucial constitutional landmark.

Did public pressure play a role in the ultimate decision in *Casey*? Did the massive marches for and against *Roe* along with the baskets and baskets of mail matter? One would assume not. The justices were mature professionals confident in their roles. The portion of the Joint Opinion addressing stare decisis spoke of the need not to betray those who had adhered to the decision, but this does not suggest that the justice felt beholden to the supporters of *Roe*. Instead, it was best understood as recognition that the law does not exist as abstractions in a law school class but rather takes on a cultural life of its own. Certain decisions such as *Brown* and *Roe* acquire an iconic significance that extends far beyond their doctrinal meaning. The plaintiff's attorney in *Casey* was able to bring this home to at least some of the justices although they probably realized this without being told. Just as the majority in *Roe* may not have fully grasped the difficulty of attempting to justify the decision to prefer abortion over potential life, the dissenters in *Casey* may not have truly understood the social and cultural disruption that the explicit reversal of *Roe* would have caused. The dissents proceed on the ordinarily reasonable assumption that establishing that a decision was illegitimate and unjustifiable should be more than enough to warrant its reversal. It is far from clear that Justices O'Connor and Kennedy would not agree that *Roe* was indeed illegitimate and unjustifiable, at least when decided in 1973. Quite possibly neither would have concurred in the decision at that time. But something more was at stake, and it was not simply respect for stare decisis. Both justices along with Justice Souter understood that *Roe* had become so much more than a constitutional decision. If Chief Justice Rehnquist and Justices Scalia, White, and Thomas understood that, then they did not care.

Did *Casey* make bad law? As with *Roe*, the answer to that question might vary according to one's views of *Roe* itself. Supporters of *Roe* should be grateful that it survived to some extent but disappointed that it no longer existed in its original and purest form. Its opponents would be crushed that *Roe* was not overruled, especially when the Court seemed to be so close. The Joint Opinion joined by Stevens and Blackmun provided some stability to constitutional doctrine in this area by endorsing both substantive due process as well as Justice Harlan's *Poe v. Ullman* analytical framework. Still in subsequent cases involving assisted suicide and gay rights, the justices would quarrel over whether Harlan's approach placed primary emphasis on history and tradition or on a balancing approach to derive and apply liberty-based rights.[102] Likewise the Joint Opinion's explanation of the constitutional justification for the abortion right, though hardly perfect, was a significant improvement over anything offered in *Roe* or in subsequent abortion cases. The undue burden standard is susceptible to Scalia's criticism that it is formless and infinitely malleable. Pro-choice advocates can justly complain that *Casey* itself demonstrated that it is capable of cutting deeply into the basic abortion right. Nonpartisan observers might conclude that *Casey* struck a fairer but still unprincipled balance between the conflicting interests. The partial birth abortion cases illustrate that the *Casey* compromise, especially with respect to the state interest in the protection of fetal life or dignity, is readily capable of divergent interpretations.

The Joint Opinion's discussion of the factors that should influence whether a prior case should be overruled was significant. Although it may not encompass every factor that might be considered, it is still the most comprehensive discussion of the question in the United States Reports and will almost certainly be cited and relied upon in the future. The discussion of why the Court should otherwise stand behind an arguably incorrect precedent is more problematic. The Joint Opinion's declaration that on occasion, the Court is warranted in calling an end to a heated national controversy through a constitutional ruling, which the public should then accept, would seem to be the height of judicial arrogance. It would be surprising and unhealthy in a democracy if the Court could in fact effectively demand such unswerving allegiance. The fact that a majority of the Court seemed to believe that this was indeed the Court's role suggests that it had learned very little from the *Dred Scott* debacle.

In the wake of *Casey, Roe* has been described as a super precedent. That is, based on the premise that because the Court thoroughly considered overruling *Roe* and then declined to do so, it now bears an extra layer of protection that almost all other decisions lack. A decision to overrule *Roe* would now require a double rejection of stare decisis in that it would entail the rejection of both *Roe* and *Casey*. For those such as Justices Scalia and Thomas who believe that *Roe* was profoundly wrong at its very core, it may never be too late to correct a constitutional error of this magnitude. Some decisions may be so deeply incorrect that they are never beyond reconsideration. Although that position is not unprincipled it would be difficult for it to attract five votes as *Casey* becomes as entrenched as *Roe*. The controversy surrounding *Roe* may be unlikely to diminish significantly in years to come; however; the decision, at least as modified, may very well be here to stay.

---

[102] *See* Washington v. Glucksburg, 521 U.S. 707, 721–22 (1997) (Rehnquist, C.J., relying on history and tradition), 765–67 (Souter, J., concurring, relying on a balance between the state and liberty interests).

"It was very likely the most profound constitutional event in our history: the dethroning of a President."[1]

ANTHONY LEWIS

19

United States v. Nixon

United States v. Nixon[2] is the very definition of the great case. It pitted the president of the United States against a special prosecutor investigating his conduct at a time when he had been named as an unindicted co-conspirator in a felony case and at a time when the House of Representatives was considering Articles of Impeachment against him. It raised at least the possibility of presidential defiance of a court order. It was litigated under extreme time pressure with intense public and press attention. It resulted in the recognition of a limited constitutional communications privilege for the president. But most significantly it resulted in the production of the "smoking gun," leading to the resignation of the president shortly after the decision was handed down.

BACKGROUND

United States v. Nixon was the culmination of the series of events known as Watergate. The central event was a foiled break-in to the headquarters of the Democratic Party in the Watergate Hotel complex during the presidential campaign of 1972, which had originated in the White House. In fact, the beginning of Watergate can be traced back to the fallout from incidents underlying another great case, *New York Times v. United States* (the Pentagon Papers Case). Disturbed by the leak of the Pentagon Papers as well as other leaks of confidential information, President Nixon ordered top aide John Erlichman to stop the leaks. Erlichman authorized the creation of the "Plumbers Unit" operating out of the Executive Office Building. Members of that unit broke into the office of Dr. Fielding,

---

[1] Anthony Lewis, *Introduction* to JAMES DOYLE, NOT ABOVE THE LAW: THE BATTLES OF WATERGATE PROSECUTORS COX AND JAWORSKI 13 (1977). Doyle was the public spokesman for the Special Prosecutors Office under Archibald Cox, Leon Jaworski, and Henry Ruth. His book provides a detailed look at the Watergate prosecutions from inside that office.
[2] 418 U.S. 683 (1974).

Daniel Ellsburg's psychiatrist, apparently searching for information to discredit Ellsburg. Nine months later, on June 17, 1972, several of the same members of the Plumbers Unit orchestrated the break-in of the headquarters of the Democratic National Committee in the Watergate building in Washington, DC. They were caught and arrested on the spot. Bob Woodward, a young reporter for the *Washington Post*, discovered that one of the individuals involved, Howard Hunt, was a consultant working at the White House, and began an intense investigation of the matter.

Four of the burglars (the Cubans) along with Hunt pleaded guilty in federal district court early in 1973. Two others, James McCord and Gordon Liddy, stood trial and were convicted. Judge Sirica, suspecting that something was amiss, withheld immediate sentencing. On March 20, McCord presented Judge Sirica with a letter explaining that the defendants had been pressured to plead guilty by higher-ups and that perjury had been committed. Shortly thereafter, White House counsel John Dean began speaking to federal prosecutors investigating the case. Within three weeks, Attorney General Kleindeist and White House aides H. R. Haldeman and John Erlichman resigned and John Dean was dismissed. After much public uproar, Harvard Law School professor Archibald Cox was appointed special counsel to investigate the case.

A Senate Committee formed to investigate the Watergate break-in and related events began holding nationally televised hearings in May 1973. In June, John Dean, who had been granted immunity from prosecution, testified at length, declaring that the White House, including the president, had been deeply involved in an attempt to cover up its ties to the Watergate break-in. The following month Alexander Butterfield informed the Committee that the president's conversations within the Oval Office were tape-recorded. Both Cox and the Senate Committee requested that the president turn over several specified tapes. President Nixon refused. Both sought to subpoena the tapes. Judge Sirica rejected the Committee subpoena but ordered the president to comply with the subpoena issued by the grand jury pursuant to Cox's request to produce the tapes for in camera inspection by the court.[3] The Court of Appeals for the District of Columbia Circuit upheld Judge Sirica's order to produce the tapes.[4] President Nixon proposed that instead of surrendering the tapes, the White House would provide summaries and partial transcripts, and Senator Stennis could listen to the tapes to verify that only non-pertinent information had been excluded. Cox rejected the proposal, noting that the courts were unlikely to accept such versions of the tapes as admissible evidence. John Dean pleaded guilty to obstruction of justice on the basis of evidence that was not derived from his immunized testimony. The president ordered Attorney General Elliot Richardson to fire Cox. In what became known as the Saturday night massacre, Richardson resigned, his deputy Donald Ruckleshaus resigned, and then Solicitor General Robert Bork dismissed Cox.[5] The firing of Cox gave rise to what White House Chief of Staff Alexander Haig characterized as a "firestorm" of adverse publicity for the president. Within 10 days, Leon Jaworski was

---

[3] *In re* Grand Jury Subpoena, 360 F. Supp. 1 (1973).

[4] Nixon v Sirica, 487 F. 2d 700 (D.C. Cir. 1973).

[5] Cox provides a firsthand account of the events in his book The Court and the Constitution 1-27 (1987). Judge Bork also described his role in the events in his book Saving Justice: Watergate, the Saturday Night Massacre, and Other Adventures of a Solicitor General (2013).

appointed to succeed Cox as special counsel and was given more independence and protection than Cox had.

Three weeks later, the White House advised Jaworski that there was an 18½- minute erasure on the tape of the meeting of Nixon and his top aides on June 20,1972, the first time they had met following the Watergate break-in. Experts indicated that the erasure had almost certainly been intentional. The White House indicated that two requested tapes could not be found but produced the others. A tape of a meeting in the Oval Office on March 21, 1973, confirmed John Dean's Senate testimony and showed that President Nixon had directed the payment of hush money to Howard Hunt in violation of several federal criminal statutes. The tape was not made public for several months.

Based on the material that had been discovered and produced, Jaworski persuaded the grand jury to indict seven officials, including Haldeman, Erlichman, and former attorney general John Mitchell. In a sealed indictment, the grand jury also named President Nixon as an unindicted co-conspirator. At the direction of the grand jury, Judge Sirica forwarded an extensive Bill of Particulars detailing the alleged conspiracy and the president's role to the House Committee that had been formed to determine whether there were grounds for impeachment.

On April 1974, Jaworski served a subpoena on the White House pursuant to Federal Rule of Criminal Procedure 17(c) for 64 more tapes needed as evidence in the upcoming trial of the seven indicted former officials. At the end of April, the White House released edited transcripts of the previously produced tapes to the House Committee, including the tape of March 21, 1973, in which Nixon had essentially led the effort to pay hush money to Hunt. This resulted in an extensive public reaction against the president. Shortly thereafter, the House Committee began consideration of whether articles of impeachment were warranted. Judge Sirica ordered Nixon to produce the 64 tapes. Nixon moved to quash the subpoena on several grounds, including presidential privilege. Jaworski asked the Supreme Court to hear the case, bypassing the Court of Appeals. Nixon's press secretary Ron Ziegler stated that the president would abide by a "definitive" ruling by the Court, which gave rise to the concern that he might not abide by a less-than-definitive ruling.

Initially, almost all of the justices were disinclined to bypass the Court of Appeals but ultimately changed their minds and decided to grant the request.[6] The Court imposed an expedited briefing and argument schedule. Not surprisingly, the nation focused on the proceeding with great intensity. Justice Rehnquist, who had been assistant attorney general in charge of the Office of Legal Counsel in the Department of Justice under President Nixon, recused himself from the case. After the Court had agreed to hear the case, defense counsel in the criminal trial leaked to the press that the grand jury had named the president as an unindicted co-conspirator. James D. St. Clair, President Nixon's attorney, asked the Court to determine whether constitutionally the president could be named as an unindicted co-conspirator. Jaworski filed a sealed brief with the Court detailing the evidence that his office had accumulated with respect to President Nixon's potential criminal liability.

---

[6] THE SUPREME COURT IN CONFERENCE (1940–1985): THE PRIVATE DISCUSSIONS BEHIND NEARLY 300 SUPREME COURT DECISIONS 184 (Del Dickson ed., 2001).

Oral argument took place on July 8, 1974. In the argument Jaworski objected to the president's claim that he had the final authority to define and apply a presidential communications privilege. Jaworski suggested that the president was attempting to place himself above the courts and the law.[7] In response, Justice Stewart noted that the president had in fact submitted himself and resolution of the issue to the judicial process.[8] James D. St. Clair, representing President Nixon, took a rather hard-line approach, proclaiming that the president had an absolute privilege with respect to the tapes and that however the Court ruled, the president would ultimately have to decide whether to produce the tapes.[9] He also maintained that every question pertaining to Watergate related to the performance of the president's official duties and that the tapes would be completely privileged even if they revealed a criminal conspiracy. St. Clair asserted that the president remained the head of the executive branch, and that there were only three branches of government, not three and one-half.[10] In rebuttal, special assistant to Jaworski Phillip Lacovara asserted that the president was precluded from asserting presidential privilege because the tapes previously produced demonstrated that he was party to a criminal conspiracy.[11] In surrebuttal, St. Clair stated that the president did not claim to be above the law, but that the law could only be applied to him through the impeachment process.[12]

DRAFTING THE OPINION

The book *The Brethren* by Bob Woodward and Scott Armstrong purports to provide an inside look at the drafting of the opinion in *United States v. Nixon*. Assuming that the account is accurate, most of the details could only have come from one of the justices, presumably Justice Stewart, who was later revealed to have been the primary source.[13] Because of the gravity of the questions and the fact that the Nixon administration had indicated that it might not obey anything less than a definitive ruling, the justices were convinced that as with *Brown v. Board of Education*, it was essential that they produce a unanimous opinion. That obviously made their tasks more difficult as it increased the leverage of any justice who might threaten to concur or dissent. Chief Justice Burger assigned the writing of the opinion to himself over the objection of Justice Blackmun, who noted that he might be called on to preside at an impeachment trial of the president.[14] Apparently, several of the justices were unhappy with the pace at which Burger was proceeding as well as with his initial drafts and began to write portions of the opinion themselves.[15] The justices were particularly dissatisfied

---

[7] Transcript of Oral Argument, *in* 79 Landmark Briefs and Arguments of the Supreme Court of the United States: Constitutional Law 844 (Philip B. Kurland & Gerhard Casper eds., 1975).

[8] *Id.*

[9] *Id.* at 871–72, 879.

[10] *Id.* at 875.

[11] *Id.* at 904–05.

[12] *Id.* at 915.

[13] John C. Jeffries, Jr., Justice Lewis F. Powell, Jr. 389 (1994).

[14] Bob Woodward & Scott Armstrong, The Brethren: Inside the Supreme Court 301 (1979).

[15] *Id.* at 310–25.

with a portion of the opinion on presidential privilege discussing the "core functions" of the president.[16] That concept was eventually eliminated. Justice Powell maintained that a subpoena served on the president for evidence should be required to meet a higher standard of proof; however Justice White objected and threatened to dissent if the Court took such an approach. At various points, Justices Douglas, White, and Powell threatened to write separate opinions but were persuaded to join the opinion of the chief justice.[17] After much bargaining and rewriting, the opinion was completed. On July 24, 1974, the opinion was issued.

Former chief justice Warren died while the opinion was being written. While the Court was working on the opinion, the House Committee across the street was debating whether to issue Articles of Impeachment against the president.

THE OPINION

The unanimous opinion delivered by Chief Justice Burger addressed several issues. Under the heading of *Jurisdiction* it concluded that there was a right to appeal from the district court's order despite the fact that the president had not explicitly refused to obey nor had he been held in contempt as it would be unseemly to require such a contempt citation against the president.[18] Under the heading of *Justiciability*, the Court concluded that despite the fact that the special prosecutor was a member of the executive branch, the parties were sufficiently adverse to create a viable case and controversy. The president had argued that as he was constitutionally the head of the executive branch, the dispute over production of the tapes was an intra-branch controversy and as such the district court's holding should be vacated and the case dismissed. The Court rejected this argument, noting that the special counsel had been appointed pursuant to an executive order that protected him against dismissal absent "extraordinary improprieties," and even then not before the president had consulted with the leaders of the House and Senate. The Court acknowledged that the president could repeal the regulation and then dismiss the special prosecutor at will, but held that until he did, he was bound by the regulation, which granted the prosecutor sufficient independence to establish a justiciable case in federal court. The next preliminary issue involved whether the requirements of Federal Rule of Criminal Procedure 17(c) had been met. The Court concluded that the special prosecutor had indeed presented evidence establishing that with respect to each of the subpoenaed tapes, the 17(c) requirements of relevancy, admissibility, and specificity had been satisfied.

The Court then turned to the central issue of the case: whether there was a constitutionally based privilege with respect to confidential communications of the president and his close advisors. At the outset, Chief Justice Burger noted that the president claimed that separation of powers precluded judicial review of the president's assertion of the privilege. In other words, the president maintained that there was in fact a constitutionally based privilege, it was absolute, and once he asserted it no further judicial review of the claim was permissible. That position had been pressed very hard by St. Clair during

---

[16] *Id.* at 329-39.

[17] *Id.* at 337, 344.

[18] 418 U.S. at 691–92.

oral argument but the Court was unwilling to accept it. Burger acknowledged that each branch of government must necessarily interpret the Constitution in the first instance in the performance of its duties. But he quoted *Marbury v. Madison* for the proposition that "'it is emphatically the province and duty of the judicial department to say what the law is.'" The Court cited and quoted from several cases in which it had resolved questions involving actions taken by other branches of the federal government and then once again quoted the same language from *Marbury*.

Turning to the specific claim of privilege raised by the president, Burger recognized that there was a legitimate need for the protection of the confidential communications between the president and his advisors to ensure that advice would not be tempered by the fear of disclosure. He declared that "the supremacy of each branch within its own assigned area of constitutional duties" provided a constitutional source for such a privilege.[19] Chief Justice Burger then concluded however that the doctrine of separation of powers did not justify an absolute privilege for confidential communications. What the Court characterized as the "broad undifferentiated claim of public interest in confidentiality in such conversations" as opposed to the protection of "military, diplomatic or sensitive national security secrets" warranted only a qualified privilege that must be balanced against competing interests.[20]

Specifically, the Court declared that an absolute privilege would interfere with the need of the judicial branch "to do justice in criminal prosecutions." It quoted Justice Jackson's observation in his *Youngstown* concurrence that the Constitution presumes "separateness but interdependence, autonomy but reciprocity." Burger noted that "[s]ince we conclude that the legitimate needs of the judicial process may outweigh Presidential privilege, it is necessary to resolve those competing interests in a manner that preserves the essential function of each branch."[21] He acknowledged the critical need for "candid, objective and even blunt or harsh opinions in Presidential decision-making."[22] However the "presumptive privilege must be considered in light of our historic commitment to the rule of law."[23] He then emphasized that "[t]he very integrity of the judicial system and public confidence in the system depend on full disclosure of all of the facts...."[24] The Court acknowledged that other testimonial privileges had been recognized, including the Privilege against Self-Incrimination and the attorney-client privilege. However, he cautioned that such privileges "are not lightly created nor expansively construed for they are in derogation of the search for truth."[25]

Chief Justice Burger repeated the need for extreme protection for military secrets, quoting from the opinion in *United States v. Reynolds*,[26] but cautioned that it has never extended "this high degree of deference to a President's generalized interest in confidentiality."[27] He then tied the right to the production of evidence in a criminal trial to

---

[19] *Id.* at 705.
[20] *Id.* at 706-07.
[21] *Id.* at 707.
[22] *Id.* at 708.
[23] *Id.*
[24] *Id.* at 709.
[25] *Id.* at 710.
[26] 345 U.S. 1 (1953).
[27] *Nixon*, 418 U.S. at 711.

constitutional values as well, citing the Confrontation Clause, compulsory process, and due process of law. Although the Court repeated again its respect for the importance of confidentiality of communications among the president and his close advisors, it nevertheless concluded that it did not believe that the occasional demands for production in the criminal process would chill the candor of such communications. However the denial of such evidence to the criminal process would "gravely impair the function of the courts."[28] It declared that the president's need for confidentiality "is general in nature," whereas the need for evidence in a criminal case "is specific and central to the fair adjudication of a particular criminal case...."[29] Thus the Court held that the president's privilege had been overridden by the special prosecutor's subpoena. It concluded the opinion by setting forth some procedures for in camera consideration of the material produced to the district court.

The Court dismissed as improvidently granted the president's petition to consider whether he could constitutionally be named as an unindicted co-conspirator.

THE IMMEDIATE IMPACT

The decision was handed down on July 25, 1974. On July 27, the House Judiciary Committee recommended an Article of Impeachment charging that the president had engaged in obstruction of justice with respect to the Watergate break-in investigation. Two days later it reported out a second Article of Impeachment focusing on the abuse of power with regard to the misuse of executive agencies. And the following day it approved a third Article concerned with the willful disobedience of the House subpoenas. The president made transcripts of the tapes available on August 6, eleven days after the Court's opinion. The transcript of conversations in the oval office on June 23, 1972, between President Nixon and advisor H. R. Haldeman, clearly revealed that the president was deeply involved in a plan to halt the FBI investigation of the break-in by recruiting Richard Helms, the director of the CIA, to call Patrick Gray, the director of the FBI, and inform him that the investigation would reveal sensitive information about CIA operations, which would not be in the best interest of the nation. Ironically in that conversation, Nixon and Haldeman assumed that Assistant Director of the FBI Mark Felt would cooperate, unaware of course that he would ultimately become "deep throat," the source who confirmed information discovered by *Washington Post* reporters Bob Woodward's and Carl Bernstein's investigation of the Watergate coverup. The tape was considered to be the "smoking gun" although it does not seem any more damaging than the previously released tape of the March 21, 1973, meeting in which Nixon had effectively orchestrated the payment of the hush money to Hunt. Nixon resigned from the presidency three days later. Consequently, the impeachment process did not go forward.

Jaworski and members of his staff argued over whether the indictment against Nixon's advisors should now be supplemented to add Nixon as a defendant. Most of the staff favored doing so; however Jaworski was hesitant.[30] The issue was resolved on

---

[28] *Id.* at 712.
[29] *Id.* at 713.
[30] Doyle, *supra* note 1, at 351–71.

September 8 when President Ford pardoned Nixon for any acts committed during the Watergate period. Jaworski departed as special counsel and was replaced by his chief deputy Henry Ruth.

The trial of the five indicted officials and aides began in October 1974. Some of the material obtained on account of the Supreme Court decision proved very helpful to the prosecution. Nixon was not called as a witness due to ill health. On January 1, 1975, the jury found Mitchell, Haldeman, Erlichman, and Mardian guilty on all counts. Kenneth Parkinson was acquitted. Mardian's conviction was reversed on appeal, and the case was dismissed. Strachan, whose case had been severed, was never tried.

It is probable that Nixon would have been forced out of office in any event but it would almost certainly have been a long and painful process. Doctrinally the opinion has had almost no impact at all. The issues presented have never again arisen, and there has been little reason to rely on the opinion or its reasoning. In that sense, though important, it is somewhat of a historical curiosity.

The Watergate episode itself led to a significant amount of legislation, especially relating to ethics in government, campaign finance, and independent prosecutors. But that would have happened in any event in the wake of Watergate with or without the Court's opinion in *United States v. Nixon*. The Court did uphold the constitutionality of the Independent Counsel statute in *Morrison v. Olsen*, but unlike the Nixon case, the counsel there was authorized by congressional statute as opposed to executive order. And following the investigation of President Clinton by Independent Counsel Kenneth Starr, Congress allowed the statute to lapse when its time expired.

NIXON AS A GREAT CASE

The Court's decision to hear the case on an expedited basis and its opinion have been the subject of withering academic criticism. Philip Kurland declared that the opinion was based on "slogans and non-sequitars."[31] Paul Mishkin declared that it was supported by "fiat" rather than "reasoning."[32] Not all of the reaction was negative however. Paul Freund, arguably dean of constitutional law scholars, published a supportive assessment of the opinion in the *Harvard Law Review*.[33]

The decision to take the case away from the Court of Appeals and to hear it immediately placed it before the Court at least several weeks before it would otherwise have gotten there, if at all. Given that the Court's term was about to end, the case would not have been heard prior to October. Some highly respected commentators have argued that the Court did a disservice to the nation by preempting the impeachment process, which was the constitutionally appropriate method for addressing serious executive misconduct. Chief among these critics was Gerald Gunther, one of the leading constitutional scholars of his time. Gunther speculated that there was no immediate need for the evidence considering that the criminal trials would probably have been delayed pending the

---

[31] Philip B. Kurland, United States v. Nixon: *Who Killed Cock Robin?*, 22 U.C.L.A. L. REV. 68, 70 (1975).
[32] Paul Mishkin, *Great Cases and Soft Law: A Comment on* United States v Nixon, 22 U.C.L.A. L. REV. 76 (1975).
[33] Paul A. Freund, *Foreword: On Presidential Privilege*, 88 HARV. L. REV. 13 (1974).

impeachment process in any event.[34] He compared the Court's apparent desire to save the nation from the trauma of a presidential impeachment to "compulsive gamblers unable to resist a piece of the action, or knights in shining armor tempted to ride to the rescue in every situation of distress."[35] Gunther feared that the more that the Court intervened in emergency situations like the Nixon tapes case, the more likely that it would feel compelled to do the same in the future, and the more that the public would come to expect it, which would in the long run be unfortunate for the democratic process. In a private letter to Gunther, Justice Powell later explained that he had cast the deciding vote to hear the case on an expedited basis out of concern that the continuing agony of Watergate was diverting "attention from pressing domestic problems" and weakening the nation's "influence on the dangerous course of international events."[36]

In retrospect, contrary to Gunther's argument, a solid case can be made that the nation was better off because the Court short circuited what would have been a painful and exhaustive process, almost certainly resulting in the removal of Nixon in any event. The Court could not have known what the ultimate outcome would be when it decided to expedite the case. It did have reason to believe that there was solid evidence of the president's guilt, and would soon learn that the grand jury had named him as an unindicted co-conspirator. It appears that initially the consensus on the Court was not to interfere with the Court of Appeals, and for reasons that remain unclear, it reversed course after discussing the matter. The expedited action was unusual but certainly not unprecedented given *Youngstown* as well as the Pentagon Papers Case. Considering that there was good reason to believe that the president was culpable in criminal activity, and considering the vigorous resistance that the White House was continuing to show to congressional and judicial investigations, perhaps the justices concluded that those investigating the Watergate matter could benefit from the prestige of a ruling by the High Court. It certainly appears that the justices did not decide to intervene oblivious to the costs and risks of such a decision. The justices no doubt recognized that any information detrimental to the president contained in the subpoenaed tapes would be utilized in impeachment proceedings.

The opinion itself is open to significant criticism. At the outset, the Court ignored one significant issue, although it had not been pressed by the president, that is, whether the president was subject to judicial process at all. The lower courts had confronted the issue in the first round of the Nixon tapes cases and had held that the president could validly be subjected to legal process in the form of a subpoena.[37] The Supreme Court did not explicitly address the issue in *United States v. Nixon*; however some 20 years later in *Clinton v. Jones*,[38] it treated the question as having been settled implicitly in the *Nixon* case.

On the issue of justiciability, the court's reasoning was questionable. There was real adversity of interest between the special prosecutor and the president. There was nothing feigned about the dispute. However that in itself may not have been sufficient. True,

---

[34] Gerald Gunther, *Judicial Hegemony and Legislative Autonomy: The Nixon Case and the Impeachment Process*, 22 U.C.L.A. L. REV. 30, 32 (1974).

[35] *Id.* at 33.

[36] JEFFRIES, *supra* note 13, at 373–74.

[37] *See* Nixon v Sirica, 487 F. 2d 700 (D.C. Cir. 1973).

[38] 520 U.S. 681, 682 (1997).

the president had agreed to permit the special prosecutor to "contest assertions of Executive Privilege," and to give him "the greatest degree of independence consistent with the Attorney General's Statutory Accountability" as well as especially strong "for cause" protection against removal.[39] But as James St. Clair argued unsuccessfully, there is only one executive branch and the president is constitutionally the head of it. William Van Alstyne noted the case could well have been styled "Nixon v. Nixon."[40] It is true that several years later in *Morrison v. Olsen* by an 8-1 margin, the Court upheld the Independent Counsel statute that was enacted in the wake of Watergate. However, that case did not pit the independent counsel against the chief executive. Given the separation created by the regulations, perhaps the Court would have found justiciability in a case in which the independent counsel and the president were at loggerheads, at least where the president was not an unindicted co-conspirator in a felony, but surely it would have been a harder case warranting greater justification than the Court provided in the *Nixon* case. Implicit in the Court's explanation in *Nixon* seems to be the assumption that under the circumstances, the president simply could not be trusted to oversee the prosecutorial function properly and fairly. Clearly he could not. However, the Court could not say that either.

The Court's reasoning on the central issue, the existence, nature, and application of the presidential privilege, has been subjected to well-deserved criticism. At the outset, the president was almost certainly overreaching in arguing that he had final authority on the initial question of whether there was a constitutionally based confidential communications privilege. The question of whether such a privilege exists at all seems to be the type of standard constitutional question that the Court regularly resolves. As such, the quotation from *Marbury* that "it is emphatically the province and duty of the judiciary to say what the law is" was appropriately cited on this point. Ultimately, the president acknowledged that he had submitted the issue to the Court for resolution. The president did not say that he had the right to conclude that there was an absolute privilege, regardless of what the Court thought. Even so, it would not have been inconsistent with *Marbury* for the Court to have concluded that the existence and scope of the privilege was indeed for the president to determine. In other words, in the course of interpreting the Constitution, the Court had determined that this was essentially a political question left to the discretion of the president.

The Court would still be "saying what the law is." The law would simply be very favorable to the president. Such an approach, though marginally defensible, would have been inconsistent with the diminishment of the political question doctrine in the wake of the relatively recent landmark cases of *Baker v. Carr* and *Powell v. McCormick*. Determining the existence, nature, and scope of a constitutionally based privilege seems quite in line with the Court's role as constitutional interpreter. Indeed not long after *Marbury*, Marshall sitting as a circuit judge had done just that with respect to President Jefferson's objection to a subpoena served on him in the context of the Aaron Burr treason trial. Contrary to the Court's declaration, *Marbury* did not demand that the Court define the privilege. But the best reading of the development of judicial review justifies the Court's approach. Perhaps

---

[39] 38 Fed. Reg. 32805, as quoted in the Court's opinion at 418 U.S. at 694 n.8.

[40] William Van Alstyne, *A Political and Constitutional Review of* United States v Nixon, 22 U.C.L.A. L. REV. 116, 131 (1974).

even more important, the crucial factor driving virtually every aspect of the Court's decision and opinion was the recognition that there was more than ample evidence that the president was a participant in a felony conspiracy. As a matter of fairness, the Court could not emphasize this factor but there can scarcely be any doubt that it loomed larger than anything else in the case. It is probable that with the demise of the political question doctrine, the Court would have been unwilling to allow even a president above and beyond suspicion to mold his own privilege. Allowing a president who most definitely was not above and beyond suspicion to do so must have seemed out of the question even with the rapidly unfolding impeachment process as a backstop.

The Court's attempt to define the scope of the privilege was fraught with difficulty however. The Constitution itself recognizes two absolute privileges: that against self-incrimination in the Fifth Amendment and the Speech and Debate Privilege of Congress. There is no room for balancing in these instances no matter how severe the cost to the judicial process might be. Moreover, perhaps the closest analog to the confidential communications privilege sought by the president, the attorney-client privilege, is also absolute in nature. In each instance, there would be a need for candid communication in order for the purposes of the privilege to be served, be it adequate representation or presidential decision-making. In each instance, information of great significance to the adjudication of criminal cases would be withheld. And yet the need for an absolute privilege for attorney-client communications is well accepted.

Likewise, the case could be made that an absolute privilege would be sensible in that the president is in the best position to assess the need for confidentiality, and as head of the executive branch can also determine whether the importance of obtaining evidence in a particular criminal prosecution outweighs that need. In concluding that the president was entitled only to a qualified privilege, the Court emphasized the needs of the judicial branch for evidence in a criminal case but that scarcely distinguishes the issue from every other absolute privilege. The fact, as noted by the Court, that separation of powers is not complete and airtight does not distinguish the Speech and Debate Privilege of Congress. The Court concluded that "the legitimate needs of the judicial process outweigh Presidential privilege." However it made no attempt beyond mere assertion to explain why that was the case. This was the point where it is most apparent that the decision was driven by the fact that the president himself was implicated. It is difficult to believe that the interests in confidentiality in the White House would not have been given far greater respect by the Court were there no suspicions as to the president's complicity.

The Court did recognize quite explicitly the need for confidentiality and privacy in presidential communications, which would seem to be an interest of great significance. But it failed to follow through and provide the degree of protection that such an important interest would seem to deserve. As one commentator noted, throughout the opinion, the Court gave lip service to the significance of the president's interests in confidentiality, but declined to adopt rules and procedures that would provide real protection.[41] In the course of analogizing to the Privilege against Self-Incrimination and the attorney-client privilege, the Court remarked that privileges "are not lightly created nor expansively construed for they are in derogation of the search for truth."[42] Be that as it may, where

---

[41] Mishkin, *supra* note 32, at 83, 88.
[42] United States v. Nixon, 418 U.S. 683, 710 (1974).

the interests at stake are substantial, absolute privileges have indeed been created or recognized. The Court distinguished the confidential communications privilege from a privilege protecting military or diplomatic secrets, suggesting that there would likely be instances in which a presidential privilege would easily override the competing interest of the production of evidence in a criminal trial. It pointed out that it had never been highly deferential toward the president's generalized interest in confidentiality, which was hardly surprising considering that the issue had never before been presented to the Court. Likewise, the Court noted that there was no explicit presidential communication privilege in the Constitution, but this should scarcely be determinative if as the Court had concluded, the privilege was grounded in constitutional structure.

In balancing the president's interest in confidentiality against the needs of the criminal process, the Court reasoned that "we cannot conclude that advisors will be moved to temper the candor of their remarks by the infrequent occasions of disclosure because of the possibility that such conversations will be called for in the context of a criminal prosecution."[43] Perhaps not, especially if the decision comes to be understood (as it probably should be) as effectively applicable only when the participants in the conversations are themselves implicated in criminal activity. However this point could be just as easily turned around to argue that if the likelihood that confidential White House communications will be relevant to criminal proceedings is indeed rare, the loss to the criminal process caused by an absolute privilege would be slight whereas the loss to candor in communications could be substantial. Accordingly, the interest in preserving the candor of such communications should prevail over the slight loss to the criminal process considering that it will often be unclear exactly how essential the evidence will be in any event. The Court reasoned that withholding relevant evidence might well frustrate the search for truth in a specific criminal trial. But that is simply a given where the material in question is protected by a recognized evidentiary privilege. If the interests that the privilege is designed to protect are sufficiently important, the trial must do without. The Court never adequately explained why the interest in confidential communication between the president and his close advisors was not that important.

The Court's conclusion that a valid prosecutorial subpoena for evidence in a criminal trial would all but automatically prevail over the assertion of presidential privilege was unpersuasive. It was not unpersuasive simply because it was poorly reasoned or written, but rather because the position itself was difficult to defend. Presumably, it was the position that the Court felt that it was compelled to take considering the fact that there was ample reason to believe that the president was attempting to conceal evidence of his own criminal culpability, and that if given any wiggle room at all, he would use it to contest and delay production of the tapes. Given that the Court could not set forth the true rationale of its decision, it was forced to provide an explanation that could not support the weight of the holding.

United States v. Nixon is a case that comes close to illustrating Justice Holmes's famous dictum. Given the intensity of public furor that had developed over the two-year period since the Watergate break-in, the Court found itself in the middle of a political crisis quite unlike anything it had ever before experienced. As the case approached the Court, new

---

[43] *Id.* at 712.

developments seemed to seize the public's attention every day. The Senate Committee had issued a voluminous report detailing the evidence it had accumulated. The House was considering impeachment. Nixon aide Charles Colson, one of the seven indicted defendants, pleaded guilty. John Erlichman was convicted for authorizing the burglary of Dr. Fielding's office. The press and public learned that four months earlier, the grand jury had named the president as an unindicted co-conspirator. The news seemed to consist of wall-to-wall Watergate coverage. And now the Supreme Court had moved to center stage.

United States v. Nixon was a great case, and it certainly did seem to result in questionable if not positively bad law. The Court was almost certainly aware of this risk and went out of its way to limit the damage. The result as one commentator noted was not that the case made bad law but rather that it made "hardly any law at all."[44] As Justice Powell's biographer notes, "Powell had hoped for, and worked for a decision that cast a very small shadow."[45] The Court carefully distinguished away almost every other context in which the question of presidential privilege might be presented, including military-, diplomatic-, or national security–based secrets as well as requests for production in civil litigation or congressional demands. That left a holding that would be limited to requests for evidence in a criminal trial, a circumstance that might never again arise. This suggests that rather than use this great case to expound principles that would resonate in the future, it was much more concerned with limiting the impact of the decision.

As is often true of great cases, the haste with which they are litigated may increase the difficulty of thinking through the issue thoroughly and producing a well-crafted opinion. *United States v. Nixon* was actually the second round of the Nixon tapes litigation. Although the Court chose to bypass the Court of Appeals, there was a detailed appellate opinion in the prior case of *Nixon v. Sirica*, which could be of use to the Supreme Court. Though briefed in haste, the case was still well briefed and was argued by highly skilled advocates. Although the Court labored under time pressure, it did take three weeks to draft the opinion, and given that it had all but completed the work of the term, there was little else to distract the justices. Solid opinions have been written in far less time. The problem was not so much lack of time as dissatisfaction with the direction that the chief justice took in his initial drafts. It is probable that Justices Brennan, Stewart, or White working alone could have drafted a better opinion. The dissatisfaction with Burger's draft led to drafting the opinion by committee, which is rarely capable of producing a coherent product. As John Jeffries has noted "too many cooks muddied the reasoning and garbled the expression."[46]

The Court was almost certainly placed under more pressure by the perceived need for unanimity in view of the possibility of presidential defiance rather than the lack of time. It is difficult to say how seriously the Court considered the prospect of defiance. At least three justices (Douglas, White, and Powell) threatened to write separately although perhaps only to gain leverage. In an interview with Bill Moyers of PBS, Justice Powell did comment that the Court was quite concerned about the possibility of defiance given that the president had the best infantry in the world at his disposal whereas the Court merely

---

[44] Louis Henkin, *Executive Privilege: Mr. Nixon Loses but the Presidency Largely Prevails*, 22 U.C.L.A. L. REV. 40, 46 (1975).

[45] JEFFRIES, *supra* note 13, at 396.

[46] *Id.* at 387.

had 50 security guards.[47] Still the Court held several aces. The president's lawyer, James St. Clair, had basically committed to submission to the Court's authority during oral argument though not without at least some wiggle room. In the event of presidential defiance, the special prosecutor might very well have returned to the grand jury and sought indictment of the president based on the evidence already presented, as many on his staff had initially counseled. Public opinion would almost certainly and overwhelmingly have favored the Court. The president's political support was collapsing and defiance of an opinion of the Supreme Court would have led to complete desertion. And most important, any defiance by the president would undoubtedly result in an article of impeachment coupled with certain conviction in the Senate. Thus the justices had to know that as a practical matter, it was the president and not the Court that was painted into a corner. The possibility of defiance was serious enough to warrant every attempt at producing a unanimous opinion, but not so severe as to preclude the justices from proceeding with a relatively high degree of confidence that the opinion would be heeded even if not unanimous. Unanimity was important not necessarily to avoid outright defiance but instead to aid in convincing the president and his remaining supporters that there was little point in continuing to fight on.

Leading critics castigated the Court for asserting an unwarranted sense of its own preeminence in *Nixon*. Professor Gunther wrote that "the Court's over broad reliance on *Marbury* was at least a non sequitur and at worst dangerous nonsense."[48] Likewise Philip Kurland boiled the Court's opinion down to the assertion that "'[t]he President cannot assert that he is the law, because we are the law.'"[49] Perhaps the *Nixon* opinion might be read as an unsettling move toward a self-perception of complete constitutional supremacy by the justices. But nothing in the *Nixon* opinion should be taken out of context. Faced with a president that the Court had every reason to believe was implicated in several criminal offenses and who might well attempt to defy a judicial mandate, it is hardly surprising that the Court should puff up its chest a bit. As with the doctrine of the case, the Court's bearing should not necessarily carry into the future. Quite arguably, the Court had concluded that it was important to the nation that it resolve the case, but hardly an instance for self-aggrandizement.

The Court could well be faulted, as indeed it was, for bypassing the Court of Appeals and expediting the decision. It is certainly a point on which reasonable people can differ. But once the Court committed itself to hearing the case with such immediacy, it was destined to produce an opinion that could only be less than satisfying. Reports of the internal struggles within the Court over the drafting of the opinion suggest that it could have been much worse. Consideration of the opinion itself and what has been learned about its drafting would suggest that it was the product of a Court that was confident but certainly not arrogant. It understood that it had chosen to place itself in historic circumstances in which the risks to itself and to the nation were very real. It proceeded firmly but cautiously. *Nixon* was a great case that did some good and very little harm.

---

[47] Bill Moyers, In Search of the Constitution, Interview with Justice Lewis Powell, Jr., April 16, 1987.

[48] Gunther, *supra* note 34, at 35.

[49] Kurland, *supra* note 31, at 75.

"[T]he interest of the outside world was reflected within the Court as well. The excitement and intense anticipation on the Court was apparent to me the instant I entered the courthouse that morning."[1]

AN UNIDENTIFIED SUPREME COURT JUSTICE IN AN INTERVIEW WITH BERNARD SCHWARTZ

20

Bakke, Grutter, Gratz (and *Fisher*)

THE CONSTITUTIONALITY OF the use of racial preferences by institutions of higher education gave rise to not one but to several great cases. *Regents of the University of California v. Bakke*,[2] where the Court initially confronted the issue on the merits, and *Grutter v. Bollinger*[3] and *Gratz v. Bollinger*[4] where it revisited the issue 25 years later, were major media events resulting in record numbers of amicus briefs. Nine years later the issue of racial preferences in education appeared before the Court again in the high profile case of *Fisher v. University of Texas*. Indeed the publicity surrounding *Grutter* and *Gratz* was so extreme that the Court deviated from its standard practice by permitting a delayed audio broadcast of the oral argument immediately after it ended. The justices in these cases were aware that their decisions would shape the admissions practices of virtually all institutions of higher learning in the nation, and would serve as crucial precedents with respect to the constitutional legitimacy of racial classifications. The massive but ambiguous decision and opinions in *Bakke* had essentially provided the foundation for the use of race as a factor in college and graduate admissions for 25 years. The prospect that the *Bakke* framework was put at risk created an extreme intensity of interest surrounding the arguments and decisions in *Grutter* and *Gratz*. There is every reason to believe that the greatness of these cases played a crucial role in their resolution.

BACKGROUND

For 20 years following *Brown v. Board of Education*, the Court was faced exclusively with challenges to state racial classifications that it tended to refer to as invidious, that is,

---

[1] BERNARD SCHWARTZ, BEHIND *BAKKE*: AFFIRMATIVE ACTION AND THE SUPREME COURT 47 (1988).
[2] 438 U.S. 265 (1978).
[3] 539 U.S. 306 (2003).
[4] 539 U.S. 244 (2003).

classifications that existed for no reason other than racial prejudice. It was only a matter of time however before the Court would have to address whether the state could constitutionally employ racial classifications for socially benign purposes. Starting in the early 1970s, governmental entities had begun using race in the context of affirmative action programs in employment, contracting, and education as a means of providing compensation or remediation for past discrimination or as a means of attempting to create more racially integrated institutions. Cases arising in the context of employment and public contracting tended to be remedial in nature. Not so with cases arising in the context of higher education.

In 1974, in the case of *Defunis v. Odegard*,[5] it appeared initially that the Court would have the opportunity to assess the use of racial preferences in higher education. There, the plaintiff Defunis had been admitted to the University of Washington Law School after having successfully challenged the school's use of race in its admissions process. The challenge evaporated however when following oral argument, the Court dismissed the case as moot after the university essentially conceded that Defunis, who was then in his final semester of law school, would be permitted to graduate even if the Court ruled in the law school's favor. Rather than dissipate the controversy however, the non-decision in *Defunis* simply added to the momentum propelling the issue toward an ultimate showdown before the Court.

Four years after *Defunis*, the issue of affirmative action in admissions returned to the Court in the blockbuster case of *Regents of the University of California v. Bakke*. Alan Bakke, a white student, had applied for admission to the University of California at Davis School of Medicine. Bakke was a middle-aged former marine with a masters degree in engineering from Stanford. The school was quite new and had never discriminated against racial minorities. Finding that few members of minority groups were being admitted pursuant to its regular admissions program, the school set up an alternative program under which 16 places in the class of 100 would be reserved for members of three specified minority groups—Blacks, Chicanos, and Asians.[6] Members of these groups could also compete for admission in the remainder of the class as well. Bakke applied twice and was denied admission twice. His age almost certainly played a significant role in his rejection.[7] In view of the fact that his objective indicators, such as college grade point and medical school test board scores, were significantly higher than some of the minority applicants admitted under the special admissions program, Bakke brought suit in the California state courts arguing that the minority admissions program violated his rights under Title VI of the Civil Rights Act of 1964, which prohibits exclusion of any person on the basis of race from any program receiving federal funds, as well as under the Fourteenth Amendment of the Constitution. He prevailed in the trial court and before the California Supreme Court. That court held that the special admissions program at the medical school was an illegal racial quota, that the school could not rely on race at all in its admissions process, and that the school had not carried its burden of proving that in

[5] 416 U.S. 312 (1974).

[6] *Bakke*, 438 U.S. at 275.

[7] HOWARD BALL, THE *BAKKE* CASE: RACE, EDUCATION, AND AFFIRMATIVE ACTION 47 (2000).

the absence of the quota, Bakke would not have been admitted. The university filed a writ of certiorari with the Supreme Court of the United States. The Court accepted review.

By the time that the Court granted certiorari in *Bakke*, racial preference admissions programs in higher education were commonplace and considered extraordinarily important by the educational community as well as civil rights groups. A decision by the Court rejecting the use of race in the admissions process was perceived as a potentially disastrous setback for the cause of racial integration in academia and society at large. Consequently, dozens of organizations interested in the matter mobilized and filed amicus briefs urging reversal. Other organizations, concerned that the use of race for even the most noble purposes was constitutionally troublesome given the nation's history, filed briefs in support of the California decision. An especially influential brief was filed in support of the medical school by Columbia, Harvard, Stanford, and the University of Pennsylvania arguing that the use of race as one of several diversifying factors should be constitutional. This approach, modeled after the program employed by Harvard College, became known as the Harvard Plan. The medical school retained former solicitor general, Watergate independent counsel, and Harvard Law professor Archibald Cox to represent it. The United States entered the case as an amicus curie. Given the political sensitivity of the issue, the Carter White House became involved in the drafting of the government's brief.[8] Ultimately, it made no clear recommendation as to how the case should be resolved.

THE ORAL ARGUMENT

Bakke was definitely perceived at the time as a "great case." Considering its significance, the oral arguments were disappointing. Archibald Cox tried too hard to avoid the troublesome fact that the medical school did employ a flat out set-aside, arguing that it was not a quota given that there was no limit on the maximum number of minority students admissible. However, he almost immediately had to concede that there was in fact a limit on the number of white students—the central argument raised by Bakke.[9] Cox arguably pushed his position too far in maintaining that there would be no constitutional problem in reserving half of the seats in the class for minority students.[10] Finally, he argued that the use of a race in this case was not "invidious." However, he was challenged by Justice Stewart as to how that concept could be applied.[11] Solicitor General McCree, appearing as amicus, argued that the federal government maintained that contrary to the holding of the California Supreme Court, voluntary reliance on race as a factor in an admissions program was constitutionally permissible.[12] He also argued that the lower court decision should be vacated and remanded to the trial court for further fact-findings.

---

[8] SCHWARTZ, *supra* note 1, at 46; JOHN C. JEFFRIES, JR., JUSTICE LEWIS F. POWELL, JR. 463 (1994) (referring to the government's brief as "a gutless waffle").

[9] 100 LANDMARK BRIEFS AND ARGUMENTS OF THE SUPREME COURT OF THE UNITED STATES: CONSTITUTIONAL LAW 627–28 (Philip B. Kurland & Gerhard Casper eds., 1978).

[10] *Id.* at 636–37.

[11] *Id.* at 636.

[12] *Id.* at 643.

Reynard Colvin, representing Bakke, got off to a decent start by emphasizing that the case was not about general principles but rather Allan Bakke's right not to be excluded from admission to medical school by race.[13] From that point, however, his argument descended into confusion, contradiction, and incoherence. To the frustration of the justices, he spent much of his argument on irrelevant quibbles about the record.[14] The justices had difficulty getting Colvin to explain exactly what his position was as to the constitutionality of the use of race in the admissions process.[15] When he did state his position, that race could never be employed in the admissions process, it was much broader than he needed in order to win the case.[16] Justice Marshall commented to Colvin that "[y]ou are arguing about keeping someone out, and the other side is arguing about getting somebody in."[17] Marshall repeated that comment several times during the justices' internal deliberations over the case.

In rebuttal, Cox urged the Court not to get involved in supervising admissions processes.[18] However he immediately had to concede that he would not maintain that position if schools were simply excluding black applicants on account of race.[19] The oral arguments seemed quite unhelpful in aiding the justices in addressing a difficult and controversial issue. Justice Blackmun was ill and did not participate in the oral arguments.

THE DELIBERATIONS ON BAKKE

Initially, after the oral argument, the justices agreed that Title VI might prove crucial in its decision. Consequently they asked the parties to file supplemental briefs on Title VI. Over the next few months, the justices exchanged memos as to how the case should be decided.

Chief Justice Burger circulated a memo in which he argued that the Court should not allow the lawyers "'(aided by a mildly hysterical media) [to] rush us to judgment [given that it would not be possible to put] this sensitive, difficult question to rest in one 'hard' case.'"[20] He indicated that he favored application of the strict standard of review.[21] Justice Powell circulated a memo urging that the Court must reach the constitutional issue and apply strict scrutiny.[22] Brennan responded with a memo arguing that there was no significant difference between the Cal-Davis approach and the Harvard Plan.[23]

In the conference held December 9, 1977, the justices essentially broke down into the coalitions that prevailed in the opinions with the qualification that Justice Blackmun was

---

[13] *Id.* at 644.

[14] *Id.* at 652.

[15] *Id.*at 653–56.

[16] *Id.* at 657.

[17] *Id.* at 656.

[18] *Id.* at 665.

[19] *Id.*

[20] Memoranda of Chief Justice Burger of October 12, 1977, quoted in SCHWARTZ, *supra* note 1, at 70-71.

[21] *Id.*

[22] Bernard Schwartz, *supra* note 1 at 80-81.

[23] *Id.* at 92.

not present and would not cast his vote for another five months. Justices Brennan, Marshall, and White were prepared to permit any use of race in admissions including an outright set-aside.[24] Justices Burger, Stewart, Rehnquist, and Stevens believed that the outright set-aside utilized by the medical school clearly violated Title VI and possibly equal protection as well.[25] At the conference, Justice Powell sketched out the intermediate position that he had suggested in oral argument that race could be a factor but approval of set-aside would cause the symbolic "effect of the Fourteenth Amendment [to be] completely lost."[26] Powell indicated that he would vote to reverse in part considering that the California Supreme Court had prohibited the medical school from taking race into account at all.[27]

Given the prominence of the case, there was a somewhat unprecedented "deluge" of memos among the justices in December.[28] Powell was acutely concerned with the potential impact of the decision and believed that it was essential for the Court to provide guidance to the hundreds of colleges and universities waiting for the opinion.[29] Justice Blackmun was recovering from surgery and appeared to have great difficulty deciding how to vote in *Bakke*.[30] Most of the delay in producing an opinion was attributable to Blackmun's absence and indecision. As John Jeffries Powell's biographer noted "[t]he greatest civil rights case since *Brown* hung fire while Blackmun spent himself on trivialities."[31] At one point, Blackmun's temperament caused Justice Brennan to worry whether he was mentally stable enough to even cast a vote in the case.[32] Blackmun finally decided the join the Brennan group on May 1, 1978, creating the 4-1-4 split that came to define the Bakke opinion.[33] The Stevens four were united throughout the process although Brennan had to struggle mightily to hold his four-justice coalition together.[34] Justice Powell produced a draft that was quite close to the opinion he published the following week.[35] In announcing the opinion from the bench Justice Powell noted that "[p]erhaps no case in modern memory has received as much media coverage and scholarly commentary."[36] Veteran Supreme Court commentator Anthony Lewis noted that "I have seen great moments" at the Supreme Court "but nothing to match the drama as five members of the court explained their positions in homely terms."[37] The decision was considered so important that network television interrupted regular programming to announce it.[38]

---

[24] THE SUPREME COURT IN CONFERENCE (1940-1985): THE PRIVATE DISCUSSIONS BEHIND NEARLY 300 SUPREME COURT DECISIONS 739–40 (Del Dickson ed., 2001).

[25] SCHWARTZ, *supra* note 1, at 97.

[26] *Id.* at 96.

[27] *Id.*

[28] *Id.* at 110.

[29] *Id.* at 111.

[30] *Id.* at 120.

[31] JEFFRIES, *supra* note 8, at 488.

[32] SCHWARTZ, *supra* note 1, at 127.

[33] *Id.* at 133.

[34] BALL, *supra* note 7, at 126.

[35] *Id.* at 133.

[36] JEFFRIES, *supra* note 8, at 494.

[37] Anthony Lewis, *The Solomonic Decision*, N.Y. TIMES, June 29, 1978, at 25.

[38] JEFFRIES, *supra* note 8, at 496.

THE *BAKKE* OPINIONS

After eight months of internal wrangling, the Court published its complicated set of opinions in the *Bakke* case. Writing for four justices, Justice Stevens issued an opinion declaring that the flat-out racial set-aside employed by the Cal-Davis medical school violated the clear text of Title VI of the Civil Rights Act of 1964, which prohibited exclusion based on race from participation in "any program or activity receiving Federal financial assistance." As such, the Stevens four did not reach the equal protection question and clearly did not believe that *Bakke* was the right case for exploring its nuances.

Justice Brennan wrote an opinion for four justices contending that the use of race by Cal-Davis, even in the form of a set-aside, was permissible. Agreeing with Justice Powell that Title VI was intended to apply the same standard as the Equal Protection Clause, Brennan devoted the bulk of his opinion to constitutional analysis. He argued that a school should be allowed to use race in its admission process in order to remedy past societal discrimination.[39] Brennan differentiated "benign" from "invidious" use of race and argued that the Equal Protection Clause did not require strict scrutiny of the former. Instead, he would employ an intermediate standard of review that would attempt to ensure that as a result of past societal discrimination, "minority under-representation is substantial and chronic" and impeding access to the institution. He argued that school desegregation and employment discrimination precedents supported this result. Moreover his approach asked whether the use of race in question stigmatized the disfavored group and concluded that it did not. Finally, Justice Brennan concluded that there were no other practical means of achieving the school's important goal of providing a remedy for past societal discrimination. The Brennan opinion followed but greatly elaborated on the approach suggested by Solicitor General McCree. The standard of review crafted by Brennan was largely an accommodation with Justice White, who favored strict scrutiny.[40]

The Stevens four and Brennan four left the Court equally divided. Justice Powell broke the tie, agreeing with each side to some extent. First, Justice Powell agreed with the Brennan opinion that Title VI was intended to follow the interpretation of equal protection. Unlike Brennan, Powell concluded that any racial classification whether invidious or benign must be evaluated under the strict scrutiny standard of review. That standard requires that the classification be justified by a compelling state interest and that the classification must be narrowly tailored to achieve that interest, and that it be established that there are no less discriminatory alternatives. Powell then engaged in a lengthy consideration of why this was so, which would prove quite influential in subsequent cases. First he emphasized that as a textual matter the guarantee of equal protection in the Fourteenth Amendment is extended to all "persons." He rejected the argument derived from footnote 4 of the famous case of *United States v. Carolene Products*[41] that racial classifications are suspect only if they disadvantage "discrete and insular minorities" that have been the subject of prejudice in the political process as being unsupported by precedent.[42] Justice Powell also rejected the argument that there should be little judicial concern when

---

[39] 438 U.S. 265, 362 (1978).
[40] BALL, *supra* note 7, at 134.
[41] 394 U.S. 144 (1938).
[42] *Bakke*, 438 U.S. at 290.

the "majority" imposes burdens on its own members, given that legislative majorities are generally not monolithic in nature but tend to be coalitions of various diverse groups.[43] He declined to rely on the concept of stigma favored by Justice Brennan in that it "has no clearly defined constitutional meaning."[44] Rather "it reflects a subjective judgment that is standardless."[45] He also argued that racial preferences may offend principles of fairness. It would be difficult to determine which minority groups were entitled to preferential treatment at any given time. Powell also disagreed with Justice Brennan's interpretation of the relevant precedents.

Justice Powell's extended discussion of why strict scrutiny is the appropriate standard for assessing all racial preferences was and still remains the most detailed consideration of the question expounded by a justice or for that matter by the Court. Although Justice Powell at this point was only speaking for himself, and Justice Brennan was speaking for four justices, Powell's approach eventually carried the day on the Court. When a majority of the Court did apply the strict scrutiny standard to "benign" racial classifications nine years later in *City of Richmond v. J. A. Croson,*[46] Justice O'Connor quoted repeatedly from Justice Powell's opinion in *Bakke.*[47] It is not surprising that Powell addressed the standard of review issue in great detail in his *Bakke* opinion. As his opinions in *San Antonio Independent School District v. Rodriguez*[48] and *Gertz v. Robert Welch, Inc.*[49] illustrate, Powell was inclined to write comprehensive opinions in doctrinally complicated areas in an effort to provide greater clarity both with respect to doctrine and foundational principle. He almost certainly recognized that although no opinion in *Bakke* commanded a majority, given the prominence of the case, even plurality opinions were likely to be taken seriously in the future. Considering his disagreement with Justice Brennan's approach to the standard of review, it was crucial to answer his arguments and set forth an alternative approach in detail.

More than any other opinion, Justice Powell analyzed the possible purposes of the Cal-Davis special admissions program in detail. He identified four justifications cited by the school. He dismissed the first, increasing the percentage of minority students in the class, summarily as unconstitutional "discrimination for its own sake."[50] As for the goal of increasing the provision of healthcare to under-served communities, Powell indicated that this might well be a compelling state interest but the special admissions program was not narrowly tailored to its achievement.

In the context of *Bakke,* Justice Powell also rejected the remedial justification as well, the justification on which the Brennan plurality placed its sole reliance. Contrary to Justice Brennan, Justice Powell rejected societal discrimination as sufficient. Rather, he would require a fact-finding of specific discrimination before a remedial approach could be employed. Absent such a finding, it would not be possible for the courts to

---

[43] *Id.* at 292.

[44] *Id.* at 294, n.34.

[45] *Id.*

[46] 488 U.S. 469 (1989).

[47] *Id.* at 494–97.

[48] 411 U.S. 1 (1973).

[49] 418 U.S. 323 (1974).

[50] *Bakke,* 438 U.S. at 307.

determine the scope of the remedy or whether it has been successful. As with Justice Powell's approach to the standard of review, his discussion of the remedial justification also proved influential and was later adopted by a majority of the Court.

That left the school's final justification, the achievement of diversity in the educational process, the justification for which Powell's opinion in *Bakke* became renowned. Powell found diversity in the student body to be constitutionally permissible, hence under his approach a compelling state interest. He derived support for this proposition from prior cases suggesting that academic freedom, including the right of a university to select its student body as it saw fit, was to some extent supported by the First Amendment. Relying heavily on the brief submitted by several Ivy League schools, Powell proclaimed that the type of diversity that a university could constitutionally employ could not be limited to racial diversity alone but must encompass all characteristics that the applicant might possess that could enrich the educational process. Under such an approach, race would be one of many factors, a plus in the applicant's file. The applicant would still be evaluated as an individual. As the Cal-Davis program involved a complete racial set-aside, it could not qualify under the diversity rationale.

There remained the question of the actual holding of the case. Powell plus the Stevens four had concluded that the special admissions program at least violated Title VI. However, Powell agreed with the Brennan four that some use of race in admissions was permissible. Consequently, section VI C of the Powell opinion joined by the Brennan four stated that

> In enjoining petitioner from ever considering the race of any applicant, however, the courts below failed to recognize that the State has a substantial interest that may legitimately be served by a properly devised admissions program involving the competitive consideration of race and ethnic origin.[51]

This was part of the holding of *Bakke*, but what did it hold? Five justices agreed that race could be used as a factor in the admissions process but they did not agree on how or why. Justice Powell limited the use of race to the attainment of student body diversity and rejected remediation of societal discrimination as acceptable, while the Brennan four relied on the remedial justification. The confusion could have been avoided had Justice Brennan been willing to endorse the diversity approach as well; however he did not really do so. Instead he dropped a footnote accepting the diversity rationale "at least so long as the use of race to achieve an integrated student body is necessitated by the lingering effects of past discrimination."[52] Thus Justice Brennan tied the diversity rationale to the remediation of societal discrimination, an interest that Justice Powell had clearly rejected. As such, the holding of *Bakke* with respect to the role that racial diversity could play in university admissions was fraught with ambiguity. Robert Dixon characterized *Bakke* "as perhaps the grandest finesse of a searing legal issue in Supreme Court history."[53]

---

[51] *Id.* at 320.

[52] *Id.* at 326, n.1.

[53] Robert Dixon, Bakke: *A Constitutional Analysis*, 67 CALIF. L. REV. 69 (1979).

BAKKE AS A GREAT CASE

The case was decided but the controversy had just begun. The *Bakke* compromise was well received by the public and the press.[54] The ambivalence of the decision reflected the views of much of the public at large on the issue of racial preferences. The extent to which universities, graduate, and professional schools could rely on race as a factor in the admissions process had been a question of extreme significance in the educational world. Schools were anxious to increase their racial diversity, but at the same time do so in a manner that did not subject them to legal liability. Although the decision itself was quite unclear in a strictly legal sense, admissions officers found the guidance that they were seeking in Justice Powell's opinion. The plus-in-the-file diversity rationale was almost universally embraced as legally safe even though its precedential status was quite debatable. Nevertheless over the next two and a half decades, Justice Powell's diversity approach became standard practice in higher education.

Bakke was a spectacular example of the great case. It involved an issue that was at the center of public debate. Public interest was intensely focused on the Court at the time. The justices were clearly affected by the atmosphere in which the case was presented. Some of the justices, especially those sympathetic to the use of race in the admissions process, hoped to provide some legal guidance to colleges and universities. Unfortunately, the medical school's flat-out set-aside did not provide a sympathetic case for resolution of the issue from the university perspective. Even so, four justices were prepared to endorse what Cal-Davis had done. Of the four justices who found a Title VI violation, at least one in Justice Stevens and possibly two in Justice Stewart may have been more inclined toward the position of the educational institutions if faced with a better factual record. Indeed, Justice Stevens would later become a strong advocate of the constitutionality of racial preferences.[55]

There is no reason to believe that the justices set out to render an ambiguous or muddled decision. The opinions that ultimately emerged seemed to be a fair reflection of the initial response of the justices to the briefs and arguments with the caveat that Justice Blackmun did not participate in the oral argument and did not cast a vote until very late in the process. Perhaps the Stevens four addressed only the statutory issue to avoid resolving the more important constitutional issue in the wrong case. Justices Powell and Brennan however almost certainly concluded that the educational community and indeed the nation were entitled to more guidance on a question that was clearly of great significance. Since after extensive negotiation they could not agree on a unified approach, each went into great detail in an attempt to exert some influence over university admissions practices and more significantly the future direction of the law. Despite the fact that Brennan was only one justice shy of a majority and Powell was speaking only for himself, Powell would ultimately carry the day.

Although the *Bakke* case reached the Court in something of a pressurized atmosphere, it did not impose unrealistic time constraints as often happens with great cases. The case was argued near the very beginning of the 1977–78 term, and the Court took nearly seven months to decide it and write the extensive opinions. Perhaps the one way in which

---

[54] JEFFRIES, *supra* note 8, at 496–97.
[55] Adarand Constructors, Inc. v. Pena, 515 U.S. 200, 242 (1995) (Stevens, J., dissenting).

the "greatness" of the case almost certainly affected the decision was with respect to the briefing. Because of the significance of the issues, the Court was swamped with amicus briefs. But one of those briefs seems to have made quite a difference. The brief of the Ivy League universities detailing the Harvard Plan caught the attention of Justice Powell. Indeed, he made it the centerpiece of his opinion, transforming it from simply one possible approach to the very key to the constitutional use of race in university admissions. Amicus briefs are often filed in constitutional litigation to be sure. But this was a case in which the educational establishment clearly believed that the stakes were extremely high. As such, it pulled out the stops in order to provide the Court with an explanation as to why race is a criteria that universities should be allowed to take into account as well as a blueprint for how that could be done in a moderate but still arguably effective manner. The fact that the brief was submitted by establishments of the caliber of Columbia, Harvard, Stanford, and Penn was intended to and certainly did have an impact. Great cases because of their greatness often provide the Court with the benefit of superb legal talent. Despite the stature of Archibald Cox, the oral arguments in *Bakke* were not exceptional, and indeed the argument on behalf of *Bakke* was quite poor. But the greatness of the case did inspire the Ivy League brief, and that in the end seemed to make the difference.

The justices did understand that they were deciding a case that had significant societal ramifications. The somewhat unusually large circulation of memos among the justices regarding the decision indicates that they clearly considered it an exceptional case. The fact that so many institutions were apparently awaiting the Court's opinion for guidance seems to have convinced Justice Powell that this was not an appropriate case for avoiding the constitutional issue and relying on statutory grounds instead, as four justices insisted on doing. Nor was it appropriate to simply strike down the Cal-Davis set-aside without addressing whether race could ever be utilized in the admissions process as schools using a Harvard-type plan would be left in the dark. As such, the very greatness of the case counseled against the traditionally conservative virtues of deciding that case on the narrowest grounds and leaving larger issues to another day. Powell believed that educational institutions were in need of greater clarity and was determined to try to provide it. Although he wrote only for himself and left many questions unanswered, he managed to provide an approach to racial diversity in higher education that prevailed for the next quarter of a century. Justice Powell considered the *Bakke* opinion the most important opinion that he wrote on the Court.[56]

THE ROAD TO *GRUTTER* AND *GRATZ*

Following *Bakke*, the Court struggled with the use of race for benign purposes. Eventually, in two opinions by Justice O'Connor involving racial preferences in public works contracting, the Court basically adopted the analytical approach proposed by Justice Powell in *Bakke*. A majority of the Court held that a racial preference could be constitutionally justified only if it survived strict judicial review.[57] Providing a remedy for general societal

---

[56] SCHWARTZ, *supra* note 1, at 1.
[57] City of Richmond v. J.A. Croson Co., 488 U.S. 469, 493–94 (1989), 520 (Scalia, J., concurring).

discrimination would not suffice. Justice O'Connor also emphasized that to be constitutional, the use of racial preferences needed to be temporary.[58]

Following *Bakke*, most universities modeled their admissions practices after the Harvard Plan endorsed by Justice Powell in *Bakke* under which race would be employed as a plus in the file as part of an individualized consideration of the applicant in an attempt to achieve student body diversity.[59] Over time, either because such an approach was too labor intensive or because it failed to produce sufficient racial diversity, some schools began to push beyond the boundaries of the Powell opinion. Litigation challenging such practices resulted. The University of Texas School of Law instituted a two-track system somewhat analogous to the Cal-Davis program in which minority applicants were essentially insulated from competition against non-minority applicants. The procedure was struck down by the United States Court of Appeals for the Fifth Circuit in *Hopwood v. University of Texas*.[60] The court went further however proclaiming that Justice Powell's opinion in *Bakke* had not been endorsed by a majority and the subsequent public contracting cases had undermined its rationale.[61] Consequently, the law school could not use race at all in the admissions process to attempt to achieve diversity. The Supreme Court declined to hear the case. The impact of this was to preclude all educational institutions, public or private, within the states of Texas, Louisiana, and Mississippi from using race in their admissions process unless they had been required to do so as part of a desegregation decree.

Other racial preference programs in education were challenged as well; however, the two cases that brought the issue back before the Supreme Court both involved the University of Michigan. After careful consideration, the University of Michigan Law School initiated a plan to increase diversity, especially racial diversity, in the student body.[62] It purported to engage in the holistic consideration of individual applicants suggested by Powell in *Bakke*, employing race as an important factor. The goal was not simply to achieve multi-faceted diversity in the student body but also to attempt to ensure that it would admit a "critical mass" of African-American, Latino, and Native American students. The school maintained that it was necessary to admit such a critical mass to avoid tokenism, to ensure that minority students did not feel isolated, and to avoid the perception that all minority students were of the same point of view. During the admissions process, the director of admissions kept a close watch on "daily reports" detailing how many minority applicants had been admitted.

Barbara Grutter, a white student who had been denied admission, filed a lawsuit in federal district court challenging the law school's admission process. After a lengthy trial, a district court for the Eastern District of Michigan struck down the program under the Equal Protection Clause of the Fourteenth Amendment.[63]

---

[58] *Id.* at 510.

[59] SCHWARTZ, *supra* note 1, at 152.

[60] 78 F. 3d 932 (5th Cir.), cert. denied, 518 U.S. 1033 (1996). *See generally* Lackland H. Bloom, Jr., Hopwood, Bakke *and the Future of the Diversity Justification*, 29 TEX. TECH. L. REV. 1 (1998).

[61] *Hopwood*, 78 F.3d at 944–46.

[62] Grutter v Bollinger, 539 U.S. 306, 314–15 (2003).

[63] 137 F. Supp. 2d 821 (E.D. Mich. 2001), rev'd, 288 F. 3d 732 (6th Cir. 2002) (en banc), aff'd, 539 U.S. 306 (2003).

At about the same time, the College of Literature, Arts and Sciences at the University of Michigan had also adopted an admissions program employing racial preferences. Perhaps because it received so many applications, the school adopted a system in which a specified number of points was assigned to each relevant factor, including grades, test scores, special talents, leadership ability, and race. Membership in a specified minority race was worth 20 points. The record indicated that this would be sufficient to ensure that all otherwise academically qualified minority applicants would be admitted. Jennifer Gratz, a white student denied admission to the college, challenged the constitutionality of the system in federal district court in the Eastern District of Michigan. A different judge from the one in *Grutter* upheld the constitutionality of the practice.[64]

Both cases were appealed to the Court of Appeals for the Sixth Circuit, which heard arguments before the court en banc. Over vigorous dissents, the en banc court upheld the admissions program of the law school in *Grutter*[65] but did not issue an opinion with respect to the undergraduate program in *Gratz*, apparently because it could not build a majority. The Supreme Court granted certiorari in *Grutter* and directed the Sixth Circuit to forward the yet-undecided *Gratz* case along as well.

If anything the public interest surrounding the *Grutter* and *Gratz* decisions was as great as that surrounding *Bakke* 25 years earlier. As of *Bakke*, the use of racial preferences in admissions was a relatively recent development. In a large part due to *Bakke*, their use had become deeply ingrained in admissions practices in higher education nationwide. The *Grutter* and *Gratz* cases raised the very real possibility that such practices might be ruled unlawful. Consequently, a multitude of amicus briefs were filed by interested groups. The cases were followed by the public with great anticipation.

The University of Michigan Law School understood that in defending its program, it faced one very severe obstacle. Michigan was one of the truly elite law schools of the nation. Its admissions process was highly selective. The pool of minority applicants with the grades and test scores that would result in admission under a race neutral standard was quite small. Thus if racial diversity was as compelling to the law school as it claimed, then why did it not simply lower its admission standards across the board, thereby increasing the size of pool of both minority and non-minority applicants? It could then admit more minority applicants without necessarily utilizing a racial preference. Michigan understood that this was a very serious argument to which it needed to respond.

Lee Bollinger, president of the University of Michigan, learned that the military had confronted a similar problem and might be able to provide some assistance.[66] That suggestion ultimately led to the Retired Officers Brief signed by over 20 well-known and high-ranking retired officers, which came to play a crucial role in the litigation. According to the brief submitted by Supreme Court advocate Carter Phillips, the military had experienced severe problems during the Vietnam War when an almost all-white officer corps was leading enlisted forces with high percentages of minority group soldiers. Because the resulting racial misunderstandings and tensions interfered with military performance, the leaders of the service branches determined that it was essential to recruit

---

[64] 122 F. Supp. 2d 811 (E.D. Mich. 2001), rev'd in part, 539 U.S. 244 (2003).

[65] 288 F. 3d 732 (6th Cir. 2002) (en banc), aff'd, 539 U.S. 306 (2003).

[66] GREG STOHR, A BLACK AND WHITE CASE: HOW AFFIRMATIVE ACTION SURVIVED ITS GREATEST LEGAL CHALLENGE 140–41 (2004).

more minority officers. This was accomplished through racial preferences in admission to the service academies as well as preparatory schools primarily for minorities who did not yet have the prerequisites for admission. The military focused on race to an extent that probably would not have satisfied Justice Powell's approach in *Bakke*. The Officers Brief emphasized that in order to produce effective officers, it needed both very high standards and racial diversity. It could not afford to sacrifice one in order to achieve the other. This was exactly the type of support that Michigan needed in order to justify the use of highly selective admissions as well as racial preferences.

ORAL ARGUMENT IN *GRUTTER* AND *GRATZ*

The oral arguments in *Grutter* and *Gratz* were scheduled back-to-back. Kurt Kolbo, the attorney for Barbara Grutter, was scarcely able to begin his presentation before the justices turned his attention to the Retired Officers' Brief and besieged him with questions about the programs used by the service academies.[67] Obviously he would rather have devoted his time to the actual case that he was arguing but virtually his entire argument was consumed by the Court's relentless questioning about the amicus brief. He must have been both mystified and disappointed when he sat down.

Solicitor General Olsen, who spoke next for the United States as amicus in opposition to the law school's admissions procedures, barely began the second sentence of his argument when Justice Stevens asked him to comment on the Retired Officers Brief.[68] General Olsen emphasized that the brief represented that of private individuals and not the United States, and that the Department of Justice was not taking a position on the constitutionality of the practices described in that brief.[69] He argued that the Michigan law school program could not be justified under the Powell approach in *Bakke*.[70]

Maureen Mahoney appeared for the law school. Justice Scalia immediately asked her why the school did not simply lower its standards if it considered racial diversity so compelling.[71] She answered that "there is a compelling interest in having an institution that is both academically excellent and richly diverse because our leaders need to be trained in institutions that are excellent, that are superior academically, but they also need to be trained with exposure to the viewpoints, to the perspectives, to the experiences of individuals from diverse backgrounds."[72] Scalia's question cut to the very core of the case. Mahoney's answer in a nutshell provided the rationale that the majority would in fact adopt. Later in the argument, Justice Scalia attempted unsuccessfully to force Mahoney into stating a specific percentage figure that would constitute a "critical mass" of minority students; however she would not be drawn into the trap designed to suggest that the school did maintain a quota.[73] Justice O'Connor expressed concern as to the apparent

---

[67] 321 LANDMARK BRIEFS AND ARGUMENTS OF THE SUPREME COURT OF THE UNITED STATES: CONSTITUTIONAL LAW 1161 (Gerhard Casper & Kathleen M. Sullivan eds., 2003)

[68] *Id.* at 1169.

[69] *Id.* at 1171.

[70] *Id.* at 1172.

[71] *Id.* at 1175–76.

[72] *Id.* at 1177.

[73] *Id.* at 1181-82.

absence of a logical stopping point. Mahoney replied that the law school program could be terminated if the number of high-achieving minority students increased or if the experience of being a member of a minority group became less relevant socially.[74] She noted that it had been 25 years since *Bakke* had been decided.[75]

The oral argument in *Gratz* followed *Grutter*. Much of Kolbo's argument in *Gratz* was spent answering the tangential question of whether a plaintiff transfer applicant had standing. The remainder was devoted to the question of whether he would allow the government to rely on race at all outside of the context of providing a remedy for past discrimination.[76] As with *Grutter*, the justices gave him very little opportunity to address the substance of his case. Solicitor General Olsen appearing next emphasized that the undergraduate program was essentially the type of two-track process invalidated in *Bakke*.[77] John Payton, representing the university, emphasized that most of the undergraduates at Michigan had little experience interacting with persons of a different race.[78] He was forced to admit that under the point system virtually every qualified minority applicant was admitted.[79]

THE *GRUTTER* AND *GRATZ* OPINIONS

GRUTTER v. *BOLLINGER*

Unlike *Bakke* where the Court spent almost the entire term developing its opinions, the opinions in *Grutter* and *Gratz* were released only two-and-a-half months after the arguments. As had been assumed, Justice O'Connor was the fulcrum of the Court and delivered the opinion in *Grutter*. At the outset, she stated that rather than enter the complicated fray over whether Justice Powell's diversity rationale in *Bakke* was a binding precedent, the Court would simply endorse it as the correct approach.[80] She noted that most universities had been relying on the Powell opinion in crafting their affirmative action programs. Relying on her opinion for the Court in *Adarand*, O'Connor concluded that the strict standard of review must be applied. She made it clear that pursuant to that standard, "the Law School has a compelling state interest in attaining a diverse student body."[81] Seven justices including Rehnquist and Kennedy in dissent seemed to agree. She noted that in order to obtain the "educational benefits of diversity" the law school had determined that it was necessary to enroll a critical mass of minority students. At that point she cited the corporate brief and quoted from the Retired Officers' Brief. She noted that the officers had explained that "'[a]t present, 'the military cannot achieve an officer corps that is *both* highly qualified *and* racially diverse unless the service academies and

---

[74] *Id.* at 1182.

[75] *Id.* at 1183.

[76] LANDMARK BRIEFS AND ARGUMENTS, *supra* note 67, at 1203.

[77] *Id.* at 1204.

[78] *Id.* at 1209–10.

[79] *Id.* at 1219.

[80] Grutter v Bollinger, 539 U.S. 306, 325 (2003).

[81] *Id.* at 328.

the ROTC used limited race-conscious recruiting and admissions policies.'"[82] The Brief continued '"[t]o fulfill its mission, the military must be selective in admission for training and education for the officer corps, *and* it must train and educate a highly qualified, racially diverse officer corps in a racially diverse educational setting.'"[83] She then quoted the Officers' Brief for the proposition that "'[i]t requires only a small step from this analysis to conclude that our country's other most selective institutions must remain both diverse and selective.'"[84] Justice O'Connor noted that a high percentage of the nation's leaders are graduates of very selective schools and emphasized that it is also important that it appear to the public that the paths to positions of prominence and leadership are open to all regardless of race.

She then turned to the narrow tailoring aspect of strict scrutiny. She concluded that the law school's emphasis on "critical mass" of minority students did not suggest that it was employing a forbidden racial quota. Justice O'Connor relied on the testimony of the law school admissions officer at trial that it was not employing a quota. Rather, the law school was engaged in the type of "individualistic" "holistic" consideration of applicants endorsed by Justice Powell in *Bakke*. Most significant, Justice O'Connor concluded that narrow tailoring "does not require a university to choose between maintaining a reputation for excellence or fulfilling a commitment to provide educational opportunities to all racial groups."[85] She declared that the Court was satisfied that the school had considered all reasonable less discriminatory alternatives. Finally, she cautioned that the law school must continue to supervise the program closely, especially to determine whether it remains necessary. On almost every point of contention in the case, Justice O'Connor deferred to the expertise of the law school and its faculty. Noting that Bakke had been decided 25 years earlier and that the reliance on race must have a logical stopping point, Justice O'Connor opined that hopefully the use of racial preferences would not be needed 25 years later.

Justice Ginsburg issued a short concurrence questioning whether the need for racial preferences would vanish in 25 years. Justice Scalia published a dissent in *Grutter* (concurring in *Gratz*) arguing that Michigan did not have a compelling state interest "in maintaining a 'prestige' law school whose normal admissions standards disproportionately exclude blacks and other minorities."[86] Thus, Justice Scalia was not persuaded by the Retired Officers' Brief.

Justice Thomas, dissenting, was also highly critical of the argument that Michigan had a compelling interest in maintaining "an exclusionary admissions system that it knows produces racially disproportionate results."[87] Indeed, he argued that a state has no compelling interest in maintaining a law school at all much less an elite one. Thus for Justice Thomas, Michigan should be forced to choose between racial diversity (which he termed its "classroom aesthetic") and "its exclusionary admissions system—it cannot have it

---

[82] *Id.* at 331 quoting from the Military Officer's Brief.
[83] *Id.*
[84] *Id.*
[85] *Id.* at 339.
[86] *Id.* at 347.
[87] *Id.* at 350.

both ways."[88] In other words, the law school does not have "a compelling interest in doing what it wants to do."[89]

He noted that the Court's "unprecedented deference to the Law School... [is] antithetical to strict scrutiny."[90] Justice Thomas argued at length that "there is nothing ancient, honorable or constitutionally protected about 'selective' admissions."[91] He maintained that preferential admissions programs such as Michigan's are a disservice to minority students by placing them in academic environments in which they tend to be ill prepared to compete. Finally, Justice Thomas interpreted Justice O'Connor's statement that hopefully racial preferences would be unnecessary in 25 years as a declaration that they would be illegal at such time.

Chief Justice Rehnquist also published a dissenting opinion. He seemed to accept diversity as a compelling state interest but argued that the means were not narrowly tailored to its achievement, given that a statistical analysis of Michigan's admission practices over a series of years indicated that its concept of critical mass was simply a euphemism for an attempt to establish racial proportionality between the percentage of minorities in the applicant pool and in the entering class. Moreover, he believed that the majority's rationale was inconsistent with narrow tailoring in that it effectively permits the employment of racial preferences in perpetuity.

Justice Kennedy produced a dissent as well. Like Rehnquist, Kennedy accepted diversity in higher education as a compelling interest but argued vigorously that the majority had failed to apply strict scrutiny to the means adopted by the law school. By according almost total deference to the admissions practice adopted by Michigan, the majority had not adhered to Justice Powell's approach in *Bakke*. For Justice Kennedy, the law school failed to carry the burden of proving that its emphasis on critical mass had not been transformed into an effective quota during the latter stages of the admissions process. Like Justice Thomas, Justice Kennedy concluded that "[d]eference is antithetical to strict scrutiny not consistent with it."[92] Essentially, Kennedy determined that the Michigan admissions process appeared to be constitutionally suspicious and that the law school had failed to carry the burden of proving that it was being operated in a permissible manner.

GRATZ v. BOLLINGER

The district courts had upheld the undergraduate school and invalidated the law school's admissions program. The Supreme Court did just the opposite. By a 6-3 vote it invalidated the Michigan undergraduate program, with Justices O'Connor and Breyer joining the four justices who had dissented in *Grutter*.

Chief Justice Rehnquist wrote the opinion for the Court. He concluded that the system of awarding 20 points to every otherwise qualified minority student was not narrowly

---

[88] *Id.* at 361.
[89] *Id.* at 362.
[90] *Id.*
[91] *Id.* at 369.
[92] *Id.* at 394.

tailored to the achievement of the type of broad-based diversity endorsed by Justice Powell in *Bakke*.[93] Rather, than providing individualized consideration, it made race determinative with respect to "virtually every minimally qualified under-represented minority applicant."[94]

Justice O'Connor offered a concurring opinion. She concluded that "the mechanized selection index score, by and large, automatically determines the admissions decisions for each applicant" essentially "preclud[ing]...[the] individualized consideration" required by *Grutter* and *Bakke*.[95] Apparently, Justice O'Connor disapproved of the reduction of "soft variables" to hard numbers, period, and not simply the fact that the index had given race an outcome-determinative weight. Justice Breyer concurred in Justice O'Connor's opinion and in the judgment of the Court.

Justice Thomas concurred proclaiming that the use of race in the admissions process should be categorically prohibited.[96] Justice Souter dissented, arguing that there was no significant difference between the two admissions programs and that the undergraduate program should be upheld as well. Justice Ginsburg, dissenting, suggested that the majority's approach would encourage schools interested in racial diversity to proceed in a surreptitious manner. This was a rather odd contention as Chief Justice Rehnquist pointed out given that *Grutter* had deferred so greatly to the good faith of the institution.

GRUTTER AND *GRATZ* AS GREAT CASES

In *Grutter* and *Gratz*, the Court provided a blueprint for schools interested in racial diversity to follow, which if adhered to, should allow them to avoid liability and possibly litigation as well. Furthermore, the holistic review process endorsed in *Grutter* and *Gratz* was sufficiently subjective to render legal review difficult, especially if the Court remained as deferential to the institution and its policies as the majority was in *Grutter*. Operating a holistic file review process is labor intensive and hence likely to be more costly than a more mechanized system, but that is simply the price of a constitutional admissions program employing race as a factor. However, three years after the *Grutter* and *Gratz* decisions, the people of Michigan passed a referendum prohibiting any agency of the state from employing racial preferences, effectively ending the admissions program upheld in *Grutter*. The Court of Appeals for the Sixth Circuit en banc struck down the referendum as unconstitutional.[97] The Supreme Court recently agreed to hear the case during the 2013–2014 term.

Between *Bakke* and *Grutter*, the large constitutional question was whether the Powell opinion in *Bakke* was the law. The Court in *Grutter* replied that it was, at least as of now. Though during oral argument in *Grutter*, Justice O'Connor declared that the Powell opinion had not "commanded a court,"[98] she rectified that immediately in her opinion by simply endorsing its rationale.

---

[93] *Id.* at 270–71.
[94] *Id.* at 272.
[95] *Id.* at 277.
[96] *Id.* at 281.
[97] Coal. to Defend Affirmative Action, et al. v. Regents of the Univ. of Mich., 701 F. 3d 466 (6th Cir.).
[98] LANDMARK BRIEFS AND ARGUMENTS, *supra* note 67, at 1172.

Like *Bakke*, a particular amicus brief seems to have had a decisive impact in *Grutter*. The prominence of the corporations that submitted the Business Brief may have caught the Court's attention. But it was the Retired Officers Brief that provided the Court with the solution to the most difficult issue presented in *Grutter*, that is, why must the Michigan Law School be so academically elite? Why did it not simply lower its admissions standards somewhat in order to enlarge the size of its minority applicant pool, thereby making it easier for it to admit a critical mass of minority students without relying explicitly on race? The Officers Brief provided the argument for why academic excellence and racial diversity combined could be a compelling state interest. At least in the context of preparing military officers, both were required. The fact that the United States' military, at its prestigious academies, employed relatively weighty racial preferences almost certainly proved quite influential with the justices. Never mind that the United States' government, through the solicitor general, was hardly willing to endorse this approach. The important point was that the military was doing it whether the Department of Justice approved or not. The analogy between the military and elite law schools was scarcely perfect but Justice O'Connor was able to build the bridge.[99] The Officers Brief was remarkable in that rarely if ever has an amicus brief so thoroughly dominated oral argument.

But the Officers Brief did not simply provide a rationale for deciding the case in the law school's favor: it inevitably changed the diversity rationale in important ways. Justice Powell's focus in *Bakke* based primarily on the Harvard Plan had been almost exclusively on the significance of diversity, especially racial diversity, in the educational process itself both in and out of class. That was not the focus of the Officers Brief and hence the O'Connor opinion. The military was far less concerned with the impact of diversity at the academies than with the production of a significant number of minority officers. The Officers Brief was more concerned with output than input. To carry through the analogy as to why racial diversity and academic excellence together was a compelling state interest, Justice O'Connor emphasized the role that elite law schools, such as Michigan, played in producing future leaders. The predominant rationale for racial diversity in admissions to elite institutions became the need to ensure that entry into the leadership strata of society was open to all and representative of all.

Arguably, there were two separate but related diversity interests recognized in the *Grutter* opinion: the classic *Bakke* value of diversity in the educational process rationale and the more recent racially diverse leadership rationale. Inevitably, the latter rationale emphasized racial, as opposed to other types of diversity, more heavily than the former. The military did not purport to care much, if at all, about the wide range of diversifying factors relied on in the Harvard Plan. Rather the service academies were concerned with academic excellence, physical capability, character, leadership potential, and race. Likewise, the leadership rationale emphasized by Justice O'Connor was concerned with ensuring that racial minorities were represented in the future among the leadership class in politics, law, and business. There seemed to be less concern that a sufficient number of oboe players, ice skaters, or farm boys would become leaders. In the process, the majority came closer to endorsing a rationale dismissed as constitutionally illegitimate by Justice

---

[99] *See* Brian Leach, Note, *Race as Mission Critical: The Occupational Need in Military Affirmative Action and Beyond*, 113 YALE L.J. 1093, 1128–33 (2004).

Powell in *Bakke*—simply increasing the number of minority medical students in order to increase the number of minority doctors. Justice Powell dismissed this as nothing more than discrimination for its own sake, but that does not really do it justice. Presumably, the Cal-Davis Medical School, the service academies, and the University of Michigan Law School each concluded that an interracial society would be better off if minority races were represented in positions of influence and power. This is not discrimination for its own sake but rather discrimination for the sake of long-term social good. Reasonable people can certainly disagree with the premise that racial preferences will in fact advance social welfare, but the rationale itself seems worthy of greater consideration than Justice Powell gave to it. Granted, the military had a more pointed justification for racial diversity than either Cal-Davis Medical School or the University of Michigan Law School. It could argue persuasively that racial diversity in its officer corps was essential to the effective functioning of the military. The analogous claims by medical and law schools were not nearly as powerful. In that sense, perhaps the officers' argument was more distinguishable than Justice O'Connor believed it to be.

Grutter did not result in the type of sustained internal debate within the Court that *Bakke* did. That in large part must be attributable to the fact that in *Bakke*, Justice Blackmun's key vote appeared to be up for grabs for most of the term whereas in *Grutter* the justices had had years to think about the broader issues of racial preferences and had probably settled in on their own basic approaches well before the case was presented. The pressure generated by the significance of the issue almost certainly did affect the majority opinion however. As the dissents demonstrated beyond any doubt, Justice O'Connor did not in fact apply anything close to traditional strict scrutiny to the question of whether the law school's means were narrowly tailored to the achievement of its ends. Instead, the majority accorded unprecedented deference to the law school's processes. This was definitely not the type of strict scrutiny that Justice O'Connor had applied in *Croson* or in her *Metro Broadcasting* dissent. Likewise, Justice O'Connor simply discarded her well-established concern that the use of racial preferences be of limited duration.

In his opinion, Justice Kennedy quite correctly explained that if the record left it unclear as to whether Michigan was employing a good faith Harvard-type plan or a disguised quota, then under the strict standard of review Michigan should lose. The implicit message of Justice O'Connor's opinion was that in case of such a tie, Michigan wins. In her oral argument for the law school, Maureen Mahoney emphasized that given the small size of the minority applicant pool, the law school could not admit a critical mass of highly qualified minority students without a fairly aggressive use of racial preferences, as the Officers had also maintained in their brief. Faced with the arguably dire social consequences of the application of traditional strict scrutiny to the facts before the Court, Justice O'Connor blinked and bent the rules. Whether the Court made good or bad law is largely a matter of legal and political perspective. For those who believe that racial preferences in higher education contribute significantly to the overall social good, *Grutter* made very good law. On the other hand for those who believe that any use of racial preferences is constitutionally troublesome, *Grutter* was a wrong turn. As will be seen, the full force of the majority opinion did not survive for long.

The great case of *Bakke* did not establish bad law but rather very little actual law and a great deal of shadow law. The great case of *Grutter* did not establish bad law but rather a disingenuous application of otherwise settled law. In each case, the hydraulic pressure mentioned by Justice Holmes was definitely at work.

FISHER v. UNIVERSITY OF TEXAS

After the Fifth Circuit Court of Appeals decision in *Hopwood v. University of Texas* in 1998 prohibited the university from making any use of race in the admissions process, the state legislature adopted a program under which the top 10 percent of the graduating class from any public high school in Texas was eligible for admission to the University of Texas at Austin. In view of the fact that many public high schools in Texas, as elsewhere, were essentially one-race schools with large minority populations, the Top Ten Percent program, though racially neutral, was intended to and did in fact result in the admission of a significant number of minority students. Indeed, by the time the *Fisher* lawsuit was initiated, approximately three quarters of the African-American and Latino students at Texas were admitted under the program.

Following *Grutter*, the university was no longer prohibited from considering race as a factor in admissions. At that point, the Board of Regents of the University of Texas commissioned the university to determine whether some use of race in the admissions process was warranted. A study indicated that presently in 90 percent of small participatory classes (5 to 24 students) there was only one or zero African-American, Hispanic, or Asian-American students. The university concluded that it had not yet reached a critical mass of minority students. Consequently, it adopted a plan closely modeled after the Michigan Law School plan approved in *Grutter* for consideration of race as a plus in the file as part of a holistic review. As a result of the new program, of 363 in-state African-American students admitted in 2008, 305 were admitted under the race-neutral Top Ten Percent program while an additional 58 were admitted either under the *Grutter*-type program or without consideration of race. Of the 1322 in-state Hispanic students, 1164 were admitted under the Top Ten Percent program and 158 either under the *Grutter*-type program or without reference to race.

Fisher, a white student denied admission to the university, challenged the addition of the *Grutter*-type program but not the Top Ten Percent Program itself. Essentially, she argued that the program taking account of race was not narrowly tailored under the strict standard of review given that the university had achieved a significant measure of diversity by race-neutral means. The district court upheld the *Grutter*-type program. In a careful and lengthy analysis Judge Higgenbotham, writing for the Fifth Circuit Court of Appeals, concluded that the challenged program was entirely consistent with *Grutter*.[100] He discussed the Top Ten Percent plan indicating that it arguably could be subjected to constitutional challenge. Judge King concurred noting that the Top Ten Percent Plan was not before the Court and need not be considered. Judge Garza wrote a lengthy and vigorous concurring opinion lambasting *Grutter* as wrongly decided and calling for its reconsideration.

---

[100] 644 F. 3d 301 (5th Cir. 2011).

Despite the fact that there was no conflict between circuit courts, the Supreme Court granted the writ of certiorari. Oral arguments were held in October 2012. In response to Justice Breyer, Bert Rein, representing the plaintiff, Abigail Fisher, conceded that he was not asking the Court to overrule *Grutter* but rather to hold that the Texas admissions program simply did not satisfy it because the university had achieved substantial racial diversity through the race-neutral Top Ten Percent program and because it had not considered other race-neutral alternatives. Justice Sotomayor responded that he was not asking the Court to overrule *Grutter* but to just "gut it."[101] Rein emphasized that the university would not define the critical mass of minority students that it was seeking, and without some definition, it was impossible to narrowly tailor a program to achieve that goal.

Several justices challenged Gregory Garre, representing the university, to define the critical mass, which he would not do, obviously for fear of suggesting that the university was employing a racial quota. He argued that the university was using a holistic process and attempting to determine whether a particular applicant would contribute to the university, including the educational benefits to be derived from diversity. Several justices indicated that the Court was being asked to defer too greatly to the judgments of the university with little judicial supervision. Solicitor General Donald Verrilli argued in support of the admissions program on behalf of the United States' government.

THE OPINION IN *FISHER*

The membership of the Supreme Court had changed since *Grutter* and *Gratz*. Chief Justice Roberts had replaced Chief Justice Rehnquist. Justice Sotomayor had replaced Justice Souter. Justice Kagan had replaced Justice Stevens. And Justice Alito had replaced Justice O'Connor. The Court reversed the Fifth Circuit by a vote of 7-1 with Justice Kagan not participating. Justice Kennedy wrote the opinion for the Court, which sounded the basic theme of his *Grutter* dissent.[102] Kennedy purported to take *Bakke*, *Grutter*, and *Gratz* as a given. He conceded that under *Grutter*, a court should defer to the university's expertise on the question of whether racial diversity contributes significantly to the educational mission of the school. However under the strict standard of review, it must not defer with respect to whether the means are narrowly tailored to achieving its ends. Considering that the Fifth Circuit did just that, it must be reversed. A court must also engage in a careful review of whether a university has seriously considered non-racial alternatives. Kennedy quoted *Grutter*'s statement that strict scrutiny was not " 'strict in theory but fatal in fact' " but added that it was neither "strict in theory but feeble in fact" as well.[103]

As the case had been decided on a motion for summary judgment, the Court remanded for a trial on the merits. Justice Kennedy purported to abide by the *Grutter* opinion but that was hardly the case. Rather, his approach echoed his *Grutter* dissent rather than Justice O'Connor's majority opinion. Justice O'Connor had applied a highly diluted version

---

[101] Official Supreme Court Oral Argument Transcript at 81.
[102] 133 S.Ct. 2411 (2013).
[103] Id. at 2421.

of strict scrutiny in *Grutter* in order to uphold the Michigan plan. Kennedy had criticized the laxity of the standard that she had in fact applied in his dissent. In *Fisher*, Kennedy took advantage of the opportunity to correct the perceived error, bringing the application of the standard into line with its language.

Justice Scalia concurred, noting that the plaintiff had not asked the Court to reconsider *Grutter*. Justice Thomas concurred and would have overruled *Grutter*. Justice Ginsburg dissented, maintaining that the Fifth Circuit opinion was consistent with *Grutter*.

Fisher attracted a great deal of attention but did not garner the extreme public interest that surrounded *Bakke* and *Grutter*. It was somewhat upstaged by the gay marriage cases argued in the same term and decided two days after *Fisher*. Still, *Fisher* followed quite readily from these previous great cases. *Grutter* would seem to be a case in which a majority of the Court, in the context of a very pressurized case, bent existing law in order to achieve a desired result. In *Fisher* in a less pressurized atmosphere, with changes in the Court's composition, the majority bent the law back again. Whether great cases make good or bad law, *Fisher* is evidence that they do not necessarily make completely enduring law.

"A no brainer! A state court deciding a federal constitutional issue about a presidential election?... Of course you take the case."[1]

JUSTICE ANTHONY KENNEDY

21

Bush v. Gore

A SUPREME COURT opinion that effectively resolves a disputed presidential election is by definition a great case. That is especially so when it is decided, as it almost certainly had to be, in a frenzied atmosphere with briefing, argument, and decision condensed into a period of four days. The case was decided with a national television audience awaiting the result in an atmosphere of vitriolic partisan charges. The Court was undoubtedly aware that a decision either way, as well as a decision to abstain entirely, would be savaged by many. The justices also understood that it was treading in territory generally not frequented by the judiciary, and as such applicable legal principles were sparse. There was at least the possibility that a judicial decision could do serious harm to the Court's credibility with the public. Despite all of these concerns, the decision to take and decide the case did not appear to be a difficult one for a majority of the justices under the circumstances.

THE BACKGROUND

The factual context of *Bush v. Gore* is complicated. It is actually the third Supreme Court decision rendered in a short period of time in response to the controversy surrounding the Florida vote count in the 2000 presidential election. The electoral college tally on election night November 2000 was extraordinarily close. It appeared that the winner of the vote in Florida would become the next president. Shortly after the polls closed in the western time zone, the major networks called Florida for Al Gore despite the fact that Bush led by over 130,000 votes at the time.[2] Later in the evening, the networks placed

---

[1] JAN CRAWFORD GREENBURG, SUPREME CONFLICT: THE INSIDE STORY OF THE STRUGGLE FOR CONTROL OF THE UNITED STATES SUPREME COURT 32 (2007).

[2] CHARLES L. ZELDEN, *BUSH V. GORE*: EXPRESSING THE HIDDEN CRISIS IN AMERICAN DEMOCRACY 2 (2010). For different perspectives on the recount and legal changles, see BILL SAMMON, AT ANY COST: HOW AL GORE TRIED TO STEAL THE ELECTION (2001), and JEFFREY TOOBIN, TOO CLOSE TO CALL: THE THIRTY-SIX DAY BATTLE TO DECIDE THE 2000 ELECTION (2001).

Florida back in the too close to call category, and then at 2:15 a.m. declared Bush the winner of both Florida and the presidency.[3] As more votes were counted however, Bush's lead diminished from over 100,000 to 1,784 votes.

The vote was sufficiently close to require a machine recount as a matter of law, which reduced Bush's lead to 229 votes. Under state law, the loser, Gore, was permitted as part of the protest phase to request manual recounts, which he did in four counties that he believed would be favorably disposed to him. Bush filed an action in federal district court to halt the manual recounts, which the court rejected.[4] Manual recounts proceeded under the glare of national television coverage with county officials unable to agree on a consistent standard for what constituted a legal vote. The counties in question were unable to complete their recounts by the statutory deadline of November 14, 2000. Florida Secretary of State Katherine Harris refused to accept untimely recounts and the Florida district court sustained her decision.[5] Under state law, the secretary of state was required to certify the winner of the election by November 18. On November 17, however, the Florida Supreme Court enjoined Secretary Harris from doing so.[6] On November 21, it issued an opinion requiring the secretary to accept returns from manual recounts up to November 26.[7] In concluding that the need to arrive at an accurate vote count superceded the statutory deadlines, the Court emphasized the centrality of the right to vote in the Florida Constitution.

The manual recounts diminished Bush's lead to 537 votes. Still, on November 26, 2000, Secretary of State Harris certified Bush as the winner of the Florida electors. Meanwhile, Bush appealed the decision of the Florida Supreme Court to the United States Supreme Court. On December 4, in *Bush v. Palm Beach County Canvassing Board*,[8] the United States Supreme Court unanimously vacated and remanded the decision of the Florida Supreme Court. It indicated that it was unclear whether the Florida Court had relied on the state constitution in reaching its decision. If it had, it may have violated Article II, Section One, clause 2 of the United States Constitution that gives the state legislatures sole authority to direct the appointment of presidential electors. Moreover, the Court was concerned that the changes in the recount procedures and deadlines mandated by the Florida Supreme Court may have constituted a sufficient alteration of the state election laws to preclude the state from invoking the safe harbor provision of federal statute 3 U.S.C. 5, which would protect its vote certification against challenge in Congress. The decision by the Court had no substantive impact on the vote totals as it focused on the protest phase of the recount, which had expired by the time of the decision.

Following the certification of Bush by Secretary Harris, Gore filed a contest action under state election law in Leon County. On December 4, 2000, Florida District Judge Sauls denied Gore all of the votes that he claimed to be entitled to in the contest action.[9] Gore appealed immediately to the Florida Supreme Court which in a 4-3 opinion in *Gore*

---

[3] *Id.* at 3.
[4] Siegel v. LePore, 120 F. Supp. 2d 1041 (S.D. Fla. 2000), aff'd, 234 F. 3d 1163 (11th Cir. 2000).
[5] McDermott v. Harris, 2000 WL 1693713 (Fla. Cir. Ct. Nov. 14, 2001).
[6] *See* Palm Beach County Canvassing Bd. v. Harris, 2000 WL 1716480 (Fla. 2000).
[7] *Id.* at 1239–40.
[8] 531 U.S. 70 (2000).
[9] Gore v. Harris, 2000 WL 1770257 (Dec. 4, 2000).

v. Harris held that Gore was entitled to 215 votes from the Palm Beach County recount and 168 votes from the Miami-Dade recount, and in addition ordered the Miami-Dade Canvassing Board to review 9000 votes that the machines had rejected as non-votes and finally ordered the district court to see that all 170,000 under-votes statewide were examined.[10] The Court reasoned that its decision was supported by a reconciliation of ambiguous and seemingly conflicting provisions of the Florida election laws. It did not respond at all to the questions that had been directed to it by the United States Supreme Court four days earlier.

Chief Judge Wells offered a blistering dissent. He predicted, quite correctly, that "the majority's decision cannot withstand the scrutiny which will certainly immediately follow under the United States Constitution."[11] He argued that the majority's decision "had no foundation in the law of Florida as in existed on November 7, 2000" and that it would propel "this country and this state into an unprecedented and unnecessary constitutional crisis."[12] Anticipating the major points to be made by the majority and concurring opinions of the United States Supreme Court, Wells indicated that the absence of a standard for determining what was a legal vote would violate equal protection. The majority's alteration of the legislature's election procedures would violate Article II of the Constitution, and there would not possibly be time to conduct a statewide recount of all 170,000 under votes prior to the December 12 federal safe harbor deadline. He concluded that "[t]his case has reached the point where finality must take precedence over continued judicial process."[13] Justice Harding filed a dissent joined by two other justices.

The counting of the under-votes began the following day, December 9. Bush filed an immediate appeal with the United States Supreme Court, which granted a stay of the recount that very afternoon.[14] The Court treated the petition as one for certiorari, which it granted, requiring briefs to be submitted the following day with oral arguments scheduled in a day and a half. Justice Stevens, writing for four justices, dissented, arguing that no irreparable harm could come from counting every legal vote. He argued that halting the recount could cast a cloud over the legitimacy of the election. Justice Scalia responded, noting that the granting of the stay indicated that a majority of the Court believed that petitioner Bush has "a substantial probability of success."[15] He contended that contrary to Justice Stevens's assertions, the question raised was whether the votes being recounted were in fact "legal" votes, and a cloud would be cast over the legitimacy of the election if illegal votes were counted.

The case of *Bush v. Gore* was argued on Monday morning, December 11, 2000. Because of the extreme public interest in the case, the Court deviated from its normal procedures and permitted the argument to be broadcast on a tape-delayed basis over the radio shortly after it had ended. The primary argument pressed by petitioner Bush was that the Florida Supreme Court had sufficiently altered the post-election procedures to violate the command of Article II, Section One of the Constitution that each state shall appoint electors

---

[10] Gore v. Harris, 772 So. 2d 1243 (Fla. 2000).

[11] *Id.* at 1263.

[12] *Id.*

[13] *Id.* at 1270.

[14] 531 U.S. 1046 (2001).

[15] *Id.*

"in such a manner as the Legislature shall direct." In a nutshell, the Florida Supreme Court had usurped the constitutional role of the state legislature. Gore's counterargument was that the Court had simply engaged in ordinary and acceptable interpretation of an ambiguous law. Petitioner's secondary argument was that re-examining ballots under divergent standards from county to county or within individual counties violated the Equal Protection Clause of the Fourteenth Amendment. Gore replied that Florida's focus on determining the "intent of the voter" provided a sufficient uniform standard. Bush responded that intent was too vague to provide adequate guidance.

ORAL ARGUMENT

Theodore Olsen, representing Bush, began by pressing the Article II argument. Much of the argument was devoted to an attempt to establish that the Florida Supreme Court had radically changed the existing election laws as opposed to merely interpreting them.[16] Eventually, the Court steered Olson toward the equal protection issue.[17] He argued that intent of the voter was too vague but despite continued prompting from the Court was unwilling to suggest a more specific standard, presumably for fear that it might undercut the Article II challenge.[18]

Olson was followed by Joseph Klock, representing Secretary of State Harris. He argued quite vigorously that a ballot was not a legal vote if the voter had failed to follow the ballot instructions and punch the chad entirely through.[19]

David Boies presented the argument on behalf of respondent Gore. He was almost immediately forced to concede that if the Florida legislature had changed the election laws as the Florida Supreme Court had subsequent to the election, it would constitute a violation of Article II of the Constitution.[20] Justice O'Connor was deeply troubled that the Florida court had failed to respond to the prior Supreme Court decision vacating its initial opinion, but had instead proceeded to "assume that all those deadlines were just fine and they would go ahead and adhere to them."[21] This comment indicated that Gore was in very deep trouble indeed before the Court. Much of the remainder of the argument consisted of Boies's attempts to explain the differences between the Florida protest and contest procedures to the Court. Turning to the re-examination of ballots, Boies admitted that the standards applied "can vary from individual to individual."[22] He attempted to defend this as involving permissible discretion in the application of the intent standard. The justices were not convinced, however, emphasizing that the ballot examiners were not attempting to focus on the minds of the voters but rather the marks on a piece of paper, which certainly could be reduced to more specific objective criteria.[23] Justice O'Connor

---

[16] 294 LANDMARK BRIEFS AND ARGUMENTS OF THE SUPREME COURT OF THE UNITED STATES: CONSTITU-TIONAL LAW 515, 520–25 (Gerald Gunther & Gerhard Casper eds., 2000).

[17] *Id.* at 526.

[18] *Id.* at 528–30.

[19] *Id.* at 533–35.

[20] *Id.* at 540.

[21] *Id.* at 542.

[22] *Id.* at 546.

[23] *Id.* at 548.

echoed Joseph Klock's argument that the ballot instructions themselves should provide the appropriate standard for assessing the legality of the vote. She declared "[w]ell, why isn't the standard the one that voters are instructed to follow, for goodness sake? I mean it couldn't be clearer. I mean why don't we go to that standard?"[24] Boies replied that Florida law required an attempt to discern the intent of the voter even when the ballot was not properly executed; however, it should have been clear by that point that this was not a satisfactory response to the equal protection concerns. Once again, Justice O'Connor had signaled that Gore's position was tenuous at best.

Ted Olsen closed with a short response. Justice Kennedy noted that Olsen's primary argument focusing on Article II, which was troublesome in that the Court would essentially be forced to determine that the Florida Supreme Court had egregiously misapplied its own law, would be academic if the Court relied on the equal protection argument instead.[25] As the argument concluded, the Court had signaled that it was deeply troubled by the approach of the Florida Supreme Court, which Gore was defending, and that it was more sympathetic to Bush's equal protection than his Article II argument.

Given that Justice O'Connor had chastised the Florida Supreme Court for ignoring the Court's opinion in *Palm Beach Canvassing Board v. Harris*, it was not surprising that the Florida court issued such a response the following day. But it was too little too late. The Florida court published a revised version of its first opinion deleting any reference to the state constitution and proclaiming that it had not rewritten the state election laws.[26]

THE SUPREME COURT OPINION

THE MAJORITY–EQUAL PROTECTION

The Supreme Court issued its opinion reversing the Florida Supreme Court the following evening. In a per curiam opinion joined by Chief Justice Rehnquist and Justices O'Connor, Scalia, Kennedy, and Thomas, the Court concluded that the election procedures at issue violated the Equal Protection Clause. Apparently, Justice Kennedy was responsible for drafting most of the opinion.[27] Relying on *Harper v. Virginia Board of Elections*,[28] which invalidated the poll tax, and *Reynolds v. Simms*,[29] the main reapportionment case, the Court explained that the right to vote can be denied by valuing one person's vote over that of another.[30] It concluded that the Florida legislature's "intent of the voter" standard was insufficiently specific "to ensure its equal application."[31] Rather, the development of more precise uniform standards was both "practicable and…necessary."[32] The Court noted that it had been acknowledged at oral argument (by David Boies) that the

---

[24] *Id.* at 551.

[25] *Id.* at 562.

[26] Palm Beach Cty. Canvassing, Bd. V. Harris, 772 So. 2d 1273, 1291 (Fla. 2000).

[27] JEFFREY TOOBIN, THE NINE: INSIDE THE SECRET WORLD OF THE SUPREME COURT 172–74 (2007).

[28] 383 U.S. 663 (1966).

[29] 377 U.S. 533 (1964).

[30] 531 U.S. 98, 104–05 (2001).

[31] *Id.* at 106.

[32] *Id.*

recount standard seemed to vary from one team to another within a given county. It cited examples from the record of changes in the evaluation standards during the course of the recounts. It pointed out that the Florida Supreme Court had ratified the inclusion of votes counted by very different standards. The Court indicated that the decision to recount under-votes but not over-votes also contributed to disparate treatment. The majority also noted that the apparent decision of the Florida Supreme Court to include votes produced by only partial recounts also raised an equal protection question. These factors led the Court to conclude that the recount process in issue "is inconsistent with the minimum procedures necessary to protect the fundamental right of each voter."[33] Placing the blame squarely on the shoulders of the Florida Supreme Court, the majority explained that "[w]hen a court orders a statewide remedy, there must at least be some assurance that the rudimentary requirements of equal treatment and fundamental fairness are satisfied."[34]

The Court then turned its attention to what should follow. It recognized that formidable obstacles lay in the path of any attempted recount in that a standard would need to be set after argument by the parties, and procedures to ensure the implementation of the standard would need to be devised, and then there would need to be an opportunity for judicial review. As the Florida Supreme Court had indicated that the legislature had intended for the state to be able to take advantage of the federal safe harbor provision of 3 U.S.C. 5, and as that in turn would require certification of the votes by December 12, 2000, the day of the Court's decision, the majority concluded that there was simply no time left to devise a constitutional recount procedure.

The opinion then noted that "[s]even justices of the Court agree that there are constitutional problems with the recount ordered by the Florida Supreme Court that demand a remedy," citing the opinions of Justices Souter and Breyer.[35] The only difference between the majority and Justices Breyer and Souter was whether Florida should be given additional time to attempt a recount. That was not a viable option from the majority's perspective given that it believed that Florida was legislatively committed to the December 12 deadline imposed by the federal statute.

REHNQUIST CONCURRENCE—ARTICLE II

Justices Scalia and Thomas joined an opinion written by Chief Justice Rehnquist arguing that the changes in the election procedures implemented by the Florida Supreme Court also violated Article II of the Constitution. At the outset, Rehnquist acknowledged that as a general rule, the interpretation of state law was beyond the authority of federal courts. This was an exception to that principle however in that Article II of the Constitution charged state legislatures with the responsibility of devising the manner of the appointment of the state's electors, and the Court had previously held that Article II left the matter "to the legislatures exclusively."[36] As such, non-legislative alternations of a

---

[33] *Id.* at 109.
[34] *Id.*
[35] *Id.* at 111.
[36] *Id.* at 113, quoting McPherson v. Blacker, 46 U.S. 1 (1892).

state's procedures for the selection of electors raised a federal constitutional issue. This in turn was bolstered by 3 U.S.C. 5, which provides that a state's selection of its electors cannot be challenged if the selection occurred pursuant to procedures in place prior to the election and the selection was completed within six days of the meeting of the electoral college. As the Florida Supreme Court had indicated that the legislature wished to take advantage of the safe harbor provision, the question of whether the recount procedures utilized were in place prior to the election presented an issue of federal law. The Court cited several instances in which it was required to interpret state law in order to decide a federal constitutional issue. As a matter of federalism, Chief Justice Rehnquist explained that this approach "does not imply a disrespect for state *courts* but rather a respect for the constitutionally prescribed role of state *legislatures*."[37]

Rehnquist then turned his attention to the alterations in the law made by the Florida Supreme Court. First, he noted that the extension of the deadline for certification during the protest phase necessarily shortened the contest phase. Moreover, the alteration of the deadline "empties certification of virtually all legal consequences during the contest."[38] In addition, the Florida Court's adoption of a de novo review standard undercut the statutory grant of discretion to the Florida secretary of state as to whether to accept vote counts. He also maintained that the Florida court's inclusion of votes submitted after certification effectively eliminated the statutory deadline. The chief justice argued that the Florida court had also deviated from the legislative definition of "legal vote" by ordering the counting of improperly marked ballots, considering that the Voting Instruction clearly directed the voter to check the ballot to ensure that it was completely punched through before submitting it, as Justice O'Connor had pointed out during oral argument. Ordering a recount of under-votes where there had been "no error in vote tabulation" contrary to established Florida practice constituted a departure from the legislative scheme. Any further recounting of votes would also jeopardize the legislature's desire for the state to take advantage of the safe harbor provision, which would in turn be yet another alteration of the legislative plan in place prior to the election.

THE STEVENS DISSENT

Justice Stevens offered a dissent joined by Justices Ginsburg and Breyer. He argued that the federal questions raised by the case "are not substantial." He maintained that consistent with Article II, legislative acts pertaining to the selection of electors were subject to judicial interpretation by state courts, just as any other state statute would be.

As for equal protection, Justice Stevens maintained that problems with respect to the uniformity of standards would be resolved by the supervision of a single judge under Florida law.[39] Most significant, given that Florida law required the legality of votes to be assessed based on the perceived intent of the voters, the appropriate disposition of the case should be to remand for further application of that standard. Stevens closed with what was indeed an extremely insightful comment as to the crux of the decision in

---

[37] *Id.* at 115.
[38] *Id.* at 118.
[39] *Id.* at 126.

Bush v. Gore. He alleged that "[w]hat must underlie petitioners entire federal assault on the Florida election procedures is an unstated lack of confidence in the impartiality and capacity of the state judges who would make the critical decisions if the vote count were to proceed."[40] He concluded that this assumption, ratified by the Court, would ultimately undermine national confidence in the judiciary.

THE SOUTER DISSENT

Justice Souter authored a dissent joined by Justice Stevens and Breyer and Justice Ginsburg in part. He objected to the exercise of review by the Court in all three instances— Palm Beach County, the stay, and the present case, and argued that but for the Court's intervention, the recount may have been resolved through the appropriate stat procedures.[41] He dismissed the statutory 3 U.S.C. 5 argument quickly, noting that the only consequence of failing to abide by the provisions of the statute was the loss of the safe harbor.

Turning to the Article II ground, Justice Souter maintained that the interpretations of the election statutes by the Florida Supreme Court were not so unreasonable as to constitute a non-judicial act. He proceeded to defend the Florida court's interpretation of its election laws as within the bounds of reason.

He conceded that there was a meritorious claim for relief on equal protection grounds.[42] He explained that he could "conceive of no legitimate state interest served by the different treatments of the expressions of voters' fundamental rights" for assessing the intent of the voters, and as such the differences appear "wholly arbitrary."[43] Unlike the majority, he would remand the case to the Florida courts to see whether they could recount the 60,000 under-votes prior to the December 18 electoral college deadline.

THE GINSBURG DISSENT

Justice Ginsburg issued a dissent joined by Justice Stevens and by Justices Souter and Breyer in part. Focusing on the Article II claim, Justice Ginsburg emphasized that the instances in which the Supreme Court interprets state law are the rare exceptions to the general rule of deference. She argued that the Article II commitment of the appointment of electors to state legislatures assumes that state courts will still interpret ambiguous provisions.

In the second half of her opinion, joined only by Justice Stevens, she rejected the equal protection challenge. As for remands, she suggested that it would not necessarily be harmful to permit Florida to continue its recounts if needs be all the way up to the determination of the electoral votes by Congress on January 6.

---

[40] *Id.* at 128.

[41] *Id.* at 129.

[42] *Id.* at 133-34. Justice Ginsburg did not concur in this part of Justice Souter's opinion.

[43] *Id.* at 134.

THE BREYER DISSENT

Justice Breyer submitted a dissenting opinion joined by Justice Souter and Justices Stevens and Ginsburg in part. He conceded that "basic principles of fairness may well have counseled the adoption of a uniform standard" for recounting disputed ballots.[44] Like the other dissenters, Justice Breyer would remand to the Florida courts to give them an opportunity to recount the under-votes prior to the meeting of the electoral college on December 18. He argued that the majority's reason for ending the recount was based on non-record evidence. He maintained that there was no reason to believe that the Florida legislature would prefer the safe harbor of 3 U.S.C. 5 over its expressed concern that the intent of the voters be determined.[45] Justice Breyer then argued that the alterations in the procedure ordered by the Florida Court hardly constituted distortions of the law. In particular, he noted that the Florida Court should not be faulted for ordering a recount that could not be completed by the December 12 deadline as it very well may have been completed by that date had the United States Supreme Court not intervened. He emphasized that the ultimate resolution of disputed presidential elections was committed by the Twelfth Amendment to Congress, not the courts. He closed his opinion with a warning that "in this highly politicized matter, the appearance of a split decision runs the risk of undermining the public's confidence in the Court itself."[46]

THE IMPACT

With the Court's decision, the 36-day impasse was brought to a conclusion. Shortly thereafter Vice President Gore conceded and the following month Governor Bush was inaugurated as president. Not surprisingly, a significant segment of the public was dissatisfied and many were enraged. Given the closeness of the election, many loyal supporters of each candidate believed that the other was attempting to "steal" the election. Rumors of treachery by both sides abounded. No matter who was declared the winner, millions of people were bound to be bitterly disappointed. Considering the razor- thin margin and the multiple disputes over the proper vote count, partisans of the loser whether Gore or Bush would have found it difficult if not impossible to believe that the opponent had prevailed fairly. The Supreme Court's termination of the recount obviously added to the frustration of Gore's supporters. Because all of the requested ballots (presumably 60,000 under-votes) were not re-examined, Gore supporters could believe that had that been done, their candidate would have closed the gap and ultimately prevailed. Moreover Gore had won the popular vote nationwide by over a half million votes.

The fact that the Supreme Court intervened and brought the recount to a conclusion increased the anger and suspicion. Although seven Supreme Court justices had been appointed by Republicans, the Court was accurately viewed as split 5-4 with conservatives generally maintaining a one-vote majority. The Court did split 7-2 with respect

---

[44] *Id.* at 145.
[45] *Id.* at 149.
[46] *Id.* at 157.

to the equal protection issue with Justices Souter and Breyer siding with the five- vote majority. However on the important question of remand, the justices split 5-4 along predictable ideological lines. This gave rise to the claim accepted by many Gore supporters that a conservative Republican majority on the Court had simply installed their preferred candidate in the White House. Bush was "selected not elected" as the slogan went. As such, the Bush presidency would never be viewed by millions as legitimate.

In response, Bush's supporters could point out that at no time from the close of the election on did Bush ever trail in the Florida vote count, however small the margin might have been. Moreover, a lengthy statewide recount by a coalition of newspapers subsequent to the election indicated that by almost all vote-counting standards, Bush would have won.[47] Perhaps most significant, had the Court stayed out of the controversy and allowed the process to proceed, Bush almost certainly had Gore in checkmate. Even if Gore pulled ahead in the recount and was declared the winner by the Florida Supreme Court, the Republican-controlled Florida legislature was prepared to stand behind Secretary of State Harris's November 26 certification of Bush as the true winner. As a result, Congress would be faced with competing claims by Bush and Gore to the Florida electors. Under 3 U.S.C. 5, the House and Senate would each vote to determine which was the legitimate set of electors. The Senate was split 50-50 and presumably Vice President Gore presiding would cast the deciding vote in his own favor. In the House, each state's vote would be determined by which party held the majority of seats. As more state delegations were controlled by Republicans, it would be safe to assume that the House would favor Bush. Under the statute, when the House and Senate disagree, the tie will be broken by the governor of the state in issue. That would be Jeb Bush, governor of Florida, the brother of George W. Bush. Any claim that Jeb Bush should recuse himself would be met with the counterargument that both Gore and Senator Lieberman should have recused themselves in the Senate vote as well. Had they done so, Bush would have prevailed before both House and Senate and there would be no need for his brother to break the tie. However, Judge Posner has argued that in view of several difficult unanswered legal questions regarding legislative resolution, it would have been quite messy with perhaps more legal challenges headed to the Supreme Court.[48] It was all but certain that George Bush was going to be the next president regardless of what the Supreme Court did or did not do.

BUSH v. GORE AS A GREAT CASE

Why did the Court decide to become involved in the election controversy, and why did it decide to halt the recount? As the dissenters pointed out, it was certainly highly unusual for the Court to become involved in a contested presidential election. There was no precedent for such action. And as Justice Breyer noted in his dissent, there was certainly a risk to the Court's prestige given that once it intervened, millions of people were likely to

---

[47] Michael W. McConnell, *Two-And-A-Half Cheers for Bush v. Gore,* 68 U. CHI. L. REV. 657, 657-58 (2001); JEFFREY ROSEN, THE SUPREME COURT: THE PERSONALITIES AND RIVALRIES THAT DEFINED AMERICA 215 (2007).

[48] RICHARD A. POSNER, BREAKING THE DEADLOCK: THE 2000 ELECTION, THE CONSTITUTION, AND THE COURTS 137–47 (2001).

resent whatever the Court might do. In addition, the legal principles on which the Court might rely to resolve the issue were quite thin in view of the lack of precedent.

One theory to explain and indeed perhaps justify the Court's intervention is that the nation was headed toward a constitutional crisis that the political system simply did not seem capable of resolving in a manner that would inspire confidence. The vote recount process in Florida had appeared chaotic and bumbling at best and there was little reason to believe that it would improve. The nation had been watching the process unfold on televison for 36 days with no finality yet in sight. Perhaps the Court concluded that for the stability of the nation, a decision by the Court would simply resolve a controversy that should have been resolved weeks before. In other words, this was the kind of crisis over which it was worth risking the Court's credibility. The recent Clinton impeachment by Congress did not necessarily inspire confidence in that institution. The fact that candidates Gore and Lieberman might well end up voting for their own election in the Senate and that Bush's brother might ultimately end up deciding the election also may have struck the justices as a less than desirable outcome.

However there is a better explanation, and it was stated by Justice Stevens in dissent when he proclaimed that "what must underlie the petitioners' entire federal assault on the Florida election procedures is an unstated lack of confidence in the impartiality and capacity of the state judges who would make the critical decisions if the vote count were to proceed."[49] In other words, George W. Bush and a majority of the Supreme Court apparently believed that the Florida Supreme Court was behaving in a partisan manner in an attempt to do all that could be done to help Gore prevail. There is every indication that Justice Stevens was correct, that a majority of the justices had lost all faith in the impartiality of the Florida court. As David Strauss put it, the Court's "actions seem to be the product of a general sense that the Florida court was illegitimately manipulating the law to ensure that Vice President Gore won" though Strauss did not believe that the Court had a sound basis for that conclusion.[50]

Justice O'Connor clearly expressed her frustration during the oral argument with the Florida Supreme Court's refusal to address the questions that the Supreme Court had posed on remand, despite the fact that the Florida court had published another opinion in the interim. Her frustration suggested that she believed that the Florida Court had shown rather extreme disrespect for the United States Supreme Court. As of that point, it is likely that as a practical matter *Bush v. Gore* was over. Justice O'Connor, often a moderate and a former state court judge herself, may have concluded that the Supreme Court was dealing with a renegade state court that must be brought to heel. Indeed she said as much in an interview a few years later.

Chief Justice Wells's stinging dissent from the opinion before the Court in *Bush v. Gore* may have gone a long way toward convincing a majority of the United States Supreme Court that the Florida court had lost its judicial bearings. His assertion that there is "no foundation in the law of Florida as it existed on November 7, 2000" for the Florida Court's decision provided some reputable Florida authority for the fact that the state court was playing fast and loose with the election rules. Indeed, the obvious subtext of

---

[49] 531 U.S. 70, 128 (2001).
[50] David A. Strauss, Bush v. Gore: *What Were They Thinking?*, 68 U. Chi. L. Rev. 737, 755 (2001).

the Wells dissent was a plea to the United States Supreme Court not to take the Florida court's statutory interpretation seriously. Both the majority opinion of the United States Supreme Court on equal protection as well as the concurrence on Article II suggest that the five justices were highly skeptical of the competence if not the impartiality of the Florida Supreme Court.

Subsequent comments by at least two justices confirm that the Court was uncomfortable with allowing the Florida Supreme Court to have the final word on the resolution of the 2000 election, either because it was concerned about the impartiality of that court or because it simply believed that if a court was to have a significant impact on the resolution of the presidential election, it needed to be a national rather than a state court. In a subsequent interview, Justice O'Connor declared that the Florida Supreme Court was "off on a trip of its own,"[51] scarcely a resounding endorsement. Justice Breyer was also troubled by the apparent partisan slant of the Florida Supreme Court's decision.[53]

In deciding *Bush v. Gore*, there was certainly little precedent on point given that no similar case had ever been before the Court. Academics were especially harsh in their criticism of the opinion[54] although it should be borne in mind that an overwhelming percentage of them tend to be liberal Democrats, many of whom were no doubt heavily invested emotionally in the prospect of a Gore presidency. The academic criticism of *Bush v. Gore* rivaled that of *Roe v. Wade*. The equal protection ground did attract seven votes, which in itself is unusual in a difficult case. The embarrassing continual shifting of standards throughout the recount procedure combined with the decision to recount some but not other votes and to submit incomplete recounts obviously convinced the justices that the approach ratified by the Florida Supreme Court was both irrational and arbitrary. The interesting question is not how seven justices could conclude that this process violated equal protection of the laws but rather how Justices Stevens and Ginsburg could possibly have thought otherwise. There was some fear that the decision might have the potential to throw open the courthouse doors to persistent constitutional challenges to close elections, especially given the disparate accuracy rate of different types of voting devices used within a particular state. The majority went out of its way to indicate that the decision was confined to its peculiar factual context. As such, the decision has not given rise to federal judicial supervision of subsequent elections, close or otherwise.

The equal protection principle set forth by the Court was not particularly intrusive or demanding. The Court simply required that if a state decides to attempt to discern the intent of the voters from the ballots themselves, it needs to provide a clear and consistent standard for making that determination. The state may choose a narrow standard,

---

[51] GREENBURG, *supra* note 1, at 31–32.

[53] TOOBIN, *supra* note 27, at 165–66.

[54] *See, e.g.*, Akhil Reed Amar, *Should We Trust the Judges?*, L.A. TIMES, Dec. 17, 2000, at M1 (the decision is not worthy of respect); Randall Kennedy, *Contempt of Court*, AMERICAN PROSPECT, Jan. 1–15, 2001 (the decision was a "hypocritical mishmash," the majority "acted in bad faith with partisan prejudice"); Jamin Raskin, *Bandits in Black Robes: Why You Should Still be Angry about* Bush v. Gore, WASHINGTON MONTHLY, Mar. 21, 2001 ("quite demonstrably the worst Supreme Court decision in history"); Cass Sunstein, WHAT WE'LL REMEMBER IN 2050, CHRON. HIGHER EDUCATION, Jan. 5, 2001, B15 (the decision was "illegitimate, unprincipled and undemocratic"). This is just a small sampling of the vitriolic academic criticism of the decision. Judge Posner was highly critical of the commentary by law professors in terms of its "quality and disinterest." POSNER, *supra* note 48, at 199.

a broad standard, or something in between as long as it is clearly articulated and consistently applied. This would seem to be little more than a requirement of elementary fairness inherent as much in due process as in equal protection. The opinion did not purport to declare that differences in the accuracy of vote counts attributable to the employment of different tabulation machinery would implicate equal protection. Rather, the principle of *Bush v. Gore* did not apply until human beings attempted to discern the intent of the voter from an incomplete ballot.

There is some reason to believe that Justices Breyer and Souter were attracted to an equal protection rationale in hopes of forging a coalition to rebuke the approach of the Florida courts and at the same time permit them to continue the recount under a clear and objective standard. That did not happen, either because all five justices in the majority had concluded that the process must be brought to an immediate end or because there was insufficient time to negotiate any further compromise. Justice Souter was later quoted as saying that he believed he could have convinced Justice Kennedy to vote for a remand had he had one more day.[55] Justice Kennedy replied that he thought that he could have convinced Justice Souter to vote against a remand given an extra day.[56]

The Article II concurrence of Chief Justice Rehnquist may have elicited more criticism than the equal protection holding even though it only represented the views of three justices. On the one hand, it was a far narrower holding in that it could apply only to presidential elections, and then only where a state court had appeared to significantly alter the legislatively provided procedure on the fly. As such, there was little danger that it would create a dangerous precedent for elections in the future. This strength could be seen as a weakness however in that a ruling that would likely apply to only one case could appear to be political in nature. There were at least three other concerns with the Article II holding as well. First, it is quite unusual for the Court to interpret state law. That is definitely the exception and not the rule, and as such suggests that the justices were behaving in an uncharacteristic manner. Second, there was disagreement over whether the Florida Supreme Court's decisions had changed the rules of the game beyond the bounds of ordinary interpretation. Finally, unlike the equal protection theory, the Article II approach inevitably required the Court, at least implicitly, to question the competence if not the honesty of the Florida Supreme Court. Obviously, that is an awkward thing to suggest even if a majority of the Court may have been driven by just that conclusion. Near the close of oral argument, Justice Kennedy acknowledged that reliance on the equal protection theory would absolve the Court of the need to question the interpretive performance of the Florida Supreme Court.[57] And that is why the equal protection theory almost certainly carried the day.

The most consistently voiced criticism of *Bush v. Gore* was simply that it was inappropriate for the Court to place itself in the position of effectively resolving a presidential election.[58] There are different faces to this argument. One point is that under a proper understanding of the Constitution, a dispute over the proper vote count in a particular state is simply a matter for that state itself to resolve and not for the federal courts,

---

[55] GREENBURG, *supra* note 1, at 177.
[56] *Id.*
[57] LANDMARK BRIEFS AND ARGUMENTS, *supra* note 16, at 562.
[58] Samuel Issacharoff, Bush v. Gore: *Political Judgments*, 68 U. CHI. L. REV. 637 (2001).

especially the United States Supreme Court. Although this point is generally valid in most elections, as Justice Kennedy acknowledged, the national interest in a presidential election is simply too great to allow a single state court to play such a decisive role whether or not there is reason to distrust its decision-making. If there is a dispute, a national body must resolve it. The answer to that concern is that in fact under the Constitution and federal law, there is a national body given authority to resolve such disputes—the Congress. Even some of the critics of the Florida Supreme Court argued that it would have been more appropriate for Congress rather than the Court to have the final say, either because that was the constitutionally prescribed procedure or alternatively that it was a political dispute that most properly should be resolved by a political body. During oral argument, Justice Scalia suggested that permitting the vote counting to proceed could undermine any subsequent political decision, whether by the Florida secretary of state, the Florida legislature, or Congress, at least to the extent that in the interim, illegal or improper votes were counted. At least some of the justices seemed to believe that permitting the recount to continue would lead to a crisis in confidence that the political branches would be unable to temper.

Perhaps the most serious concern over Supreme Court intervention was that expressed by Justice Stevens: that the Court's credibility, its moral capital as it is often called by legal scholars, would be seriously damaged if a significant portion of the public believed that a majority of the Court had essentially decided a presidential election whether consciously or not for partisan or ideological reasons. Based on traditional assumptions about public perceptions of judicial behavior, this seemed like a serious concern. And yet there is no evidence that the decision did in fact have an adverse impact on the Court's standing with the public once the dust had settled.[59] There may be a number of explanations for this. Arguably, once the Court undertakes to resolve troubling issues that it might not have resolved in the past, the public comes to expect fairly aggressive judicial behavior in the future, and as such is not disturbed when it occurs. Second, the public at large had grown weary of the seemingly endless dispute over the election and simply welcomed a definitive resolution to it regardless of whether it was by the Court or some other entity. Finally, given that Bush had never fallen behind in the vote count in Florida, and as such Gore was perceived as the challenger attempting to reverse the course of events, a majority of the public over time came to accept Bush as the legitimate winner and simply did not believe that the Court had awarded the presidency to an undeserving candidate, despite efforts of the Gore campaign to create that impression.

Another significant dispute centered around whether the Court should have remanded to give the Florida Supreme Court the opportunity to decide whether to continue the recount up to December 18, the electoral college deadline, rather than December 12, the safe harbor deadline. This was the point on which the seven-vote majority decreased to five. The majority was able to argue that the Florida Supreme Court had in fact indicated that the legislature intended for the state to be able to avail itself of the safe harbor of 3 U.S.C. 5. Indeed the Florida Supreme Court indicated this most clearly in its eventual

---

[59] BARRY FRIEDMAN, THE WILL OF THE PEOPLE: HOW PUBLIC OPINION HAS INFLUENCED THE SUPREME COURT AND SHAPED THE MEANING OF THE CONSTITUTION 363 (2009) (a 2006 Gallup Poll indicated that 60 percent of the public approved of the Court as compared to 29 percent approval of the Congress and 39 percent approval of the president).

response to the United States Supreme Court issued the day after the oral argument in *Bush v. Gore*, of which the United States Supreme Court was apparently unaware.[60] If so, time was up, as the majority of the Supreme Court held. The alternative as expressed by Justice Breyer was why not simply remand to the Florida Supreme Court and permit it to decide whether the safe harbor was more important as a matter of state law than continuing the recount. One advantage of such an approach would be to take much of the heat off of the United States Supreme Court. The Court could not readily have been accused of ending the election dispute as the final judicial action would take place in Florida.

The justices in the majority may have had at least three reasons for rejecting that approach. First, if the majority believed that the Florida Court was playing fast and loose with the legislatively prescribed rules in order to give Gore every conceivable chance to pull ahead, it may simply have concluded that the lower court was unworthy of further deference. Second, the majority may have concluded that if the recount were to continue, the election would ultimately be determined almost certainly in Bush's favor by the Congress under the Twelfth Amendment and that a Florida court decision asserting that Gore had won would not change that result, but would instead create an unnecessary crisis of confidence and legitimacy. Finally, the Court may simply have concluded that enough was enough—the dispute had roiled the nation for too long. It was simply time to end it.

Like many, perhaps like most great cases, *Bush v. Gore* brought the Court into a relatively unique controversy. The Court was required to decide an issue that had never come to it before and was unlikely to ever present itself again. It was a dispute that the Court could have easily avoided without significant criticism. And yet a majority of the Court entered the dispute twice (three times if the stay is counted) without hesitation. Some would contend that *Bush v. Gore* is a classic example of a great case that made very bad law, bad in the sense that it was unprincipled and bad in the sense that it was designed to have little if any precedential impact. It is probably more accurate to conclude that like *United States v. Nixon*, it is an example of a great case that made almost no law at all. Rather it simply resolved a temporary national crisis. Perhaps it is most importantly understood as further evidence that a confident Court is not the least bit intimidated by the prospect of resolving a great case regardless of the pressurized context in which it is presented or the potential threat to the Court's own stature.

---

[60] 772 So. 2d 1273 (Fla. 2000).

"The Supreme Court decision in NFIB v. Sebelius (NFIB) achieved a level of media coverage and public salience reached by very few Supreme Court decisions. It represented a political moment, if not a constitutional one."[1]

ANDREA LOUISE CAMPBELL AND NATHANIEL PERSILy

22

National Federation of Independent Business v. Sebelius

RARELY IF EVER has there been a case that has attracted as much attention as *National Federation of Independent Business v. Sebelius*.[2] The case presented a constitutional challenge to the Patient Protection and Affordable Care Act of 2010, the signature legislation of the Obama presidency. The legislation, which imposed massive structural changes to the healthcare and health insurance industries, had been enacted on a strictly partisan basis. Feelings about it were intense. At the time that the case was argued polls indicated that a majority of the public disapproved of it and favored its repeal.[3] Oral arguments in the case extended over four days. Public clamor over the potential decision was relentless during the three-month period between the argument and the publication of the decision. A majority of the justices accepted the primary argument raised by the challengers to the legislation; however Chief Justice Roberts, joining with four other justices, voted to uphold the law nevertheless on a basis that few had anticipated. From what can be gleaned about the decision-making process as well as the opinion itself, *Sebellius* would seem to be an example of a case in which the hydraulic pressure of the great case was indeed a factor.

BACKGROUND

President Obama chose to make reform of the healthcare system the primary issue on his legislative agenda. With Democratic control of both the Senate and the House during the first two years of his presidency, after much debate, Congress passed the Patient Protection

---

[1] Andrea Louise Campbell & Nathaniel Persily, *The Health Care Case in the Public Mind, in* THE HEALTH CARE CASE: THE SUPREME COURT'S DECISION AND ITS IMPLICATIONS 245 (Nathaniel Persily, Gillian E. Metzger & Trevor W. Morrison eds., 2013).

[2] 132 S. Ct. 2566 (2012).

[3] Campbell & Persily, *supra* note 1, at 255.

and Affordable Care Act (ACA), a massive piece of legislation designed to significantly alter both health insurance and the delivery of healthcare in the United States. The Act was extremely complicated and covered a great variety of issues. A primary goal of the Act was an attempt to extend health insurance coverage to millions of uninsured Americans. Congress concluded that many were uninsured either because they were too poor to purchase insurance, were unable to purchase insurance because of preexisting medical conditions, or simply chose not to purchase health insurance because they were healthy and did not see the need. At the heart of the Act were three interrelated provisions. First, the Act provided for "guaranteed issue," that is, health insurers were required to provide coverage to everyone who applied. Second, health insurers could not base the cost of insurance on the preexisting medical conditions of the insured but must instead rely on "community rating," that is, the larger pool of insured individuals. Then to ensure that the young and healthy especially do not simply forgo purchasing health insurance until they need it, thus driving up the cost for everyone else, Congress enacted an individual mandate requiring most uninsured individuals to either purchase health insurance or pay a fee on their federal income tax return. In addition, the Act provided for interstate health insurance exchanges, which would presumably be able to bargain for lower cost policies for the uninsured. Moreover, the Medicaid program would be expanded to provide health insurance coverage to persons whose income was up to 133 percent of the poverty level. Initially, the federal government would pay 100 percent of the cost of the expansion although eventually its share of the cost would drop to 90 percent with the states supplying the additional 10 percent.

The very day that the Act was signed into law several legal challenges were filed. All of the challenges argued that Congress did not have the authority under the Commerce Clause to impose the individual mandate to purchase health insurance. Moreover, they maintained that the mandate could not be justified under the taxing power either as Congress intended the payment to be a penalty, justified if at all by the Commerce Clause rather than a tax based on the taxing power. Some of the challenges also argued that the Medicaid expansion was unconstitutional in that it was unduly coercive. District Courts and Courts of Appeals in the Fourth,[4] Sixth[5] and District of Columbia[6] Circuits rejected all challenges to the Act. However in a case brought by the attorneys general of 26 states, a federal district court in Florida struck down the mandate as exceeding the scope of the Commerce Clause in that it was an unprecedented attempt to regulate inactivity.[7] The district court also explained that the mandate could not be justified under the taxing power as Congress had gone out of its way to treat the mandate as a penalty. The Court of Appeals for the Eleventh Circuit affirmed the decision of the district court by a 2-1 vote.[8] The Supreme Court granted the petition for certiorari on all issues raised by the litigation and scheduled the case for four days of oral argument during the final week of March 2012. Over 150 amicus briefs were filed.[9]

The oral arguments considered all significant issues raised by the challenges to the Act including whether the litigation was barred by the statute prohibiting the issuance of

---

[4] Liberty Univ. Inc. v Geithner, 671 F.3d 391 (4th Cir. 2011).

[5] Thomas More Law Ctr. v Obama, 651 F. 3d 529 (6th Cir. 2011).

[6] Seven-Sky v Holder, 661 F. 3d 1 (D.C. Cir. 2011).

[7] 780 F. Supp. 2d 1256 (N.D. Fla. 2011) clarified, 780 F. Supp. 2d 1307 (N.D. Fla. 2011).

[8] 648 F. 3d 1235 (11th Cir. 2011).

[9] Marcia Coyle, The Roberts Court: The Struggle for the Constitution 341 (2013).

injunctions against the collection of federal taxes, whether the expansion of the Medicaid Act unconstitutionally coerced state compliance, whether the mandate could be sustained under either the Commerce Clause or the taxing power, and whether the remainder of the Act was severable if the Court did find the individual mandate to be unconstitutional. The centerpiece of the oral argument took place on the second day when the Court considered the constitutionality of the individual mandate under the commerce power. In a nutshell, Paul Clement, arguing on behalf of the state plaintiffs, maintained that Congress was attempting to regulate inactivity and that Congress simply did not have the authority to create commerce in order to then regulate it. Solicitor General Verrilli responded that the decision not to purchase insurance, or to self-insure as the government characterized it, was in itself an economic decision that had a substantial effect on the interstate market in healthcare. Several of the justices appeared to be quite skeptical of if not hostile to the government's argument. In particular, they seemed to be sympathetic to the states' contention that there was nothing constitutionally unique about healthcare and as such, if the government was permitted to force a citizen to purchase health insurance then there would be absolutely no limit on the scope of congressional power, contrary to the federal structure of limited governmental authority. When the solicitor general argued that the mandate penalty was in fact a tax authorized by the taxing power, Chief Justice Roberts, Justice Scalia, Justice Ginsburg, Justice Sotomayor, and Justice Kagan all expressed skepticism.[10] Justice Scalia noted that President Obama had denied that the penalty was a tax.[11] The tone of the oral argument seemed to suggest that a majority of the Court was inclined to invalidate the individual mandate.

The case was of such extreme public interest that the Court released tapes of the oral arguments shortly after they ended. Following the arguments while the case was under consideration by the justices, defenders of the Act conducted a relentless campaign in the media aimed particularly at Chief Justice Roberts, arguing that the credibility of the Court would be destroyed if it invalidated such a monumental piece of legislation.[12] In late June, the Court announced that it would be delivering its opinion on the Healthcare Act. Most observers were stunned on learning that although five justices did conclude that the individual mandate was not authorized by the Commerce Clause, and although four justices were prepared to invalidate the Act in its totality, Chief Justice Roberts joined four other justices to sustain the Act on the ground that it could have been passed pursuant to the taxing power, despite the fact that Congress explicitly characterized the payment requirement as a penalty rather than a tax. The decision evoked high praise from the defenders of the Act and intense criticism form the opponents, especially considering the eccentric justification provided by the chief justice for sustaining the Act.

THE ROBERTS OPINION

Chief Justice Roberts issued an opinion that was joined by Justices Ginsburg, Breyer, Sotomayor, and Kagan upholding the Act as an exercise of the taxing power, an opinion

---

[10] Oral argument transcript at 44–52.

[11] *Id.* at 46.

[12] COYLE, *supra* note 9, at 347.

joined by Justices Breyer and Kagan concluding that the Medicaid expansion was unduly coercive, and an opinion only for himself maintaining that the mandate could not be justified under the Commerce Clause. The four dissenters, Scalia, Kennedy, Thomas, and Alito, agreed that the mandate was not justifiable under the Commerce Clause and that the Medicaid expansion unduly coerced state participation by threatening to deny the states all Medicaid funds; however the dissenters did not join the Roberts opinion. At the outset, perhaps in response to those who were upset that the Court did not invalidate the Act, Chief Justice Roberts proclaimed "[i]t is not our job to protect the people from the consequences of their political choices."[13]

Initially, Chief Justice Roberts, writing for the Court, rejected the argument that the lawsuit was precluded by the Anti-Injunction statute. The opinion reasoned that Congress had clearly designated the payment for failing to purchase insurance as a penalty and as such it was not a tax within the meaning of the Anti-Injunction Act.

Then writing only for himself, Roberts addressed the constitutionality of the individual mandate under the Commerce Clause. He observed, as had often been noted during the litigation, that Congress had never before attempted to require an individual to purchase a product. He concluded "that the power to regulate commerce presupposes the existence of commercial activity to be regulated."[14] Roberts accepted the principal argument of the challengers that permitting Congress to regulate inactivity would destroy any meaningful limitation on congressional power. He pointed out that the exercise of congressional power in this case went well beyond what Congress had done and what the Court had approved in *Wickard v. Filburn*, generally considered the most extreme extension of the commerce power. He cited the oft-repeated hypothetical that under the government's theory, individuals could be required to purchase vegetables in order to improve public health and thereby decrease healthcare costs. He maintained that a country in which the government could "use its commerce power to compel citizens to act as [it] would have them act. . . is not the country the framers of our Constitution envisioned."[15] Paraphrasing language used by Justice Kennedy during oral argument, Roberts declared that the government's theory would fundamentally change "the relationship between the citizen and the Federal Government."[16] He noted that "the Framers gave Congress the power to *regulate* commerce, not to compel it."[17] Nor can Congress regulate individuals on the theory that they will engage in interstate commerce at some point in the future. He also rejected that government's argument that healthcare is unique and thus does not create a slippery slope, as well as its argument that the delivery of healthcare and the maintenance of health insurance are so closely integrated that regulation of the former necessarily encompasses the latter.

Roberts then turned to the Necessary and Proper Clause. He reasoned that even if the individual mandate was necessary to effectuate the goals of the Act, it was not "proper" as the clause only permitted Congress to provide the means for carrying out legislative ends otherwise authorized by the underlying enumerated power. As the Commerce Clause did

---

[13] 132 S. Ct. 2566, 2579 (2012).
[14] *Id.* at 2587.
[15] *Id.* at 2589.
[16] *Id.*
[17] *Id.*

not authorize Congress to regulate inactivity, imposing the mandate on such activity would not be constitutionally proper. He concluded that "[t]he commerce power thus does not authorize the mandate," citing the dissent of Scalia, Kennedy, Thomas, and Alito for the same proposition.[18]

In section III B of the opinion, Chief Justice Roberts turned to the taxing power. At the outset he declared that "[t]he most straightforward reading of the mandate is that it commands individuals to purchase insurance."[19] The question then became whether "the government's alternative reading of the statute—that it only imposes a tax on those without insurance—is a reasonable one."[20] The question according to Roberts was whether that was a "'fairly possible'" construction of the statute.[21]

In section III C, he then argued that "the exaction...looks like a tax in many respects."[22] He noted that the penalty produces some revenue, is collected through the income tax form, and is based on the taxpayer's taxable income, and the requirement to pay is found in the Internal Revenue Code. Though he conceded that it is characterized as a penalty and not a tax, that alone does not preclude considering it as authorized by the taxing power even if that characterization nullifies the application of the Anti-Injunction Act. Citing several precedents, Chief Justice Roberts argued that the label that Congress attached to the measure was not conclusive in determining whether it could be enacted pursuant to the taxing power.

He cited three reasons that "the shared responsibility payment may for constitutional purposes be considered a tax, not a penalty."[23] First, the amount would often be less than the cost of insurance. Second, there was no intent requirement. And third, it was collected by the Internal Revenue Service. The fact that it was intended to influence conduct did not render it any less a tax, citing the examples of taxes on cigarettes, marijuana, and illegal weapons. He argued that penalties are usually imposed as punishment for committing illegal acts, and Congress did not make the failure to purchase health insurance illegal. As a result, Chief Justice Roberts concluded that "Congress had the power to impose the exaction...under the taxing power [and]....[t]hat is sufficient to sustain it."[24]

Treating the payment requirement as a tax, Roberts then determined that it was not a direct tax requiring apportionment among the states as it was based on a specific individual decision not to purchase insurance as opposed to simply being imposed on everyone.

Speaking for a majority, Roberts proclaimed that "[t]he Court today holds that our Constitution protects us from federal regulation under the Commerce Clause so long as we abstain from the regulated activity. But from its creation, the Constitution has made no such promise with respect to taxes."[25] He argued that there was nothing new or unusual about using taxes as incentives to encourage conduct. At some point, such use of tax incentives could become unconstitutional if unduly coercive. However, this tax

---

[18] *Id.* at 2593.
[19] *Id.*
[20] *Id.* at 2594.
[21] *Id.*
[22] *Id.*
[23] *Id.* at 2595.
[24] *Id.* at 2598.
[25] *Id.* at 2599.

incentive could not mandate the underlying conduct given that the individual could simply choose to pay the tax instead.

In response to Justice Ginsburg, Chief Justice Roberts explained that it was necessary to analyze the Act under the Commerce Clause as the most natural construction of the mandate was as a penalty rather than a tax. Only upon concluding that it could not be authorized under the Commerce Clause did it become necessary to consider whether it could be justified as a tax. As such, the Commerce Clause analysis was not simply gratuitous dicta.

Then in section IV. A of the opinion, joined by Justices Breyer and Kagan, Roberts addressed the challenge by the states to the Medicaid expansion. At the outset, he noted that "[t]here is no doubt that the Act dramatically increases state obligations under Medicaid."[26] That was so because it expanded coverage of the program to all adults under 65 with an income at or below 133 percent over the poverty line. In addition, it required the states to provide an "essential health benefits Package" to all new Medicaid beneficiaries, which provided far more benefits than anything the states had previously been required to offer.[27]

Chief Justice Roberts explained that although Congress has wide latitude to engage in conditional spending, that is, to grant funds to the states with strings attached, the Court has recognized that such a program will be unconstitutional if as a practical matter, the states do not have a free choice to decline to accept the funding. Otherwise, the federal government could avoid political accountability by shifting the focus to the states. Roberts concluded that Congress had indeed crossed the line in this case by authorizing the denial of existing Medicaid funds to states that did not consent to the expanded coverage as opposed to simply denying the funds appropriated with respect to the new coverage. He concluded that the states were correct in maintaining that "this threat serves no purpose other than to force unwilling states to sign up for the dramatic expansion in health care coverage effected by the Act."[28] As noncompliance with the expansion would cause states to lose over 10 percent of their average budget, the condition amounts to "a gun to the head," giving the states no effective choice.[29] Although the states did agree to accept alterations to the program, Roberts argued that the expansion was "a shift of kind, not merely degree" considering that it required coverage of entirely new classes of individuals.[30] In summary, the opinion concluded that "Congress is not free to...penalize States that chose not to participate in the new program by taking away their existing Medicaid funding."[31]

In the final section of his opinion, Roberts explained that he was not rewriting the Medicaid Expansion provisions but merely invalidating that aspect that was unconstitutional. He also concluded that there was no reason to believe that Congress would have preferred for the entire Act to fall because this particular section was unconstitutional.

---

[26] *Id.* at 2601.
[27] *Id.*
[28] *Id.* at 2603.
[29] *Id.* at 2604.
[30] *Id.* at 2605.
[31] *Id.* at 2607.

JUSTICE GINSBURG'S CONCURRENCE AND DISSENT

Justice Ginsburg, joined in part by Justices Breyer, Sotomayor, and Kagan wrote an opinion that concurred in the portion of Chief Justice Roberts's opinion sustaining the Act under the taxing power and dissented from the rest. They did not independently discuss the taxing power however. She began with a lengthy discussion of the healthcare problems facing the nation and maintained that the states that had attempted to expand coverage to the uninsured had learned that they could not effectively do so without requiring all individuals to carry health insurance. She argued that Congress had a rational basis for concluding that the uninsured have a substantial effect on interstate commerce. She accepted the government's contention that an individual's failure to purchase health insurance was an "economic decision" that Congress had the authority to regulate under the Commerce Clause.

She then turned her attention to Chief Justice Roberts's analysis of the Commerce Clause issue. Ginsburg argued that the uninsured do directly affect interstate commerce as a solid majority of them do utilize healthcare services on an annual basis and not simply in the distant future. Like the government, she emphasized the inevitable and unpredictable nature of healthcare. She also argued that there was an interstate market in both healthcare and health insurance; therefore Congress was not simply creating commerce in order to regulate it. Justice Ginsburg rejected the claim that the Court had never allowed Congress to regulate inactivity under the Commerce Clause, arguing that as a practical matter the Court permitted the regulation of inactivity in *Wickard* by effectively forcing the farmer to purchase wheat in interstate commerce by limiting the amount he could produce for home consumption. She asserted that the political process would preclude Congress from imposing mandates to purchase products with any regularity.

Justice Ginsburg then contended that the individual mandate was justified as a necessary and proper means of effectuating the guaranteed issue and community rating provisions of the Act. She emphasized that it did not unduly intrude on the states but operated directly upon individuals.

With only Justice Sotomayor concurring, Justice Ginsburg also challenged the holding that the Medicaid expansion unduly coerced state compliance. She noted that this was the first time in history that the Court had found an exercise of the spending power to be unduly coercive. She pointed out that Congress has amended the Medicaid statute over 50 times; thus alteration was nothing unusual. Thus, she characterized the expansion as simply an ordinary addition to the program rather than an extraordinary change in its character. Consequently, she maintained that the chief justice's principle would require the federal government to create a new and separate program rather than simply expand an existing one, and that there was no basis for such a distinction. Ginsburg contended that as the Medicaid Act permitted Congress to alter or amend the program, Robert's principle must be that Congress can "alter *somewhat*" or that it can "amend *but not too much*."[32] She maintained that determining when federal spending conditions become too coercive involves a political rather than a legal judgment. She agreed with Chief Justice

---

[32] *Id.* at 2639.

Roberts that if the Medicaid expansion was to some extent unconstitutional, that those elements were severable from the remainder of the Act.

JUSTICES SCALIA, KENNEDY, THOMAS, AND ALITO DISSENTING

Justices Scalia, Kennedy, Thomas, and Alito wrote a lengthy dissent signed jointly by all four. They would have invalidated the Act in its entirety. Their dissent largely ignored the opinion of the chief justice, focusing instead on the arguments raised by the government. At the outset, the dissent declared that the government's theory makes "mere breathing in and out the basis for federal prescription and... extend[s] federal power to virtually all human activity."[33] Like the chief justice, the dissent argued that Congress did not have the authority to create commerce. The dissent emphasized that Congress could have addressed the problem in several constitutionally uncontroversial ways, including subsidizing health insurance, placing a surcharge on the uninsured when they seek healthcare, or providing preferential tax treatment to the insured. It noted that at oral argument, the government could not identify a single type of private conduct that could not be reached under its theory.

The dissent rejected the government's argument that everyone is a participant in the healthcare market, declaring that it is simply not true and cannot be made true by declaring that everyone will participate at some point in the future. As the dissent put it "if every person comes within the Commerce Clause *power* of Congress to regulate by the simple reason that he will one day engage in commerce, the idea of a limited Government power is at an end."[34] It dismissed Justice Ginsburg's conclusion that the failure to insure was an economic decision as "wordplay."[35] The dissent also observed in response to Justice Ginsburg that the Constitution does not enumerate "federally soluable *problems*, but federally available *powers*."[36]

Turning to the taxing power, the dissent argued that an exaction must either be a penalty or a tax, but under well-accepted precedent simply cannot be both. It concluded that the fee imposed for failing to purchase health insurance was by the clear terms of the Act a penalty and could not reasonably be construed as a tax. Contrary to the chief justice, the dissent reasoned that the exaction is imposed for violation of the law and therefore is a penalty rather than a tax. It observed that the Act refers to the exaction as a penalty 18 times. Moreover, Congress had deliberately changed the language of prior versions of the Act, which had described the fee as a tax, to describe it as a penalty in the bill as enacted. The dissent characterized the government's (and hence the chief justice's) arguments that the fee could be considered a tax as "flimsy" and "feeble."[37] Consequently, the government was asking the Court not to interpret but rather to rewrite the statute. The dissent also criticized the meager analysis of the difficult question of whether if it was a tax, it was a direct tax. As for the Anti-Injunction Act, the dissent charged that the

---

[33] *Id.* at 2643.
[34] *Id.* at 2648.
[35] *Id.* at 2649.
[36] *Id.* at 2650.
[37] *Id.* at 2654.

government was engaging in sophistry by arguing that the exaction was not a tax for statutory purposes but was a tax for constitutional purposes.

As for the Medicaid expansion, the dissent found this to be a clear case of coercion given that the states could not realistically decline to participate considering the penalty they would suffer. It noted that the federal government was threatening to withhold $233 billion dollars, or 21.86 percent of all state expenditures combined. The fact that Congress failed to include a backup plan for insuring the uninsured if a state declined to participate revealed that Congress was of the view that no state could afford to so decline. As the goal of the Act was to provide universal coverage, Congress would not have left such a gap had it believed that states actually had a choice.

Considering that Congress effectively believed the Medicaid expansion to be mandatory, reading the statute to render it optional was simply judicial rewriting of the statute. Even if a state opted out, its citizens must still pay extensive taxes, which will benefit only the citizens of other states that choose to participate.

Turning more generally to the issue of severability, the dissent argued that once the two major pillars of the Act—the individual mandate and the Medicaid expansion—were declared unconstitutional, the entire Act must fall as well. To determine severability, the Court must ask whether the remainder of the statute will operate as Congress intended, and even if so whether Congress would have passed the remaining sections as such. The dissent argued that the Act was a highly integrated piece of legislation, and if these two crucial pieces were removed, the remainder of the Act would impose enormous costs and risks on the healthcare system and its participants. The dissent explained why this would be so in some detail.

In summary, the dissent charged that the Court "decides to save a statute that Congress did not write."[38] That in turn is not an act of "judicial modesty" but instead amounts to a vast "judicial overreaching."[39] It has the effect of creating "a debilitated, inoperable version of health-care regulation that Congress did not enact and the public does not expect."[40] The dissent concluded with a reminder that the structural provisions of the Constitution are as essential to the preservation of liberty as is the Bill of Rights.

THE HEALTH INSURANCE LITIGATION AS A GREAT CASE

Few great cases better support Justice Holmes's claim that the hydraulic pressure of the great case can have a decisive impact on the result. That almost certainly happened in *Sebelius*. Only one justice, Chief Justice Roberts, seems to have been affected by the pressure, but he turned out to cast the decisive vote. As briefed, argued, and understood by the profession and the public, the case would almost certainly turn on the congressional commerce power. Had the Court rested the decision on either Robert's rejection of the Commerce Clause justification or Justice Ginsburg's endorsement of it, the case would presumably be one more great case in which the Court disappointed a lot of people but developed constitutional doctrine in a plausible manner. By turning the decision on an

---

[38] *Id.* at 2676.
[39] *Id.*
[40] *Id.*

eccentric and unpersuasive rationale that at most had been on the margins of the dispute, Roberts introduced a legal rationale that was fraught with uncertain consequences. It seems unlikely that in the future, the Court would stretch and bend to such a degree to sustain legislation under one head of power that was quite clearly enacted pursuant to another. Nor to be more specific is the Court likely to labor so hard to construe what was certainly intended as a penalty to be justified as a tax. As with some of the great cases such as *United States v. Nixon* or *Bush v. Gore*, the approach taken by Chief Justice Roberts may be confined to the peculiar circumstances of the case. As such, perhaps it will not do a great deal of damage as precedent although it is too soon to know. But far more seriously, the decision suggests that at least one key justice was simply unwilling to strike down a major piece of congressional legislation that presented very serious constitutional questions, for fear that the Court's reputation would be damaged as a result. Ironically, the implication that the Court is fearful and subject to manipulation by the threat of public and political disapproval may in the long run do more harm to its prestige than the backlash that might follow the invalidation of legislation that did not even seem to have majoritarian public support. It should be noted however that four justices were quite prepared to invalidate the entire Act even though credible arguments could be made to sever both the individual mandate and the Medicaid expansion. The four justices who joined the chief justice in sustaining that Act almost certainly did so based on their own doctrinal predispositions rather than on account of any public pressure.

As Professors Herbert Wechsler, Alexander Bickel, and Gerald Gunther argued so eloquently over 50 years ago, the Court's strong suit is the principled nature of its constitutional decision-making.[41] If the Court does not proceed in a principled manner in spite of the consequences, it simply becomes another political institution subject to all of the pressures and vacillations of other political bodies. Professor Bickel argued that because the Court cannot afford to always proceed in a principled manner, it needs to be able to employ various avoidance devices, which he called the "passive virtues." in order to duck issues that could not be resolved in a constitutionally principled way at least at the time they were presented. Professor Gunther disagreed and maintained that the Court must always proceed based on principle regardless of the consequences. Arguably, Chief Justice Roberts chose to decide *Sebelius* on an unprincipled basis on the constitutional merits in an attempt to preserve the Court's moral capital in the long run, violating the advice of Wechsler, Bickel, and Gunther. If so that in itself may diminish the respect in which the Court is held by a significant segment of the population.

Credible reports indicate that initially Chief Justice Robert was prepared to invalidate at least the mandate if not the entire Act under the Commerce Clause.[42] At some point, he changed his mind and decided that although the Commerce Clause could not justify the mandate, nevertheless the Act must be upheld. The best and probably most likely explanation for his change of mind was a deep-felt concern for the reputation of the Court. It was a presidential election year. Had the Court invalidated the most prominent

---

[41] *See* Herbert Wechsler, *Toward Neutral Principles of Constitutional Law*, 73 Harv. L. Rev. 1 (1959); Alexander M. Bickel, The Least Dangerous Branch: The Supreme Court at the Bar of Politics (1962); Gerald Gunther, *The Subtle Vices of the Passive Virtues—A Comment on Principle and Expedience in Judicial Review*, 64 Colum. L. Rev. 1 (1964).

[42] Coyle, *supra* note 9, at 350, referring to a report by CBS correspondent Jan Crawford on July 1, 2012.

accomplishment of the Obama administration during its first term, it is likely that the Court would have become the target of vigorous attacks during the campaign. Regardless of the results of the election, the Court's prestige might have suffered, perhaps greatly. Had these attacks been successful in contributing to an Obama victory, the damage may have been even greater, convincing perhaps a solid majority of the public that the Court was indeed responsible for denying the nation the opportunity to reach a political solution to the healthcare crisis. Under this view, perhaps Roberts engaged in an act of judicial statesmanship that was justified, although no one can know what the true risks to the Court's reputation actually were. If a large segment of the public believes that the Court must decide even great and hard cases on the basis of legal principle with little if any concern for public criticism or disappointment, then the perception that the Court, or at least the chief justice pulled his punches, might in itself sully the Court's reputation. Public opinion polls do suggest that the reputation of the Court did decline somewhat following the *Sebelius* decision although it is not necessarily clear why that happened.[43]

A less charitable view is that Chief Justice Roberts was simply intimidated by the barrage of threats from the defenders of the Act, including the president, especially after the case had been submitted and it appeared that the Court might strike the Act down. Only two weeks before the Court was expected to announce its decision prior to the end of its term, the volume and intensity of the speeches warning Chief Justice Roberts not to invalidate the Act increased significantly. This struck observers of the Court as unusual considering that the decision by the Court would have been reached weeks before and the opinion itself would almost certainly be in its final stages of completion. That caused seasoned court watchers to wonder why politicians believed that they could have any influence whatsoever on the chief justice at this late stage of the proceedings, if at all. It seemed especially strange given that the conventional wisdom was that Justice Kennedy, not Chief Justice Roberts, would be the most likely fifth vote to uphold the Act were that to happen. Why was the focus so entirely on the chief justice? Apparently, there was a leak from inside the Court indicating that Roberts had initially voted to invalidate the Act but was now was leaning toward sustaining it. The rash of public commentary seemed to be intended to persuade him to stick with his change of mind given that the justices who favored invalidation were lobbying hard to bring the chief justice back into the fold. There is no evidence or reason to believe that the chief justice initially changed his mind, assuming that he did as the result of public pressure or that he stayed the course because of such pressure. It is quite plausible, however, that his concern with keeping the Court out of the center of political conflict guided his thinking. Of course this is all speculation. No one outside of the Court knows, at least not yet.

It can be argued that Roberts's embrace of an arguably implausible ground for sustaining the Act was consistent with his overall jurisprudential approach.[44] In *Northwest Austin Utility District 1 v. Holder*,[45] which Roberts cited in his opinion in *Sebelius*, he adopted an improbable interpretation of section 5 of the Voting Rights Act to avoid the issue of its constitutionality. It should be noted however that four years later, the chief justice did

---

[43] Campbell & Persily, *supra* note 1, at 271.

[44] Jonathon Adler, *Judicial Minimalism, the Mandate and Mr. Roberts*, in THE HEALTH CARE CASE, *supra* note 1, at 171.

[45] 557 U.S. 193 (2009).

face up to the constitutional issue and did write an opinion invalidating the provision in question. Thus he was hardly prepared to avoid confronting the constitutionality of a significant federal statute no matter what.

A penchant for avoiding constitutional issues does not necessarily explain why the chief justice would initially commit to invalidation, if in fact he did, and then change his mind late in the game. Moreover, presumably, there are limits as to how far a statute can be twisted or rewritten in order to avoid unconstitutionality. The dissent argued vigorously that those limits had been disregarded by the chief justice.

In any event, having determined that the Act must be saved, Roberts adopted the taxing power as the only viable alternative. This led to an opinion that few could take seriously. The fee in question was explicitly characterized as a penalty, and understood by Congress, the lower courts, and the public to be a penalty. Even Chief Justice Roberts understood that the most plausible reading was that in fact it was a penalty. The Act was sustained on the assumption that it could have been passed or could be considered a tax—not that it was. The Court was subjected to criticism but almost certainly not to the degree that it would have been, at least by the political elites, had it invalidated the Act. Most of the criticism was directed not at the Court per se but rather at the chief justice who was perceived, at least by the Act's challengers, as having had a failure of nerve. Roberts wrote that "[i]t is not our job to protect people from the consequences of their political choices." It will be interesting to see how far the Court may be willing to press this principle of deference in the future. Taken seriously in other areas of constitutional law it would lead to a far more docile Supreme Court. Is the principle of deference relevant only to the exercise of enumerated powers, or does it carry over to congressional action that poses a threat to provisions in the Bill of Rights and civil rights as well? If not, why not? The dissent argued that enforceable restraints on the affirmative powers of Congress are just as important to the protection of individual liberty as the negative constraints of the Bill of Rights. Certainly the framers so believed.

Time passes, and whatever damage may have been done to the Court's prestige will likely fade. It was predicted that Bush v. Gore would have a devastating impact on the Court's reputation and that did not turn out to be the case. The rationale relied on by Chief Justice Roberts may not bear any fruit. Congress may recognize that the Court's forbearance was little more than a response to this particular case as opposed to a new level of deference to congressional legislation. This is particularly true given that the approach was only the product of one justice seemingly desperate to avoid a confrontation with a relatively popular and aggressive president determined to wage a no holds barred re-election campaign. And as Chief Justice Roberts noted in his opinion, reliance on the taxing power as a source for controversial legislation raises serious political obstacles. So perhaps there is a more viable political check against abuse of the taxing power than of the commerce power.

Did Sebelius make bad law? It is simply too soon to tell for two reasons. First, there has been insufficient time to determine whether any of its principles or doctrine will be followed and will have a long-term impact. Second, like Bush v. Gore, the partisan divide on both the underlying question as well as the legal approach was so sharp that it is difficult if not impossible to uncover much analysis that does not seem to be largely influenced by ideology. Sebelius presented the Court with two clearly defined and contrasting views of the Constitution as well as the role of the Court. Defenders of the Act believed that aggressive use of enumerated powers by Congress was easily consistent with the constitutional understanding settled by the New Deal revolution of 1937. The appropriate role of the Court was to defer to such legislation, relying upon the political process as the sole check against abuse. The challengers to the Act believed that Congress was bound to stay within boundaries of its enumerated powers to ensure that the government is indeed limited. The role of the Court is to enforce those limits if transgressed. A decision one way or the other was bound to appear profoundly wrong to the losing side. As the underlying issue, an extreme reconfiguration of the healthcare and health insurance system, would have a direct impact on so many people, what might otherwise be simply an obscure debate among law professors was transformed into a controversy of extreme public interest. At least some students of constitutional law may be capable of evaluating the doctrinal impact of *Sebelius* quite apart from whether they like the Act. However, for much of the public the two are inseparable. Despite these difficulties, it is worth trying to engage in a preliminary evaluation of the law that *Sebelius* made.

The issue that had been at the vortex of the health insurance litigation throughout was whether Congress had the power under the Commerce Clause to impose the mandate to purchase insurance. Every other issue had been secondary. It had been assumed that the Act would stand or fall on the resolution of that issue. In fact there had been some surprise initially that the Court was even interested in devoting substantial time in oral argument to any other question. The positions of the parties had been staked out clearly during litigation in the lower courts and in oral argument. Throughout the litigation, the parties waged a war of characterization. Arguably the case would turn on the way in which the congressional action was perceived. From the challengers' perspective, Congress was attempting to regulate inactivity, the failure to purchase health insurance, something that it had never done and something that it did not have the power to do. From the government's viewpoint, Congress was regulating the economic decision to self-insure, an activity well within its power. The majority (on the Commerce Clause question) accepted the former characterization while the Ginsburg four accepted the latter.

There was general agreement that Congress had never before required a person to buy a product pursuant to the Commerce Clause, and as such the question of constitutionality was open. Although partisans would maintain that the law was clear one way or the other, in fact plausible arguments could be raised both for and against the constitutionality of the mandate, and Chief Justice Roberts and the four dissenters on the one hand and Justice Ginsburg on the other developed those arguments and counterarguments thoroughly. The central argument for the challengers to the Act pressed hard by Roberts and the dissent was that if Congress could require a person to purchase health insurance, then there was no limit on its authority to regulate under the Commerce Clause, contrary to the well-accepted design of the constitutional structure. Justice Ginsburg picked up the government's argument that healthcare was unique and distinguishable and that the mandate to purchase was closely linked to the interstate market in both healthcare and health insurance. The decision on the issue ultimately came down to a judgment as to whether there was a need for judicially enforceable limits on the congressional commerce power and whether a decision not to recognize such limits would, as Justice Kennedy noted in oral argument and as Chief Justice Roberts stated in his opinion, fundamentally alter the relationship between the federal government and the individual. Five justices concluded that this would indeed be the case. On the commerce power, *Sebelius* presented a cutting edge or hard case. A decision either way would have been defensible.

It is not clear how much of an impact the rejection of the Commerce Clause justification will have in the future. Justice Ginsburg argued that this conclusion was mere dicta as a majority would ultimately uphold the law pursuant to the taxing power. Chief Justice Roberts responded that because the mandate read more like a Commerce Clause–based penalty rather than a tax, he never would have addressed the taxing power issue without first rejecting the Commerce Clause claim. The line between holding and dicta is fuzzy and as a practical matter the precedential status of the rejection of the mandate under the Commerce Clause will be determined by future courts. There is simply no way of knowing at present whether it will be treated as precedent or mere dicta. At the very least, the fact that five justices in very strong language and great detail rejected the Commerce Clause approach should carry substantial weight. Moreover, the recognition of the limitations of the Commerce Clause by five members of the Court should cause a future Congress to pause before pressing its Commerce Clause authority beyond traditional boundaries. Given that this was the first instance in which Congress had ever attempted to regulate inactivity under the Commerce Clause, the decision does not upset settled precedent or represent a change of direction. Rather, it is simply additional proof that five justices were prepared to enforce constitutional boundaries in this area.

Chief Justice Roberts also rejected the government's reliance on the Necessary and Proper Clause to sustain the Act. From *McCulloch v. Maryland* on, the Court has given a spacious construction to the word "necessary," construing it to mean convenient or one reasonable means of accomplishing a legitimate congressional objective. For the most part the Court has neglected the word "proper." Roberts and the four justices who also rejected the Act concluded that requiring a person to purchase health insurance was not proper. Roberts maintained that the mandate was not proper as it was an attempt to regulate something (inactivity) that was wholly beyond congressional authority to regulate. As such, sustaining it under the Necessary and Proper Clause would demolish the limitations of the enumerated powers. This emphasizes that the Necessary and Proper Clause should not be considered a wild card permitting the government to legislate wholly beyond the scope of the enumerated powers. This clarified the limits of the Necessary and Proper Clause and may prove to be a significant addition to constitutional jurisprudence if followed.

Although a decision either way would not have been surprising on the Commerce Clause issue, the decision to uphold the law under the taxing power was startling. Hardly anyone anticipated such a result. The taxing power issue was in the case to be sure but it had been solidly rejected by the lower courts and had been largely ignored in the briefs and oral arguments. There was a near consensus that Congress considered the fee for failing to purchase insurance to be a penalty rather than a tax. Of the eight lower court judges who had addressed the taxing power issue, seven concluded that the payment in question was a penalty, which could not be upheld as an exercise of the taxing power, and most did not consider it a close case.[46]

---

[46] The following rejected the taxing power justification: Thomas More Law Ctr. v. Obama, 651 F. 3d 529 (6th Cir. 2011), (Sutton, J., concurring), *id.* at 550–54 (Graham, J., concurring and dissenting), *id.* at 566; Fla. v. Dep't of Health & Human Servs., 648 F.3d 1235, (11th Cir. 2011) (majority), *id.* 1313–20; Fla. v. Dep't of

To argue, as Chief Justice Roberts did, that the payment requirement seemed to be a Commerce Clause–based penalty but nevertheless could be justified as a tax, but even so must be thought of as a penalty for purposes of the Anti-Injunction Act, was bizarre. Contrary to the rest of his opinion, this section simply lacks conviction. It reads as if the author clearly recognized that he was making an implausible argument that would persuade very few. Justice Ginsburg and the three justices who joined parts of her opinion concurred in Chief Justice Robert's taxing power argument but made no independent effort to support it. The dissent offered a devastating critique of the argument, explaining that a payment requirement could be either a tax or a penalty but not both. The text of the Act and its legislative history showed that Congress intended the payment to be understood as a penalty. As such, Roberts taxing power rationale appeared to the professional reader as well as the casual observer as a desperate attempt to avoid overturning such a major piece of legislation, even at the cost of judicial honesty and integrity.

The long-term danger in the Roberts approach is that it could encourage Congress to attempt to conceal unpopular tax increases as penalties to avoid political resistance. Indeed, the district court in *Sebelius* criticized the government for characterizing the payment as a penalty to make the legislation politically palatable, then defending it as a tax in court.[47] As that court noted, this undermines political accountability, which is generally understood to be the primary check against abuse of the taxing power. There are limits under Robert's approach as to when the Court can construe an apparent penalty to be a tax. At the very least, the fee in question must be sufficiently modest in comparison to cost of the otherwise mandated conduct to provide the individual with a legitimate choice. If the fee is too substantial, it must be regarded as a coercive penalty as opposed to a tax imposed on a voluntarily chosen activity or inactivity. It is unclear whether Congress would be tempted to use the same tactics in the future or whether the Court would be as accommodating in a different case. It is at least possible that a majority would not be nearly so sympathetic in a case that did not involve the potential invalidation of such a major piece of legislation. The Roberts opinion may have created a dangerous precedent with respect to the exercise of the taxing power, although that remains to be seen. Quite possibly, it is an isolated case.

More troublesome than the taxing power argument as such was the effort by the chief justice to avoid invalidating an Act that he did not believe could be sustained on the primary theory on which it was enacted and defended through a strained and unpersuasive rationale. Throughout the Court's history, it has tended to decide great cases forthrightly. Sometimes as with *Dred Scott*, the Court was too willing to confront the most troublesome questions. Roberts's opinion in *Sebelius* has been compared to Marshall's opinion in *Marbury* in that both chief justices relied on strained readings of congressional legislation

---

Health & Human Servs., 716 F. Supp. 2d 1120, 1143–44 (N.D. Fla. 2010); U.S. Citizens Ass'n v. Sebelius, 754 F. Supp. 2d 903, 909 (N.D. Ohio 2010); Liberty Univ., Inc. v. Geithner, 753 F. Supp. 2d 611, 629 (W. D. Va. 2010); Virginia v. Sebelius, 728 F. Supp. 2d 768, 782–88 (E.D. Va. 2010); Goudy-Bachman v. Dept. of Health & Human Servs., 764 F. Supp. 2d 684, 695 (M.D. Pa. 2011); Mead v. Holder, 766 F. Supp. 2d 16, 41 (D.D.C. 2011). The only lower court judge to accept the taxing power argument was Judge Wynn in Liberty Univ, Inc. v. Geithner, 671 F. 3d 391, 415–18 (4th Cir. 2011).

[47] Florida ex rel McCollum v. U.S. Dept of Health & Human Servs., 716 F. Supp. 2d 1120, 1142 (N.D. Fla. 2010), aff'd., 648 F. 3d 1235 (11th Cir. 2011), rev'd., 132 S. Ct. 2566 (2012).

to avoid a showdown with a popular president. In the process, Marshall established the concept of judicial review of both congressional and executive action. Roberts provided the fifth vote for important limitations on the scope of the Commerce Clause. It should be noted, however, that the position of Marshall and his court was far more precarious than that of Roberts. Unlike the Marshall Court, the Roberts Court has 200 years of judicial review and a vast reservoir of goodwill behind it. Roberts, unlike Marshall, would scarcely have risked impeachment with a decision against the government. For the most part, the modern Court does not tend to be bashful. It has consistently invalidated congressional limitations on campaign finance, struck down a historic provision of the Voting Rights Act of 1965, and is willing to wade into the middle of contemporary controversies on gay marriage and racial preferences. There is little if any reason to believe that the Roberts approach in *Sebelius* signaled a new reticence. It may be a reminder that at least for the chief justice, the turmoil of 1936 and 1937 is always in the back of the judicial mind.

The decision, especially by a 7-2 margin, to invalidate the Medicaid expansion as unduly coercive under the Spending Clause was also surprising. This argument had been rejected by every single lower court that had addressed it. To some it was even surprising that the Supreme Court had agreed to consider it given that there was no circuit split on the issue. Chief Justice Roberts and the dissenters produced solid arguments as to the inevitably coercive nature of denying the states all Medicaid funds if they failed to accept the expansion. Despite Justice Ginsburg's dissent, the majority was able to establish an approach that could easily prevail as mainstream jurisprudence in the unlikely event that Congress should ever employ the Spending Clause in such a heavy-handed manner again.

It is obviously way too soon to assess the doctrinal or institutional impact of the healthcare decision. For whatever it establishes, it is a precedent that may be employed in the future for good or quite possibly for ill. *Sebelius* would seem to be an instance in which at least the chief justice was indeed affected by the hydraulic pressure of which Holmes spoke. Whether in the process the Court made bad law remains to be seen.

23

Do Great Cases Make Bad Law?

DO GREAT CASES make bad law? As noted at the outset, asking that question necessarily requires a definition of terms as well as several subjective and speculative judgments. Holmes assumed that the great case was distinguishable from the hard case, which he also indicated makes bad law. It is unclear whether Holmes was suggesting that great cases and hard cases were mutually exclusive. There is no reason that should be so unless by definition, a great case is indeed an easy case that has been unduly complicated by the publicity and pressure that surrounds it. Arguably, that may be what Holmes was suggesting. If so, the universe of such cases is quite small and scarcely worth discussing. The better view is that there is in fact room for substantial overlap between the great case identified by unusual public interest in its outcome and the hard case marked by the absence of clear legal rules for its resolution. The overwhelming number of hard cases are not great cases, but most great cases are in fact hard cases at least at the time decided although they might not seem so hard in retrospect. That complicates analysis. If a case that was both great and hard made bad law, did it do so because of greatness, hardness, some combination of the two, or for other reasons instead?

As also noted in the Introduction, the great case as discussed herein, is not the same as the landmark case although many great cases do become landmark cases. The great case is recognizable at the time that it is presented to the Court. Whether a case is a landmark depends on how it is received in the future. The great case would seem to be the case in which either the public at large or at least the legally informed public have taken an extraordinary interest in the decision of a case by the Supreme Court, either because of the celebrity of the parties involved or because of the public or political significance of the issues at the heart of the case. For a brief period of time at least, the eyes of the nation are focused on the Court. Most of the cases discussed in this volume clearly fit this description. A few cases have been included however such as the *Slaughter-House Cases* and the Reapportionment Cases that do not fall into the classic great case pattern but where it was at least obvious to the justices themselves that they were confronting an issue of extraordinary and long-lasting importance. Arguably at least, the internal pressure generated in such cases would be somewhat equivalent to the external pressure that accompanies the more typical great case.

The central question is whether the circus-like atmosphere that often accompanies the great case, what Holmes described as hydraulic pressure, distorts the judicial process in an adverse manner. If so, is it possible to identify such distortions? Do great cases interfere with the Court's decision-making process itself? Are the adverse effects of the greatness of the case discernable from the most significant artifact of the decision, the Court's opinion? Can it be determined that the decision or its reasoning was in some sense deficient, and can that deficiency be attributable to the greatness of the case? Does the long-term precedential status of the decision support the claim that the greatness of the case had either a positive or negative impact?

The cases detailed in each of the preceding chapters provide at least some data for addressing these questions. This study has not discussed every great constitutional case ever decided by the Supreme Court but it has attempted to review the greatest of the great, which should provide a fair sample.

THE DYNAMICS OF THE GREAT CASE

Tolstoy wrote that happy families are all alike but unhappy families are each unhappy in their own way.[1] It may not be true that all ordinary cases are ordinary in the same way but great cases tend to be great for different reasons. That is not surprising given that by definition they are the relatively rare cases that focus the attention of the nation on the Court, present the Court with a question of monumental significance, or both. The circumstances under which the great case finds its way to the Court will play a role in how it is decided. Rarely is a great case simply thrust upon the Court. The Court had every opportunity to avoid the great cases that seem to have landed on its doorstep with some immediacy such as *Youngstown*, the Pentagon Papers Case, *United States v. Nixon*, and *Bush v. Gore*. The Court could have either avoided those cases entirely or at least considered them only after they had wound their way to the Court through the normal appellate process. Had the Court taken the latter approach, the controversies would have dissipated or been resolved before reaching the Supreme Court. The Court heard these cases with expedition simply because it chose to, thereby playing a significant role in the creation of the great case. The Court may have played a role in expediting the process in *McCulloch v. Maryland* as well.

Often, the great case receives more extended deliberation than the ordinary case. Of course during the Marshall Court era before written briefs were submitted, the cases were argued for days rather than hours with minimal if any questioning of the attorneys by the justices. Several great cases have been argued more than once, generally in consecutive Court terms, including *Dred Scott*, the *Slaughter-House Cases*, *Pollack v. Farmers Home Loan*, *Brown v. Board of Education*, *Baker v. Carr*, and *Roe v. Wade*. *Hepburn v. Griswold* and *The Civil Rights Cases* sat on the Court's docket for years before they were decided, and there was no oral argument in the latter.

---

[1] LEO TOLSTOY, ANNA KARENINA 1 (1859).

Sometimes the Court creates the momentum for the great case by consolidating several cases presenting the same issue, as occurred in the *Legal Tender Cases*, the *Slaughter-House Cases*, *The Civil Rights Cases*, *Pollack v. Farmers Home Loan*, *NLRB v. Jones & Laughlin Steel*, *Brown v. Board of Education*, *Reynolds v. Simms*, *Miranda v. Arizona*, and *Roe v. Wade*. Some great cases present unique circumstances such as the Pentagon Papers Case, *United States v. Nixon*, and *Bush v. Gore*. Every great case is unique in terms of the glare of publicity and/ or the momentousness of the questions.

Great cases, because of their greatness, tend to attract highly talented counsel. Several of the most renowned members of the Supreme Court bar have appeared in great cases, including Daniel Webster, William Wirt, Luther Martin, William Pinckney, John Campbell, Joseph Choate, John W. Davis, Thurgood Marshall, Archibald Cox, Erwin Griswold, Herbert Wechsler, Ken Starr, Ted Olsen, and Paul Clement. The arguments have often been quite enlightening though not always. Certainly the Court's approach to oral argument has changed significantly over time. In the days when written briefs were not submitted, attorneys were permitted to deliver extended and often eloquent dissertations with little if any interruption from the bench. In the modern era, the attorney in the great case is peppered with questions from the very outset of the argument. Perhaps John W. Davis was the rare exception in that he was permitted to speak with little interruption in *Youngstown*, which he won handily, and in *Brown*, which he lost unanimously.

Oral argument is not always enlightening in the great case however. In the Pentagon Papers Case, two very distinguished lawyers, Erwin Griswold and Alexander Bickel, were unable to be as helpful as one would ordinarily expect given the limited time to prepare. *Roe v. Wade*, though argued twice, is perhaps the most outstanding example of a great case in which the attorneys on both sides were not up to the task, while in *Bakke*, Archibald Cox clearly outclassed the attorney for the challenger. On occasion, the justices become entangled in peripheral issues during oral argument and scarcely focused on the larger issues presented and to be decided by the Court. That seems to have happened in *Reynolds v. Simms*. There are instances however in which the oral arguments or briefs seem to have played a crucial role. Marshall quite obviously relied heavily on the oral arguments in drafting his opinions in *McCulloch* and *Gibbons*. *New York Times v. Sullivan* may be the most outstanding example in Supreme Court history of a brief and argument having an extremely positive impact on the opinion. Had it not been a great case, Herbert Wechsler almost certainly would not have been involved to present the argument that Justice Brennan so heavily relied upon. In the modern era, great cases lead to an avalanche of amicus briefs. Most are probably ignored by the justices; however, the Harvard brief in *Bakke* and the Retired Officers Brief in *Grutter* clearly had a crucial impact on the decisions and opinions. There can be little doubt that on balance, the justices have the benefit of excellent counsel in great cases, which cannot help but have a beneficial effect.

DOES THE GREATNESS OF THE CASE HAVE AN ADVERSE EFFECT ON THE COURT'S DECISION–MAKING PROCESS?

One difficulty with assessing the impact on the decision-making process itself is the general absence of material pertaining to that process prior to the middle of the twentieth century. Perhaps there is too much evidence of the process since that point.

We know almost nothing as to how the Marshall Court decided the great cases of *Marbury*, *McCulloch*, and *Gibbons*. The Court heard lengthy arguments and then published lengthy and polished opinions shortly thereafter. Marshall almost certainly wrote the opinions himself, although he was living in a boarding house with the other justices so there may well have been some interaction. There is every reason to believe that the other justices held Marshall in the highest esteem and almost certainly accorded his opinions great deference. The speed with which he prepared the opinions in *Marbury* and *McCulloch* suggests that he may have started drafting at least during the oral arguments. The greater delay in the preparation of the *Gibbons* opinion may be attributable to Marshall's fall and injury during the interim. In all three cases, Marshall probably factored the political context into the decision. That was almost certainly the case in *Marbury*. Marshall probably underestimated the political opposition that was to materialize with respect to *McCulloch*. The contemporaneous congressional debates on federal power as well as the fact that Marshall's control of the Court might have been declining probably played a role in how *Gibbons* was decided.

If anything should be clear however, it is that Marshall was not afraid of the great case. Instead he welcomed the opportunity that it provided him both to influence the future development of the law and strengthen the Court's relative position. Marshall was quite adept at transforming great cases into landmark cases. He had the intellect and the confidence to do so as well as the ability to carry a unanimous or near unanimous court along with him.

Justice Story rather than Chief Justice Taney controlled the Court in *Prigg v. Pennsylvania*, but it was a tenuous control at that. The publicly explosive controversy surrounding the issue of fugitive slave rendition along with the difficulty of holding a majority together probably influenced the decision-making process in *Prigg* although there is no direct evidence.

The *Dred Scott* Case would almost certainly provide the single most persuasive example of what Holmes had in mind with his famous remark in *Northern Securities*. Due to a leak to a reporter as well as the correspondence of some of the justices, there is a fair amount of information regarding the decision-making process in *Dred Scott*. It is plain that the boiling political cauldron surrounding the decision did seem to play a significant role in transforming what could and should have been a relatively inconsequential case into the most catastrophically bad decision in the Court's history. The justices allowed themselves to be caught up in the most divisive political controversy of the time, apparently divided among themselves along partisan lines, and seemed to convince themselves that they could resolve an issue beyond the Court's capacity and perhaps beyond the capacity of any form of peaceful settlement. At least two justices in the majority were intent on assisting the new president, and one of the dissenters was intent on attempting to become the next president. The chief justice seemed willing to defend the existing order even at the expense of the Court as an institution. *Dred Scott* is the most extreme example of how the great case can infect the Court's decision-making process and lead the Court astray. It occurred in an overheated political context in which few on or off the Court were able to keep their heads about them, so perhaps it is not so surprising that the justices were swept up in the political firestorm.

Dred Scott was followed by *Hepburn v. Griswold* and the *Legal Tender Cases*, another example of how the hydraulics of the great case can cause the justices to deviate from the relatively objective decision-making process that they would ordinarily follow. Chief Justice Chase and apparently some of his colleagues concluded that as a matter of economic policy, it was so important to obliterate the concept of paper money as legal tender that reliance on the concurrence of a justice who was no longer in his right mind was necessary in order to decide the case before the president could install justices of a different point of view to the Court. The public clash between two of the justices following *Hepburn* with respect to its precedential status on pending cases certainly did not help the public perception of the Court. By the same token, the new majority created by the two new appointments was so convinced that *Hepburn* was wrongly decided that it proceeded to overrule the decision even scarcely before the ink had dried. Although the reaction of the justices in the *Legal Tender Cases* is probably more excusable than the initial action of the Court in *Hepburn*, the decisions illustrate that when the Court departs from its ordinary decision-making process, it may well create a chain reaction that makes it more difficult to return to normalcy. The apparent abnormalities in the process seemed to have discredited these cases with the public and the bar to a greater extent than the results. As with *Dred Scott*, both *Hepburn* and the *Legal Tender Cases* suggest that the hydraulics of the great case can have an adverse effect on judicial behavior.

Despite the importance of the case, there is nothing to suggest that anything unusual occurred during the decision-making process in the *Slaughter-House Cases*. It was reargued due to a 4-4 split after Justice Nelson took ill and stepped down. The *Civil Rights Cases* is unusual among great cases in that some of the consolidated cases lingered for years on the Court's docket before being decided, and this was the only great case decided without oral argument. The Court's decision invalidating the Civil Rights Act of 1875 met with widespread approval. Perhaps the justices wanted to put a certain amount of distance between their decision and the end of Reconstruction.

There seemed to have been some unusual internal activity within the Court during the decision-making process in the *Pollack* cases but historians have been unable to determine exactly what occurred. In the first *Pollack* opinion the Court seemed to be split evenly on the question of whether a tax on the income from personal property was a direct tax. Despite the return to the Court of a justice who did not believe that it was, a month later the majority nevertheless found it to be a direct tax, suggesting that a justice had changed his mind in the interim. *Pollack* was definitely a case not unlike *Dred Scott* and the *Legal Tender Cases* in which the political and economic views of at least some of the justices seemed to play as much if not more of a role than legal doctrine. Whether this was influenced by the fervor surrounding the case or was simply the result of the long-standing ideology of strong willed justices is unclear.

One of the great historical debates regarding the Court is whether the preparation or announcement of President Roosevelt's court packing plan caused Justice Roberts to change directions in either *West Coast Hotel v. Parrish* or *NLRB v. Jones & Laughlin Steel* in 1937. The evidence would seem to suggest that Justice Roberts's decision to change course was not prompted by the specific announcement of the plan itself. It is more plausible however that the general political turmoil surrounding the Court's decisions during the three-year period leading up to *West Coast Hotel* and *Jones & Laughlin Steel* may have prompted Roberts to rethink his jurisprudential approach. The changes of direction have been justified on doctrinal grounds. Still Roberts was not a judge of the firmest of convictions and it is likely that a lengthy period during which the Court found itself deciding one great case after another, usually against the grain of elite opinion, probably took a toll. Every attempt was made by both Roberts and Chief Justice Hughes to portray the shift in direction as legally rather than politically driven.

Youngstown Sheet & Tube v. Sawyer and *Dennis v. United States* are sterling examples of great cases, both decided in a relatively short time of each other. In each case, the justices had difficulty agreeing on clear doctrinal principles. Justices Frankfurter and Jackson wrote important concurrences challenging the plurality in *Dennis* and the majority in *Youngstown* to some extent. There are conference notes in both cases however, and they seem to indicate that the ultimate decisions tracked the initial votes and discussion rather closely. *Youngstown* would seem to be an instance in which confident justices, recognizing that they benefited from substantial public support, were able to impose constitutional limits on a politically weakened president. In *Dennis* however, the majority either lacked the confidence to stake out a position adverse to heated public opinion or even more likely was caught up in and swayed by that opinion. In both cases, there is every reason to believe that the political context influenced the decision-making process.

Brown v. Board of Education is one of the most prominent examples of the greatness of a case having a profound, though not adverse impact, on the decision-making process. There may be no other case in the Court's history in which so much material regarding the decision-making process is available. *Brown* presented one of the rare instances in which most of the justices agreed that a unanimous opinion on a very controversial question was crucial. That in turn led to a significant amount of internal negotiation to persuade the justices with reservations to come aboard. Unanimity was achieved through the leadership of recently confirmed Chief Justice Warren, and more debatably that of Justice Frankfurter. A compromise as to the appropriate remedy seems to have been the price of unanimity. From the outset, the justices realized that it would be counterproductive to take a conference vote early in deliberations and apparently delayed such a vote for at least a year and a half. Unlike most great cases, the justices in *Brown* took their time reaching a decision, partially due to the need for unanimity, partially due to the question of how to deal with original understanding and precedent, and partially due to the difficulty of devising an appropriate remedy.

The Reapportionment Cases, including *Baker v. Carr*, provide examples of great cases that may have been somewhat below the public's radar but were nevertheless understood to be of monumental importance by the political class and by the justices themselves. The significance of the issue in *Baker* led to an inability to decide on the part of Justice Stewart, resulting in re-argument. Justices Frankfurter and Harlan considered the Court's foray into legislative apportionment a mistake of the most egregious nature and fought a determined but ultimately unsuccessful battle to turn back the tide. The initial indecision of Justice Clark in *Reynolds v. Simms* led to a broader opinion than appeared feasible at the outset. The magnitude of the issues clearly played a role, especially in *Baker v. Carr*, in the deliberations of the Court and the extent to which a decision marked a significant and possibly radical change in the Court's conception of its role. *Reynolds v. Simms* was decided by a very self-confident court that was not as affected by the greatness of the case as perhaps it should have been.

The stakes could hardly have been higher in *New York Times v. Sullivan* both for the press and the civil rights movement. Libel law as traditionally understood had become a weapon capable of possibly crushing both. The result was never in doubt. There was no possibility that the Court would allow the half million dollar libel award against the *Times* to stand; however, the Court needed to revise 150 years of defamation law in order to establish a First Amendment defense. Despite the fact that all of the justices would vote to reverse, Justice Brennan was unable to build a majority opinion until quite late in the process. The dramatic factual context almost certainly was a driving force behind the decision itself and prompted the justices to design an opinion under which there was no possibility that the same result could be reached on remand.

The Court, through its confusing decision in *Escobedo*, and then its determination to provide clarification with an omnibus opinion in *Miranda*, basically created a great case out of whole cloth. Chief Justice Warren seemed to have strong views on police interrogation. He all but single-handedly took charge of the drafting of the opinion in *Miranda v. Arizona*, ultimately delivering one that was far broader than it needed to be, in turn resulting in a political backlash against the Court contributing to the election of Richard Nixon in 1968. *Miranda* is a prime example of a case in which the hydraulic pressures of public and professional opinion seemed to have had little if any effect at all but quite probably should have. Warren and the Court would have been wise to have taken greater account of the weight of public opinion opposed to the direction in which the majority was determined to move.

The Pentagon Papers Case, like *Youngstown, United States v. Nixon*, and *Bush v. Gore* is an example of the great case that was litigated at such warp speed that the abbreviated decision-making process was bound to have an impact. Of the great cases litigated on such an expedited basis, the Pentagon Papers Case is the only one in which the Court declined to make any attempt to produce an opinion for the Court, relying instead on separate opinions for all nine justices. The immediate harm attributable to prior restraint was understood as demanding such an approach. The inevitable result was a lack of clear guidance although in an area where continual recurrence was unlikely. Perhaps the greater cost, as explained by Justice Harlan in dissent, was a near complete inability of the justices to digest the complicated factual record. Highly skilled counsel were unable to provide much assistance given that they too seemed to be overwhelmed by the pace of the litigation. The fact that much of the record and some of the briefs were filed under seal also took the Court out of its normal procedures of adjudication. The Court did resist the request to conduct the oral arguments in camera. The Pentagon Papers Case illustrates that there is a practical limit on how quickly a multi-member court can function effectively.

The decision-making process in *Roe v. Wade* was quite troubled and dragged on for the better part of two years. Despite exhaustive records of the deliberations, it is unclear whether the delay was the product of pressure stemming from the moral and political sensitivity of the underlying question of abortion rights, the inadequacy of the briefing and argument, internal squabbles among the justices, or simply the indecisiveness and slow pace of Justice Blackmun. It seems likely that Justice Brennan could have produced an opinion that a majority of the justices would have joined in a fraction of the time taken by Blackmun, and it almost certainly would have been a stronger opinion though certainly not beyond vigorous criticism. *Roe* is testament to the fact that the competence and confidence of the justice preparing the opinion in a great case is a crucial factor as to whether the pressures brought to bear will have an adverse impact on the decision-making process.

Two decades later when the Court agreed to reconsider *Roe* and determine whether it should be overruled, the hydraulic pressure of the great case appeared to exert a determinative impact. Initially, a majority appears to have agreed that *Roe* should be rejected; however the social dislocation and backlash that might occur as a result seems to have prompted Justice Kennedy to succumb to the entreaties of Justices O'Connor and Souter and to vote in favor of limiting rather than overruling *Roe*. *Casey* would appear to be a textbook example of the type of pressure that can be exerted by the very dynamics of the great case.

United States v. Nixon presented unique problems for the Court. The justices understood that the president was almost certainly implicated in serious criminal conduct and that its decision might very well lead to his removal from office. Never had the stakes in a constitutional case been so high. Considering the seriousness of the case as well as rumors of potential defiance of an order, the justices understood that this was a case, like *Brown*, where unanimity was essential. Moreover, most of the justices were dissatisfied with the approach taken by the chief justice in drafting the opinion for the Court. The combination of these circumstances led to an unusual amount of internal communication and negotiation over the shape and scope of the opinion. This would seem to have resulted from a combination of the pressures inherent in the case as well as a lack of confidence in the leadership of Chief Justice Burger.

According to Justice Powell, the *Bakke* case produced an unprecedented amount of internal memoranda circulated among the justices. The justices were deeply divided as to how to respond to the challenges of racial preferences in higher education. The case placed the Court in the public spotlight, and the justices were quite aware of its ramifications. The resolution of the case dragged on throughout the term due less to its momentousness and difficulty than to the absence and indecisiveness of Justice Blackmun.

Twenty-five years later when the meaning of the divided opinions in *Bakke* was before the Court in *Grutter* and *Gratz*, Justice O'Connor, who had been the Court's primary spokesman in the area of affirmative action, brokered the majority and produced the opinion of the Court. It would appear that the public consequences of the decision, brought to bear on the Court through amicus briefs, played a decisive role in her approach. When 10 years later the 7-1 majority in *Fisher v. Texas* cut back on the O'Connor approach, the justices did not appear to be as concerned with the reaction of the political elites as at least Justice O'Connor had been in *Grutter*.

Bush v. Gore thrust the Court into the center of the month-long dispute over the outcome of the 2000 presidential election. It is likely that the Court has never decided a case in such a glare of public and media attention. It was simply a given that no matter what the Court did, millions of people would be extremely angry. The Court proceeded in a more expedited manner than in any other great case besides the Pentagon Papers. There was apparently some internal lobbying among the justices but scarcely enough time for much beyond the drafting of the opinions. The justices, like the rest of America, could not help following the developing crisis over the election on television, and there is reason to believe that their positions on the case had congealed even before oral argument. It would have been difficult if not impossible for the momentousness of the case not to have affected the decision-making process.

Sebelius was yet another great case in which the Court was at the very epicenter of a national media spectacle. It is too soon to know the impact of the public pressure on the Court's decision-making. There is reason to suspect that the gravity of potentially invalidating an Act of such political importance weighed upon at least the chief justice and may very well have led to a reversal of direction at some point.

The information that exists as to the impact of the hydraulics of the great case on the Court's decision-making process is too incomplete to justify definitive conclusions. It would be fair to conclude however that the gravity of the issues that are often at the heart of great cases and their likely impact on the future of the law and the nation itself does cause at least some of the justices to resist drastic change in the law and doctrine. The expedited manner in which at least some great cases are litigated almost certainly has at least some adverse impact on the decisional process, making reflection and agreement all the more difficult.

The information available with respect to the decision-making in great cases suggests that perhaps the single most important factor in the manner in which these cases are decided is the strength of the leadership on the Court and the confidence of the other justices in that leadership. It would appear that the Court struggles most severely with the decision of great cases either when the chief justice or a key justice in the composition of the majority is either indecisive or lacks the confidence or ability to draft an opinion that resolves the question in a principled manner capable of gaining support within the Court.

The Marshall Court, though from a bygone era, can be contrasted with virtually everything that followed. Even then, there is some reason to believe that Marshall was beginning to lose his sway over the Court by *Gibbons v. Ogden* in 1824.

Justice Story was one of the greatest intellects to ever sit on the Court. It is likely that his opinion for a majority in *Prigg v. Pennsylvania* is best understood as the price of holding together a tenuous majority, although even that is unclear.

It would certainly appear that the *Dred Scott* and *Legal Tender Cases* Courts suffered from internal turmoil driven at least to some extent by the greatness of the cases. Neither Chief Justice Taney nor Chase was capable of stabilizing the institution, and indeed both made the situation significantly worse. It is also likely though less clear that internal struggles were an issue in *Pollack*, the Income Tax Case, as well.

Although the indecisiveness of Justice Roberts had been a contributing factor to the crisis surrounding the Court in the 1930s, once the Court changed directions in 1937 in *Jones & Laughlin Steel*, the confident leadership of Chief Justice Hughes made the transition appear as seamless as possible under the circumstances.

The two great cases of the early 1950s were the product of a weak chief justice surrounded by several strong, indeed overbearing, associates. That led to an opinion in *Youngstown* by Justice Black, one of the strongest of the personalities, that purported to represent the majority view but only in a simplistic way, and a plurality by Chief Justice Vinson in *Dennis* that could not even garner majority support. The internal dissension on the Stone and Vinson Courts is legendary and made it near impossible for the Court to respond in a unified manner in great and often not so great cases.

Strong leadership returned to the Court with the appointment of Chief Justice Warren and Justice Brennan. The successful efforts to build unanimity in *Brown* is arguably one of the Court's finest hours. If anything however the leadership skills and confidence of Chief Justice Warren led to judicial overreaching with a popular but sloppy opinion in *Reynolds* and a doctrinaire opinion quite oblivious to the risks undertaken in *Miranda*. Justice Brennan's skill as both a legal craftsman and as a leader were well displayed in both *Baker v. Carr* and *New York Times v. Sullivan*.

The great decisions of the Burger Court are marked by a lack of leadership and confidence. The Pentagon Papers Case may be attributable to the warp speed with which it was litigated and decided. *Roe, Nixon*, and *Bakke* were all plagued by Chief Justice Burger's failures of leadership, or Justice Blackmun's indecisiveness, as well as the limited ability of either to write a coherent and principled opinion capable of commanding the support of a majority.

Two of the great cases of the Rehnquist Court, *Casey* and *Grutter*, were unsuccessful attempts to overrule great cases of the Burger Court. The center of power on the Court had shifted to two or three centrist swing votes who brokered the decisions, aligning with coalitions that took a more doctrinaire and ideological approach. The same pattern was present to a lesser extent in *Bush v. Gore*. Although Rehnquist was a far more successful chief justice than Burger he was unable to control the Court in the great cases of *Casey, Grutter*, and *Bush*.

In *Sebelius*, it would appear that Chief Justice Roberts determined that it was most important to protect the Court from vigorous political challenge even if that meant producing an opinion that few could find persuasive. It seems likely that Roberts withstood extreme pressure from four other justices in so doing.

THE IMPACT OF THE GREAT CASE ON THE OPINION

The single most significant piece of evidence of the potential impact of the great case is the Court's opinion itself. That is the document from which the legal implications of the case flow, and it is the Court's attempt to provide a reasoned legal explanation for its holding. If the greatness of the case has an impact on the law that it yields, then the opinion would seem to be the first place to search for it. The signs that the greatness of the case had at least some impact on the opinion are usually evident.

Marbury v. Madison can readily be cited as a case in point. No one will ever know for certain why Marshall wrote the opinion the way he did in *Marbury*. Perhaps he simply called it as he saw it and there was nothing more to it than that. That is possible but unlikely. The more conventional interpretation of *Marbury* seems more plausible. Marshall found himself in a tight spot. Jefferson was likely to disobey a mandate to issue Marbury his commission. Marshall lacked the support on the Court to invalidate the repeal of the Judiciary Act of 1800 in *Stuart v. Laird*. Marshall sincerely believed that Jefferson had essentially declared war on the judiciary. Thus Marshall did what he could. He wrote an opinion that to some extent reasoned backward, first declaring that the Court could adjudicate at least some questions involving the responsibilities of Cabinet officers but then failed to do so for lack of jurisdiction, recognizing the power of judicial review over an inconsequential provision of an Act of Congress in the process. Under this standard interpretation of *Marbury*, the justly famous opinion was driven by the hydraulic pressures brought to bear on the Court. In other words, a great case provided a great justice the opportunity to write a great and enduring opinion.

McCulloch is another example of an opinion that was driven by the greatness of the case. The primary legal question in *McCulloch*, whether a state could tax a federally chartered instrumentality, was in itself an explosive political issue. But Marshall saw the case as representing something far larger—the very nature and origin of the Constitution, the relationship between the federal government and the states, and the judicial understanding of congressional power. Marshall thus transformed what was unquestionably a great case into a monumental case. Unlike *Marbury* where Marshall seemed to retreat in the face of pressure, Marshall charged forward into the very teeth of the controversy, determined to provide a judicial statement on the most significant questions of his time. Arguably, Marshall underestimated the resistance that his opinion would encounter but it seems likely that it would not have mattered to him in any event. *McCulloch* is proof that great cases are what the Court makes of them and that a confident and ambitious court can take full advantage of the stage that the great case provides. It may take the nation quite some time to fully appreciate the opinion in a great case, as was true of *McCulloch*.

The pressures of the great case are apparent in the opinion in *Gibbons v. Ogden* as well. The controversy at the heart of *Gibbons* was nearly as long-standing and well publicized as that in *McCulloch*. In addition, unlike *McCulloch*, Marshall was in the position to decide the case in accordance with majoritarian sentiment. Nevertheless, *Gibbons* resulted in an opinion that was both confident and ambivalent. As with *McCulloch*, Marshall established important and enduring principles of constitutional law. But as with *Marbury*, he was reluctant to carry them to their logical conclusion in the case, deciding the ultimate issue under a strained preemption approach rather than the muscular reading of the Commerce Clause. Marshall's reluctance to rest the decision on the dormant Commerce Clause may have been driven by an inability to muster a majority under that theory. But his decision to endorse a bold theory of congressional power to regulate commerce and a limited authority of the states to do so would, as in *McCulloch*, be driven by a desire to judicially weigh in on larger political disputes, including the constitutionality of pending internal improvements legislation and quite possibly legislation affecting slavery as well. *Gibbons* is yet another example of Marshall producing an opinion that capitalized on the opportunity presented by the great case.

The opinion in *Prigg v. Pennsylvania* has always been a puzzle for scholars of the Court. Clearly, Story could not have built a majority to save the Pennsylvania liberty act. The votes simply were not there. But why did he go well beyond the demands of the case before him to federalize the law of rendition? Perhaps that was necessary to hold a majority against the demand of Taney to invalidate only those state laws that disadvantaged slave catchers. Or perhaps he believed that federalization and uniformity would in some way benefit the cause of freedom, as he later asserted. Or perhaps it was a means of otherwise pressing his nationalist ideology. Or perhaps he believed that this approach was most likely to quiet the controversy over fugitive slavery, and at the same time hopefully remove the Court from the fray. It is likely that the red-hot controversy over fugitive slave rendition did affect the Court's opinion, and yet it is difficult to know exactly how or why.

Dred Scott may well be the greatest of the great cases in the sense of a minor private dispute expanding into a controversy of truly monumental proportions. The collected opinions in the case are among the longest in the Court's history. The opinion of Chief Justice Taney is quite arguably the worst in the Court's history in view both of its incoherence and its devastating impact on sensitive issues that hardly needed to be discussed at all. It is surely the prime example of a justice who became so enmeshed in the most heated political controversy of the day that he lost all semblance of an impartial judicial officer. For the most part, the concurrences, which often fail to explain in exactly what they concur, augment the confusion. Justice Nelson stuck with the modest approach, which should have prevailed assuming that the Court would affirm. Justice Curtis did produce a remarkable cogent and persuasive dissent. *Dred Scott* is the cautionary tale of what can go terribly wrong in a great case. The Court seems to have been caught up in the political controversy and either attempted unsuccessfully to impose a judicial solution or simply got carried away and launched an internal no holds barred debate on an issue well beyond the Court's ability to resolve. To be sure there was significant political pressure urging the Court to address the question of slavery in the territories—pressure that the justice would have been wise to resist. For a lengthy period of time, at least some historians blamed the dissenters for baiting the majority into addressing the politically explosive issue of the constitutionality of the Missouri Compromise. It is hardly clear that that was why the majority chose to discuss the issue. In any event the responsibility should still rest with Taney and the majority given that they were in no way compelled to take the bait. The tragedy of *Dred Scott* is that the massive opinions should never have been written. *Dred Scott* should have remained a relatively insignificant dispute between private parties.

Hepburn v. Griswold, striking down the Legal Tender Act, is another instance of a justice, Chief Justice Chase, becoming embroiled in the underlying political and economic controversy and producing an opinion that scarcely met the minimum standards of professional competence. The constitutionality of the Legal Tender Act was certainly an issue that demanded resolution by the Supreme Court, although the wisest approach would have been to designate it as a political question, thereby effectively upholding it as the Court essentially did in *Juillard* several years later. As Justices Field and Clifford illustrated in their lengthy dissents in the *Legal Tender Cases*, powerful legal arguments could be raised against the constitutionality of paper money as legal tender. Those were not the type of arguments that Chase set forth in *Hepburn* however. And in any event, even if the dissenters were correct, the massive circulation of legal tender during the Civil War had almost certainly altered the constitutional landscape for good. The Court simply needed to accept that change, however unconstitutional and wrongheaded it may have seemed. The dispute though seemingly legal in nature was no longer within the Court's competence.

As noted above, the *Slaughter-House Cases* was quite untypical as a great case in that the public was scarcely paying attention. And yet all of the justices clearly recognized that they were deciding one of the most significant cases ever presented. As such, their opinions were influenced by the gravity and likely consequences of the decision. The opinions of the justices were thorough and scholarly. The crucial difference between the majority and dissents turned on divergent conceptions of the recently ratified Fourteenth Amendment. Justice Miller's opinion for the Court seemed at bottom to be based on his fears of the consequences that would follow from a dynamic reading of the substantive protections of the Amendment. He understood that the interpretation endorsed by the plaintiffs would significantly, perhaps radically, change the structure of the relationship between the federal governments and the states. Miller could not believe that that was the correct understanding of the Amendment, despite the fact that the dissenters made a convincing case that indeed it was. It would appear that the larger political and legal consequences that a decision in favor of the plaintiffs would entail persuaded the majority to reject that possibility.

The Civil Rights Cases challenging the ability of Congress to extend protection against discrimination into some aspects of the private sphere pursuant to the Fourteenth Amendment presented the Court with an issue of significant public controversy. The majority had the luxury of writing an opinion that was legally defensible and probably correct while at the same time coming down on the side of dominant political and social opinion. Justice Harlan, unconcerned with contemporary approval, wrote a vigorous dissent that helped to earn for him the endorsement of subsequent generations but caused him to be characterized as an eccentric in his own time.

Pollack v. Farmers Home Loan, the Income Tax decision, was the most prominent of several decisions in which the Court reacted negatively to the reforms of the progressive era. The opinions of the majority may have been driven by ideology more than law. The attorney for the plaintiffs had certainly made a political as well as a legal argument to the Court. Still the justices had the legal ammunition to construct a solid argument based on original understanding as to the unconstitutionality of a tax on the income derived from real or personal property. However that argument had been rejected by a solid line of precedent dating back to the very beginning of the nation and it had gained momentum over time. The majority's determination to reach its result in the very teeth of almost 90 years of Supreme Court case law to the contrary certainly suggests that the passions evoked by the income tax issue got the better of the majority's sound legal judgment.

The decision in *NLRB v. Jones & Laughlin Steel* in 1937 was the fulcrum on which modern constitutional law turned. It would be difficult to overestimate its significance. It opened the Court to the charge that it had been bullied into submission by the president's threats. That was probably not the case, at least in such a stark manner. But the Court well understood that it was deciding a case that would have a significant impact on the future of the Court and on the nation as well. The press and the public were focused on the Court as an institution. With the exception of *Dred Scott*, the stakes had never been higher. Chief Justice Hughes was up to the task responding with a masterful opinion that significantly changed the direction of the Court while at the same time making it appear that the decision was little more than the ordinary progression of precedent. Rarely has a justice responded more gracefully and effectively under the pressure of a great case.

Dennis v. United States placed the Court in the center of the public controversy regarding the potential communist threat to American government and society. It would seem that the opinions of the Vinson plurality as well as the Frankfurter and Jackson concurrences, all of which diminished the strength of First Amendment protection, were influenced by the Red Scare in one way or another. First Amendment protection for subversive speech had certainly not obtained full protection by the time of *Dennis* but it had been moving in that direction. *Dennis* was a temporary setback. The opinions upholding the convictions suggest that the members of the majority were either caught up in the public hysteria over the possible communist threat or that they believed that the question was best left to Congress given its complexity, or perhaps that it was simply not an opportune time to advance the cause of civil liberties considering the climate of public fear. Whatever the explanation, the opinions reveal a timid Court. Justice Douglas's dissent illustrates that it was at least possible for one justice, often eccentric to be certain, to recognize that the threat to national security was minimal to nonexistent. There is a consensus that *Dennis* was hardly the Court's finest hour.

The Vinson Court was faced with another great case in *Youngstown Sheet & Tube v. Sawyer*. The diversity of the opinions favoring the steel company, despite pro forma agreement with Justice Black's opinion for the Court, may to some extent be attributable to the expedited nature of the litigation. It is more likely however that it was the result of a lack of strong leadership coupled with several confident justices with divergent viewpoints. The majority opinion was too simplistic to be of great utility. Justice Jackson did produce a concurrence that provided the basic framework for subsequent separation-of=powers adjudication, and Justice Frankfurter provided a significant insight. Considering the crisis atmosphere in which the case was heard, the opinions, at least of the concurring justices, made a significant contribution to constitutional jurisprudence.

Brown is by any measure one of the greatest of the great cases. The opinions in both *Brown I* and *II* have been criticized for providing little guidance or theoretical justification for the holding. Considering the need for unanimity as well as the very real fear of political backlash, they can just as easily be considered works of judicial genius. The opinions are quite likely among the finest examples of the Court responding positively to a highly pressurized environment. Chief Justice Warren understood that this was an occasion to put aside lawyers' talk and to appeal directly to the American public, and at the same time avoid inflaming the defenders of segregation any more than necessary. The opinions in *Brown* stand as constitutional and historic landmarks. They were shaped significantly by the hydraulic pressures of the case but not in a negative way.

The Reapportionment Cases had as large of an impact on American society and government as almost any other case ever decided. *Baker v. Carr*, addressing the political question issue, involved a question of lawyers' law and as such may not have been of great interest to the public at large. The justices however understood that it was truly a watershed case, and the majority opinion of Justice Brennan, as well as the dissent of Justice Frankfurter, was written with full recognition that a great case was being decided. They are both examples of Supreme Court opinions at their finest. It was the final opinion of Justice Frankfurter's long and distinguished career and seems to be written with recognition that an era was coming to a close.

Rarely has such a weak opinion been so well received as that of Chief Justice Warren in *Reynolds v. Simms*. Warren certainly understood that he was on the right side of history and scarcely bothered to justify in traditional constitutional terms a decision that was bound to be publically accepted as eminently just and fair. Justice Harlan's dissent demolished Warren's reasoning. *Reynolds* illustrates that the Court can employ the momentum of a great case brought before the Court at the right historical moment to change the constitutional paradigm.

Rarely has a case been likely to have such a profound impact on three divergent areas—the civil rights movement, freedom of the press, and the law of libel—as did *New York Times v. Sullivan*. The *Times* understood *Sullivan* to be a great case and litigated it as such. There was no question that the *Times* would prevail, almost certainly with no dissents. And yet the legal challenges facing the *Times*, its attorneys, and the Court were formidable. The greatness of the case led to the employment of a superb lawyer who in turn filed a brilliant brief that the Court relied upon to write a landmark opinion. *Sullivan* is an example in which the magnitude of the case was responsible for leading the Court to produce an opinion that was far grander than could have been expected under more ordinary circumstances.

In many respects, *Miranda v. Arizona* was the Warren Court's bridge too far. The rules for custodial interrogation developed in *Miranda* have stood the test of time. The case itself is justly considered a landmark decision. And yet the opinion itself was so insensitive to the concerns of law enforcement, as well as the traditions of constitutional adjudication, that it contributed in a very significant way to a political reaction that helped bring the Warren Court era to an end. *Miranda v. Arizona* was a great case; however its greatness was entirely manufactured by the Court itself. The Court threw the world of police interrogation into a state of chaos with its unusual decision in *Escobedo v. Illinois* and then attempted to restore order in one monumental decision addressing every conceivable issue instead of through traditional case-by-case adjudication. The exhaustive opinion in *Miranda* reeks of both hubris and impatience. More than any other decision, it branded the Warren Court with the label of judicial activism. Even if Chief Justice Warren's basic instincts for dealing with the custodial interrogation issue were correct, and perhaps they were, his methods for implementation probably did more harm than good to the Court as an institution.

The Pentagon Papers Case is the sterling example of the public legal controversy that can arise almost instantaneously and focus the attention of the nation on the Court. The Court is hardly equipped to respond adequately to a controversy of this complexity and magnitude as swiftly as the Court believed that the law of prior restraint seemed to require. The inability to even attempt to produce a majority opinion was testimony to the extreme time pressures that the Court imposed upon itself. Consequently, the Court was able to do little more than resolve the particular dispute before it. There was wisdom in the suggestion of the dissents that the Court should have taken a deep breath and proceeded in a more traditional and deliberate manner. The opinions provided little guidance. However considering the Court's strong stance against prior restraints by injunction, future controversies in this area would rarely arise.

Roe v. Wade has become one of the great events in constitutional law of the twentieth century. The momentum built throughout the litigation and the two sets of oral arguments before the Court. Justice Blackmun acknowledged at the outset that the Court understood that it was deciding a question of great political, social, and moral controversy, although it is almost certain that the justices failed to recognize the extent to which that decision would envelop the Court in conflict for decades to come. The opinion itself is testament to the Court's indecision, lack of confidence, and ultimately inability to justify its result. Very strong opinions in great cases, such as *McCulloch v. Maryland*, have been subject to vigorous challenge by critics. Like *Dred Scott*, the inherent weakness of the *Roe* opinion made it relatively easy for the public and professional critics to make the case that the Court had no business deciding the case in the first place. The labored opinion of Justice Blackmun was to some extent influenced by the tremendous pressure that he internalized from the controversy over abortion itself, to some extent the result of his very limited ability as a legal craftsman, and to a large extent the result of the impossibility of justifying the decision in a constitutionally principled manner. A better opinion could have been written but almost certainly not a satisfactory opinion.

If anything the pressure on the Court was even more intense two decades later when it formally considered whether *Roe* should be overruled in *Casey*. The unusual joint opinion saving while altering *Roe* was almost a direct result of the recognition by at least some of the justices that reversing *Roe* at this point would saddle the Court with an unacceptable degree of public disillusionment. The Joint Opinion was quite obviously a negotiated compromise, as many judicial opinions are. As such, it was an easy target for criticism by the dissent. The Opinion purported to defend itself on the basis of principle while arguably taking an unprincipled approach. The Joint Opinion in *Casey* is one of the most striking examples of an opinion that was heavily influenced if not created by the hydraulic pressures surrounding a great case.

United States v. Nixon was as unique of a case in as pressurized of an atmosphere as the Supreme Court will ever consider. The fate of a presidency hung in the balance. The hydraulics of the case obviously had a significant impact on the opinion itself. The Court understood that unanimity was essential and there was internal disagreement regarding the appropriate approach. Moreover a decision needed to be produced on a relatively expedited basis. In addition, given the singular nature of the case, including the fact that there was ample reason to believe that the president was implicated in felonious conduct, there was every reason not to produce an opinion that would attempt to provide a precedent for dissimilar future circumstances. All of these factors combined ensured that the Court was almost certain to produce an opinion lacking coherence and subject to vigorous professional criticism. *Nixon* was a prime example of the great case in which the circumstances overwhelm the ordinary judicial process and make the production of a solid opinion all but impossible. Internal dissatisfaction with the approach of the chief justice added to the difficulty. *Nixon* was perhaps the ultimate example of opinion by committee, a task almost definitely likely to disappoint.

The *Bakke* case was decided in the midst of a media circus. Rarely has a Supreme Court case evoked as much publicity. The Court was badly split and unable to agree on very much. The opinions in *Bakke* are almost unique in that the crucial opinion of Justice Powell, which for the most part was not joined by any other justice, became the legal foundation for affirmative action in higher education for the next 25 years. Apparently, Justice Powell believed that higher education was sorely in need of guidance as to the legality of the use of racial preferences in admissions. It is likely that the pleas of several of the most distinguished educational institutions in the nation presented to the Court by former solicitor general Cox convinced Powell that a thorough discussion of the underlying legal principles was warranted. As such, the greatness of the case almost certainly influenced the decision of Justice Powell to discuss the issues in depth. The inability of Powell to assemble a majority behind his approach was probably attributable to the difficulty of the issues and legitimate disagreement as to the correct approach, along with a poor factual setting for testing the legal limits of affirmative action in higher education.

When the Court reconsidered the constitutionality of racial preferences in higher education 25 years later in the *Grutter* and *Gratz* cases, the momentousness of the issues quite clearly had an impact on the opinion of the Court. The defenders of racial preferences built a coalition of major corporations as well as of leading retired military officers to file briefs in support. These efforts paid off as Justice O'Connor relied upon these arguments quite explicitly in the opinion for the Court. In the process, she significantly altered the applicable legal principles in order to validate a fairly generous use of racial preferences. Grutter is a stunning example of how the pressure brought to bear in a great case through a careful and deliberate litigation strategy can significantly influence both the outcome and the opinion. *Fisher v. Texas* decided 10 years later illustrated that the doctrinal approach taken in a great case, at least by a very closely divided court, is not immune to subsequent revision.

Like the Nixon tapes case, *Bush v. Gore* was also a unique case. Just as the potential removal of a president results in extraordinary public interest in the litigation, so does a case that may result in the ultimate selection of the president. The opinions plowed new ground and were quite controversial. The fact that seven justices coalesced around the equal protection theory may suggest the attraction of relying on doctrine that had some familiarity, and as such might seem slightly less manufactured for the situation. The equal protection theory, unlike the Article II theory, held out at least some potential for continuing the Florida recount, which would have been attractive to Justices Breyer and Souter. The dividing line in the case was over whether the process should be brought to an immediate conclusion or whether it should be allowed to continue for at least another week. The determination of the majority to bring it to an end was almost certainly not dictated by clear legal mandates. Rather it was based on the dynamics of the controversy. The justices in the majority may have believed that the continuing uncertainty of the election's outcome with the potential that both candidates might well be certified as winners by competing institutions was having or was likely to have too great of a destabilizing impact on the nation and its political process. Alternatively, some of the justices apparently concluded that the Florida Supreme Court simply could not be trusted to supervise a fair recount process. Perhaps the cleanest resolution of the case was the Article II approach offered by the Rehnquist concurrence; however, it could not garner a majority as it embroiled the Court in the interpretation of state law and entailed the conclusion that the Florida Supreme Court had egregiously misinterpreted its own election law, perhaps willfully.

There can be no question that the opinions in *Sebelius* were significantly affected by the magnitude of the case. The surprising decision of Chief Justice Roberts to rest the opinion on the highly questionable taxing power rationale after thoroughly demolishing the government's primary Commerce Clause justification cannot be explained by anything other than the hydraulic pressure attributable to the magnitude of the issues in their political context. The unusual style of the dissent with no specified author, an unwillingness to join those portions of the Roberts opinion with which it fully agreed, and the focus on responding to the government rather than Roberts where there was disagreement also suggests that something unusual was occurring. Either the dissent had originally been the majority opinion, perhaps even drafted in part by Chief Justice Roberts, or bad blood had developed between the dissenters and the chief justice over the result. It is too soon to know what occurred, although it is likely that there will be some information in the future, with the eventual publication of internal memoranda as now seems to occur regularly. It would be fair to conclude however that the dynamics of the case did indeed have a profound impact on the nature of the opinions.

It is clear that the circumstances and pressures of the great case almost always have an impact on the nature of the opinion although in very different ways. Sometimes the pressures inherent in the great case cause the Court, or at least one or more justices, to trim their sails and either duck an issue or reach a decision that would not have been reached under more normal circumstances. *Marbury*, *Sebelius*, and possibly *Dennis* are examples of this. On other occasions, the great case will present the Court with the opportunity to write a more comprehensive opinion than might otherwise occur. *McCulloch*, *Gibbons*, *Dred Scott*, *Jones & Laughlin Steel*, *Baker v. Carr*, *Reynolds v. Simms*, *New York Times v. Sullivan*, and *Miranda* illustrate this to some extent. Sometimes the dynamics including the expeditious nature of the great case make agreement behind a coherent opinion difficult. *Dred Scott*, *Dennis*, *Youngstown*, the Pentagon Papers Case, *Bakke*, and *Casey* are illustrative. In a few instances, such as *Brown* and *Nixon*, the necessity for unanimity greatly constrains the nature of the opinion. Sometimes, though not often, the political controversy swirling around the great case may cause the justices to lose their impartiality and descend to political argument. That seems to have been the case in *Dred Scott* and *Hepburn*, and may have been the case in *Pollack*. The critics of *Bush v. Gore* would charge that it was the case there as well.

Great cases by definition attract an extreme amount of scholarly attention. Criticism is a central component of that attention. Consequently, there is no great case, even if it has become a landmark case, that escapes often harsh criticism. From an abstract perspective, it is always possible to show how a Court could have done a better job, removing the decision from its pressurized context as well as from the necessity of building a majority out of strong-willed life-tenured colleagues. Scholars have attempted to poke holes in the opinions in landmark cases such as *Marbury* and *Brown* for instance, although it is hardly evident that they could have done as well if placed in the shoes of Marshall or Warren at the time. Judicial opinions are written in circumstances imposing a variety of constraints, not the least of which is that the justices usually have much other business to attend to as well. The pressures brought to bear in the great case are often severe and unique, and it is hardly surprising that those pressures to some extent influence the resulting opinions of the Court. If anything, it is surprising that so many excellent opinions have been produced in the peculiar circumstances of the great case. *Marbury*, *McCulloch*, *Gibbons*, *Jones & Laughlin Steel*, the *Youngstown* concurrences, *Brown*, *Baker*, and *Sullivan* might be cited as examples.

DO GREAT CASES PRODUCE UNQUESTIONABLY BAD LAW OR FAIL TO HAVE A LONG-TERM IMPACT?

The two evaluative criteria—(1) do the cases clearly produce bad law, and (2) do they have a long-term impact on the jurisprudence—are treated together as it is often difficult to discuss one without discussing the other as well. With the exception of cases at the extremes, determining whether a case created bad law requires subjective judgement. At least some commentator will be willing to argue that any great case has created bad law. Still it is usually possible to determine whether the critiques of a decision are well grounded or eccentric. It is far easier to assess the long-term impact of a case, which may speak to whether it produced bad law though not necessarily decisively.

It has been easy to criticize *Marbury* ever since it was decided for discussing issues that should have been avoided and for providing an imperfect justification of judicial review of congressional action. Even so, it is a powerful opinion and the justification that Marshall did offer, despite its shortcomings, remains a masterwork of the greatest justice. Its prestige has grown over time. It provides the foundation not simply for judicial review of congressional legislation, but its often criticized dicta provides the underlying support for judicial review of executive action as well. *Marbury* did not simply produce good law but rather the structure under which constitutional law would develop over the next 200 years. *Marbury* produced profound and enduring law.

McCulloch v. Maryland has often been described as the greatest and most important opinion in the history of the Supreme Court. It established the nationalistic narrative of constitutional origin, declared an expansive conception of congressional power as well as judicial deference to its exercise, established protection of the federal government and its institutions against state incursions, introduced the political safeguards of federalism arguments, and provided one of the best examples of structural and textual interpretation in the United States Reports. The doctrinal test for resolving issues under the Necessary and Proper Clause is still relied on by the Court almost 200 years later. *McCulloch* did not simply make good law but probably some of the best law ever.

Gibbons v. Ogden remains the seminal case in affirmative Commerce Clause jurisprudence. Marshall's analysis is frequently the starting point when there is a challenge to a congressional exercise of that power. The opinion itself was conflicted and indecisive with respect to the dormant Commerce Clause, and even Marshall himself failed to develop his dicta with respect to congressional exclusivity. Still, *Gibbons* is not simply a landmark but rather *the* landmark with respect to the congressional commerce power.

Prigg v. Pennsylvania tried but failed to establish enduring law. Justice Story's case for congressional exclusivity over fugitive slave rendition was unpersuasive, based more on assertion than logic. In retrospect, any decision that tilted in favor of slavery, as did *Prigg*, would seem to produce bad law, and yet there was no other realistic option considering the composition of the Court. If the goal of the Court was to minimize the political and legal controversy over fugitive slave rendition, it certainly failed in that endeavor. However considering the degree to which the nation was torn apart over the issue, it is difficult to see how the Court could have succeeded

Dred Scott is the very epitome of the notion that great cases make bad law. It made bad law in so many ways. The Court reached out to decide crucial issues that it could have and should have avoided. It rendered incredibly bad decisions on both the power of Congress to prohibit or regulate slavery in the territories as well as the possibility that an African American could be a citizen. The opinion of the chief justice was intemperate, disingenuous, and filled with factual and legal error. It certainly contributed to the deep partisan divide that erupted in secession and the Civil War a few years later. It was largely reversed by a constitutional amendment a decade later. No other case decided by the Court suffers such an indictment. There was no possibility that *Dred Scott* would win his freedom but the Court could have decided against him in a way that rendered the decision a historical footnote rather than the greatest embarrassment in the Court's history.

Hepburn v. Griswold is also a great case that made bad law. A respectable legal argument could be made that the Legal Tender Act was unconstitutional, but that was not the type of analysis that Chief Justice Chase made. Instead, he relied largely on policy and unconstrained "spirit" of the constitution argumentation. Even if legal tender was constitutionally suspect, it was practically impossible for the Court to effectively reverse the trend, and it would have been well advised to have steered clear of the matter. The manner in which Chase rushed the case along by relying on the vote of a justice who was no longer in control of his faculties contributed to the aura of impropriety. The decision was reversed almost immediately with the addition of two more justices. Although reversal was appropriate, the means by which it was accomplished subjected the Court and the president to as much if not more criticism than the decision in *Hepburn* itself. The entire business was viewed as a most unfortunate episode in the Court's history.

The *Slaughter-House Cases* was one of the great turning points in American constitutional law. There is a consensus that Justice Miller misinterpreted the Fourteenth Amendment but anything but a consensus as to how it should have been understood. It is certain however that the shape of constitutional law would be quite different had the dissenters prevailed. Unlike the opinions of Taney in *Dred Scott* or Chase in *Hepburn*, Miller wrote a solid legally grounded opinion in the *Slaughter-House Cases*. It would simply appear that he misunderstood or wanted to misunderstand the meaning of the Privileges or Immunities Clause and the significance of the impact of the Fourteenth Amendment on the traditional conception of federalism. Miller wrote a powerful opinion though not as powerful as Field's dissent. The *Slaughter-House Cases* made bad law though not in a careless or haphazard way.

From the standpoint of the quest for racial equality, *The Civil Rights Cases* made very bad law. Even so, the majority opinion would seem to be a solid reading of the constitutional text, and as such an arguably correct decision. Justice Harlan's vigorous dissent has gained followers as times have changed but was dismissed as strange and eccentric at the time. The movement to expunge racial injustice would have been easier had *The Civil Rights Cases* come out the other way. From that standpoint, the case made bad law. But even now, the principles of the case control and have long withstood the test of time.

The *Pollack* case invalidating the income tax, like *Dred Scott*, was reversed by constitutional amendment. That in itself suggests that in a large sense it made bad law. Both the majority opinions and the dissents wrote detailed and scholarly opinions. The majority made a forceful case that under the original understanding that taxes on income from real and personal property were direct. The dissent made an even stronger case that that understanding had been rejected by the Court early in its history, and that the overwhelming weight of the precedent was inconsistent with the majority's approach. The majority made a respectable legal argument but arrived at the wrong result nevertheless. As such the *Pollack* cases made bad law.

The decision in *Jones & Laughlin Steel* changed the Court's approach to congressional power in a permanent manner. It is one of the hinges of American constitutional law.

Chief Justice Hughes had the opportunity to decide the case on a narrower stream of commerce theory but instead chose to rely on the broader effects on commerce approach. Hughes wrote a careful opinion in which he changed the direction of the law significantly while seemingly adhering to existing precedent. It was a brilliant opinion when written and 75 years later remains a cornerstone of modern affirmative Commerce Clause jurisprudence.

In *Dennis v. United States*, a solid majority of the Court affirmed the convictions of the leaders of the Communist Party of the United States under the Smith Act; however Chief Justice Vinson could not produce an opinion that a majority of the justices would endorse. The opinion of the plurality adopted a balancing test that significantly limited the protection for subversive speech. Once the crisis was over and the communist threat faded, the Court corrected the damage first through statutory and later through constitutional interpretation, eventually adopting the approach of the famous Brandeis concurrence in *Whitney v. California*. Defenders of freedom of speech understood at the time that *Dennis* had made bad law. A majority of the justices soon recognized as much and corrected the mistakes, depriving *Dennis* of any lasting precedential authority.

Like *Dennis, Youngstown* featured concurrences by Justices Frankfurter and Jackson that stole the thunder of the majority in the latter as they had done with the plurality in the former. The majority opinion of Justice Black stated solid principles but was too simplistic to be of great use in the future. Justice Frankfurter made an important observation regarding the significance of unopposed custom in the area of separation of powers. Justice Jackson upstaged the majority with an elegant and nuanced opinion that took hold as if it had been the majority and has been relied upon ever since. The Jackson concurrence has come to represent the starting point for separation of powers analysis and must be consider one of the most influential opinions of the twentieth century.

Brown v. Board of Education is without question the most important case of the twentieth century and arguably the most socially significant case in the Court's history. The opinion in *Brown I* is different than most opinions in its brevity and informality, as well as its non-accusatory nature, considering the great wrong that it was addressing. In retrospect, many would have liked to have seen more vigor or perhaps more doctrinal and theoretical justification. But Chief Justice Warren understood that that would have been inappropriate. The Court was faced with one of the most challenging tasks in its history, and the opinion in *Brown I* met the challenge with grace and wisdom. The Court was slightly more candid in the companion case of *Bolling v. Sharp* where it did conclude that there was no legitimate justification for racial segregation in public schools, something that it assumed but did not quite say in *Brown*. The gradualism endorsed in *Brown II* has been widely criticized; however it seems to have been the inevitable price of unanimity in *Brown I*. As such, it could not really be helped, and was quite probably the soundest strategy at the time in any event. *Brown* was a great case and the opinions were constitutional landmarks of the first order. *Brown* provided little doctrinal guidance. As such it did not make great law so much as light the way to it.

Baker v. Carr opened the door to aggressive judicial interpretation not simply in the area of reapportionment but well beyond. In a sense it was a formal announcement by the Warren Court that it had little use for judicial restraint in the future. It was a rejection of the philosophy that Justice Frankfurter had nourished over the previous 20 years and his anguished dissent recognized that he had lost the battle. Justice Brennan's opinion for the Court is a masterpiece of precedential analysis. Justice Frankfurter's reply in dissent, his final opinion, is also a classic of legal reasoning. *Baker* has survived and remains the foundational modern opinion on the political question doctrine.

Reynolds v. Simms revolutionized the political system by largely abolishing malapportionment at almost all levels of elective government. It has stood the test of time and is celebrated as one of the Warren Court's greatest decisions. By throwing its weight behind majoritarian democracy, it could not help winning popular approval. Even so, it is a very poorly reasoned opinion doing little more than assuming its central conclusion. From a legal standpoint, Justice Harlan provided a devastating critique. In addition to his commentary on great cases, Holmes also noted that experience can trump logic in the advancement of the law. *Reynolds v. Simms* is proof of that axiom, perhaps as modified to privilege intuition over logic. Or to employ Professor Bickel's metaphor, Warren bet on the future and won (although at the time Bickel seemed to believe that Warren had actually lost his bet in the Reapportionment Cases).

New York Times v. Sullivan brought the law of libel into the domain of the First Amendment. It established a doctrinal test that still governs libel actions brought by public official plaintiffs. It made it difficult, if not impossible, to use libel actions as a means of suppressing dissent or criticism of public officials. It provided the best theoretical explanation of the protection of freedom of expression ever offered in a Supreme Court majority opinion. As such it made extraordinarily good law.

Miranda v. Arizona was the Supreme Court's biggest event in the history of constitutional criminal procedure. The Court consolidated several cases raising the issue of the legality of the admission of confessions obtained through custodial interrogation. It then delivered an opinion unequaled in the extent to which it addressed and decided issues well beyond those raised by the facts of the cases. Moreover, Chief Justice Warren offered only the thinnest precedential support for the Court's bold venture. The reaction against the decision was intense and arguably had serious political ramifications. *Miranda* became ingrained in the popular culture. Over the next three decades the Court stuck with the core of *Miranda* but limited its expansion. It eventually declined to reject it outright when given the opportunity. Opinion remains divided as to whether *Miranda* made good or bad law. There is no question however that it has become part of the permanent legal landscape.

The Pentagon Papers Case landed in the Supreme Court with unprecedented speed. Given the demands of the law of prior restraint, the justices believed that they were compelled to decide the case as swiftly as possible. That prevented the justices from delivering an opinion for the Court. As such, the Court could provide little institutional guidance beyond cautioning that prior restraints against the press will almost never be permissible. Perhaps that was enough. The Court was required to attempt to work out the details of prior restraint doctrine in other contexts in subsequent cases with the Pentagon Papers Case looming in the background. The Pentagon Papers Case delivered a strong message as to the near impossibility of restraining publication by injunction. That was significant and positive. However, it made very little law in the doctrinal sense.

Roe v. Wade is the most controversial case that the Court has decided since *Dred Scott*. Given the nature of the issue, the assault on *Roe* has not subsided despite the fact that the Court has stood behind it though in modified form. There is a consensus that Justice

Blackmun wrote a very bad opinion. Whether the decision itself was right or wrong, a matter of extreme controversy, the legal justification was wholly inadequate. The attack on *Roe* would continue regardless of how well written the opinion had been but its obvious defects made the challenge easier. Arguably, there is almost certainly something terribly wrong with a judicial decision that so polarizes the nation for decades on end with no relief in sight.

The Joint Opinion in *Casey*, modifying yet sustaining *Roe*, was better reasoned than *Roe* itself. Still it was incapable of defusing the conflict. The Joint Opinion argued that it is sometimes the role of the Court to bring closure to divisive national controversies, a debatable proposition and one on which the *Casey* Court was unable to deliver. *Casey* was an improvement over *Roe*, but that is faint praise.

United States v. Nixon was unique and such a strange case that it could scarcely be expected to produce much law of long-term significance, and it did not. The likelihood that President Nixon was guilty of a felony and was attempting to conceal evidence hung over the decision but could not be explicitly referenced by the Court. Consequently, the Court labored to draft an opinion that would at least seem to have some general application but was likely to have very little. The opinion was highly qualified, designed to exclude most other instances in which executive privilege might arise. The Court resolved the issue before it without doing much long-term damage, and that may be the most that could be expected. Like the Pentagon Papers Case, *Nixon* is notable for creating very little law as opposed to bad law.

The divided Court in *Bakke* produced very little of precedential value as a technical matter as there was not much that five justices agreed on except that institutions of higher learning could take some account of race in the admissions process, but could not impose a quota or set-aside. Justice Powell accepted the demands of educational institutions for guidance and attempted to provide it although no other justice concurred in the core reasoning of his opinion. Nevertheless, the *Bakke* decision was so crucial to the future of affirmative action in higher education that virtually all educational institutions latched on to Powell's diversity theory as if it were a legal safe haven, even though a competent attorney would understand that it represented the view of only one justice. *Bakke* may stand for the principle that if a segment of the Court's audience is determined to receive some affirmative guidance from a great case, they will find it if at all possible even if it does not really exist. Although the wisdom of the Powell approach remains subject to debate, the fact that is was so widely embraced is some testament to its propriety and value.

The challenge to the *Bakke* approach presented by *Grutter* and *Gratz*, some 25 years later, attracted as much public attention as *Bakke* itself. Powell's diversity justification had become deeply entrenched in the educational world and an attempt to alter or reject it was seen as an extreme threat. The effort to preserve *Bakke* proved successful with Justice O'Connor endorsing the Powell approach while expanding its theoretical basis. Justice O'Connor's opinion suffered from serious doctrinal flaws, as the critics noted; however it preserved the developed status quo for at least the time being. Ten years later, *Fisher v. Texas* attempted to correct the major error in O'Connor's analysis, the utilization of far too much deference to educational institutions, while purporting to leave the doctrine of the opinion untouched.

Bush v. Gore like *United States v. Nixon* was a great case of singular uniqueness. It was intended to resolve one specific crisis—the unsettled presidential election of 2000, and seemed to say as much. At the same time, the Court found it necessary to attempt to bolster the propriety of its decision through reliance on principles of some general applicability. As such, there was an inherent tension in the opinions as the Court declared that well-accepted doctrine supported its result; however, the instant case was unique and probably would have little future impact as precedent. And indeed it has been noted by commentators that courts almost never cite or rely on *Bush v. Gore*. That is generally stated as a criticism of the case, and yet it may simply be recognition of the fact that some great cases are indeed unique factually so that it is quite unlikely that they will create a doctrinal wellspring. As with *United States v. Nixon*, the legal doctrine was to a large extent manufactured for the particular situation and then quietly laid aside thereafter. It is perhaps impossible to separate assessments of *Bush v. Gore* from partisan commitments. It was and almost always will be a very polarizing decision. Like the Pentagon Papers Case and *Nixon*, it seems to have had little long-term doctrinal impact.

Sebelius is almost too recent to assess. It is fair to say that the Roberts opinion on the taxing power was surprising and largely unpersuasive. It seemed to be a desperate attempt to save a major piece of legislation that suffered from serious constitutional defects. As such, the opinion appeared to be unprincipled but that is a charge that could be leveled at other great cases as well. It is too soon to determine whether the Commerce Clause holding of five justices or the taxing power holding of a largely different five will have any long-term impact. That will depend to a significant degree on whether Congress chooses to press either of these legislative powers to their margins in the future and whether if it does, subsequent courts will treat *Sebelius* as an honored precedent or as an eccentric decision.

So have great cases tended to make bad law either in a subjective sense or in their long-term impact? The answer must be partially yes but mainly no. Great cases have made bad law and certainly can make bad law, but that is hardly inevitable. The three examples from the latter half of the nineteenth century that Holmes probably had in mind and that Hughes characterized as the Court's self-inflicted wounds are prime examples of the great case making bad law. In all three at least some of the justices appear to have been caught up in the partisan struggle at the center of the cases and decided the cases on political rather than legal grounds. Two of these were rejected by constitutional amendment, and one was overruled scarcely a year later. However, these three cases do stand out as almost unique. Critics of *Bush v. Gore* assert that the same happened in that case. Perhaps ironically, Justice Jackson justified his vote to overturn segregation in *Brown* as a political rather than a legal decision.

The impact of the hydraulic pressures of the great case almost certainly have some impact on the decision-making process, the opinion, and the doctrine, though not necessarily an adverse impact. *Marbury, Jones & Laughlin Steel, Nixon, Bakke*. and *Sebelius* would seem to be cases in which the pressures of the great case had an effect on at least one crucial justice. Whether it was a positive or an adverse impact is for the most part a matter of debate. Taking the context and the pressures of the great case into account is quite different however from getting caught up in the underlying political struggle. The former is understandable and often desirable; the latter is likely to lead to serious error. More often than not the justices have resisted or managed the pressures of the great case and have produced solid and in many instances memorable opinions that have had a positive impact on the law.

The three great cases that Holmes may have had in mind and that Hughes criticized, *Dred Scott, Hepburn* and Legal Tender, and *Pollack*, were examples of the political trumping the legal. But more great cases have produced good and enduring law as opposed to bad and rejected law. The three Marshall Court decisions discussed have become constitutional landmarks of the first order. *Brown v. Board of Education, NLRB v. Jones & Laughlin Steel*, and the Reapportionment Cases are seminal turning points in constitutional law, though *Brown* is of such significance that it seems inappropriate to include anything else in its class. The *Slaughter-House Cases* is an example of a wrong turn in the Court's jurisprudence that has prevailed over time, whereas *Dennis* is a wrong turn that was quickly ignored and undermined. *The Civil Rights Cases* probably were correctly decided but perhaps unfortunately so in terms of societal impact. *New York Times v. Sullivan* and *Miranda v. Arizona* have become deeply entrenched in constitutional jurisprudence and in both instances expanded doctrine far beyond its prior boundaries. The Pentagon Papers Case, *United States v. Nixon*, and *Bush v. Gore* resolved specific controversies of the first magnitude without significant doctrinal impact. *Youngstown Sheet & Tube v. Sawyer* resolved a similar crisis while making a lasting impact on the law. *Bakke* and *Grutter* reached a compromise that resolved a controversial issue, at least for a while. *Sebelius* saved an important piece of legislation through questionable reasoning. *Roe v. Wade* remains the most controversial decision of the twentieth century. Both its supporters and detractors remain committed to their positions with little prospect of compromise or consensus. Some would consider it this century's *Dred Scott*. Others would be deeply offended by such a characterization. It is certainly the most problematic great case of the past century however.

Most great cases have been driven to a large extent by strong willed and confident justices. Confidence was the hallmark of the Marshall and Warren Courts. Often strong leadership and confidence can lead to landmark decisions. However, overconfidence can also lead the Court over the cliff, as it did in *Dred Scott, Hepburn*. and *Pollack*. Humility and moderation would have served the Court better in these instances. Arguably, Chief Justice Warren suffered from overconfidence in both *Reynolds v. Simms* and *Miranda*. In each a more limited and nuanced decision would have been preferable.

The Court in *Dennis* suffered from a lack of leadership leading to a failure to build a majority and at least a temporary setback for freedom of speech. The chief justice could not construct a majority. The four strong-willed concurring and dissenting justices were scarcely capable of agreeing among themselves. *Roe* and *Nixon*, decided in close proximity, are clear examples of a leaderless Court attempting to muddle through. In *Nixon*, the justices were trying hard to correct and respond to the chief justice's inadequacies. In *Roe*, the majority seemed so relieved that Justice Blackmun could finally produce anything at all that they were willing to turn a blind eye to its significant deficiencies.

The inability of the Court to decide much of anything in *Bakke* has been considered a blessing by some. With a bad record, the Court was split. Justice Powell took charge and provided important guidance though in an opinion of questionable precedential impact. Universities were given direction, and yet the Court was not truly locked in. *Bakke, Casey*, and *Grutter* are examples of leadership from the center. In these cases, neither of the ideological extremes could muster a majority. Rather the more centerist justices took control and determined the outcome, usually with a compromise. Perhaps something similar occurred in *Sebelius* as well. Leadership on the Court does not necessarily flow from the chief justice or even from the most strong-willed and ideologically committed.

Great cases by definition are unusual. They take the Court out of its routine and its comfort zone, placing it on center stage and magnifying the possibility of serious error. They also provide the Court with the opportunity to proceed boldly and stake out new ground. Fortunately although great cases can make bad law, for the most part they have not.

INDEX

A.L.A. *Schechter Poultry Corp v.United States* (1936), 169, 175
abortion law. *See Roe* and *Casey*
Abrams v. United States (1919), xiii, 184, 264
ACA. *See NFIB v. Sebelius* (2012)
ACLU, 271, 287
Adams, John, 1, 2, 256
Adarand Constructors, Inc. v. Pena (1995), 350
affirmative action. *See* Racial Preferences in Education Cases
Affordable Care Act. *See NFIB v. Sebelius* (2012)
African Americans
    confessions of, 268
    in Louisiana legislature, 116
    Slaughter-House Cases and, 131
    See also Brown v. Board of Education (1954); *The Civil Rights Cases* (1883); Racial Preferences in Education Cases; *Scott v. Sanford* (1857); slavery
Akron v. Akron Center for Reproductive Heath (1983), 114–15
Alien and Sedition Acts, 30, 256, 259, 263
Alito, Samuel
    Grutter and, 357
    McDonald and, 134–35

Sebelius and, 378, 379, 382–83
Allgeyer v. Louisiana (1897), 129, 168
amicus curiae/briefs
    Bakke, 339, 346
    Brown, 217
    expansion of the, xvi, 393
    Grutter and *Gratz*, 337, 348–49, 350–51, 354, 355, 393, 398, 407
    Miranda, 271
    Reynolds, 242
    Roe, 302, 318
    Sebelius, 376
    Webster, 309
    Youngstown Steel, 199
The Amistad (1841), 65, 70
Article I, 31, 32, 152, 162, 241
    See also Specific clauses
Article II, *Bush* and, 360, 362, 363, 364–67, 370, 371, 407
Article III, 10–11, 21
Article IV, 236
Articles of Confederation, 31, 39, 79, 85, 118
Asian-American students, 356
Associated Press v. Walker (1967), 261, 263, 265